I0891153

AFRICA YEARBOOK

AFRICA YEARBOOK

Volume 6

Politics, Economy and Society South of the Sahara in 2009

EDITED BY

ANDREAS MEHLER

HENNING MELBER

KLAAS VAN WALRAVEN

SUB-EDITOR

ROLF HOFMEIER

TUTA SUB AEGIDE PALLAS · 1683 ·

BRILL

LEIDEN • BOSTON
2010

For free access to the online version, go to www.brillonline.nl/tokenaccess

This book is printed on acid-free paper.

ISSN 1871-2525
ISBN 978 90 04 18559 3

Contents

Preface

In May 2003, the Africa-Europe Group of Interdisciplinary Studies (AEGIS) encouraged some of its member institutions to publish an *Africa Yearbook* with a wider international appeal. The African Studies Centre in Leiden (ASC), the Institute of African Affairs in Hamburg (IAA) and the Nordic Africa Institute in Uppsala (NAI) – all very active AEGIS centres sharing similar profiles – accepted this challenge and their joint efforts first bore fruit in the initial volume of the series in 2004. In 2007, the Dag Hammarskjöld Foundation in Uppsala (DHF) joined this international project, while the NAI ended its involvement with the fifth volume published in 2009. For this current volume Rolf Hofmeier once again joined us as sub-editor for the Eastern Africa section.

The country-specific articles cover domestic politics, foreign affairs and socioeconomic developments in the states of sub-Saharan Africa during the calendar year under review. While we recognise the impossibility of finding fully objective indicators for the relative importance of each of the states covered by the *Yearbook*, the length of the country-specific articles aims to reflect the approximate weight of each country. The four sub-regions are also introduced by means of an overview article. Further overviews summarise general continental developments, European-African relations and the United Nations and Africa.

The *Yearbook* is based on scholarly work, but oriented towards a wider target readership, including students, politicians, diplomats, administrators, journalists, teachers, practitioners in the sphere of development cooperation and business people. Without forcing the individual contributions too much into a straitjacket, the volume is primarily concerned with providing factual (though not necessarily neutral) information. Each issue, in focusing almost exclusively on developments during the particular calendar year, provides a completely fresh annual overview of events and thereby adds to the cumulative record of ongoing developments.

We wish to express our gratitude to all the contributors for their collaboration in this endeavour and to the partner institutions in AEGIS for encouraging us to embark on this ambitious project. With this volume, the Yearbook has entered a new phase and left behind the initial "probation period" of five years. Carol Rowe as language editor and Bas van der Mije as coordinator have joined the team. We thank them for their solid support, as well as Brill Publishers for their continued commitment. Last but not least, we note with appreciation and gratitude the ongoing support of our three institutions, remaining loyal to turning the original idea into reality.

The Editors
(Hamburg, Leiden and Uppsala, June 2010)

List of Abbreviations

ABN	Autorité du Bassin du Niger (Niamey)
ACP	African, Caribbean, and Pacific Group of Countries (Lomé/Cotonou Agreement)
ADF	African Development Fund (Tunis)
AfDB	African Development Bank (Tunis)
AFD	Agence Française de Développement (Paris)
AGOA	African Growth and Opportunity Act
AI	Amnesty International
APRM	African Peer Review Mechanism
AU	African Union (Addis Ababa)
BCEAO	Banque Centrale des Etats de l'Afrique de l'Ouest (Dakar)
BEAC	Banque des Etats de l'Afrique Centrale (Yaoundé)
CAR	Central African Republic
CBLT	Commission du Bassin du Lac Tchad (N'Djaména)
CEEAC	Communauté Economique des Etats de l'Afrique Centrale (Libreville) = ECCAS
CEMAC	Communauté Economique et Monétaire de l'Afrique Centrale (Bangui)
CEN-SAD	Community of Sahel-Saharan States (Tripoli)
CEPGL	Communauté Economique des Pays des Grands Lacs (Gisenyi/Rwanda)
CFAfr	Franc de la Communauté Financière Africaine (BCEAO; BEAC)
COMESA	Common Market for Eastern and Southern Africa (Lusaka)
CPLP	Comunidade dos Países de Língua Portuguesa
DAC	Development Assistance Committee (Paris)
DDR	Disarmament, Demobilisation and Reintegration
DFID	Department for International Development (London)
DRC	Democratic Republic of the Congo
EAC	East African Community
ECA	Economic Commission for Africa (United Nations; Addis Ababa)
ECCAS	Economic Community of Central African States (Libreville)
ECOWAS	Economic Community of West African States (Abuja)
ECOMOG	ECOWAS Ceasefire Monitoring Group
EDF	European Development Fund (Brussels)

EIB	European Investment Bank (Luxemburg)
EPA	Economic Partnership Agreement
ESAF	Enhanced Structural Adjustment Facility (IMF)
EU	European Union (Brussels)
FAO	Food and Agricultural Organisation (Rome)
FTA	Free Trade Area
GDP	Gross Domestic Product
HDI	Human Development Index (UNDP)
HIPC	Heavily Indebted Poor Countries
HRW	Human Rights Watch
ICC	International Criminal Court
ICG	International Crisis Group
IDA	International Development Association (Washington)
IDP	Internally Displaced Person
IFAD	International Fund for Agricultural Development (Rome)
IFC	International Finance Corporation (Washington)
IGAD	Intergovernmental Authority on Development (Djibouti)
ILO	International Labour Organisation (Geneva)
IMF	International Monetary Fund (Washington)
IOC	Indian Ocean Commission (Quatre Bornes, Mauritius)
IORARC	Indian Ocean Rim Association for Regional Cooperation (Port Louis)
MDGs	Millennium Development Goals
MDRI	Multilateral Debt Relief Initiative
MRU	Mano River Union (Freetown)
NEPAD	New Partnership for Africa's Development
NGO	Non-Governmental Organisation
OECD	Organisation for Economic Cooperation and Development (Paris)
OIC	Organisation of the Islamic Conference (Jeddah)
OIF	L'Organisation Internationale de la Francophonie
OPEC	Organisation of Petroleum Exporting Countries (Vienna)
PALOP	Países Africanos de Lingua Oficial Portugesa
PPP	Purchasing Power Parity
PRGF	Poverty Reduction and Growth Facility
PRSC	Poverty Reduction Support Credit
PRSP	Poverty Reduction Strategy Paper
SACU	Southern African Customs Union (Pretoria)
SADC	Southern African Development Community (Gaborone)
SAF	Structural Adjustment Facility (IMF)
SDR	Special Drawing Right (IMF)

TI	Transparency International
UAE	United Arab Emirates
UEMOA	Union Économique et Monétaire Ouest-Africaine (Ouagadougou)
UMA	Union du Maghreb Arabe
UN	United Nations (New York)
UNCTAD	United Nations Conference on Trade and Development (Geneva)
UNDP	United Nations Development Programme (New York)
UNEP	United Nations Environment Programme (Nairobi)
UNESCO	United Nations Educational, Scientific and Cultural Organisation (Paris)
UNGA	United Nations General Assembly
UNHCR	United Nations High Commissioner for Refugees (Geneva)
UNICEF	United Nations Children's Fund (New York)
UNSC	UN Security Council
UNSG	United Nations Secretary-General
USAID	United States Agency for International Development (Washington)
WFP	World Food Programme (Rome)
WHO	World Health Organisation (Geneva)
WTO	World Trade Organisation (Geneva)

Factual Overview (as of 31 December 2009)

West Africa

Country	*Area (in sq km)*	*Population (in m)*	*Currency*	*HDI*	*Head of State*	*Prime Minister*
Benin	112,622	8.9	CFA Franc	0.492	Boni Yayi	
Burkina Faso	274,122	15.2	CFA Franc	0.389	Blaise Compaoré	Tertius Zongo
Cape Verde	4,033	0.52	Cape Verdean Escudo	0.708	Pedro Pires	José Maria Pereira Neves
Côte d'Ivoire	322,462	21.1	CFA Franc	0.484	Laurent Gbagbo	Guillaume Kigbafori Soro
Gambia	11,295	1.7	Dalasi	0.456	Yahya Jammeh	
Ghana	238,500	23.8	Cedi	0.526	John Attta Mills	
Guinea	245,857	9.8	Guinean Franc	0.435	General Sékouba Konaté	Kabiné Komara
Guinea-Bissau	36,125	1.58	CFA Franc	0.396	Malam Bacai Sanhá	Carlos Gomes
Liberia	111,370	4	Liberian Dollar	0.442	Ellen Johnson-Sirleaf	
Mali	1,240,000	14.3	CFA Franc	0.371	Amadou Toumani Touré	Modibo Sidibé
Mauritania	1,030,700	3.3	Ouguiya	0.520	Mohamed Ould Abdel Aziz	Moulaye Ould Mohamed Laghdaf
Niger	1,267,000	14.7	CFA Franc	0.340	Tandja Mamadou	Ali Badio Gamatié
Nigeria	923,768	149.3	Naira	0.511	Umaru Yar'Adua	
Senegal	197,192	12.5	CFA Franc	0.646	Abdoulaye Wade	Souleymane Ndéné Ndiaye
Sierra Leone	71,740	5.6	Leone	0.365	Ernest Bai Koroma	
Togo	56,785	6.6	CFA Franc	0.4799	Faure Gnassingbé	Gilbert Fossoun Houngbo

Central Africa

Country	*Area (in sq km)*	*Population (in m)*	*Currency*	*HDI*	*Head of State*	*Prime Minister*
Cameroon	475,442	19.5	CFA Franc	0.523	Paul Biya	Philemon Yang
Central African Republic	622,984	4.3	CFA Franc	0.369	François Bozizé	Faustin Archange Touadéra
Chad	1,284,000	11.3	CFA Franc	0.392	Idriss Déby	Emmanuel Nadingar
Congo	342,000	3.6	CFA Franc	0.601	Denis Sassou-Nguesso	Isidore Mvouaba
DR Congo	2,344,855	64.3	Congolese Franc	0.389	Joseph Kabila	Adolphe Muzito
Equatorial Guinea	28,051	0.7	CFA Franc	0.719	Teodoro Obiang Nguema Mbasogo	Ignacio Milam Tang
Gabon	267,667	1.5	CFA Franc	0.755	Ali Bongo	Paul Biyoghe Mba
São Tomé and Príncipe	1,001	0.2	Dobra	0.651	Fradique de Menezes	Joaquim Rafael Branco

Eastern Africa

Country	*Area (in sq km)*	*Population (in m)*	*Currency*	*HDI*	*Head of State*	*Prime Minister*
Burundi	26,338	8.3	Burundi Franc	0.394	Pierre Nkurunziza	
Comoros	1,862	0.7	Comoran Franc	0.576	Ahmed Abdallah Sambi	
Djibouti	23,200	0.9	Djiboutian Franc	0.520	Ismail Omar Guelleh	Dileita Mohamed Dileita
Eritrea	124,320	4.9	Nakfa	0.472	Isaias Afewerki	
Ethiopia	1,121,900	73.9	Birr	0.414	Girma Wolde-Giorgis	Meles Zenawi
Kenya	569,259	39.8	Kenya Shilling	0.541	Mwai Kibaki	Raila Odinga
Rwanda	26,338	10.0	Rwanda Franc	0.460	Paul Kagame	Bernard Makuza
Seychelles	455	0.1	Seychelles Rupee	0.845	James Michel	
Somalia	637,600	9.1	Somali Shilling	n.d.	Sheikh Sharif Sheikh Ahmed Dahir Riyale Kahin (Somaliland)	Omar Abdirashid Ali Shermarke
Sudan	2,505,805	42.3	Sudanese Pound	0.531	Omar Hassan Ahmad al-Bashir	
Tanzania	945,087	43.7	Tanzania Shilling	0.530	Jakaya Kikwete	Mizengo Pinda
Uganda	197,000	32.7	Uganda Shilling	0.514	Yoweri Kaguta Museveni	Apollo Nsibambi

Southern Africa

Country	*Area (in sq km)*	*Population (in m)*	*Currency*	*HDI*	*Head of State*	*Prime Minister*
Angola	1,246,700	18.5	Kwanza	0.564	José Eduardo dos Santos	Paulo Kassoma
Botswana	581,730	1.9	Pula	0.694	Ian Khama	
Lesotho	30,344	1.9	Loti	0.514	King Letsie III	Pakalitha Mosisili
Madagascar	592,000	19.5	Ariary	0.543	Andry Rajoelina (contested)	Albert Camille Vital
Malawi	118,484	15.3	Kwacha	0.371	Bingu wa Mutharika	
Mauritius	2,040	1.3	Mauritius Rupee	0.804	Sir Anerood Jugnauth	Navinchandra Ramgoolan
Mozambique	799,380	22.9	Métical	0.402	Armando Guebuza	Aires Bonifácio Ali
Namibia	824,269	2.2	Namibian Dollar	0.686	Hifikepunye Lucas Pohamba	Nahas Angula
South Africa	1,219,090	49.1	Rand	0.683	Jacob Zuma	
Swaziland	17,364	1.2	Lilangeni	0.572	King Mswati III.	Sibusiso Dlamini
Zambia	752,614	12.9	Kwacha	0.481	Rupiah Banda	
Zimbabwe	390,580	12.5	Zimbabwe Dollar	n.d.	Robert Gabriel Mugabe	Morgan Tsvangirai

I. Sub-Saharan Africa

The effects of the global financial crisis, resulting in the slow down of most economies in the industrialised countries, continued to have a negative impact, especially on the resource-rich economies in the region. Most countries registered a marked decline in their economic growth rates, albeit still managing to maintain modest economic growth. Low oil prices and dramatically lower world market prices for copper, diamonds and other primary export commodities left their mark on trade balances. The emerging economies of China, as well as India and Brazil, managed to use this to create new opportunities by consolidating their ties with African countries and extending their economic relations. The regional interim EPAs the EU sought to impose on African partner countries remained contested and provoked massive dissent and resistance.

Continental policies were confronted with new calls for conflict mediation in countries such as Madagascar and remained occupied with matters concerning Guinea, Guinea Bissau, Mauritania and Zimbabwe as some of the more prominent hot spots. The ICC indictment of Sudanese President al-Bashir initially met with a seemingly united front against what was declared to be selective external interference in African affairs, but it soon became obvious that Africa did not speak with one voice. Similarly, differences also emerged in response to the continued initiatives of the Libyan leader Kadhafi with regard to his Pan-African visions and ambitions. A series of elections in eight countries brought no political changes but reinforced the trend towards dominant party systems, which consolidated and further entrenched the political control of specific elites running parties and states.

The further decline in the relevance of NEPAD indicated that what had originally been considered a new chapter in African collective responsibility and political enlightenment was in fact more of the same, despite several further efforts to maintain the APRM as a new tool enhancing best practice.

Africa in the Global Economy

Gloom over the world **economic downturn** led to pessimistic forecasts about Africa's ability to weather the storm. While fears were expressed that Western countries would cut development spending, African governments called on both Western and Asian powers to allocate portions of their economic stimulus measures to poorer countries. The World

Economic Forum on Africa, held in Cape Town on 10–12 June, added demands for better terms of trade and enhanced market access (not encouraged by the US-EU moratorium on such concessions introduced the previous year after the collapse of the WTO's Doha round). The World Bank and IMF warned at their spring meetings that 55 to 90 m more people in the world might become trapped in poverty and a total 1 bn could face hunger, with Africans disproportionately represented in both cases. Assessments about the effects of the global economic downturn nevertheless varied, with the IMF predicting overall output growth for Africa at 1% (down from 3%). This still amounted to a 1% per capita decline, and fears that the earlier advances in reducing poverty could be reversed were not put at rest. Indeed, figures published during the first quarter of 2010 showed that average economic growth in Africa plummeted to 2.5% according to the OECD, as compared with an overall growth figure of 5.9% the previous year. Petroleum exporting countries were hard hit, as oil prices fell to $ 34 a barrel (though then climbing back to around $ 59 at mid year). Countries that felt the downturn more than others were those better linked to the world financial system, such as Kenya and Ghana, and Southern Africa experienced the strongest effects because of the importance of the mining sector. Copper prices halved as compared with the previous year (causing unemployment in Zambia and DRC), diamond sales were down (hurting mainly the economies of Namibia and Botswana), and asset prices on the Johannesburg stock exchange fell.

In early 2010, the IMF said there had been a 16.4% drop in 2009 trade volume/value. The World Bank warned that private capital flows were drying up, and in a preliminary estimate the OECD reported that foreign direct **investment** fell by more than a third in 2009. As Africans in the diaspora faced salary and job cuts, remittances decreased by 6.6% according to a World Bank study published in the spring of 2010. Surprisingly, official **development assistance** (ODA) remained more or less at pre-crisis levels and countries, such as Italy, that cut back on development spending were the exception. In contrast to the overall gloomy picture, the IMF expected Africa to rebound to ca. 4% growth in 2010.

Domestic prices for rice, maize, millet and sorghum in sub-Saharan Africa were by April still significantly higher than in the previous year. The WFP estimated that **food prices** were above the five-year average in 19 out of the 20 countries studied. Eastern Africa in particular faced food insecurity. The EU released some € 394 m from its food facility, created in the wake of the 2008 African food riots and to be disbursed to numerous countries in and outside Africa. The FAO called on donor countries to devote 17% of ODA to **agriculture**. With 80% of African smallholdings confined to 2 hectares or less and fertiliser use limited to 13 kg a hectare (against 73 kg in the Middle East and 190 kg in east Asia), a lot remained to be done, not least in the area of transport. Thirty per cent of Africans were said to be suffering from chronic hunger and malnutrition. Numerous countries continued to be net food importers (though countries such as Malawi and Rwanda had undergone remarkable 'green revolutions', which made them bread baskets in the sub-regions). Thus, there was enough food for talk at the World Food Security Summit in Rome, 16–18 November, boycotted by Western countries due to the attendance of Zimbabwe's Robert Mugabe. For their part, Asian countries complicated the picture by continuing the purchase of land for commercial agriculture in countries such as Madagascar and Tanzania. The Rome summit resolved to renew efforts to achieve the first MDG (halving hunger by 2015). African initiatives in the field of food security involved, among other things, a new partnership between NEPAD and the Alliance for a Green Revolution in Africa.

Demographic developments showed the importance of the issue, with the population of sub-Saharan Africa this year estimated to have exceeded 1 bn. With an overall **population growth** of 3% during the previous two decades, Africans were deemed to be poorer than in the mid 1970s. Most GDP growth rates have been below the 6%-8% mark needed to diminish poverty. Thus, **migration** to Europe remained an option for many, marred by incidents such as the drowning of more than 300 Africans who were trying to reach Italy from Libya at the end of March, and the flight of more than 900 immigrants from a southern Italian town in January after mafia-led vigilante violence against African farm workers. Italy, like Spain, the UK and other industrialised countries, cut foreign worker quotas in response to the downturn.

With rich countries $ 20 bn behind on their 2005 Gleneagles aid pledges, the results of this year's **G8** summit proved less of an earthquake than the one that had rocked the conference's venue (the Italian town of L'Aquila). World leaders said they would commit $ 20 bn in farm aid over three years as part of a Food Security Initiative. It was unclear, however, how much of this money was new. The **World Bank** sought to fast-track $ 42 bn of its 2008 $ 100 bn bailout package for developing countries and to channel this in the form of IDA grants and interest-free loans to Africa. The Bank's director lobbied rich countries for a vulnerability fund to be fed by 0.7% of their fiscal stimulus spending, but the response from the North was poor. The **IMF** disbursed more aid from its Exogenous Shocks Facility. A new framework for loans was announced for the poorest countries, involving resources that would boost concessional lending to $ 17 bn until 2014. The Fund was also more flexible about African governments boosting budget spending in response to the crisis. In February, the Bank agreed that Africa should get a third seat on its Executive Board. While this still left the region under-represented, the Committee on IMF Governance Reform agreed that 12 out of the 20 seats on the IMF Council would be reserved for developing countries. IMF quotas were to be reviewed but, with European countries standing to lose most out of this, results were not likely to come fast. African finance ministers created a new institution, the African Investment Bank (AIB), with Nigeria, South Africa and North African countries owning 50% of the shares. To be based in Tripoli, Libya, it was to complement the activities of the AfDB with a projected capital base of $ 4 bn. The G20 summit in London (2 April), preceded by a high-level conference of African development ministers in Dar es Salaam on 10–11 March, promised an increase in lending to poor countries of $ 100 bn by multilateral development banks. Meeting on 24–25 September in Pittsburgh, the group of leading and emerging economies (including South Africa) reiterated calls for institutional reform of the IMF.

China made it clear that the economic crisis was a particularly Western phenomenon, pledging that it would not cut aid or backtrack on past debt waivers. During a four-nation tour in January, President Hu Jintao laid the foundation stone of a bridge in Senegal, and also granted $ 22 m in aid to Tanzania, besides visiting Mali and Mauritius. At a meeting of the Forum on China-Africa Cooperation (FOCAC) in Sharm el Sheikh, Egypt (8–9 November), the Chinese offered Africa $ 10 bn in concessional lending over the next three years. They also promised to improve market access to China (zero tariffs for 95% of goods from the least developed African states, beginning with 60% by 2010), cancellation of debt and increased social responsibility on the part of Chinese companies active in Africa. African delegates responded enthusiastically and China's economic weight was underlined by the fact that, for the first time, the country became the continent's prime trading partner, surpassing the US – the value of whose imports from Africa plummeted as a result of the collapse in oil prices.

India expected that its trade with Africa would reach the value of $ 100 bn in the next five years, identifying mining, chemicals, infrastructure, information technology and agriculture as the principal areas for expansion. Several of these issues were discussed at the India-Africa Business Partnership summit in New Delhi (21 January), attended by 14 African leaders. At the 4th Tokyo International Conference on African Development (TICAD, at ministerial level), on 21–22 March, **Japan** announced $ 500 m in new aid, on top of an older pledge to double aid to Africa. Most of the new money would be spent on food assistance and fighting AIDS, tuberculosis and malaria. Japan's motivations were influenced by concern over Chinese dominance of African trade and the desire to secure a seat at a reformed UN Security Council. **South-South cooperation** led, among other things, to a summit of African and Latin American countries in Lomé, Togo (27 September), where it was decided to establish a 'Bank of the South'. The bank, with a start-up capital of $ 200 bn, would finance joint projects.

The annual United States-Sub-Saharan Africa Trade and Economic Cooperation Forum, held under the **AGOA**, took place in Nairobi on 4–6 August, attended by US Secretary of State Hillary Clinton. Discussions focused on an extension of the Act, affording African nations preferential access to US markets beyond the expiry date of 2015. The conference also recommended the US scale down subsidies, notably to its own cotton farmers, which heavily damaged cotton producers in West Africa. While more than 6,400 products could enter the US duty-free under the AGOA, a report of the Brookings Institution made clear that the Act principally benefited oil exporting countries, such as Angola and Nigeria. Energy-related products accounted for some 96% of AGOA-covered African exports to the US. As a result of the economic downturn, US imports of non-oil products fell by 22%. At year's end President Obama ended trade benefits for Guinea, Madagascar and Niger – all three embroiled in political crises – for not meeting AGOA demands on good governance and the rule of law. By contrast, Mauritania was reinstated in the programme and Kenyan exporters were given an extension, although the US was still not satisfied with Kenyan reforms.

African Union

At the first summit, held in Addis Ababa from 1 to 4 February, Libya's leader **Kadhafi** was elected to the chairmanship of the Assembly, a post that had eluded him in the past. Kadhafi entered the conference hall accompanied by a retinue of chiefly rulers from various countries, who formed part of the 'Forum of Kings, Sultans, Princes, Sheikhs and Customary Chiefs' established by Libya the previous year and who had bestowed on Kadhafi the title of 'king of kings'. The heads of state bore the spectacle with patience, although Uganda's President Museveni threatened to arrest traditional leaders who spoke in Kadhafi's name – he had already cancelled a forum of traditional leaders in Kampala that was financed by Libya. Libya's leader retorted that he would destroy Museveni 'like he had destroyed Mbeki'.

Having set the tone, the Union got embroiled in the perennial debate on **institutional reform**. AU Commission President Ping tried to limit discussion of Kadhafi's new plan for a 'United States of Africa', but the maverick leader re-launched the issue during the summit's last day. His plan had already led to heated exchanges, with several countries, notably in Southern Africa, having opposed his election to the Assembly chair – in vain, because it was North Africa's turn and Libya, as one of the Union's principal funders, could not be ignored. So-called 'gradualist' countries (Kenya, Nigeria, Uganda, South Africa, Namibia) pointed out that peace and security issues had to precede the immediate continental government Kadhafi was said to be craving and that the sub-regional communities were stepping stones in this process. Uganda dismissed Kadhafi's ideas as impractical. South Africa largely agreed with Museveni, who extracted the concession that the AU should not dispatch the Libyan leader to the G20 summit in London on his own but that he should be accompanied by his predecessor, President Kikwete of Tanzania, and Museveni himself.

Libya's plans were supported by Déby of Chad and President Wade of Senegal, although the latter also presented an alternative plan in which 20 countries (mainly from West and North Africa) would commence the project of continental integration. Wade explained to Kadhafi that he could not have his way and the debate ended in the compromise decision that the Commission would become the AU's **'Authority'**, of which Ping would continue to be the president but with the current Commissioners renamed cabinet 'secretaries', responsible for 'areas of shared competence'. Kikwete emphasised that the new 'secretaries' would receive portfolios different from those they had held before to make the change more real. He spoke in generalities without setting any time schedule. Moreover, it was agreed that the Authority would not be introduced until the next summit and Ethiopia, Uganda and South Africa managed to impose the condition that the reform could only be introduced by a modification of the Constitutive Act, requiring ratification by all member states.

The Executive Council met in extraordinary session on 15–16 April in Tripoli in an effort to make the institutional reform more tangible. However, many of these issues remained matters of dispute and, in typical AU fashion, were deferred to the next summit (1–3 July), which again became the scene of heated exchanges. With the venue changed from Antananarivo to Sirte in Libya because of the unconstitutional takeover in Madagascar, Kadhafi presented a text on the Authority that differed completely from what had been discussed in Tripoli. He tried to rush it through, but the diplomatic Ping openly expressed disapproval. Nigeria became involved in a sharp exchange with the Libyans, and Tanzania and Ethiopia refused to discuss the revised text. Angola was also vehemently opposed (Uganda's Mueseveni had refused to attend the summit altogether). An insulted Kadhafi left the conference hall for his mid-day prayer and, when he was urged to come back by the presidents of Mali and Gambia, the heads of state hammered out a **compromise**, which involved, among other things, the decision that the Authority would have a defence coordinator, in addition to the nine secretaries, president and vice-president. However, the institution's new 'powers' still depended on an explicit mandate from the member states and the changes would still have to be ratified. Kadhafi typically presented the outcome as a success – raising the possibility of putting the idea of continental government to a referendum in all member countries.

Other institutional matters concerned the **Pan-African Parliament** (PAP), which asked the Addis summit for an increase in its budget but saw its funding cut from $ 12.9 m to $ 9.5 m. There was dissatisfaction about the expenses of MPs and the cut in funds meant that the PAP would have to reduce its election missions to member states, one of its prime areas of work. On 29 May, it elected the Chadian Idriss Ndele Moussa to succeed the parliament's chairperson Gertrude Mongella, whose performance in the role had not helped the institution. Four new vice-presidents were elected and it was hoped this would ameliorate relations between the PAP, headquartered in South Africa, and the overall Union.

Several **conflicts** were on the summit agendas, including the perennial conflagration in Somalia, the Darfur mission and several unconstitutional takeovers (Guinea, Madagascar, Niger). On 2 February, the EU and the AU signed the new Africa Peace Facility, involving European funding to a value of € 300 m for the period up to 2010 and the development of an early response mechanism. The AU's peacekeepers (AU Mission in Somalia – AMISOM) were still not at full strength (4,300 at the start of the year instead of the maximum

8,000), although Nigeria, Sierra Leone and Malawi made new troop offers. In order to emphasise its support for the official president, the Somali head of state was invited to participate in the Union's first summit, which also called on the UN to impose a sea blockade and no-fly zone on Eritrea for its help to Somalia's insurgent forces. In July, the AU accepted a recommendation by IGAD to beef up the mandate of the Union peacekeepers and lift the ban on peacekeepers from neighbouring countries.

A **special summit** in Tripoli on 31 August–1 September discussed a range of conflicts, including the political turmoil in Guinea, Guinea-Bissau and the Great Lakes area. The leaders once more threatened Madagascar with sanctions if its new leader would not come to a transition arrangement with other political forces. The response to developments in Mauritania was weakened by Kadhafi's support for its coup leader, which complicated the role of Commission President Ping. The problems in Guinea were tackled by way of a special PSC meeting on 8 July, among other measures. On 19–23 October, the AU convened a special summit in Kampala, sponsored by the UNHCR, where member states adopted a convention on IDPs.

Member states' commitment to the international legal order was marred by selective political attitudes. Senegal continued backtracking on the AU-sponsored trial of the former Chadian dictator, Habré. The Senegalese representative at the Addis summit claimed his country required some CFAfr 18 bn (more than € 27 m) to pursue the case. The **ICC**'s case against Sudan's President Omar al-Bashir for his role in Darfur continued to produce disagreement with Western powers. The Sirte summit refused to act on the arrest warrant against Bashir and complained that the AU's request to the Court to defer the indictment had been ignored. Although around 30 African countries are party to the ICC statute, many felt the Court's prosecutor was biased towards pursuing African cases. Exceptionally, Botswana did not agree with this majority opinion, which risked tarnishing the Union's image in the same way as that of its predecessor, the OAU.

Governance

The 20th summit of the **NEPAD** Heads of State and Government Implementation Committee (HSGIC) was held on 31 January at the AU headquarters in Addis Ababa ahead of the 12th AU summit. It dealt mainly with the integration of NEPAD into the structures and processes of the AU and the appointment of the new chief executive for the NEPAD secretariat. In his opening address, Ethiopian head of state Meles Zenawi emphasised the need to further eliminate dysfunctionality and to embrace change. He urged the implementation of the decision already taken at the AU's 10th ordinary session a year earlier to integrate NEPAD into AU structures. AU Commission President Ping noted that significant strides had been made towards the integration of NEPAD. The initiative's only remaining autonomy was confined to the continued physical location of its secretariat in the South

African city of Midrand (between Pretoria and Johannesburg) with the status of an AU office outside headquarters. With Ibrahim Hassan Mayaki from Niger, NEPAD had a new CEO whose task was to finalise the integration of NEPAD into AU structures and processes and to implement NEPAD as a programme of the AU. The remaining issue to be solved was the future financing of the NEPAD secretariat, whose budget of $ 6 m a year was never met. Ping therefore identified the need for the HSGIC to secure its financing. The year basically brought an end to the once highly applauded initiative, which had been seen as an alternative and innovative way to promote good governance and NEPAD was effectively demoted to become an economic agency integrated into the AU headquarters.

Nonetheless, the **APRM** continued to be considered as the NEPAD flagship, although no further countries joined the queue of those registered for the review process during the year. Cape Verde will become the 30th country to have signed up once formalities are completed. Three APRM missions were undertaken during the year: in Mali, Mozambique and Lesotho. In mid-year the APRM secretariat launched a project to "streamline and fast-track" the APRM. According to its annual report, bi- and multilateral partners had contributed almost $ 13 m at continental level between 2003 and 2009, compared with $ 20.5 m contributed by member states. Algeria, Nigeria and South Africa paid more than half of this amount, while many countries remained in arrears on their minimum annual contribution of $ 100,000. In January, Nigeria's elder statesman and experienced international civil servant Adebayo Adedeji was re-confirmed in the rotating chairmanship for another full year. This decision by AU chairperson Meles Zenawi raised eyebrows over the lack of respect for constitutional principles. For most of the year, the APRM secretariat was as negatively affected as the overstretched NEPAD secretariat, and was mainly preoccupied with internal power struggles, bickering and other destructive in-fighting (including controversies over the appointment of the members of the panel of eminent persons and efforts to compromise their autonomous role), and intensified efforts by governments to discredit the legitimacy of the peer review process and its results by manipulating the reports. As a result, inefficiency and delays in delivery of reports increased and the APRM was as paralysed as the NEPAD secretariat. Even the supportive 'APRM Monitor', published by the Partnership Africa Canada, noted with concern in its June issue: "The slow pace of renewal of the membership of the Panel of Eminent Persons and of the staff at the APRM Secretariat, and the lack of transparency of both processes, does a disservice to the APRM. Moreover, the fact that the APRM Secretariat chooses not to have an efficient and open communications strategy only compounds the problem."

The year provided a new development with regard to the ranking of African countries on their **governance performance**, when a split occurred between the Mo Ibrahim Foundation and a team from the Kennedy School of Government at Harvard University, previously tasked to compile the Mo Ibrahim Index of African Governance. Rival reports were presented, on 1 October in Johannesburg by the latter, and by the former on 5 October in

Cape Town. The controversies seemed to be over ownership and control of the compilation, which highlighted the partly political nature of such assessments. In substance, however, few differences were visible in the rankings. Somalia remained the worst-governed country in terms of human rights, with Equatorial Guinea, Eritrea, Libya and Sudan close behind and the CAR competing for bottom place with regard to health, education and freedom from poverty with Zimbabwe, and Chad not far after. Southern Africa was the sub-region with the most positive aggregate figure and had six countries among the top ten performers, while Central Africa was the worst average scoring of the sub-regions.

According to Mo Ibrahim, some 26 to 27 countries on the continent had improved in general governance. As the regional office of the International Federation of Journalists warned in its annual report for the year, however, **press freedom** had never been so threatened on the continent, adding that elections did "not necessarily guarantee that the political protagonists and stakeholders do respect press freedom".

Elections

The year provided for some crucial elections and referendums. Not a single election could be considered as a breakthrough on the path to democracy. It became rather clear that the many hybrid and authoritarian regimes were about to stabilise their rule. Frequently, results produced between a two-thirds and a three-quarters majority (whether elections were openly manipulated or not). An established pattern of easy wins for former liberation movements was in train in Southern Africa. Arguably most international attention was paid to legislative elections in the Republic of **South Africa**. The result was a disappointment for all those who had expected that the defections from the ruling African National Congress (ANC) would alter its position of dominance. The 65.9% of votes it gained also permitted the indirect election in parliament of Jacob Zuma as the new president to succeed Thabo Mbeki. The similarly dominant position of the South West African People's Organisation (SWAPO) in **Namibia** was also not challenged in presidential and parliamentary elections, with the ruling party and presidential candidate Hifikepunye Pohamba receiving more than 74% and 75% of the votes respectively. Likewise, elections in **Mozambique** produced "more of the same". President Guebuza received a slightly higher percentage of votes in the presidential elections (76%) than his ruling Frelimo (75%) in parliamentary elections. Democratic standards were arguably higher in Botswana and Malawi, although without bringing about change in the ballot box. In **Malawi**, Bingu Wa Mutharika, who was accused of becoming increasingly authoritarian, could rely on his solid popularity with the poor in his country and won elections with 66.2% of the votes against John Tembo with 30.5% (which was well below expectations, particularly in his stronghold) and five competitors who received less than 1% each. Tembo refused to accept the results and challenged them in court, while EU election observers gave an overall positive judgement on the quality of the voting process. Bingu's Democratic Progressive Party (DPP) received a smaller share of the vote in the parallel legislative elections (58.9%), but this still led to a comfortable majority in the National Assembly (113 out 192 seats), with independents taking 32 seats, ahead of the 27 won by Tembo's Malawi Congress Party (MCP). In **Botswana**'s legislative election, the ruling Botswana Democratic Party (BDP) was able to augment its lead from 51.7% to 53.3% of the vote, while the two main competing parties, the Botswana National Front (BNF) and the Botswana Congress Party (BCP) fared differently, the former losing 4.1% (21.9% in total), and the latter boosting its votes by 2.5% (to 19.1%). This was translated into small gains in seats for BDP and BCP and a damaging loss of six seats for the BNP. Botswana confirmed its role as one of the best established democracies on the continent.

In Central African politics, there was equally no major change: In **Congo** (Brazzaville), after contested results, Denis Sassou Nguesso again emerged as the winner of the presidential elections with 78.6% of the votes. Even less competitive presidential elections were held in **Equatorial Guinea**, with results that could have been forecast: 95.8% for President Obiang Nguema. After the death of Omar Bongo Ondimba, a kind of dynastic succession was engineered in **Gabon**, with Bongo's son Ali winning his first election with 41.7% of the vote (a relative majority in one round of elections being sufficient).

Comoros' parliamentary elections confirmed the rule of Union president Abdallah Sambi, with his Baobab coalition securing 19 out of 24 seats. An earlier referendum with a particularly low turnout of about 50% permitted changes to the constitution favouring the union government over the individual islands' administrations. Sambi and the presidents of Grande Comore and Mohéli increasingly appeared to be on a collision course. In March, a referendum in the only French possession in the Archipelago produced an overwhelming vote of 95% in favour of becoming France's fifth overseas department in 2011 (from its former status as overseas collectivity).

Coups and Unconstitutional Rule

Extra-constitutional changes of government, as well as extra-constitutional governmental behaviour, occurred more frequently than in previous years. West Africa saw a number of problematic developments that had repercussions in the electoral field. Coup leader Mohamed Ould Abdel Aziz in **Mauritania** was elected president by a slight margin (52.6%). **Niger**'s increasingly authoritarian leader, Mamadou Tandja, instigated a constitutional referendum to allow him to extend his mandate. Described by his opponents as a "coup from above", Tandja's move to change the country's constitution set the stage for him to continue his rule and subsequently run for new full terms. The existing constitution had expressly banned him from doing so. Tandja organised a referendum in August, which was declared illegal by the Constitutional Court. Tandja therefore dissolved the

Court, and held the referendum, which showed an overwhelming majority in favour of his plans but threw the entire polity into a deep crisis. In October, parliamentary elections were held – boycotted, like the referendum, by the opposition, which allowed Tandja's MNSD to take 76 out of 113 seats. Tandja was of course not the only African president bending the rules, but this was probably the most visible case.

Elections in **Côte d'Ivoire** were further postponed, President Gbagbo was about to extend his rule to an entire second five-year term without being elected since 2000. However, heads of state could also be victims of political murder: in **Guinea Bissau** President Vieira was shot by soldiers seeking revenge for the killing of the army's chief of staff in a bomb explosion only hours before. In an apparent quick return to constitutional rule, the speaker of the National Assembly, Raimundo Pereira, was sworn in as interim head of state only three days later, and new elections were announced. Political violence marred the pre-election phase with further political assassinations. In the second round, the candidate of the ruling 'Partido Africano da Independência da Guinea e Cabo Verde' (PAIGC), Malam Bacai Sanhá, won a clear victory (63.3% to 36.7%) over former president Kumba Yala of the 'Partido da Renovação Social' (PRS). At least no further incidents had overshadowed the election of Sanhá.

Madagascar's President Marc Ravalomanana was overthrown in a coup after weeks of popular protest in the capital Antananarivo. His main challenger and mayor of the capital, Andry Rajoelina, was sworn in immediately. Ravalomanana resigned when he realised that he had lost the support of the military hierarchy, but did not renounce his ambitions. International mediators brokered a power-sharing deal to end a long period of violence, but a sustainable consensus between the main actors was not tangible at year's end.

Even more dramatic was a series of political crises following the coup d'etat by Capt. Moussa Dadis Camara in **Guinea** in 2008. Initial popular support faded when Camara showed keen interest to stay in power instead of returning to the barracks as initially announced. A major opposition demonstration ended with the massacre of scores of opposition supporters by junta soldiers in a Conakry stadium in September. In December Camara was shot in the head by one of his own bodyguards, who had apparently been designated to take responsibility for the stadium killings. While Camara's injuries were being treated in a Moroccan hospital, more moderate officers seized the opportunity to take control. It soon became clear that they did not want Camara to resume power, so that their action was effectively a new coup d'etat.

Peace and War

Overall, the level of violence in on-going armed conflicts was lower than before, with Somalia the obvious exception. Nevertheless, the need to keep peacekeeping missions in place was as strongly resented as ever, pointing to the on-going risk of re-escalation in most former arenas of war. Six UN missions (DRC, Chad/CAR, Liberia, Côte d'Ivoire and Sudan, plus Western Sahara) and the hybrid AU/UN mission in Sudan were maintained on African soil. The AU mission in Somalia, the CEEAC mission in the CAR and the EU forces in Chad and the CAR (until March) had to be added, plus the 1,800 French soldiers deployed in Côte d'Ivoire under the 'operation Licorne' label – a total of nearly 66,000 troops.

As fragile as ever, the **CAR** witnessed new attacks by rebel movements in the north and the east throughout the year, while the Lord's Resistance Army (LRA) attacked villages in the south-east. Ugandan government forces intervened with limited success. Neighbouring **Chad** saw further serious rebel activity, but repulsed a rebel attack on Goz Beida in early May. In spite of this, the country looked more stable than in many previous years. The newly formed alliance between the governments of the **DRC** and Rwanda was taken as good news for peace in an unstable sub-region and allowed for a joint operation against rebel movements in North Kivu, although this failed to halt the violence. In fact, new scores of civilians were forced to leave their villages.

In comparison with previous years, Sudan's **Darfur** province saw also fewer confrontations, except in the month of May. Several rounds of peace talks were, however, inconclusive. When the Justice and Equality Movement (JEM) held discussion rounds with the government facilitated by the government of Qatar in Doha, the second important rebel movement, the Sudan Liberation Movement (SLM) chose not to participate. Libya hosted further talks in October, aimed at bringing a number of smaller factions together. The associated tensions between the governments of Chad and Sudan continued, despite fresh rounds of talks starting in May. In parallel, tensions grew in **Southern Sudan** ahead of the referendum for independence scheduled for 2011, but appeared to be mostly ethnically tainted violence between groups in the south. An estimated 2,500 people were killed in various clashes, with the epicentre located in the major town of Malakal (Upper Nile). In the nearby state of Jonglei, armed Murle, Bor Dinka and Lou Nuer militias engaged in fresh fighting. In addition, two branches of the Nuer group fought each other. And, in October, forces loyal to Paulino Matip (Nuer) and the Dinka-dominated SPLA forces battled in the oil-producing area of Bentiu, necessitating intervention by the UN Mission in Sudan (UNMIS). The mixture of local land disputes and cattle raids, sometimes intensified by the return of demobilised soldiers and displaced people, plus the prospect of new oil discoveries, again turned the south into a powderkeg.

Somalia was the only country at war in Africa with more or less unchanged high levels of violence, including terror attacks perpetrated by al-Shabaab and Hizbul Islam that led to the killing of several top members of the transitional government. One attack targeted the AU peacekeeping mission's compound, killing almost a dozen people, including the Burundian deputy force commander. In May, a new battle for Mogadishu led to the conquest of a greater share of urban territory by al-Shabaab. Suicide bombings and reports of foreigners and diaspora Somalis participating in terror missions again drew international attention to the conflict. Shifting alliances between members and leaders of the warring groups characterised the year in southern Somalia. Somaliland, while on the whole peaceful, also experienced violent incidents. In November, a top military commander was shot and killed. The low-intensity border conflict in the Sanaag-Sool and eastern Togdheer regions between Puntland and Somaliland saw no major change.

Terrorism and Piracy

Al-Qaida in the Islamic Maghreb (AQIM) significantly raised the level and intensity of its activity in **Mauritania**, as well as in **Mali**. On 22 January, AQIM operatives abducted four Europeans along the Mali-Niger border and demanded ransoms plus the release of a Palestinian cleric held in the United Kingdom. A British tourist in this group was killed when the demands were not met. A US citizen and NGO worker was later shot in Mauritania. A suicide bombing near the French embassy in Nouakchott was a further signal of AQIM vitality in this country. Finally, on 29 November, three Spanish aid workers were kidnapped. In Mali, an army convoy was attacked by AQIM-related fighters in July and several soldiers were killed. In Niger, three Saudi tourists were killed in late December.

The **US military presence** on the continent, very much related to the self-assigned mission to combat terrorism, was more indirectly felt than directly seen. The decision on whether to move the Africa command (**AFRICOM**) from Stuttgart (Germany) to Africa was postponed until 2012, officially to allow the command to gain greater understanding of its long-term operational requirements. In reality, few African governments were eager to host a large US military installation within their borders and SADC had even publicly denounced AFRICOM. The South African government said it would not tolerate the presence of an American military structure on its soil. Nigeria, Libya and Botswana made similar statements. The US administration had internal discussions about the obvious failure to create sympathy for AFRICOM in African capitals.

In the Sahel, the Obama administration sought increased funding for the Trans-Saharan **Counter-Terrorism** Program ($ 20 m in 2010) and begun a special security assistance programme for Mali to provide the country with all-terrain vehicles and communications equipment worth $ 5 m, and 300 special forces advisers carried out training exercises with the Malian army. In addition, the administration requested an extra $ 60 m in the 2010 financial year to pay for the operations of the Combined Joint Task Force-Horn of Africa (CJTF-HOA), as well as $ 249 m to pay for the operation of the 500-acre base at Camp Lemonier in Djibouti, plus $ 41.8 m for major improvement construction projects at the base. CJTF-HOA, operating under the aegis of AFRICOM, provided logistical support and supplies to the French-led training of 500 soldiers of the official, but weak, Transitional Federal Government in Somalia. The meteorological (and oceanographic) department of the task force was deployed to Uganda from 28 September to 3 October in preparation for the humanitarian exercise "Natural Fire". More importantly, the CJTF-HOA was expanding its range to include Comoros, Mauritius and Madagascar in the Indian Ocean. In January, the US Navy inaugurated a Combined Task Force 151 (CTF-151), and on 3 May handed over the command to Turkey. CTF-151 was primarily meant to combat piracy and free CTF-150, operating since 2002 and currently under French command, to combat terrorism, its original task. Together with NATO and the European naval operation Atalanta, the vessels at the disposal of the two CTFs made up for an impressive armada. They were able to report some success, but did not manage to halt pirate activities.

In fact, the International Maritime Bureau (IMB) reported that there were 406 reported **incidents of piracy** and armed attacks on the high seas during the year, the highest level in six years, and that attacks were becoming more frequent and violent: 217 attacks on vessels were recorded with 47 of them successful. Attacks remained concentrated in the Gulf of Aden between Yemen and the northern cost of Somalia and along Somalia's eastern coastline. The threat from piracy in the Indian Ocean arguably increased because additional resources were being committed to piracy by Somali and Yemeni 'investors' and because of the increasing sophistication of the tactics and technology available. Pirates operating off the coast of Somalia also expanded their forays into an area stretching to the Seychelles and even Madagascar. The business of piracy flourished with seaborne gangs seizing several cargo ships and demanding millions of dollars in ransom. Among the most spectacular acts was the hijacking in January of a German-owned tanker carrying liquefied petroleum gas in the Gulf of Aden. In April, Somali pirates also seized a US-flagged container ship with 20 American crewmembers on board. The ship's cargo was 400 containers of food aid, including 232 containers belonging to the World Food Program and destined for Somalia and Uganda. On 19 October, a Chinese coal carrier with 25 Chinese crewmembers aboard was kidnapped. A US super tanker, carrying crude oil from Saudi Arabia to the United States worth more than $ 20 m, was also seized. But **West Africa**'s coasts became increasingly dangerous, too. On 24 November, pirates attacked a German-owned oil tanker off the coast of Benin, robbing the tanker and killing a Ukrainian officer onboard. However, most attacks occurred along the Nigerian coastline. The Nigerian authorities recorded more than 40 pirate attacks on tankers, barges, oil-industry back-up vessels and oil platforms involving robbery, damage to vessels, and the injury and kidnapping of ships' crews, as well as the hijacking of vessels. According to the IMB, the waters of Nigeria became the second most dangerous in the world, after Somalia. Attacks were also recorded all along the Gulf of Guinea in the waters stretching from Angola in the south to Guinea in the west. Equipped with new technology, seaborne rebels and pirates also continued to operate in coastal towns. In February, pirates attacked **Equatorial Guinea's** island capital, where they tried to storm the country's presidential palace. Motivations were not always clear as some groups carrying out attacks in the Gulf of Guinea described themselves as freedom fighters, while others were clearly nothing but well organised criminal gangs.

Epidemics and Disasters

People continued to suffer from **natural disasters**. Heavy seasonal rainfall caused floods in many parts of West Africa and Chad (July-August). Among the rivers that broke their banks and caused destruction were the Niger, Volta and Senegal rivers. About 1 m people were affected by the consequences of torrential rainfall in Benin, Burkina Faso, Côte d'Ivoire, Ghana, Guinea, Niger, Nigeria, Senegal and Sierra Leone; about 200 people died. In Burkina Faso alone, about 150,000 people had to take shelter. Despite the floods, irregular rainfall in parts of northern Nigeria and Niger shortened the crop season and led to malnutrition in certain areas. Earlier, floods had hit Southern Africa (March-May) with Namibia, Zambia and Botswana most affected. The Zambezi carried enormous quantities of water, raising its level to unprecedented heights in many places. Despite the loss of crops, food security in Southern Africa improved compared with previous years. The effects of global climate change were most visible in Eastern Africa where Kenya experienced another very dry year.

The severe **cholera** outbreak in Zimbabwe continued, with 55 out of 62 districts in all ten provinces affected. The infection rate declined slowly between February and May, but Mozambique and Zambia became equally heavily affected during the year. The WHO World Malaria Report 2009 recorded progress in the containment of **malaria** in the endemic countries, despite massive shortfalls in international disbursements to these countries. In 2008, 80% of external funds were targeted at the African region.

Figures on the **HIV/AIDS** pandemic did not differ much from previous years. According to UNAIDS figures based on data for 2008, sub-Saharan Africa remained most heavily affected, with 67% of all people with HIV and 72% of AIDS-related deaths. It accounted for an estimated 1.9 m or 68% of new infections among adults and 91% among children. More than 14 m children had lost one or both parents to AIDS. The number of new infections on the continent decreased over time, but the number of people living with HIV increased, partly because of better treatment leading to longer life expectancy: 44% of those in need of antiretroviral therapy had access to treatment (in contrast to only 2% five years earlier). Significant variations in infection rates between countries and sub-regions continued, with most rates having stabilised, though at very high levels, especially in parts of Southern Africa. Women and girls remained disproportionally affected, with 60% of all infections.

Andreas Mehler, Henning Melber & Klaas van Walraven

II. United Nations and Sub-Saharan Africa

The work by the UN and the AU concerning the norm of a global '**Responsibility to Protect**' (R2P) was in the spotlight during the year. On 21 July, the UN Secretary General Ban Ki-moon presented his January report entitled 'Implementing the Responsibility to Protect' to the UN General Assembly (UNGA). Following this, an unprecedented UNGA plenary debate on the R2P took place (23–24 and 28 July). African state leaders, but also the five permanent members of the UN Security Council (UNSC), spoke in support of the R2P. African states called for a global consensus on R2P because of the prevalence of wars in sub-Saharan Africa. Their support also sprang from the fact that African institutions in this area are at the forefront of normative and institutional developments. This global meeting of 92 governments offered African states a rare occasion for positive attention: they upheld the continent's contributions in adopting strong provisions for the prevention and halting of mass atrocity crimes and, in turn, received promises regarding assistance and capacity-building.

Africa in the UN

African states earned recognition at the highest levels for the importance of their assistance in ongoing efforts to **protect African civilians**. Eighteen African states spoke at the July UNGA debate on the R2P. Among the stronger supportive voices were Benin, Ghana, Nigeria, Rwanda and Sierra Leone, but also previous R2P sceptics, such as Algeria and South Africa. Sudan failed to convince other states that the purpose of the debate was to renegotiate the R2P. However, African states together helped ensure a continued important role for the UNGA in considering the norm and its implementation. This was to counter what some states, such as Sudan, consider a politicised Security Council control over the agenda, which might enable violations of sovereignty principles. On 14 September, the UNGA adopted by consensus a first-ever resolution on this topic, ensuring that body's continued consideration of the R2P. Prominent Africans, such as Mohamed Sahnoun, Desmond Tutu, Kofi Annan and Ngugi wa Thiong'o, spoke in favour of the norm throughout the year, as did African parliamentarians and representatives from African civil society.

There was a critical sub-Saharan response to the **indictment of Sudanese President** Omar Hassan Ahmed al-Bashir for war crimes and crimes against humanity. The process was officially initiated in April by Chief ICC Prosecutor Luis Moreno-Ocampo. The AU, at its July Summit in Sirte, Libya, regretted that the UNSC had not acted on the AU's request to defer the indictment of al-Bashir, which had been made on the grounds that the case against the Sudanese leader might undermine the delicate peace process underway in Sudan. In Sirte, African leaders decided to refuse to extradite al-Bashir to stand trial, pursuant to the provisions of Article 98 of the Rome Statute of the ICC relating to immunities of state officials. The only country to disagree with the decision was Botswana, while Chad "expressed reservations". Nonetheless, representatives of South African civil society recalled that, as a State Party to the Rome Statute, South Africa was obliged to cooperate fully with the ICC in the arrest and transfer of al-Bashir to the ICC. The decision to refuse stood in conflict with South Africa's constitution and laws. While African leaders did not achieve a deferral of the indictment process, a debate began at the highest levels to examine the ICC's role in relation to Africa. It raised strong concerns with the "abuse of the principle of universal jurisdiction", despite the existence of immunity for state officials. However, despite the AU's defiant position, the organisation was at pains to stress its commitment to combating impunity and promoting democracy and the rule of law throughout Africa. In this context, it condemned the gross violations of human rights in Darfur and appointed an **AU High-Level Panel on Darfur** (AUPD). This investigatory panel symbolised the African view of Darfur as a case where the efforts of the AU, in cooperation with the UN, should be allowed to bear fruit and where peace talks and reconciliation (preferably indigenous) might produce a better result than penal justice as understood and carried out by a Court based outside of the continent. The AUPD's intense efforts between March and October were endorsed at the AU Peace and Security Council meeting on 29 October. The AU initiated the implementation, through the existing AU-UN meditation framework and Chief Joint Darfur Mediator Djibril Bassolé, of a 'roadmap' towards a Global Political Agreement (GPA) for Sudan.

A rare show of force and unity in global negotiations by African countries, together with other developing countries, helped mark the **world summit on climate change** in Copenhagen, Denmark, in December. The Copenhagen Conference of Parties to the UN Framework Convention on Climate Change (UNFCCC) ended in chagrin. A non-binding accord was ultimately brokered by the US, China, India, South Africa, Brazil and the EU. It put in place a 'pledge-and-review' process, in which individual nations make voluntary commitments on emission cuts, to be verified by an international mechanism to be developed by the UNFCCC secretariat. This was unsatisfactory from a sub-Saharan African viewpoint. The African position on climate change built on the Nairobi Declaration from the Special Session of the African Ministerial Conference on the Environment (AMCEN), in collaboration with UNEP, in May. The African delegation pushed a **'carbon justice' agenda**, demanding compensation for the damage to its economies caused by global warming on the grounds that Africa had contributing virtually nothing to it, and ensuring that the resource flow to Africa was not reduced. The Africa group, supported by the Group of 77 and China, walked out of negotiations in protest at what they saw as a move by developed countries away from commitments under the Kyoto Protocol, and away from binding stipulations for the reduction of greenhouse gas emissions and penalties for defaulters. This brought about a serious stalemate in negotiations, and put the focus on the lack of political will among richer states. Africa wanted carbon emission cuts to be raised to 40% by 2020 and developed countries to strengthen the institutional capacity of developing countries to adapt to the impact of climate change. AU Climate Negotiator, Ethiopian President Meles Zenawi, controversially asked for $ 10 bn a year in global short-term finance, with 40% of this for Africa, and long-term financing that would reach $ 50 bn by 2015 and $ 100 bn by 2020. He was criticised from within the African delegation, as his proposal did not press developed countries to commit themselves to capping greenhouse gas emissions. South Africa was also unhappy with Zenawi's request, considering that at least double the amount of finance would be appropriate.

Peace and Security

A stronger **AU-UN partnership** was promoted by the UN Secretary General and his Under-Secretary General for Peacekeeping Operations, Alain Le Roy, as well as the AU and the African Group in New York. Ban Ki-moon issued a report on 18 September about support to UN-authorised AU peacekeeping operations. It included a detailed assessment of the recommendations of the 'Prodi panel' (headed by former Italian prime minister Romano Prodi), released on 31 December the previous year. Ban Ki-moon's report bore signs of intense consultation between the UN Secretariat and the AU Commission and relayed the AU's request for the UNSC to discuss the Prodi report and to consider ways to ensure predictable, sustainable and flexible funding for **AU-led peacekeeping operations**. And, specifically, to examine, within the context of Chapter VIII of the UN Charter, the possibility of funding, through the UN's assessed contributions, peacekeeping operations undertaken by the AU or under its authority. The Secretary General noted that using UN-assessed funding for AU-led and UN-authorised peacekeeping operations on a case-by-case basis (for up to six months, to be provided mainly in kind, and when there was an intention to transition the mission to a UN peacekeeping operation) would underline the political support of the UNSC for peacekeeping operations at the regional level. However, such a proposal as a general rule remained sensitive. In a presidential statement in October, the UNSC merely agreed to consider all options. It recognised the AU's view that, in deploying UN-authorised peacekeeping operations, the AU was contributing towards maintenance of international peace and security. Even so, some UN member states were concerned that UN-funded regional operations could dangerously put the the UN's credibility at risk unless the AU implemented 'appropriate' political and security objectives. The UNSC called upon the AU to speedily develop a comprehensive capacity-building road map in consultation with the UN and other international partners. In addition, the

UN Security Council welcomed the intention of the UN Secretariat and the AU Commission to set up a joint task force on peace and security to review immediate and long-term strategic and operational issues. The UNSC also reiterated the importance of establishing a more effective strategic relationship with the AU Peace and Security Council, and between the UN Secretariat and the AU Commission, as had also been expressed in an AU-UN joint communiqué in May.

Under the auspices of the 2006 AU-UN ten-year **capacity-building programme**, the UN Departments of Political Affairs, Peacekeeping Operations and Field Support worked with Africa on a number of initiatives, including capacity-building in mediation, elections, conflict resolution, early-warning, peacekeeping planning and operations, rule of law and security sector reform. Plans were made to better integrate the UN Secretariat presence in Addis Ababa. In order to more effectively engage the UN Secretariat and member states on the African peace and security issues on the UNSC agenda, the AU Commission also agreed to enhance the capacity of the Office of the Permanent Observer of the AU to the UN.

On several occasions, the UNSC chose to defer to **regional initiatives** on specific situations. One example was ECOWAS's response plan to the increasing drug trafficking and organised crime in West Africa. The AU Commission, in collaboration with the UN and its Specialised Agency on Drug Control (UNODC), as well as ECOWAS and other Regional Economic Communities (RECs), agreed to intensify the fight against drug trafficking in Africa, particularly in West Africa. The issue was raised during the year by Ugandan Ambassador Ruhakana Rugunda, chair of the Ad Hoc Working Group on Conflict Prevention and Resolution in Africa, by UN Special Representative and head of the UN Office for West Africa (UNOWA), Said Djinnit, as well as by UNODC. Another example was that the UN Security Council supported the actions taken by the AU and ECOWAS, and the mediation undertaken by Burkina Faso's President Blaise Compaore with regard to political instability in **Guinea**. The UNSC and ECOWAS agreed to establish an international commission of inquiry to investigate the events that saw members of the army open fire on civilians attending a rally. The UNSC noted the decision by the AU Peace and Security Council to impose targeted sanctions against the president of the National Council for Democracy and Development (CNDD) and other individuals, and the decision of ECOWAS to impose an arms embargo on Guinea. Adding weight to the issue, the UN Security Council determined that Guinea might pose a risk to regional peace and security following the killings that occurred in Conakry on 28 September.

Moreover, in a May presidential statement, the UNSC articulated its support for the AU's condemnation of the resurgence of **coups d'état**. This built on a Ugandan draft presidential statement which had been circulated to support the AU's February decision to condemn the coups that took place in Mauritania in August 2008 and Guinea in December 2008, and the attempted coup in Guinea-Bissau in August 2008. However, the UNSC chose not to comment specifically on the AU's sanctions on countries such as Mauritania.

At the end of the year, it decided to impose arms sanctions and an asset freeze on **Eritrea** for its rejection of the Djibouti Agreement and for its actions undermining peace and reconciliation in Somalia. This action had been requested at the July AU Summit. Additionally, Djibouti's Permanent Representative to the UN had warned at the UNGA against 'appeasing' Eritrea's 'dangerous regime'.

The UN Department of Peacekeeping Operations (DPKO) had six out of a total of 15 peacekeeping missions and one out of two political missions deployed in sub-Saharan Africa. 2009 marked the tenth year of the deployment of the UN Mission in the **DRC** (MONUC). The mission endeavoured to protect civilians and to assist DRC government armed forces in their struggle against foreign armed groups, notably the Forces Démocratiques de Libération du Rwanda (FDLR) and the Lords Resistance Army (LRA), as well as home-grown militias. MONUC was severely criticised for its joint operations with government armed forces in taking on the FDLR. The 'Kimia II' campaign, launched in North and South Kivu, led to grave humanitarian consequences, such as reprisal attacks against civilians. Elements within the army were also involved in attacks on civilians. Such outcomes made MONUC a case in point as the UN Security Council reinvigorated its commitment to the protection of civilians and to the promotion of respect for the principles of international humanitarian law, human rights law and refugee law, in a November resolution – a timely decision, since it was the tenth anniversary of the theme 'protection of civilians in armed conflict' as a distinct consideration by the UNSC. The resolution made a clear link to African contributions, taking note of the AU's adoption of the AU **Convention for the Protection and Assistance of IDPs**.

The AU-UN Hybrid Operation in **Darfur** (UNAMID) was the years' costliest and the second largest in terms of personnel. The mission encouraged greater dialogue between local Sudanese authorities and IDPs and provided round-the-clock security patrols at IDP camps. UNAMID tried to enhance the capacity of the government and police to address human rights violations and inadequacies in the local judicial services, and it set up a gender crimes special investigation unit. The security situation remained volatile and the political process complex. Kidnappings, tribal clashes, banditry and attacks against peacekeepers complicated the mission's work. Nine peacekeepers were killed in hostile actions. The humanitarian obstacles worsened following the ICC indictment of President al-Bashir: Sudan expelled 13 international NGOs from the country and shut down many national NGOs. By the close of 2009, the mission still lacked the requested 18 utility and five tactical helicopters, two surveillance aircraft and two heavy transport units.

In response to an unusually violent and politically unstable year in **southern Sudan**, the UN Mission in Sudan (UNMIS) undertook a proactive approach to peacekeeping. It defused tensions in the aftermath of violent clashes in several hotspots in the area of deployment through 'robust patrols' and by airlifting in leading members of the Sudan People's Liberation Movement (SPLM). As inter-tribal turmoil escalated, the mission implemented a stabilisation programme in Jonglei State to curtail the fighting. Some progress was achieved towards implementing the 2005 Comprehensive Peace Agreement (CPA) in areas such as voter registration, police training and child protection, and on the issue of the disputed boundaries of the oil-rich area of Abyei. The National Congress Party (NCP) and the SPLM accepted the 22 July ruling by the Permanent Court of Arbitration in The Hague on the Abyei boundary dispute. UNMIS helped launch the Sudan disarmament, demobilisation and reintegration (DDR) programme. Marauding bands of gunmen belonging to the LRA continued terrorising communities living near southern Sudan's border with the DRC and the Central African Republic (CAR).

The UN Mission in the **CAR and Chad** (MINURCAT) was endowed with a military component as it assumed responsibilities from the EU force (EUFOR) on 15 March. The UNSC had authorised the deployment of 5,200 troops in January, tasking the mission to help create conditions conducive to a voluntary, secure and sustainable return of refugees (263,000 from neighbouring Darfur) and 180,000 IDPs encamped in eastern Chad at the start of the year. In mid-January, clashes between rebel factions and the CAR government resulted in a new influx of refugees from north eastern CAR into the Salamat region of Chad. The UNHCR estimated that approximately 16,000 new refugees arrived, bringing the total number of refugees receiving humanitarian aid in Chad to approximately 320,000. However, MINURCAT struggled to consolidate its presence, with just over 2,000 troops deployed. Force Commander Major-General Elhadji Mouhamedou Kandji (Senegal) directed the troops to advise and deploy the special Chadian security force, the Détachement Intégré de Sécurité (DIS) of around 820 men and women, to maintain law and order in refugee camps, IDP sites and surrounding towns.

A new addition to field operations was the UN Support Office for the AU Mission in **Somalia** (AMISOM), dubbed UNSOA. This unique operation was headquartered in Nairobi, Kenya, since Mogadishu remained at security level 5 for the UN (meaning no international staff can live there). In Nairobi, UNSOA and AMISOM cooperated and liaised with the UN Political Office for Somalia (UNPOS) and the UN country team. UNSOA began implementing its mandate to deliver support packages to AMISOM similar to those of a traditional UN peacekeeping mission. Such logistical support was part of the UN's 'three-phase plan' in Somalia: to strengthen the security sector of the Somali Transitional Federal Government (TFG), to create a 'light footprint' for the UN and, when conditions allow, to transition from AMISOM to a UN peacekeeping operation, pending SC approval. The AU has pushed strongly for such a transition, but the year merely saw continued discussions on bringing AMISOM's force levels of just over 5,000 troops from Burundi and Uganda up to the mandated strength of 8,000. By the end of February, a newly elected government relocated to Mogadishu. AMISOM helped in holding strategic positions and government installations against threats from Somali extremists, aided and abetted by foreign fighters. One of the worst security incidents occurred on 17 September, when Al-Shabaab insurgents attacked the AMISOM force headquarters, killing 21 people including four Somali civilians and five Ugandan and 12 Burundian peacekeepers.

Ahmedou Ould-Abdallah, head of UNPOS, urged world leaders to provide AMISOM and the TFG with stronger diplomatic support and increased financial backing. In April, donors pledged around $ 200 m at a UN-EU sponsored conference in Brussels in support of AMISOM and Somali security institutions. Later in the year, over two-thirds of pledges had been collected.

The UN Operation in **Côte d'Ivoire** (UNOCI) assisted the process leading up to national elections, which had been postponed but were expected for early 2010. It lent its boats, helicopters and land vehicles to carry equipment for use in a population identification and voter registration operation, reaching difficult to access localities. More than 6 m people registered throughout the country during the operation, which lasted from September 2008 to June. The UNSC and the Secretariat continued the process of a phased downsizing and demilitarisation of the UN Mission in **Liberia** (UNMIL). In September, the mission was extended for one more year, which is hoped to be the last. Liberia officially ended its DDR programme on 15 July. In less than five years, some 101,000 ex-combatants were disarmed and demobilised.

The UN **Peacebuilding Commission** (PBC), Fund and Support Office were active in Burundi, CAR, Guinea-Bissau and Sierra Leone. The Fund also supported peacebuilding projects in Côte d'Ivoire, Guinea, Liberia, the DRC, Kenya, Comoros and Somalia. The UN Integrated Peacebuilding Office in Sierra Leone (UNIPSIL) worked with the government on implementing its Agenda for Change and the supporting UN joint vision for Sierra Leone. The PBC engagement in Sierra Leone was bolstered by approximately $ 37 m from the Peacebuilding Fund. Political missions in CAR (BONUCA) and Guinea-Bissau (UNOGBIS) are expected to transform into integrated peacebuilding offices in early 2010. Guinea-Bissau's Prime Minister Carlos Gomes Jr. told the UNGA in September that his government deemed it essential to determine who was responsible for a series of assassinations of senior political and military figures earlier in the year, which had been condemned by the UNSC and the AU. He pledged on behalf of his government, which he said had come to power in recent elections that had been deemed free, fair and transparent by international observers, to facilitate the work of the committee tasked with finding out who carried out the killings. The UN Integrated Office in Burundi (BINUB) focussed on DDR activities and on assisting in the country's preparations for elections next year. During Uganda's presidency of the UNSC in July, a debate was held at ministerial level on **post-conflict peacebuilding**. The debate resulted in a presidential statement, reiterating the UNSC's commitment to more effective and efficient peacebuilding, and sustainable development in post-conflict situations.

Economic Performance and Development

In May, the **Economic Report on Africa** by the AU Commission and the ECA outlined the impact of the global economic crisis on African nations. The report set out the year's priorities for sub-Saharan Africa: modernising agriculture for development and industrialisation in Africa, ensuring food security, sustained poverty reduction, and integration of Africa into the global economy. It noted that Africa was heavily dependent on the agricultural sector for providing employment, generating economic growth, foreign exchange earnings and tax revenue. Though Africa was the continent with the largest agricultural potential per hectare and per capita, it remained a net food importer. To address these priorities, the report recommended working through the **Comprehensive Africa Agriculture Development Programme** (CAADP), adopted by the AU in 2003. Similarly, the theme of the AU Summit in July was 'investing in agriculture for economic growth and food security'. African leaders re-enforced the 2003 Maputo Declaration commitment, to set aside 10% of their annual budgets for the agriculture sector, which has to date seen uneven implementation. They stated that the principal way to tackle the global food crisis was to offer assistance to small farmers.

African states grew more outspoken on world economic affairs after the **G8 Summit** on 8–10 July, to which they were invited, revealed that the world's richest nations were failing to meet their landmark pledge, made at the 2005 Gleneagles summit, to double to $ 50 bn a year by 2010 their aid to the poorest countries. The US and Britain were on course to meet their target shares, but Italy and France were falling short. Italian Prime Minister Silvio Berlusconi was perceived as failing to give a lead on aid at the L'Aquila summit. The meeting resulted in G8 leaders merely 'reaffirming' their Gleneagles promises. They agreed to review in 2010 the progress they had made towards meeting the MDGs by the 2015 deadline. With regard to food security, G8 leaders did agree to **a food security initiative**: a $ 20 bn package to tackle world hunger, including a switch from emergency relief to long-term agricultural projects. This was $ 5 bn more than planned, some of it 'new' money. African leaders wanted a follow-up and implementation of the G8 Summit decisions on Africa, but welcomed the food security initiative and the commitment of the UN High Level Task Force on Food Security to strengthen CAADP and to operationalise agricultural investment through it.

The 64th UNGA centred on themes pertinent to sub-Saharan Africa, namely climate change, the MDGs and guiding principles of international cooperation, especially equity and democracy. At the UNGA annual high-level debate (23–30 September), African states including Lesotho and Benin urged donor countries to deliver on past pledges for **official development assistance** (ODA). They argued that this was even more necessary than before, given the context of a global financial crisis, which had had adverse effects in Africa, such as increased poverty and acute hunger, especially since the crisis was hitting hardest those who had no part in causing it. Using the same argument, Ban Ki-moon urged the simultaneous G20 meeting in Pittsburgh on 24–25 September to fulfill their aid pledges, beginning with the $ 50 bn for the poorest, pledged by the G20 summit in 2008. Earlier in the year, the G20 had pledged a $ 1.1 tr stimulus package for the world economy, the bulk of which was for developing countries. They had also agreed to give emerging and developing economies a greater voice and representation in international financial institutions. This was partly a result of efforts by South Africa, being the only country from sub-Saharan Africa with a seat on the G20 gathering. South Africa argued at the UNGA that the major international financial and institutions, including the World Bank and the IMF, needed reform so as to include representatives of the developing world in the process of forging a more equitable and stable global economic system. Ethiopian Prime Minister Meles Zenawi, the only representative from Africa outside of the G20, in his capacity as chair of NEPAD, asked for special funds to be made available for Africa immediately. Several African countries argued in the UNGA that the global trade system should be rectified to remove hindrances to poor nations' participation in the global economy, and that G20 'commitment' should translate into action on finalising the Doha Development Round of world trade talks. President Robert Mugabe of Zimbabwe, supported by AU and SADC, strongly condemned the 'illegal' **sanctions against Zimbabwe** by the US and the EU, adding that they were especially harmful in the midst of the current global economic crisis.

In November, UN Deputy-SG Asha-Rose Migiro reiterated at a meeting of the ECA Regional Coordination Mechanism (RCM) that Africa's efforts to meet the **MDGs** by 2015 were threatened by the impact of the global financial crisis. Participants examined how the UN system, international donors and African states might collaborate to implement the recommendations issued in July 2008 by the MDG Africa Steering Group chaired by Ban Ki-moon. The Group, once again, called for investments in agriculture, reforms of the global trade regime and short-term funds from donors to help the continent meet short-term needs that have arisen as a result of soaring food prices. It also urged African governments to work with global partners to launch a Green Revolution on the continent. Earlier in the year, UNCTAD had also recommended African states to build more resilient economies through deepening regional integration. Its report released in June, 'Economic Development in Africa 2009: Strengthening regional economic integration for Africa's development', said that better links between countries, ranging from paved roads to banking cooperation, were needed to spur mutual economic growth, because weak physical and institutional infrastructure constituted key obstacles to increasing intra-African trade and investment.

Towards the end of the year, agriculture and the **food crisis** were high on the global agenda. At a High-Level Expert Forum in October on How to Feed the World in 2050, FAO Director-General Jacques Diouf called on governments to ensure enhanced agricultural productivity if it were to feed a growing world population as well as respond to the environmental challenges ahead. He said the combined effects of climate change could reduce potential agricultural output by up to 30%. Recommendations relevant to Africa included a special focus on smallholder farmers, women and rural households, and their access to land, water and high quality seeds and other modern inputs, increasing yield growth and improving cropping intensity by turning to organic agriculture rather than farming more land, despite the fact that there are still ample land resources with potential for cultivation in sub-Saharan Africa. The attention to these issues culminated at the **World Summit on Food Security** on 16–18 November in Rome. The FAO unveiled a $ 60 m five-year programme to encourage sustainable low-emission agriculture in developing countries. The FAO found that, while agriculture is responsible for 14% of greenhouse gas emissions, the sector has the potential to slash output by removing carbon dioxide from the atmosphere. Methods such as smallholder agriculture, conservation, organic agriculture, no or low tillage and use of compost or mulch, may account for almost 90% of agriculture's potential to curb or remove emissions from the atmosphere. In addition, a $ 1 bn agreement was signed in Rome by the FAO, the Islamic Development Bank (IDB) and a leading Brazilian university. The agreement covers funding for agricultural development in 26 least-developed countries that are members of both the Bank and the FAO. The total investment in the IDB-FAO programme amounts to $ 5 bn by 2012. The guiding insight is that sustained investment in agriculture – especially **smallholder agriculture** – is acknowledged as the key to food security. This came as the FAO was warning that critical food insecurity was affecting 31 countries, the situation being particularly acute in East Africa, but also serious in West Africa. After the continuous attention on food security throughout the year, it was a disappointment that the more than 60 world leaders meeting at the food summit in Rome, agreed on a declaration without measurable targets or specific deadlines for eradicating world hunger. The summit unanimously adopted a declaration 'renewing a commitment' to eradicate hunger sustainably and at the earliest date. It did not go along with the FAO proposal to set a target of 2025 for total eradication of hunger from the face of the earth and increasing ODA to agriculture to $ 44 bn per year for investment in developing-country agriculture and rural infrastructure. It did, however, sign up to a 'Global Partnership for Agriculture, Food Security and Nutrition', committed to renewed efforts to achieve the first MDG of halving hunger by 2015, improved international coordination through broadened participation by the public and private sector, international funding for agriculture in developing countries, and new investments in agricultural production there. To mitigate the impact of high food prices, the WFP launched an Emergency Market Mitigation Account initiative and allocated a total of $ 181 m to 18 priority countries in Africa alone to assist governments to meet the urgent call for high food price assistance through new and enhanced social safety nets.

Governance/Human Rights

The African group in New York, and particularly South Africa, participated actively in the **Durban Review Conference** in Geneva, Switzerland (20–24 April). This was a follow-up meeting to the 2001 UN World Conference against Racism, Racial Discrimination, Xenophobia and Related Intolerances. African states were content that the meeting resulted in the adoption by consensus, by 182 states, of an outcome document that reaffirmed the political commitment to the implementation of the Durban Declaration and Programme of Action (DDPA) of 2001. The document highlighted the continued existence of victims of many different sorts of racism and intolerance; it reaffirmed the positive role of freedom of expression in the fight against racism, while also deploring derogatory stereotyping and stigmatisation of people based on their religion or belief; and it launched a process to examine how the prohibition of incitement to hatred, as reflected in Article 20 of the International Covenant on Civil and Political Rights, has been implemented in various parts of the world. African leaders' influence was seen in how the document acknowledged the economic basis of racism; that the transatlantic slave trade and slavery were crimes against humanity; and that the descendants of those victims were owed compensation (reparations). The AU's July Summit threw its weight behind the process to further review the progress of implementation of the DDPA by all national, regional and international stakeholders. The AU welcomed the resolution passed by the US Senate in which it apologised for the slave trade and the racism that evolved from it. But this apology did not stop the AU from keeping the door open for reparative claims, a priority set, for example, by the expert group meeting on slavery in Banjul, Gambia, in June of the previous year. The AU deplored the boycott of the meeting by states such as Israel and the US. A related and positive surprise was that the US for the first time sought and achieved a seat for a three-year term on the UN Human Rights Council.

Botswana and Namibia were leading in the process of getting the **Declaration on the Rights of Indigenous People** adopted by the UNGA in 2007. It was therefore significant that Botswana was one of the first countries to be reviewed by the UN Special Rapporteur on the situation of human rights and fundamental freedom of indigenous people. In March, the Rapporteur disclosed that Botswana's indigenous peoples still struggle to gain access to health services, education and employment opportunities, despite national efforts to improve their situation. Botswana was advised to renew efforts to take into account the language, culture and heritage of those most affected, to ensure better recognition and less discrimination. The non-binding declaration sets out the individual and collective rights of indigenous peoples, as well as their rights to culture, identity, language, employment, health and education, and other issues.

Namibia argued at the UNGA that it should take a tougher line against **undemocratic transfers of power**, highlighting what it called the AU principle position of not recognising governments that come to power through military coups. Namibia had been leading in the 25 September UNGA ruling to deny permission to address the high-level segment of the Assembly's 64th session to a delegation from Madagascar, where violent political unrest earlier this year led to the ousting of the president. The AU has suspended Madagascar and African governments threatened to walk out if Madagascar were allowed to speak. More controversially, Namibia called for governments that come to power through coups d'état to be banned from participating in all UN institutions. Present in the chamber, of course, were many other governments that had come to power through undemocratic means. At the UNGA on 28 September, the DRC and Niger called for proper **African representation on the UNSC**. They advanced the AU's position, which is that the UNSC should be reformed and enlarged, particularly since two thirds of the issues it addresses concern the continent of Africa.

In February, an **AU gender policy** was adopted, pursuant to the Maseru Declaration from the meeting of ministers in charge of Gender and Women's Affairs held in Maseru, Lesotho, in December of the previous year. AU Chairperson, Jean Ping, said, "This will ensure gender issues remain a permanent policy on Africa's development." The policy provided for the setting of a target of reserving at least 30% of all government positions in every country for women.

At year's end, the RCM reviewed the AU-UN ten-year **capacity-building programme**, which aims to enhance the capacity of the AU Commission and African regional and sub-regional organisations to act as effective partners in addressing political, peace and security, and socioeconomic challenges in Africa. The participants agreed to re-examine and reprioritise the framework, to include, for example, issues such as climate change, and to improve on AU ownership.

A UNICEF campaign to bring **education to African children** announced in September that it was expanding to reach millions more after exceeding its initial target by raising more than $ 50 m. The Schools for Africa partnership, set up in 2004 by UNICEF, the Nelson Mandela Foundation (NMF) and the Hamburg Society, helps over 4 m children in Angola, Malawi, Mozambique, Rwanda, South Africa and Zimbabwe to access the basic human right to basic education. Having amassed $ 71 m to date, phase II of the scheme will expand to Ethiopia, Madagascar, Mali, Niger and Burkina Faso. The funds will be used to provide new classrooms, textbooks, chairs, desks and tables, safe drinking water, health checks, school meals, immunisation, etc.

Humanitarian Assistance /Refugees/Environment

The 2009 **humanitarian appeal** by the UN Office for the Coordination of Humanitarian Affairs (OCHA) raised the record-sum of $ 7 bn. The most serious humanitarian crises were in sub-Saharan Africa: CAR, Chad, Côte d'Ivoire and DRC, and regions in Kenya, Somalia, Sudan, Uganda, the West African region and Zimbabwe. In the Horn of Africa, UN agencies responded to the severe and prolonged **drought** that was causing acute humanitarian needs in Kenya and in neighbouring Somalia. Food insecurity in Kenya deepened, and its refugee camps saw a new influx of Somalis. Floods in north-eastern Kenya in November worsened the situation. In Somalia, the number of displaced people was swelling. Fears were expressed that the wider Horn of Africa region would experience devastating **floods** in the next few months as a result of the El Niño weather phenomenon. In Uganda, the situation was becoming stable and resettlement programmes continued. Zimbabwe had a generally good harvest, which slightly reduced the number of severely food-insecure people. At the same time, humanitarian operations in the country increased because the power-sharing government facilitated humanitarian action and access. The biggest appeal was for Sudan, at just over $ 2 bn, with the appeal for the DRC up from $ 600 m in 2008 to $ 830 m. UNICEF reported thatmore than 100,000 children in the DRC were on the run in North Kivu and South Kivu provinces, either with their families or separated from them. There was a spike in recruitment of children by armed groups and sexual violence had increased. In Somalia, while the hijacking of ships by pirates was galvanising media attention, UNICEF struggled to amass the funds to assist some 180,000 acutely malnourished children. In West Africa, over a 160 people are thought to have died as a result of floods. In September, the UN faced a $ 5 bn shortfall in funding for their operations. During the year, two flash appeals were made following disasters in Namibia and Madagascar, the latter emergency stemming from a combination of drought and civil unrest. African crisis situations continued to be dangerous places, and the UN Emergency Relief Coordinator John Holmes told the UNSC that he was particularly concerned for humanitarian personnel in Chad, the DRC and Somalia.

African heads of state adopted an AU convention for the **protection and assistance of IDPs** at a special summit on refugees, returnees and IDPs in Africa, in October in Kampala, Uganda, where the AU tabled the world's first legal framework to prevent or mitigate, prohibit and eliminate root causes of internal displacement, as well as to provide for durable solutions, through regional and national measures. The convention includes obligations upon states, international organisations and humanitarian agencies. When the convention is applied, state parties will respect several obligations relating to the protection and assistance of IDPs and avoid situations that create forced displacement. According to the AU, forced displacement in Africa is mostly attributable to the acts or omissions of the state, such as human rights violations, political and socioeconomic marginalisation, and conflicts over natural resources. At the start of 2010, the UNHCR congratulated Africa because 25 states had already signed the convention and the Ugandan government became the first to ratify it. Bahame Tom Nyanduga, AU Special Rapporteur on Refugees, Asylum Seekers and IDPs in Africa, called on African states to accept responsibility for addressing human rights abuses faced by IDPs, deploring the fact that armed combatants in Somalia, Liberia, Sierra Leone, northern Uganda, Darfur and eastern DRC had violated the Geneva Convention's protocol on civilian protection with impunity. NGOs in Africa were content that the adopted convention was now legally binding, but they want to see implementation and a determined AU role concerning effective enforcement.

In January, the **UNHCR Regional Liaison Office** in Addis Ababa was split into two offices: the Representation in Ethiopia and the Representation to the AU and the ECA

(RAUECA). The RAUECA continued diplomatic negotiations geared to influence Africa's policies on refugees. The priority of the year was to mobilise support and resources for the AU Special Summit on Refugees, Returnees and IDPs in Africa, within the context of the AU-UN ten-year capacity-building programme. The UNHCR made monetary contributions of $ 170,000 to support the development of the AU's IDP convention, and an additional $ 350,000 towards organising the AU Special Summit on forced displacement.

At the beginning of the year, an estimated 11.6 m people were IDPs as a result of **conflict in Africa**, nearly 45% of the world's IDPs. There are more IDPs in five African countries – Algeria, the DRC, Somalia, Sudan, and Uganda – than there are refugees in the rest of the world, reported the Internal Displacement Monitoring Centre (IDMC). Sudan has the world's highest number of IDPs, with an estimated 4.5 m people affected, including 2.7 m in Darfur. At least 250,000 have fled their homes due to inter-communal violence in Southern Sudan. In Somalia, an estimated 1.3 m were displaced mainly by violence, including 700,000 who have fled the capital, Mogadishu. In the DRC, since the start of military operations against militia in the east in January, nearly 900,000 people have fled their homes. This brought the total of those displaced across North and South Kivu and Orientale Province to at least 2 m, as at July. In Kenya the government ordered a closure of all IDP camps in October, which has made assessment difficult. Most IDPs were victims of post-election violence in 2008, which displaced an estimated 600,000. Inter-ethnic tensions over pasture have also displaced families in the north, while flooding has affected some communities in the west. During the autumn, John Holmes drew attention to the link between **climate change, disasters, displacement and migration**, especially in Africa. Despite a decline in the worldwide number of refugees in recent years, the continent still has around 2.3 m refugees. The UNHCR Representation in Ethiopia as at 31 May was caring for 98,483 refugees, mainly from Somalia, Eritrea, Sudan and Kenya.

The AU put the fight against **trafficking in human beings** on its agenda when the AU Commission's Department of Social Affairs launched the AU.COMMIT campaign on 16 June. AU.COMMIT aims to prevent trafficking and prosecute traffickers through a number of actions and activities 2009–2012. It has been designed to implement the 2006 Ouagadougou Action Plan on Trafficking in Human Beings. Various agencies in the UN system (UNHCR, UNODC, UNICEF, ECA) expressed commitment to the implementation of this campaign.

Winners of the **UNEP award** 'Supporting Entrepreneurs for Environment and Development (SEED)' included an association of small-scale women farmers in Zimbabwe; civil society organisations in Southern Africa developing bio-cultural procedures; and institutions in Niger establishing sustainable solid waste management systems.

Linnea Bergholm

III. African-European Relations

The global financial and economic crisis, which hit both Africa and Europe hard in 2009, dominated relations between the two continents. European foreign direct investment (FDI) in Africa dropped sharply, while fiscal pressures on governments started to have an impact on official development assistance (ODA). Western aid traditionally slips in the years following a recession, but this time middle income countries have emerged from recession faster and have stepped into the gap left by European donors. Concerns resurfaced in Europe about competition with China for influence in Africa, and the supposedly waning global influence of the EU.

Global summitry in 2009 was dominated by questions about how to address the global economic downturn and how to minimise its effects on the world's poorest countries. At the G-20 summit held in London (2 April) Africa was represented by South African President Kgalema Motlanthe and Ethiopian Prime Minister Meles Zenawi in his capacity as head of NEPAD. In preparation for the Summit, British Prime Minister Gordon Brown hosted a meeting with African leaders, finance ministers and Central Bank governors (16 March) in order to hear the views of African nations on the global economic crisis and African contributions to the debate on how to deal with it. However, Africa did not feature prominently on an agenda concentrated mostly on efforts to repair international finance and resurrect the global economy, and the Summit's conclusions offered little in concrete measures for the continent. Nevertheless, the G-20's commitment to supporting global finance, refraining from competitive deflationary measures and maintaining trade openness arguably prevented an even greater economic catastrophe, which would have impacted even more heavily on Africa.

African vulnerability was discussed in more detail at summits held later in the year. At the G-8 Summit in L'Aquila, Italy (8–10 July), national leaders and the European Commission committed to a food security package that promised $ 20 bn over three years to support agricultural development. These commitments were increased to $ 22 bn at the G-20 Summit held in Pittsburgh (24–25 September), and more European countries joined the initiative. Meanwhile in Africa, food prices continued to increase, albeit more slowly than in 2008.

A second major global issue of 2009 with direct implications for Europe-African relations was **climate change**. The deal brokered between China, South Africa, India, Brazil and the US at the UN Climate Change Conference held in Copenhagen (7–18 December) disappointed both African and European governments. Leaders from both continents had wanted deeper, verifiable cuts in greenhouse gas emissions, and were effectively shut out from influencing the Conference's non-binding outcome. Although the EU was committed to implementing binding legislation to reduce carbon emissions even without a satisfactory deal in Copenhagen, exclusion from the deal caused great consternation among European leaders and commentators alarmed at Europe's lack of international influence in a world supposedly dominated by the 'G-2'. Prior to the summit, the EU lent its support to an AU proposal for a $ 30 bn 'fast start fund' to help poor countries cope with the effects of climate change, but the spirit of cooperation was short-lived. During the summit, developing countries responded with fury to a leaked draft agreement that threatened to sideline the UN process and set different per capita emission targets for developed and developing countries. Africa took the moral high ground at Copenhagen, but ended the talks divided between leaders willing to accept European leadership on emissions reductions and leaders committed to demanding deeper cuts from the rich world.

In the EU, institutional changes brought about by the **Lisbon Treaty** were likely to influence diplomacy with African countries and multilateral organisations during the next few years. Following ratification by referendum in Ireland, the long-awaited Treaty came into force on 1 December. The Lisbon Treaty created two new posts: former Belgian Prime Minister Herman van Rompuy was appointed President of the European Council, and British peer and former EU Trade Commissioner Baroness Catherine Ashton was appointed to the 'double hatted' position of High Representative for Foreign and Security Policy and Vice President of the Commission. Meanwhile the European Parliament re-elected José Manuel Barroso as the President of the European Commission for a second five-year term on 16 September, while the Commission itself was named on 27 November, although its commencement of office was delayed until after European Parliament hearings scheduled for January 2010. Unlike the first Barroso Commission, the development and humanitarian aid portfolios were split between two commissioners who were assigned the additional responsibility of coordinating policy and programmes with the high representative. The **European Parliament elections** that took place between 4 and 7 June were noteworthy for low turnout, losses for the centre-left and gains for the far-right. Nevertheless, the outcome was likely to mean business as usual during the next five-year term, especially with regard to Africa. The Parliament's influence on EU external relations has grown in recent years and it has been especially successful in maintaining a high profile for Africa in the EU's global development policy debates. It gained additional external relations powers under the Lisbon Treaty and appeared likely to remain a strong partner for Africa in the EU, particularly in its monitoring and oversight roles of the Joint Strategy for Africa and the Economic Partnership Agreement negotiations. Norwegian born French MEP (Member of the European Parliament) Eva Joly, who had a past career as a corruption-battling lawyer, became chair of the European Parliament's Committee on Development.

Bilateral Relations

2009 was a quiet year for bilateral diplomacy between European and African countries. In **Germany**, Chancellor Angela Merkel emerged victorious from the 27 September general elections, but her centre-right Christian Democrats (CDU) formed a coalition with a new partner. The new German development minister, Dirk Niebel, hailed from the Free Democratic Party (FDP) and said before taking office that he believed the German Development Ministry should be abolished. Niebel later earned praise from Africa lobbyist Bob Geldof for saying that German aid should be concentrated on Africa rather than China and India. The new German government expressed an interest in encouraging African ownership of the continent's development and security, and multilateralism in Africa. Negotiations on development cooperation between the AU and the new German government were held in Addis Ababa (18 November). Germany committed € 30 m in additional funding for the period 2009–2010 to assist the AU in pursuing its strategic objectives: the establishment of the African Peace and Security Architecture (APSA), the Sharm el Sheikh Water Agenda and the Charter for Democracy and Elections. Special emphasis was put on developing regional infrastructure, for which Germany would contribute € 10 m to the Infrastructure Project Preparation Facility at the AfDB. The talks also focussed on shared values, development, integration and cooperation, and institutional transformation.

Italian Foreign Affairs Minister Franco Frattini visited several African countries in 2009. He stressed the strategic importance of Africa for **Italy** and the EU, especially regarding the creation of the APSA and the economic integration of the African continent. Nevertheless, Italy's main interests in Africa remained north of the Sahara. In August, the Italian government agreed a Treaty of Friendship, Partnership and Co-operation with Libya, including stronger provisions for bilateral efforts to combat illegal migration – mostly of citizens of sub-Saharan countries taking the risky route to Europe through Libya and across the Mediterranean.

Relations between **France** and the African continent were unusually quiet in 2009, perhaps due to the need to consolidate rather than launch new initiatives during the global economic downturn. There were no major state visits or bilateral summits between African and French heads of state. As if to confirm the consolidation theme, French Secretary of State for Foreign Trade Anne-Marie Idrac visited South Africa in May as a follow-up to the state visit made by President Nicolas Sarkozy in December 2008. Such a quiet year may reflect the lack of personal ties between President Sarkozy and African leaders, but it did not, of course, signify that Africa became any less important to France. In February, Sarkozy announced the renegotiation of defence agreements with eight African countries dating from the early post-independence period, which contain secret clauses that committed France to providing military assistance to partner governments in times of crisis. President Sarkozy promised to pay more attention to democracy and human rights in Africa and said that France would henceforth emphasise collective security rather than bilateral support. The first two revised agreements were signed with Togo (14 March) and Cameroon (22 May).

Similarly, bilateral relations between the **UK** and African countries were a lot less prominent than in previous years. Tony Blair's strong engagement with the African continent has not been continued by his successor, Gordon Brown, despite the latter's commitment to development issues evident from the high-level meeting held in London in March before the G8 Summit. British politics was in any case dominated by the economic downturn and the survival of an unpopular government amid scandals over MP's expenses. In Europe – and especially in Britain – the media devoted extensive coverage to new South African President Jacob Zuma's private life, particularly his polygamous marriages and estimated 20 children. In November, Buckingham Palace announced that Zuma would be making a state visit to the UK in March 2010.

European governments continued to view **South Africa** as the leading country in Africa that has even greater potential to be at the forefront of an African emergence on the world stage. Zuma, who became president of South Africa in May, hosted the Cape Town EU-South Africa Summit (11 September). The EU was officially represented by the Swedish Presidency, High Representative Javier Solana and Development Commissioner Karel De Gucht. The meeting sought to build convergence between European and South African positions on a number of issues, from coping with the global economic crisis to regional peace and security. The agenda also included preparations for the G-20 summit in Pittsburgh. De Gucht and South African Trade and Industry Minister Rob Davies launched a € 100 m Employment Creation Fund aimed at increasing employment opportunities and skills development in the South African economy. As an adjunct to the summit, Swedish Prime Minister Fredrik Reinfeldt held bilateral meetings with Zuma, during which the leaders discussed climate change and security issues and afterwards spoke of their desire to strengthen the relationship between the two countries.

Effects of EU Reforms

The **Lisbon Treaty** was likely to have a long-term effect on EU policy towards Africa. Article 208 of the Treaty states "Union development cooperation policy shall have as its primary objective the reduction and, in the long term, the eradication of poverty. The Union shall take account of the objectives of development cooperation in the policies that it implements which are likely to affect developing countries." Essentially, this Article required the EU to ensure coherence in development, external relations and foreign policy and to focus on the MDGs. The practical implications of the Treaty for the coordination of development, diplomatic and security goals in Africa were yet to be seen – some commentators praised the EU for bringing foreign and development policy closer together, while others raised the spectre of development's sub-ordination to short-term foreign policy and the economic and security concerns of EU institutions and some EU member governments. Such concerns were probably overstated, as clauses in the Financial Regulations governing the EDF and Development Cooperation Instrument (DCI) ensure that operations funded by these instruments comply with development standards defined by the DAC of the OECD. Nevertheless, at the end of the year it was unclear whether EU development policy would be as strongly ring-fenced as it was before the Lisbon Treaty came into force.

High Representative Baroness Ashton's first task was to build the new **European External Action Service** (EEAS), a *de facto* foreign ministry which was set to become one of the world's largest diplomatic organisations with a major presence in Africa. The Lisbon Treaty stated only that the EEAS would support the High Representative's work, and left decisions over the details of the service's purpose and structure to be negotiated after the Treaty had entered into force. The EEAS represented a major reshuffle of external relations policymaking power in the EU with long-term implications and, as 2010 dawned, the European Commission, Parliament and member states were gearing up for a major battle over the distribution of policymaking responsibilities, budgets, key staff appointments and other administrative details.

The EU's development budget is the largest set of operational financial instruments for use outside Europe, and it quickly became apparent that programming for the EU's major ODA instruments for Africa, the member state-funded **EDF** and the community-funded DCI, would be at the centre of intra-EU negotiations. The outcome of these negotiations was not clear by the end of the year, but there were several open questions regarding the potential politicisation of development policy in the EEAS, the allocation of country and regional desks between the EEAS and the Commission's DG Development, and the role of Development Commissioner Andris Piebalgs in development policymaking. With the entry into force of the Lisbon Treaty on 1 December, the Commission Delegations, including several in Africa, became **EU Delegations**. At year's end there remained open questions about the staffing of delegations, especially the issue of whether delegation heads would be political appointees pushed by member states. Given the continent's colonial history, this question was particularly salient in the African context.

The Lisbon Treaty did not completely remove the six-month rotating presidency from the international stage. For the first six months, the **Czech presidency** showed up the inherent weaknesses in this system. Like most rotating presidencies, the Czech Republic promoted national priorities while in the chair of the EU's various committees, and unsurprisingly the Eastern dimension of EU external relations had a higher priority than EU development policy or relations with Africa. Moreover, much of the Czech presidency's political capital was spent on internal debates about a shaky government, its collapse on 24 March and the formation of a 'technocratic' interim government in Prague.

In the second half of the year, the **Swedish presidency** placed a greater emphasis on development issues and on the African continent. Outcomes of the Swedish presidency included the adoption of an operational framework to help the EU live up to international development undertakings made in Paris and Accra ahead of the MDG review summit to be held in 2010. The migration issue remained a high priority for the EU during the Swedish presidency, and the Draft Stockholm Programme was presented on 16 October under the aegis of the EU's freedom, security and justice policy. The **Stockholm Programme** is a declaration of intent to strengthen border controls, establish standardised technology and procedures, and facilitate information-sharing between border agencies across the EU for the period 2010–2014. The initiative has met with mixed responses ranging from guarded praise to accusations that it is another step towards 'fortress Europe'.

EU-AU Relations

Muammar Kadhafi was elected to the AU chair in February and the organisation survived despite the controversial Libyan leader's willingness to ruffle feathers with outlandish statements, including a call for the immediate establishment of a **"United States of Africa"** in his inaugural address. Arguing that African countries are not strong enough to negotiate bilaterally with the EU and other international partners, Kadhafi proposed replacing the AU Commission with an "African Authority" charged with bringing about a longstanding vision of a "union government" for Africa. Kadhafi's plan was not supported by other key African governments, including South Africa, Kenya, Ethiopia and Nigeria. Nevertheless, supporters gathered at an international symposium on uniting Africa held in Dakar (27–30 July) pointed out that, just as European citizens benefit from their Union, Africans could also. Senegalese President Abdoulaye Wade argued that "large unions", such as the United States and the EU, could provide inspiration (although not models) for African efforts to build common institutions.

Relations between the EU and the AU continued to deepen, especially between the AU Commission and the European Commission, which signed an agreement on 6 November aimed at capacity building and enabling the exchange of officials. A mid-term review of the implementation of the Joint Africa EU Strategy (JAES) and its First Action Plan was undertaken during the EU-AU ministerial troika meeting in Addis Ababa on 14 October. The review highlighted progress made since 2007, identified some areas where progress had not met expectations, and reasserted the intention of both the EU and the AU to continue to work towards deeper multi-level and multi-issue cooperation. Areas of progress that were noted included cooperation on peace and security and regional integration in Africa, where the EU could offer its technical expertise and the benefits of its own experiences. Also singled out for praise was cooperation on climate change, although following the outcome of the Copenhagen summit it was believed that this might not be the case in the next review. Areas where improvements could be made included the desire to establish common negotiating positions in key international forums such as Copenhagen and the MDG review summit scheduled for 2010. Given some fundamental conflicts of interest on specific aspects of trade negotiations (see below), the disappointment of Copenhagen was no surprise after all.

Dialogue between the EU and AU on **human rights** protection continued with a fifth round held in Addis Ababa (20 November). The dialogue covered a wide range of issues of interest to both parties and was judged to be a success by those present. Conclusions noted progress during the year, including the abolition of the death penalty in Togo and Burundi. Concerns were raised about the rights of children affected by conflict and the rights of migrants and asylum seekers in African as well as in European countries. Delegates promised to work on an AU/EU declaration on preventing torture, possibly with input from the Council of Europe and the African Commission on Human and People's Rights. Disagreements over human rights issues also surfaced. The NGO Human Rights Watch wrote an open letter to EU foreign ministers on 10 February lamenting the EU's silence over the Ethiopian government's adoption of the Charities and Societies Proclamation, which bars foreign NGOs from working on human rights or security sector issues. European reactions to Uganda's anti-homosexuality bill (proposed 13 October) were much stronger. If enacted, the bill would mean that people convicted of certain offences against the country's anti-gay laws could face the death penalty. Both the European Parliament and German Development Minister Niebel threatened to cut aid to Uganda if the bill became law.

Security and Development

The EU made several statements about the need for Africans to address security concerns if sustainable development is to accelerate across the continent. On 12 October, the AU Peace and Security Council and the EU Political and Security Committee met in Addis Ababa in the context of the **EU-AU Partnership on Peace and Security**. The AU and the EU have adopted a joint strategy with the objective of establishing APSA and making the African Standby Force operational for peacekeeping deployments in 2010. By late 2009, procedures had been developed, forces identified and exercises mounted, and evaluation was underway. Nevertheless, it was deemed unlikely that such an ambitious endeavour would proceed without difficulty and high expectations were bound to lead to disappointment, given the magnitude of the continent's security challenges and the very limited capacities at hand.

As part of its Conclusions on the European Security and Defence Policy (ESDP), the European Council on 17 November welcomed the progress of the EU's peace and security partnership with Africa and reminded Africans and Europeans that seeking security in Africa is first and foremost an African responsibility. Notwithstanding the fact that most of the continent's large-scale conflicts have been brought under control, the externalities of the ongoing wars in DR Congo and Somalia, together with the fragility of several post-conflict states such as Liberia and Chad, meant that more dialogue was needed on how the EU and its members could support Africa's long-term efforts to address insecurity. For the EU, supporting such endeavours was not without controversy due to the policy of neutrality of some member states. The APSA support was funded by the intergovernmental **African Peace Facility** rather than the community-funded Instrument for Stability. This controversy was mostly due to the prevailing separation of the EDF and the EU budget, which was set to persist until at least the end of the current EU budgetary period in December 2012.

Piracy off the coast of Somalia became a major international issue following several high-profile hijackings, most notably that of the supertanker Sirius Star, which was released in January after the payment of a ransom estimated at $ 3 m. European Union Naval Force (EUNAVFOR)-Atalanta, the EU's anti-piracy mission in the Gulf of Aden and Indian Ocean, reached full operational capacity in February. In December, the European Council decided to extend the mission's mandate for another year. Together with the UN mission that began in September 2007, EUNAVFOR has been able to claim some successes – the EU escorted dozens of vessels carrying UN World Food Programme aid to ports in Somalia, and not one of these ships was attacked. Nevertheless, the vast area of ocean off Somalia's coast presented a massive challenge for naval patrols and hijackings of commercial shipping continued. Naval missions were unable to address illegal fishing and toxic waste dumping off the coast of Somalia, which was unconstrained due to the lack of sovereign governance over Somalia's 200-mile Exclusive Economic Zone. Arguably, this 'tragedy of the commons' functioned as an immediate push-factor for piracy. Nevertheless, the greatest challenge lay in addressing the conflict in Somalia itself – as AU Commission President Jean Ping said, "pirates were not born in the ocean and they don't live there. They come from Somalia. If you want sustainable peace you have to go where they come from, which is on the land." The European Council meeting on Somalia held in July concluded that a comprehensive approach to resolving Somalia's problems was needed, but the EU – like the wider international community – was unable to do more than support the AU's efforts to protect the beleaguered Transitional Federal Government in Mogadishu. By the end of the year, plans were being discussed to provide EU training to Somalian security forces in Uganda.

The 18-month **EUFOR mission to Chad and Central African Republic** (CAR) ended in March with a medal parade in Mont Valérien (France) and the official handover of peacekeeping duties to the UN. The mission involved 3,700 troops from 23 EU member states, including around 2,000 from France. It had a mandate to protect civilians, improve the general security situation, facilitate the delivery of humanitarian aid, and ensure the safety of UN personnel, but not to address any of the factors behind the conflicts in Chad, CAR and the neighbouring Darfur region of Sudan. Moreover, the mission was constrained by the magnitude of the task of deploying to an area with poor infrastructure, thousands of kilometres from the nearest ports. Accordingly, the mission was able to successfully protect UN personnel and facilitate aid delivery, but the general security of the region and the situation of civilians in the refugee camps of eastern Chad remained dire.

Although its original condemnation of the December 2008 coup in **Guinea** was largely rhetorical, a serious deterioration of the situation prompted the EU to react. In late September, more than 150 people were killed by soldiers firing live bullets at protesters against the junta government. International condemnation of the atrocity was swift. EU High Representative Javier Solana called for the immediate release of detained opposition leaders, and on 21 October the European Council imposed sanctions on the junta, including an arms embargo, travel restrictions and the freezing of European bank accounts. In December, junta leader Captain Dadis Camara survived a serious assassination attempt, after which he was treated in Morocco before going into exile in Burkina Faso. French Foreign Minister Bernard Kouchner warned in December that Guinea faced the prospect of civil war if Captain Camara were to return home.

European efforts to assist in the resolution of ongoing African security issues continued. EU Special Representative to Sudan Torbyn Brylle attended peace talks on **Darfur** held in Doha, and re-iterated the EU's support for AU efforts to bring about a political solution to the conflict. The situation in **Zimbabwe** improved somewhat as the economy stabilised following the replacement of the Zimbabwe dollar with the US one, but the record of the power-sharing government was mixed at best, with co-opted opposition politicians alleging continued harassment from supporters of President Robert Mugabe. A visit on 12–13 September by a high-level EU delegation, including the Swedish and Spanish development ministers and Development Commissioner Karel de Gucht, signalled a slight thawing in relations, but sanctions against Zimbabwe's leaders were maintained, despite calls from southern African states for them to be lifted.

Elections were held in **Guinea-Bissau** in June and July to elect a new president following the assassination of incumbent João Bernardo Viera in March. **Electoral observers** from the EU were present across all 27 constituencies and visited 80 of the 2,700 polling stations. Tensions were high in the days leading up to the first poll on 28 June, and there was considerable relief that the polls themselves proceeded smoothly. The head of the EU mission, Johan Van Hecke, said that, although turnout was low, voting was calm and orderly and not a single incident or complaint was reported to the election observers. The election was won by Malam Bacai Sanhá in the second round (26 July). He promised to deal with organised drug trafficking through Guinea-Bissau, which has become a major transit point for cocaine-smuggling from South America to Europe.

Development Cooperation

The **European Development Days** (EDD), held in Stockholm on 22–24 October, have evolved into a high profile annual event. The more than 5,000 delegates attending the fourth EDD included European Commission President Barroso, European Parliament

President Jerzy Buzek, EU Development Commissioner de Gucht, Liberian President Ellen Johnson-Sirleaf, Sierra Leone President Ernest Bai Koroma, Kenyan Prime Minister Raila Odinga, Burkina Faso Prime Minister Tertius Zongo, UNDP Administrator Helen Clark, Arab League Secretary General Amr Moussa, IMF Managing Director Dominique Strauss-Kahn, World Bank Managing Director Ngozi Okonjo-Iweala, Nobel laureates Mohammed Yunus, Rajenda Pachauri and Mario Molina, philanthropist George Soros and musician Youssou N'dour. Four broad themes were debated: how to respond to the global economic downturn, democracy and development, citizenship and development, and, given the upcoming Copenhagen Conference, climate change. Within these debates, the Development Days were an opportunity to highlight several 'hot issues' currently attracting the attention of development experts. The inaugural European Report on Development 2009, published by the European University Institute, Florence, was presented at this event. The Report, entitled "Overcoming Fragility in Africa", called for a reassessment of EU development policy towards fragile states in sub-Saharan Africa and a renewed focus on investing in human capital and institution-building. The issue of aid effectiveness also received a great deal of attention at the Stockholm event. A report was presented that estimated that some € 3 bn per year are being wasted due to the volatility of aid flows, the proliferation of donors and implementing organisations and the fragmentation of programmes into tens of thousands of sometimes competing projects. Development Commissioner de Gucht subsequently called for a European approach to managing aid policy, actions and projects more effectively, and reinvesting the savings in better development.

Policy Coherence for Development (PCD) was also a major issue for discussion, particularly as the Lisbon Treaty included a clause on coherence aimed at improving this key area of development cooperation. In September, DG Development's Forward Looking Studies and Policy Coherence team published its second report on PCD. The report (which was also on the Development Days' agenda) included a case study of the JAES, which was meant to encourage cooperation between the Europeans and Africans not just on development, but on a wide range of political and economic issues at multiple levels of engagement. The report concluded that JAES had had a limited impact on PCD thus far, but that both partners needed to be realistic about their expectations and patient in their wait for concrete outcomes. The report highlighted the EU's claim that it can bring a wide range of instruments to support developing countries' battle against poverty.

The European Commission launched the **second Revision of the Cotonou Agreement** on 29 May. The review, undertaken every five years, focussed on several aspects of the Agreement, including regional integration, state fragility, food security and the progress of negotiations on the Economic Partnership Agreements (EPAs) with sub-regional groups of African, Caribbean and Pacific countries. Results were due to be published in March 2010. On 17 December, the European Parliament Development Committee published a report on the 2nd revision. The report deplored the fact that the European Parliament, the ACP-EU Joint Parliamentary Assembly, the national parliaments of ACP States and civil society organisations were not involved in the decision-making process that led to the identification of areas of the Cotonou Agreement for revision. The European Parliament called for greater transparency and renewed focus on climate change, renewable energy, addressing the effects of the food and financial crises, and migration.

In April, the European Commission, in recognition that the global economic downturn was hitting the poorest countries hardest, issued a **Communication to the European Parliament and the Council** entitled "Supporting developing countries in coping with the crisis". The paper argued that the gains of the past decade were at risk and that there was a real prospect of people falling back into poverty. Recognising that aid was an integral part of the recovery package, the Commission called upon member states to honour existing commitments and to step up efforts to raise new development-related finance. While the Communication advanced 28 recommendations, there was very little that was new – rather, ideas were re-iterated, such as for more attention to be paid to improving aid effectiveness and that the aid for trade agenda should be stepped up.

Despite the Commission's urgings, the recession appeared to have bitten into **EU member states' development spending**. Short-term community financial commitments to Africa have not been boosted to meet the extra demands posed by economic downturn. Multilateral commitments to the EU did not suffer due to a time-lag in the setting of aid budgets, but EU member states' promises to meet the UN's Monterrey goal of devoting 0.7% of national income to ODA came no closer to being realised, while some countries – such as Ireland and Italy – actually reduced commitments. On 4 November, the Commission submitted a proposal for a Council decision establishing the ceiling of the financial contributions to be paid by member states to finance the EDF in 2011. According to the Commission's estimations, EDF contributions for 2011 would consist mostly of funds coming from the 10th EDF (to which all 27 member states contribute) and to a lesser extent from the leftover of the 9th EDF (to which only 15 member states contribute). The Africa, Caribbean and Pacfic Working Party met several times to discuss the Commission proposal and, on 20 November, reached aunanimous agreement on a compromise that set the ceiling for 2011 at € 3.9 bn: € 3.69 bn for Commission programmes and € 210 m for the EIB. This represented a reduction of the 2011 EDF cash flow for the Commission by € 260 m.

Africa continued to occupy a central position in the development cooperation programmes of several smaller European countries. In May, the Danish Commission for Africa released its final report, which called for greater focus on private sector-led growth, entrepreneurship and education. The Netherlands was one of the few countries to surpass the UN's ODA target of 0.7% of Gross National Income (GNI). Around half of Dutch ODA was provided to African partners. Despite reductions in ODA, Ireland made some progress towards the goal of focussing on Africa expressed in its 2006 White Paper on development cooperation. Seven out of Irish Aid's nine 'priority countries' were in Africa.

The **EIB** and the IMF agreed in December to enhance capacity building cooperation across Sub-Saharan Africa. Under the agreement, the EIB would support the IMF Regional Technical Assistance Centres. The funds involved were relatively small, but the agreement – which links the EIB's efforts to foster the growth of the financial sector with the IMF's work on macroeconomic governance – was hailed as 'landmark' by the two financial organisations. In 2009, the EIB provided over € 1.1 bn in loans, guarantees and risk capital to sub-Saharan Africa, targeted at projects that can deliver sustainable economic, social and environmental benefits.

Ahead of the September 2010 MDG review summit, comparisons between European development cooperation with Africa, and that of **emerging donors**, were becoming more common. A senior officials meeting of the Forum on China-Africa Cooperation (FOCAC) held in Sharm-el-Sheikh, Egypt (8–9 November) concluded with China making several pledges to Africa in the core MDG areas of health, education and agriculture. **China** also promised financial support (more than $ 10 bn in concessional loans as well as debt relief), research cooperation, clean energy projects and intercultural dialogue. Individual recipient countries were not specified beyond those with diplomatic relations with China. Some European critics have raised concerns at China's hunger for natural resources and 'no strings attached' engagement with some of Africa's less democratic governments, but Chinese pledges were helping Africa's progress towards the MDGs. Chinese news reports indirectly berated Europeans for their envy of China and for continuing to view Africa as "their own back yard".

Trade and Development

During the 2009 economic downturn, the erudite arguments of prominent economists about the danger of beggar-thy-neighbour trade policy during a recession appeared to have been noted by governments world wide, and a catastrophe like that of the 1930s was avoided. Nevertheless, opportunities that exist in crises were not seized and the Doha round came no closer to resolution in 2009. Trade between Europe and Africa continued to grow, despite the lack of a global deal: in December, EuroStat and the AU Secretariat's Statistics Unit for the first time jointly published figures on African economic indicators, trade and investment. These showed that nominal average African GDP increased faster between 2000 and 2008 than the GDP of the EU. Furthermore, Africa's trade surplus with Europe – € 38 bn in 2008 – was growing year by year. The statistics also confirmed that South Africa was the continent's economic power-house and Europe's most important economic partner in Africa. The country dominated African trade in services with the EU, and was by far the continent's largest recipient of European FDI.

In Africa, considerable concern was expressed at the uneven progress of the negotiations on **EPAs** between the European Commission and African countries and sub-regional organisations. In previous years, African suspicion about Europe's motives has not been eased by former EU Trade Commissioner Peter Mandelson, whose vigorous negotiating style and insistence on restricting domestic trade policy tools was sometimes seen as pushing African governments into agreements they were unprepared for, and abrogating the spirit of an equal partnership. Malawian President Bingu wa Mutharika has said that his country would not be part of the EPAs in their current format, since the intention of Europe was to divide Africa and thereby secure access to natural resources also coveted by China. Baroness Ashton, who replaced Lord Mandelson as trade commissioner in October 2008, proved a less abrasive negotiating partner for Africans. Commissioner Ashton stressed that her priority was to build trust and confidence in the process of negotiations. She visited several African countries and built a reputation as an efficient and receptive negotiator.

Aid for Trade (AfT), development assistance provided support of partner countries' efforts to increase their capacity to trade, has become a major topic of discussion in EU development policy in recent years. The profile of the EU's AfT instruments grew in 2009, especially with regard to Africa and the contribution of aid to supporting regional integration and the ongoing EPA negotiations. The EU and its member states were collectively the world's largest AfT donor, with commitments of around € 7 bn per year. In 2007, the European Commission had committed to providing € 2 bn per year in AfT programmes by 2010. African leaders expressed concern at the potential effects of the 2009 global recession on AfT, and called for the EU and its members to maintain their commitments. ECOWAS Executive Secretary Mohammed Ibn Chambas said that Europe had a duty to increase AfT with Africa, since the bulk of African trade was with Europe and lifting trade would assist the recovery of both continents. On 6–7 July, the Second Global Review of Aid for Trade was held at the WTO Headquarters in Geneva, Switzerland. The meeting scrutinised how AfT was being operationalised in the field. In the lead up to the Global Review, high level AfT meetings were held in Lusaka, Zambia on 6–7 April, jointly hosted by COMESA, EAC and SADC.

Mark Furness

IV. West Africa

The global economic downturn had a significant effect on the sub-region, as commodity prices, with the exception of gold, fell sharply and remittances declined, though the latter not always as much as forecast. Floods in numerous countries compounded the situation for many people. Guinea and Guinea-Bissau continued to experience high levels of instability marked by killings, including among members of the military cliques, which put the southwestern forest zone at risk. The cocaine trade maintained its growth, so that the sub-region as a whole accounted for almost half of European cocaine imports. While Mauritania once again returned to civilian rule, ending its international isolation, Niger went the opposite way as its president staged a constitutional coup d'état in a bid to cling on to power. The Tuareg rebellions in Mali and Niger went into a downturn as their governments managed to push rebel groups, which suffered from internal divisions, onto the defensive or closer to some sort of settlement. This, however, did not improve security in the desert zone, which was marked by kidnappings and killings of Westerners across the sub-region, usually by groups acting on behalf of al-Qaida in the Islamic Maghreb (AQIM). As always, various forms of violence continued to rock Nigerian society without seemingly endangering the integrity of the federation, although the prolonged illness of the head of state and constitutional ambiguity over his replacement put stability at risk. Côte d'Ivoire was largely calm but, while some slow progress was made on the contentious issue of voter identification (and less on disarmament), the long-awaited presidential elections – which should complete the return to a normal constitutional order – continued to recede below the horizon. Political life in other countries, including Ghana, Liberia, Mali, Burkina Faso and Benin, remained fairly quiet.

Coups and Electoral Politics

Volatile **Guinea-Bissau**, which had experienced coup attempts and an attack on the president the previous year, was again rocked by incidents. In March, the country's chief of staff was killed in a bomb blast, which prompted soldiers to assassinate President Vieira in reprisal the following day. Although the parliamentary speaker was sworn in as interim president in conformity with constitutional requirements, new violent incidents later cost the lives of two politicians who had been close to Vieira. Much of the violence was representative of persistent infighting in the country's state elite (civilian and military), sharpened by the rising stakes provided by Guinea-Bissau's growing role in cocaine trafficking. Nevertheless, internationally approved presidential elections followed in June–July and, with the victory of an ally of the incumbent prime minister, a semblance of order was restored – at least for the time being.

Guinea hardly fared better. Suspended from the AU as a result of the military's seizure of power in the wake of the death of President Lansana Conté in December 2008, the country initially appeared on track towards a return of normal civilian rule by 2010, as promised by the junta leaders. However, a campaign of criticism about abuse and corruption on the part of military and civilian politicians quickly turned sour as its initiator, junta leader Moussa 'Dadis' Camara, sent signals that he might wish to stand in presidential elections, contrary to earlier promises. As his behaviour became increasingly erratic, unrest grew, culminating in a day of mass protest in late September to which military forces responded with premeditated mass killings and gang rapes of protesters in the capital's sports stadium. More than 150 people died (some by electrocution) and more than 100 women were sexually assaulted. An international outcry prompted Camara to put the blame on his aide de camp, who then tried to kill the junta leader, seriously wounding him and forcing one of Camara's deputies to take over. Regional fears about the potential overspill of Guinea's simmering instability (besides the country's mineral wealth) limited international reactions.

While in **Togo** stability was more solid, infighting in the ruling elite as represented by the Gnassingbé family showed that domestic politics had heated up considerably ahead of the presidential elections scheduled for 2010. Divided between so-called modernisers and conservative hardliners, the Gnassingbé clan witnessed the arrest, preceded by a shoot-out, of the president's younger half-brother Kpatcha Gnassingbé, who had already been deposed from the post of defence minister the previous year and was now accused of plotting a coup. While the president's personal security forces were beefed up and the army chief of staff was removed from office, there was concern about the upcoming elections and the risks posed by the cracks in the ruling elite, which, besides the Gnassingbé family, was made up of the ruling party and security services.

Niger plunged into a deep crisis as President Tandja was unwilling to step down and staged a constitutional coup d'état by dissolving the Assembly and Constitutional Court and then forcing through a referendum on a new constitution that allowed him to renew his candidature indefinitely after a transitional three-year term without an election. Enjoying the backing of high-ranking officers and popular support in rural areas, thanks to small-scale development projects initiated under his presidency, Tandja braved the international community, a divided political class and a vociferous urban civil society. Expected proceeds from increased uranium mining and oil production, in addition to pressure from his personal entourage and a lack of personal democratic culture, all played a role in the confrontational course on which the head of state was embarked. The clash with the republic's institutions indicated considerable resistance to the autocratic direction the country was taking, but the divisions in the political class forced civil society to lead protests that culminated in boycotts of the referendum and subsequent parliamentary and municipal elections, whose validity was rejected by the international community.

In contrast, **Mauritania** completed a transition period towards civilian rule. The previous year's coup d'état, followed immediately by the military's announcement of elections, set a by now predictable trajectory of political transition. A special consultation on democracy did not preclude the possibility of members of the military standing for election and, despite pro-democracy rallies, the 2008 coup leader, Gen. Abdel Aziz managed to gain the upper hand in the presidential elections, which were held in July and sanctioned by the international community. The military thus remained the power behind the throne.

In other countries, electoral schedules were absent or of minor importance. Ghana and Nigeria went through a **post-electoral wind-down**, marked in Ghana by scandals concerning emoluments provided to former government officials, including the former head of state, while Nigeria was typically embroiled in petition procedures over the 2007 polls. **Pre-electoral manoeuvring** dominated politics in Benin, where many politicians crossed the floor in both directions and computerisation of the electoral register was the subject of politicking. Similarly, Burkina saw pre-electoral power games, while the opposition remained splintered ahead of presidential elections in 2010, to which purpose a new electoral code brought in many changes without, however, revising constituencies (currently demarcated in favour of the ruling party). In Togo, too, a new electoral code was adopted while a new electoral commission came into being, and it was agreed to update the deficient electoral register ahead of the 2010 polls. In Mali, an extensive national registration process was begun in March with the objective of establishing a reliable civic register. The long-drawn-out process of identifying citizens and voters in Côte d'Ivoire witnessed substantial progress, but without managing to keep within the deadlines, which forced another deferral of presidential elections beyond year's end. **Minor electoral contests** took place in Cape Verde, where the parties represented in the Assembly held internal leadership polls, and Mali and Senegal, which both witnessed local elections. In the former, these were won by parties grouped around the president, while in Senegal the ruling party received a painful beating, losing control of the country's major cities, including the capital.

Human Rights and the Rule of Law

As always, the human rights record proved mixed. The worst performer was probably Guinea, with its military purposely targeting civilian protesters with rape and death. However, the public applauded draconian anti-crime measures, including plans to burn to death robbers caught *in flagrante delicto*. In Guinea-Bissau, too, violations of human rights took place, developing into a veritable climate of **impunity**. A lawyer was beaten up by soldiers for criticising the military leadership, as was a government auditor, while a local human rights league, the attorney-general and an MP became the target of various threats. In Gambia a witch-hunt in which alleged wrongdoers were forced to drink damaging hallucinogenic concoctions involved members of the ruling party, indicating the repression of groups both inside and outside the government alliance. A number of citizens were held **incommunicado**. In Liberia, the head of the Public Procurement and Concessions Commission was shot dead and his body cut in pieces and burnt, after he cancelled numerous dubious contracts signed by a previous administration. Mauritania's human rights record was marred by a report on the continued existence of cases of slavery, while Niger witnessed the arrest of several politicians and journalists charged with various offences in the wake of opposition to the president's constitutional coup. Women participating in a protest sit-in in the capital were violently dispersed.

Countries where there was still a wider freedom to oppose and criticise the government and ruling groups included Ghana, Mali, Burkina, Benin, Nigeria and Senegal. However, in Mali an attempt to legislate better rights for women and children by way of a **family code** had to be stopped after massive protests, spurred on by Muslim clerics, forced the president to send the bill back for another parliamentary reading. In Senegal, homosexuals were subjected to temporary arrest or sentenced to jail terms that were scrapped on appeal, while women journalists campaigning in Sierra Leone against female genital mutilation were attacked by crowds and forced to march naked through the streets of a local town. Togo abolished the death penalty, although this did not affect one of the country's major human rights problems, i.e. extra-judicial killings. The country also witnessed the establishment of a truth and reconciliation commission, but its lack of powers turned the new institution into a paper tiger. The Special Court for Sierra Leone, while continuing its case against former Liberian President Charles Taylor in The Hague, handed down long prison sentences for the senior surviving leaders of the former rebel Revolutionary United Front (RUF), responsible for many of the atrocities committed in the country's civil war. The prison terms, for **crimes against humanity** and war crimes, ranged from 25 to 52 years, and the convicted men were immediately transferred to Rwanda, where they began their spell in jail in conformity with an agreement between the two countries (Sierra Leone not being able to meet international standards in this respect).

In many countries, anti-**corruption** campaigns took place, frequently as part of infighting between members of the political class. Benin was rocked by corruption scandals involving the finance minister, the customs sector and Hajj tour operators, among others. An ombudsman was appointed. A final APRM report pointed to corrupt practices in Burkina Faso, and rebel forces controlling the northern part of Côte d'Ivoire continued to levy 'taxes'. Ghana's new administration announced plans to prosecute corrupt officials of the previous government and, apart from the emoluments scandal, there were revelations about corrupt deals in the oil sector. However, during the year three ministers of the incumbent administration became involved in allegations of corruption and were forced to resign. A new anti-corruption campaign in Mauritania led to the dismissal or imprisonment of several senior officials, although opposition parties alleged that their supporters were disproportionately targeted. That such campaigns could be politically motivated was particularly evident in Niger, where the president, engaged in a running war against the opposition, began a massive operation targeting more than 120 politicians who were charged with misappropriation of funds. To be sure, an inspection of the accounts of the National Assembly, a known source of privilege, had already shown that many millions of euros had gone missing. Guinea's anti-corruption campaign, targeting drugs trafficking among other things, led to arrests, while in Guinea-Bissau the civilian government found itself confronted by the army when attempting to take measures to combat trafficking. Several foreign companies in Guinea were forced to renegotiate mining contracts signed by the previous administration and deemed to be unduly disadvantageous to the country. As in Guinea-Bissau, corruption remained rampant. In Liberia numerous government officials continued to be under investigation. The government introduced a whistle-blower act to protect people reporting on corrupt practices. The danger involved in anti-corruption work was made clear by the death not only of the head of the Public Procurement and Concessions Commission, but also by an assault on the deputy auditor general in the office of the ministry of public works when he was asking for information. In Sierra Leone, the fight against corruption followed more normal paths, with the Anti-Corruption Commission pursuing numerous cases against officials in the courts, besides continuing the battle against 'ghost workers' in the health and education sectors and offering a whistle-blower incentive of 10%. In September, youths and police were involved in clashes over police corruption, leading to a couple of deaths. Anti-corruption work in Nigeria targeted numerous former politicians and officials, but many still avoided prison terms, partly because the Economic and Financial Crimes Commission lacked good staff to produce sufficient evidence. Nevertheless, some high-profile cases were successful, recuperating billions of naira, while corruption cases in Switzerland and the US involving Nigerians or companies working in Nigeria led to convictions.

A few incidents took place in the area of **media** freedom. Gambia and Niger were among the worst performers. The Gambian authorities continued their habit of harassing newspapers. By June, nine journalists were under arrest accused of publishing seditious material related to the unresolved case of the murder of an editor in 2004. Six were sentenced to jail terms, and later pardoned. In Niger, several journalists and newspaper directors were pursued for publishing critical stories on President Tandja's actions, or those of his family. By contrast, a court case brought by the president of Nigeria against a newspaper accused of criminal defamation the previous year was adjourned *sine die*. A minor incident marred press freedom in Benin, which has a relatively good record in this respect, but a broadcast deemed politically sensitive was nevertheless banned.

Conflict, Instability and Violence

As usual, most violence took place in populous **Nigeria**, although the government, after months of fighting with militias in the volatile Niger Delta, introduced an amnesty in June. Plans were launched for talks, disarmament and social reintegration. Hostage taking had previously got completely out of hand, with over 500 people, both Nigerians and foreigners, falling victim to such acts up to July. The proposed amnesty for Delta militias was preceded by a large-scale assault on their strongholds in May in which dozens of militants were killed. Clashes between security forces and Islamic sectarian groups occurred in the Middle Belt and the north, the most serious being in northeastern Maiduguri, where over 700 people died and thousands were left homeless after several days of battles between police forces and members of the 'Boko Haram' sect, which had also spread to other cities. Some of the sect's leaders fell victim to extrajudicial execution after their arrest. Clashes of a communal nature (between different ethnic groups or herders and peasants) occurred in several of the federation's states and cost the lives of dozens of people. The previous year's fighting in the city of Jos, in which more than 400 people died, was the subject of several investigations. Criminal violence continued unabated and on a large scale, notably characterised by robberies, kidnappings and the deaths of policemen killed in the line of duty – more than 100 in the capital alone. The problems over the replacement of the ailing head of state hardly contributed to the stability of the Nigerian polity.

The kidnapping and killing of foreigners also rocked the **Sahelian-Saharan zone** of the sub-region and, while this never involved more than a handful of people, it managed to turn the entire Saharan region into a no-go area for Westerners. Most of the incidents were in some way related to AQIM and affected Mauritania, Mali and Niger, as well as Algeria. One British hostage was murdered in the course of the year, while others were freed. African leaders condemned the payment of ransoms, widely suspected to have occurred before the liberation of some of the victims. The intermittent violence of the Tuareg rebellions in Mali and Niger, both more or less on the downturn, had potentially fewer international repercussions, although the political stability of Niger as such received a blow as a result of the presidential coup d'état, which gave rise to some violent incidents in the city of Dosso and also led to tensions among the lower ranks of the armed forces.

The other node of instability concerned the **southwestern forest zone**. The violent actions of security forces in Guinea against civilian protesters in September was the worst incident that took place, although as shown above, Guinea-Bissau was also regularly the scene of killings and other violent incidents linked to infighting in the civilian-military elite. While Liberia and Sierra Leone continued to enjoy relative peace, both countries had their own security concerns. Despite the presence of UN peacekeepers in Liberia, police forces and the justice system remained underdeveloped. As a consequence, rape and robbery continued to be serious problems, in part countered in the rural areas by vigilante groups or more traditional forms of justice. In Sierra Leone, fighting between supporters of the two main political parties in March stood out. Dozens were wounded and three women were allegedly raped. Much of the violence was the result of youths having been recruited into the parties' protection squads – a dangerous practice in view of the past role of youngsters in the civil war. Guinea was again seen as posing potentially the greater danger to the stability of the forest region, although tensions diminished when the erratic Dadis Camara was removed from power at year's end. Tellingly, however, the witch-hunt that led to political problems in Gambia had its origins in Guinea, an indication of the many cross-border interactions in the forest zone. Senegal's army crossed into Guinea-Bissau in October in an attempt to crack down on rebels in the Casamance region, which was on the whole fairly quiet this year. The secessionist problem, compounded by internal splits, was hardly over, though, and the instability of neighbouring Guinea-Bissau provided Casamance fighters with greater room for manoeuvre. Small-scale violent incidents therefore persisted, and the expansion of cocaine trafficking in the forest zone hardly contributed to long-term stability, as shown by the dramatic events that took place in Guinea-Bissau.

By contrast, although **Côte d'Ivoire**'s stability remained severely constricted as long as the problems of (rebel) disarmament, voter registration and presidential elections were not resolved, calm reigned in the country for much of the year. In Burkina Faso, the social situation remained tense, leading to strikes and riots involving university personnel, traders and retired soldiers. Similar problems occurred in Senegal and Benin.

Socioeconomic Developments

The plunge in commodity prices affected economic activities in many countries. Overall, **growth** rates decreased, on average hovering around 3%, with Guinea as the worst underachiever (zero growth) and Gambia and Ghana higher – the latter with an estimate of 5.9%. In practically all cases (with the notable exception of Côte d'Ivoire), this represented a decline in growth, certainly when set against demographic developments, and the trend did not help in the long-term effort to reach MDG goals such as a reduction in poverty. On the positive side, the reduction in growth went hand in hand with an overall fall in inflation, helped by a decline in fuel prices. Ghana and Sierra Leone had the higher inflation rates, though in the latter case the figure dropped below 10%.

Almost all countries suffered from the collapse in **commodity prices**. Marked exceptions were those producing gold and uranium, whose prices continued to be high thanks to international worries over the economic crisis and the renewed popularity of nuclear energy. Niger thus benefited as market prices for uranium rose by 35% up to June (the government having the right to sell 900 tonnes on its own account, the rest being part of long-term contracts with French Areva), while it could also cash in somewhat on gold prices – as did Mali, Ghana and Burkina. Most countries, including Sierra Leone, significantly increased their output of the precious metal. Iron ore production fell, however, and new projects were put on hold, thus damaging the economic interests of Senegal and more especially Liberia, though Chinese investors persevered with new joint ventures with Mauritania and an agreement for the expansion of the country's port facilities. Diamond and bauxite production faced problems, which affected the economy of Sierra Leone, exacerbated by the absence of taxation on artisanal production of diamonds, most of which were smuggled across state boundaries. Construction of an aluminium factory in Guinea slowed down. Phosphates production in Togo continued to stagnate, despite plans for the modernisation of the industry. The gradual recovery of oil prices did not allow Nigeria, which also suffered a systemic banking crisis, to cash in sufficiently, partly because of stagnant production in the Niger Delta, which was beset by militia violence. Nigeria's foreign reserves fell from $ 52 bn to $ 10 bn at year's end. By contrast, oil prospecting in Ghana continued unabated, feeding expectations.

International **cotton** prices remained low, thus damaging the interests of several countries in the sub-region, and notably of their peasant population. Farmers in Benin, which depends on cotton for nearly half of its foreign exchange earnings, turned to other (food) crops, partly also because of domestic management problems. In Mali, too, production continued to fall, continuing the patterns of the preceding years. In Togo, production declined by 25%, to an historic low of 30,000 tonnes. By contrast, in Burkina, prices recovered to pre-crisis rates, modestly boosting overall production. Small and unstable Guinea-Bissau suffered from the decline in prices for **cashew kernels**, the country's major export crop. **Cocoa** farmers in Côte d'Ivoire, beset by bad state management, temporarily withheld beans in attempts to boost prices, while their counterparts in Ghana benefited from an expansion of production and the rise in the crop's international price in September, part of which was transferred to the farmers.

In many countries, prices of imported **food crops,** such as rice, fell, benefiting the population, at least in the urban areas. Thanks to government fertiliser programmes, rice production in Mali rose, as in Gambia, where it doubled, while Togo heralded plans for another 'green revolution' focusing on a boost in cocoa, coffee and rice production, as well as fish. Generally, the economic situation in the Sahelian countries benefited from better food production, though this was not the case in Niger. In Senegal, production of cereals, including groundnuts, grew as a result of good rainfall.

On the downside, **remittances** fell, in some countries more than in others. The sub-region was also struck by occasional **epidemics**, in addition to natural disasters. An outbreak of bacterial meningitis in Central and West Africa, which particularly affected the Sahelian zones, led to some 2,500 deaths in the two sub-regions by April. Nigeria was the worst affected, followed by Burkina and Niger. It was the worst outbreak since 1996. Nigeria needed millions of doses of vaccine, though vaccination had been held up by several factors including poverty and ignorance, fed partly by local cultural suspicions about immunisation. This had been worsened by the flawed anti-meningitis drug test by American pharmaceutical conglomerate Pfizer in 1996, which killed more than 50 children. The company this year finally reached an out-of-court settlement with the state government of Kano. Cape Verde was hit by an outbreak of Dengue fever in the autumn, affecting more than 20,000 people. Several countries in the sub-region were affected by **floods** as a result of torrential rains, including Burkina Faso, Niger, Benin, Senegal, Ghana, Gambia, Sierra Leone, Guinea and Mauritania. In total, an estimated 350,000 people were confronted with the consequences, including several deaths and the destruction of infrastructure and homes. A **plague** of crop-destroying army worms (the caterpillar stage of moths) affected 400,000 people in Liberia, but its spread into Côte d'Ivoire was contained.

The international **drugs trade** continued to use the sub-region as a hub for the transport of cocaine to Europe. Guinea-Bissau reinforced cooperation with the UN Office on Drugs and Crime and Venezuela to combat the trade. One spectacular incident underlining its expansion in West Africa took place in Mali, where a Boeing 727 was found in the northern desert zone after having transported vast amounts of cocaine from Venezuela. It had landed on an illegal airstrip but crashed during take-off after offloading its freight.

The traffickers and their cargo had disappeared, showing the importance of the Sahara in smuggling operations.

The expansion of the **power sector**, whose deficiency, as in other sub-regions, continued to hinder development, took some very small steps forward. While Nigeria did not even reach half of its production target of 6,000 MW of electricity, in Niger a beginning was made with the construction of the Kandadji dam, which would help boost power. In Sierra Leone, a 50 MW hydro-dam began producing electricity for the capital.

Sub-regional Organisations: Cooperation and Conflict

Intelligence became the subject of increasing cooperation, with regard to the issue of both drugs trafficking and smuggling and, more broadly, terrorism and money laundering. West African defence chiefs met in Lomé early in the year to look for common approaches in this area, while in September the governments of Mali, Niger, Mauritania and Algeria discussed terrorism and cross-border crime – issues that had become more important as a result of the rise in kidnappings of Westerners. The intelligence agencies of these countries were already cooperating with each other in efforts to fight this new plague. Plans were made for the establishment of a geopolitical and strategic 'watchdog' (think tank) in Bamako. In May, West African countries set up a Committee of Chiefs of Security Services in Dakar, which would also include customs and immigration services. An ECOWAS meeting in March recommended that immediate steps should be taken to address drugs trafficking, for which Guinea, Guinea-Bissau and Cape Verde were to serve as pilot countries.

Defence and security were also the subject of various cooperation initiatives. In June, an exercise took place in Benin together with members of the US Africa command (AFRICOM). Earlier in the year (12 February) that country witnessed joint exercises between Belgian soldiers and members of the military from Niger, Benin and Togo ('Dassa 2009'), as a result of a defence agreement between Benin and Belgium signed in 2000. Military observers from various countries, including Nigeria, Burkina Faso and Côte d'Ivoire, were present. AFRICOM held training courses on navy ships to fight piracy and drugs smuggling in the framework of the 'Africa Partnership Station', a naval component of AFRICOM. To this purpose, exercises took place in Nigerian waters. ECOWAS went ahead with the development of its ECOWAS Standby Force (ESF). A training exercise ('Jigui 2009') for its logistic component, involving 1,270 troops from seven countries, began on 12 June in Burkina Faso. Defence chiefs of the organisation approved the structure of the ESF's Main Brigade and, on 21 November, an ordinary ECOWAS summit in Abuja authorised the release of $ 2 m for the start of one of the sub-regional logistics depots in Sierra Leone to support peacekeeping operations. The ESF was now also to comprise a flexible force of 2,500 for deployment within 14 instead of

30 days to conform to AU standards. On 20 November, the ECOWAS Convention on Small Arms and Light Weapons came into force.

ECOWAS mediation took place in various conflicts, notably Guinea, Guinea-Bissau and Niger. More generally, ECOWAS defence chiefs called for a review of the 1999 protocol on conflict prevention with a view to addressing flash points that could develop into violent conflicts. **Guinea-Bissau** was the subject of continued attention and, while ECOWAS could hardly be expected to significantly ameliorate the country's stability, at least it contributed to the return of some normality in the course of the year. ECOWAS chair, President Yar'Adua of Nigeria, responded to the killing of President Vieira with the announcement that a delegation of foreign ministers (Nigeria, Burkina, Cape Verde, Gambia and Senegal) plus the president of the Commission would travel to Bissau for discussion with stakeholders. Sharp language was used to denounce the political killings and pressure the country's armed forces to uphold the rule of law. The meeting of the Committee of Chiefs of Defence Staff of ECOWAS members on 4–6 March decided to deploy a multidisciplinary group to coordinate Guinea-Bissau's security sector reform. The ECOWAS summit in Abuja on 22 June discussed this issue, deciding among other things to provide $ 3.5 m to pay the salary arrears of members of Guinea-Bissau's armed forces, while also granting some money for the presidential elections held that month to complete the political transition process. The ECOWAS chair announced a donor conference for after the elections (at a roundtable for Guinea-Bissau's security sector reform in Cape Verde on 19 April ECOWAS had already pledged $ 13.5 m), and the summit urged the international community to begin investigations into the several political killings that had beset the country during the first half of the year.

Guinea's membership in ECOWAS was suspended on 10 January in reponse to the unconstitutional takeover in that country by the military the previous year. The organisation's influence on the developments in Guinea was weakened by resistance from Senegal and Libya to the hard ECOWAS line. When the organisation asked President Compaoré of Burkina Faso to mediate between Guinea's political forces, its influence was hardly boosted as a result of the pro-junta stance taken by the Burkinabè head of state. However, ECOWAS pursued peace in the broader framework of the International Contact Group on Guinea, and the atrocities in Conakry's sports stadium at the end of September met with a sharp response that included the imposition of an arms embargo under the Convention on Small Arms and Light Weapons (17 October). The organisation also insisted on an international inquiry.

While the effectiveness of these measures was smothered by the violence within the leadership of the Guinean military itself, the ECOWAS stand on **Niger** hit the brick wall of President Tandja's obstinacy. Neither the Council of the Wise, the Mediation and Security Council, an ad hoc committee to confer with stakeholders, nor a delegation led by Liberia's President Sirleaf, could dissuade the head of state from his collision course.

Tandja's decision to go ahead with the parliamentary elections after ECOWAS had explicitly asked him not to do so, led to a furious reaction from the West African body, which suspended Niger's membership the day after the elections were held "in total disregard of the Authority of Heads of State and Government". ECOWAS warned that it would not recognise the outcome of the parliamentary polls, and went as far as to deny the legitimacy of the president's tenure after expiry of the constitutional deadline on 22 December. This only led to the breaking-off of negotiations by Niger's government and, while the failure of ECOWAS mediation could be laid squarely at Tandja's door, it left the West African institution without influence and the crisis in the country unresolved.

ECOWAS boosted its cooperation with Spain in the area of illegal **migration**, for which it received € 10 m of Spanish funding. A special ECOWAS-Spain summit took place immediately following the 36th ECOWAS summit on 22 June, and was attended by the Spanish prime minister. It covered a range of issues, such as sub-regional integration, professional training and the development of the ECOWAS Agricultural Policy (ECOWAP).

ECOWAS also announced as part of ECOWAP a five-year programme of food security, for which a sub-regional fund on **agriculture** totalling $ 900 m was planned. A new public-private sector partnership called the West Africa Seed Alliance was launched on 5 October with the objective of boosting yields by improving access to better and locally adapted seed varieties. As noted, rice production had already significantly increased in several countries, benefiting from New Rice for Africa (NERICA) varieties introduced by the West Africa Rice Development Association, among others. West African experts came together in Lomé on 15–16 September to hammer out a common sub-regional stance on **climate change**, ahead of a common AU position for the Copenhagen climate conference in December.

Not unexpectedly, in the area of **monetary cooperation** there was a setback. The members of the West African Monetary Zone (the non-CFAfr countries Nigeria, Ghana, Guinea, Gambia and Sierra Leone) extended to at least 2014 the take-off date for their common currency, the ECO, which should have been introduced this year as a step towards one sub-regional currency at a later date. Only Gambia had reached the conditions set out for the currency's introduction. In September, the Francophone UEMOA came up with concrete steps to boost the interconnection between banks in its member states so as to reduce costs. In each member state, three banks would participate in a network to be developed to this purpose.

ECOWAS approved a revision of its Common External Tariff with the creation of a fifth band of 35% to be levied on certain goods imported into the sub-region. Efforts to harmonise value added taxes in member states were endorsed. Discussions about EPAs with the EU continued – ECOWAS calling on the Europeans to finance plans to increase the competitiveness of West Africa's economies.

New **infrastructural projects** servicing the sub-region included an agreement for the construction of the West Africa Cable System linking West Africa and Europe by way of a submarine fibre-optic cable, which would allow more internet connectivity. The AfDB was involved in co-funding the (private/public) project, which was worth a total of $ 240 m. The AfDB also approved a grant of $ 17.6 m for the ECOWAS Network of African Institutions of Science and Technology project aimed at improving the supply of engineers and scientists. This area of cooperation also included the ECOWAS Technical and Vocational Education and Training Initiative, for which Spain made available € 240 m over a three-year period. On 3 July, Nigeria, Niger and Algeria signed an agreement for the building of a trans-Saharan gas pipeline to transport natural gas from Nigeria to North Africa and Europe. Finally, ECOWAS called on donors to help fund existing initiatives to address sub-regional power shortages.

Klaas van Walraven

Benin

The promises of presidential and parliamentary elections in 2011 dominated the political agenda. The year was marked by political struggles between government and opposition. President Boni Yayi faced strong opposition in the National Assembly as well as growing dissatisfaction within his own majority camp. The government pushed ahead with its ambitious programme to improve the reliability of the electoral register in preparation for the 2011 polls. Growth slowed, despite economic measures and initiatives to promote the private sector and boost the economy. The socioeconomic situation for most of the population remained precarious, adding to growing popular disenchantment with the politics of change promoted by Boni Yayi since 2006.

Domestic Politics

Without an outright majority in parliament, President Boni Yayi encountered important difficulties in governing. At the same time, a growing **division** within the presidential camp emerged. A few MPs in the ruling coalition, 'Force Cauris pour un Bénin Emergent' (FCBE), left the presidential camp to join other parties or coalitions (such as G13), showing discontent and rivalries within the 'mouvance présidentielle'. By contrast, MPs from other political parties negotiated moves towards the FCBE.

Thus, several MPs **crossed the floor**, which had particular significance for the balance between the FCBE and G13, and was especially linked to the race for the March 2011 presidential and parliamentary elections. In order to secure his re-election, Boni Yayi actively tried to broaden his political base and open up access to his camp for more parties and associations (under the plural majority agenda). On 2 April, one of the FCBE MPs joined the G13, following the example of another FCBE parliamentarian the year before. On 30 April, some MPs collectively resigned from the FCBE to create a new parliamentary group while they still claimed to belong to the presidential majority. On 16 May, in his opening speech on the occasion of the formation of a new political coalition (the 'Union pour la Majorité Présidentielle Plurielle') in Cotonou, Boni Yayi addressed over 180 parties and 150 associations, inviting them to unite. This attempt at unification around the figure of the president was intended to heal divisions among his supporters and increase his chances in the next polls. Unofficially, Boni Yayi had already been challenged by various candidates and an opposition coalition called 'L'Union Fait la Nation' made up of 'Force Clé', G13 and G4 (G4 itself composed of the 'Renaissance du Bénin', 'Mouvement Africain pour le Développement et le Progrès', 'Parti du Renouveau Démocratique' and 'Parti Social-Démocrate').

Many influential politicians moved in the opposite direction, from the opposition to the presidential wing. On 21 April, MP Rachidi Gbadamassi (former mayor of Parakou and hostile opponent of Boni Yayi since 2006) left G13 to join the ruling FCBE, followed on 16 July by MP Joachim Dahissiho. Media and civil society organisations criticised this political 'nomadism' and the predominant role of money as serious ethical problems for the National Assembly. The defection of opposition politicians to the presidential camp also increased the number of rivals within the ruling party, contributing to tension in the FCBE. Several FCBE MPs also tended to abandon the president (though unofficially) for his rivals, among whom was Abdoulaye Bio Tchané. Bio Tchané is president of the 'Banque Ouest Africaine de Développement' (BOAD), as Boni Yayi had been before entering the 2006 presidential elections. Like Boni Yayi, Bio Tchané is from northern Benin and represented a serious, though undeclared, challenge to the head of state in the upcoming race.

In this context, the computerised **electoral register,** called the 'Liste Electorale Permanente Informatisée' (LEPI), and the census, the 'Recensement Electoral National Approfondi', became major subjects of debate. The National Assembly had been plunged into crisis the previous year (with the vote of the LEPI bill postponed several times), but legislation on both issues was finally examined on 30 April. Pressed by civil society groups joined in the 'Front des Organisations de la Société Civile pour la Réalisation de la Liste Electorale Permanente Informatisée', the National Assembly finally passed the bill to approve the new register on 4 May by a majority of 64 votes to nil with 1 abstention. While this was considered a step forward for the transparency of elections, the conflict between the president's opponents and supporters was not over. With major worries about potential fraud and manipulation, the ruling FCBE and the opposition coalition of G4, G13 and Force Clé battled to take over the institution in charge of supervising the computerisation of the voter registry (the 'Comité Politique de Supervision de la LEPI'). A further step was taken on 23 November, when the head of state launched the national electoral census. The computerised permanent electoral project has been supported by most of Benin's financial partners, among them the EU, the US, France, Spain and the Netherlands. The cost of the LEPI was estimated at CFAfr 25 bn.

Several **corruption** scandals rocked the public sector. In July, a major case (called 'CEN-SAD gate') involving two ministers was discussed in successive extraordinary cabinet meetings chaired by the president himself. Finance Minister Soulé Mana Lawani and Minister of Urban Development François Noudégbessi were suspected of embezzling CFAfr 2–6 bn allocated to the restoration of the International Conference Centre and the 'Palais des Congrès' in Cotonou. Noudégbessi was first suspended and then reinstated in the government after being found innocent. Following investigations by the 'Inspection Générale d'Etat', the finance minister was charged with irregularities in relation to building contracts and procurement of heavy equipment. He was dismissed and replaced on 9 June. Other corruption cases emerged in the customs sector, involving more than CFAfr 12 bn, and also in the port of Cotonou. On 9 December, the 'fourth national day' in the fight against corruption was held in Cotonou, chaired by Minister of Administrative and Institutional Reform Joseph Ahanhanzo. The government recognised that corruption was a serious challenge and that Benin's public finances suffered from fiscal and customs fraud. According to TI, Benin was ranked the 106th most corrupt country in the world, with a score of 2.9, indicating that corruption was perceived as rampant (very close to the score of 3 that denotes that corruption is perceived as a serious challenge by businessmen). In comparison with the previous year, Benin regressed in its score. On 21 August, the president appointed for the first time in Benin an ombudsman, whose five-year mandate includes receiving citizens' complaints about the functioning of the central administration, local government and public institutions. Corruption also affected the private sector, notably tour operators organising the Hajj to Saudi Arabia.

On 26 June, at a press conference in Porto Novo, National Assembly Questor Sacca Fikara, also a member of the G13 Alliance, criticised the government for its record on **press freedom**. He questioned the impartiality of the state media organisation, which had refused to broadcast his televised statement, recorded on a private channel, on the grounds that he had made inflammatory allegations against the government and the head of state and that his statements did not aid national unity. The dispute was related to Bio Tchané's supposed intention to stand in the next presidential polls. It was feared that the fact that two politicians from the north (Bio Tchané and Boni Yayi) would contest the elections could divide the northern electorate. The independent mass media regulatory body, the 'Haute Autorité de l'Audiovisuel et de la Communication', summoned the director of state television, Julien Akpaki, who explained he could not broadcast statements that might cause trouble. On 29 October, the 'Union des Professionnels des Médias du Bénin' expressed its regret about the decline of press freedom. According to 'Reporters sans Frontières', Benin fell to 72nd place out of 168 countries worldwide – in 2006 Benin was the highest-placed African country, ranked 23.

On 13 May in Cotonou, Boni Yayi launched an award in memory of the late Beninese prelate, Cardinal Bernardin Gantin, who died in 2008 at the age of 86. Cardinal Gantin was the dean of the College of the Cardinals of the Vatican and occupied top posts in the **Catholic Church.**

Foreign Affairs

External relations were dominated by negotiations related to the computerised electoral register and development programmes. In view of its dependence on investment by foreign partners, the government engaged in a diplomatic offensive, resulting in a number of bilateral and multilateral agreements.

On 2 December, Boni Yayi visited the Bretton Woods Institutions in Washington DC. He obtained CFAfr 52 bn in temporary funding from the World Bank to address the difficult situation that confronted Benin and to support economic and financial reforms. Foreign Affairs Minister Jean-Marie Ehouzou attended the UN General Assembly on 15–30 September, pointing out that the world financial crisis had jeopardised the success of government measures tackling marginalisation and poverty and promoting human rights. He also stressed that Benin suffered from drought and coastal erosion due to rising sea levels and called for the establishment of a multilateral investment fund under the aegis of the UN and AU to combat environmental problems resulting from climate change. Benin also participated in the UN Climate Change Conference (COP15) in **Copenhagen** on 7–18 December.

On the **Asian front**, Boni Yayi travelled to India (March 3–7), where he signed several agreements on financial, economic, technical and political cooperation. Following this visit, it was decided to open a new embassy in New Delhi. On 29–31 July, the government organised the first 'Journées de l'Inde' in Cotonou, followed on 22 October by the first session of the 'Commission Mixte de Coopération Bénino-Indienne'. On 23 October, Benin received a $ 15 m loan from India. China also provided support to Benin through various programmes including infrastructure construction, including the Godomey interchange in Cotonou and Parakou hospital, among others. On 24 August, Boni Yayi officially received a South Korean donation of CFAfr 1 bn worth of equipment for Dantokpa market and the modernisation of the 'Société de Gestion des Marchés Autonome'. Japan provided financial support for the restoration of the 'Hôpital de la Mère et de l'Enfant'.

Benin also received diplomatic visits from various European countries (Finland, France), African countries (Equatorial Guinea, Liberia) and the Middle-East (Kuwait, Iran). Benin strengthened its partnership with **Brazil**, where a Beninese cultural week was organised in Salvador de Bahia (19–22 November) and a first session of the 'Commission Mixte de Coopération Bénino-Brésilienne' was held in Cotonou on 12–13 March. Jean-Marie Ehouzou, head of the ministry of foreign affairs, visited Canada, Cuba and Mexico. Benin and the US continued their cooperation through the Millennium Challenge Account and other programmes, notably in health and education, supported by USAID. USAID provided three grants to support livestock markets.

Boni Yayi travelled several times to **Europe**, specifically to the Netherlands (20–24 January), France (governmental visit and UNESCO on 14–30 April), and Spain (8–10 December) to consolidate cooperation agreements and negotiate financial support for the electoral register. New embassies were opened, one in Rome and one in the Vatican as well as one in Doha (Qatar). The government received a working visit from France's minister of immigration, integration and national identity on 8–9 January. Former President Chirac was received to discuss health projects initiated by the Chirac Foundation, together with the presidents of Senegal, Burkina Faso, Niger, Togo, DRC and CAR. The government created a special commission of reflection to evaluate the prospects of cooperation with France. There were bilateral annual meetings with France, Denmark, Germany and Canada.

Benin hosted several international and sub-regional **meetings**, including the 'Comité Technique de l'Observatoire des Fonctions Publiques Africaines' on 12–13 February; a conference on Sino-African ties on 23–27 April; and the 28th ordinary session of the Council of Ministers of the ABN on 24–29 September. Benin also participated in meetings of the Entente, ECOWAS and AU. Boni Yayi visited neighbouring countries, including Niger (8 January), Togo (10 February) and Nigeria (June 9, August 4) and also went to Mali (10 May), Côte d'Ivoire (22 May) and Burkina (23 May).

From 30 June to 2 July the government organised a national forum on the management of Benin's **international borders**. A national commission of frontiers was established, while on 7 September Burkina Faso and Benin signed a resolution to submit their disagreement over the Koualou Kourou region to the International Court of Justice. A similar issue was discussed with the president of Nigeria in August.

Socioeconomic Developments

Responsible for 40%–45% of total foreign-exchange earnings, **cotton** continued to be the most important cash earner for the economy. As a consequence of the fall in international cotton prices, internal crises in the cotton sector and failed government efforts to support the sector (including a project to boost production and reimburse arrears to producers of about $ 18 m), cotton farmers preferred to produce corn, rice and other cereals. The decline, which has affected cotton, cotton oil production and exports, reduced national growth. GDP was estimated at about $ 6.4 bn (or $ 1,500 per capita), a growth rate of 3.2%. An IMF mission that took place 14–28 September concluded that the external current account deficit, excluding grants, was expected to widen to about 13% of GDP, reflecting the decline in cotton exports, which more than offset the improvement in the terms of trade.

A large part of Benin's trade remained informal and unrecorded, especially cross-border exchanges with Nigeria (fuel, commercial crops, re-exportation of imported goods). Because of the informal character of this trade, the state has been losing several CFAfr billions in taxes and customs duties. Moreover, **illegal trade in fuel** between Nigeria and Benin continued, despite police attempts to stop trafficking. Thousands of people are involved in the illicit distribution of fuel, on which motorised transportation largely depends. Import, transportation and sale of the illicit gasoline called 'kpayo' caused several accidental fires and explosions leading to several deaths and injuries throughout 2009.

Inflation reached 4%. At the beginning of the year, the inflation rate was pushed up by the rise in the price of domestic rather than imported goods. Inflation then declined because of lower agricultural prices, thanks to a good cereal harvest, and lower international food and fuel prices.

Several strikes took place in the **health** sector, which remained in crisis, despite important investments (CFAfr 56 bn were allocated in the budget). Basic healthcare remained extremely poor because of the lack of medical equipment and competent, motivated staff. Strikes were motivated by disparities and inequities in payments owed to workers, as well as unfulfilled commitments regarding professional reclassification. On 25 May, opposition leaders accused Boni Yayi's government of indifference toward the strikes, which paralysed the system. Successive meetings between a governmental team and health workers' unions in June led to an exceptional agreement according to which special bonuses were allocated and paid to more than 8,000 workers (though this expenditure had not been planned in the 2009 national budget). The payment of 50% of the amount (about CFAfr 1.8 bn) was decided by a cabinet meeting on 9 June. Other intermittent strikes started in the summer and paralysed the **education** sector until the end of the year. Following these strikes, the government, pushed by donors and opposition parties, proposed a reform of the civil-service pay structure, which was characterised by a system of bonuses and benefits, making it discriminatory and non-transparent and a source of frustrations and claims undermining economic development.

Higher bonuses for civil servants, recruitment of new staff in public administration and a carryover of capital expenditure commitments caused slippages in government **expenditure**. At the same time, government revenue declined because of a reduction in customs collection in the context of a slowdown in imports, lower levels of tax collection and embezzlement of public resources. This led to a worsening fiscal position during the first quarter. In that situation, the authorities were encouraged to continue the implementation of reforms already under way (tax collection, customs, control of expenditure in the public sector including the reform of bonus allocations and other fringe benefits to civil servants, civil service reform). An IMF mission noted progress in the implementation of structural reforms (privatisations), but asked the government for more control of public expenditure, which was contributing to a structural fiscal deficit estimated at about CFAfr 416 bn for 2009 (CFAfr 101 bn more than in 2008). **Fiscal policy** was therefore geared toward maintaining a balanced overall fiscal position, including grants. It focused on improving tax administration (especially in customs) and better public resource utilisation while, on the expenditure side, the goals were to ensure that spending reflected government priorities for the private sector, the social sector and infrastructure. Structural reforms under the programme focus on the government plan to promote private investment, expand social programmes, and reduce poverty.

The government decided to partially privatise the 'Société Industrielle du Bois du Bénin' in order to continue reducing state involvement in production and commercial activities. Related to this were plans to develop a regulatory framework promoting competition in sectors to be privatised. These reforms also concerned the **port of Cotonou**. On 10 September, the government signed a 25-year concession agreement for the South Wharf Container Terminal with Bolloré Africa Logistics, led by the Bolloré Group of France, which won the bid to invest in and manage container handling. The Bolloré Group's proposal included a commitment to pay fees of $ 200 m over the first eight years and to invest $ 256 m in operating equipment and civil works over the life of the concession. This should improve Cotonou port performance and security, expand capacity and increase government revenues and trade by cutting costs and delays, developing markets for Benin's agriculture and fishing industries, and increasing trade opportunities for West Africa's landlocked economies.

According to a World Bank survey, Beninese companies faced various obstacles caused by long delays in securing permits and licences from corrupt government officials. Benin's **microfinance** sector has also been encountering serious difficulties. Levels of deposits, outstanding loan portfolios and loan arrears showed a degenerating situation. The growth of lending activities, inadequately controlled and managed, continued, despite endemic fraud and loans arrears. Yayi Boni's intervention, using microfinance as a political weapon, went against World Bank warnings (29 June) and aggravated the situation. Looming elections could exacerbate this.

The government intended to continue **decentralisation** reforms, agreeing on a new territorial organisation with 29 'départements' instead of 12.

In May, the EU granted Benin **budgetary aid** to the value of € 50.5 m (about CFAfr 33 bn) for the period 2009–2011. This aid was aimed at supporting implementation of the current poverty reduction and growth strategy in a bid to meet the MDGs. The same month, BOAD granted Benin a CFAfr 8 bn loan towards the construction of the road linking Djougou-Ouaké to the Togo border. The head of BOAD and undeclared presidential contender, Bio Tchané, originated from Djougou. Jointly financed by the Regional Integration Fund and UEMOA, the project would help open up the north-central part of the country. The project was supplemented by two other **road construction** programmes in the northern region. The first links the northwestern Atacora and Donga departments to the main national Cotonou-Niamey road. On 21 October, Boni Yayi inaugurated the 126 km Djougou-N'Dali road. The CFAfr 1 bn costs were supported by the national budget and loans from BOAD, the 'Fonds Africain de Développement' and the 'Fonds Spéciaux du Nigéria'. A second project linking N'Dali-Biro-Nikki-Chicandou to the Nigerian frontier was also launched, supported by Abu Dhabi, in order to improve east-west connections and increase trade between Benin and its neighbours in the subregion. In the same context, the government in April also approved an emergency programme of road reconstruction, maintenance and repair for the period up to year's end. BOAD granted Benin several other loans, including CFAfr 4 bn for a sanitation project (the 'Programme d'Assainissement d'Abomey') on 13 May, CFAfr 9 bn for a food security project on 25 August, and another CFAfr 4 bn on 9 September for a sanitation project in the capital Porto Novo.

Eric Komlavi Hahonou

Burkina Faso

The political, social and economic situation became more settled during the year. Heading towards the virtually certain re-election of President Compaoré in November 2010, both the presidential and opposition camps tried with modest success to strengthen their political standing. The mixed performance did not result in significant changes in the political landscape, largely defined by the predominance of the presidential party and continued fragmentation of the opposition, in part co-opted by the government. Heavy flooding had disastrous consequences for Ouagadougou's infrastructure and proved a burden for the national budget, in addition to the world financial crisis. Meanwhile, President Compaoré enhanced his sub-regional diplomatic standing by mediating in Guinea.

Domestic Politics

By mid-year, both the presidential and opposition camps launched early **pre-campaign activities** for the 2010 presidential elections. The major goal was to close ranks. While the ruling 'Congrès pour la Démocratie et le Progrès' (CDP) sorted out some of its leadership problems in order to achieve this, the leading opposition party 'Union pour la Renaissance/Parti Sankariste' (UNIR/PS) tried to bring about more unity between the bickering adversaries of President Compaoré. The CDP used its fourth ordinary congress in Ouagadougou on 23–25 July to restructure its leadership, and many leading positions were reshuffled after the departure of dissidents. In addition, the executive committee ('Bureau Exécutif National', BEN) was enlarged from 22 to 37 members in order to include more loyal personnel. Previously, the party had suffered from several occurrences of internal strife.

Six former leaders of the 'Convention Nationale des Patriotes Progressistes' (CNPP), which had merged into the CDP in 1996, left the BEN ahead of the party congress on 23 April. This group of senior politicians, headed by CDP's second vice president Marc Yao, had repeatedly denounced the party leadership's authoritarian style, but also felt marginalised. Their departure followed their suspension from all party functions in June 2008 and thus forestalled their possible formal exclusion by the congress. In August, the dissidents organised the founding congress of **a new party**, the 'Convention Nationale du Progrès du Burkina' (CNPB). About 400 delegates – many more than expected – attended the meeting and elected Moussa Boly as the CNPB's president. He immediately declared the CNPB to be part of the opposition. The party's name clearly alluded to the politicians' former political home and underlined their aspiration to reactivate old popular loyalties.

Meanwhile, Salif Diallo lost the first vice presidency of the **ruling party**, the CDP, as the result of an interview he had given to the 'Observateur Paalga' newspaper on 7 July, in which he called for more democracy and profound reforms of Burkina's political system. In particular, he suggested the abolition of the presidential system of government in favour of a parliamentary one, thus implicitly questioning the position and role of President Compaoré. Diallo was said to have been one of the president's closest allies until he was dismissed from the government and sent to take up a diplomatic post in Vienna in March 2008. Diallo's statements provoked sharp protest from leading CDP members, including the party president Roch Marc Christian Kaboré, who told him to exercise self-criticism. Since Diallo refused to apologise or acknowledge that he was mistaken, the CDP suspended him from all party positions on 16 July. During the CDP congress, Kanidoua Naboho, a former head of the parliamentary party, replaced Diallo as the first vice president. Simon Compaoré, the mayor of Ouagadougou, replaced Yao as the second vice president, ceding his own function as the party's secretary general to Achille Tapsoba.

In a more inclusive style, the 'Union pour la Renaissance/Mouvement Sankariste' welcomed new adherents from other **Sankarist parties**, particularly from Ernest Nongma Ouédraogo's 'Convention Panafricaine Sankariste' (CPS) and parts of the 'Front des Forces Sociales' led by Nestor Bassière. At a conference in Ouagadougou on 21–22 March, the party was renamed 'Parti' instead of 'Mouvement', in order to highlight the process of enlargement. Several new members were integrated in the executive committee, which Bénéwendé Stanislas Sankara continued to head as party president. However, they failed to achieve the aim of uniting all the so-called Sankarist parties, which form a major part of the fragmented opposition, though they all refer to the politics of late President Thomas Sankara (no relation of Bénéwendé).

Other politicians also began **political manoeuvres** ahead of the 2010 polls. On 10 October, the president of the 'Parti pour la Démocratie et le Progrès/Parti Socialiste' (PDP/PS), François Kaboré, confidently announced that his party wanted a unified opposition bloc, presenting a common candidate for the presidential race. However, the proposal came months after the UNIR/PS congress in March had proclaimed Sankara to be the presidential candidate. Kaboré was therefore implicitly challenging Sankara's leading role in the opposition. Sankara had won 4.9% of the votes cast in 2005, ending as runner-up. While he had failed to seriously threaten the incumbent, he had been well ahead of the PDP/PS party's then president, Ali Lankoandé, who had received 1.7%. When it was led by the famous historian Joseph Ki-Zerbo, PDP/PS was Burkina's most important opposition party, but his successors could not maintain the party's achievements, which eventually resulted in several splits and resignations. On 31 January, another of the most important opposition politicians, the country's first president's son Hermann Yaméogo, hinted at a possible electoral boycott by his party ('Union Nationale pour la Démocratie et le Développement') because of the – in his view – unacceptable conditions in which President Compaoré's previous re-elections had been secured. In 2005, Yaméogo had withdrawn his candidacy so shortly before election day that his name still appeared on the ballot paper.

The **second largest party** in parliament, the 'Alliance pour la Démocratie et la Fédération/Rassemblement Démocratique Africain' (ADF/RDA), which Yaméogo had headed until 2003, was expected to support President Compaoré in the 2010 election as it had in 2005. Simultaneously, ADF/RDA claimed to belong to the parliamentary opposition against the CDP. However, due to ADF/RDA's continued participation in government – party president Gilbert Ouédraogo continued to be minister of transport – it officially lost its status as an opposition party when the opposition law was amended in mid-April. From then on, UNIR/PS's Bénéwendé Sankara enjoyed the formal position of leader of the opposition, since he led the largest party in parliament that did not support or participate in government.

Also in mid-April, the **electoral law** was amended without touching crucial questions such as the composition of the Independent National Electoral Commission or the size of constituencies, currently favouring the ruling party. The reforms lowered the requirements for access to public funding for political parties and for the admission of presidential candidates. They also introduced a 30% quota for women candidates in parliamentary elections, tightened security measures with regard to the issuing of voter cards, and prohibited the use of images of national heroes in party logos. Another amendment aimed to ban so-called 'floor crossers' or 'political nomads'. MPs who change their party affiliation in the course of a legislative term, thus unilaterally altering the voters' choice, lose their parliamentary seat. Significantly, Burkinabè living abroad were now enfranchised. While their voting preferences are unknown, the inclusion of millions of diaspora citizens – estimates vary from 3–6 up to 12–13 million – could have a deep impact on future elections. However, with a large majority of them living in neighbouring countries, particularly Côte d'Ivoire, the registration process constituted a challenge to the authorities and was not expected to be completed by the date of the 2010 contest.

In May, prominent citizens founded the 'Forum des citoyens de l'alternance' (**citizens' forum** for alternation in power). The initiators included Augustin Loada, the country's leading political scientist and head of the think-tank 'Centre pour la Gouvernance Démocratique' (CGD); Prosper Farama, a renowned human rights lawyer; and Zéphirin Diabré, a highly-placed employee of French nuclear giant Areva, former senior CDP government minister and former deputy head of UNDP. About 250 participants attended the forum, mostly critics of President Compaoré's prolonged stay in power. Only a small number of them represented political parties. The forum's implicit call for a change and an interview Diabré gave to the 'Observateur Paalga' in January gave rise to speculation about the latter's political ambitions. However, Diabré denied any intention to run for presidential office.

Meanwhile, on 9 March, the president of the CDP group in parliament, Mahama Sawadogo, refuelled debate on **presidential term limits** by rebutting the position of the Burkinabè bishops, who advocated preservation of the two-terms clause introduced into the Constitution in 2002. On 30 November, in a guest contribution to the parastatal newspaper 'Sidwaya', Sawadogo reaffirmed that this limit would deprive the sovereign people of their right to pronounce upon the president's record. Although Compaoré had already served two electoral terms at the time of the 2005 presidential elections, in addition to his four years as unconstitutional military leader, his supporters as well as the courts argued that the term limit would only commence with the first five-year period from 2005–2010. Consequently, his expected re-election in 2010 would be constitutional. However, the new debate on the relevant article 37 of the constitution was probably launched with an eye on the 2015 polls. On 11 June, the CGD published survey results according to which 53% of the Burkinabè favoured the term limit.

The social situation remained tense, although unrest and violence did not reach the same alarming levels as the previous year. University teachers, trade unions, retired soldiers and traders took part in **strikes and riots** to express their dissatisfaction with government policies. Lecturers, researchers, workers and soldiers mainly called for better working and living conditions, higher salaries and pensions, as well as tax relief. While workers organised short stoppages, academic staff blockaded the University of Ouagadougou for three months (April to June). This followed extensive student strikes the previous year, thus further impairing the country's higher education sector. However, working conditions at the university were so unacceptable that even government concessions offering a 30% salary increase could not bring the strike to an early end.

Government reactions to **other protests** were less conciliatory. Traders in all three major towns clashed with police, accusing police officers of malpractice. First, frequent police checks provoked riots in the central market in Ouagadougou in late June. Violence escalated when a young trader died in police action on 7 July. Second, riots erupted in Koudougou after the police sanctioned merchants who failed to pay market rents. Eventually, the local authorities agreed to reduce fees by a fifth. Finally, traders complained about police inaction against frequent thefts in Bobo-Dioulasso. Suspecting that the police benefited from connivance with delinquents, the situation led to violent incidents (24 July). A demonstration by retired soldiers in Ouagadougou was violently dispersed by gendarmes on 27 August after permission for their march had been abruptly revoked.

Foreign Affairs

Relations with **Côte d'Ivoire** remained central to foreign policy. Compaoré's continued efforts to mediate in the neighbouring country's internal conflict were closely related to the desire for stability – Burkina being largely dependent on Côte d'Ivoire's trade channels and millions of its citizens living and working there. However, Compaoré's involvement led to ambiguous results at best. Political deadlock in Abidjan continued. Following several meetings the previous year, Burkina's president again met the chairman of the Ivorian electoral commission on 4 July without any significant outcome, since the elections were neither organised nor rescheduled at year's end. Talks with UN officials (Special Representative of the UN Secretary General on 10 February and 22 October, UN Under-Secretary General for Peacekeeping on 11 June) also failed to contribute to visible progress. Neither did the first official visit of President Compaoré to Abidjan since the beginning of the Ivorian crisis (15–18 September). However, the visit confirmed the further improvement of bilateral relations, coming in the wake of the ratification of a treaty of friendship and co-operation by the Ivorian parliament in August. Hope intensified that the treaty would further facilitate trade relations.

By contrast, the fact that the northern **Ivorian rebels** of the 'Forces Nouvelles' (FN) have been dependent on channelling their exports through Burkina led a UN group of experts to conclude that "certain elements within Burkina Faso may have little cause to welcome the rapid political and administrative reunification of Côte d'Ivoire", since this "would jeopardize a lucrative transit trade through Burkina Faso". In the same report, dated 9 October, the experts also expressed deep concern about a systematic transfer of weapons and ammunition across the Burkinabè-Ivorian border. The group urged Ouagadougou to take the necessary measures and put a stop to the violation of the international arms embargo against Côte d'Ivoire. Accusations that Compaoré's government supported the FN during the Ivorian civil war persisted.

Compaoré also continued mediating on behalf of ECOWAS in **Togo**. On 28 June, he attempted to renew dialogue between the authorities, opposition and civil society prior to the 2010 presidential elections. Delegates from several foreign and international bodies hailed Compaoré's efforts, including the presidents of the Pan-African, Rwandan and Senegalese parliaments on 30 September, the OIF on 25 October and the European

Commissioner for Development on 28 October. Thus, his appointment by ECOWAS on 2 October as official mediator for **Guinea** could be seen as a personal and diplomatic success. On 5 October, Compaoré travelled to Conakry for the first time. Several more talks followed. On 19 November, the mediator presented a draft memorandum of understanding ('protocole d'accord globale'), which proposed three options. Guinean media and opposition criticised the suggestions which, in their view, all favoured the head of the military junta, President Dadis Camara.

On 9–11 October the 7th World Sustainable Development Forum was held in Ouagadougou. Ahead of the UN Climate Change Conference COP15 in **Copenhagen** on 7–18 December, the Forum produced a common position of African countries. The 'Ouagadougou Declaration' called for the North to contribute more financial and technological aid to vulnerable African countries, which suffered disproportionately from climate change in comparison with their contribution to pollution. Compaoré attended COP15 from 16–18 December.

On 24 June, the chief of mission of the APRM, Mohamed Seghir Babès, presented Compaoré with a **peer review report** on Burkina. The final review report, written by a panel of external African experts and dated May 2008, contained few surprises. On the one hand, it lauded what it called "political stability" and Burkina's "role as a hub in the resolution of sub-regional crises" as well as efforts in the development of agrarian and cultural potential. On the other hand, it criticised prevalent economic and political deficits, such as rising inequalities, biased contracting and other forms of corruption, and "the mode of 'blocking' the democracy and multiparty system, which is somewhat stifled by the omnipresent weight and domination of the majority party".

France remained Burkina Faso's most important European partner and the country's largest bilateral donor. At the end of the year, Ouagadougou emphasised their good political relations by signalling that the country was ready to sign an agreement on the control of migration. The agreement was prepared by the French ministry of immigration and vigorously debated in the West African sub-region. The **US** continued calmly to expand its good relations with Ouagadougou. With military cooperation against Sahelian terrorism activities and Burkina Faso's current inclusion in the US Millenium Challenge Corporation – worth $ 480.9 m over five years – the importance of bilateral relations steadily increased.

On 25 February, Niger and Burkina Faso decided to settle their long-standing disagreement over their common border peacefully by submitting to the adjudication of the International Court of Justice concerning a 650 km demarcation line.

Socioeconomic Developments

Burkina ranked 177th out of 182 countries in the 2009 Human Development Report, with a slight increase of the index value to 0.389 compared with the previous report. Niger was the only country performing worse with regard to education. The World Bank's report 'Doing Business in 2010' ranked Burkina 147th out of 183 countries, with 23 other African countries ranking more highly.

On 1 September, torrential rainfalls, the heaviest in 90 years, brought 263 mm of precipitation within 12 hours. At least 16 people died and some 180,000 lost their homes. **Floods** damaged important parts of Ouagadougou's infrastructure, including houses, bridges, roads, dams and power lines. On 24 November the minister of economics and finance reported to the IMF that preliminary estimates put the damage at € 125 m, which was about half the value of the year's gold production. Various countries pledged support. Neighbouring countries sent envoys, but only the Ivorian government could afford financial help in the sum of CFAfr 500 m (approx. € 0.76 m, offered on 10 September). The West African Development Bank offered CFAfr 100 m (approx. € 0.15 m) and France promised € 1.06 m additional help.

The world financial crisis assailed the economy, with rising costs and decreasing demand for cotton. However, globally falling food prices contributed to a significant reduction in domestic **inflation**. The average increase in the consumer price index was expected to reach between 2.7% ('The Economist') and 3.8% (IMF) in 2009, which would be significantly below the 10.7% of the previous year.

Diminishing inflation somewhat eased the social crisis that the rising cost of living had provoked in 2008. However, the slight improvement in the economic situation hardly proved sustainable and did little to help the poorer parts of the population to face their daily challenges. In this context it was good news when the government announced a 41% increase in domestic agricultural **food production**. However, this sharp variation in annual production figures underlined the dependence on weather conditions and the unreliable food supply. Many agricultural products, such as rice, a staple food, must be imported – the country being unable to produce more than a third of its own rice needs.

At the end of the year, the Economist Intelligence Unit forecast a 3.3%, and the IMF a 3.5%, real GDP **growth** rate for 2009. The indicators thus fell behind earlier achievements. Growth is mainly dependent on cotton production and world market prices, as well as on the gold mining sector, and therefore remained highly vulnerable to external shocks.

Cotton prices recovered during the year from a long-time low to pre-crisis rates. According to data from the US Foreign Agricultural Service, Burkina's production in the 2008–09 season improved from a low in 2007–08 to the expected level, i.e. about two-thirds the all time high of 2006–07. Only a moderate further increase of about 3% was estimated for the 2009–10 season.

Following massive foreign investment which led to the opening of several industrial mines during the preceding few years, the **gold sector** significantly increased output to an estimated 12 tonnes in 2009. The previous year's production only reached 5.5 tonnes. In addition, driven by high international prices, gold earnings surpassed cotton earnings for the first time and were projected to reach some € 245 m. Investment in the mining sector continued, although without leading to new contracts. Nevertheless, growth in earnings was expected to slow down after the opening of two more mines announced for 2010, unless gold prices continued to surge.

The **IMF** completed two reviews under the 2007 PRGF arrangement. The report on the fourth review – completion announced on 22 June – commended the country for "prudent macroeconomic policies" and efforts towards more investment-friendly administrative procedures. The main concerns focused on tax policy. On 14 December, the IMF Executive Board completed the fifth country review. It approved an increase of access of SDR 33.1 m (about € 37 m) due to the exceptional costs the government had to deal with following the global financial crisis and the domestic flood disaster. Government estimates said that the impact of the flooding amounted to about 2% of GDP. The Board repeated its praise for "good macroeconomic management in a challenging external environment", as well as its concerns about the tax administration and diversification of the economy.

Victor Tiendrébéogo successfully advocated the production of **biodiesel** by planting 'Jatropha curcas' on a large scale. A deputy in the National Assembly, Tiendrébéogo, is president of the 'National Union for the Promotion of the Jatropha Sector' and owner of 'Belwet Biocarburant', a Jatropha oil producing company. In 2009, his company invested € 50,000, in cooperation with the German company 'DBD Deutsche Biodiesel', in a pilot plantation, which should reach an annual production capacity of 375 tonnes of oil. As in neighbouring Mali, power supply for rural villages could improve by operating generators with agrarian fuel. However, local experts remained sceptical about the social and environmental consequences and the German investor. On 17 December, DBD filed for insolvency at a court in Munich. At year's end, it was unknown whether this would affect a projected € 2 m investment in a larger plant.

In mid-April, the Rood Woko market in central Ouagadougou reopened. Fire had destroyed the multi-storey facility in May 2003. Controversies about the renovation ended when the French development agency AFD agreed to bear large parts of the costs. On 30 April, the national telephone company 'Onatel', which had previously been part-privatised, became the first of Burkina's companies to be listed on the sub-regional stock exchange in Abidjan. On 31 December, a new high-voltage line connected Ouagadougou to an additional 86 MW of power generated in neighbouring coastal countries. The same day, President Compaoré's New Year address included an announcement that free antiretroviral treatment would be provided to all Burkinabè suffering from HIV/AIDS. However, it remained unclear how the government would defray the costs.

Alexander Stroh

Cape Verde

The political scene was marked by the comeback of Carlos Veiga, the former prime minister and leader of the 'Movimento para a Democracia' (MpD), who was elected uncontested as new leader of his party. At the same time, Prime Minister José Maria Neves was re-elected leader of the ruling 'Partido Africano da Independência de Cabo Verde' (PAICV). During a visit to the archipelago, US Secretary of State Hillary Clinton praised Cape Verde as an African success story. Tourism, the mainstay of the economy, was affected by the global economic crisis, but recovered in the second half of the year.

Domestic Politics

In the second half of the year, the three parties represented in the National Assembly held **leadership elections**. On 24–26 July, the small opposition party 'União Caboverdeana Independente e Democrática' held its 15th Congress in Mindelo, São Vicente. The executive committee was extended from 11 to 19 members. The 128 delegates re-elected António Monteiro as party leader. Monteiro declared that his party's objective was to extend the parliamentary representation from the current two deputies to five in the legislative elections of 2011.

On 4 October, Prime Minister José Maria Neves was re-elected uncontested for another three-year term as leader of the **ruling PAICV**. In the PAICV's first direct leadership elections, Neves received 22,047 votes from the 28,682 registered party members. Altogether 78% of the party membership participated in the election, with 98.7% of the votes cast in favour of Neves. Voter turnout reached 99% in Santa Catarina, Santa Cruz and Tarrafal (Santiago), while in São Vicente, Praia, São Filipe (Fogo) and Sal the turnout ranged between 62% and 80%. In contrast, in Brava and Maio only 30% and 44.5% of party members respectively went to the polls. On 11 November, the PAICV decided to postpone its 12th party congress (scheduled for 20–22 November) to January 2010 due to the outbreak of dengue fever.

On 11 October, the **opposition** MpD elected Carlos Veiga, a former prime minister (1991–2000), uncontested as new party leader with 69% of the votes in a direct vote. All over the country, 22,646 of the 32,838 registered members participated in the election. Veiga, who had been party leader while he was prime minister, had declared his intention to return to the party leadership in April, but only on 3 July did he publicly present his candidature. Former party leader Jorge Santos, who had announced his own candidature on 2 April, finally withdrew from the election in early September arguing that his decision was inspired by the party's common interest. Another competitor, José Luís Livremento, a former minister of education who had announced his candidature in January, had already withdrawn it in August to support Veiga. Immediately after his election, Veiga declared that the MpD's objective was to win the legislative elections in 2011 and to recapture government power, lost to the PAICV in 2001. During the 9th convention of the MpD on 30 October–1 November former party leader Jorge Santos and Úlisses Correia e Silva, the mayor of Praia, were elected party vice presidents, while Agostinho Lopes, another ex-party leader, was elected secretary general of the party.

For months, the two principal parties debated a revision of the country's **Constitution**. On 4 February, the National Assembly constituted a 13-member commission for the amendment of the Constitution, composed of members of the three parties represented in parliament. Initially, the key proposals included the financial and administrative autonomy of the Supreme Judicial Magistrate Council ('Conselho Superior da Magistratura Judicial') in order to reinforce the independence of the judiciary; the recognition of the local Creole language 'Crioulo' as the country's second official language; the introduction of a national minimum wage; and legal questions such as night searches by the police of suspected homes and the extradition of Cape Verdean nationals to foreign countries.

On 26 November, following consecutive controversial debates, the delegations of the PAICV and MpD, headed by the leaders José Maria Neves and Carlos Veiga respectively, finally signed a **memorandum** of understanding on the proposed revisions. The two parties agreed on several amendments, including the country's recognition of the jurisdiction of the ICC; the possible extradition of nationals who had committed serious crimes abroad; the possibility of night-time home searches in restricted cases; the new composition of the Supreme Judicial Magistrate Council; the elimination of the need for approval by the Council of the Republic of the dissolution of the National Assembly by the head of state; and the composition of the Council of the Republic itself. However, no consensus was reached on several other issues, including the introduction of a minimum wage and the promotion of Crioulo as the second official language, proposed by the PAICV, as the MpD argued that the conditions for this move had not yet been met.

Foreign Affairs

While Cape Verde strengthened longstanding ties with **Portugal** and China, the visit of US Secretary of State Hillary Clinton stood out in particular. On 12–14 March, the Portuguese Prime Minister José Sócrates paid an official visit to Cape Verde with a huge 120-member delegation comprising six ministers, seven secretaries of state, dozens of Portuguese business people and 14 journalists. The Portuguese delegation expressed its appreciation for the longstanding co-operation with Cape Verde in traditional sectors such as defence, security, justice, civil service and public works, and pleaded for co-operation in new areas, including new communication technologies and renewable energies. Prime Minister Sócrates donated Portuguese laptop computers 'Magalhães' to the pupils of a primary school in Fazenda, which marked the beginning of the project 'Novu Mundu', aimed at distributing 150,000 computers to local students of all educational levels the following years. The Portuguese prime minister announced a plan to hold biannual summits between the two countries in the future. During the visit, the two governments signed a series of agreements on co-operation to a value of € 170 m.

On 18 March, a delegation of the opposition MpD headed by party leader Jorge Santos arrived in Portugal for a four-day working visit. The delegation was received by the Portuguese President Cavaco Silva and the speaker of the parliament, Jaime Gama. In addition, the delegation held meetings with representatives of the municipalities of Lisbon, Oeiras, Amadora, Cascais and Sintra and with Cape Verdian associations in these cities, where a large part of the Cape Verdian community live. On 25 March, Prime Minister José Maria Neves left for a four-day visit to Portugal, where he held meetings with the Cape Verdian communities in Greater Lisbon. Together with Prime Minister José Sócrates, Neves also went to Lisbon's 'Centro Cultural de Belém' to attend the debut of the Cape Verdean opera 'Crioulo', a work on the archipelago's Creole culture.

On 19 June, **Britain**'s ambassador, Christopher Tott, and defence minister Cristina Duarte in Praia signed, aboard the British warship HMS Gloucester, a memorandum of understanding on the fight against drug-trafficking in the Atlantic Ocean. The memorandum involves, among other things, joint surveillance missions between the British and Cape Verdean law enforcement authorities on Royal Navy vessels and airplanes.

On 13 August, **US** Secretary of State Hillary Clinton arrived for a 24-hour visit to Cape Verde, the last country on her seven-nation Africa tour begun on 5 August. Clinton was received by Foreign Minister José Brito and met Prime Minister José Maria Neves. The secretary of state praised Cape Verde as an unparalleled success story in Africa and stressed the country's advancement in terms of good governance, transparency, poverty reduction and economic development. Clinton and the prime minister discussed bilateral co-operation in the areas of renewable energies, agriculture, maritime security, and the ongoing US Millennium Challenge Account programme. On 9 December, the Executive Board of the Millennium Challenge Corporation (MCC) honoured the country's successful implementation of an MCC Compact agreement signed in 2004 by approving the selection of Cape Verde as the first country eligible for a second five-year Compact agreement worth $ 110 m.

On 24 August, Foreign Minister José Brito and **China**'s ambassador Li Chunhua signed in Praia an agreement on a Joint Commission of Economic, Commercial and Technical Co-operation. The Joint Commission was a new bilateral mechanism to process Chinese loans and investment projects worth some $ 240 m, including $ 100 m for the construction of social housing units in Santiago, São Vicente, Boa Vista, Maio and Sal; a cement factory at Santa Cruz estimated at $ 65 m; the renovation of the Cabnave dockyard, budgeted at $ 65 m; and the modernisation of the Praia power plant, an investment of $ 10 m. On 22 December, Defence Minister Cristina Fontes Lima and Ambassador Li Chunhua signed a biannual renewable protocol on military co-operation, particularly the supply of military equipment worth Yuan 5 m. During the signing ceremony, the defence minister announced for early 2011 the arrival of the Zhi-9 helicopters, the Chinese version of the French Dauphin II, purchased for about € 34 m from Beijing and destined for the coast guard and to be used for rescue and emergency operations.

Socioeconomic Developments

The government continued the implementation of macroeconomic policies recommended by the IMF, while investments focussed on the improvement of the country's infrastructure. On 12 January, the government and the ECOWAS Bank for Investment and Development signed an agreement on a loan of € 3.5 m, equivalent to 15% of the total amount budgeted, for a project to reinforce the production and distribution capacity of **electricity** on Santiago island. The project consists of the extension of the Palmarejo power station by two generator groups of 10 MW each, the construction of 40 km of 60 kV supply lines and the reinforcement of the electricity distribution network. Finance Minister Cristina Duarte expected the project to increase the archipelago's electrification rate from the current 76% to 90%.

On 14 April, at the end of a two-week 6th review mission of the country's three-year Policy Support Instrument (PSI), Lamin Leigh, the IMF mission chief, declared in Praia that Cape Verde's **macroeconomic performance** continued to show robustness and that the impact of the global economic crisis had remained controllable, thanks to the accumulation in previous years of comfortable buffers created through prudent macroeconomic management. The IMF approved a one-year extension to July 2010 of the PSI signed in July 2006. On 23 September, the 7th PSI review mission arrived in Praia. The IMF again praised the government's macroeconomic performance and concluded that the international crisis had only slightly affected the country's financial sector.

On 1 October, the 'Agência de Regulação Económica' (ARE) presented a new mechanism for **fuel price adjustments**, based on new legislation passed in June that became effective on 29 August and was the result of the three-year PSI signed with the IMF. By law, the ARE's maximum resale prices are revisited every two months in order to reflect the real prices on the international energy market. As a result, the ARE consecutively increased fuel prices on 29 August, 8 October and 8 December.

On 15 May, the newly established company Cabo Verde Fast Ferry launched the public sale of 1,500,000 shares worth nominally CVEsc 1,000 each at the stock exchange 'Bolsa de Valores de Cabo Verde'. With the capital generated, the company ordered two ferry boats from the Dutch Damen Shipyard for the rapid inter-island **ferry services** expected to start in mid-2010. On 24 July, the last day of the subscription period, Veríssimo Pinto, head of the 'Bolsa', declared that the sale had been a success. The municipality of Brava subscribed to 51% of the shares, providing it with a controlling interest in the company.

According to figures presented by the 'Instituto Nacional de Estatística' (INE) on 30 September, **tourist arrivals** in the country's hotels numbered 163,125 in the first half of the year, 2.8% less than in the same period in 2008. In the same period, a total 989,354 overnight stays were recorded, an increase of 8.7%. Portugal (16.2%), the United Kingdom (16.0%), Italy (13.1%) and Germany (12.7%) were the visitors' principal countries of origin. Sal island received 46.1% of the tourists, while 23.7% and 17.1% of the travellers spent their holidays in Boa Vista and Santiago respectively. On 22 December, the INE reported 81,951 tourist arrivals for the third quarter, a 7.5% increase compared with the same period in 2008. The principal countries of origin were the UK (18.3%) followed by Portugal (17.5%), Italy (16.3%) and Germany (9.4%).

On 24 November, the majority of the ruling PAICV in parliament approved the 2010 **budget**, which expected revenue of CVEsc 44 bn (€ 399 m) and expenditure of CVEsc 61 bn (€ 553.2 m). Public investments were expected to increase by CVEsc 7 bn to CVEsc 31 bn. Investments in infrastructure represented 62.9% of the total, of which 20.7% in roads, 20.1% in the extension of ports and 9.5% in energy production and supply. Education, health, and professional training represented 5.3%, 2.9% and 1.7% of public investments respectively, while 7.4% was scheduled for the promotion of competitiveness in the private sector. The national budget reduced income tax by 3%, equivalent to a revenue loss of CVEsc 25 m. The loss of another CVEsc 30 m of revenue was expected as a result of the increase in tax deductions for health and education expenditure. The public deficit accounted for 12% with a 23.8% increase in public debt totalling CVEsc 117.1 bn – representing 77% of GDP.

On 22 December, the 'Empresa Nacional de Aeroportos e Segurança Aérea' inaugurated the new international **airport** of São Pedro, situated 8 km from Mindelo, São Vicente. With an investment of CVEsc 3 bn (€ 27.2 m) over three years, the existing aerodrome at São Pedro was transformed into the country's fourth international airport, after Sal, Praia (Santiago), and Boa Vista. The new airport's three-storey terminal has a capacity of 500 passengers an hour. It was expected that the new international airport, whose official opening had been delayed several times, would stimulate tourist development in São Vicente and the neighbouring islands of Santo Antão and São Nicolau.

By November, the health authorities had registered almost 14,000 cases of **dengue fever** since the month of October, predominantly in the capital Praia. By the end of the year, 21,000 dengue cases had been recorded.

Gerhard Seibert

Côte d'Ivoire

Because of the impossibility of holding elections in what was still a divided country, the presidential election initially due in October 2005 was still awaited in 2009, this being the ninth year President Laurent Gbagbo was in office. Although normalisation was slowly taking place, the northern part of the country, disconnected from Abidjan since the outbreak of civil war in 2002, remained isolated from developments in the south. Two years after the Ouagadougou Peace Agreement (OPA) signed by Ivorian political forces, the disarmament of the former combatants, dismantling of militias and reunification of Ivorian security forces were still pending, as were the redeployment of the state administration across the territory, identification of citizens and voters, and the preparation of electoral lists. The Ivorian people, struggling to maintain their day to day life in a context of increasing poverty, suffered from a strong sense of fatigue. Developments were bogged down in an endless process of determining who was an Ivorian national and thus eligible to vote, and in repeated justifications for rescheduling the polling date. The proposed date of 29 November was also postponed, preparations for presidential elections becoming an object of pure speculation.

Domestic Politics

The year began optimistically with voter identification in full progress, in spite of very little clarity on the new schedule, which had not been released by the Independent Electoral Commission (CEI), as requested by the last 'Cadre Permanent de Concertation' (CPC) meeting on 10 November 2008 in Ouagadougou. The UN Secretary General's representative to the country, Young-Jin Choi, told reporters on 9 January that, despite some technical problems, "3 m people [had been] identified and that in a few months the identification process would be complete". This was confirmed on 21 January by an official CEI communiqué, which said that nearly 3.5 m people had been accounted for in the **census**, which reported a total of 12 m nationals both at home and abroad, including 9 m voters. The CEI boldly said that voter identification would be wrapped up by the end of February.

However, **disillusionment** quickly set in. The target completion date of 28 February passed with 3 m people still unregistered. It was quickly realised that the other objectives had also been missed: the process of redeploying the public administration in the north, initially foreseen for 15 January, had not really started, and the disarmament of fighters remained symbolic, with only a couple of units destroying their small arms.

Both international observers and average citizens started to feel that the country was once again at risk of disintegrating, and this increased on 18 March, when Anaky Kobenan, leader of the 'Mouvement des Forces de l'Avenir' (MFA), a party participating in the coalition government, said in an interview on state television that what had happened in Madagascar should serve as food for thought for President Gbagbo and the Ivorian people. Kobenan was arrested and questioned by the country's territorial surveillance agency but was released after 24 hours. On 23 March, he announced that the MFA was leaving the governing coalition, where it was represented by Bamba Hamza, the reconstruction minister and only MFA member. Kobenan urged the other coalition members to do the same. The 'Forces Nouvelles' (FN), the former rebels and members of the coalition government since the OPA, whose leader, Guillaume Soro, held the position of prime minister, followed suit a few weeks later, on 15 April. They urged Soro to step down, accusing Gbagbo and his 'Front Populaire Ivoirien' (FPI) of stalling the elections. FN delegates said that, with his resignation as prime minister, Soro could be part of "the vanguard of the Ivorian people's struggle to improve its lot".

Fears increased with the release of the semi-annual UN panel of experts report on arms, financial and travel sanctions and the embargo on trade in rough diamonds imposed since Resolution 1572 (2004). The report, transmitted to the Secretary General on 20 March and made public in mid-April, warned of the risks of escalating violence, particularly in the north, which were increased by constant verbal attacks between the parties. In their letter to Ban Ki-moon, the experts stated that "despite the **arms embargo**, the parties to the conflict remain[ed] sufficiently heavily armed to engage in sustained armed hostilities and some [were] rearming". The panel noted that it had obtained "physical evidence that suggested a consistent pattern of violations of the arms embargo". Funding for arms purchases was provided by the control of natural resources, notably in the western regions.

In this critical context, on 13 April, Robert Mambé Beugré, president of the CEI, requested specific support from UNOCI (UN Operation in Côte d'Ivoire) in order to complete the process of identifying the remainder of the Ivorian population. On 22 April, in his latest report on the situation in the country, the UN Secretary General called for a realistic timetable for the holding of credible and transparent elections, pointing out that this was now a matter of urgency in order to capitalise on the gains achieved so far in the peace process. In response, on 28 April, the country's UN ambassador, Ilahiri A. Djedje, told the Security Council meeting on the situation in Côte d'Ivoire that the first round of the presidential elections would be held no later than 6 December 2009.

The **new schedule** was confirmed on 15 May by Prime Minister Guillaume Soro, who said the nation would hold the election on 29 November, after more than four years of delays since the expiry of Gbagbo's mandate. On 19 May, Burkina Faso's President Blaise Compaoré, 'Facilitator' of the OPA and official mediator, congratulated the government and the parties for this new schedule, just before a new round of mediation talks, saying that Gbagbo's government was committed to holding the poll. At last, in a handover ceremony on 26 May in the ex-rebel capital of Bouaké, former rebel forces started to relinquish territory to civilian administrators appointed by the government, which constituted a decisive step towards presidential elections. Gbagbo had repeatedly said that they could not be held until the central government's rule was restored throughout the country.

Identification and voter registration was formally completed on 30 June and, on 23 July, the CEI published the **timelines** of the electoral process including: the publication of the provisional electoral list on 29 August and then the final list, following the appeals process, between 15 and 21 October; the production of identification and voters cards by 20 October and their distribution by 26 November; and the electoral campaign from 13 to 27 November. In his address at the country's independence celebrations on 7 August, Gbagbo reaffirmed that there would be no more political obstacles to holding the election as scheduled.

On 8 August, Gbagbo appointed Paul Yao N'dré head of the Constitutional Council, the supreme institution in charge of verifying the eligibility of the presidential candidates, the legality of the elections, and the declaration of the results. N'dré, a high level member of the FPI and former interior minister in the government led by Pascal Affi N'Guessan in the early 2000s, was also known as a long time comrade of the president and part of his inner circle. Many observers and the opposition parties pointed to the risks related to such a **biased appointment** if there were a political crisis, and many referred to what had occurred in Kenya in the aftermath of the last presidential elections.

On 9 August, the Facilitator convened the 7th **meeting** of the 'Cadre Permanent de Concertation', attended by Prime Minister Soro, to review progress in the implementation of the OPA. The markers of the electoral process were confirmed and participants called for the resolution of all the pending security-related issues, notably the harmonisation of the status and benefits of the 5,000 FN personnel who were to join the national army, their confinement to barracks and the deployment of mixed brigades by the Integrated Command Centre.

However, the deadline for publishing the provisional list on 29 August was missed. On 20 August, the CEI deplored the delay in the **verification of voters**, saying it was yet to receive the register from the National Commission for the Supervision of Identification. On 1 September, the CEI announced that the "slight technical readjustment on the publication date…would not have any repercussion on the 29 November date" and that the list would be published on 15 September. The deadline was missed again, owing mainly to technical issues, as well as a strike by unpaid workers. Nevertheless, the CEI announced that 95% of the provisional electoral list had been processed and that its publication had been "moved forward a few days". While speculation was mounting that the latest poll deadline would not be met, Young-Jin Choi, the UN's special envoy, said the focus had to be on progress made rather than on remaining obstacles. But Blaise Compaoré, paying his first official visit to the country since the start of the civil war, warned of the dangers of further postponing the presidential elections.

The completion of the provisional voter **registration list** was announced on 26 September by Jean Baptiste Gomis, the vice chairman of the CEI, who said the list was held on a CD soon to be presented to the Commission by SAGEM, the French company commissioned as an independent agency to identify the electorate and publish the voter registration list. The register was presented to Gbagbo on 6 October, even though the identity of 2.7 m out of the 6.3 m registered voters remained unconfirmed. Gbagbo said he was "very optimistic" about holding the presidential election "in 2009", although he made no reference to the official date of 29 November. He stated that "there were no obstacles for the holding of the plebiscite".

In the meantime, on 29 September, the UN Security Council had **warned** of dire political consequences if the presidential elections failed to take place. Ban Ki-moon gave a reminder that the slow pace of disarmament and demobilisation of former combatants was indeed a cause for concern.

General Robert Guei, former leader of the 1999 coup that deposed President Henri Konan Bédié, and head of state in the transition, was reburied on 2 October in his home village near Man, in the western part of the country, more than seven years after his death in 2002. He had been mysteriously killed during the failed 2002 coup, which sparked off the civil war, and had initially been buried in Abidjan. Gbagbo attended the **funeral**, having over the previous months been patiently trying to poach the main leaders of Guei's party, the 'Union pour la Paix et la Démocratie en Côte d'Ivoire'.

On 16 October, Gbagbo, FPI candidate for the presidential elections, officially registered his candidature with the CEI under the banner of 'La Majorité Présidentielle' (LMP), the grouping of FPI allies. The **president's campaign** relied on a high-level communication team with international consultants and prominent members of the international media – such as Stéphane Fouks, CEO of the French Havas company (Bolloré group) and joint president of Euro RSCG Worldwide. Locally, the leader was Nady Bamba, Gbagbo's second wife and chair of Cyclone, her communication agency. She started to distribute contracts among loyal supporters, such as Charles Blé Goudé, nicknamed "Général la Jeunesse", who was not only the chief of the 'Congrès PanAfricain des Jeunes et des Patriotes' (Young Patriots – COJEP), but also campaign director for the youth wing of the LMP candidate and CEO of Leader's Team Associated, which would manage Gbagbo's commercials.

However, the **election schedule headache** quickly returned. As expected by everyone and despite progress in the confirmation of voters (only 1 m names remained to be validated out of the 2.7 still pending early October), the CEI announced on 11 November that the first round of the presidential election would have to be postponed. On 20 November, the Constitutional Council endorsed 14 out of 20 candidates for the presidential election. The list of candidates included Henri Konan Bédié for the 'Parti Démocratique de Côte d'Ivoire' and Alassane Ouattara for the 'Rassemblement des Républicains'. The latter's right to participate had already been stipulated in the 2005 Pretoria agreement. The provisional electoral list was eventually released on 23 November and the appeals process was launched the following day and was intended to be completed in early January 2010.

Henri Konan Bédié said that any new election date in Côte d'Ivoire should be set by broad political agreement and not by the whim of Gbagbo. The president retorted that he was not in charge of the election schedule, which was the business of the CEI, and that the CEI was equally controlled by the opposition parties through the representation of all parties on the Commission. The CPC, chaired by the Facilitator, met on 3 December and the parties to the peace process endorsed a **new timeline**. They agreed on publication of the final electoral list in January 2010, the distribution of identity and voters' cards in February, and the presidential elections by the end of February or early March. By 28 December, the CEI had approved 328,836 appeals on the provisional electoral list. 12,000 FN combatants were yet to be demobilised.

Foreign Affairs

The **UN** confirmed its routine management of the situation by the adoption of its three yearly Security Council resolutions: two for the six-month renewal of the mandate of UNOCI and the French 'Licorne' force supporting it (Resolutions 1865 and 1880 adopted on 27 January and 30 July), and one (Resolution 1893 on 29 October) for the one-year renewal of the arms, financial and travel measures imposed by Resolution 1572 (2004) and the measures preventing the export of rough diamonds imposed by Resolution 1643 (2005). Among the 48 Security Council resolutions, Côte d'Ivoire remained, however, among the main UN concerns along with Sudan and Somalia. UN Secretary General Ban Ki-moon, as well as his special envoy and representative in the country, Young-Jin Choi, called throughout the year for a realistic electoral timetable, encouraging the country's electoral commission, and urging the government to respect the schedule.

Local stakeholders tried to soften UN sanctions. In a first attempt, a group of Young Patriots protested on 20 March in front of the **UNOCI headquarters**, calling for the lifting of the sanctions imposed against their leader, Charles Blé Goudé, in 2006. However, they did not attack the UN premises, as had occurred in January 2006.

The government also intensified its campaign to have the UN Security Council partially lift the arms embargo imposed since 2004. The request was first made by Defence Minister Michel Amani N'Guessan and reiterated on 12 May when the government met Young-Jin Choi. The Interior Minister, Désiré Tagro, explained that a **partial lifting** of the embargo would enable the country to equip the 8,000 policemen and gendarmes, whose redeployment had begun the previous week. The request appeared ill-timed, however, since the UN panel of experts had released its reports a couple of weeks earlier (mid-April).

Resolution 1880 in July reiterated its full support for the Ouagadougou process, particularly expressed its appreciation of the Facilitator's continued efforts, and urged the signatories of the OPA to support the remaining tasks before the presidential election on 29 November. However, preparation for **Resolution 1893** clearly appeared to raise more tension. On 29 September, referring to the 22nd progress report of the UN Secretary General on UNOCI released the same day, the Security Council expressed its real concern. Susan Rice, the US's ambassador to the UN and Council's president for the month, said in a press statement that further delays in publishing a provisional voters list might endanger the timeline and that, if necessary, the Council would take appropriate action against those blocking progress. However, and surprisingly, the Resolution itself on 29 October only referred to the "planned presidential elections", showing thereby some resignation on the part of the UN body.

At the end of the year, **UN forces** in Côte d'Ivoire, still led by major-general Fernand Amoussou from Benin, comprised 7,391 military personnel and 1,138 police, which represented a slight decrease compared with 2008. The force continued to be mainly composed of Bangladeshis (25%) and a further 25% made up of a joint contingent from five ECOWAS countries (Benin, Ghana, Niger, Senegal, and Togo), followed by smaller contingents from Jordan, Pakistan, and Morocco. The major change occurred on the part of the **French forces**. On 28 January, following the announcement made one year earlier by President Sarkozy (February 2008, Capetown) about the revision of all France's defence agreements with African states, French Prime Minister François Fillon announced in

Paris, in a Chamber of Representatives special session dedicated to overseas military operations, that the military presence in Côte d'Ivoire would be reduced and the military base closed. The base was effectively dismantled in June, almost secretly and without problems from the Young Patriots. The strength of the Licorne force was reduced to 900 troops (from 1,800 in 2008 and 5,200 in 2004). French forces were now only in position in Abidjan.

Relations with **France** continued to improve and, in his 31 March speech, Gbagbo recognised the French contribution in bringing about negotiations with the IMF and World Bank on debt management and budgetary support. This optimism, strengthened by growing French private investment, was obviously tarnished by the adjournment of the presidential elections, which led to two successive postponements of a visit by Claude Guéant, the powerful Secretary General of the Elysée.

Civil society and political party representatives, as well as delegates from ECOWAS and the West African Civil Society Forum, met on Gorée Island, Senegal, on 6–8 April, for discussions on the theme: "Civil society and the media's contribution to the election process and peace consolidation in Côte d'Ivoire". The meeting was hosted by the Gorée Institute, managed by South-African-born artist and writer Breyten Breytenbach.

On 10–14 August, Rev. **Jessie Jackson**, the American civil rights activist and former nominee for the Democratic Party's presidential candidacy, visited Côte d'Ivoire to promote its fragile march towards democracy. He was greeted as a head of state and had a series of high-level meetings with Gbagbo, Soro, representatives of the opposition, and religious and youth leaders. In Krindjabo, capital of the south-eastern Sanwi kingdom near the Ghanaian border, he was crowned Prince Nana by the Agni King of Sanwi. Jackson participated in a meeting of COJEP and in a youth rally in Yopougon, an important suburb of Abidjan. During the rally, a makeshift stage, where he was moving to the music, collapsed and his wife and other participants were injured.

At the regional level, Côte d'Ivoire was visited on 7 April by the newly elected president of **Ghana**, John Atta Mills. After the announcement of the possible discovery of a new oil field near the maritime border between the two countries, the common border as defined by the 1893 Anglo-French Treaty was the subject of discussion. Following on from this, on 3–4 November, Gbagbo made an official visit to Ghana, where it was decided to reactivate the Ivorian-Ghanaian boundary commission. On 16–18 September and reciprocating Gbagbo's visit to **Burkina** in 2008, Blaise Compaoré visited Côte d'Ivoire. He was received in Mama, Gbagbo's home village near Gagnoa, in the centre-west of the country.

The president participated in the 36th **ECOWAS** meeting in Abuja, Nigeria, on June 22, followed by the Spain-ECOWAS special summit. He also took part in the 64th session of the **UN General Assembly** in New York on 25 September, where he advocated an increased role for sub-regional organisations in conflict management.

Socioeconomic Developments

2008 had ended with the release of a study carried out for the national planning ministry for the preparation of the PRSP. It served as a reminder of the country's harsh socioeconomic reality, with almost 50% of the population living in absolute poverty and growing social and regional inequalities, worsening conditions in the north and an impoverished countryside. This situation was especially caused by the discrepancy between low economic **growth** (1%–2% of GDP in real terms) and a population increasing by a minimum of 2.4% a year. As a consequence, GDP per capita hovered around $ 1,000, having slightly decreased over the preceding years. The macroeconomic situation continued to improve, however, with a GDP estimate of 3.8% (against 2.3% in 2008), but this did not suffice to keep pace with the demographic challenge. With around 20 m people, the country's population was expected to increase by 10 m in the next 15 years and the yearly cohort of new job seekers to surge from 430,000 to more than 600,000 by 2025.

Fortunately, relations with international donors continued to improve. The country had won eligibility for assistance under the HIPC initiative in December 2008 and, on 27 March, attained the so-called 'decision point' as a result of the progress achieved in economic reform. However, to reach the HIPC completion point (when **debt relief** becomes irrevocable), Côte d'Ivoire would have to achieve annual GDP growth of 4.2% so as to cut its overall budget deficit and reduce inflation. To help with this challenging objective, while dealing simultaneously with the consequences of the global economic downturn, the IMF immediately approved a three-year $ 565.7 m loan under the PRGF to support the country's recovery. As part of the HIPC initiative, the World Bank and IMF agreed to write off $ 3 bn of Côte d'Ivoire's total $ 12.8 bn debt (the equivalent of 70% of GDP). Gbagbo said the weight of debt had become a "grave mortgage on the very future" of the country. Dominique Strauss-Kahn, IMF director general, visited the country in May, showing the commitment of the international community to resolving the Ivorian crisis.

The "grands travaux" of the government **infrastructure** programme continued to develop in spite of their reintegration in the national budget, which was a precondition for donor reengagement. They included extension of official buildings in Yamoussoukro, continuation of the toll motorway, beginning of construction of Abidjan's third bridge, extension of the port and the start of Jacqueville's bridge (40 km west of Abidjan).

In the meantime, the **cocoa sector**, representing 40% of export revenue and supporting the livelihood of more than 7 m people, continued to focus attention because of the longstanding crisis in its management. The main leaders of the sector had been jailed in June 2008 on charges of corruption and the former governance bodies (the 'Bourse du Café et du Cacao', 'Fonds de Régulation' and the 'Fonds de Développement et de Promotion des Activités des Producteurs de Café et de Cacao') had been dismantled. New ad hoc committees, including the 'Comité de Gestion de la Filière Café-Cacao' (CGFCC) and the 'Comité de la Réforme Café-Cacao' (CRCC), had taken over and their activities were subject to World Bank scrutiny, as the sector's reform was part of the HIPC reform programme. Early in the year, the CGFCC launched a CFAfr 3 bn Quality, Quantity and Growth Operation to bring about major improvements in the income of cocoa farmers. In mid-October, cocoa farmers started to withhold beans to demand higher than official farm-gate prices. The sector was threatened at the beginning of the year by caterpillars ravaging the north of Liberia, which threatened to cross the border. Luckily, little damage was caused, though a few attacks were listed, notably in the locality of Danane, near the border.

In the north of the country, regional "guichet unique" offices grouping customs, fiscal and registration services were progressively installed as part of the normalisation process. However, the FN continued to levy and collect taxes. The release of the second UN panel of experts report in October shed new light on the business of the 'Com'zones' (FN district commanders). They continued to act as feudal lords organising **smuggling networks** with or from Burkina Faso, notably the city of Bobo Dioulasso. Thus, the north, where cocoa does not grow, was reputed to be the world's seventh cocoa producer.

On 30 March, at least 22 people were killed and more than 130 injured in a **stampede** at the Houphouët-Boigny football stadium in Abidjan during the Côte d'Ivoire–Malawi World Cup qualifier. On 21 September, after a three-year long procedure, the London-based oil trading firm Trafigura, agreed to pay more than $ 46 m compensation to people who had fallen ill as a result of **toxic waste** dumped in 2006. The company said 30,000 people would each receive $ 1,546, this amount coming in addition to the nearly $ 200 m disbursed by the company to the Ivorian government in 2007, which had been used in part to pay compensation to the families of 16 people killed.

Bruno Losch

Gambia

The year closed with the Gambia National Television broadcast of President Yahya Jammeh's speech to the nation. Jammeh restated honesty, hard work, self-reliance and justice as the founding values of his political vision. A promised 20% increase in government salaries accompanied the ritual call for patriotism. Jammeh announced reforms to improve the efficiency of public administration and criticised civil servants' corruption and lack of commitment to the public good. Political liberties and civil rights remained under siege. Heavy floods during the rainy season were expected to have compromised the annual agricultural output.

Domestic Politics

An epidemic of **witch-hunting**, which led to the harassment of hundreds of people, brought the Gambia to international attention in the first part of the year. Witch-hunters from Guinea swept the regions of Fogny, Kombo and Barra, and reached the outskirts of the capital Banjul. Alleged evildoers were detained and forced to drink a hallucinogenic concoction, causing severe psychological and physical distress. A number of them died as a result. Government supporters minimised the event (by stressing the long-term historicity of this practice, an assertion that was unsupported by sufficient evidence). Critics remarked on the presence of state agents, policemen and young supporters of the ruling Alliance for Patriotic Re-orientation and Construction (APRC), who were alleged to have orchestrated the so-called healers' tour.

Halifa Sallah, secretary general of the People's Democratic Organisation for Independence and Socialism and co-ordinator of the National Alliance for Democracy and Development – a coalition of **opposition** parties formed to contest the 2006 elections – was arrested in the first week of March after having denounced the witch-hunts as a gross violation of human rights and having visited one of the villages involved with the aim of gathering a petition. Sallah, who is also a board member of 'Foroyaa' (the only opposition newspaper still published), was charged with 'spying', 'control of processions' (he led a procession in Makumbaya) and 'seditious intentions', but was released unconditionally after almost a fortnight. News of his arrest aroused the concern of AI.

Far from being yet another manifestation of supposed African irrationality, the events pointed to the **climate of fear** and general mistrust built up by Jammeh over the previous 15 years. Some of the alleged witches, such as Al Haji Tabora Manneh, former Chief of Lower Niumi, were notables and businessmen known to be strong supporters of the APRC, a detail that indicated underground conflicts and struggles for prominence within the ranks of the ruling party.

On 19 June, the **media** reported the re-arrest of Halifa Sallah. Eight other journalists were already in custody, including Pap Saine, editor of 'The Point' newspaper and Reuters correspondent for Gambia, who had just been cleared of other allegations made against him early in February. The nine were accused of publishing seditious material after having supported the Gambia Press Union's criticism of Jammeh's remarks about the unsolved murder of prominent Gambian editor, Deyda Hydara, who was ambushed and killed in 2004. On national television, Jammeh had not only denied any government involvement, but had also implied that an extra-marital affair was the cause of the assassination. Pap Saine and five other colleagues were sentenced to two years' imprisonment by the High Court. The president's pardon arrived during Ramadan and was officially presented as an example of the forgiving attitude that Muslims should display during the month of fasting. Media and international pressure on the government nonetheless played a role.

On 27 January, the Independent Electoral Commission announced the registration of a **new party**, the Gambia Moral Congress. The leader is barrister Mai N.K. Fatty, a human rights lawyer, and the party's economic platform is strongly oriented to the development of the private sector. On 8 August, on the occasion of his birthday, Ousainou Darboe, the leader of the United Democratic Party (UDP) and Jammeh's historical opponent, spoke during a private gathering of his followers, denying that the opposition was in disarray and announcing mobilisation for the scheduled 2011 elections. However, Gambians remained sceptical about the possibility of significant change. The authorities deemed illegal a UDP rally on 25 October, reportedly attended by up to 700 people. A permit had been refused but Darboe declared that "the days when the party will fail to hold a rally simply because they are not given a permit by the police are gone". The UDP campaign manager, Femin Peters, was arrested on the same day. Limited financial resources, restricted access to the media and government persecution seriously compromised whatever effort the UDP and other opposition parties could make to counter the hegemony of the APRC.

Fears of retaliation have curbed political discussions in Gambia, widening the gap between the active civic engagement of some sections of the **diaspora** (which uses the Internet to denounce the government's shortcomings) and what goes on within the country. Internal criticism has been confined to private circles and the difficulty of checking Internet news has undermined the reputation of the major electronic media as reliable sources. Government supporters espouse the thesis that any information spread by the diaspora is biased.

The "Dialogue with the People Tour" (a constitutional requirement aimed at increasing communication between the state and the populace) took place in May. Jammeh and his entourage met the major rural communities and witnessed a big display of **organised popular support**, with provincial governors and traditional authorities heavily involved in the preparations. The slogans "no more elections" and "thank you Mr Jammeh" resonated during the celebrations of the fifteenth anniversary of the 22 July military take-over in 1994, which for the first time saw active participation by some Gambians abroad. For the occasion, the government announced the implementation of the new Biometric Identification System, meant to develop security, and a system of identity-based services, such as credit references and income tax clearance certificates. Towards the end of the year, other rallies tested the APRC's powerful consensus-building machine. In the rainy season, presidential farms (established throughout the country with the official development target of enhancing food self-sufficiency and providing an example of rural capitalism) attracted numerous volunteers, including a procession of top rank civil servants from the capital. About 5,000 members of the Mouride brotherhood responded to their Khalifa General's appeal for assistance for Jammeh during the harvest. National television and other pro-government media provided extensive coverage of the event.

Cabinet reshuffles and **sacking of civil servants** continued to take place as a result both of Jammeh's efforts to streamline the public administration and of increased competition within civil service ranks. Interpersonal grievances and struggles for positions played their part in the yearly wave of dismissals and re-appointments, with the president easily misled by negative reports. An assessment carried out in the framework of the civil service reform measures (which the National Assembly adopted on 8 April) observed significant losses of professional senior staff and high vacancy rates at the same level. Staff increases had been concentrated at the semi-skilled and unskilled levels, with the parastatal and private sectors offering educated young people more secure and better-paid jobs than government. The 20% salary increase that the president announced in his New Year's Eve speech was explicitly directed at raising public officials' motivation alongside their earning power.

Five senior **government members** were sacked in June, including Yankuba Toureh (the last of the 1994 five coup plotters still serving the government). Toureh was minister of fisheries, water resources and national assembly affairs and, most notably, head of APRC national propaganda. Not having displayed the same rhetorical and persuasive skills as Toureh, his successor, Ansoumana Sahno, was replaced towards the end of the year by Yankuba Colley, a charismatic personality and mayor of one of the largest Gambian municipalities.

In October, the demotion and arrest of Lt General Lang Tombong Tamba from his position as **chief of staff** of the Gambia Armed Forces on initial charges of corruption and embezzlement, besides other minor changes, caused public surprise. The dismissal followed an unexpected presidential visit on 10 October to the military barracks near Yundum Airport, which were found to be in a deplorable state. Other senior officers in the armed forces, including the commanders of the Republican National Guards, the National Army and the Military Training Institute, were fired, together with Tamba. The wave of dismissals also hit the National Intelligence Agency. Tamba, who like the president belongs to the Jola minority, had won the latter's confidence during the 2006 attempted coup. Popular in the army, he also enjoyed a reputation for extreme loyalty. Rumours of a **coup plot** spread immediately after the events and were reinforced by Jammeh's call for loyalty on the part of the army on the occasion of the swearing in of Tamba's successor in the first week of December.

Political liberties and civil rights remained under siege, with the government well aware of its negative international reputation. At year's end, a number of citizens were detained incommunicado. Besides the pending case of Deyda Hydra, no light was shed on the fate of his colleague Ebrima Manneh, who had disappeared after his arrest in 2006.

Foreign Affairs

In October, the president's speech at the UN General Assembly provided an opportunity to display his **anti-Western stance** and simultaneously champion the cause of Taiwan, one of the major financial supporters of the APRC government. Jammeh described international companies as "locusts who ravage the African continent". Relations with Iran, Venezuela and Cuba remained strong. Attendance at the 22 July celebrations by President Kadhafi reaffirmed historical links with **Libya**. Addressing a youth gathering, Kadhafi touched on the hot topic of illegal migration to Europe. His visit was reciprocated by Jammeh's attendance at the fortieth anniversary of Kadhafi's coup d'état in Libya on 1 September 1969.

At the end of the year, relations with **Senegal** cooled following the publication by the 'Daily Observer' of a letter that Kukoi Sanyang allegedly wrote to Senegal's president urging him to help overthrow Jammeh in the name of democracy. Sanyang was the leader of the bloody 1981 coup attempt against Sir Dawda Jawara's government. However, neither the Gambian nor the Senegalese authorities issued any official reaction. A meeting between Jammeh and Senegal's chief diplomat in December re-opened the dialogue between the two countries with a view to preparing President Wade's scheduled visit in the first week of 2010. Official estimates put the number of Senegalese expatriates in Gambia at 500,000, although their real number is probably higher.

Socioeconomic Developments

Heavy **floods** during the rainy season were said to have compromised annual agricultural output, though official estimates were not yet available at year's end and output benefited from good weather the previous year. The floods also highlighted poor conditions in some historical neighbourhoods of Banjul. The government promptly distributed rice to the victims and announced a presidential plan for the restoration and modernisation of the city.

IMF teams visited Gambia to assess the progress of the three-year project financed under the aegis of the Extended Credit Facility. Besides the fiscal target, all the quantitative criteria were satisfied. However, the IMF expressed concern about the country's indebtedness and urged structural measures to reduce the debt. As a side-effect of the global downturn, economic **growth** dropped to an estimated 4.5%–5%. Remittances from abroad declined less than forecast, although the flow of passengers through Banjul airport fell by 7%.

Good weather conditions in 2008 (after three years of drought) boosted the **agricultural sector**, thus reducing the impact of the economic crisis. Rice production almost doubled (from 34,000 tonnes in 2008 to 64,500 in 2009) and production of groundnuts, an important cash crop, also increased due to an extension of cultivated land and investment by migrants returning from Europe. Re-established state control of the Gambian Groundnut Corporation (GGC), currently the biggest groundnut buyer in the country, and government distributions of seeds and fertilizer, brought partial relief to farmers, after years of difficulties and smuggling of produce across the Senegalese border. Nevertheless, the situation was far from rosy. The GGC could not completely pay back its 2008 bank loans and this led to closure of credit in the course of the year. The 2009–2010 trading season opened with farmers returning home empty-handed or with credit notes instead of cash after selling their harvest to the GGC.

Undocumented **migration** to Europe continued to capture public attention due to the death of a number of Gambians en route between Libya and Italy, the repatriation of 41 clandestine migrants from Italy, and the signature of a bilateral agreement with Spain to regularise migratory flows. The media stigmatised the case of a certain Ebrima Jaiteh (who sought asylum in Italy by claiming that an Islamic court had sentenced him to death for homosexuality) as a fabrication that tarnished the national image. But the real social problem, immigration into Gambia, was still to be addressed by the government. The 2009 Human Development Report gave Gambia an emigration rate of 3.6 and an immigration rate of 15.2. Peaceful living conditions (in comparison with other African countries) continued to attract migrants and settlers from destabilised areas in southern Senegal and several other West African countries, mainly Nigeria, Ghana, Sierra Leone and Guinea. Although the government has tried to foster amicable diplomatic ties with each of these countries (Nigeria is Gambia's major partner for technical co-operation) and has also spoken in favour of religious collaboration between Muslim and Christians, latent tensions between citizens and the large number of foreigners living in the peri-urban areas of Banjul were a feature of social conditions in the capital.

Alice Bellagamba

Ghana

The year ushered in the administration of the National Democratic Congress (NDC), previously in opposition, following a tightly fought election that saw the exit of the incumbent National Patriotic Party (NPP) after eight years in power. The new government met a challenging fiscal balance and had recourse to the IMF, but vowed to bring transparency and accountability to oil dealings. Oil appeared to be a resource from which all political programmes could be supported, having whetted local and international appetites alike. In line with its aim to fulfil campaign promises, the government sought to justify the continuation of existing projects and, among other things, got to grips with the delicate and politicised task of handling conflicts in the northern part of the country. US President Barack Obama visited Ghana on his Africa foreign policy trip.

Domestic Politics

The December 2008 presidential and parliamentary elections were completed on 2 January after a run-off. The new president, John Atta Mills, defeated his opponent by a mere 40,586 votes nationally, in an election that was certified by observers as the freest and fairest to date in Africa, prompting the international community to praise the country's democratisation process, and earning Ghana the privilege of being chosen as the venue for US President Obama's first official visit to Africa. Attention soon turned to how domestic politics would pan out, particularly in key areas of electoral concern, such as jobs and the economy. Hence the budget, **appointments** and justice became three testing areas. Signs that the new administration was not a government-in-waiting began to show in difficulties with both national and international appointments. Diplomatic appointments were not finalised until as late as August.

In the interim, the government's attempt to redress the status quo was naturally viewed as the politics of vengeance, and this, rather than national priorities and real government business, appeared to take centre stage in popular perceptions during the first half of the year. In particular, there was turmoil about the purported ex-gratia **emoluments** for the former president, which constituted a long list including two houses, six cars, 60 days of overseas travel each year, and over $ 1 m in annual expenses. President Mills suspended disbursement of the emoluments and, in March, appointed a committee on emoluments chaired by Ishmael Yamson to review the basis for the entitlements determined by the previous presidential committee on emoluments chaired by Mrs Chinery-Hesse. In July, the Ishmael Yamson committee concluded that it could not establish the authorship of the two unsigned final reports of the Chinery-Hesse committee, and furthermore could not determine which of the unsigned reports was approved by the ex-president and parliament.

The new government pledged to fight corruption and prosecute the previous administration's corrupt officials. The attorney general was tasked to prepare a list, to which directive the NPP replied that they were not intimidated. The Ghanaian obsession with cars became a huge problem for the government to handle. On 9 January, the government ordered a return of all **state vehicles** in the possession of former ministers and government appointees, and suspended with immediate effect the re-registration of such vehicles with the drivers and vehicle licensing authority. The government also demanded a list of all state vehicles transferred into private ownership since June 2008, and directed that any further transfers be subject to the approval of the chief director at the office of the presidency.

All **security operatives** of the previous administration from 2001 to 2008 in the intelligence services, police, army and foreign service were laid off by the new security bosses. In a tit for tat measure for what occurred when the NPP took office in 2001, political appointees were instated across sectors where applicable, seeing to the exit of the appointees of the previous administration.

A series of **corruption** revelations about the NPP administration began to surface, especially the sale of Ghana Telecom to Vodafone UK, and the acquisition of the Kosmos Energy stake in the Jubilee Oil Field. Both revelations directly implicated the former president and his cronies. However, the new government's zealous anti-corruption campaign received a setback when, on 25 June, the sports minister, Mohammed Muntaka

Mubarak, resigned over allegations of corruption and was replaced in a government reshuffle with Akua Sena Dansua, who was the minister for women and children's affairs. Furthermore, in September, a British Serious Fraud Office investigation indicted Dr Sipa Yankey, the minister of health, and Amadi Seidu, a minister of state at the presidency, over allegations of taking bribes from the British construction company Mabey & Johnson. The two ministers resigned on 9 October, even though the transactions in question occurred in 1996, when they were both serving in different capacities under an NDC government. The British court that handled the case ordered Mabey & Johnson to pay a package including reparations of £ 658,000 to the Ghanaian government.

Despite the change in government and signs of uncertainty in some quarters, the **central bank** enjoyed stability and integrity under the firm hand of its experienced governor Dr Paul Acquah, who had won the Banker of the Year – Africa award in 2008. He retired in September. But the position of his **deputy** Dr Mahamudu Bawumia became immediately untenable after the elections, since he had stood as vice-presidential candidate on an NPP ticket. He resigned in January and took up appointments first, in May, as visiting professor at the University of British Columbia, and subsequently, in November, as a senior associate member of St Antony's College and visiting senior research associate at the Centre for the Study of African Economies at the University of Oxford.

High among the government's challenges were uncompleted national projects, empty coffers and a huge budget deficit of 14.9%. Hence, the 2009 **budget** attracted extensive debate, including whether it could be the effective instrument for delivering on the key electoral promise of creating jobs, or at least engineering their creation in the medium and long term. The government got locked in protracted talks with civil servants over salary increases, arrears and the implementation of the new single spine salary structure. These funds were later allocated in the 2010 budget, announced on 19 November.

The government inherited an existing proposal to divide the **Northern Region** into two administrative regions. On 28 October, Vice President John Mahama received presentations in Accra from a delegation of the Northern Regional House of Chiefs, and decided to set up a technical committee that would prepare the case for carving up the region, in accordance with provisions in the Constitution. While it did not intend to cultivate a special focus on the underdeveloped north, the new administration found itself grappling with **conflicts** in this area, particularly in Bawku and Dagbon. A string of curfews was imposed on the Bawku municipality and environs because of renewed clashes in the longstanding conflict between Kusasis and Mamprusis. In Dagbon, both the Andani Gate and the rival Abudu Gate also made their impressions. On 16 January, the Andani Gate officially commenced lobbying to reopen the case of the murder in 2002 of the former regent of Dagbon, Ya-Na Yakubu Andani, alleging that the Wuako commission of the previous NPP government had failed to identify the culprits. The Andanis had voted massively for the NDC in the December 2008 elections. The president promised, in his 20 February state of the nation address, to bring justice to the resolution of these armed crises. Amidst the complexity of the security situation, the vice president warned, in a speech on 7 March in Tamale, that the ban on possession of weapons would be enforced irrespective of political, ethnic or other affiliation.

The conflicts already had a history of **politicisation**. At a news conference in Tamale on 20 May, the Abudu Gate called on the president to remove the Northern Regional minister, Stephen Nayina, from office on the allegation that he was interfering in the Dagbon chieftaincy dispute and not abiding by the roadmap to peace as drawn up by the committee of eminent chiefs. Furthermore, as chair of the Northern Regional Security Council, he had provided security for an elder of the Andani Gate to renovate a sacred room in the Gbewaa Palace. The nature of the political minefield prompted Mills to state, in a speech during an official visit to Wa on 30 May, that the government would not interfere in chieftaincy issues. The Alliance for Accountable Governance had warned the president to proceed cautiously and with circumspection on the Dagbon case, which featured in his state of the nation address. In parliament, on 15 September, the NPP called for the minister of interior and national security, Cletus Avoka, to be reassigned because he was a Kusasi and too attached to the Bawku conflict to implement an impartial solution. The president summarily assured citizens, in a Yendi speech on 6 December, that the government was working seriously behind the scenes to bring justice to the Dagbon and Gusghiegu crises. Gushiegu is among townships on which curfews were imposed during the year.

Foreign Affairs

The highlight of Ghana's foreign affairs was **President Obama**'s visit to Accra on 10 July. Ongoing areas of cooperation with the US included projects under the Millennium Challenge Account and military exercises with the US Africa Command in relation to maritime security for the oil industry and drugs trafficking. The Ghanaian online media reported on 16 September that Ghana had placed orders for four air force planes and other defence equipment worth $ 680 m from the US Defense Security Cooperation Agency. Obama used his speech in Accra to outline US foreign policy on Africa.

There were no dramatic foreign policy shifts. The new government continued with Ghana's **longstanding policy** of maintaining itself in good standing with its neighbours, pursuing Pan-Africanism passionately, interacting positively with all well-meaning international partners, and in the process remaining unaligned to any superpower, while recognising international law and the centrality of the UN in global governance.

The controversial **appointment** of the inexperienced Alhaji Mohammed Mumuni as foreign minister made headlines, and the government took too long over the appointment of representatives to the biggest missions abroad – an ambassador to the US and a high commissioner to the UK – both of which took effect in September. President Mills made an official visit to the UK from 4 to 9 May before appointing Danso Boafo as high commissioner. The offices of the ministry of foreign affairs caught fire on 21 October, forcing the department to relocate temporarily. The Chinese government offered to construct a new office complex, to be situated close to the Accra airport junction.

On 25 March, the vice president held wide-ranging trade and political discussions in Ouagadougou with President Blaise Compaoré of **Burkina Faso**, during which Compaoré called for the resumption of the Joint Commission for Cooperation to take forward a number of projects, including the proposed rail link between Ouagadougou and Kumasi which would facilitate trade between the two countries. The sensitive issue of the rise of water levels at the Bagre Dam in Burkina Faso, which leads to flooding in northern Ghana, was included in the discussions. When the Bagre Dam was opened on 4 September, it took just two days to flood the White Volta in northern Ghana and its tributaries, and prompted the rapid response team of Ghana's National Disaster Management Organisation, and a team from the 48th Engineer Regiment of the Ghana Army, to attend to the situation on 8 September.

In response to Mills' visit to **Côte d'Ivoire** in April, his Ivorian counterpart President Laurent Gbagbo met with him in Accra on 4 November, when both leaders agreed to reactivate the Ghana-Côte d'Ivoire Permanent Joint Commission for Cooperation, and Mills pledged Ghanaian assistance towards a peaceful presidential election in Côte d'Ivoire. One issue in Ghanaian-Ivorian cooperation has been the problem of cocoa smuggling. A more sensitive problem concerned demarcation of the common sea border, because of recent oil prospecting in this part of the Gulf of Guinea. This was in tandem with the agreement at the 13–14 February ECOWAS ministerial meeting to define national ocean and sea boundaries in accordance with the UN Convention on the Law of the Sea, and Ghana's own procedures with the UN Commission on the Limits of the Continental Shelf for an extension beyond the mandatory 200 nautical miles. On 6 November, the Ivorian government donated $ 60,000 to Ghana's future foreign office complex.

Relations with **Togo** resumed normality at various levels. On 19 June, the Ghana Water Company announced the launch of the Sogakope-Lomé Water Project with the Togo Water Company for the construction and operation of a water treatment plant and pipeline that would transport water from the Volta River to Lomé. The Togolese authorities aired their displeasure about Ghana permitting opposition leader Gilchrist Olympio to interact with President Obama during his visit to Accra. However, at a meeting in Accra on 26 August, Mills and his Togolese counterpart agreed to reconvene the Joint Border Demarcation Commission, which would facilitate the implementation of the ECOWAS protocol on the free movement of people, goods and services.

On 19 June, Mills visited **Nigeria**. A deal brokered to increase Nigerian oil supplies from 45,000 to 60,000 barrels a day could not be implemented. There was general concern about the influx of Nigerians and crime levels in Ghana. The Nigerian high commissioner to Ghana announced on 9 July that 300 Nigerians were serving jail terms in

Ghanaian prisons. From 23 November to 2 December, Ghanaian naval security intercepted and returned a Nigerian oil vessel, which had been hijacked by pirates in the Gulf of Guinea.

EU aid included a € 175 m MDG contract facility, approved on 2 July. Ghana also hosted several **meetings**. From 24–25 August, the ECOWAS Small Arms Programme conference took place to identify armed violence reduction projects. Subsequently, on 2 September, the Ghanaian authorities agreed to ratify the ECOWAS Convention on Small Arms and Light Weapons and the Convention on Cluster Munitions. From 16 to 21 November, the First Pan-Africa Trade Fair and Investment Conference took place in Accra. From 23 to 27 November, the International African Coffee Organisation held its annual General Assembly in the Ghanaian capital, coinciding with the Eighth General Meeting of the African Coffee Research Network. From 7 to 8 December, Accra was the venue for the All Africa Energy Summit.

Socioeconomic Developments

A Comprehensive Food Security and Vulnerability Analysis (CFSVA), launched by the UN's World Food Programme in Accra on 6 May, outlined that 1.2 million people were insecure, with limited access to sufficient and nutritious **food**. Some 0.5 million in the rural areas of the three northern regions were determined to be at risk, while up to 1.5 million in the remaining seven regions faced comparable problems. The CFSVA cited the Upper West Region as the most affected area, where 34% of the population were food insecure, followed by the Upper East Region with 15%, and the Northern Region with 10%. The main causes of food insecurity included reliance on traditional and often inefficient agricultural practices, limited markets for farm produce, high food prices, lack of education and hazards such as weather conditions. On 13 November, two state-of-the-art laboratories sponsored by the Swiss government through the UN Industrial Development Organisation's Trade Capacity Building Project were opened at the Ghana Standards Board, to be used to test Ghana's agricultural exports. The accredited laboratories would assist Ghanaian exporters to ensure food safety, detect pesticide residues and reduce costs of testing, in order to boost consumer confidence in Ghanaian export products.

The new administration resolved to restructure the beleaguered National **Health** Insurance Scheme. The government responded to the demands of doctors for higher salaries, instituted the decentralisation of administrative processes that compelled health workers to travel to the capital, and promised to upgrade existing health training institutions or establish new ones. On 6 August, the Upper East Region director of health services, Dr Awoonor-Williams, expressed concern that none of the 57 newly qualified medical doctors nationwide chose postings to the region, adding that the doctor to patient ratio was 1:34,000. UNICEF also raised concerns about maternal deaths in the Upper West Region. According to the Zabzugu/Tatale District director of health, UNICEF and the Danish

International Development Agency donated 16,000 insecticide-treated mosquito nets for free distribution to motivate pregnant women to attend district health facilities for delivery. The results of a survey conducted in six communities of the Birim Central Municipality and the Birim South District revealed that about 10% of teenagers between the ages of 11 and 14 were sexually active, either because of the influence of sex videos or driven by hardship. In the course of the year, the National Health Insurance Authority suspended two private hospitals in Kumasi for faulty prescriptions and over-billing.

The government signed an agreement with the Ghana National Association of Teachers for a 17% salary increment for teachers (as reported in July), while awaiting implementation of another salary structure early in the next year. On 3 August, it announced cabinet approval for senior high school reforms, reducing **education** by one year. On 24 August, the government announced an increase in grants for school meals, while it also began implementing distribution of free school uniforms to poorer pupils. On 19 November, the government announced an initiative to provide permanent buildings for schools currently operating under trees, and to expand facilities in schools still running on a shift system. The 19 November budget statement made provision for constructing and furnishing 165 school buildings to accommodate primary and junior high schools, and 250 structures for kindergartens, in the next three years.

The GDP **growth** rate for 2008 was over 7%, but being cognisant of the global credit crunch and the decline in remittances, plus an inherited budget deficit of 14.9%, the new government proposed a modest and realistic target of 5.9% growth in 2009. This was the first time in nine years that the annual growth rate of GDP was expected to fall below the level for the previous year. Inflation had skyrocketed from 18.1% in December 2008 to 20.5% in March 2009, and to 20.7% in June. With the budget deficit and financial difficulties ahead, the government went to the IMF and obtained a three-year $ 1.2 bn interest-free package to support the budget, in addition to World Bank support. The package came with conditions and other triggers, such as a jobs freeze in the public sector, except for teachers, nurses and doctors, for at least two years, and a halt to subsidising petrol prices – both measures that were in sharp contrast with campaign promises. Experts viewed the move as a setback for the country's development and a reminder of similar IMF conditions for structural adjustment during the 1980s and 1990s under the previous NDC administration, which had failed to work. The NPP administration had worked very hard to wean the country from such arrangements by raising sovereign bonds from the international capital market. The government, however, achieved 4.7% GDP growth for 2009 and set a more aspirational 6.5% GDP target for the next year. **Inflation** was reduced to 17% at the end of the year, on the basis of which the government set a 14.5% target for 2010. The reduction in inflation, coupled with a sharp decline in the depreciation of the cedi against the US dollar from 5.4% in January to 0.9% in July, and a subsequent steady appreciation of the cedi from July, became the first real signs of macroeconomic stability. In December, the cedi appreciated by 0.2% against the US dollar, 1% against the British pound, 1% against the euro, and 1% against the South African rand.

Gold exports for the first half of the year increased by 1.2%, from $ 1,199 m in 2008 to $ 1,213 m, but diamond exports declined significantly from $ 29.5 m in 2008 to $ 3.1 m. Exports of **cocoa** and related products for the first half of the year amounted to $ 1,060 m, an annual growth of 16.6% compared with $ 910 m in 2008. The cocoa harvest for the full season of 2008/09 was 703,000 tonnes, up by 3% from the preceding year's figure of 680,000 tonnes. In September, the price of cocoa rose on the London international market to its highest since 1989 and, in response, the government increased the producer price with effect from 14 October. On 3 September, the Ghana Cocoa Board announced that the crop year bonuses from the last season had been released to the Licence Buying Companies for payment to all cocoa farmers. On 3 November, Cadbury Ghana and Cadbury Canada donated 5,000 bicycles to be distributed to school children in deprived cocoa growing communities to increase access to education.

In order to ensure more efficient revenue administration, the president, himself a **tax** expert, welcomed representations from the Chartered Institute of Taxation on 10 September. Subsequently, on 19 November, the government announced that the three revenue collection agencies would be amalgamated under a single commissioner general. New software was also introduced to facilitate the prompt preparation and submission of tax returns.

On 7 September, the deputy director-general of the Ghana Atomic Energy Commission announced the International Atomic Energy Agency's agreement to assist Ghana in performing a training needs assessment for its nuclear capacity. On 7 October, Ghana signed a memorandum of understanding with Brazil to construct a 9,000 MW capacity hydroelectric dam on the River Oti, at Juallay near Pwalugu in the Upper East Region. On 20 November, the Volta River Authority (VRA) confirmed that the West African Gas Pipeline Company would deliver enough gas to power the VRA's 110 MW turbines and distribute **energy** supplies in Ghana. Furthermore, Ghana progressed with plans to supply its own natural gas, and announced on 4 October the selection of Nigeria-based Oando as a partner to the Ghana National Petroleum Corporation (GNPC), to develop the natural gas infrastructure from the offshore Jubilee Oilfields, a project worth $ 1 bn. The VRA also announced plans on 23 November to establish a wind farm in Ada that would add 50 MW-80 MW of electricity to the national grid.

Oil prospecting became the busiest hub of the energy sector and several institutions, both national and international, called for transparency and accountability. The new administration therefore took comprehensive steps to streamline the initiatives of the previous government. On 27 February, Mills announced the government's decision to review the previous government's draft oil law in order to ensure the better regulation and transparency of oil deals. Kosmos Energy's stake in the Jubilee Oilfields was alleged to have been negotiated under a deal too generous for the national interest, and became subject to investigation. On 9 March, the Revenue Watch Institute congratulated the Mills administration on its decision to publicly disclose all present and future contracts with oil companies and expressed the hope that Ghana would incorporate the oil sector into the Ghana Extractive Industries Transparency Initiative. On 29 September, Mills met with World Bank President Robert Zoellick in Washington DC and announced plans to set up a growth fund to manage oil revenues. On 12 October, the president announced that a petroleum revenue management bill was being drafted to ensure prudent use of the expected revenue from the oil and gas sectors. Finance Minister Kwabena Duffuor announced on 18 November that the government would establish an oil industrialisation plan to ensure judicious application of the expected revenues. International interest in Ghana's oil industry also arose. On 13 July, India's state-run Oil and Natural Gas Corporation expressed interest in putting in a formal bid to buy a 30% stake in the Jubilee Oilfields. On 20 September, the GNPC announced plans to collaborate with the China National Oil Offshore Corporation to provide the GNPC with financial and technical support in exploration.

The Corporate Social Responsibility Movement organised a two-day meeting from 17 March for stakeholders in the oil and gas industries to discuss the ecological and economic impacts of oil production. The fishing industry was particularly concerned and the director of petroleum at the ministry of energy pledged to set up a team to examine the concerns of the fisheries sector. The universities have been no exception to the impact of the **oil boom**, and on 4 March, Brong Ahafo Regional Minister Kwadwo Nyamekye Marfo reaffirmed government commitment to upgrade the Faculty of Forest Resource Technology of the Kwame Nkrumah University of Science and Technology (KNUST) in Sunyani to a fully-fledged University of Energy and Natural Resources. On 27 August, the GNPC's communications manager announced that there had been a huge increase in the number of geology students graduating from KNUST, from 15 to 100 per year. On 9 November, the dean of the Engineering Faculty of the University of Ghana announced that the premier university was holding discussions with oil companies about training the requisite human resources.

The Tema Oil Refinery (TOR) suffered a string of shutdowns due to technical faults. The TOR refines about 45,000 barrels of oil, i.e. 75% of the daily consumption of 76,500 barrels. It was estimated that capacity should increase to about 145,000 barrels to meet national demand. Plans were therefore announced for the building of new refineries. The TOR's capacity problems became politically sensitive as they helped to push up **petrol prices** – a hot campaign issue for the new government. On 9 March, the government's National Petroleum Authority (NPA) made a political move and effected decreases in fuel prices at a total cost of almost $ 50 m in government subsidies. The government subsequently bowed to the global crude market and an IMF requirement to halt the subsidies. A series of petrol price hikes then occurred, culminating in a 5% price increase by the NPA in October.

As **job creation**, especially for young people, was a hot campaign issue, the 19 November budget statement announced that 14,700 jobs would be created for masons, carpenters and other skilled workers by the massive school building programme outlined above. On 25 November, it was announced that the National Youth Employment Programme (NYEP) was launching its recruitment drive for 2009/2010 to create productive employment opportunities in all sectors of the economy, and that it had plans to recruit 44,000 young people by December. The Youth in Agriculture module of the NYEP was also expected to recruit 50,000 young people by December. On 30 November, the deputy minister of lands and natural resources, Henry Kamel, announced in parliament that 30,000 jobs were to be created in 100 districts through the implementation of a National Forest Plantation Development Programme. Some 100 targeted districts were to benefit, with 300 jobs each. The government therefore still had some way to go in making an impact on the job creation front, particularly at the grass-roots level, where the pinch of the credit crunch was felt the most, and to which constituency the election promises had been directed.

There were **floods** during the year, which displaced a number of citizens of northern Ghana, damaging large areas of farmland and crops, and stretching national and UN relief services.

Michael Amoah

Guinea

Guinea experienced one of the most dramatic years in its history since independence. The military junta 'Conseil National pour la Démocratie et le Développement' (CNDD) that took over in the last days of 2008 continued to rule. President Moussa 'Dadis' Camara became increasingly erratic and authoritarian over the course of the year, and by October was accused of command responsibility in the massacre of 150 to 200 unarmed civilians protesting against the regime, as well as over 100 instances of (gang) rape that accompanied the massacre. Dadis's aide de camp, Aboubacar 'Toumba' Diakhité, was accused of direct oversight, and when he felt that he was being prepared to take full blame for the killings and rapes, he attempted to assassinate Camara, shooting him in the head. The wound required Camara's medical evacuation to Morocco in December. Minister of Defence and effective number two Sékouba Konaté took over as interim president. At year's end, negotiations were underway to begin a civilian-led transition toward elections in which the military would not be involved.

Domestic Politics

With the death of former president General **Lansana Conté** and the coup that followed at the end of December 2008, Guineans entered 2009 hoping that the CNDD would bring the democracy and development that the junta's name promised. Many Guineans cheered the first appearances of Captain Moussa Dadis Camara as much because he represented the departure of Conté and his disastrous government as because of Camara's fiery speeches promising reform. They knew that Conté had come to power in exactly the same way, taking power in a coup after the death of the country's first president, Sékou Touré, who died in office after 26 years in power. Although Conté promised reforms that would open the political and economic fields and bring prosperity, those promises had gradually slipped away over the course of his first decade in power.

Still, almost all Guineans joined in Camara's scathing criticism of both the abusive soldiers and greedy civilians who had betrayed popular faith in government. They especially applauded his promises to dismantle networks that had brought Latin American **narcotraffickers** to Guinea. Commander Tiégboro Camara was named as Minister for the Fight against Grand Banditry and Narcotraffic, and soon made a number of arrests. He also called upon the mayors of Conakry's five communes to take armed robbers caught *in flagrante delicto* and burn them to death on the spot. Despite the draconian nature of their methods, many Guineans appreciated the intention of eliminating crime in a city that had become dangerous and where society and politics were becoming contaminated by drug money.

By late February, Camara, who became known throughout Guinea simply by his nickname, 'Dadis', began conducting the business of the state from the antechamber outside his bedroom in the Alpha Yaya Diallo military camp. Emerging some time between 18h and 20h, Dadis met with government ministers, foreign ambassadors and businessmen, and members of the Conté government, all on live television. Camara's unscripted and intemperate interactions fascinated Guineans over the three months that they were an almost nightly fixture on national television. They even became minor hits on YouTube, where diasporic Francophone Africans watched the **Dadis show** in large numbers.

The trust Guineans were willing to place in Camara and the CNDD was built upon his promise that he was there simply to clean up the affairs of government, and that neither he nor any member of his government would run for elected office at the end of a one-year transition. Given that he took a **solemn oath** to this effect on live television with one hand on the Bible and the other on the Qur'an (Camara was raised a Catholic by his mother, though his father was Muslim), Guineans took him at his word, as many assumed that breaking such an oath would bring great calamity or even death upon him.

Nevertheless, Guineans noted many warning signs and contradictions in the behaviour of the junta from the beginning. Although it immediately banned the National Assembly and the Supreme Court and suspended the Constitution – everything that in French is called 'the republican institutions' – Camara simultaneously proclaimed himself 'Président de la République', and insisted that everyone address him by this title. Similarly, though the junta promised free and fair elections within a year, members of the junta attacked the residence of **opposition leader** Cellou Dalein Diallo on 1 January, threatening the inhabitants with violence, destroying property and accusing him of stockpiling weapons, which were never found but that allegedly were part of a plot to take power by force. Many Guineans saw in these acts the same techniques that the Touré and Conté governments had used to intimidate and silence those they considered to be their most credible political competitors.

As the televised Dadis Show went forward, Camara extracted **public confessions** from the former president's son, Ousmane Conté, arrested on 24 February on the grounds that he had been involved in dealings with the cocaine traffickers. Camara similarly acted as interrogator, judge and jury in the cases of former ministers accused of theft and fraud, particularly in the case of the ministry of mines. In that department, successive ministers had negotiated mining contracts that were increasingly unfavourable to Guinea, as control of public finances became nonexistent and the interest of international mining companies was growing. While the forthright and righteous tone of Camara's monologues thrilled many Guineans, who had not heard such impassioned rhetoric since the socialist period (1958–1984), some quickly became sceptical of the junta's claims, wondering whether they were moving the former criminalised elements out of their way in order to monopolise the same sectors.

Support for the junta began to collapse in April, when Camara gave a speech during the opening of a renovated mosque in the Boulbinet neighbourhood of Conakry. During the speech, he harshly criticised the political class, warning politicians to "put some water in their wine" and show him more respect, and threatening to take off his uniform and **run for president** as a civilian. This threat solidified suspicions that many had begun to develop that Dadis might have become too fond of the attention, wealth and power that accompanied the presidency to walk away from them.

Adding to this suspicion was the way in which Camara had seemed to **centralise power** by marginalising, and even arresting, other members of the junta for diverse (real or imagined) infractions. On 26 January, the president had Colonel Aboubacar 'Idi Amin' Camara, arrested for unspecified reasons. During one of the first Dadis Shows, he accused him of going forward with plans to take over the ministry of which he had been named head without asking Dadis's permission regarding the date. Dadis called this an unacceptable act of insubordination, but many wondered whether the minister, who was considered one of the more progressive members of the CNDD, was being put on warning not to act too independently. Several weeks later, Minister of Security and nominal number two in the Junta, Mamadouba 'Toto' Camara (no relation to Dadis Camara) was viciously humiliated by Dadis on live television. On 22 July, Camara was publicly beaten up by members of the presidential guard and left semi-conscious by the side of the road.

By June, Camara was organising oaths of allegiance amongst all police and armed forces personnel. These oaths were "to respect the flag, defend the nation, and to remain loyal to Camara himself and his Minister of Defence, Sékouba Konaté". Despite the promises to protect Guineans, the period from March onward showed a steady **increase**

of insecurity, with petrol stations, money changers, shops and restaurants, as well as private citizens, all targeted for theft, carjacking, and even murder and rape, with the assailants usually being uniformed military. Most Guineans agreed that the level of insecurity was the worst they had ever experienced.

By September, the junta had lost almost all of the support and legitimacy it had ever had, and Guineans had grown increasingly impatient to see the CNDD leave power. Voices in the press, from opposition leaders, and amongst the population increasingly expressed the fear that, having placed military officers at the head of almost all significant ministries and in all of the positions of the territorial administration (Governors, Préfets, and Sous-Préfets), Camara could easily rig elections in his favour if he were to run – just as Conté had done before him.

All of the major opposition parties announced a **protest march**, demanding assurances that neither Camara nor members of the junta would run for elected office in the upcoming elections. The date was fixed for 28 September, the historic day when Guinea voted 'No' to France's offer of semi-autonomous status for its colonies, choosing immediate independence instead. The year before, Guinea had celebrated the 50th anniversary of the 28 September vote and independence a few days later. The date thus lent the march an air of political seriousness and patriotism.

What followed was a **bloody reprisal** that left at least 156 dead and 109 women raped. All investigations suggest that the killings were premeditated. Once marchers had entered Conakry's main stadium for the rally, for example, the metal gates were chained shut, and attached to metal cables that would later electrocute several of the marchers who tried to escape after members of the presidential guard opened fire. Most of the opposition leaders were badly beaten. Cellou Dalein Diallo, Jean Marie Doré and Sidya Touré all sustained serious injuries that required hospitalization. Some of those who escaped made video footage of the killings and rapes, using their cell phones. Oral testimonies gathered by HRW, AI and a UN Commission of Inquiry in the six weeks after the killings produced consistent versions of the events from eyewitnesses and survivors.

In addition to the killings, which were allegedly undertaken by presidential guards, gendarmes and ordinary soldiers, much of the sexual violence consisted of **public gang rapes** that appeared to be calculated to terrorise the protesters. There were also reports that members of an ethnic militia were involved in the killings. Many Guineans attested to the fact that an ethnic militia, made up of roughly 80% Kpelle speakers (Dadis Camara's ethnic group), and numbering at least 4,000, had been recruited over the course of the junta's year in power. Eyewitnesses said they were trained by white mercenaries at Kaliah, a village near the town of Forecariah that had once hosted a large refugee camp for Sierra Leoneans.

International reaction was swift and unanimous, and it was under this pressure that the government entered into **negotiations** with the opposition under an ECOWAS-mandated mediation by Burkinabè President Blaise Compaoré on 5 October. Camara, who claimed that neither he nor his government bore any responsibility for what had happened (and initially claimed that only 50 to 60 people had died, most of them suffocated in a panic stampede for the exits), invited an international investigation, which did take place from 15 November to 5 December.

On 3 December, the UN commission of inquiry was to have interviewed Aboubacar 'Toumba' Diakhité, Dadis' aide de camp. Diakhité was accused by many of having overseen the massacre. He refused to meet with the commission, and lured Camara to Camp Koundara, a military base at the tip of the Conakry peninsula, which Diakhité had controlled since shortly after the CNDD took power. Once Camara arrived, Diakhité attempted to kill him, shooting him in the head, but only grazing his skull. Diakhité's men also threw a hand grenade at Tiegboro Camara, wounding him and killing his driver.

In the fight that ensued, Dadis Camara was brought back to the Alpha Yaya Diallo military camp with Tiegboro, while Toumba Diakhité escaped. That night, Dadis and Tiegboro were both medically evacuated to **Morocco**, where General Toto Camara was already undergoing treatment unrelated to the events of 3 December. Sékouba Konaté, officially the number three in the CNDD, but always considered to be the true second-in-command, returned to Guinea from Lebanon and took over as the country's interim leader. At the end of the year, Dadis and Tiegboro remained in Morocco, Toumba Diakhité had yet to be found, and Konaté was consolidating his authority as interim president.

Foreign Affairs

On 10 January, **ECOWAS** voted to suspend Guinea until constitutional order was re-established. The AU had done the same on 29 December 2009. Despite the suspension, ECOWAS expressed its intention to 'accompany' Guinea throughout what it hoped would be a peaceful transition toward a legitimately elected government. Amongst African leaders, several broke ranks with this position. Senegalese President Abdoulaye Wade publicly castigated the ECOWAS and AU positions, travelling to Conakry on 11 July and referring to Capt. Camara as his 'son'. Kadhafi also supported the junta, and visited Conakry on 3 January. In a more discrete vein, **Burkina**'s President Blaise Compaoré, a long time associate of Kadhafi's who (as a friend and associate of Charles Taylor's and Foday Sankoh's) was persona non grata in Guinea during the Conté years, visited Conakry on 21 April. By summer, reports were circulating that Compaoré had secured financial interests in the port of Conakry; a no-bid contract for its operation had been granted to GETMA-International, run by Richard Talbot, a long-time associate of Compaoré's.

Nevertheless, many other African countries took a dim view of the junta, especially after the **Ghanaian ambassador** to Guinea found himself the object of the carjacking of his designated 'Chief of Diplomatic Mission' vehicle on the week of 3 August. The Ghanaian ambassador was robbed of his money, cell phone and clothing, reportedly being left in his underwear at an intersection by the presidential guards who had robbed him. Similarly, the Malian ambassador to Guinea was arrested, beaten and had his diplomatic vehicle stolen on the night of 28–29 September.

The UN echoed the initial pro-forma condemnation of the junta. As with the African reactions, the rest of the world was less united in its initial views of the junta than a cursory view would reveal. Initially, the US and Japanese governments took the most negative view of the unconstitutional succession. The **US** publicly announced that it was suspending all aid to Guinea that was not tied to humanitarian assistance or democracy support. In part because of a long-term prior reduction in aid to Guinea, this did not amount to major changes in funding, but it did send a strong and unambiguous message to both the junta and the Guinean public. Both European diplomats and many Guineans criticised this position as being too much based on principle and not enough on an understanding of Guinea as an exceptional place with a unique history.

Although constrained to suspend most aid to Guinea, the **EU** privately took a more flexible position until after the Boulbinet speech in April, when all donor nations began to align their positions. This position became still more negative after the dressing down Camara gave German ambassador (and representative of the EU chair at that time) Karl Prinz. He had asked whether he planned to run in the 2010 presidential elections (recently postponed from December 2009 to January 2010), but Camara continued to state very carefully that he would not run for election in 2009. **France**, which had been the most conciliatory of the European countries toward the junta, continued security sector cooperation programmes up to the September massacre. French MP Patrick Balkany, a member of France's governing party, returned from a September trip to Guinea and gave interviews the day before the massacre, arguing that Dadis Camara had as much right as any other Guinean to run for the presidency.

After the massacre, a significant number of countries imposed **travel bans** and asset freezes on members of the junta, and it is clear that the preliminary report by HRW and a UN Commission of Inquiry created the internal pressures that led to the assassination attempt on Camara. The CNDD, in its attempts to prop up some remaining legitimacy, announced on 12 October that it had signed a \$ 7 bn resources-for-infrastructure deal with the **China** International Fund (CIF), a Hong Kong based investment company with complex but fairly clear links to the Chinese and Angolan governments. This announcement, which appeared to be embarrassing to the Chinese government, drew reactions from Beijing insisting that the CIF was not owned by the government, and that it did not represent Chinese foreign policy. CIF released only an initial sum of \$ 100 m, and even that had evidently not been made available to the CNDD or the Guinean government by year's end. In the discussions leading up to the constitution of the UN Commission of Inquiry, China did not block the creation of the Commission or its work, or lend the CNDD any other support. At the end of the year it was unclear whether the deal would move forward.

During this period, other supporters, including Presidents Wade and Kadhafi, became mostly silent on the subject of Guinea. When ECOWAS and the AU sought a **West African intermediary** to negotiate a way out of the political impasse created by the massacre, they reportedly first contacted Amadou Toumani Touré ('ATT'), president of Mali and viewed by many as an ideal honest broker in this situation, especially since Camara had publicly announced that 'ATT' was his model for taking power to restore order and then return it to civilians. Touré declined, however, and ECOWAS therefore approached Blaise Compaoré. He took the position, though many in Guinea already suspected him of a pro-CNDD bias because of his close ties to Kadhafi and his rumoured business interests in Guinea. When Compaoré listened to both sides of the conflict, and then proposed a 'compromise' that granted almost all of the junta's demands from the start, he lost credibility with most Guineans, and only the assassination attempt on Camara, and the latter's subsequent arrival in Ouagadougou brought Compaoré back into the negotiations.

From late January through the December negotiations in Ougadougou, some of the hard core of pro-Dadis supporters used a series of techniques borrowed from Côte d'Ivoire in order to try to sway public support toward the junta. These techniques included a strong nationalist rhetoric, claims that French and other foreign policies were motivated only by the desire to sabotage Guinean sovereignty and lay hands on the country's mineral wealth, and populist techniques of mobilising supporters, especially youth in Conakry. The formation in January of the Young Patriots of Guinea, and the overheated rhetoric of press secretary Idrissa Chérif (himself Ivorian), resembled politics in Abidjan more than Conakry, and for the most part, Guineans were unconvinced.

Socioeconomic Developments

The beginning of the year saw the promise of significant improvement in the economy, as both Guineans and foreign investors demonstrated their optimism that the end of the Conté era of mismanagement and grand theft meant a real possibility for Guinea's economy to get back on track. By the end of the year, the situation was, in fact, worse. The global economic downturn and falling commodity prices hit the economy hard. Furthermore, the CNDD's **erratic management** scared off new investment, and caused most businesses already in the country to go into 'wait and see' mode.

Locally driven economic growth was also limited to one or two companies which established the same kinds of relationships to the junta that Italian Guido Santullo and Guinean Mamadou Sylla had enjoyed during the Conté period. One entrepreneur who came suddenly onto the scene was Kerfalla Camara, owner of Guicopress, a Guinean construction company. This company gained many **government contracts** over the course of the year. Some estimates of the junta's year in power placed **expenditure** at \$ 800 m, most of it spent either as discretionary expenses or in no-bid ('gré à gré') contracts. Guinea owed some \$ 70 m to outside lenders and was in arrears to the World Bank and AfDB. The government also reportedly owed another $ 5 m-$ 10 m to Guinean entrepreneurs.

Initial estimates of economic **growth** indicated that it was flat, with an end-of-year **inflation** rate of 8.5%. Given inflation and population growth, most Guineans saw their standard of living fall. Average GDP per capita was $ 418. For the first time in several years, there was a significant gap between the official exchange rate (for the dollar, $ 1=5,200 GF) and the black market rate ($ 1=6,300 GF) by the end of the year.

As soon as it took power, the junta lowered **petrol prices** from 7,800 GF per litre to 5,500 GF/litre. At year's end, the small provincial town of Siguiri (population 28,000), near the Malian border, was consuming the same amount of petrol as the capital, Conakry (population around 1.5 m). The reason was presumably because the price of Guinean petrol was set significantly lower than in any of the neighbouring countries, and so there was a thriving cross-border trade from Siguiri into Mali. At the end of the year, donors were placing strong pressure on the Guinean government to bring prices up to somewhere near those prevailing in neighbouring countries. Further pressure came from oil retailers, who were reportedly owed some $ 20 m by the government, which had set the retail prices below what it cost the oil companies, but had not paid the agreed difference. Such payments were largely a cost of continuing to do business under the junta, and this was reflected in the country's ranking of 168 of 180 countries worldwide in TI's **corruption** index. Only Chad, Sudan and Somalia ranked lower in Africa.

Camara's promise to revisit **mining contracts** that many Guineans believed to have been negotiated to the detriment of the people was popular. Russian aluminium giant Rusal came under early scrutiny. AngloGold Ashanti was also singled out in part for failing to send a representative to a public meeting called by Camara. The British giant Rio Tinto had lost half of its Simandou iron ore concession to the Israeli-owned Beny Steinmetz Resources Group (BSRG). Although this deal was opaque and controversial when it took place in the last year of the Conté presidency, Camara seemed to ratify it. At year's end, BSRG even announced that it had been granted permission to ship ore out via Liberia, rather than bringing it across Guinea to a deep water port near Conakry, which would require building a trans-Guinean railway and new port. This was the deal that other iron ore mining companies had tried for over the last 30 years. Thus it seemed that Camara was willing to negotiate away the final infrastructural benefits that Guineans had long demanded from successive companies.

The American 'wildcat' **oil** firm, Hyperdynamics, which had gained the exploration rights to 100% of Guinea's offshore shelf in 2005, succeeded in retaining exploration rights to only 34% of the whole. In principle, the rest would go to CIF, if the deal with the Chinese company in fact went forward. International consortium Global Alumina began building an **alumina refinery** during the year. Progress has been slower than expected, and the projected opening was moved back to 2015.

Guinea claimed 170th place of 182 on the Human Development Index. According to the Human Development Report, Guinea received $ 151 m in **remittances**, or about $ 16 per person. However, as most Guineans send money home through clandestine and informal networks, it is likely that this figure is substantially higher. Years of neglect had diminished the capacities of the health and education sectors, but there was nevertheless good news in some quarters. Guinea's **HIV infection** rate remained low, estimated by UNAIDS at 1.6% of Guineans aged 15 to 49, 59% of those being women; 31% of HIV positive Guineans received antiretrovirals, and 33% of pregnant HIV-positive women received treatment to prevent transmission to their babies.

Mike McGovern

Guinea-Bissau

The year was marked by politically motivated violence, which erupted regularly as a result of sharp divisions within the state elite. Both the chief of staff and the president were assassinated in March, followed by the killing of two high-ranking politicians in an alleged coup attempt in June. The subsequent presidential elections passed off smoothly, but stability remained dubious as a result of an unruly military. Human rights violations and drug-trafficking continued, possibly also affecting the state and army apparatus. Little was done to end the impunity of traffickers, shielded by interference from the military – who have a major financial stake in the trade – and the limited capacities of the police and judiciary. These issues also largely dominated the conduct of foreign affairs. Socioeconomic developments were marked by attempts to improve the country's ageing infrastructure. The global economic crisis had a negative impact on exports and remittances, while easing the price of imported staple foods.

Domestic Politics

On 2 January Carlos Domingues Gomes jr. was inaugurated as the **new prime minister**. His 'Partido Africano da Independência da Guiné e Cabo Verde' (PAIGC) had won the parliamentary elections in 2008. The government programme was approved by parliament on 18 March. The prime minister announced a cabinet reshuffle on 18 September.

The **defamation case** against Kumba Yala, leader of the main opposition party 'Partido da Renovação Social' (PRS), was suspended on 5 January for medical reasons. Yala had accused President Vieira of playing a leading role in drug-trafficking.

On 6 January, an **attack** was launched on chief of staff General NaWaie at the presidential residence. While the presidential guard called it an accident, a spokesman of the 'Movimento Nacional da Sociedade Civil' attributed responsibility to the 'Aguentas' – a group of adolescents who fought for Vieira during the military conflict of 1998–99. They had been integrated into the guard put at the disposal of interior minister Cipriano Cassamá. The 'Aguentas' were immediately disbanded.

While the January attack had failed, on 1 March General NaWaie died in a bomb blast at army headquarters. Obviously in a **revenge killing**, the following day, a number of soldiers loyal to NaWaie killed President Vieira at his residence in front of his wife, who fled to the Angolan embassy. According to a police source, eight soldiers subsequently entered a judicial police building and freed military detainees arrested after the attempted coup against Vieira in 2008. Vieira and NaWaie had reportedly been at odds for many years. Both had been accused of involvement in drug-trafficking.

The UN Security Council, AU, EU, CPLP, ECOWAS and several countries condemned the assassinations and called for compliance with the rule of law. Both the government and general staff declared their respect for constitutional order. After an emergency meeting, the CPLP decided on 3 March to send Portuguese Secretary of State for Foreign Affairs João Gomes Cravinho and CPLP Executive Secretary Domingos Simões Pereira to Bissau. They were accompanied by an ECOWAS mission. Cape Verde considered evacuating its citizens, most of them resident in Guinea-Bissau since colonial times. Also on 3 March, Guinea-Bissau reopened its borders and public life returned to normal. In accordance with the Constitution, Raimundo Pereira, the parliamentary speaker, was sworn in as **interim president**, and assigned the task of preparing for presidential elections within 60 days.

By a 2 March government order, the attorney-general set-up a **fact-finding commission** to investigate the violent incidents. A parallel fact-finding commission to investigate the bomb attack on NaWaie was set up by the army on 6 March. The next day, its spokesman announced the detention of three suspects. According to a statement on 19 March by José Zamora Induta, naval chief of staff, the bomb that killed NaWaie had come from abroad. Induta declared on 8 April that those responsible for the bomb blast had been identified, and on 8 May, an army source stated that five suspects had been detained. A number of parties considered the upcoming nomination of Induta as **new chief of staff** to be illegitimate but, although the Constitution did not allow for decrees by the interim president, Induta was appointed by presidential decree on 6 April.

On 5 June, Guinea-Bissau was rocked by **further violent incidents**: presidential candidate and former minister Baciro Dabó and former minister Hélder Proença (both

PAIGC members and close allies of the late President Vieira), as well as two other individuals, were shot by the army. Dabó was reportedly killed at his home, while Proença was shot near Bula, both reputedly having resisted arrest. The international community condemned the assassinations. On 5 June, the army arrested former Prime Minister Faustino Fudut Imbali, who later accused the military of having beaten him as he was being detained. According to declarations by the government and army, Imbali, Proença, Dabó and 11 other co-conspirators had planned a coup d'état, with Proença as the alleged mastermind. On 12 June, in response to doubts over the veracity of this accusation, the government made public an incriminating video and telephone recording. On 25 June, the Portuguese secretary of state for foreign affairs appealed for a quick solution of the case, saying the alleged conspirators had been illegally detained by the army since 5 June.

On 23 March, with the backing of the ruling PAIGC and the opposition PRS, parliament elected Desejado Lima da Costa as the new chairman of the national election commission. **Presidential elections** were scheduled for 28 June, thus for technical reasons exceeding the time limit specified by the Constitution. The presidential elections were funded by the EU, Portugal and ECOWAS, amongst others. The high court of justice announced on 29 April that 20 contenders had filed their candidatures. Induta repeatedly accused unnamed politicians of mobilising the support of certain army officials to gain political power. Although the electoral law stipulated the postponement of the election date if any candidate were prevented from standing, the date remained unchanged after the incidents of 5 June and the polls passed off without violence. Voter turnout of 60% (of an electorate of 593,765) was relatively low by Bissau-Guinean standards. Malam Bacai Sanhá (PAIGC), an ally of Prime Minister Gomes jr., won 39.5% of the votes, Kumba Yala (PRS) 28.9% and former head of state Henrique Pereira Rosa 24.1%, while another eight candidates (among them one woman) won only very few votes. In the run-off on 26 July, Bacai Sanhá beat Yala, with 63.3% of the votes. Voter turnout in the second round was 61%. The EU, CPLP, ECOWAS, UEMOA and Portugal, amongst others, expressed their approval. Even before his official investiture on 8 September, Bacai Sanhá paid visits to Angola and Cape Verde. His visit to Portugal in December had to be postponed when he suffered a diabetic crisis, which led to the president's being taken to Dakar for treatment on 3 December, and his subsequent relocation to Paris.

Human rights violations continued. On 27 March it became known that, after criticising the military leadership, Pedro Infanda was arrested, beaten by soldiers and later handed over to the judicial police. Infanda was the lawyer of former naval chief of staff José Américo Bubo Na Tchuto, who had fled the country after being accused of planning to overthrow President Vieira in 2008. On 1 April, the president of auditors and former prime minister Francisco Fadul was beaten and robbed in his home by 15 uniformed and armed assailants. Just before, Fadul had criticised Induta's nomination as chief of staff and the government's de facto subordination to the army. That same day an armed civilian penetrated the offices of the 'Liga Guineense dos Direitos Humanos' (LGDH) in search of its chairman, Luís Vaz Martins. In late August, the attorney-general and head of the governmental fact-finding commission into the March incidents announced publicly that he had received death threats. The LGDH declared on 12 August that the human rights situation was going from bad to worse. On 15 August soldiers attempted to detain Francisco Conduto de Pina, an MP who the previous day had been exonerated by the public prosecutor of charges related to the alleged coup attempt of 5 June. The international community condemned Guinea-Bissau's climate of impunity.

On 28 January, the public prosecutor's office announced that the case concerning two airplanes grounded since 2008 for alleged **drug-trafficking** had been shelved for lack of evidence, but the case was reopened following protests. In response, the army filed a libel suit against the judicial authorities on 30 January, asserting that one plane had only carried pharmaceuticals, not illegal drugs, as claimed by the prosecutor's office. At year's end, the prime minister announced that the remaining plane had been confiscated. On 6 May, Justice Minister Mamadu Djaló Pires announced that, since traffickers increasingly used waterways to transport their drugs, the UN Office on Drugs and Crime (UNODC) would try to arrange the purchase of at least one speedboat. According to UNODC and other sources, cocaine arrived in Guinea-Bissau from Brazil and Colombia mainly by sea. On 23 June, US sources stated that Colombian guerrillas were also involved in drug-trafficking in Guinea-Bissau. On 20 October, the government signed a cooperation agreement with Venezuela on the issue. Former naval chief of staff Na Tchuto, who had been exiled in Gambia, clandestinely returned to Bissau on 28 December. After his discovery, the supposed drug-trafficker fled to the local UN headquarters.

The first **census** since 1991 was conducted from 1 to 15 March, supported by the international community.

Guinea-Bissau's first head of state (1973–80), **Luís Almeida Cabral**, died in exile in Portugal on 30 May.

Foreign Affairs

Against the background of the **violent incidents,** the ECOWAS chiefs of defence staff met in Praia, Cape Verde, for a regular meeting on 4 March, receiving a report by the Special Committee on Guinea-Bissau that had been set up in December 2008. AU President Kadhafi paid a brief visit to Bissau on 12 March, announcing an **inquiry** into the incidents by the AU and CEN-SAD. On 6 April, a press report disclosed that an Angolan diplomat, João Bernardo de Miranda, had been appointed special envoy for Guinea-Bissau by the AU. On 4 June, Attorney-General Luís Manuel Cabral said that Guinea-Bissau had officially requested the UN to set up an international commission to investigate the March assassinations. The UN mandated the AU and ECOWAS to carry out this inquiry. On 18 September, the prime minister declared that the government was still waiting for the support promised by ECOWAS, the CPLP and the AU.

On 31 March, the Portuguese foreign minister, Luís Amado, declared that the CPLP was willing, in support of an ECOWAS initiative, to commit troops to Guinea-Bissau if the government so desired. Under a mandate of the UN and the AU, they would serve to restore security and maintain a presence throughout the electoral process. The government denied any need for **foreign troops**, but Maria Luiza Ribeiro Viotti, president of the UN Peacebuilding Commission, nevertheless considered the reinforcement of the UN presence to be essential. After the incidents of 5 June, Portugal and the CPLP repeated the troop offer.

Following these violent incidents, the international community urged the intensification of **security sector reform**. The Roundtable on the Restructuring and Modernisation of the Defence and Security Sector in Guinea-Bissau, co-organised by the government, ECOWAS, CPLP and UNOGBIS (UN Peacebuilding Support Office in Guinea-Bissau) and held in Praia, Cape Verde, on 20 April, discussed further measures for the reform process that had been started in 2006. These included the (re-)construction of prisons, the fight against corruption and drug-trafficking, the creation of training facilities, demobilisation of soldiers and the completion of a legal framework for the security forces by December. However, in October parliament had not yet passed ten reform laws drafted by the EU and only a handful of soldiers had been retired. In November the Council of the EU approved an extension of the EU mission in support of the security sector reform in Guinea-Bissau for six months until 31 May 2010.

On 12 March, **Colombia**'s interior minister, Fabio Valencia Cossio, declared his willingness to assist West African countries in their fight against drug-trafficking. The country's poorly equipped authorities received cars, motorcycles, generators and cameras, financed by Portugal and the EU. The Colombians also promised to pay for the reconstruction of the judicial police building that had been wrecked in 2008. On 26 June, the UN Security Council agreed to extend the mandate of **UNOGBIS** until 31 December. It was to be succeeded by the UN Integrated Peacebuilding Office in Guinea-Bissau (UNIOGBIS) from 1 January 2010.

From July, rumours persisted that insurgents from neighbouring **Guinea** were coming into the country to seek refuge. The prime minister dispelled accusations brought forward by parts of the Guinean leadership while on a visit to Conakry on 7 August. A military source stated on 14 October that **Senegal**'s army, cracking down on Casamance rebels, had violated the border in September, occupying territory and impeding border patrols. The defence minister, Artur Silva, paid a visit to Dakar on 15 October to discuss the issue. On 28 November the authorities arrested 45 boat people, mostly from the **Gambia**.

Lusophone cooperation continued. Guinea-Bissau co-founded the CPLP forum of local authorities in late March. A CPLP entrepreneur confederation was founded in Bissau on 13 December. On 23 November, parliament approved the Portuguese Language

Orthographic Agreement of 1990 creating a reformed, unified orthography for the Portuguese language.

Socioeconomic Developments

In January alone three wooden passenger boats capsized with the loss of at least 80 lives, highlighting Guinea-Bissau's increasingly ailing **infrastructure**. The AfDB that month granted a € 2.3 m loan to support the fishing industry's infrastructure and capacity. Moreover, the bank approved a grant worth € 1.6 m to finance the integrated water resources management in the Kayanga-Geba basin by the Organisation for the Development of the Gambia River, formed by the Gambia, Guinea, Guinea-Bissau and Senegal. On 19 June, an EU-funded bridge over the Rio Cacheu was inaugurated. In February, the capital went without tap water for one week because of a damaged pump. In general, many wells were contaminated, contributing to outbreaks of disease. The World Bank financed repair and development works on the water system. One of the many problems continued to be the collection of subscribers' payment for electricity and water. On 24 September, the World Bank approved a grant worth $ 5 m as part of the rural community-driven development project, aimed at increasing access to basic social and economic infrastructure and services.

Corruption continued to be rampant. Guinea-Bissau ranked 158, compared to 147 the year before, in TI's corruption index. Two top officials of the national service for surveillance and control of fishing activities were arrested in December on charges of embezzlement. While the country's **health** system was almost totally dependent on foreign aid and partnerships, some progress was made in the fight against malaria. The poor state of the **education** system was underlined when the new education minister, Artur Silva, announced on 17 December that 780,000 of the country's inhabitants were illiterate (out of a population of 1.7 million). Portugal invested in bilateral education projects worth about € 5.5 m.

Following the visit by the prime minister to Luanda, Angola opened a credit line worth $ 30 m (27 January). On 30 March, the EU adopted projects within the EU food facility worth € 8.4 m. On 19 June, the IMF approved a third raft of purchases worth $ 2.7 m under the emergency post-conflict assistance programme, designed to promote administrative capacity building. The World Bank approved a grant of $ 8 m for economic governance reform. On 15 July, the AfDB approved $ 12 m for the administrative capacity building project. As in the past, teachers and other civil servants were repeatedly on strike during the year in protest against salary arrears. The government paid delayed salaries in January and August. On 24 October, ECOWAS decided to grant $ 3.5 m to cover soldiers' pay. On 23 December, the EU supported the country's budget to the tune of € 17 m.

China strengthened its presence: the 'Banco da África Ocidental', whose anchor shareholder was the Macauan Geocapital holding, enlarged its capital five-fold to € 8 m. The Bank of China also looked for cooperation partners in Guinea-Bissau. The country boosted trade with the People's Republic in spite of the economic crisis.

As a result of the **global economic crisis**, prices for cashew kernels – the main export product – and migrants' remittances decreased. However, the population benefited from falling prices (about 40%) for imported rice, the country's staple food. The IMF drew a positive picture for 2010, predicting a growth rate of 3.5%.

Christoph Kohl

Liberia

Economic setbacks, including delays to major investments in mining and agriculture, were compounded by violent reactions to anti-corruption efforts. The conclusions of the Truth and Reconciliation Commission (TRC) appeared to threaten stability by sanctioning President Ellen Johnson Sirleaf and key figures associated with the country's violent past. The global financial crisis forced badly-hit Arcelor Mittal to scale back investments in the country. Early in the year, the government declared a state of emergency in response to a plague of crop-destroying army worms. The prospects of implosion of dictatorship-wracked neighbouring Guinea remained a source of anxiety. By year's end, however, the government appeared to be gaining traction, and Sirleaf announced that she would stand for re-election in 2011. Violent crime, in particular gender violence and armed robbery, remained high despite desperate counter-measures and efforts, including the imposition of the death penalty for robbery and the work of the Special Court for trying rape the previous year. UNMIL (United Nations Mission in Liberia) stayed put with some 10,000 troops.

Domestic Politics

The most significant political event was the release of the final **TRC report** in July. After more than two years of work and close to $ 9 m spent, the TRC issued a controversial and badly written report which recommended that 98 people, some of them highly influential and powerful in the post-war establishment, be prosecuted for violations of international humanitarian law and war crimes committed during the civil war. Among them were a powerful senior senator, Prince Yormie Johnson; several other sitting members of the country's legislature; a number of wealthy businessmen and public officials; and a professor at the University of Liberia, Alhaji Kroma, who during the war was a leader of one of the more powerful factions, the United Liberation Movement of Liberia for Democracy. The TRC also recommended that a further 50 people, including President Sirleaf, be barred from public office for 30 years on account of the support they had given to various warring factions. If accepted as provided by law, this would mean that Sirleaf – internationally praised as a model African leader, and the continent's first elected female head of state – would be forced to resign and confined to the political wilderness for the rest of her life.

Reaction to the report was predictably swift and brutal. A group of former warlords, led by Prince Yormie Johnson – the militia leader who tortured to death former President Samuel Doe but now a staunch senior senator – called a press conference in Monrovia and warned, none too subtly, that the report would undermine the country's fragile peace and possibly return it to war. Many of the TRC's Commissioners received **death threats**, and at least two went into hiding. President Sirleaf was initially tight-lipped on the report, and then finally said that her government was carefully studying it for further action. The report remained the key issue of public debate for months, but the **embarrassment** it caused to the international community – which had been enthusiastic in its support for Sirleaf – was such that when US Secretary of State Hillary Clinton visited in August, she carefully avoided any mention of it. Clinton appeared at a press conference with the president and declared that the US unreservedly supported her government. After this, few in Liberia entertained any hope that the report's recommendations would be implemented and by year's end President Sirleaf appeared fully embarked on her re-election campaign. Prince Johnson, too, announced he would contest the 2011 polls.

Corruption remained a major concern throughout the year, as previously. Information Minister Lawrence Bropleh said by year's end that the justice ministry was probing more than 100 corruption-related cases, many of them involving officials in Sirleaf's administration. Many of the investigations, including the presidential enquiry launched the previous year into an email scam indicating the high-level theft of over $ 1 m, were inconclusive by year's end, while most of those implicated still retained their positions. In many cases, an impression of impunity could not be avoided. For example, Winsely Nanka, deputy auditor general on the General Auditing Commission – which claimed among other things that corruption in the government was more widespread than in the graft-ridden previous administration – was physically assaulted in the offices of the deputy minister for public works, Roderick Smith. The deputy auditor general and his team of auditors were evicted from the latter's offices when they called for audit-related information.

Far worse was to come. On 1 November, Keith Jubah, the head of the Public Procurement and Concessions Commission, was **shot dead**, and his body cut to pieces and burned in Kakata, 35 kilometres north of the capital Monrovia. Jubah's commission had cancelled most of the contracts and concessions signed by the National Transitional Government of Liberia (NTGL), which steered Liberia to elections from 14 October 2003 to 16 January 2006, as well as those of the Taylor government before that. Jubah was known to have taken his job rather seriously, making sure that contracts awarded by the government were transparent and economically justifiable, and that they met the standards set by the Governance and Economic Management Assistance Programme, a key instrument steering the country's recovery.

A few months before Jubah's murder, corruption cases against the chairman of the defunct NTGL, Gyude Bryant, and a key figure in the Taylor regime, Edwin Snowe (who was Managing Director of the Liberian Petroleum Refining Company) were thrown out by a Monrovia criminal court. The unanimous not guilty verdict did not appear to have come as a surprise to the former officials. Liberian newspapers reported that Snowe had planned a 'victory celebration' days before the verdict was announced. The government's anti-graft posture remained undaunted. On 22 December, President Sirleaf issued a **whistle-blower act** as Executive Order No. 22. The Act was intended to protect anyone who disclosed information about improprieties and corruption involving a public official or institution. A whistle-blower whose disclosure resulted in the recovery of any amount of money would receive a reward of 5% of the money recovered. By year's end, TI reported that Liberia had made progress in the fight against corruption. It ranked Liberia at 13th out of 47 countries in sub-Saharan Africa, compared with 30th in 2008, an improvement of about 13 places. It noted, however, that "recent scandals affecting government procurement and financial management, and the perception that too many government officials are political appointees, continue to undermine transparency, accountability and public trust in the political leadership."

Security concerns were high, accentuated by a number of high profile killings, including that of a clergyman and senior government official Jubah. Armed robbery and rape remained persistent, and security forces appeared incapable of checking crime. In fact, there was a dismal lack of coordination between the various arms of state security. On three separate occasions – in February, April, and May – members of the 2,000-strong Armed Forces of Liberia attacked personnel of the Liberian National Police (LNP). Also at the beginning of the year, the deputy commissioner of the LNP was facing criminal investigations and the chief of narcotics was indicted for theft and making false statements. Public trust in these institutions was not enhanced as a result. In Monrovia, mob violence was common. On a number of occasions young men burnt down police stations and court houses to get to criminals they believed would escape justice. In rural Liberia, where there is hardly a police presence, vigilante activities were also common, as was the reliance on traditional forms of justice, such as trial by ordeal, in order to combat criminal activity and settle disputes. In trials by ordeal accused persons are made to drink certain herbal concoctions called sassywood and, presumably if guilty, would immediately confess their crimes: on a number of occasions, however, they died as a result of drinking the sassywood. The Emergency Response Unit within the LNP, meant to combat armed robbery and mob violence, grew to 207 officers of its planned strength of 500 officers, but was still logistically constrained and during the year its activities were not very visible.

By year's end the political future of President Sirleaf appeared to be priority number one, with politics as usual – in the name of 'reconciliation' – apparently taking precedence over the president's previous rhetoric of transparency and accountability. On 1 October, Sirleaf appointed Benoni Urey and Christmas Lawrence, associates of Charles Taylor, as mayors of two minor rural towns. Urey, now a wealthy businessman, was still banned by the UN from travel abroad and was also sanctioned by the TRC report. In December, the governing Unity Party's candidate for a major senatorial **by-election**, in Montserrado County (the largest in Liberia, and the county in which Monrovia lies), was soundly defeated by the candidate for the opposition Congress for Democratic Change, headed by ex-football star George Weah (who was earlier defeated by Sirleaf). There were signs of desperation in the presidential camp. Finally, there was little apparent interest in the ongoing trial of former President Charles Taylor in The Hague. Only one newspaper – the 'New Democrat' – consistently and prominently covered the trial on its pages.

Foreign Affairs

A key concern throughout the year was **Guinea**, which was under an unstable junta. Anxieties were high that the country would implode, destabilizing its fragile neighbours, Liberia and Sierra Leone. The AU, ECOWAS and the MRU, which was chaired by President Sirleaf, all suspended Guinea pending a return to constitutional rule. Sirleaf announced Guinea's suspension from the MRU at a press conference in Monrovia on 12 January. By year's end, however, with Captain Dadis Camara, the erratic Guinean junta leader, out of the picture, tensions decreased somewhat.

On 19–20 May, as a mark of its support for the Sirleaf government, a special delegation of the UN **Security Council** to Liberia was led by Susan Rice, Permanent Representative of the US to the UN. The delegation included ten permanent representatives of the Security Council and five Deputy Permanent Representatives or senior officers of the other five member states on the Council. The delegation met with President Sirleaf and discussed, among other things, the "impact of sub-regional factors on the situation in Liberia", and explored ways to strengthen sub-regional cooperation, including measures to counter the threat of illegal drug trafficking. After the meeting, the UN extended the mandate of **UNMIL**, and proposed to beef up its police component and to include more female officers. With a budget of $ 561 m, the UN mission maintained a total of 10,427 uniformed personnel, including 8,982 troops, 127 military observers, 1,318 police, 448 international civilian personnel, 998 local staff and 205 UN Volunteers. UNMIL, noting "with concern the threats to sub-regional stability, including to Liberia, in particular posed by drug trafficking, organized crime, and illicit arms", pledged to remain "seized of the situation" in Liberia, and to review the mission in August 2010.

On 7–8 March, to coincide with International Women's Day, Liberia hosted nearly 1,000 women leaders from across the world. The **colloquium**, co-chaired by Sirleaf and President Tarja Halonen of Finland, discussed women's empowerment and leadership roles, and provided a forum for discussing global issues such as climate change. There was also an exhibition of wearable arts and Liberian women's entrepreneurship. The colloquium also sought to realise the aims of Security Council Resolution 1325 on women, peace and security, aimed to ensure that women are protected from the worst abuses in times of conflict and "to empower them to play their rightful and vital role in helping their countries prevent, end and recover from conflict".

But by far the most heralded visit for the government was that of Hillary Clinton, the American Secretary of State, on 12 August. The **US** continued to be Liberia's most important bilateral partner, exerting enormous influence in the country's popular imagination. During her visit, Clinton appeared at a press conference with President Sirleaf, where she announced that her government was very pleased with the "great achievements" of the Liberian leader. "President Sirleaf has been a very effective leader of the new Liberia," she said. "The US officially supports what this government is doing. We think that Liberia is on the right path, as difficult as that path may be." The unambiguous endorsement effectively killed the TRC's recommendation that the president be barred from holding public office for 30 years.

China, another important bilateral partner, announced the completion of a barracks for the Liberian army at Gbarnga, in the hinterland of the country. It was also building campuses for the degraded University of Liberia, the country's premier university.

Socioeconomic Developments

Gains made in 2008 in the form of investments and job creation were significantly reversed as a result of the **global financial crisis**. By year's end, the central bank reported to the IMF that: "The global financial crisis has impacted Liberia severely through job losses in the export sector, an investment slowdown and a weakening of the exchange rate. Nonetheless our monetary and fiscal policies remain broadly on track and we have made significant progress in implementing our economic reform program."

The key issue was the decision by Arcelor Mittal, which before the financial crisis had planned to increase its **iron ore production** to two-thirds of its steel output by investing $ 1.5 bn over 25 years in Liberia's huge iron ore reserves, to scale back its investment in the country. The company signed a deal with the government in 2007 to mine the iron ore around Yekepa and then transport it by rail to the port city of Buchanan, from where it would be exported to Arcelor Mittal steel mills around the world. It was one of the best deals that Liberia had ever brokered for its rich mineral reserves, and the government was helped by legal advice arranged by American billionaire George Soros, a friend of Sirleaf's. Under the deal, the Liberian government owns 30% of the mining company and would receive 4.5% in royalty fees. Arcelor Mittal also promised to spend $ 3 m annually for community development projects in the three counties where it operates, and had since been reconstructing hospitals, clinics and schools. By the beginning of 2009, some 2,800 people were working on the derelict railway, and the company had announced it would create a total of 3,500 direct and 20,000 indirect jobs as a result of its investment. A few months later, however, Arcelor Mittal announced that it needed to make "temporary adjustments to protect [its] long-term goals". It was cutting its steel production by nearly 50%. About 1,600 jobs were immediately terminated. Worse yet, the government was left scrambling to adjust its budget projections for 2009/10, which it had pegged at $ 347 m. It had hoped to raise $ 67 m of this in taxes mainly from Arcelor Mittal.

Early in the year, the government declared a state of emergency in response to a plague of crop-destroying **army worms**. Liberia's agriculture ministry reported that some 400,000 residents in 80 villages had been affected, a statistic the FAO Resident Country Representative confirmed. This did not dampen foreign investor interest in the sector, however. The government in mid-year said that it had signed an $ 800 m agreement with Malaysian conglomerate Sime Darby Berhad to restore and expand the country's third-largest **rubber** plantation, as well as to invest in the **palm oil** industry. By year's end, however, little activity was reported in this regard.

Another promised investment was that made by the billionaire and former prime minister of Thailand, Thaksin Shinawatra, who visited the country on 21 April and said that he would like to share Thailand's success in agriculture and poverty eradication with Liberia. He expressed interest in oil and mineral exploration and extraction, agriculture, telecommunication licences and the lottery business. Not much activity was reported on this after the visit, however.

The 2009/10 **budget** was criticised in many quarters for its apparent lack of pro-poor focus. It allocated about $ 9 m for the purchase of cars for government officials. Wages/personnel costs made up 31% of total proposed expenditure, though the government had downsized its work force from 54,826 employees (2008–09 fiscal year), to 53,097 employees for the proposed 2009–2010 budget year. But important areas such as the Family Assistance Programme, under the Ministry of Health, were allocated only $ 10,000 and the Center for Vulnerable Children only $ 15,000. The critical Youth Rehabilitation Centre gained only $ 9,000, while the Chief Justice got $ 10,000 for domestic travel alone.

By year's end, formal sector employment remained at 15%. Few people had access to mains electricity or running water, and over 70% of the country's population was reckoned to live below the **poverty** line, earning less than a dollar a day.

Lansana Gberie

Mali

Several abductions of Westerners and increased drugs and arms trafficking indicated the deterioration of security in the northern regions. Another major issue that preoccupied many Malians citizens concerned a legislative proposal by the government to improve women's and children's rights. Mobilised by religious leaders who claimed some of the articles contradicted Islamic traditions, tens of thousands of people demonstrated against the legal proposals, forcing President Touré to withdraw the bill. The government continued to considerably scale up its investments in the agricultural sector with support from international donors, with the object of reducing vulnerability to potential food crises in a sustainable manner. Alongside the continued importance of relations with Western donors, Mali strengthened its diplomatic ties with a number of (relatively) new partner countries, such as India, Venezuela, Qatar and China.

Domestic Politics

Polarised debate remained exceptional due to the country's consensual political system, in which all major parties rally around the president. However, the third **local elections**, organised on 26 April in Mali's 703 municipalities, provided an important arena for political competition. The majority movement in Mali, which had rallied behind President

Touré in 2007, consolidated its position and won the vast majority of municipal council seats. The two major parties, the 'Alliance pour la Démocratie au Mali' and the 'Union pour la République et la Démocratie', secured almost half of the 11,000 available seats between them. The main opposition party, the 'Rassemblement pour le Mali', lost more than 5% of its votes as compared with the 2004 elections, which mostly benefited the 'Convergence pour le Développement du Mali', a party whose star had recently begun to rise. The fragmentation of the party system was further increased by the localised support bases of most of them. The available seats were divided amongst 38 different political groupings. Independent candidates secured around 10% of the seats, thereby reflecting their presence in the National Assembly. With a turnout of over 43%, political participation was still modest, but relatively high in comparison with national elections.

An issue that generated fierce debate throughout the year concerned a government move to regulate family and women's rights, popularly referred to as the **family code**. Although appearing on the political agenda for over ten years, the bill was only formally adopted by cabinet on 13 May. The bill aimed to: set a minimum age of 18 for marriage to protect the majority of young girls, who still marry before that age; improve women's rights in general and inheritance rights in particular; increase the rights of the many children born out of wedlock; and formally recognise civil marriage. The bill was presented to parliament during its first session of the year and finally adopted by a clear majority on 3 August, amidst persisting popular discontent. Women's associations congratulated MPs for having adopted the bill, but other organisations, notably religious ones, expressed anger. The 'Haut Conseil Islamique du Mali' attacked the government and parliamentarians for having surrendered to donor pressure and dishonoured Mali's cultural and religious values. They began to organise demonstrations and, on 22 August, around 50,000 people gathered in the national football stadium. In mosques all over the country, imams continuously attacked members of parliament and cassette recordings were sold containing arguments against the proposed changes. A day after the massive protests, President Touré underlined the importance of continued dialogue with the Islamic community and, on 26 August, he announced that he would not sign the bill but send it back to the Assembly for a second reading. The issue had become too polarised. In an interview, Touré stressed that a new version of the code would require the approval of the religious associations. When the code was tabled during the Assembly's second session of the year, starting in October, MPs considered it an issue too sensitive to handle. They did not address it further and postponed it until the next parliamentary session, which would start in 2010. In September, an EU delegation issued a press statement reassuring Malians that no link existed between its financial support and the failure to pass the bill.

A second major issue dominating the political agenda concerned the **northern rebellion**. Following years of negotiations, the army attacked what still remained of the Tuareg rebel groups in January. On 22 January, the government wiped out their main bases near

Tinsalak and a peace settlement was subsequently agreed between the state and the rebels in early February. During the year, however, the main threat came from the Maghreb branch of al-Qaida. Following the abduction of two Canadian diplomats on 14 December 2008 in Niger, a Briton, a Swiss and two Germans were kidnapped on Malian territory on 22 January. The **kidnappings** were strategically timed and executed on behalf of al-Qaida in the Islamic Maghreb (AQIM) on the eve of the long-planned regional conference on security and peace in the Sahel, which was subsequently cancelled. On 22 April, the government, with strong support from the Burkinabè president, was able to negotiate the release of the two Canadians, one of whom was the special UN envoy to Niger, as well as one German and the Swiss hostage. On 31 May, however, news was released that the British hostage had been killed. Ten days later, the last Western detainee, a German, was released. On 17 June, the army attacked one of the AQIM groups, killing 26 men and, on 22 June, Touré also tabled the issue during an ECOWAS heads of state summit and once again underlined the need for strong regional cooperation in this area. On 25 November, a French citizen living in Menaka (Gao region) paid a high price for ignoring his embassy's instructions to leave the area due to increased insecurity, when he became the next victim of an abduction. Most Westerners and NGOs left the area during this period. Western governments, like the larger travel agencies, informed their citizens of increased insecurity in the northern regions. This negatively impacted on tourism and overall development.

In the vast northern zone, the **smuggling** of drugs, weapons and other contraband also appeared to increase significantly. On 2 November, the remains of a burned-out Boeing 727 were found some 200 km north of Gao, next to an illegal desert airstrip. Almost two weeks later, a UN representative stated that the plane had been carrying vast amounts of cocaine on a flight from Venezuela to Mali and that it had crashed after trying to take off again. Investigators later concluded that the plane had been set on fire in order destroy evidence. This deserted area seems to have become an important hub in international drugs trafficking. Several members of parliament from the northern regions warned of the role played by drugs money in domestic politics.

During the year, the last preparatory phase of Mali's **constitutional reform process** was completed. A small committee led by former minister M. Daba Diawarra was mandated by Touré to draft a constitutional review bill, as well as legal reform texts on specific issues, to strengthen the country's democratic system. The committee finalised its work at year's end and was expected to officially present its report to the president in January 2010. With a view to establishing a reliable **civic register**, an extensive national registration process was launched in March. Each citizen was to be given a national identification number. The final results were expected to provide accurate demographic information that would also allow for the creation of a consistent electoral register enjoying the confidence of political stakeholders.

Foreign Affairs

The official state visit by the **Chinese president** on 11–12 February underscored the intensification of diplomatic ties between the two countries. During the China-Africa Summit in 2006, Touré had presented seven specific development projects to his counterpart. During this state visit, the heads of state lay the foundation stone of the third bridge over the river Niger in Bamako. Additional agreements were signed in the areas of infrastructure, agriculture and scholarships. At year's end, a supplementary agreement was signed for the construction of a new hospital in the capital. On 29 July, the cabinet decided to open an embassy in **India** and Indian diplomatic representation in Mali followed soon after.

Relations with the **EU** also continued to be of importance. On 18 March, Mali and the EU signed an agreement under the Third Economic Development Fund, focusing on improved infrastructure in the northern regions and a cultural development programme worth CFAfr 213 bn, amongst other things.

The importance of mutual cooperation between **Latin America** and Africa increased gradually. At the end of September, Touré attended the second Africa-South America Summit in Venezuela, where reforms of the UN Security Council, food security and the establishment of a Southern development bank were discussed. Mali benefited from the opportunity to sign a bilateral cooperation agreement with Venezuela. On 22 October, a delegation led by the Brazilian minister of foreign affairs visited Mali in order to strengthen mutual cooperation and trade.

One of the more important **bilateral exchanges** involved the state visit of President Touré to Qatar on 22–23 November. Its objective was to strengthen cooperation in mining, oil exploration, tourism and trade. An agreement with the French government on the position of illegal Malian migrants in France remained pending. Despite the visit of the French minister for immigration on 28 March, the countries still disagreed on the approach to be taken towards migratory flows. Mali greatly benefits from remittances and naturally prefers the legalisation of their compatriots' presence in Paris to their repatriation.

Mali participated in the **peer review** work of the APRM framework, and a report generally lauded the country's performance as positive.

Socioeconomic Developments

Real GDP **growth** slowed down but still reached 4.3%. Mali's balance of trade profited from rising gold prices on the world market and reduced fuel and food prices, which compensated for decreased direct foreign investment. However, the limited extent of remaining reserves in some of the principal mines was beginning to become a serious challenge for the sustainability of export revenues, of which almost two-thirds depend on gold. While inflation figures rose above 10% in 2008, they dropped to 2% by the end of 2009. The country's fiscal deficit remained under the 1.5% GDP threshold. Mali slightly improved its ranking in the 'doing business' index developed by the World Bank. The 2010 GDP growth rate was expected to reach 4.8% and the budget deficit predicted to further decrease, thanks to increased fiscal revenues.

The **agricultural season** profited from good rains and total food production reached approximately 6 m tonnes. Cereal harvests exceeded the 4.6 m tonnes objective by 0.4 m tonnes and had never witnessed such an annual increase. It is Touré's ambition to achieve 10 m tonnes production in 2012. In addition, the ambitions for improved rice production (a 1.6 m tonnes target) were almost entirely realised. Producers were assisted under the 'Initiative Riz' programme launched by the prime minister. Fertiliser subsidies were made available, as well as soft loans for agricultural equipment, technical assistance and training. Based on this success, the government indicated its objective of enlarging the support programme to other crops, such as corn, grain and cotton, in 2010. The initiative was supported by a wide variety of donors (notably Western countries, China and Libya) and, on 9 April, Touré appointed a deputy minister in the office of the prime minister to coordinate the international support provided for the development of the 'Office du Niger', Mali's main irrigation scheme in the interior Delta of the Niger River. Despite increased output, however, agricultural prices only decreased for a very short period of time. This was particularly caused by the fact that many producers did not sell much of their harvest on the regional market but stored part of it and sold larger shares to international traders, who exported it to other countries in the sub-region where prices were higher. The lack of impact of improved agricultural production on food prices is probably a good explanation of why 78% of Malians still rated the government's performance in providing food security as bad or very bad in an Afrobarometer poll in December.

Mali's **cotton production** also faced numerous challenges. The countries that are members of the CFAfr zone used to be responsible for 5% of global cotton production, but this was more than halved in the 2008/2009 season. In Mali, cotton production decreased for three consecutive years and the 2009/2010 output was expected to be 7% lower than production in the 2008/2009 season. The privatisation of various parts of the parastatal cotton company, the 'Compagnie Malienne du Développement des Textiles', which produces substantial losses, was expected in 2010. On a positive note, efforts to diversify the agricultural sector were slowly generating results, as mango exports, for example, increased from 4,000 tonnes in 2007 to 10,000 tonnes in 2009.

Other parastatals were already privatised in the course of this year. Maroc **Telecom** bought 51% of the national telephone company, 'Societé des Télécommunications du Mali', which generated an additional CFAfr 180 bn in revenue. Touré allocated these funds to various sectors without consulting parliament, which generated a lot of protest, notably from opposition MPs. On 6 November, the president therefore organised a formal meeting, together with the speaker of the National Assembly, the budget minister and other cabinet representatives, in order to clarify how he intended to use the additional resources. However, the calculations presented by the budget minister during the meeting added to the confusion as they did not seem to add up correctly. The opposition subsequently demanded that the additional funds be included in the 2010 budget and the revised 2009 budget. Although the budget minister stated that these special funds could be spent outside the official budget, they were later partly included in a revised 2009 budget and in the 2010 budget.

The national **oilseed** crushing factory, 'Huilerie Cotonniere du Mali', got into serious difficulties following its privatisation. Mainly because of a 65% fall in cotton production over the preceding three years and also as a result of increased domestic competition, production almost came to a standstill. More than half the workers became unemployed in each of the three production sites in Koulikouro, Kita and Koutiala. On 10 November, these workers began a sit-in protest near the trade unions centre, which lasted until the end of the year. On 15 December, the opposition asked a number of critical questions, addressing the lack of professional management and the need to come up with a redundancy plan.

Progress in **infrastructure** development continued to be significant. Numerous road construction and improvement schemes were undertaken in order to expand access for various cities and villages to regional markets. The renovation of the national airport, under the US Millennium Challenge Cooperation, was embarked upon, as well as the construction of the third bridge over the Niger River in Bamako, funded by the Chinese.

In 2009, as a result of much quantitative progress in school enrolment in the preceding decades, 90% of Malian boys and 70% of girls were attending school. Under the 'Programme Décennal de Développement de l'Éducation' the government and donors aimed to increase the enrolment rate to 95% by 2010 (from 21% in 1990!). However, a report presented by OXFAM in July pointed to various problems, such as the poor quality of **education**, high drop-out rates and large classes (over 60 children on average). Mali still had a very high illiteracy rate (ranked 176th out of 177 countries with adult literacy at 24%).

On 20 April, the ministry of health and no less than 35 international partners signed a joint agreement increasing efforts to bring realisation of the **health**-related MDGs closer. It was decided to extend the 10-year health policy cooperation framework, which should have ended in 2009, to 2011. The operational plan for 2009 covered approximately CFAfr 121 bn, whereas it had been calculated that CFAfr 182 bn would be necessary annually in order to achieve the health care-related MDGs. With one in five children still dying before the age of five, combating malaria, malnutrition and tuberculosis are important priorities identified in the agreement, as well as scaling down the levels of maternal mortality. Vaccination figures for tuberculosis had gone up considerably in previous years, but malaria was still reported to be responsible for more than half of child deaths. Mali therefore submitted another five-year malaria application to the Global Fund to Fight AIDS, Malaria and Tuberculosis.

Malian **tourism** was affected by the world economic downturn, but also, more specifically, by the hostage drama in the northern region. Various international tour operators registered the country on the 'red list' of risky destinations. Some Western governments counselled nationals not to travel to areas north of the Niger River. Most Western NGO staff left the cities of Gao, Kidal, Menaka and Tombouctou in November. The Malian government and members of parliament for the relevant regions tried to play down the risks (and safeguard tourist incomes) by travelling to the region with Western journalists. They claimed that many areas in Western cities were much more dangerous. Despite these difficulties, tourist facilities continued to improve. At the year end, the number of hotels had increased to 500 – a doubling in only a few years.

At the start of the year, on 24 January, an important **cultural event** took place when Touré, together with South African Vice President Montlanthe and former President Mbeki, inaugurated the renovated Centre Ahmed Baba in Tombouctou. The centre protects and safeguards a great number of ancient manuscripts. In **sport**, there were two particularly outstanding successes. On 5 December, the football club 'Stade Malien de Bamako' became the first ever Malian team to win a continental competition, the African Confederation Cup, and there followed a long night of festivities. Mali's female youth basketball team (under 16) had won the Africa Cup in September.

Martin van Vliet

Mauritania

Following the presidential elections in July, the country returned to constitutional rule. Although the election results were contested by the majority of the opposition candidates, foreign governments quickly acknowledged the elected president, Mohamed Ould Abdel Aziz, as the winner. He could rely on a comfortable majority in the National Assembly, where a new party under the banner of 'Union pour la République' had 83 out of 151 members. The return to constitutional rule led to improved relations with most Western powers, which had either frozen or threatened to freeze aid in response to the military coup of the previous year. Spain and France considered Mauritania as a key partner in their strategies to reduce illegal immigration and combat terrorist activities. The Bush administration in the US had been particularly critical about the military junta but accepted the outcome of the elections and resumed anti-terrorism co-operation immediately, as did NATO. Relations with China, now Mauritania's largest trading partner, became closer. Mining, fisheries and oil continued to dominate the industrial sector. The rural sector, vulnerable to climatic conditions, especially drought, was estimated to employ 40% of the labour force. The global economic crisis and the resulting drop in world market prices affected the economy. As a consequence of the political stalemate, the business climate deteriorated and the country was ranked 166 out of 183 countries on the World Bank's Doing Business report. The potential threat posed by the regional terrorist group, al-Qaida in the Islamic Maghreb (AQIM), continued to increase. Proceeds from tourism remained depressed as a consequence of this, as well as of the economic crisis in Europe.

Domestic Politics

From 27 December 2008 to 6 January 2009, the special **consultation on democracy** or 'États généraux de la démocratie' took place. Its recommendations included advice to hold the presidential election in late May (subsequently postponed to early June and then 18 July) and to allow members of the armed forces to put up their candidatures, provided that they first resigned from their military posts. The largest political party, 'Rassemblement des Forces Démocratiques' (RFD), and the 'Front National pour la Défense de la Démocratie en Mauritanie' (FNDD – a coalition formed to support ousted president Sidi Mohamed Ould Cheikh Abdallahi) opposed the candidature of former military personnel.

Ahead of a meeting in Paris on 21 February with European and African leaders, the military rulers lifted a ban on **demonstrations**. On 20 February, thousands of Mauritanians participated in the biggest pro-democracy rally since the coup in August 2008. On 23 April, the FNDD and RFD announced they would boycott the elections and mobilise supporters to protest in Nouakchott. On 24 April, three cars owned by high-level government officials were set alight. Security forces accused an unknown opposition group of being responsible. Protests again took place in May.

On 4 June, Mauritania's political and military leaders signed an agreement in Dakar, Senegal, on creating a **transitional government** before the presidential elections. Senegal's President Abdoulaye Wade, designated by the AU, facilitated the negotiations. He was supported by the International Contact Group on Mauritania, composed of representatives of the AU, Arab League, EU, OIF and UN. As part of the deal, ousted President Abdallahi handed over power to a transitional government on 27 June and formally stepped down. The 2008 coup leader and now president, Mohamed Ould Abdel Aziz, appointed the transitional prime minister, Moulaye Ould Mohamed Laghdaf, and 14 other ministers. The remaining 15 ministers – including of the interior, finance and information – were put up by the FNDD and RFD.

President Aziz also announced his own presidential candidacy. The other main **presidential candidates** were Jemil Ould Mansour, leader of the moderate Islamist party 'Rassemblement National pour le Renouveau et le Développement', Messaoud Ould Boulkheir, standing as joint candidate of the FNDD, the 'Alliance Populaire Progressiste' and 'Union des Forces du Progrès', Ahmed Ould Daddah, representing the RFD, who came second in the 2007 presidential election and, finally, Colonel Ely Ould Mohamed Vall, the retired military leader who had led the 2005 military coup that restored democratic rule to Mauritania. All candidates appeared to have full access to the media.

The **elections** were monitored by a total of 300 observers from various organisations and countries, including the AU, France, Spain, the OIF, Arab Maghreb Union, Arab League and CEN-SAD. Voter turnout was 61%. Aziz was declared the winner with 52% of the votes. Messaoud Ould Boulkheir won 16% and Ahmed Ould Daddah 14%. The results were contested, however, and the chairman of Mauritania's electoral commission, Sid'Ahmed Ould Deye, resigned on 23 July because of doubts over the reliability of the vote. However, on the same day, the results were confirmed by the Constitutional Council. International observers concluded that, despite a certain number of irregularities, the declared results reflected the general will of the people. Laghdaf resigned as prime minister, but President Aziz reappointed him to lead a new, 27-member government on 11 August. The opposition decided not to participate in the government. Naha Mint Hamdi Ould Mouknass was the first woman to be appointed foreign minister. Five other **women** were also appointed as ministers.

A partial election involving 18 of the 56 **senate seats** took place on 8 and 15 November. The ruling 'Union pour la République' won 13 of the contested seats, while allied parties and nominal independents took the rest. The opposition failed to win any of the new seats. Prior to the election, 80% of the senators supported President Aziz, and the poll results further consolidated his control of parliament.

An increased threat was posed by AQIM. A first attack took place on 23 June, when unidentified gunmen killed a US citizen. The second attack was carried out on 8 August when a suicide bomber detonated himself, just outside the French embassy, injuring three embassy staff. This was the first suicide bombing in Mauritania and took place only days after President Aziz was sworn into power. The bomber was a Mauritanian national and evidence was presented that he had been trained in AQIM camps. As a consequence of the **attacks**, the US Peace Corps decided to suspend operations on 12 August since it could not guarantee the security of its volunteers. Attacks increased at the end of the year. On 29 November, three Spanish aid workers were seized by gunmen believed to be linked to al-Qaida. The authorities were unable to catch the kidnappers and the national police chief, Colonel Ahmed Ould Bekrine, was sacked on 2 December. The number of Western **hostages** in Mauritania increased further on 18 December, when two Italian nationals were kidnapped some 20 km from the Malian border.

On 14 December, the government introduced tough **anti-terror legislation** to be voted on in parliament before the end of the session in January 2010. The draft law provided for closer cooperation with other countries concerning extradition, exchange of information and telephone taps without judicial approval. Opposition groups were concerned that the new efforts to combat terrorism could set back the country's human rights record.

On 4 November, the UN special rapporteur on **slavery**, Gulnara Shahinian, released a report showing that in some parts of the country slavery continued, 28 years after the practice had been abolished. The 2007 law criminalised slavery, but mechanisms to help former slaves had so far been lacking.

The repatriation of Mauritanian **refugees** from Senegal, started in 2008, continued during the year. On 27 October, the UNHRC announced that a total of 14,955 refugees had returned since the operation began, following the tripartite agreement signed by Senegal, Mauritania and the UNHCR in November 2007. Altogether, 24,000 people fled to Senegal and 6,000 to Mali as a result of instability and ethnic clashes in Mauritania in the late 1980s and early 1990s.

Foreign Affairs

As a consequence of the military coup, relations with the AU and Western powers were deteriorating seriously. The US blocked $ 15 m in military cooperation, more than $ 4 m in peacekeeping training and $ 3 m in development assistance. On 5 February, the AU barred delegates from Mauritania from attending its summit. Targeted **sanctions** were imposed, including a travel ban and a check on bank accounts. A few weeks after his election as AU chair, the Libyan leader Kadhafi decided to try to mediate. He visited Mauritania on 9 March. Kadhafi's legitimacy as a mediator was dismissed by the FNDD and the RFD after he publicly stated that all political parties should accept that ousted President Abdallahi would not return to power. There were indications of a split between Kadhafi and the AU, when the continental body announced on 24 March that it would maintain sanctions on Mauritania, despite Kadhafi's suggestion that they should be lifted. Nevertheless, on 1 July, the AU finally decided to end the sanctions, following the appointment of the transitional government on 27 June and the scheduling of the presidential elections to take place on 18 July. The country resumed its full AU membership.

Mauritania has been one of only three Arab countries to have had full ties with **Israel**, but diplomatic relations were severed in response to the Israeli offensive in Gaza. Massive protests took place in Nouakchott on 4 January, where at least ten civilians and several policemen were injured. Mauritania's ambassador in Tel Aviv was ordered to return "for consultations" and on 6 March staff left the Israeli embassy in Nouakchott. The majority of Arab countries welcomed the move by Mauritania, which expected greater financial and diplomatic support as a result.

After the military coup in 2008, the **EU** continued its financial commitments worth $ 128 m, notably for a fisheries agreement. But it suspended its cooperation programme for 2008–2013, worth $ 223 m. On 8 August, an EU evaluation team announced that constitutional rule had been restored. This step was necessary under article 96 of the Cotonou accords, which regulate EU cooperation with developing countries, and made it possible for the EU Council to take a decision on renewed cooperation. The Union had not sent any observers to the presidential elections but took account of the view of other international observers. On 21 December, the EU and Mauritania agreed to completely restore cooperation, freeing $ 223 m in aid. On 29 September, **NATO** and Mauritania also resumed full cooperation within NATO's Mediterranean Dialogue security forum, aimed at improving regional security by linking the group's 28 members with the non-NATO countries – Algeria, Egypt, Israel, Jordan, Morocco, Tunisia, and Mauritania.

Following the presidential elections, bilateral ties with **France** were normalised and, on 13 October, French chief of staff Jean-Louis Georgelin met President Aziz to discuss co-operation in the fight against terrorism and drug trafficking. On 27 October, Aziz met President Sarkozy in France to discuss security matters and sign an agreement on technical assistance for the Mauritanian army. In order to tackle the growing regional security threat, the army chiefs of staff of **neighbouring countries** – Algeria, Mali and Niger together with Mauritania – held several meetings in mid-August and agreed to mobilise 25,000 troops and increase co-operation in their common border areas.

Despite enhanced relations with Western powers, President Aziz was keen to improve ties with those countries that had supported him after the military coup, particularly Qatar and Libya. The visit on 21–23 December of **Sudan**'s President Omar al-Bashir together with his foreign minister, Tidjani Saleh Fadil, resulted in an agreement on wide-ranging co-operation, despite the fact that Bashir was wanted under an international arrest warrant. As Mauritania was not a signatory to the ICC treaty, it was under no obligation to execute the warrant. Bashir's visit was the first by a foreign leader since Aziz was sworn back into office.

Socioeconomic Developments

China strengthened its position as principal trading partner. A greater share of iron ore was sold to Chinese companies. On 12 January, Mauritania and China signed an agreement on investments of $ 282 m to expand the port of Nouakchott. The deal came after Western and African governments threatened sanctions against Mauritania following the military coup. The previous government had been reluctant to reach major financial agreements with China in view of the latter's demand for substantial mineral and oil production in exchange. On 12 June, China Minmetals, a joint venture with Mauritania's majority state-owned 'Société Nationale Industrielle et Minière' and the world's seventh-largest steel producer, announced it was looking for acquisition targets in Mauritania.

After the return to constitutional rule, contacts with **Western business partners** were intensified. On 8 October, French oil company Total announced it would begin drilling new sites in the Taoudeni Basin. On 4 December, the 'Société Nationale Industrielle et Minière' announced that it had secured financing totalling $ 710 m to expand the mine at Guelbs and build a new port for mineral exports at Nouadhibou. Multilateral institutions contributing to this were the AfDB, the Islamic Development Bank, the EIB and the AFD. Several commercial banks also participated: BHF-BANK and KfW IPEX-Bank of Germany, as well as two French banks, BNP Paribas and Société Générale.

The Western freeze on aid, with the exception of humanitarian assistance, affected implementation of the public investment programmes prepared by the previous government. The implementation of the three-year PRGF agreed with the IMF in December 2006 was suspended in early October 2008 and expired on 17 December 2009. **Donor assistance** restarted following the return to constitutional rule. An IMF mission headed by Boileau Loko visited Nouakchott on 2–17 December to carry out the 2009 Article IV consultations and discuss a new three-year arrangement supported by the PRGF. In particular, the Fund sought to promote the independence of the central bank.

Real GDP **growth** was estimated at 1.5% compared with 3.5% in 2008, reflecting the international crisis and decline in iron ore prices. A slowdown in oil production caused a decline in revenues and a relatively high budget deficit. Falling international food prices and prudent monetary policy allowed **inflation** to decrease from 7.3% in 2008 to 2% in 2009.

Mauritania ranked at 130 of 180 countries on TI's 2009 corruption perception index. The government initiated an offensive against **corruption**, welcomed by foreign donors and investors. However, the opposition parties claimed their supporters were disproportionately targeted. Several senior public officials, both present and former, were dismissed from their posts or imprisoned. On 19 November, budget director Zeine Ould Ahmed El Hadi was sacked. Sid'El Moctar Ould Nagi, former central bank governor and government minister, was detained, allegedly having embezzled funds to a total of $ 56 m.

On 3 March, a government commission acknowledged that 6,000 tonnes of donated food had gone unconsumed due to possible corruption. The country imports more than half of its **food stock** and was estimated to be facing a shortage of more than 60,000 tonnes over the year. The general **poverty** level remained high with more than 46% of the population estimated to be under the poverty datum line.

Mauritania was on track to reach education-related **MDG targets** for gender equality and primary school enrollment. In the health sector, some improvements were recorded in the areas of maternal health, particularly the level of maternal mortality, with the ratio reduced from 747 to 686 deaths per 100,000 live births.

Claes Olsson & Helena Olsson

Niger

Concerns that President Tandja might extend his mandate by tampering with the constitution finally materialised. He dissolved the National Assembly and Constitutional Court, which had declared illegal a referendum on a three-year extension of his mandate. The plebiscite on the constitutional revision, boycotted by the opposition, was pushed through, as were parliamentary elections. Tandja's measures amounted to a constitutional coup d'état and split the political class, isolated Niger internationally and brought to an end a decade of stability under a multi-party dispensation. At year's end, rumours surfaced about tensions in the armed forces, amidst efforts to tighten surveillance and appease the officer class with gifts. The Tuareg rebellion went into a downturn as a truce was announced in May, but this could not be consolidated. Kidnappings of Western nationals pointed to rising insecurity in the Saharan zone.

New calculations of growth in 2008 reported a record rate of 9.5%, thanks to a boost in agricultural output – much higher than previously calculated. The growth rate for 2009 was expected to decline significantly, in part as a result of the global economic downturn. The UNDP again put Niger at the bottom of its Human Development Index. Aid flows came into doubt as a result of Tandja's refusal to step down, although economic links with France and China remained solid.

Domestic Politics

Tandja's supporters in the ruling 'Mouvement National pour la Société du Développement' (MNSD) continued campaigning for a **third term** under the slogan 'Tazarce' (Hausa for 'continuity'). A memorandum was published calling on parliament to extend Tandja's second term by another three years. His supporters had initially aimed at a change in the constitution to allow for a full third term. They argued that the president needed time to resolve the Tuareg rebellion and to complete infrastructural projects. The new strategy would allow a continuation of his second term, while MPs would be given a similar **extension**. Initially, other parties declined to respond to the challenge of Tandja's kingmakers. These included the MNSD's coalition partner, the 'Convention Démocratique et Sociale' (CDS) of National Assembly chairman Mahaman Ousmane, and the opposition 'Parti Nigérien pour la Démocratie et le Socialisme' (PNDS) of Mahamadou Issoufou. In this vacuum, civil society organisations decided to take the lead, following on the establishment towards the end of 2008 of a coalition of 26 civic groups, parties and union federations called the 'Front Uni pour la Sauvegarde des Acquis Démocratiques' (FUSAD). Led by human rights campaigner Marou Amadou, it pledged to continue with its action.

One of the first moves by Tandja's supporters was to oust Hama Amadou from the MNSD chairmanship (21 February). Amadou, Tandja's rival presidential contender, was dismissed as prime minister in 2007 and imprisoned in 2008 on charges of embezzlement. Prime Minister Seyni Oumarou succeeded as MNSD chair, supported by new general secretary Albadé Abouba, the interior minister. On 27 March, during a visit to Niamey by French President Sarkozy, Tandja spoke against a change in the constitution. Despite this, on 5 May, two days after Tandja's meeting in Agadez with Tuareg rebels (the first since the conflict) and one day after his launch of the construction of the Imouraren uranium mine in the presence of France's development minister and the director of Areva (France's nuclear power company), the president called for a **constitutional referendum**. Behind this decision lay the fact that the current constitution exempted the article limiting presidential terms from revision by parliamentary vote or referendum. On 2 June, Tandja appointed a drafting committee, which proposed a presidential form of government instead of the existing semi-presidential one: the president would be the sole holder of executive power, appointing the cabinet and prime minister, formerly appointed by the Assembly. Tandja himself would have a transitional three-year term without an election, after which he would be allowed to renew his candidature in presidential polls indefinitely.

On 9 May, the 'Alliance Nigérienne pour la Démocratie et le Progrès' withdrew its support for Tandja, followed later by Mahaman Ousmane's CDS. Eight ministers resigned in the process. Mahamadou Issoufou's PNDS had already reacted early May, with a **demonstration** in Niamey that drew between 20,000 and 30,000 people. On

25 May, Tandja received a serious blow when the Constitutional Court ruled that a referendum about a third term was illegal. The following day, a furious Tandja dissolved the Assembly. On 29 May, the president broadcast to the nation that he would not be bound by the opinions of the Court or the Assembly but, on 12 June, the Court, undaunted, annulled as illegal a decree of 5 June calling the referendum. This reminded Tandja that any constitutional revision required the approval of fourth-fifths of the Assembly. A few days later, some 40,000 people demonstrated in the capital against the presidential plans and, on 24 June, Tandja submitted a request to the Constitutional Court to reconsider its position. However, when the president assumed **emergency powers** on 26 June, the Court again rejected his request, pointing out the necessity of parliamentary approval for a referendum, and bringing the number of negative rulings to three. At the end of the month, Tandja dissolved the Court and one week later appointed a new one.

If the titanic clash between the republic's institutions showed that the rule of law could not be done away with at a whim, the outcome amounted to a **constitutional coup d'état**. Tandja's behaviour showed that democratic values had not penetrated the political culture, especially among politicians who traced their origins to careers in the military. From 23 June, the army began to patrol the streets of the capital and, on 7 July, the chairman of the electoral commission announced the referendum for 4 August. Opposition parties, united in an umbrella organisation called the 'Front pour la Défense de la Démocratie' (FDD), withdrew their representatives from the commission. Legislative elections, which by law should take place within 90 days of the Assembly's dissolution, were set for 20 August but were subsequently postponed till 20 October.

In early June, the country's seven union federations decided to combine forces in the 'Intersyndicale des Travailleurs Nigériens'. Tandja knew that he could rely on support in the rural areas, where his regime enjoyed popularity as a result of small-scale development projects. Nevertheless, at the beginning of June, protests rocked the city of Dosso, south-east of Niamey, as demonstrators sacked government offices and vehicles and tried to attack the provincial chief's palace. The PNDS called for a referendum **boycott**, but the opposition failed to mobilise enough people for a 'pays mort' campaign on 1 July. On 13 July, Niger's lawyers staged a one-day strike to protest against the dissolution of the Constitutional Court and two days later about 100 women protesters were dispersed with batons and tear gas during a sit-in at the Court. Tandja's supporters began to organise increasing numbers of counter-demonstrations. Mahamadou Issoufou of the PNDS was briefly detained by the gendarmerie on 30 June when he called on the army to disobey Tandja's orders, while FUSAD leader Marou Amadou was arrested about the same time on charges of sedition. A number of high-ranking officers assured Tandja that the military would remain neutral. On 3 July, the president issued a decree by which judges opposed to his plans were transferred to remote posts in the countryside.

The state media began a 'Yes' campaign, to which trade unions responded by calling a **general strike** on 23–24 July. On 4 August – referendum day – numerous demonstrators were arrested in the city of Tahoua, in the centre of the country. On 30 July, prosecutors issued an international arrest warrant for Hama Amadou, who had gone abroad (he had been provisionally released to undergo medical treatment in France). Marou Amadou of FUSAD was rearrested on 10 August for having called for the overthrow of the Tandja regime. The **referendum** itself was a non-event, as so often in the modern history of the country. According to the electoral commission, turnout was 68%, of which 92.5% approved the new constitution. The 'Coordination des Forces pour la Démocratie et la République' (CFDR), a body now combining unions, civic groups, the CDS, ANDP and PNDS into an extra-parliamentary opposition force, claimed the turnout barely reached 5% and that the outcome was null and void. The new Constitutional Court confirmed the results.

Ahead of the parliamentary elections on 20 October, the government began investigations targeting dozens of MPs on suspicion of **corruption**. An inspection of the accounts of the Assembly (known to be a rich source of perks) showed that millions of euros had gone missing, but the investigations were obviously an attempt to silence Tandja's opponents. Over the course of several weeks, more than 120 politicians were charged with misappropriation of funds, including Mahamadou Issoufou of the PNDS and Assembly chair Mahamane Ousmane. At the time, the latter was presiding at a session of the ECOWAS parliament in Abuja and was therefore driven into exile – like Hama Amadou. All three were **political tycoons** with long-standing careers and a dislike of each other, but they were now driven into each other's arms. Issoufou left Niger for ECOWAS-sponsored talks. When he returned home on 30 October, he faced an arrest warrant, but was not arrested. It was not only opposition politicians who fell victim to harassment, but also members of the independent media. Abdoulaye Tiémogo of the private 'Le Canard Déchaîné' was given a three-month jail sentence on 18 August for "casting discredit on a judicial ruling" and, during the same month, the directors of eight weeklies were questioned over articles accusing the president's son of taking bribes.

The CFDR forum called for a boycott of the **legislative elections** and for a protest gathering on 26 September in Niamey. On 21 September, Prime Minister Seyni Oumarou and two of his colleagues – staunch Tandja supporters – resigned in order to stand in the parliamentary elections. The president appointed Ali Badio Gamatié, a former finance minister and World Bank technocrat, to replace Seyni Oumarou. The MNSD took 76 of the 113 seats and five smaller parties allied to the MNSD took another 25. Eleven independents also gained seats, a disappointment for Tandja's opponents since they represented the only opposition in the Assembly. The Constitutional Court validated the results. The alleged turnout was 51.3%; some reports suggest that turnout in the countryside was high, but this was disputed by the opposition and some international observers, who reported an overall low turnout. The military, who voted one day ahead of the polls, abstained in massive numbers – as had happened during the referendum.

A CFDR-sponsored meeting in Niamey on 13 December drew thousands of demonstrators. Two days later, Tandja retaliated with a counter-demonstration, and a union-sponsored gathering at the university later that month underlined the high level of political **tensions**. On 24 December, the government delegation to ECOWAS-mediated talks with the opposition walked out after the West African body stated that 22 December marked the end of Tandja's legal tenure. The opposition had agreed to talks as a concession when the government suspended the arrest warrants on Hama Amadou and Mahamadou Issoufou. The warrants were reactivated and Mahaman Ousmane also became subject to arrest. New talks were scheduled for 7 January. On 27 December, Tandja completed his constitutional coup with **local elections**, which were boycotted by the opposition and disapproved of by the international community. Representatives for 265 councils were elected and the MNSD predictably captured over half the seats, the remainder taken by parties participating in the ruling coalition.

Security in the north remained a problem. On 22 January, four Western citizens returning from a festival on nomad culture were kidnapped in the border zone with Mali. Rumours continued about the **kidnapping** the previous December of the UN special envoy to Niger, Robert Fowler, his aide, Louis Guay – both Canadian, and their local driver, in the vicinity of the capital. A video showing the three captives was released in Bamako on 30 January. Niger's government pointed the finger at Tuareg rebels, but the main 'Mouvement des Nigériens pour la Justice' (MJN) denied responsibility. Another rebel faction, the 'Front des Forces de Redressement' (FFR), had first claimed responsibility but later retracted. Fowler's driver was released in Mali in late March. His kidnappers, sub-contractors, had handed the three over to members of 'Al-Qaida in the Land of the Islamic Maghreb', the Algeria-based group of Islamist activists, which on 28 March demanded the release of 20 of its members by Mali and other countries in exchange for Fowler and the other five Westerners. Fowler and his fellow Canadian, together with two of the Western tourists captured in January (a German and a Swiss woman) were released on 22 April. A ransom may have been paid, although the Canadian government denied this. Later in September, Fowler suggested that the Niger government might have been involved in his kidnapping, since it deeply resented his mediation mission in the Tuareg rebellion and his capture had occurred in a safe zone. If true, this would exacerbate the already grim picture of Tandja's regime. In the course of the year, one of the hostages taken in January, a Briton, was murdered by his captors; they had demanded the release of a Jordanian from a UK prison, which the British refused. The remaining Westerner was released later, but another incident rocked Niger on 28 December: roughly in the same area where the other incidents took place, three Saudi tourists were killed by gunmen, while several others were injured. Three suspects were arrested.

The splintering in the ranks of the **Tuareg rebels** continued. In March, Aklu Sidisidi led a group of rebels to leave the MJN and form a third faction, the 'Front Patriotique

Nigérien' (FPN). In April, possibly encouraged by the weakening of the rebel ranks, the government sent a security official to Libya to negotiate a truce – a clear softening of its line. The previous week, a group of rebels had announced that it planned to surrender its weapons after a call for a truce by Libya's leader Col. Kadhafi. These manoeuvres led to direct talks between Niger's government and Tuareg rebels – the first since the eruption of the conflict – in Tripoli on 5–6 April. Interior Minister Abouba met representatives of all three factions. While all sides agreed to make peace, the accord, which involved rebel disarmament, a general amnesty, the lifting of the state of alert and release of detainees, was stalled. The MJN questioned Niamey's commitment to peace and reiterated demands, such as a greater share by the Tuareg population in the country's uranium proceeds. On 3 May, Tandja himself met in Agadez with representatives of the three rebel factions, who, before the meeting, announced the release of the last government soldier still held hostage. Tandja promised the rebels an amnesty in exchange for laying down their arms, but no date was set for the signing of an accord or the disarmament process. On 15 May, after talks with the prime minister, the MJN and FPN agreed to a ceasefire, but the FFR boycotted these talks.

Disagreement within the rebel ranks thus beset the elaboration of an agreement. On 31 August, the MJN, which called on the other factions to regroup, announced that it had deposed its own leader, Aghaly Ag Alamba, accusing him of spending too much time in Libyan hotels. The other factions reiterated demands, such as the release of prisoners, posts in the armed forces and a share in uranium proceeds. On 5–6 October, several rebels, deprived of Libyan support, felt forced to agree to a formal ending of the conflict at Sabha in Libya. The MJN said that Libya had exceeded its powers as mediator, and both MJN and FFR, disappointed by the government's refusal to concede a bigger share in uranium proceeds and more jobs for Tuaregs in the army and the mining sector, swore to continue the struggle. With only the FPN and the MJN's deposed Aghaly Alambo as signatories, the accord's future remained dubious. Nevertheless, the government announced an amnesty and the lifting of the state of alert. Around 800 rebels in Libya were planning to return home. So far, the conflict had cost the lives of some 400 people, wounded many more and displaced some 20,000 civilians.

Towards the end of the year, reports trickled in about tension in the **armed forces**. On 10 November, with soldiers dissatisfied about the sharp reduction in pay brought about by a decrease in mission indemnities earned during the Tuareg rebellion, the chief of staff warned them not to engage in politics. Pamphlets circulated asserting that the president's tenure after 22 December was illegitimate. Although Tandja had increased gifts to the military, rumours of coup plots surfaced and a dozen young officers were questioned. The assistant chief of staff of the army, who had resisted presidential bribes, had already been replaced. With a presidential guard increased to 600 men, commanded by a fellow easterner, the president's security was stepped up considerably.

Foreign Affairs

Foreign policy was dominated by the fall-out from Tandja's takeover. On 15 May, a delegation of the Council of the Wise of **ECOWAS** pointed out to the president that he had signed a protocol banning electoral reform without majority support within six months of an election. The following day, ECOWAS issued a sanctions threat and, on 24 August, its Mediation and Security Council in Abuja expressed concern over the violation of Niger's constitution, establishing an ad hoc committee of four countries (Nigeria, Benin, Burkina Faso and Sierra Leone) to confer with Nigérien stakeholders. A special summit in Abuja on 17 October called for postponement of the parliamentary elections, also banning Niger from putting up candidates for posts in international organisations and hosting ECOWAS meetings. A delegation led by Liberia's President Sirleaf could not dissuade Tandja from his collision course and, when the elections went ahead, Niger's membership was suspended. However, mediation continued. On 10 November, the ECOWAS mediator, Nigerian Ret. General Abubakar, met a 22-member delegation of Niger's government in Abuja, followed by a similar meeting two days later with opposition representatives, and, on 13 December, Abubakar travelled to Niamey for a dialogue with all parties concerned. With the passing of the 22 December constitutional deadline, ECOWAS issued its statement on the end of Tandja's legal mandate, to which the government responded with a walkout.

In November, the **EU** froze non-humanitarian development aid to the value of € 458 m. The **US** also reacted sharply, but not being Niger's principal trading partner and focusing strongly on anti-terrorist issues in the Sahara, Washington's influence was circumscribed. When the 22 December limit of Tandja's tenure passed, it refused to recognise the president's legitimacy. The next day it suspended non-humanitarian aid and imposed travel restrictions on members of the regime. If the result of these measures was limited, their symbolism in terms of Niger's international isolation was powerful. **Nigeria**, one of Niger's principal trading partners, also expressed concern, temporarily closing the border in November. Since transport through Nigeria is of crucial importance to Niger's landlocked economy, this could be interpreted as a warning signal.

Tandja, however, could rely on support from Libya, France and China. **Libya**'s leader, Kadhafi, having been asked to help end the rebellion, put pressure on rebel factions. On 12 March, he made a stopover in Niamey, handing over army soldiers held hostage by rebels. He facilitated the talks between the government and rebel factions in Tripoli in April. However, he clearly went too far in pressing the rebels, and some later repudiated the peace deal. Tandja visited Libya in person early in September. **France** trod a delicate line between disapproval of Tandja's moves and not wishing to endanger imports of Niger's uranium – representing 38% of French uranium imports (expected to rise to 50% by 2012). During his visit to Niger on 27 March, Sarkozy said that he did not favour life presidencies but also made it clear that he would not interfere. The fact that Tandja made his referendum call the day after the launching of the construction of the Imouraren uranium mine in the presence of the French development minister and Areva's director showed that French support was crucial. Some sources suggested Tandja secured discrete backing from Sarkozy, though this may not have been more than reluctant acquiescence. The **Chinese** felt no compunction in maintaining ties with Niamey, the vice president of the China National Petroleum Corporation visiting Niger on 30 July and being received with full honours. Chinese comments on political events remained moderate.

Other issues in foreign relations included the rising insecurity in the Saharan zone. On 6 September, the press reported a meeting of army representatives of Niger, Mali and Mauritania with their counterparts in **Algeria** to discuss plans to counter terrorism and cross-border crime.

Socioeconomic Developments

New calculations of GDP **growth** in 2008 yielded a much higher figure: 9.5%, mainly caused by a growth of 25% to 30% in cereal produce. However, forecasts for 2009 warned of a sharp drop in growth. It was estimated that inflation would fall from a year-on-year rate of more than 10% to around 5% due to lower import prices and the excellent 2008 harvest (4.96 m tonnes of cereals), but this year's **harvest** was far poorer than in 2008. Confronted with erratic rainfall (there was flooding in some regions, destroying some 3,500 homes), many areas saw disappointing crop yields, presaging malnutrition or starvation in the coming year.

The **uranium** sector saw the start of the construction of the Imouraren mine, with 67% owned by Areva and the remainder in the hands of the Nigérien state. Uranium exports for 2009–2010 were predicted to increase in value as a result of the higher contract price negotiated with Areva in 2008. Market prices also increased – 35% up by June – as a result of the new global popularity of nuclear energy. This could boost Niger's overall growth.

On 3 July, Niger, Nigeria and Algeria signed an agreement in Abuja on the building of a gas pipeline across the Sahara for the export of Nigerian gas to North Africa. Work started on the Kandadji dam, intended to produce power and water for irrigation. The Chinese were awarded the first major contract in this huge project; they also began work on the construction of the oil refinery in Zinder, to be fed by the Agadem block near the Chadian border, and were already working on the second bridge across the Niger river in Niamey. In 2008, **Chinese trade** with Niger increased fivefold.

In the course of the year, Niger was granted **development aid** by various donors but it was unclear whether these plans would be affected by the political developments. Some of the programmes that were hit included the money to be provided by the EU, with which Niger signed six agreements in May worth some $ 300 m in terms of budget support.

The government renationalised the national telecommunications company, SONITEL, after a Chinese-Libyan consortium owning a stake of 51% had failed to abide by the contract, notably with regard to modernisation of the network. Despite its mining attractions, the 'Doing Business Report' of the World Bank ranked Niger at 174 out of 183 countries in terms of its **business environment**. Its poor rating was affected by the degree of red tape and strict labour regulations. Some hope was placed in the peace deal with Tuareg rebels and the boost this could give to tourism, which depends on the attractions of the northern region.

The UNDP again put Niger at the bottom of its Human Development Index. With life expectancy at 50 and school enrolment stalled at 27.2% and adult literacy at 28.7% – low even for West Africa, Niger was statistically a worse place to live than Afghanistan. The government claimed the report was based on erroneous population estimates. In March, around 30 people died after an outbreak of meningitis, which began in neighbouring Nigeria. Casualties climbed to over 200. The EU donated € 4.7 m to assist in coping with the epidemic.

Klaas van Walraven

Nigeria

The ill-health of President Umaru Yar'Adua and his physical absence during the last weeks of 2009 exacerbated the power struggle within the ruling People's Democratic Party (PDP) and the federal executive council. Brinkmanship, manipulation and deliberate misinterpretation of various constitutional provisions prevented the seemingly hapless Vice President Goodluck Jonathan from immediately assuming presidential powers, so that towards the end of the year a military coup seemed possible. With some delay, the international financial melt-down also reached the Nigerian economy, although the serious banking crisis, which forced the central bank to inject huge amounts of money to avert a systemic crisis, was almost entirely home-made. In the wake of an unprecedented increase of violence, attacks and counter-attacks by security forces and the militias in the Niger Delta, the government eventually offered an amnesty programme, thereby making a surprising political U-turn in an effort to break the long-lasting deadlock in the oil and gas producing region.

Domestic Politics

When President Umaru Musa Yar'Adua travelled to Saudi Arabia on 23 November for follow-up medical checks, nobody thought that he would not be back by the end of the year. Ever since he had become governor of Katsina state in 1999, a position he occupied twice, it was common knowledge that he suffered from recurring **health problems,** but he was nevertheless elected president in 2007 and went abroad on several occasions for temporary medical treatment. This time, however, the situation was different because, when he arrived in a Saudi Arabian hospital in Jeddah, it was announced that he had acute pericarditis, or inflammation of the lining around the heart. His ill-health then became the focal point of domestic politics for the rest of the year, raising serious legal and constitutional issues in respect of the president's powers.

During the month of December, continuing doubts surrounding Yar'Adua's ill-health led to a period of great uncertainty, as scheming politicians and godfathers outside of government and parliament prepared for the possibility that he might be too sick to remain in office. Unfortunately, although Vice President Goodluck Jonathan had presided over cabinet meetings, articles 144, 145 and 146 of the 1999 **constitution** prevented him from assuming executive powers, a situation which led to questions over the legality of government decisions. According to the Constitution, the vice president assumes the role of president if the president sends a written declaration to the president of the Senate and the speaker of the House of Representatives, indicating that he is going on vacation or that he is otherwise unable to discharge his office, until such time as he sends a written declaration to the contrary. Moreover, the president or vice president ceases to hold office if a resolution passed by a two-thirds majority of all members of the executive council of the federation declares that the president or vice president is medically incapable of discharging his office. This declaration must be verified by a five-man medical panel, appointed by the Senate president, of whom one should be the personal physician of the office-holder concerned.

By the end of the year, however, the president had sent no such written declaration to the Senate leadership nor had the executive council of the federation passed any resolution, thus creating a serious power vacuum in which rumours of an imminent military coup were rife. Throughout December, while published opinion called for Yar'Adua's resignation, the cabinet unanimously and vigorously maintained its view that there were no grounds on which to seek his resignation. Against this background, it became apparent that the ruling PDP was engaged in a quiet power struggle, horse trading behind closed doors and grappling with the question of whether to transfer executive power to Vice President Jonathan to make him acting president. Interestingly, while this **power vacuum** brought politics at the federal level almost to a standstill, the state governors consolidated their position, forcing the National Assembly to work on a modus operandi that would empower Jonathan to become acting president, thereby preventing a possible military coup.

The controversy over the vice president's constitutionally weak position took a further twist when the chief justice of the federation, Idris Legbo Kutigi, was expected to retire at the end of the year, having reached the mandatory retirement age of 70, with his successor, Alloysius Katsina-Alu, already having been confirmed by the Senate. On 30 December, the president's absence and the vice president's lack of powers forced the outgoing chief justice to conduct the swearing-in ceremony of his successor himself, breaking with the tradition that all previous chief justices had been sworn in by the head of state. This situation prompted further scathing remarks from legal practitioners and the public concerning the **state of the nation**. On 12 March, Kutigi had already sworn in two new supreme court judges, among them a woman, Olufunmilola Adekeye, bringing the number to 17. She thus became the court's second female justice after Aloma Mariam Mukhtar. Isa Ayo Salami became president of the court of appeal, the second highest court in the land.

Despite his ill-health, President Yar'Adua made several **strategic appointments**. In a minor cabinet reshuffle, the minister of interior, retired Maj. Gen. Godwin Abbe, swapped his portfolio with the minister of defence, Shettima Mustapha (14 July). On 23 July, Ogbonnaya Okechukwu Onovo, an ethnic Igbo, became inspector-general of police in place of Mike Okiro, whose tenure had expired. This appointment, however, reminded the public of Onovo's rather dishonourable demotion to his former rank as deputy inspector-general after just three days in charge of the police force in 2007. At that time, in a contentious move, the new president had revoked his previous decision in favour of Okiro. In June, the managing director of First Bank, Lamido Sanusi, replaced Chukwu Soludo as governor of the central bank, and Steve Oronsanye, permanent secretary at the ministry of finance, became head of service of the federation, succeeding Ms Ama Inyingiala Pepple, who had reached the mandatory retirement age of 60. Soon after taking over, Oronsanye implemented new rules within the federal civil service, which provide for a four-year tenure renewable only once for permanent secretaries and an eight-year tenure for directors. In August, the new comptroller-general of the Nigeria customs service, Abdullahi Dikko, took over from Bernard-Shaw Nwadialo, who had been in charge only since January. Christopher Uloneme Anyanwu emerged as new director-general of the privatisation agency Bureau of Public Enterprises on 10 March, succeeding Irene Chigbue. In October, Samuel Ukura became auditor-general of the federation. Timi Alaibe became special presidential adviser on the Niger Delta, while on 8 August Mudashiru Atoyebi was appointed executive secretary of the Nigerian press council. In addition, the president approved new boards for several parastatals and agencies, such as the Nigerian Television Authority, Federal Radio Corporation of Nigeria, the News Agency of Nigeria, Airports Authority, Civil Aviation Authority and the Niger Delta Development Commission, to mention only the most important, paving the way for hundreds of lucrative positions within the public sector. Within the Nigeria Electricity Regulatory Commission, however, the chairman Ransom Owan and his commissioners were sacked in February, following allegations of corruption.

Within the **military**, Maj. Gen. Babagana Monguno assumed command of the defence intelligence agency (10 July), while his predecessor Musa Sa'id retired after 36 years' service. In October, the army promoted 261 majors and lieutenant colonels to their next rank, and in November the air force followed suit, promoting another 105 officers with the rank of squadron leader, equivalent to major, to air commodore, equivalent to brigadier. To avoid any discontent among non-commissioned officers, the military leadership also promoted more than 9,600 soldiers to their next rank. A number of army officers, implicated in the non-payment of allowances to 27 soldiers on the peace-keeping mission in Liberia the previous year, were demoted in January after they were found guilty of diverting more than $ 68,000 meant for peace-keeping troops to another military unit. Eventually, they suffered the consequences and were compulsorily retired. The soldiers, however, who had been openly protesting in Akure, Ondo state, the preceding year, were subsequently charged with mutiny and sentenced to life imprisonment by a court-martial on 27 April. On 29 August, the army headquarters commuted the sentences to seven years' imprisonment and eventually released the records of proceedings in the cases to the convicts and their counsels, who appealed the sentence at the court of appeal.

The legal aftermath of the 2007 elections was still taking its toll, although all but five of the pending gubernatorial election appeals (Ekiti, Delta, Imo, Ogun and Sokoto states) were closed at the appeal court in favour of the incumbents. On 17 February, the court of appeal sacked Olusegun Oni, governor of Ekiti state, ordering him to hand over to the speaker of the state house of assembly and ordering fresh elections in ten out of the 16 local government areas. The re-run between the candidate of the Action Congress (AC), Kayode Fayemi, who had successfully filed an appeal against the ruling of the **election petitions tribunal**, and the formally declared winner, Olusegun Oni of the PDP, was won by the latter on 25 April. The runner-up, however, again challenged the outcome at the tribunal, which was still out on a decision at year's end.

Apart from the gubernatorial elections, the courts still had to deal with petitions regarding the **National Assembly** election results in various senatorial districts and federal constituencies in Ekiti, Anambara and Oyo states. Interestingly, as in the previous year, not a single actor, party or public institution dared to sue a rival or a candidate for committing a breach of the law in the run-up to, or during, the election. However, bye-elections in Ondo for the Senate and in Adamawa state for the House of Representatives were won by the candidates of the Labour Party, Debo Olugunagba, and the PDP, Abubakar Mahmud Wambai, respectively.

To the great surprise of public and legal experts, the **supreme court** ordered the presidential election petitions tribunal to establish a fresh panel of justices to hear, *de novo*, the election petition filed by Ambrose Owuru, the candidate of the Hope Democratic Party, a rather small political grouping (27 March). It accepted his appeal and set aside the tribunal's ruling, which had dismissed the petition on the grounds that it lacked merit, although the same court, by a narrow decision of 4–3, upheld the tribunal's ruling that the challenge by Chukwuemeka Ojukwu, presidential candidate of the All Progressive Grand Alliance, was incompetent (24 April). On 17 November, however, the newly established tribunal, like the previous one, struck out the petition filed by Owuru.

After months of fierce fighting, attacks and counter-attacks by militias and security forces in the oil producing **Niger Delta**, Yar'Adua offered a presidential pardon and an amnesty programme to gunmen in the area, trying to end years of bloody unrest that had cost billions of dollars in lost revenues (24 June). The previous day, a high-ranking government delegation, led by retired Maj. Gen. Godwin Abbe and the then inspector-general of police, Mike Okiro, paved the way by meeting prominent militia leaders to discuss the amnesty terms. These included setting up 27 collection and reintegration centres for disarming the fighters, mostly in Bayelsa, Delta and Rivers states, where the violence had been at its worst. In addition, the disarmed militants would be paid 20,000 naira ($ 135) a month during the rehabilitation programme, along with a daily 1,500 naira for food. Such action had been strongly recommended by the Niger Delta Technical Committee the previous year and the fixed time frame of 60 days, from 6 August to 4 October, was supposed to offer a small window of opportunity to break the vicious circle of organised violence, crime and human rights abuses. In addition, the federal government was ready to release from prison a leader of the Movement for the Emancipation of the Niger Delta (MEND), Henry Okah, who was standing trial in a federal court for alleged gun-running and treason.

On 13 July, soon after the announcement, Okah accepted the **amnesty offer** and was set free, despite the fact that MEND had set fire to the 'Atlas Cove Jetty' in Lagos the previous day, leaving five workers dead and endangering the fuel supply to other depots. On 19 October, he was even received by the president. On 7 August, more than two dozen MEND militia members led by Victor Ben Ebikabowei met the president, who had also agreed to a dialogue with other militia leaders, such as Ateke Tom, Farah Dagogo and Government Ekpemupolo, alias Tompolo. At the end of October, Yar'Adua approved the sum of $ 1.3 bn in federal funding to build roads, hospitals and schools in the Niger Delta. Despite these good intentions and the **voluntary disarmament** of some 15,000 militia members, by early November, the promised rehabilitation and reintegration camps being set up to receive the fighters were not ready to process them. Furthermore, the ill-health of the president and his subsequent absence almost brought the peace and reconciliation process to a standstill. Notwithstanding, on 16 December, the government, represented by the vice president, inaugurated a presidential committee and four sub-committees on the Niger Delta. Shortly thereafter, however, MEND claimed to have attacked a major pipeline in Rivers state as a 'warning strike', a claim which security forces and oil companies denied. Furthermore, in Yenegoa (Bayelsa state), and Warri (Delta state) heavily armed police forces were deployed to disperse former militants protesting over the non-payment of amnesty allowances (22/23 December), claiming that they had been promised some $ 2,000 each in return for laying down their weapons earlier in the year, but that the government had failed to pay.

Prior to that, there were strong indications that this volatile situation, exacerbated by **hostage-taking** and piracy, was about to get completely out of hand, causing a further serious shortfall in oil production and revenues and leading to the deaths of dozens of security personnel, militia members, oil workers and civilians. In addition, the growing crisis had led to a massive increase in security expenditure, the oil companies having spent an estimated $ 3.7 bn the previous year. As before, the main oil companies such as Shell, Chevron and Agip, operating in a joint venture with the Nigerian National Petroleum Corporation (NNPC), had been the main target of organised attacks and had to shut down oil and gas production several times. In addition, within the first seven months of the year more than 500 people from Nigeria and countries such as Britain, Russia, Lebanon and Lithuania were taken hostage. Most of them were released almost unharmed after militants and criminals had collected ransoms from the companies or extorted money from the victims' families. Some of the hostages were freed by security forces. Virtually all of the kidnappings took place in the southeast and the Niger Delta. Two Britons, Robin Barry Hughes and Matthew Maguire, who had been taken hostage in September the previous year, were released by MEND on 20 April and 12 June respectively.

In a major reorganisation of the security forces in the Niger Delta, 'Operation Flush Out III' was merged with 'Operation Restore Hope' in March. Led by Maj. Gen. Yakin Bello and his deputy, Brigadier Nanvem Rintip, the more centralised task force eventually started a large-scale **military assault** in May, killing dozens of militants and destroying a number of strongholds, such as the notorious Camp 5. The principal militant groups, however, declared an 'all-out war', and several military personnel fell victim to their counter-attacks. At this time, the federal government back-pedalled and presented its amnesty programme, which, however, did not convince local analysts.

On 8 June, Royal Dutch **Shell** agreed a $ 15.5 m out-of court settlement in the Ogoni case, initiated 13 years earlier in the US. Shell had been due to go to trial, accused of complicity in the show trial and subsequent execution of human rights activist Ken Saro-Wiwa and eight of his comrades-in-arms in Nigeria in 1995. Moreover, at year's end, a district court in The Hague in the Netherlands ruled that it was competent to handle a case brought against Royal Dutch Shell and its Nigerian branch by Nigerian farmers in the Niger Delta and the environmental group Friends of the Earth Netherlands, who were suing for compensation for alleged damage caused by oil spills.

While the proposed amnesty and disarmament exercise in the Niger Delta brought the violence at least temporarily to a standstill, the Muslim north and the eastern part of the Middle Belt experienced a wave of **sectarian clashes** between security forces and Islamic sects such as 'Boko Haram' (meaning 'western education is forbidden'), 'Kalo-Kato' (meaning 'a layman says') and the 'Nigerian Muslim Brothers', also known as the 'Islamic Movement', sympathetic to the Iranian revolution but wrongly called Shi'ites. On 26 July, violence broke out in Bauchi, the capital of the state of the same name, when some members of 'Boko Haram' were arrested on suspicion of plotting to attack a police station. Within 48 hours, the unrest had spread to the sect's stronghold in the Borno state capital, Maiduguri, and to Yobe and Kano states, where the sect clashed with police forces, leaving dozens of militants and several policemen dead and a police station burnt to the ground. More was to come, and security forces including army personnel were deployed to quell the uprising, which turned Maiduguri into a battlefield for days, leaving at least 700 people dead and thousands homeless. The leader of the sect, 39-year-old Mohammed Yusuf, and scores of his followers, including former state commissioner for religious affairs and the sect's alleged financier, Buji Foi, were killed while in custody, highlighting the fact that extrajudicial killing was still practised by the security forces. A high-ranking delegation, led by the justice minister and attorney-general Michael Aondoakaa, hypocritically apologised to the UN in Geneva for the killings and promised to punish those responsible. By year's end, no investigation, let alone any punishment, could be reported.

The 'Boko Haram' **sect** had been fighting against Western education and for the implementation of strict Islamic law for years and was known to the security agencies under various names. Its leader Mohammed Yusuf, thought to be a theology undergraduate drop-out from the Islamic University of Medina, was considered a charismatic preacher. He attracted illiterate and jobless youths, as well as educated people and school and university drop-outs, who felt betrayed by mainstream Islam. In November of the previous year, he, along with some of his followers, was arrested for public incitement through preaching and charged in court in the capital Abuja but, on 20 January, they were granted bail. In 2006, the federal government had charged Yusuf with belonging to an international terrorist network, but the charges never reached court.

On 21 February, the 19th **Shehu of Borno**, Mustapha Umar Ibn El-Kameni, died at the age of 85 in an Egyptian hospital in Cairo and was buried in his palace in Maiduguri. His successor, 51-year-old Abba Kyari Abubakar Ibn Umar Garbei El-Kanemi, was turbaned on 4 March and received his staff of office on 30 May, formalising government recognition of his unique position, which traces its authority back to the ancient Kanem-Borno Empire.

Towards the end of the year, in the city of Bauchi, the Islamic sect 'Kala-Kato', which rejects modernity, Western education, radio and television, and adheres only to the Qur'an, clashed with security forces, who had intervened in an intra-sectarian power struggle. Some 40 persons died during the two-day **uprising**, including security personnel. The incidents around the 'Boko Haram' and 'Kala-Kato' sects recalled the Maitatsine uprising in 1980, which left several thousand people dead. The remnants of the movement, founded by the self-proclaimed prophet Mohammed Marwa Maitatsine (meaning 'the one who curses'), were thought to have kept alive his ideas, which are inspired by Mahdism.

In the aftermath of the clashes with 'Boko Haram', a puritanical Darul-Islam community near Mokwa in Niger state came to limelight. It had been founded some 16 years previously to live and practise pure Islam. Although there was no proof that the community had any relationship with the sects mentioned above, the federal and state governments sacked the settlement in a joint action and dispatched the approximately 4,000 members to their respective states of origin or home countries.

On 11 September, the 'Nigerian Muslim Brothers' under the leadership of its founder Ibrahim El-Zakzaky were marking the annual Quds (Jerusalem) day in their stronghold Zaria, in Kaduna state and in other northern cities, in solidarity with the plight of the Palestinians. The procession in the ancient **city of Zaria**, however, clashed with police forces who opened fire, killing at least two people and injuring three. According to police sources, armed members of the group had shot at police, confirming the suspicion that the radical Islamic group was in possession of weapons. Ever since the group was founded in the late 1980s, its aim had been to establish a theocratic state, by force if necessary, and the number of its followers had grown steadily. In the meantime, it had established a formidable network all over the country's far north, rejecting the formal introduction of shariah law as half-hearted.

As in previous years, there were several violent **communal clashes** in a number of states. In Gada and Kasanga village in Mashegu local government (Niger state), at least half a dozen people were killed in February in a clash over the relocation of the village market. At least four people lost their lives and almost a dozen were injured at the end of March in a controversy between pastoralists and farmers in Marke and Boyoni villages in Miga and Kaugama local governments (Jigawa state). In Okene (Kogi state), the army had to help restore peace in early July following the inability of the police to bring under control a crisis that had claimed no fewer than eight lives and involved the destruction of several properties. For years, Okene had been plagued by recurring violent clashes arising from political differences and disagreements between clans. In mid-July, a crisis broke out between the Nyieva and Uyough communities in Kwande local government (Benue state), leaving six people dead and hundreds displaced. In mid-August, five people were killed as a result of a boundary dispute in villages along the administrative border between Abia and Akwa Ibom states. And in December, fighting between cattle herdsmen and peasants in Udeni village in Nasarawa local government (Nasarawa state) led to the death of some 30 people.

In most of these clashes the culprits were not brought to book. The violent unrest in Jos in November of the previous year, however, in which more than 400 people were left dead, saw not less than six **investigations**, examining both the immediate and indirect causes. While the federal government inaugurated the nine-member panel of inquiry on

5 February, chaired by retired Maj. General Emmanuel Abisoye, the Plateau state governor had already set up another panel in January, chaired by the former attorney-general of the federation Bola Ajibola. In addition, both chambers of the National Assembly, as well as the house of Plateau state Assembly and the defence headquarters, set up their own inquiries behind the scenes. The ex post review and the question as to who had the authority to probe such an issue, said much about how the Nigerian political elite ran public affairs. This case proved for the umpteenth time that, in the still unstable Nigerian political system, the elite could set aside almost any rule and pursue different agendas whenever it saw fit. While Ajibola submitted his as yet unpublished report on 27 October, within the period under review, the Abisoye panel could not wind up its sittings until the year's end.

When Jacob Gyang Buba, former comptroller-general of customs, became the fourth Gbong Gwom of Jos, the paramount ruler of the Berom Kingdom in Plateau state (1 April), it underlined once again how more and more high-ranking officers were cleverly occupying the positions of traditional leaders, which offered the possibility of utilising for their local political interests an institution corrupted and discredited by successive military regimes. His predecessor, the late Victor Dung Pam, had been a retired deputy inspector-general of police.

The **anti-corruption campaign** slowed down again, partly reflected in the poor ranking of TI, which placed Nigeria 130th of 180 countries in the corruption perception index. Most of those charged were released on bail or even had their cases dismissed. Only in a few instances did the court sentence respondents to imprisonment. For example, Attahiru Bafarawa, former governor of Sokoto state, was granted bail in December, soon after he had been arrested. The same applied to former comptroller-general of customs, Hamman Bello Ahmed, in August. The trials of the Rivers state chief of staff, Ezebonwu Nyesom Wilke (17 July), the ex-chairman of the police equipment foundation, Kenny Martin (24 November), and the former health minister, Adenike Grange, and her ex-minister of state, Gabriel Aduku (10 December), as well as that of the former governor of Delta state, James Ibori (17 December), were even quashed, indicating that the Economic and Financial Crimes Commission (EFCC), mainly financed by Western donors, generally lacked the competent and independent personnel to provide sufficient evidence. In the cases of Martin and Ibori, however, the commission appealed the verdict.

Bode George, former chairman of the Nigerian ports authority and ex-vice-chairman of the PDP, was sentenced to two years in prison along with five other board members (26 October). They were found guilty of inflating contracts and abusing public funds worth some $ 500 m. Bode George's was the highest profile conviction since Yar'Adua had taken office in 2007. The EFCC was also able to hand over assets worth naira 44 bn, including a hotel in Abuja, to the Bayelsa state government (9 July) as part of the property recovered from the state's former governor Diepreye Alamieyeseigha, who was briefly jailed for **corrupt practices** in 2007. The judicial annulment of the right of occupancy of a valuable piece of land in Port Harcourt reminded the Nigerian public that the family of the late military dictator, Sani Abacha, still owned property and a lot of money, siphoned off while he was in power. The supreme court revoked the unlawful occupancy and returned the land to the original owner. In addition, Abba Abacha, a son of the deceased, was convicted in Switzerland of being a member of a criminal organisation and had assets worth $ 350 m seized (20 November). Switzerland had already returned some $ 700 m to Nigeria during Obasanjo's presidency. Against this background, it became clear in March that the former subsidiary of the US construction company Halliburton, Kellog, Brown and Root (KBR), had been bribing Nigerian officials in connection with the construction of liquefied natural gas facilities in the Niger Delta between 1995 and 2004. While Halliburton and KBR agreed to pay heavy fines in the US, at year's end the Nigerian authorities had not brought any charges.

As in previous years, in most states, including the Federal Capital Territory, Abuja, **security** generally deteriorated and the number of policemen and civilians killed increased significantly, although the figures did not include those who fell victim to the violence in the Niger Delta. Well over 100 policemen lost their lives on duty and Abuja and other urban centres in the far north became new hubs of organised crime. On 19 March, gunmen raided a foreign exchange office in the Kano metropolis, killing six policemen in the Wapa area, where hundreds of moneychangers do business. In Kabba, Kogi state, three policemen were shot dead on 6 August; two local government chairmen were also kidnapped, but were freed two days later. In the city of Kaduna, a Canadian, Julie Mulligan, was kidnapped on 16 April while visiting Nigeria for a conference. She was released after two weeks and the ring-leader of the kidnap gang was arrested soon afterwards. This was one of the rare occasions when the police arrested a member of an organised criminal gang. On 3 April, a Sokoto state civil servant, Mustapha Isa Tela, was murdered, and on 7 July in Bauchi state, businessman Michael Ogboh was killed by unknown assailants.

In the southern parts of the country, the **crime** rate continued to be high. In two incidents in Edo state alone, 15 policemen lost their lives. On 11 February, a gang of robbers killed seven policemen and, on 25 March, eight policemen attached to the convoy of the Delta state commissioner of police also fell victim to armed robbers. In October, the president approved a joint military/police patrol in the state in response to the extraordinarily high crime rate. In Abia state, five policemen died on 30 June when a gang attempted to abduct expatriates working for a bottling company in Aba and, on 8 October, the Delta state police command lost five of its staff in an attack by a kidnap-syndicate operating within and outside the state. Many more people were killed during raids on long-distance buses and bullion vans and others were assassinated or kidnapped. But the killing of football star Abel Tador, captain of Bayelsa United, which had just clinched the Nigerian championship, caused a nationwide outcry (14 June). Two other famous stars were luckier and escaped death after being kidnapped. 'Nollywood' star Pete Edochie was taken hostage on 16 August in Anambra state but was set free unharmed two days later, while retired Capt. Elechi Amadi, the author of the famous 'The Concubine' and other novels, was kidnapped on 5 January in Rivers state but released shortly after. On 20 September, Bayo Ohu, editor of the 'Guardian' newspaper (Lagos), was shot dead in his apartment in Lagos. On 21 November, Charles Nsiegbe, who was close to the Rivers state governor, died from gunshot wounds in Port Harcourt and, on 20 December, the former ambassador to the Ukraine, Hakaire Ignatius Ajuru, fell victim to highway robbers in Abia state. In July, against the background of the **worsening security** situation the police service commission approved the recall of almost 1,600 police officers who had unilaterally and without due process been sacked in 2008.

With regard to **human and civil rights abuses**, the situation improved slightly. A court in Abuja adjourned *sine die* the criminal defamation suit initiated by the president against the 'Leadership' newspaper the previous year (18 June). Moreover, a law that had forced hospitals to withhold emergency treatment for victims of gunshot wounds until a police report had been filed was lifted in October. On 8 April, the verdict against Lateef Sofolahan and Aminu Mohammed, who were given long prison sentences for conspiracy and the attempted murder of the late Afenifere, Abraham Adesanya, reminded the public that a number of well-known people close to the late Sani Abacha, such as former chief security officer Hamza Al-Mustapha, were still on trial, proceedings having begun in 1999. On 5 September, Gani Fawehinmi, one of the most outspoken human rights lawyers and democratic activists, died at the age of 71. Under military rule, he had defended many political dissidents and been arrested, detained and charged more than 30 times.

Foreign Affairs

Since Yar'Adua came to power in 2007, Nigeria's close relationship with the **United States** had cooled considerably. This relationship was not helped by the flawed elections in 2007, or by the fact that new US President Barack Obama snubbed the Nigerian leadership on his first African trip as president (10–11 July) by visiting Ghana rather than the sub-region's leading country. The critical remarks by Secretary of State Hillary Clinton during her two-day visit to Nigeria (12–13 August) about its reputation for corruption aggravated the situation and were subsequently strongly condemned by leading politicians. In addition, the Nigerian president's absence from the annual meeting of the UN General Assembly in September was seen as a deliberate diplomatic protest against the attitude of the US, which the federal government considered to be unfair. This discomfort had been reinforced by the rejection of the newly appointed ambassador to the US, Tunde Adeniran, a retired professor of political science and former education minister and ambassador to Germany. He was meant to succeed retired Brigadier Oluwole Rotimi, who had been recalled in February for gross insubordination. The US-government's refusal to accept Adeniran's appointment was said to hinge on the arrest of his son, who lived in the US and had been charged with having raped a girl in Baltimore a short time before. As a result, shortly before he left for Saudi Arabia for medical treatment, Yar'Adua nominated Adebowale Adefuye, who had served as deputy high commissioner in Jamaica and Britain. But bilateral relations almost hit rock bottom when, on 25 December, 23-year-old Nigerian Umar Faruk Abdulmutallab attempted to blow up a Delta Airlines flight on its final approach to Detroit. The suspect's close relations with al-Qaida in Yemen soon came to light and the anchorless Nigerian embassy was weighed down by the challenge of handling the case in accordance with international diplomatic conventions.

Despite diplomatic irritations, the assistant secretary of state for Africa, Johnnie Carson, pointed out in May that Nigeria remained a **strategic partner**, supplying the US with almost 50% of its oil and a significant amount of liquefied gas. Furthermore, US investment in Nigeria was well in excess of $ 15 bn. This statement was mirrored in the ongoing efforts to boost maritime security in the Gulf of Guinea, which was plagued by raids on oil facilities, piracy and drug smuggling. To this end, the US navy was holding training courses on board the USS Nashville, including in hand-to-hand combat and intelligence gathering, for partners from around the Gulf within the framework of the 'Africa Partnership Station', a naval component of the US-Africa command AFRICOM. The exercises in Nigerian coastal waters took place in March and June, and Rear Admiral William Loeffler visited Lagos in March as part of his Africa tour. In early September, chiefs of naval staff from Ghana, Kenya and South Africa met in Uyo, Akwa Ibom state, for a conference on maritime security. Towards the end of the year, Nigeria and São Tomé and Príncipe agreed to set up a joint maritime military commission. On 11 June, Delta Airlines started twice-weekly flights between Abuja and New York, the first direct route between the Nigerian capital and the US. On 3 June, the former secretary of state, Colin Powell, attended a conference to celebrate ten years of democracy in Nigeria and, in October, Nigeria was given a clean bill of health for its drugs control programme.

Over the years, Nigeria has been a focus of the activities of the **UK**'s DFID. In February, the department confirmed its former commitment and unfolded a six-year development agenda worth £ 500 m to aid development targets and comprehensive health schemes and to combat malaria. The focus of bilateral relations during the year turned on the question of repatriation of the more than 800 Nigerians serving various terms in British jails for sex, drugs, immigration and various minor offences. Nigerians were second only to Jamaicans in the numbers of foreign inmates. Britain was even willing to refurbish Nigerian prisons in order to allow Nigerians to serve out their sentences at home. However, Nigerian law would have to be amended to allow prisoners to be transferred without the individual's consent.

On 19 November, the **European Union** signed an agreement worth € 677 m for the period 2009–13, which was designed to help Nigeria tackle development challenges in three main areas. The fund, financed through the EDF, was intended to be distributed as follows: € 166 m for peace and security; € 297 m for governance and human rights;

€ 105 m for energy and regional integration; € 99 m for miscellaneous issues such as facilitating health, cultural and technical cooperation. In addition, the EU sponsored the anti-corruption agencies, the EFCC and the Independent Corrupt Practices and Other Related Offences Commission, to the tune of some 85% of their annual budget, but threatened to cut funding the following year should the government fail to produce clearer results in its fight against corruption.

Relations with **China** focused on resuming ambitious technical projects. In February, the 'China Great Wall Industry Corporation' finally agreed to replace the communication satellite NIGCOMSAT 1, which had disappeared in space in 2008 after being launched into orbit by a Chinese company in 2007. In addition, and after a lot of bickering, the federal government eventually gave the go-ahead to continue with the contract, worth $ 8.3 bn, to modernise the north-south rail route, which had been suspended the previous year. When, in early October, Sinopec (China Petroleum & Chemical Corporation) acquired the Canadian Addax Petroleum Corporation through its subsidiary 'Mirror Lake', China eventually made its long expected move into the direct exploitation of Nigeria's oil and gas fields. On 28 November, the Nigerian ambassador to China acknowledged that Nigerians accounted for about 90% of the crimes committed by Africans in China. At that time, more than 100 Nigerians were serving various jail terms and more than 300 were awaiting deportation. Some were even on death row. More than two dozen had died in jail or had been executed. However, an estimated 20,000 Africans were believed to be living in Guangdong province, many of them students and traders from Nigeria.

When **Russia**'s President Dmitry Medvedev visited Nigeria in June and Gazprom and the NNPC agreed a joint investment of at least $ 2.5 bn, it became obvious that another heavy-weight global player in the energy sector had finally arrived in the country (24 June). The new company, Nigaz, a 50/50 joint venture, proposes to build pipelines, refineries and gas power stations in various parts of the country. Moreover, the planned giant gas pipeline across the Sahara, agreed by Nigeria, Niger and Algeria on 3 July, also offered long-term perspectives for Russian capital. Yet another global player, **Brazil**'s state-run Petrobas, which owned 20% of the deep offshore oilfield Akpo, revealed that plans were under way for long-term investments in Nigeria second only to those in the Gulf of Mexico. The increasing economic cooperation was underlined politically by a three-day state visit by President Yar'Adua (29–31 July) to Brazil. At the second Africa–South America Summit in Caracas, Venezuela, in late September, however, he was represented by the vice president. Finally, in June, the Indian energy giant ONGC Mittal Energy announced its readiness to start exploration of its own deepwater block.

As for relations with African states, Yar'Adua chaired an **ECOWAS** meeting in Abuja on 15 October amidst concern over the crises in Guinea and Niger, which resulted in an arms embargo on Guinea on 17 October and the suspension of Niger on 20 October. In July, the president had already taken part in the 15th summit of the Non-Aligned

Movement in Egypt, but was conspicuously absent at the AU summit in early February and at a follow-up summit in July in Libya, where nearly half of Africa's leaders were discussing a proposed 'African government'.

As in previous years, Nigeria was heavily engaged in the crisis-ridden **Darfur** region and continuously involved in training courses for several hundred military personnel and police forces at the peacekeeping centre Jaji, in Kaduna state. Shortly before his term ended on 31 August, the outgoing commander of the joint UN/AU UNAMID force, Nigerian Martin Luther Agwai, said he believed that the Darfur region was no longer in a state of war. He maintained that the conflict was of low intensity and had descended into banditry, reflecting the increasing fragmentation of the rebel groups. On 29 October, the 15-member AU Peace and Security Council met in Abuja to consider the report on Darfur by a team of African 'wise men' led by Thabo Mbeki. The Sudanese government was represented by its vice president, after President Omar al-Bashir had had second thoughts and decided to stay away, thus avoiding possible arrest following the issue of a warrant by the ICC. Despite Agwai's rather optimistic view, UNAMID staff were still experiencing rebel attacks, kidnapping and killings by rebels and, on 2 December, the controversial Nigerian diplomat Ibrahim Gambari was appointed as the new head of the UNAMID mission and expected to take up his post on 1 January of the following year.

Ever since Nigeria's independence, relations with **Israel** have been controversial, with diplomatic ties having been broken off in 1973 and restored only in 1992. However, for Nigerian Christians a pilgrimage to Israel or Rome is seen as the equivalent of the Islamic hajj, and Nigerian military and intelligence services have made use of Israel's competence in these fields for years. In addition, more than 100 Israeli companies have been doing business in Nigeria. In that context, Avigor Lieberman, who doubled as deputy prime minister and minister for foreign affairs, visited Nigeria in early September as part of his Africa tour; he met his counterpart and the vice president and signed a trade agreement. The two governments also concluded a deal for the manufacture and delivery of patrol boats worth some $ 25 m.

Last but not least, on 15 October, Nigeria was elected to serve on the UN **Security Council** for the period 2011–12, and in July the president attended the G-8 summit in Italy.

Socioeconomic Developments

The international oil and gas price recovered over the course of the year to some $ 77 per barrel at the end of December, up from $ 40 at the beginning of the year. Foreign reserves, which stood at $ 52 bn in January, fell by some $ 10 bn by December, mainly triggered by the aftermath of the international financial melt-down the previous year and a shortfall in oil production during the first six months caused by the unrest in the Niger Delta. By early February, the naira had depreciated by more than 20% within two months. As a result, regulators announced tighter controls on the more than 1,100 bureaux de change (25 February), to which the central bank makes a weekly sale of some $ 200 m. They were eventually split into class A and class B sections to allow easier supervision. Class A was allowed to import and transfer foreign exchange provided they had a minimum paid-up capital of naira 500 m at all times and a minimum deposit of $ 200,000 with the central bank, while class B was permitted to sell a maximum of $ 5,000 per transaction. Despite these actions, the local currency fell to naira 188:$ 1 on the **parallel market** within two weeks before recovering to naira 160:$ 1 towards the end of March. Shortly before the end of his five-year term on 29 May, however, central bank governor Charles Saludo announced that the bank would lift the restrictions and would return to a fully liberalised foreign exchange market within three months. At year's end, the naira rebounded and was trading at 150:$ 1.

Against the background of these controversial regulations, the president finally signed the 2009 **budget** into law on 10 March. The budget, totalling naira 3.101 trillion ($ 21.2 bn) had eventually been approved by both chambers of the National Assembly on 18 February. However, the budget left key benchmarks unchanged, despite the reality on the ground. While the assumed exchange rate was put at naira 125:$ 1, the projected oil price per barrel was $ 45 and the expected oil output 2.3 m barrel a day.

On the eve of his departure to Saudi Arabia for medical treatment, Yar'Adua presented a 2010 budget proposal of naira 4.079 trillion, an increase in spending of 31.5%. A supplementary budget, however, passed by parliament shortly thereafter, did not come into force because the vice president refused to sign it into law, having taken the position that he would not sign anything that required the president's approval. Despite this issue, which could have raised sensitive constitutional problems, the 2009 budget was not fully implemented until March of the following year, highlighting the fact that in early November the government had only implemented some 30% of the budget, underlining its own lack of competence in handling this central political issue.

In an unprecedented move, the central bank, under its new governor, Lamido Sanusi, injected naira 400 bn ($ 2.6 bn) into five undercapitalised banks on 14 August and sacked their top management in an effort to prevent a systemic **banking crisis**. While the 24 Nigerian banks accounted for more than 60% of the market capitalisation of Nigeria's stock exchange, the five affected banks accounted for as much as 40%. On 2 October, the central bank intervened again, providing yet another naira 200 bn ($ 1.3 bn) to four more banks expected to face a grave liquidity crisis, and dismissed their chief executives and some of their staff. Hardly had they been removed from their posts than the EFCC arrested and detained all those it could get hold of, and prosecuted them on multiple fraud charges. Within a rather short period of time, the EFCC recovered some $ 300 m of bad debts, but an estimated $ 10 bn were still outstanding. In mid October, the central bank released a list of major bank debtors, including such powerful people as former vice president Atiku Abubakar, who owed $ 730,000. However, towards year's end all detainees were granted bail and set free. Despite the banking crisis and its legal implications, the external **debt** portfolio was kept stable at some $ 3.75 bn, while domestic debts rose to the enormous amount of some $ 17 bn. In November, however, the World Bank estimated an inflow of almost $ 10 bn of foreign exchange from Nigerian citizens abroad, representing 4.7% of Nigeria's GDP and making the country the sixth highest recipient of diaspora remittances of all developing nations.

The growth of the **telecommunications** sector continued and the number of mobile phone subscribers was put at some 67 million. Notwithstanding the sector's success story, the saga of the former state monopoly, Nigerian Telecommunication Limited (NITEL), took a new twist when, on 1 June, the government resumed control of the fixed line operator and its mobile subsidiary M-TEL, of which a majority stake had been taken over by the local Nigerian Transnational Corporation Limited in 2006. The government justified its action by citing lack of investment and unpaid debts and tried to find a new investor. On 8 December, however, it extended the deadline for a third time, allowing another month for prospective bidders after two previous deadlines had lapsed without any bids being made.

The government totally failed to reverse the disastrous trend in the **power** sector, which produced less than 3,000 MW instead of the promised 6,000 MW. Moreover, it continued to subsidise fuel, mostly imported, to the tune of some $ 4 bn and put the oil sector reform bill on hold.

In July, US-based Nigerian writer E.C. Osondu won the 'Caine Prize for African Writing', and in early November the two-day 'African Media Leaders Forum' took place in Lagos, with some 100 publishers from almost all countries participating. Shortly before, 50 years of television in Nigeria had been celebrated, recalling the introduction of the new media on 31 October 1959 by the government of the then Western Region. These minor achievements contrasted sharply with the surprise defeat of Nigeria, the defending FIFA U17 champion, by the maverick Switzerland in the final in Abuja on 15 November.

On 30 July, after years of litigation, the Kano state government signed an out-of-court settlement worth $ 75 m with US pharmaceutical company **Pfizer** over an unregistered drug test in 1996, in which several children had died, while others had developed mental problems and/or physical deformities. $ 30 m were to go to the victims and their families and the same amount was to be used to provide health projects in the state. $ 10 m were to pay for litigation and $ 5 m for settling sundry expenses. This settlement did not affect charges against Pfizer filed by the federal government, which was seeking billions of dollars in damages. In November, however, Pfizer insisted on DNA tests to ensure that the real victims benefited from the settlement, thereby shifting the responsibility for the payment to a settlement team led by retired supreme court judge Abubakar Wali, and delaying full payment till at least 2010.

Heinrich Bergstresser

Senegal

The global economic crisis affected the country, particularly through pressure on migrant remittances, a key stimulant of the economy. Nevertheless, international assistance and foreign direct investments maintained satisfying levels, saving the economy from a slump. These uneasy economic traits combined with problems in the energy sector, seasonal floods in the suburbs of Dakar, Kaolack and Saint-Louis and difficulties concerning education. Social protests were the result. This was a key factor behind the beating received by the ruling coalition (and by extension President Wade) in the local elections in March, in the course of which it lost control of most of Senegal's large cities. These results were a clear blow to Wade's son's bid for succession to the presidency. The Casamance conflict grew somewhat more heated, while Senegal maintained high-profile, though not evenly successful, diplomacy at both the sub-regional and international levels.

Domestic Politics

The political high point of 2009 came with the **local elections**. Initially planned for May 2008, they finally took place in March. The campaign was bitterly fought, both within the 'Sopi' coalition led by the ruling 'Parti Démocratique Sénégalais' (PDS) and between the

PDS and the broader public. The rifts that divided the PDS and the galaxy of movements that supported its various figureheads resulted in occasional local violence in the run-up to the elections and the preparation of the lists of candidates. More spectacular still were expressions of popular anger at worsening socioeconomic conditions and at the gap between President Wade's extravagant promises and his achievements, in a context of global economic crisis. In many cities, Wade and his campaigning ministers were met by protesters wearing red arm-bands, a now established gesture of defiance in Senegal, and also with stones. Turnout was low (a little above 55%). The ruling 'Sopi' coalition came first, with almost 39% of the votes, and won in 296 of the 543 local authorities, a number of them in rural areas where it stood unopposed. The main opposition force, the 'Bennoo Siggil Senegal' coalition, which succeeded in presenting joint lists of candidates, won more than 30% of the votes and took over most of Senegal's large cities, including Dakar, Saint-Louis, Kaolack and Diourbel. Dakar was fiercely contested, as the 'Sopi' list led by the incumbent PDS mayor, Pape Diop, included none other than Karim Wade, the president's son and putative heir. Two former Wade prime ministers who had fallen from grace won in their local fiefs: Idrissa Seck in Thiès and Macky Sall in Fatick – the latter had not bowed to accusations of money-laundering conveniently brought against him in January, which were quickly dropped. The only good news for Wade came from Ziguinchor, the main city in the southern region of Casamance, where Abdoulaye Baldé, the secretary general of the presidency and a close associate of Karim Wade, defeated a political dinosaur, the ex-socialist Robert Sagna, mayor of the city since the mid-1980s.

A clear expression of the mounting criticism of Wade's government and growing socioeconomic tensions, these elections were also a testimony to the unpopularity of local PDS elites and their **factional divisions**. Factional divisions also tore apart 'And Jëf/Parti Africain pour la Démocratie et le Socialisme' (AJ/PADS), a leftist party that had been associated with the PDS since 2000. A splinter group hostile to the PDS alliance and established in May 2008 under the name 'Yoonu Askan Wi/Mouvement pour l'Autonomie Populaire' was officially registered as a party on 27 January. Tensions between AJ/PADS' two figureheads, Landing Savané and Mamadou Diop Decroix, came to a head after the local elections, and Decroix organised a party conference which designated him as the new secretary general, to Wade's applause.

Wade appointed a new prime minister in April to replace technocrat Cheikh Hadjibou Soumaré; the new appointee was a politician and longstanding PDS member, Souleymane Ndéné Ndiaye. Ndiaye undertook a thorough **cabinet reshuffle**, with 13 ministers leaving the cabinet and a number of key advisers to President Wade being forced to step down, including Serigne Diop, Landing Savané and Abdoulaye Faye. Among the most notable newcomers was Karim Wade himself, whose ministry was quickly expanded to cover International Cooperation, National Planning, Air Transport and Infrastructure. The cabinet, however, continued to suffer from instability, a sure sign of intrigue and tensions between personalities within the ruling coalition. A number of ministers were sacked, including Mamadou Abdoulaye Sow, the budget minister (on 10 June) and Moustapha Sourang, the justice minister (on 26 December), apparently for following legal rules too closely. Minister of Foreign Affairs Cheikh Tidiane Gadio, who was the only minister to have kept his post since 2000, was finally sacked on 1 October over a disagreement concerning Wade's handling of the situation in Guinea. Soon after, another minor reshuffle took place. Minister of the Interior Cheikh Tidiane Sy left and Aminata Tall, a stalwart of the PDS with a long history of opposition to Wade, entered the cabinet. Abdoulaye Baldé took over defence, a Casamançais ministry since 2000. Towards the end of December, Modou Diagne Fada became minister of health.

In order to strengthen his political grip, Wade took a number of other measures. On 15 May, the Assembly accepted his proposal to create a **vice presidency**, whose holder was to be designated by the president. Although this nomination was still pending by the end of the year, the expectation that the post would be given to Karim Wade remained the talk of the town. This also went some way towards explaining why a number of PDS representatives refused to vote in favour of the bill. In a letter addressed to the opposition on 13 June, Wade called for renewed political dialogue. He also tried to regroup some of his former associates, making conciliatory gestures in the direction of both Seck and Sall. Seck showed interest. This raised eyebrows inside the PDS, and such key figures as Abdoulaye Baldé and Farba Senghor openly declared themselves to be against Wade's move. In July, the idea of the creation of a broad presidential party was raised. Possibly in an attempt to get around his son's persistent political failure and limit PDS factionalism, Wade announced in September that he would stand in the 2012 election. The president's entourage floated the idea of suppressing the second round in the presidential elections, but Wade rejected this. In November, Moustapha Touré, the head of the electoral commission, was forced to resign, apparently because of his rigorous management of the municipal polls. In one notable episode, the electoral commission under Touré had refused to register Sopi lists for the local elections in the localities of Ndindy and Ndoulo because they had been submitted after the official deadline, a decision soon overruled by the minister of the interior. Touré's replacement by Doudou Ndir, whose wife is a close associate of Viviane Wade, the president's wife, was widely commented on. In November, the president announced he was considering a constitutional reform establishing full gender parity for all elective functions. On 5 December, works began for a huge mosque in Dakar – President Wade, known for his affiliation to the Muridiyya, an important Islamic Sufi order, pledged to contribute no less than CFAfr 500 m.

The completion of the **'Assises nationales'** as well as a series of scandals and controversies, guaranteed that public criticism of the government continued. The 'Assises nationales', a forum created in June 2008 by a coalition of opposition parties, trade unions and civil society organisations critical of the regime, published the results of its nation-wide consultations on 24 May. As might be expected, it represented a biting critique of Wade's government. Delegates of the 'Assises' decided to extend the movement until June 2010 in order to publicise the results of its investigations, and a final report was under preparation. On 25 January, Wade lost a dedicated adversary and Senegal a great historical figure with the death of Mamadou Dia, who had been the first prime minister of independent Senegal.

Throughout the year, **controversies** erupted. Wade's admission in February that he had been a freemason in his youth raised some eyebrows in a country where freemasonry is viewed by many as a dubious and irreligious secret society. The latest book by the investigative journalist Abdou Latif Coulibaly on Karim Wade's management of the 2008 OIC summit in Dakar was released in August and widely commented on. So was the building of the 'Monument de la Renaissance Africaine' – a huge bronze statue symbolic of African Renaissance on a hill north of Dakar. People were critical of its cost, the complex financing (the construction company was paid by the transfer of state land to a Senegalese entrepreneur connected to both the Muridiyya and the ruling party) and Wade's claim to a personal share in the eventual touristic profits from the statue. Wade made clear that his share would go to a foundation, but this did not prevent a public outcry. Muslim activists condemned the statue as a heretical abomination, and Wade's clumsy attempt to justify it by reference to statues of Christ in churches caused outrage in the Catholic community. Archbishop Théodore Adrien Sarr expressed his unhappiness at the comment and, over Christmas, some young Catholics briefly fought the police in Dakar. Wade sent his son to apologise on his behalf to Archbishop Sarr. Controversies about Wade had echoes beyond Senegal's borders. In November, a civil society organisation based in France, 'Le moment de se lever pour l'Afrique', filed a case against Wade (and a number of other African heads of state) for corruption and illegal acquisition of property in France. Wade replied with a statement authorising French local authorities to confiscate any property he was proved to own in France.

In the southern region of **Casamance**, the beginning of 2009 was relatively peaceful, as the separatists of the 'Mouvement des Forces Démocratiques de Casamance' (MFDC) kept a low profile. The Senegalese army used the opportunity to intensify their hearts and minds campaign. However, things got out of hand from May on, as separatist groups went on the offensive, attacking Senegalese soldiers and robbing civilians in the northwest of Casamance, along the Gambian border. They soon expanded their activities southward, to the Buluf district. Additional Senegalese troops were dispatched in May. In June, separatist hardliners killed Youssouf "Rambo" Sambou, an MFDC commander closely connected to the 'Comité des Sages du MFDC', a mediation group supported by the Senegalese state – Sambou was apparently not well-received on his mission to persuade fellow fighters to adhere to the ceasefire. In July, a group of the Comité led by Lamine Cissé went to meet the fighters with the same objective, but ended up being robbed. Later in the year, the town of Bignona fell victim to a MFDC raid. The **separatist groups** settled south of the Casamance River and initially kept to defending their zone of control, particularly cashew plantations, but from August, they too went on the offensive, attacking the army on the outskirts of the regional capital, Ziguinchor. Several hundred civilians were displaced as a result. Violence also affected the interior of Casamance, between the city of Sédhiou and the Bissau-Guinean border. There, on 2 October, six Senegalese soldiers were killed and others wounded in an ambush. The brutal killing, earlier in the year, of the Bissau-Guinean chief of staff General NaWaie, who had subdued separatist fighters along the common border, surely played a part in giving the separatists a freer rein.

But the fundamental motivations lay elsewhere. While the MFDC militants do not agree between themselves on their views and objectives, many want to force the authorities into accepting serious negotiations. The peace process remained stalled, however, and Dakar did not seem enthusiastic to talk, despite repeated calls by various civil society groups for serious dialogue between the MFDC and Dakar. Tensions were rife between Farba Senghor, Wade's middleman in the Casamance dossier, and the 'Collectif des Cadres Casamançais' (CCC) led by the Casamançais entrepreneur Pierre Atépa Goudiaby, an advisor to Wade. On 6 May, Senghor's right hand man in Casamance, Moustapha Bassène, was tried and sentenced for threats against Goudiaby. The CCC met President Wade on 18 September with a proposal for peace, and Wade announced that an amnesty and incorporation within paramilitary forces would be offered to all MFDC fighters renouncing violence. The nomination of the mayor of Ziguinchor, Abdoulaye Baldé, as minister of defence on 14 October may have been a move to establish the state's presence in Casamance, but Baldé remained very cautious on the issue, rejecting the idea that he was now Wade's man in charge of the Casamance dossier. All this seemed to have little impact on the ground, as **violent incidents** persisted throughout the last months of the year.

Foreign Affairs

Senegal remained an active diplomatic player, and Dakar's latest scandals troubled relations with donors only briefly. In October, Alex Segura, the departing **IMF representative** in Senegal, who had never shied away from voicing his criticisms of the regime's governance, made it public that he had received a briefcase full of cash from the Senegalese presidency. The presidency's explanations that it was merely a leaving present in the African tradition, and that € 100,000 and $ 50,000 could buy nothing anyway, did little to calm tempers. However, the scandal did not fundamentally affect the government's good working relationship with donors. The projected sale of the government's profitable shares in Sonatel, Senegal's telecommunications company, and the disputed funding of the 'Monument de la Renaissance Africaine' were other occasions of tension with donors, but these remained minimal and Senegal was still one of the West's favoured partners. Indeed, the country made efforts to improve economic governance and satisfy donors.

Wade continued his outspoken statements on **North/South issues**. In March, soon after the ICC issued its warrant against Sudanese President Omar al-Bashir, he pointed out that "the Court gives the impression it was created for the Africans [only]". In October, he decried the unsatisfactory management and poor results of the Digital Solidarity Fund, and in December, at the Copenhagen climate summit, he denounced the West for its unkept pledges.

France remained a key partner, though there seemed to be growing unease between the two countries. Around the beginning of the year, allegations of tensions between the presidency and French ambassador Jean-Christophe Rufin, who was said by the press to have criticised Senegal's addiction to aid, were denied by Paris and Dakar. The media also noted Wade's absence from President Sarkozy's press conference in Copenhagen, a sign of Wade's increasingly pluriform diplomatic profile. On 25–26 March, French Minister Eric Besson paid a visit to Dakar to discuss the management of Senegalese immigration. Ségolène Royal, the Dakar-born defeated socialist candidate in the French presidential elections of 2007, visited Senegal, and on 6 April she apologised to Africans for Sarkozy's infamous 2007 speech at Dakar University. The Senegalese presidency prudently declined to meet her.

Thanks to both old and new diplomatic friends, the list of **grants and gifts** for 2009 remained impressive. The most significant was the US Millennium Challenge Account grant, worth more than $ 500 m over a five-year period, which Wade announced in September. It is to be used to build roads and rural markets, support agriculture and create economic enterprise zones. With a growing involvement in agricultural development, USAID also significantly increased its support, from $ 52 m to $ 88 m. International financial institutions continued with their various efforts, and in June it was made public that the IMF would provide CFAfr 48 bn using the Exogenous Shocks Facility. The AfDB confirmed its growing role in Senegal, and announced in April a $ 45 m loan for the development of access to water, and in July a $ 70 m loan for the Dakar-Diamniadio motorway.

But Senegal maintained its diversified portfolio. Significantly enough, it was among the four countries visited by **China**'s President Hu Jintao during his Africa tour, and one of the two African countries where Iranian President Mahmud Ahmadinejad made an appearance, on 26 November, in his quest for support for **Iran**'s nuclear programme. On that occasion, Wade expressed unambiguous support for Iran's access to nuclear power for civilian purposes. Earlier in the year, a deal was struck for the provision of 1,000 Iranian tractors for Senegal's agricultural development, and discussions were under way for Iranian investments in the energy sector.

At the sub-regional level, the situation was less easy. The twin murders in March of **Guinea-Bissau**'s President Nino Vieira, and his chief of staff General NaWaie, both close partners of Dakar in the struggle against Casamance separatists, created tensions between the two countries. Senegal felt frustrated over the passiveness of Guinea-Bissau's new leadership with regard to the Casamance rebels. In June, the Bissau authorities announced that a coup attempt involving a number of Dakar-based associates of former president Vieira had been foiled – Dakar's own involvement in the coup was hinted at. Senegal tried to redevelop its influence in Bissau, backing Malam Bacai Sanhá's campaign for the presidency. But despite Sanhá's victory in the July election, relations between the two countries remained tense. In October, Bissau-Guinean troops were deployed at the border, apparently over a territorial dispute with Senegal. Ministerial-level meetings were quickly held to settle the issue.

With **Gambia** the year started better, as Gambian soldiers took part in Senegal's national festivities. However, relations went through a new round of tensions towards the end of the year. In November and December, Gambian state media fiercely denounced Wade's support for Kukoi Sanyang, a Gambian opposition figure who stood accused of planning a coup against Gambian President Jammeh. Senegal's Minister for Foreign Affairs Madické Niang made a trip to Banjul on 22 December for discussions.

Wade played a part in **Mauritania**'s political transition. He had been quick to come to the support of General Ould Abdel Aziz to help him normalise his diplomatic standing after his successful 2008 military take-over and now helped him in contesting the presidential elections in July. The two regimes maintain close relationships, and the repatriation of black Mauritanian refugees based in Senegal continued. Faced with another sub-regional coup, in **Guinea-Conakry**, Wade tried to play the part of mediator for Guinea's new military ruler, Captain Moussa 'Dadis' Camara, whom he called his 'son'. He made several trips to Guinea, on one occasion bringing the Liberian President Ellen Johnson-Sirleaf with him. This proved a rather ill-timed move, for soon after a visit by Wade to Conakry, on 28 September, a massacre by the military ruined Dadis' credentials and tainted Wade in the eyes of the Guinean public. Senegalese citizens in Guinea were apparently endangered by Wade's pro-Dadis activism.

Socioeconomic Developments

The economy continued to struggle in an unfavourable global context. Economic **growth** did not pick up, standing at around only 1.2%, and the country went through a brief spell of deflation: yearly inflation settled at around –1%. While state revenues fell short, the state attempted to mitigate the damage by keeping expenditure higher than programmed. Public investment rose to 10.5% of GDP, and the budget deficit predictably increased. Taking this into account, the budget voted for 2010 was rather prudent. The pillars of the economy were unevenly affected by the global crisis. While international assistance maintained high levels, migrant remittances (which officially amount to around $ 1 bn annually) were affected. According to UNDP estimates released in June, the growth in remittances, which had slowed in 2008, might well become a drop in the course of the year. The agricultural sector had a good year, and the increase in foreign direct investment persisted.

The **energy** sector remained a major issue, as the national power company Senelec remained unable to satisfy needs. In July, it had to ask a number of industrial firms to use their own power groups to reduce the burden on the network.

In April, Wade announced a 'green revolution' and the creation of a 'green bank'. To this end, the (small) resources of the 'Caisse Nationale de Crédit Agricole du Sénégal' were augmented. Cash crop production increased as a result of good rainfall as well as support from the state and donors, although it remained unclear whether markets could absorb the production of some commercial crops, such as groundnuts. Groundnut production increased from 0.7 m tonnes in 2008 to 1.1 m tonnes in 2009, corn from 397,000 tonnes to 544,000 tonnes, millet from 678,000 tonnes to 759,000 tonnes, and rice from 408,000 tonnes to 508,000 tonnes.

Royal Air Maroc finally withdrew from the crisis-ridden 'Air Sénégal International' (ASI) **airline**, which stopped flying in April. Under Karim Wade's direction, plans were drawn up to create 'Sénégal Airlines', a new company with private capital and a state minority share (31%). Capital was raised from private investors and discussions ensued for the purchase of six Airbus planes. In the meantime, the UAE company Emirates agreed to lend two Airbuses, gaining in exchange a share of the state's participation. The company was expected to begin flying in 2010. The collapse of ASI, combined with the global economic crisis, was damaging news for the **tourist industry**, and in the first quarter the sector's turnover was 30% lower than in the same period the previous year. The crisis in Dubai called into question the capacity of Dubai Ports World to go ahead with the redevelopment of Dakar's **harbours**. Some headway was made, however, and the renovation of the old terminal and the building of a new one were due to be completed in 2011.

In the **mining industry**, news was mixed. In June, Arcelor Mittal confirmed that its $ 2 bn ore mine project in eastern Senegal was suspended, but that same month, Mineral Deposits Limited's (MDL) Sabodala mine produced its first gold ingot – yearly production was expected to be around 4.2 tonnes for the next ten years. Another project by MDL was also under way, with a CFAfr 90 bn project to exploit zircon on the coast north of Dakar. In November, Goldstone Resources received a licence for exploration in the Tambacounda region, and a Chinese company was to develop a marble-processing site in the east. Chinese investors were also prime movers in the encouraging signs of industrial development.

In November, President Wade inaugurated a bus assembly plant in Thiès. The Chinese firm King Long took it over from Indian company Tata Motors, which had run it from 2005 to 2008. That same month, agreements were signed with Chinese firms for the building of three factories (including a glass factory). Other **Chinese projects** went ahead, such as the construction of the CFAfr 190 bn Kawsara business city in Rebeuss (north Dakar).

The overall uneasy economic situation formed the background to persistent **social unrest**. People protested about living conditions, flooding in Dakar, Saint-Louis and Mbour, power cuts and rises in electricity prices. Senegalese cities went through the usual bouts of student protest. Conditions in the newly created regional universities (Thiès, Ziguinchor and Bambey) were additional causes for recurring student mobilisation. The controversy over **homosexuality** also continued, stirred up by the 'Collectif des Associations Islamiques du Sénégal', a group of reformist Muslim activists with a critical stance towards Wade, who took the opportunity to denounce the immoral leniency of the state and its submission to Western norms. On 6 January, nine gay AIDS activists were sentenced to jail terms of up to eight years for indecency, but the Court of Appeal rejected the judgment on 20 April. International opinion had been very critical, with President Sarkozy himself commenting on the issue. Homosexuals were arrested in December in Saly, but were quickly released.

Vincent Foucher

Sierra Leone

President Koroma entered his third year office and undertook some major ministerial reshuffles. The Special Court for Sierra Leone handed out long sentences to the three rebel commanders accused of war crimes and crimes against humanity, closing another chapter in the country's violent past. International donor support remained significant for the country as it emerged from a decade-long conflict which ended in 2002. The Bumbuna hydroelectric dam, under construction for over 30 years, finally started to produce electricity for the capital by the end of the year.

Domestic Politics

The year started with a number of **cabinet changes**. At the end of February, a major and long-awaited ministerial reshuffle was announced by President Ernest Bai Koroma and the changes were approved by parliament on 17 March. There were a number of new appointments: Dr Dennis Sandy was appointed minister of lands, country planning and the environment, replacing donor favourite Benjamin O. Davies; and Dr Samura Kamara – the former governor of the central bank – became minister of finance and economic development. This was the third change in a short period of time within this ministry: David Carew, the previous minister of finance, took the post from Afsatu Kabba, who was implicated by the Anti-Corruption Commission (ACC) in a dubious energy contract. Curiously, Kabba was then appointed minister of marine resources and fisheries, leaving some to question how forcefully Koroma was pursuing his fight against corruption. Prof. Ogunlade Robert Davidson was appointed minister of energy and power, while Allieu Pat Sowe became minister of transport and aviation. Mines and mineral resources minister Abubakar Jalloh lost his ministry because the president considered that he had underperformed: the ministry kept its reputation for corruption and a promised review of existing contracts did not materialise. Jalloh was replaced by Alpha Kanu, Koroma's close aide during the 2007 presidential election campaign. Minister of trade and industry Alimamy Koroma (not related to the president) moved to housing and infrastructure. His ministry was taken over by David Carew, the former finance minister and former partner in the accountancy firm KPMG.

During the All Peoples Congress (APC) **party convention** held on 16–18 April in the northern town of Makeni, Koroma was re-elected as national leader and party chairman. His supporters were able to persuade the party to defer the party leadership contest until a year after the next elections, scheduled for 2012. Chukuma Johnson was elected deputy leader of the party. John Benjamin, recently elected leader of the opposition Sierra Leone Peoples Party (SLPP), addressed the APC convention to show his commitment to stability and peace.

On 4 November, President Koroma, whose victory in the 2007 presidential elections was partly based on his promise to stamp out **corruption**, sacked minister of health and sanitation Sheku Tejan Koroma and minister of state in the vice president's office, Leonard Balogun Koroma (not related to the president), who was replaced by Dr Komba Kono. On the same day that Sheku Tejan Koroma was dismissed, he appeared in court on three charges of abuse of office and financial mismanagement brought against him by the ACC. Other major cases for the ACC – still part of the ministry of justice – included the prosecution of the former executive director of the Sierra Leone Road Transport Authority, Sarian Finda Bendu and the managing director of the Mabela Industry Ltd, Amza Alusine Sesay. By half way through the year, the ACC had recovered 1.1 bn leones (approximately $ 330,000), about 30% more than the total amount recovered in 2008. The ACC focused resolutely on limiting the plague of 'ghost-workers' in the education and health sector. In another move to stimulate people to step forward with cases of (suspected) fraud and corruption, the ACC offered 10% of the proceeds to whistle-blowers. Nevertheless, corruption remained a highly sensitive issue. In September, police in the western town of Rotifunk shot a number of youths who were protesting against police corruption. According to a government's spokesman, three died and 11 were wounded, but witnesses claimed that far more people were injured. In November, at a Trade and Investment forum in London, Ireland pledged € 200,000 to the ACC to support its activities.

On 25 February, the **Special Court for Sierra Leone** handed down its third collective judgement. Issa Hassan Sesay, Moris Kallon and Augustine Gbao, the three most senior surviving commanders of the Revolutionary United Front (RUF) were found guilty on most of the 18 counts of war crimes and crimes against humanity. On 8 April, the Court announced the prison sentences: 52 years for Sesay (guilty on 16 counts); 40 years for Kallon (guilty on 16 counts); and 25 years for Gbao (guilty on 14 counts). Previously, three senior commanders of the Armed Forces Revolutionary Council (AFRC) had been sentenced to nearly 50 years in prison, while three senior figures in the Civil Defence Forces (CDF) were sentenced to 15–20 years. The trial of former Liberian dictator Charles Taylor, who is charged with aiding the RUF and the AFRC and 11 counts of war crimes and crimes against humanity continued throughout the year; it is convened in The Hague for security reasons. However, international human rights monitors warned early in the year that, unless the more than $ 5 m shortfall in funding for the Court were addressed – the Court being dependent on donations, there was a risk that Taylor would have to be released. Within two months, the Court received $ 6.5 m of the $ 28 m needed in total for 2009. On 14 July, after the prosecution presented 91 witnesses, the defence started to present its case, denying all charges. The United Kingdom (UK) had already given assurances that, if found guilty, Taylor could serve his prison sentence in Britain. The CDF, RUF and AFRC convicts were transferred to Rwanda on 30 October to serve their sentences in Mpanga Prison, following an agreement between the Court and the Rwandan government. No prison in Sierra Leone met the required international standards, reflecting the dire state of the judicial system. The international Centre for Transitional Justice estimated that about $ 23 m was spent on the case of each Special Court defendant.

In addition to the Special Court, Sierra Leone established a Truth and Reconciliation Commission to deal with the history of the armed conflict. Among its recommendations to the government were **reparation payments** to victims, which began to be made in the course of the year. The National Commission for Social Action took charge of a reparations programme. This year, $ 3 m was received from the UN Peace Building Fund as a start-up fund, with the Sierra Leonean government also contributing. By the end of the year the programme had registered nearly 30,000 applications.

In mid-March, five days of **fighting** – the worst since the 2007 election violence – between APC and SLPP supporters left dozens wounded, three women allegedly raped and the SLPP headquarters ransacked. Cars were burned, including those of the newly elected SLPP Chairman John Oponjo Benjamin, who had been secretary general under the wartime National Provisional Ruling Council military regime (1992–96), which had deposed the APC government and that of SLPP Secretary General Jacob Jusu Saffa. The direct cause was the unveiling of the restored clock-tower in eastern Freetown. SLPP supporters accused the Freetown City Council of corruption and of not respecting the original stone-built base of the clock-tower, which was now fully covered with white marble tiles. The conflict escalated rapidly, in part because of the employment of large groups of youths (including many ex-combatants) by both political parties as so-called youth protection squads. Michael von der Schulenburg – the recently appointed executive representative for the UN Integrated Peacebuilding Office in Sierra Leone – and his aides rescued about 20 people who were trapped on the roof of the SLPP office when an angry mop in the street below attacked the building. Police dispersed the crowds with tear gas.

Foreign Affairs

Following the provisional approval of an **ECOWAS** Standby Force Main Brigade by West African Defence Chiefs at a meeting in Ouagadougou on 11 June, its creation was later fully endorsed during a meeting in Freetown held on 9–12 December. This initiative further underscored the sub-regional stand on the threat of armed conflicts and violence and the risk of the West African coast becoming a zone for international drug traffickers. In November, ECOWAS provided $ 2 m for the commencement of a regional logistics depot in Sierra Leone as part of the sub-regional body's Peace Support Operations programme.

Following an announcement on 12 July by **Guinea**'s junta leader, Capt. Moussa Dadis Camara, that his country was facing the threat of an armed attack by mercenaries funded by drug cartels, President Koroma, who was in Conakry at the time for a Mano River Union working visit, announced that not an inch of Sierra Leonean territory would be used to destabilise another country in the region. On 21 December, 53 (of a projected total of about 130) well-equipped Sierra Leonean **peacekeepers** arrived in southern Darfur to join the AU-UN mission. The government would receive more than $ 1,000 a month for each blue helmet.

Socioeconomic Developments

Despite the global economic downturn (resulting in a fall in mining revenues, particularly from the diamond and bauxite sector), economic **growth** was still estimated to be around 5.5% to 6% (with real GDP growth put at around 4%). This was about 1% less than the growth figure for the previous year. The next step would be to translate these growth figures into job creation, particularly for the young. According to President Koroma's 2008 Agenda for Change, youth **unemployment** – estimated to be around 70% – was considered to be one of the three most significant security risks, together with drug trafficking and corruption. Over 200,000 jobs each year would have to be created to satisfy demand. Inflation was expected to fall to just under 10%, down from 13.4% in 2008.

The reduction of **inflation** to a single digit is one of a number of criteria put in place by the members of the West African Monetary Zone to enable a single currency, the Eco, to take off. The new launch date was now postponed until June 2014.

In the **mining sector**, gold production boomed, in contrast to diamonds and bauxite. Up to June, Sierra Gold Corporation increased its production to a level equal to more than 75% of the entire production of the previous year. In May alone, 75 troy ounces of gold were mined. Artisanal diamond mining employed an estimated 100,000 people and was, according to the World Bank, the country's second-biggest employer, after subsistence farming. The government's focus has traditionally been on the foreign-owned industrial mining sector, leading to a loss of the tax revenue that could be generated by the artisanal mining sector. It was estimated that the government received 0.65% instead of a potential 3% in royalties from the labour-intensive artisanal mining sector, with most diamonds being smuggled to neighbouring countries. Formulating community development rules to increase benefits for local communities was just one of the aims of the new Mines and Minerals Act 2009. The Act, which was passed by parliament in November, required provisions for health and safety and environmental protection. Licence holders failing to meet the requirements would have one year to comply and commence operations or lose their rights. The act was intended to prepare the country for membership of the international Extractive Industries Transparency Initiative. The act also stipulated an increase of government royalties in diamond production (from 3% to 6.5%, plus a 15% tax on the most valuable diamonds) and for precious metals (from 4% to 5%), while it was to remain at 3% for all other minerals.

The **agricultural sector** is responsible for about half of GDP (estimated at $ 1.7 bn), although the country was still not capable of producing more than two-thirds of its requirements for rice, its staple food. A grant worth $ 40 m from the International Development Fund for Agricultural Development, promised at a forum in London in November, may have some positive effects on agricultural production.

The country made improvements with regard to the business environment. According to the World Bank's annual survey, the country ranked 148 out of 183 economies, an improvement of eight places compared with 2008. Between 24 March and 7 April, an **IMF** mission visited the country to conduct discussions for the fourth review under the PRGF arrangement. By the end of December 2008, all performance indicators had been met, with the exception of the government domestic revenue target. This was to be partly addressed through a $ 15 m AfDB/ADF grant awarded in May under the Supplemental Support Window of the Fragile States Facility. The grant will finance the country's Economic Governance Reform Programme (I), aimed at the improvement of economic governance through greater transparency, accountability and efficiency in the use of public resources. A $ 20 m IDA **credit**, agreed in October, was also aimed at supporting decentralised delivery of basic services, among other things. In June, the IMF completed the fourth review, which paved the way for a disbursement of nearly $ 19 m. The UK promised to increase its support from £ 40 m in 2008 to £ 50 m in 2010. The UN Peacebuilding Commission promised to put another $ 35 m in the country.

Commitment by international **donors** to the country's second PRSP was still strong. The second PRSP required nearly $ 2 bn and would be running until 2012. This year, donors supplied nearly half of the government's budget and about 12% of GDP. The $ 200 m in foreign reserves would serve the country's import needs for a maximum of four months. In September, however, the IMF allocated the country Special Drawing Rights equivalent to nearly $ 130 m, which boosted its international reserves significantly. On 21 January the Board of Directors of the AfDB agreed in Tunis that Sierra Leone had qualified for $ 112 m worth of assistance under the Fragile States Facility programme. $ 41 m of the total amount was allocated for water supply and sanitation projects aimed at providing rural areas with drinking water and sanitation facilities.

The capital Freetown would also be benefiting from improvements in this area. $ 39 m was earmarked for upgrading 65 km of road between Port Loko and Lungi, thus improving the connection between Lungi international **airport** and the rest of the country. Currently, only 8% of the roads in the country are paved. To further enhance Lungi airport, the Investment Climate Facility for Africa announced on 3 April that it would support a two-year airport transfer project. In collaboration with the government, the project was planned to improve the IT and office infrastructure, improve terminal and jetties facilities and set up an Airport Transfer Unit to monitor transfers to and from the airport. Prior to the war, more than 70,000 **tourists** visited Sierra Leone every year, but in 2009 the number did not even reach 5,000. On 15 July, the European Commission published its 11th blacklist of national airline companies banned from flying to Europe, with Sierra Leone as one of the countries concerned. Tellingly, British former Prime Minister Tony Blair, whose African Governance Initiative has nine advisors in the country, and rock star campaigner Bob Geldof did not use a Sierra Leone registered plane when they arrived in the country on 28 April with a portfolio of proposals to promote tourism. The potentials of tourism were also discussed by President Koroma and philanthropist George Soros.

Soros' Economic Development Fund was already supporting BRAC (Bangladesh Rural Advancement Committee – now international), a non-governmental micro-finance organisation, which started lending in rural Sierra Leone in June. Towards the end of the year, a UK development financing group launched a private equity **investment** in the country worth $ 5 m. The so-called Sierra Investment Fund would provide funding to small and medium-sized companies and was the first of its kind in the country. At a Trade and Investment forum held in London in November, Finance and Economic Development Minister Dr Samura Kamara told donors that the country needed about $ 900 m to implement President Koroma's Agenda for Change. Contributions were pledged by various countries.

The dire medical situation was again brought into the spotlight by the WHO. In February, ministry of **health** figures showed that there were only 75 state medical doctors for a population of more than 5.5 m. Even with the country's additional 23 public health workers and 25 medical specialists, the nation's requirements for medical care could not be met. As a short term measure, the government made a request for 110 doctors from countries such as Cuba, Sudan, Egypt and Nigeria. Some of these health specialists would without doubt be confronted with the health implications of **female genital mutilation** (FGM). FGM remained a taboo. Back in 2002, the incumbent President Kabbah refused to speak out against it ahead of the presidential elections. Seven years later, in February, four female journalists who reported on a campaign against FGM were attacked and marched naked through the centre of Kenema by angry crowds.

In July, Indian engineers started an 18-month project to improve **telecommunications**. The improvements would allow the creation of a tele-medicine project, linking the city's main hospital to India, as part of a medical exchange programme. Once completed, the improved telecommunication facilities will also allow universities and colleges in Freetown to have online access to courses in other African nations and in India.

Serious **flooding** in Freetown, following heavy rains, killed dozens of people. Most died in the so-called green belt zones (undeveloped land), where slum dwellers have built their house. In the north of the country, the Bumbuna hydro-dam started to produce **electricity**. After being under construction for 30 years, the power plant – with a capacity of 50 MW – was finally switched on by President Koroma at the beginning of November. It started to supply energy to the capital – which has an energy consumption of around 100 MW – saving about $ 2 m per month on diesel imports for the city's large generators. However, another $ 400 m was needed to complete the Bumbuna Hydro project and increase production to 300 MW. DFID promised to put £ 50 m into a World Bank trust fund over a five year period. The money was to be used to increase access to electricity beyond Freetown.

Krijn Peters

Togo

Domestic politics was dominated by preparations for the decisive 2010 presidential elections and by the escalation of a feud within the ruling Gnassingbé clan, which culminated in April in an alleged plot to stage a coup, led by Kpatcha Gnassingbé, the younger half-brother of the head of state. It was claimed that the alleged plot also involved other members of the family, who were still in detention without official arraignment at the end of the year. The international donor community rewarded political reforms. Economic growth was negatively affected by the global economic and financial crisis.

Domestic Politics

At the start of the year, Togo's political heavyweights were keen to take a lead position in the race for the decisive **presidential elections** scheduled for early 2010. The upcoming elections were considered a litmus test of the sincerity of the regime's commitment to democratisation. The rigged presidential elections of 2005 had brought acting President Faure Gnassingbé to power by means of a constitutional coup and massive repression, accompanied by widespread violence and the displacement of some 40,000 political refugees. In a barely disguised pre-election campaign, the head of state and leader of the ruling 'Rassemblement du Peuple Togolais' (RPT) travelled the country in January and tried to gain the support, including that of the traditional chiefs. Following his father's example, he announced in a meeting of 329 district chiefs at Kara on 29 January the doubling of the annual allowances for these influential 'guardians of customary law', a decision widely applauded.

However, Gilchrist Olympio, the head of the main opposition party, the 'Union des Forces du Changement' (UFC), also expected to increase his chances of winning the race. Unlike the parliamentary polls of 2007, each vote in the presidentials will have equal weight, thus not favouring the RTP in their sparsely populated northern strongholds. The latter were lost by the opposition in the legislative elections mainly because of the then newly introduced **voting system** of proportional representation, with medium and small constituencies tailored to meet the interests of the ruling party. Thus, the opposition coalition of the UFC and the 'Comité d'Action pour le Renouveau' (CAR), which came first in 2007 with 45% of the votes (made up of UFC 37% and CAR 8%, compared with 39% for the RPT), will stand a good chance of winning, provided they rally behind a single candidate. In January, both opposition parties agreed in principle to back a common candidate, as in 2005, when, however, Olympio was barred from taking part. The RPT parliamentary majority had effected changes in the constitution of 2002 and in the electoral code of 2005 in order to prevent a show-down between Gnassingbé's clan and his major adversary, the son of the first Togolese president Sylvanus Olympio, allegedly assassinated by Eyadéma Gnassingbé in 1963. In February the parties involved started to negotiate the removal of the strict residence and single nationality requirements from the electoral code, which had barred the head of the UFC and other opposition aspirants from standing as presidential candidates.

A dialogue forum called the 'Cadre Permanent de Dialogue et Concertation' (CPDC), created in 2006 to bridge the long-standing cleavages between government, ruling party and opposition, met again on 4 February to resolve this and other controversial issues. However, this was of little avail in view of the CPDC's domination by the ruling party. Negotiations ended in a stalemate after a month of fruitless haggling, but after considerable donor pressure the opposing parties finally arrived at a partial consensus mediated by the president of Burkina Faso. The controversial appointment of Henri Kolani as head of the new 'Commission Electorale Nationale Indépendante' (CENI) was revoked in favour of the independent candidate Issifou Taffa Tabiou, and on 8 August a **new electoral code** was presented in Ouagadougou. The Togolese parliament unanimously adopted the code two weeks later (21 August), opening the way for Gilchrist Olympio to stand as a presidential candidate.

The electoral code allowed the creation of a new electoral commission with a more balanced membership. Its 17 members, sworn in on 1 September, quickly announced the calendar for the upcoming elections to be held on 28 February 2010. The schedule included the crucial revision of the chronically deficient **electoral register** (delayed by one month to 10 January 2010 because of the quarrel about the new CENI chief). However, there was still one lingering controversy, which was still not resolved at year's end, not least because the opposition put it on the agenda rather late. According to an amendment of the 1992 constitution, pushed through by the RPT majority in 2002, the presidential election was to be held in one single round, contrary to internationally recognised standards that favour two rounds in order to give the opposition the chance to unite behind a single candidate in the run-off. The major opposition parties repeatedly issued threats to boycott the elections, but to no avail.

This led to disagreement between opposition parties over a common candidate, thereby reducing their chances of beating the ruling RPT. The CAR declared on 21 October that it would not accept the candidature of G. Olympio, who – although an experienced and charismatic politician – was said to polarise politics through his hostile relations with the Gnassingbé clan. The latter were responsible not only for the murder of Olympio's father, but also for the attempted assassination of the leader of the UFC himself during an election campaign in northern Togo in 1992, when 12 members of his staff were killed. In the autumn, other **opposition leaders** announced their intention to stand, including Kofi Yamgnane. He is a Togolese citizen born in Bassar, northern Togo, who lives in France, where – because of his political career as the first African migrant to become a mayor in France and later secretary of state for social affairs under President Mitterrand (1991–93) – he seemed to be the favourite presidential candidate of the Quai d'Orsay. At about the same time, veteran opposition leader Léopold Gnininvi of the 'Convention Démocratique des Peuples Africains', the only remaining opposition member in the cabinet, resigned from his post as minister of state for industry and health in order to be able to stand for president, as he had done in 1998.

The split among the opposition was more than matched by the long-standing and hostile feud within the ruling **Gnassingbé clan**, where so-called modernisers and conservative hardliners intent on preserving the prerogatives of the Eyadéma regime oppose each other. On 12 April, as the president was about to leave for a tour of China, his most powerful younger half-brother Kpatcha Gnassingbé, who had been deposed as defence minister the previous year, allegedly plotted a **coup**. According to the government, a foreign intelligence service (not publicly named) alerted the president in advance. A night-time **shoot-out** ensued at Kpatcha's residence in Lomé between his bodyguards and the Rapid Intervention Force, under the command of Colonel Abalo F. Kadanga, an Ewe from Atakpamé whose wife was from the Eyadéma family, who remained loyal to the president. Several of Kpatcha's guards were killed. The armed intervention of another half-brother of the president, lieutenant-colonel Rock Gnassingbé, commander of a reconnaissance tank regiment close to Kpatcha, saved him, but only temporarily. As Kpatcha sought asylum at the gates of the US embassy three days later, he was arrested along with two other family members (Essolizam, a third brother, and Captain Bagou-Badgi Gnassingbé, a cousin of the president) and other presumed coup plotters (18 soldiers and ten civilians).

That same day they were charged by public prosecutor Robert Bakaï with fomenting rebellion and undermining state security. Kpatcha and others denied the accusation, claiming to be victims of a conspiracy to sideline them in the context of the ongoing power struggle. Even within the opposition there were concerns that the coup plot was not genuine and that basic human rights of the accused to a fair trial had been violated. Although army chief of staff General Zakari Nandja had remained loyal to the president, he was removed and offered the newly created post of minister for water and sanitation, and General Essofa Ayeva, former chief of staff in the president's office, succeeded him. Other high ranking officers, as well as the secretary general of the RPT, publicly announced their support for the government, but the **cracks in the ruling elite**, composed of the Gnassingbé family, the RPT and the security services, became apparent once more, posing a serious threat to the transition process. It could not be ruled out that hardliners would derail the ongoing democratisation process if they foresaw defeat in the upcoming polls.

Faure Gnassingbé took the precaution of creating a special 'Force Sécurité Election Présidentielle 2010' in order to have at his disposal a **personal military force** separate from the army, which could be crucial if a conflict broke out between the modernisers and hardliners. Its official task was to "guarantee security before, during and after the elections". As head of this force, he nominated the chief of the Gendarmerie National, Lieutenant-Colonel Yark Damehane. The latter was notorious for his involvement in the brutal repression of opponents during the 2005 presidential elections, figuring on the index of a UN report on human rights violations in Togo.

On 12 November Ernest Gnassingbé, eldest son of Eyadéma and a hardliner, died. He had been commander of the 'red berets' parachute battalion of Camp Landja (Kara), renowned for its brutalities in the transition process in the early 1990s, when it was involved in extra-legal killings of opposition leaders and the attempted assassination of Gilchrist Olympio and his entourage. The **burial** of Ernest in Pya, the home village of the Gnassingbé family, in the absence of detained members such as Kpatcha Gnassingbé and the other assumed coup plotters again highlighted the deep division within the clan.

The **human rights** situation improved further. On 23 June parliament voted unanimously for the abolition of the death penalty. Togo thus became the 15th member state of the AU and the 94th country worldwide to renounce the death penalty for all crimes. However, the bill was rather symbolic since in practice legal executions had ceased 30 year earlier. The thorny problem that remained was the extra-legal killings committed or condoned by the state in the course of political persecution. A technical team, supported by the UNHCR, toured the country from March to July to gather opinions on human rights violations in the past. A truth and reconciliation commission ('Commission

Vérité, Justice et Réconciliation', CVJR) was established on 29 May. Meant to investigate human rights violations from 1958 up to the bloody persecutions of 2005, it proved to be a paper tiger right from the start as the CVJR had neither the power to lift the immunity from prosecution of perpetrators of human right violations, nor the ability to offer amnesty or reparations – tasks that remained prerogatives of the state. The CVJR's 11 members represented different groups of civil society (excluding political parties) and notably involved religious leaders. In early December its president, Mgr. Nicodème A. Barrigah, Catholic bishop of Atakpamé, announced the suspension of the commission's hearings till further notice in order that it should not be accused of interference in election politics.

Foreign Affairs

On 13 March **France** and Togo signed a new defence and security agreement. It followed the policy announced the year before by French President Sarkozy of a 'rupture' with the past. It was also meant to stop the practice of inserting secret clauses permitting France to intervene to support the incumbent regime, as stipulated in the defence pacts of 1958 and 1963. The new military cooperation focused on training, equipment and support of UN and AU peacekeeping operations. In addition, in October Paris cancelled Togo's bilateral trade finance debts ($ 104 m). On 7 December, however, the traditionally close ties between Paris and Lomé temporarily came under pressure when Foreign Affairs Minister Koffi Esaw expelled a high ranking French diplomat – the first time this had occurred since independence. Éric Bosc, first secretary of the embassy, was accused of interference in internal affairs, more particularly of backing Kofi Yamgnane, who was put forward as a Francophile politician of dual nationality (French and Togolese), born in Bassar (northern Togo), and considered a rival candidate to the president, whose power base is also in the north. Following the usual diplomatic tit for tat, Paris retaliated by expelling a Togolese diplomat.

A five-day state visit by the president to **Germany** on 16 to 21 June heralded a new chapter in German-Togolese relations. Chancellor Angela Merkel praised Togo's political reforms. On 12 March the German ambassador to Togo had announced the cancellation of bilateral debt to the tune of € 18 m within the HIPC framework and the Paris Club negotiations.

The outgoing head of the **EU** commission's delegation in Togo, Filiberto Sebregondi, commended democratic efforts and the spirit of dialogue between political actors. The new head of the EU in Lomé, Patrick Spirlet, made it clear in December that the EU would remain neutral on the issue of one-round elections because it considered this to be an internal matter. On 3 December the **UN** Human Rights Office Togo, established in 2006 in the wake of the 2005 elections, announced its strategy to contribute to peaceful elections. This included training programs for the security forces and the installation of election monitoring centres all over the country. Already beforehand, in early November the UN office had already started a training programme for 960 young 'promoters of non-violence' in the Kara region (home of the Gnassingbé clan), whose task was to propagate respect for human rights during the election period.

China and Togo once more pledged to enhance their cooperation, including upgrading relations between the two militaries, during a six-day visit to China by army chief Essofa Ayeva at the invitation of his Chinese counterpart, chief of the General Staff of the People's Liberation Army Chen Bingde (15 November). In early November the minister of economics and finance, Adji Othèth Ayassor, signed a loan agreement with the China Exim Bank worth $ 165 m to be paid back in 20 years (with a seven-year grace period) allocated to the building and renovation of road infrastructure in Lomé (a dual-carriage ring-road connecting the harbour with the Ghanaian border and the national motorway to the north). The works would be carried out by the China Road and Bridge Corporation, which had already built the bridges of Togblékopé, Iilikopé and Amakpapé. In March it was announced that a China parastatal, Sinohydro, had won a $ 282 m construction contract for the 96 MW Adjarala dam, the second largest dam on the Mono River, jointly owned by Togo and Benin. The China Exim Bank had pledged $ 24 m to contribute to the financing of the dam in exchange for supply contracts. International rights organisations cautioned against the negative impacts of the project, including the displacement of over 8,000 people (75%–25% in Togo and Benin respectively) and increased coastal erosion.

Early in September the president paid a two-day visit to **Ghana**. His counterpart, John Atta Mills, promised to assist Togo in the conduct of the elections, citing Ghana's proven record as a model for democratic elections in West Africa. This indicated an improvement in bilateral ties, which had been particularly strained in the era of Atta Mills' mentor, Jerry Rawlings. In December 2008 the latter had accused Lomé of interference in the Ghanaian presidential elections. By contrast, relations with **Burkina Faso** continued to be excellent. On 28 July Burkina's president, Blaise Compaoré, visited Lomé in the course of his efforts to mediate between Togo's government and opposition. Relations with other neighbouring states also improved. On 29 December six West African countries (Benin, Burkina Faso, Côte d'Ivoire, Ghana, Mali, Togo) met in Lomé to ratify the **Volta basin charter**, which envisaged the sharing and development of the water resources of the Volta in order to reduce potential environmental and socioeconomic problems with transnational implications and to avoid potential conflicts over the use of the basin's resources. In August, Faure Gnassingbé participated in a special AU summit on conflict settlement in Tripoli, after attending the celebrations of the 40th anniversary of the Libyan revolution. Kadhafi – an old friend of the Eyadéma family – had already tried in vain to mediate in the row between Kpatcha and Faure Gnassingbé.

Socioeconomic Developments

Economic **growth** was influenced by the global economic downturn, which caused exports, remittances and investment to diminish. Real GDP grew by about 1.8%, while inflation was down to 2.1%. Specially affected were so-called re-exports, which constitute more than one-third of total exports because of the country's position as a transit hub. However, **cotton** production, a major export earner, also declined – by 25%, to an historic low of 30,000 tonnes. Stagnant farm gate prices and unfavourable weather made farmers reluctant to plant: acreage plunged by 23% to 42,579 ha. The impact was especially felt by the rural poor. Togo ranked 144th out of 160 countries worldwide on a listing of the Economist Intelligence Unit. Nevertheless, the donor community was satisfied with **economic policy** as the government honoured its obligations under the PRGF (April 2008 to April 2011). In its third review (November) an IMF mission reported that the country was on track and so the IMF released a further $ 14 m, increasing its PRGF loans to $ 93 m out of a total of $ 141 m earmarked for the whole three-year period. Other donor missions followed suit. Remarkably, in November the EU granted unconditional budgetary aid to the value of $ 22 m. Overall, donor funding of the budget was estimated to rise from 2.2% of GDP in 2009 to 4.3% in 2010. Donors accepted the estimated budget deficit of 2.9% of GDP in 2009 in view of the country's overall compliance record.

The government pledged to invest $ 178 m for a second **'green revolution'** with a view to boosting the income of the agricultural working population (4 million according to the 2006 census). Donors were reminded at a meeting in Kara on 30 January to honour their pledges and they agreed to provide $ 57 m in 2009 with a focus on boosting cocoa, coffee, fish and rice production. During the official launch of a rice-rehabilitation programme in the Zio river valley (35 km north of Lomé) on 26 August, the minister for agriculture, K.M. Ewovor, announced that the programme was aimed at boosting domestic rice production from 27,000 to 52,000 tonnes. Whether such an ambitious agenda would work was doubtful in view of the failure of the first 'green revolution' in the 1970s and 80s.

Other ambitious plans involved the revitalisation of the moribund **phosphate** sector, still the fifth-largest in Africa. The government aimed to attract $ 193 m over the next five years in order to rehabilitate machinery and infrastructure, open new mines and build a phosphoric acid plant that could increase the added value of phosphate exports. Although phosphate production and export earnings rose by an estimated 7% in 2008 to 842,000 tonnes, they remained at a low level when compared with the peak of 3 m tonnes in the mid 1990s. In January 600 workers had to be laid off. In view of past experience with corruption, nepotism and the inefficiency of the parastatal 'Société Nouvelle des Phosphates du Togo' and its predecessors, the key challenge remained the search for private investors, especially since the failure of the public-private partnership with Brifco (Tunisia) in 2005.

In the autumn about one-third of **mobile phone** users were deprived of a functioning network because of a quarrel between the ministry of post and telecommunication and the private operator Moov (Atlantic Telecom) over licence payments and free international access. Moov, which had attracted about 600,000 subscribers since its entry to the market in 2006, had become a tough competitor for Togocel, a subsidiary of state-owned Togo Telecom.

In January construction work started on the new 110 MW **power plant** in Lomé, built and managed by the US group, Contour Global. It was meant to start production in 2010, powered by Nigerian gas via the West African Gas Pipeline, and would put an end to the chronic power cuts in the capital.

Dirk Kohnert

V. Central Africa

The global financial crisis particularly affected oil-producing countries of the sub-region, but largely spared those without notable incomes from the oil sector (Central African Republic, DR Congo). In general, the sub-region proved less vulnerable than feared because of its weak integration in the global economy. A relative decline in armed encounters between government troops and rebel movements was noted and some glimmers of hope for more peace were recorded. Indeed, the prospects for peace in eastern Congo were better than they had been for 15 years after the formation of an alliance between Kigali and Kinshasa to neutralise both Laurent Nkunda's wing of the 'Conseil National pour la Défense du Peuple' (CNDP) and the 'Forces Démocratiques pour la Libération du

Rwanda' (FDLR) rebels, who fought against the respective regimes. However, the security situation in Chad and Central African Republic remained volatile despite continued international engagement, including the deployment of peacekeepers. The Copenhagen conference on climate change urged decision-makers in the region to better coordinate positions on shared interests. With the death of Omar Bongo Ondimba, Gabon's president, the single most active player in international relations from the sub-region suddenly disappeared. The consequences were mixed: while concerns were raised about the lack of suitable mediators in some of Africa's violent conflicts (even beyond the sub-region), it also permitted an acceleration of necessary reforms within sub-regional organisations dominated by Gabon.

Democracy and Elections

National elections were held in three of the eight countries. The death of Omar Bongo necessitated early elections in **Gabon**. Surprisingly, his son Ali won comfortably with 41.7% of the vote. After he managed to become the candidate of the ruling 'Parti Démocratique Gabonais' (PDG), most observers presented him as the likely winner by a small margin, but his main challengers, Pierre Mamboundou and André Mba Obame, unexpectedly received only 25–26% of the vote each. The electoral legislation fixed a single round of voting, and so a relative majority was sufficient to win. Only comparatively small and symbolic observer missions under the auspices of the AU (35 members), OIF (5) and CEEAC came to Gabon and issued mostly reassuring statements, pointing to a couple of technical problems. People were killed during post-election riots, although numbers of casualties varied between sources, with the government admitting just three deaths. The PDG had won nearly a three-quarters majority in senatorial elections already held on 18 January (75 out of 102 seats), but those were indirect elections by municipal councils and departmental assemblies, making it difficult to judge whether the party enjoyed a much higher popular legitimacy than its new strongman. More solidly established were the 'electoral autocracies' in both **Congo** and **Equatorial Guinea**. Denis Sassou Nguesso and Obiang Nguema had no serious challengers at all in their respective elections, receiving 78.6% and 95.8% of the vote respectively, and observers found little interest in those polls. Local observers mainly deployed in Brazzaville noted a low participation rate, in contrast to the official 66% turnout in the Congolese elections, and a number of organisational shortcomings. From unreliable voter registers to unfair media coverage over the sabotage of opposition rallies, the authorities made sure that the presidential elections in Equatorial Guinea would not – even approximately – look like a democratic process. Upcoming elections in 2010 or 2011 already cast their shadows on the political game in Cameroon, CAR, Chad, DRC and São Tomé and Príncipe, with incumbents invariably preparing for re-election.

Human Rights

Evidence from various government and NGO reports showed that serious human rights violations were committed in the entire sub-region, with one notable exception: in São Tomé and Príncipe there was nothing to report. In contrast, **Chad** and DR Congo were almost invariably characterised in the worst terms by a variety of sources. This was linked to on-going violent conflicts in both countries, as was already evident from the title of AI's report "No place for us here. Violence against refugee women in eastern Chad", which covered the hopeless situation of endless victims exposed to all sorts of threats, including rape and forced marriage. Similarly, HRW focused on IDPs, but particularly those who tried to re-establish themselves in the country (report entitled "The risk of return"). The majority of refugees preferred to stay in their displacement sites than risk their lives in the perpetually unsafe countryside. Both reports implicitly questioned the success of the EUFOR and MINURCAT missions, which focused specifically on the security of refugees and internally displaced people in Chad (and Central African Republic), but were not able to secure return areas. Both asked for a full and more rapid deployment of the MINURCAT mission. The 'Fédération Internationale des Droits de l'Homme' (FIDH) issued a report on the increasingly authoritarian behaviour of the regime in **DR Congo**. Its report ("La dérive autoritaire du régime") listed a series of actions restricting civil rights and liberties. Dissident voices were suppressed, judicial organs tightly controlled and the security forces given complete freedom of action. Human rights campaigners were also interested in the impact on the ground of the trial of Congolese warlord Thomas Lubanga before the ICC. Intimidation of witnesses was particularly feared. US human rights campaigners used Secretary of State Hillary Clinton's Africa visit in August to launch a series of reports and appeals, not least on the Democratic Republic of the Congo. The Committee to Protect Journalists had singled out the country as the scene of some of the worst cases of intimidation and attacks on press freedom on the continent.

Cameroon earned an AI report ("Impunity underpins persistent abuse"), although the organisation continued to be prohibited from entering the country. The report listed the main human rights violations over the preceding years, with specific focus on the response to the 2008 riots. FIDH was most concerned by acts of intimidation against journalists and human rights campaigners in Cameroon. In **CAR**, FIDH expressed concern that the death of human rights campaigner Goungaye Wanfiyo, who died in a suspicious car accident on 27 December 2008, was not appropriately investigated. Serious human rights violations were committed by the government army and rebel movements during their sporadic fighting in the north-east of the country. In **Equatorial Guinea**, nine opposition politicians (plus a number of Nigerian fishermen) were detained and some of them allegedly tortured after the February attack on the presidential palace. President Obiang had publicly hinted at the potential collaboration of nationals with the attackers.

Charges against former DRC vice president, Jean-Pierre Bemba, were mostly confirmed by the **ICC** on 15 June. The pre-trial hearing confirmed two counts of crimes against humanity (rape and murder) and three counts of war crimes (rape, murder and pillage), but rejected the counts of torture and outrages against personal dignity as crimes against humanity and/or war crimes (as originally requested by the prosecution). The beginning of the trial was set for July 2010. Taking its cue from this decision, FIDH reiterated the call for more indictments of those presumably responsible for crimes against humanity in CAR, including former president Patassé, current president Bozizé and rebel leader Abdoulaye Miskine. On 26 January, the ICC had already opened its first trial in the case against Congolese warlord Thomas Lubanga (see above) and proceedings took place throughout the year.

Instability, War and Peace

CAR continued to have its usual share of instability, with several attacks by rebel movements (or splinter groups thereof) in the northern and eastern border zones. This was arguably linked to frustrations with the at best lukewarm implementation of the results from both the peace and the dialogue processes conducted in 2008. Fighters of the Lord's Resistance Army (of Ugandan origin) terrorised villages in the south-eastern part of the country and provoked the intervention of Ugandan government forces with the explicit permission of Bangui; results were unconvincing. The situation in neighbouring **Chad** eased only gradually. On 4 May, Chadian rebel groups launched an attack from Sudan on Goz Beida. The army conducted air strikes against the rebel columns and engaged in a fierce battle on 7 May, pushing back the attackers. Tensions between Chad and Sudan remained high, with Chadian aircraft dropping bombs on locations in west Darfur. The transfer of responsibility from the EU peacekeeping mission operating in both countries to a UN mission worked more or less as scheduled. The peace process in eastern DR Congo made clear progress after the harmonisation of views in Kigali and Kinshasa on both the sidelining of rebel leader Laurent Nkunda (CNDP) and the disarmament of FDLR rebels. Joint Congolese-Rwandan operations against the FDLR led to only a few direct clashes in north Kivu, as the FDLR retreated most of the time. At a second stage, the UN peacekeeping mission MONUC entered the action. Civilians paid a high price, with more than 100,000 people displaced by mid-year and an estimated 125 civilians killed in north Kivu during the latter operation alone. Clashes in Goma between the two main CNDP factions were reported in June.

A surprise maritime attack on **Equatorial Guinea**'s capital, Malabo, by a group of Nigerian gunmen, allegedly linked to the sinister Movement for the Emancipation of the Niger Delta (MEND), was defused by the security forces on 17 February and a couple of attackers were arrested. This served as a pretext to arrest several opponents of the regime, who were held 'incommunicado' for some days (see above). Acts of violence sparked off by the announcement of election results that favoured Omar Bongo's son in **Gabon** were quickly managed. Pirates continued to pose a threat in the Gulf of Guinea, but staged no further spectacular actions comparable to the previous year's events.

Socioeconomic Developments

While the IMF World Economic Outlook, published in April 2010, asserted that sub-Saharan Africa would weather the global crisis well (and its recovery would be expected to be stronger than after past global downturns), this was in fact not so evident for the sub-region, with its high dependence on export commodities such as timber and oil. In general, oil exporters experienced sharp deceleration or contractions of production during the year. Oil producer Congo (Brazzaville) apparently managed the crisis best. The IMF predicted a quick economic recovery in Africa as a whole. The reasons given resonated well in the sub-region: relatively limited integration of most low-income economies into the global economy, limited impact on their terms of trade, rapid normalisation in global trade and commodity prices, and the use of countercyclical fiscal policies. On closer inspection, the countries of the sub-region fared quite differently with regard to main economic indicators. While Gabon and Chad even had negative **GDP growth rates** (–1.6% and –1.4% respectively), Congo and Equatorial Guinea still showed solid positive growth (7.6% and 5.3% respectively), and all other countries recorded slim to moderate growth: CAR (1.7%), Cameroon (2.0%), DR Congo (2.8%) and São Tomé and Príncipe (4%). While these figures looked generally promising with regard to an expected upturn in 2010, **strong inflationary trends** hit ordinary consumers and were recorded particularly in São Tomé (17%) and in DR Congo with a staggering 46.2% inflation rate according to the IMF. Inflation was also high in Equatorial-Guinea (7.1%) and Chad (10.1%). All other countries recorded moderate inflationary trends between 2.1% and 4.3%. High deficits in the balance of current accounts were recorded, particularly in São Tomé and Príncipe and Chad (both at 32% of their GDP).

UNDP's **Human Development Index** showed the familiar picture of the sub-region's socioeconomic status, with Gabon ranking best at (an improved) position 103. Together with Equatorial Guinea (ranked 118), São Tomé and Príncipe (131), Congo (136) and Cameroon (153), it shared the "medium human development" classification, while Chad (175), DR Congo (176) and CAR (179) ranked towards the end of the list of 183 countries and in the "low human development" category. Poverty levels according to the **Human Poverty Index** (HPI-1) showed the same pattern. Only São Tomé and Príncipe, ranking 57 out of 135, had a significantly better ranking than in the HDI, pointing to less extreme social inequality in this country. The UN-sponsored **MDG monitor** showed a bleak outlook for the sub-region as a whole. It presented (again) mostly positive views on

Equatorial Guinea and Gabon; both were considered "on track" for four or five of the eight goals, though none was achieved (with the deadline drawing nearer). By contrast, CAR and DR Congo had not a single MDG "on track". Chad was "off track" on five MDGs and Cameroon, DRC and São Tomé and Príncipe continued to be considered "off track" for three of them. Goals 3 (promote gender equality and empower women) and 5 (improve maternal health) were both very unlikely to be achieved in four countries of the sub-region. For many MDGs, the information was deemed insufficient to draw clear conclusions.

Sub-regional Organisations

On 30 January, **CEMAC** held an extraordinary summit in Libreville, "principally" on the ramifications of the global financial crisis for member countries. Most presidents attended the meeting (Biya, Bongo, Bozizé, Obiang, Sassou Nguesso), the exception being Déby (represented by Prime Minister Abbas). Obiang presented a further report on institutional reforms, which suggested among other things the immediate establishment of the CEMAC parliament. As on many previous occasions, the heads of state verbally supported the acceleration of the process to allow for free movement of persons in the Community. Later, immigration ministers, at their meeting on 23 May in Douala, stated progress had been made on this front in only some member states. The conference decided *inter alia* that projects identified within the sub-regional economic programme should be implemented immediately, including the establishment of a fund for small and medium enterprises, the adjustment of some norms for banks to encourage long term financing, and the establishment of follow-up monitoring of the business environment and a supervisory committee for the implementation of these and other measures. A sense of crisis was apparent with regard to the sub-regional central bank, BEAC, for which conference participants demanded a general audit and other measures to "preserve the credibility and stability" of the bank. The perennial topic of the establishment of a sub-regional airline ('Air Cemac') was also on the agenda, with participants urging the CEMAC commission to pursue the current negotiations with South African Airlines as a potential strategic partner in this endeavour. The summit accepted additional financial assistance of CFAfr 8 bn to CAR for the country's DDR programme, i.e. CFAfr 1 bn per member state plus a BEAC loan for the remainder. The official reason for staging the summit was more intensely dealt with in an ad-hoc ministerial meeting in Douala (Cameroun) on 6 March, when participants exchanged views on the significant negative impact of the crisis on exports of raw materials (mining, timber). Recommendations included fiscal, monetary, budget and business environment measures (e.g. tax relief for affected companies, lowering interest rates). A number of further ministerial meetings were organised, but the ordinary summit was postponed from December to January 2010. The much-wanted, but symbolic first CEMAC day was celebrated on 16 March; acting chairman Bozizé (CAR) gave the official speech on the occasion.

Ramifications of a **financial scandal** at the sub-regional central bank BEAC (for the CFA currency zone) rocked the community after several revelations by the Paris-based weekly 'Jeune Afrique' in September. 'Jeune Afrique' reported that € 30 m had been embezzled from BEAC's Paris office between 2004 and 2008 via forged cheques, the embezzlement of cheques and forged statements. Partial responsibility was attributed to BEAC's former governor Mamalepot (from Gabon). The Paris office has a particular status as the only branch (together with the main office in Yaoundé) that reports directly to the BEAC governor. Irregularities had been known about internally for years, but inquiries began only in December 2008, after an investment scandal when the current governor, Philibert Andzembe (also from Gabon), filed two complaints against 'x' before a court in Paris. An audit committee issued its first report to Obiang on 22 May, and two further reports on 20 July and 24 October, providing a list of 139 names of suspects, a list of forged cheques, and explanations of the role the governor, vice governor and other personnel had played in the scandal. The committee could prove the embezzlement of CFAfr 16.6 bn. On 26 October, the bank's executive board issued a declaration explaining the situation and listing measures including judicial prosecution, and administrative, organisational and disciplinary measures. Pressure had grown with the IMF's suspension of disbursements and programmes concerning all member states, which was only lifted on 12 November, after all conditions had been met. The need to reform CEMAC, and particularly BEAC, was underlined by these developments and the chances to do so were deemed higher than ever with the disappearance of the perpetual gate-keeper Omar Bongo.

CEEAC held the 14th ordinary session of its conference of heads of state on 24 October in Kinshasa, with seven heads of state attending (Equatorial Guinea, Chad, São Tomé and Príncipe, CAR, Gabon, DRC, Congo). Burundi was represented by Vice President Yves Sahinguvu, Cameroon by Prime Minister Philemon Yang and Angola only by the minister of foreign affairs. On the agenda were security and sub-regional integration issues. The increase in piracy in the Gulf of Guinea, plus a rising concern that CEEAC governments would be sidelined in the management of their "vital interests at sea", put pressure on the member states to accelerate the establishment of a sub-regional centre of maritime security in Central Africa (with the French acronym CRESMAC) in Pointe-Noire (Congo) and of a standing international maritime conference. Cross-border criminality was to be fought by integrating existing efforts to collect small arms and light weapons into a broader police co-operation scheme. CEEAC's instruments in the field of conflict prevention and management were also on the agenda, with the conflict prevention mechanism (COPAX) lacking an appropriate institutional framework and the 'Mission de Consolidation de la Paix en Centrafrique' (MICOPAX) peacekeeping force in CAR needing an adaptation of its manpower (potentially to last until 2013). Gabon's new president Ali Bongo was designated responsible for the latter aspect and thereby inherited a dossier dear to his father. CEEAC sent a small number of election observers to Gabon for elections held on 30 August. The delegation was led by Apollinaire Malu Malu, president of the independent electoral commission in DRC. A preliminary statement mentioned some technical problems, including long delays in opening polling stations. On 6 September, when turmoil erupted after the election, acting CEEAC President Kabila invited Gabonese stakeholders to refrain from any actions that might disturb the peace and to respect the appeal procedures laid down by electoral laws. No official report of the mission was published.

The elaboration of a Central African common position for the Copenhagen UN climate change conference (7–18 December) was left to a CEEAC council of ministers responsible for forestry, environment and planning. They met on the occasion of the launch of the second edition of 'Etat des Fôrets du Bassin de Congo 2008', a status report on the Central African tropical forest, on 15 September in Kinshasa. In fact, this was turned into an **extraordinary session** of CEEAC-COMIFAC ('Commission des Forêts d'Afrique Centrale') ministers of the six 'forest countries', Cameroon, Congo, Gabon, Equatorial Guinea, CAR and DRC. The Kinshasa Declaration on the preparation of negotiations for a new international climate regime was later adopted at the aforementioned summit. French President Sarkozy met Sassou-Nguesso (Congo), Biya (Cameroun), Deby (Chad), Bozizé (CAR) and Ali Bongo (Gabon), as well as officials from Angola, Burundi, DRC, Equatorial-Guinea and Rwanda, on 16 December in Paris, ahead of the final round of the Copenhagen summit. This meeting was preceded by a meeting between Sarkozy and Africa's coordinator, Prime Minister Meles Zenawi of Ethiopia, when a joint French-African text was elaborated. Earlier, a **South-South** Coordination meeting comprising delegates from COMIFAC, the Amazon Cooperation Treaty Organization and the Association of Southeast Asian Nations, plus a number of resource persons mainly from donor organisations, was held in Montreal (Canada), where the Secretariat of the Convention on Biological Diversity is based (8–10 July). Participants agreed to pursue discussions in anticipation of the World Forestry Congress in Buenos Aires in October 2009. A general trend towards more South-South cooperation emerged with these events.

The **Gulf of Guinea Commission** held a summit in Luanda (Angola) on 21 January with four heads of state attending (Angola, Congo, Equatorial Guinea and São Tomé and Príncipe). Participants elected São Tomé's former president, Miguel Trovoada, as the Commission's new executive secretary. Trovoada explained in May that the budget of the organisation could not be fully executed due to financial constraints. The new Luanda headquarters of the organisation were inaugurated on 14 September.

Andreas Mehler

Cameroon

Throughout the year in Cameroon, there was an awareness of the 2011 presidential election being on the horizon. President Biya and his party, which continued to dominate the political scene, seemed to be already preparing for election day, as public criticism emerged for the first time about the president's wealth. As a consequence of the global financial crisis, the economy tended to slow down, with a sharp drop in oil revenues. No major social unrest was recorded.

Domestic Politics

In January, the main opposition party, the Social Democratic Front (SDF), demanded the revision of the membership of **Elections Cameroon (ELECAM)**, the new institution created by law in 2006, whose responsibility is to organise and supervise elections, although all its members were from the ruling 'Rassemblement Démocratique du Peuple Camerounais' (RDPC). A few weeks later, the (EU) expressed regret that "most of the members" of ELECAM, named at the end of 2008 by Biya, belonged to the ruling party. The authorities did not react to this publicly, but in an address to the members of the diplomatic community gathered in his ministry, the minister of external relations, Henri

Eyebe Eyebe Ayissi, admonished them to respect Cameroon's sovereignty and asked them to refrain from making comments that would discredit ELECAM. The last six months of the year were marked by a strong **mobilisation of the RDPC** and its chairman, President Paul Biya, apparently already on the starting-blocks for the 2011 presidential election. As with the 25th anniversary celebrations of the Biya regime (2007) and the change in the Constitution (2008), mobilisation started with a large increase in the notorious 'motions of support' for the head of state, asking for his candidacy in 2011, and these were reported daily by the public media. The RDPC, though weakened by factional divisions, also organised numerous meetings throughout the country as if the electoral campaign had already begun. Some party members insisted that the poll should be brought forward from 2011 to 2010. In November, on the occasion of the 27th anniversary of his accession to power, 76 year-old Biya thanked his supporters for their 'calls' in an open letter, but remained elusive about his plans, not stating clearly whether he would run for the presidency. However, he implied that he wanted to stay in power by asserting to the Cameroon people that he would "go the whole way to find solutions to the painful problem of unemployment of young people" and to improve moral standards and fight against corruption and the embezzlement of public funds.

A few months before, the RDPC had been on the defensive because of a heated argument that directly affected Biya. For the first time, the national media discussed his wealth and his use of public funds. The controversy was first caused by a report written in June by the French NGO 'Comité Catholique Contre la Faim' about the "dishonestly acquired property" of several African heads of state, including Biya. The RDPC strongly defended its chairman, but the debate was reactivated in August with articles in the French media about the cost of **Biya's vacation in France**. According to these reports, the president had stayed for three weeks in August at the coastal resort of La Baule, with a delegation of 40 people, occupying 43 rooms in two prestigious hotels at a cost of about € 900,000. The government and the RDPC denounced the reports as a "media conspiracy". The opposition parties, who were largely absent from the political scene throughout the year, took the opportunity to react. John Fru Ndi, chairman of the SDF, said Biya's stay in La Baule would amount to a true scandal, adding, "Since his accession in power in 1982, Paul Biya and his acolytes are only ransacking the Cameroonian people." Bernard Muna, Chairman of the 'Alliance des Forces du Progrès', an SDF splinter party, was equally outspoken and criticised the president's behaviour in the middle of an economic crisis.

A **cabinet reshuffle** took place on 30 June: Biya sacked Prime Minister Ephraïm Inoni, who had been appointed in 2004. Philemon Yang, 62, a magistrate from the Anglophone North West region who had been minister and deputy secretary general at the Presidency, was appointed as his successor. Inoni, a native of the South West region, was dismissed, as his name had often been mentioned in connection with corruption during recent years. Equally significant was the removal of Defence Minister Rémy Ze Meka. He was replaced by the chief of police, Edgar Alain Mebe Ngo'o, a long-time ally of President Biya. Seven other ministers also lost their jobs.

The **February 2008 riots** were still a matter of controversy. In February, the 'Observatoire National des Droits de l'Homme du Cameroun' (ONDH), a federation of human rights NGOs, deplored the absence of an official inquiry into responsibility for the violence and condemned the excessive use of force by the army and the police, accusing them of serious human rights violations. The ONDH also maintained that at least 139 people had been killed. The government replied that the final death toll was 40 and that the ONDH's figures were "not true and not credible". In January, the mayor of Njombé-Penja (South) and member of the ruling party, Paul Eric Kingué, was sentenced to six years' imprisonment for his alleged participation in the riots in his city against a French-owned banana plantation, the Plantations du Haut Penja (PHP). He was also condemned with 17 others to pay the company € 1.2 m in damages. Some NGOs said his condemnation was related to his ambition to break up a corruption network involving the PHP and another French-owned banana plantation company in his home area. In June, the singer Lapiro de Mbanga, very famous in the early 1990s, was sentenced on appeal to three years' imprisonment. He had been arrested in April 2008 and subsequently charged with looting during the riots.

Corruption remained an important topic of public debate. An old case returned to the political scene in October, when a new trial for corruption was launched against Titus Edzoa, already condemned in 1999. Former secretary general at the Presidency and formerly Biya's personal physician for many years, Edzoa was sentenced in 1999 to 15 years in prison for embezzlement. He had been arrested in 1997, a few days after his resignation as health minister and his announcement to stand as a candidate in the 1997 presidential election. In the new case, Edzoa and his co-accused, including a former minister in the president's office, were charged with embezzling a total of CFAfr 61 bn (€ 91 m). Edzoa claimed that he was the victim of a "political conspiracy".

The government's **anti-corruption campaign** 'Epervier' seemed to slow down, compared with spectacular arrests carried out in the previous year. In August, the former head of the state-owned petroleum distribution company 'Société Camerounaise des Dépôts Pétroliers' (SCDP), Jean Baptiste Nguini Effa, and six of his aides were arrested, all suspected of having embezzled public funds. A few months before, Nguini Effa had been ordered to repay € 1.4 m and to pay a fine of € 3,000 for misappropriating funds while managing SCDP. In July, seven finance officers and cashiers employed by the city government in Douala were arrested on charges of embezzling € 3 m. Former energy minister Alphonse Siyam Siwé, initially condemned to 30 years in prison in 2007, was sentenced to life on appeal in June for the embezzlement with 12 other people of € 53 m when he was head of the 'Port Autonome de Douala'. A former high official at the health ministry, arrested in 2006, was sentenced in July to 15 years in prison for having embezzled funds provided by donor organisations to fight the spread of HIV/AIDS. Former ministers

Polycarpe Abah Abah, Urbain Olanguena Awono and Jean-Marie Atangana Mebara, who were arrested in 2008, were still awaiting trial.

Despite these actions, critics questioned the will of the authorities to seriously fight corruption. The case of the **'Association Citoyenne de Défense des Intérêts Collectifs'** (ACDIC) raised most attention in the media. In May, Bernard Njonga, chairman of ACDIC, was given a suspended two-month sentence for "illegal demonstration". He was accused of having held a meeting at the ACDIC headquarters in Yaoundé in December 2008, to protest against the embezzlement of funds at the ministry of agriculture. According to an ACDIC report, 62% of a € 1.8 m grant to support the production of maize had been misappropriated in 2008 by civil servants in the ministry. Faced with the strong mediatisation of this affair, the head of the 'Commission Nationale de Lutte contre la Corruption' (CONAC), a state body mostly inactive since its creation in 2006, had launched an inquiry into the embezzlements. Its report confirmed the ACDIC data and highlighted the culpability of 47 individuals, most of them employees at the ministry, but the CONAC document was never published. In September, ACDIC decided to lodge a complaint against the 47 employees to avoid the affair being entirely forgotten.

Domestic **insecurity** remained a matter of concern. Pirate attacks at sea were numerous off the Bakassi peninsula. In March, four employees of Tidewater, a multinational firm that provides maritime services to the oil industry, were kidnapped off the Bakassi peninsula. They were freed in July. According to the Cameroonian media, a large ransom was paid to the kidnappers. No public information was given by the authorities, who even denied the incident had taken place. In the same period, three Filipino fishermen and two Ukrainian mechanics were seized from a trawler off the Cameroon coast and were later released, apparently without a ransom being paid to their captors. The abduction was initially blamed on the Nigerian guerilla group Movement for the Emancipation of the Niger Delta, but this group, active in Nigeria's oil-rich south, denied any involvement. In October, the new defence minister, Edgar Alain Mebe Ngo'o, said that Cameroonian troops had killed four armed pirates who had attacked a private boat off Bakassi, and one person was killed in a different attack on a trawler. In late December, a policeman was killed by pirates in an assault on a boat. Some media reports said that responsibility for the attack was claimed by the Bakassi Freedom Fighters, a small armed group from the peninsula, who had kidnapped nine French oil company workers in 2008. At the end of the year, attacks by bandits were also frequent in the Northern regions. In November, seven people were killed by bandits armed with automatic weapons in less than a week. Several jailbreaks took place during the year, proving that **prison conditions** remained poor and worrying. In June, 51 prisoners escaped from the prison in Yagoua (Far North), and only 33 of them were recaptured. In July, 17 prisoners escaped from the prison in Meri (North). In October, two prisoners were shot dead and two others wounded during an attempted jailbreak at Bafoussam (West). A report by the 'Commission Nationale des Droits de l'Homme', an official body, denounced the delays in the justice system. Preventive detention, i.e. imprisonment before trial, accounts for 62% of all those held in Cameroonian prisons and can last up to nine years. Conditions in detention were "draconian, inhuman, degrading", it added. A report published in January by Amnesty International (AI) caused quite a stir: The report, 'Impunity underpins persistent abuse', registered numerous human rights violations "approved or committed" by the authorities and whose perpetrators escaped with "almost total impunity". AI complained that its inquiry teams had not been permitted to visit Cameroon for 10 years.

Two **journalists** were sentenced during the year. The first was Lewis Medjo, the publisher of the weekly 'La Détente Libre', who has been imprisoned in the southwestern city of Douala since 26 September 2008 for publishing a report about an alleged ploy by President Biya to force the President of the Supreme Court to retire early. A court sentenced him on 7 January to three years in prison and a fine of CFAfr 2 m on a charge of disseminating false news. In December, Jean Bosco Talla, managing editor of the weekly 'Germinal', was sentenced to a one-year suspended term and a fine of CFAfr 3.15 m for insulting the head of state. Talla had been arrested and jailed a few days after publishing passages from a book alleging that, before becoming president, Biya pledged fidelity to his predecessor, Ahmadou Ahidjo, in a secret pact that was sealed by "a homosexual act". The French NGO 'Reporters Sans Frontières' urged the Cameroonian authorities to decriminalise press offences. This position was shared by associations of Cameroonian journalists who, at the same time, pointed to the lack of a sense of responsibility among many of their colleagues. At the end of the year, the employees of 'Le Messager', the country's oldest private daily newspaper, went on strike to demand their salaries, which had not been paid for seven months. The chairman of the 'Syndicat National des Journalistes Employés du Cameroun', Norbass Tchana Ngante, stated that there were constant problems with the payment of salaries in all the private media and questioned their directors' probity.

In November, Cardinal Christian Tumi, archbishop of Douala, retired. He was well-known for his constant critical stance against the Biya regime, and for speaking out against corruption and the lack of justice and democracy. In contrast, during the three-day visit of Pope **Benedict XVI** in March, Biya and his wife attended popular masses celebrated in the Yaoundé stadium and in the historical Mvolyé basilica, and the Pope avoided addressing any of Tumi's major concerns with Cameroonian politics. This disappointed many Catholic believers, but confirmed the support of the majority of the local Catholic hierarchy.

Foreign Affairs

The government continued working to strengthen the special relationship with **France**, which remained Cameroon's principle trading partner and a main source of private investment and foreign aid. On 24 July, President Biya met President Nicolas Sarkozy at the

Elysée during a state visit to Paris. A few weeks before, French Prime Minister François Fillon paid an official visit to Yaoundé and was received by Biya. Both signed a new defence partnership agreement, putting an end to a set of partially secret agreements concluded in 1974, which had provided for automatic French military assistance if Cameroon was attacked. Fillon also signed a bilateral migration agreement regulating the access of Cameroonian migrants to the French labour market. In March, the French secretary of state for cooperation, Alain Joyandet, also came to Cameroon and made a notable visit to the French-owned banana plantation PHP in Njombé-Penja.

Biya attended the funeral of **Gabon**'s President Omar Bongo Ondimba in Libreville in June. The government followed closely the presidential election in Gabon on 30 August, but did not side with any of the candidates. Former interior minister André Mba Obame, who officially came third in the elections, spent three weeks as a refugee in the Cameroonian embassy in Libreville immediately after the poll, claiming that he feared for his life. The first official visit made by the newly elected president, Ali Bongo Ondimba, son of Omar, was to Cameroon, on 11 September. He was welcomed with full honours at the airport by Biya himself. Relations between the two countries had been characterised by fierce competition over the past decades.

At the end of his mandate in December, the **EU** representative in Yaoundé, Javier Pujol, criticised the government's fight against corruption. In particular, he deplored the fact that the constitutional requirement for a declaration of property by ministers and members of parliament had not been implemented. He complained about the lack of desire for reform and criticised the excessive number of ministers (about 60). Pujol also expressed his doubts as to the credibility and neutrality of the members of ELECAM. This was a rare show of outspokenness within the diplomatic corps.

No ceremony was held in August to mark the first anniversary of the official handing over of the Bakassi peninsula to Cameroon by **Nigeria** on 14 August 2008, in line with an international court ruling. In December, a first boundary stone was erected at Banki-Amchide in north Cameroon in the presence of Cameroonian and Nigerian officials, foreign diplomats and UN officials. About 1,950 km have to be marked. The EU said there were more than 3,000 boundary stones to be erected and that the EU had contributed € 4 m to the project. The **Chadian** President Idriss Deby Itno visited Biya in Yaoundé on 28–29 October. Deby thanked Biya for his support when Chad was attacked by rebels in May. Asserting that the relationship between the two countries was "excellent", they also spoke about insecurity in northern Cameroon, including attacks by bandits and kidnappings for ransom. Biya said he wanted a "permanent dialogue" on this matter.

The relationship with **Equatorial Guinea** remained strained. President Biya did not attend the swearing-in ceremony of President Teodoro Obiang Nguema in December, after his easy re-election. In January, the media reported that three Equato-Guinean soldiers had been arrested and detained for a few days on the southern border. One of them was accused of having killed a Cameroonian fisherman. According to the national media, he was kept in jail and the other two were freed. In May, about 300 Cameroonian illegal immigrants were expelled from Malabo to Douala. Four months later, 100 more illegal immigrants, including 71 Cameroonians, met the same fate.

Socioeconomic Developments

The 2009 **budget** stood at CFAfr 2,301 bn, an increase of 1.1% compared with 2008. Oil revenues were estimated to have decreased from CFAfr 593 bn to CFAfr 519 bn. About 59% of expenditure was devoted to government spending, 26% to investment and 15% to servicing debt. The government chose to renew the suspension of customs duties on several imported consumer goods. This measure was initially taken in response to the February 2008 riots. The global financial crisis had a clear impact on the Cameroonian economy. In his end-of- year speech, President Biya himself recognised that exports of wood, aluminium, cotton and rubber had fallen and the decline would be aggravated by the fall in prices of raw materials on the world market. The slow-down in economic activity would also result in a decline in tax and customs revenues and a loss of jobs. Some earmarked foreign investments were postponed. Oil revenues in particular decreased to a significant degree. Credit transfers to the public treasury from the state-owned 'Société Nationale des Hydrocarbures' (SNH) had fallen to CFAfr 331.76 bn from CFAfr 651.75 bn in 2008. Volumes of oil sold by the SNH had fallen to 17.624 m barrels against 20.231 m barrels in 2008. According to SNH, insecurity in the Bakassi area was also partly responsible. In April, the IMF warned that the growth of GDP would slow down because of the crisis and the fall in crude oil prices. It forecast a growth rate of 2.5% instead of 3.4% in 2008 and instead of 4% as projected by the 2009 budget. The IMF granted a loan of $ 144.1 m to help the country face the crisis in July. The World Bank signed two agreements worth $ 100 m in September for the development of agriculture and health, education, water, transport in rural areas.

In November, the government published a new **growth and employment strategy** paper ('Document de Stratégie pour la Croissance et l'Emploi'), replacing the PRSP adopted in 2003 and developed at international donors' request. The new plan is intended to help the country towards a GDP growth rate of 5.5% per year for the next 10 years. The government also expected to bring the rate of unemployment from more than 13% down to less than 7%. According to Prime Minister Yang, PRSP had allowed positive growth rates but had not helped to reduce poverty substantially. The business climate in Cameroon was termed "noxious" by the **World Bank**. The country was ranked 173 out of 183 countries by the Bank's yearly 'Doing Business' report, falling four places compared with the previous year. A representative of the World Bank declared that government reforms would not encourage substantial investment, and asked for limitation on corruption, a better tax system and a more impartial justice system. In December, the World Bank found Cameroon's growth achievement disappointing. The country would not be on-track to meet most of the MDGs. The report associated the extremely high under-employment with risks of social unrest and instability. In this regard, the impact of a decade of fiscal austerity, poor governance and unequal distribution of public services was found to be particularly problematic. The World Bank also noted that there was one doctor per 583 people in Biya's home region (South) compared with one doctor per 20,662 in the North region and the report described around one-third of all children as chronically malnourished. The World Bank's vice president for Africa, Obigieli Ezekwesili, said that, thanks to its debt reduction, Cameroon should be able to invest money in important sectors such as health, education and important economic infrastructure. "Unfortunately (...), what has happened is that Cameroon, unlike countries like Ghana which used the opportunity to generate strong growth of 5–6%, has the whole period been growing at levels of 2–3% on the average, which is well below expectations," she said.

Energy supply continued to be a matter of concern throughout the year. Although Cameroon was still planning to spend CFAfr 6 bn to increase electricity output from 1,000 MW to 3,000 MW by 2020, no real progress was observed in 2009, apart from the start-up of a new thermal power station (86 MW) in Yassa-Dibamba, close to Douala. The construction schedule for the Lom Pangar dam, which was supposed to supply more than half of the planned increase in capacity, was also still unclear. In May, about 20 organisations protested against the increase in power cuts. The assessment of the privatisation of the 'Société Nationale d'Electricité' would be calamitous, the NGOs said, asking for an end to the private monopoly on the public power service. In 2001, the government granted this monopoly to an American group, AES Sirocco, which held 51% of the capital of the company, the rest being held by the State (44%) and employees (5%).

Serious problems also emerged with the **railway company** Camrail, a concession of the French group Bolloré Africa Logistics: in August, a train carrying 1,000 people from Ngaoundéré (Adamaoua) was derailed in Yaoundé. Five people were killed and 303 injured. A few days later, another train carrying oil products from Douala was also derailed in Yaoundé and caught fire. One person died.

Some strategic decisions were taken in the **oil sector**. In December, Cameroon's state-owned oil refinery, the 'Société Nationale de Raffinage' (SONARA) signed a CFAfr 45 bn loan agreement with the Cameroon-based private Afriland First Bank, which also has branches in Equatorial Guinea, Democratic Republic of the Congo and São Tomé and Príncipe. This loan was intended to be used to raise the production capacity of SONARA from 2.1 to 3.5 m tonnes a year. The project should also enable the refinery to process the heavy crude that Cameroon produces. SONARA, which has been operational since 1981, has so far only refined light crude oil imported from Angola, Equatorial Guinea and Nigeria. Cameroon signed four new contracts with oil companies. In April, China's Yan Chang

Logone Development Holding Company Ltd signed a $ 62 m production sharing contract for oil exploration on two onshore blocks in northern Cameroon. In July, Cameroon gave the French oil group Total-E&P (which already controlled about 65% of the country's oil production) the right to explore an off shore block in the Rio del Rey basin (South West), off the Bakassi peninsula. The Swiss firm Glencore was also given a permit to carry out offshore explorations in the same area. Noble Energy Inc. and Petronas Carigali Gas Ltd jointly won a contract to explore and drill for oil in the Campo basin (South). The two firms are already partners in Cameroon oil investment, and Petronas is a shareholder in the Chad-Cameroon Pipeline.

Some new trends became evident in the **mining sector**. In September, Australia's Legend Mining Ltd acquired a 90% interest in two permits for iron ore exploration in Ngovayang (South) and Mayo Binka (North). In October, Cameroon Alumina Ltd (a joint venture set up in 2008 by Dubai Aluminium Company Ltd and India's Hindalco Industries, along with US firm Hydromine Inc.) announced having found 550 m tonnes of bauxite deposits at their Ngaoundal and Minim-Martap properties (North). According to the company, the site could produce 4.5 to 9 m tonnes of bauxite per year starting in late 2014. Cameroon Alumina Ltd was projected to build an aluminium refinery with a capacity of 1.4 to 3 m tonnes and was discussing with the authorities the upgrading and extending of existing railway links from the mines to the Kribi deep-sea port. Australia's Sundance Resources, which has a permit for iron ore exploration in Mbalam, announced a two-year delay in starting production at the $ 2.46 bn project (i.e. until 2013). Once operational, Sundance hopes to produce some 35 m tonnes of ore per year. Geovic, which expects to produce 4,200 tonnes of cobalt per year and 2,100 tonnes of nickel per year for 21 years in Nkamouna (East), also said in early 2009 that, because of the global financial crisis, production would be delayed until 2012 and that investment had been cut to $ 250 m from $ 370 m. As in 2008, the government did not publish any reports on the framework of the Extractive Industries Transparency Initiative.

Fanny Pigeaud

Central African Republic

The political atmosphere of the somewhat promising end of 2008 could not be maintained for long. Few of the concessions made by President Bozizé during the inclusive political dialogue (IPD) forum were eventually implemented. New armed encounters all over the country marked the year, while the president's camp was already preparing for the 2010 elections. Rebel movements fought mainly for material gains, but had also good reason to suspect the regime of not fulfilling its earlier promises and some real grievances related to the blatant disregard of minority group rights. The export-oriented economy (diamonds, timber) suffered from the global economic downturn.

Domestic Politics

President Bozizé dissolved the government on 18 January and immediately reappointed Prime Minister Touadéra the following day. His newly formed **'government of national unity'**, meant to include representatives of both opposition parties and rebel movements, fell far short of expectations. Only second-rank members of those contesting parties made their entry into the government and occupied mostly medium-weight positions. This was particularly true for the representative of the opposition alliance, the 'Union des Forces Vives de la Nation' (UFVN), André Nalke Dorogo, who was made minister of public health. His party, the 'Mouvement pour la Libération du Peuple Centrafricain' (MLPC) excluded him from its ranks after he accepted this position. Moïse Kotaye, contested leader of the 'Front Patriotique pour le Progrès' (FPP), supposed to represent the second opposition alliance simply called 'Autres Partis', was made minister of small and medium-sized companies. His participation in government was also dismissed by those he was deemed to represent. Equally second-rank were those ministers representing the armed movements, such as François Naoyama of the 'Armée Populaire pour la Restauration de la Démocratie' (APRD) and Djomo Didou of the 'Union des Forces Démocratiques pour le Rassemblement' (UFDR), who were made ministers of the environment and housing respectively.

Key ministries were still held by staunch **presidential supporters**. In particular, Cyriaque Gonda, leader of the 'Parti National pour un Centrafrique Nouveau' (PNCN), saw his powers increased and was now made state minister for communication, civic affairs, national reconciliation and the follow-up of the IPD. Sylvain Ndoutingaï continued to manage the ministry of mines, energy and water, and Col. Anicet Parfait Mbaye the ministry of transport and civil aviation. Sylvain Maliko headed the plan, economy and international cooperation department. Former chief of staff Gen. Antoine Gambi became foreign minister. As the opposition had criticised the fact that Bozizé combined his function of head of state with that of minister of defence, he introduced a cosmetic move promoting his son Francis from junior minister within the ministry to full defence minister, while preserving his control over the strategic post. Hopes that Bozizé would share substantial parts of his power were therefore futile.

Obviously related to the ensuing frustration were new outbursts of **violence**. In fact, serious setbacks in the peace process were recorded, despite some progress in 2008 with the signature of a global peace accord by most of the main rebel movements. Only Zacharia Damane's UFDR, dominated by ethnic Gula, respected the peace agreement with government forces. However, it came increasingly under attack in its stronghold of Birao (north-east) from competing Kara militias, leading to serious confrontations at its Birao base in June on two separate occasions. Four UFDR combatants were killed against about 15 of the attackers. After UN mediation (1–4 July), the UFDR agreed to leave the destroyed and deserted town for its base in Tiringoulou. Earlier skirmishes between armed groups occurred in mid-January in Ndélé (Bamingui-Bangoran prefecture). In retaliation, the armed forces attacked the nearby village of Sokoumba and killed at least 18 male civilians, including the village chief. In February, an armed group attacked the prison of Bossembelé, 160 km north of Bangui, freed all prisoners and seized weaponry and ammunition. Responsibility for the attack was claimed by the newly created 'Convention des Patriotes pour la Justice et la Paix' (CPJP), led by the ominous political entrepreneur Charles Massi, who had agreed to become UFDR coordinator (i.e. political spokesperson) the year before.

Subsequently, CPJP was involved in further attacks in the north-east, including in Ndélé in June. **Retaliation** by government forces reportedly caused the displacement of 5,000 civilians. The army also allegedly killed 30 civilians during the operation. The CPJP stayed outside any peace framework through the entire year. Massi was arrested by Chadian authorities when trying to cross the border from Chad into CAR to join CPJP troops based near the border, but was released in July for unknown reasons. After a short occupation of Ndélé by about 400 CPJP troops on 26 November (11 people were killed), the town was recaptured by the army two days later. Massi was arrested by the Chadian army again in mid-December and was then handed over to the CAR authorities, who transferred him to the prison in Bossembélé where he was allegedly tortured (and killed, though his death was not officially confirmed).

The **north and north-west** were equally theatres of combat. In late February, rebels attacked a gendarmerie post in Bataganfo, 500 km north of Bangui, stealing weaponry and equipment. Two armed groups claimed to have staged the attack, the 'Front Démocratique du Peuple Centrafricain' (FDPC) and the 'Mouvement des Libérateurs Centrafricains pour la Justice' (MLCJ). Both organisations had suspended their participation in the peace process. However, on 31 May, MLCJ leader Abakar Sabone returned to Bangui and agreed to work within the framework of the peace process. On 3 July, FDPC leader Abdoulaye Miskine signed the Libreville peace accord on the sidelines of the AU summit in Sirte (Libya), but later (on 2 October) declared that he would step out of the peace process, sparking a split within his movement. The APRD, though officially sticking to the peace process, was involved in several incidents. Stockbreeders accused local traders in Paoua of selling 170 cattle that had been stolen by bandits ten days earlier. The ensuing clashes left 22 dead and 52 injured. Only a few days later a top representative of the cattle breeders, Soule Garga, was killed by APRD rebels. Jean-Jacques Démafouth, coordinator of the APRD, thereafter replaced the local APRD commander as he feared losing some of the existing sympathy of the local population.

Chadian rebel leader Baba Laddé, opposed to the Déby regime in N'Djaména and initially allied to the APRD, operated with his men in the APRD strongholds around Kaga Bandoro, claiming to fight the dreaded 'Zaraguina' highway robbers. He was declared persona non grata in October, arrested and deported. His 'Front Populaire pour le Redressement' (FPR) and **Chadian forces** had clashed in the border town of Sido on 3 October. Laddé's supporters now threatened to wage a 'jihad' against the government and the peacekeepers of CEEAC's 'Mission de consolidation de la paix' (MICOPAX). This added to the more and more religiously loaded confrontations Bozizé had with groups of Muslim origin. In November, two French aid workers were kidnapped near Birao by rebel fighters who apparently belonged to the 'Mouvement National du Salut de la Patrie' (MNSP), a break-away faction of the MLCJ under hardliner Hassan Ousman, who fell out with Sabone and reportedly took with him most of the fighters.

The government authorised the Ugandan army to conduct military operations on CAR territory together with Southern Sudanese and Congolese troops following repeated attacks and looting by the Ugandan rebel movement **Lord's Resistance Army** (LRA) in the south-east (around Obo and Mboki), which displaced an estimated 4,500 civilians. The Ugandan army was subsequently reported to have rescued 100 kidnapped children and young adults, killing one senior and four junior commanders and capturing a senior LRA commander; 46 LRA fighters would have surrendered to Southern Sudanese forces. Nevertheless, LRA attacks continued in late November, when 24 people were abducted and 11 killed in new attacks. Additionally, confrontations between ethnic Sango and Ngbubu made more than 500 inhabitants of Mobaye-Banga (South) flee over the River Oubangui into DR Congo in September, where both groups cohabited peacefully.

In the light of these events, any **disarmament**, demobilisation, and reintregration (DDR) process looked intrinsically unrealistic. After some preparatory work, Bozizé nevertheless officially launched the DDR programme in Paoua (north-west) after provisional lists of ex-combatants had been submitted to the UN. Initial funds of $ 4 m were released from the UN Peacebuilding Fund. In addition, a new round of collection of small and light weapons was launched shortly afterwards. A three-year plan to disarm 6,000–10,000 fighters was announced in December, but apart from a couple of information meetings little had been achieved by year's end.

Without tangible success in the DDR process, it looked difficult to conduct peaceful **presidential elections** in 2010. Bozizé nevertheless prepared his re-election by all possible means. His 'Convention Kwa Na Kwa', hitherto a platform of movements supporting the president, formally registered as a political party (simply 'Kwa Na Kwa', literally 'work, nothing but work') after an inaugurating meeting in Boali on 29 August. It later held a first congress in M'baiki (13 November). Gonda's PNCN reiterated its support for Bozizé.

The National Assembly adopted a new **electoral code** after controversy over the nomination process of the independent electoral commission ('Commission Electorale Indépendante'; CEI). The two opposition alliances, which had boycotted the vote, suspended their participation in the selection process of the commissioners, while the Constitutional Court had declared some provisions of the text anti-constitutional. Pierre Buyoya, Burundi's former president and chief mediator in the IPD, former archbishop Paulin (the head of the National Council for Mediation) and the new Special Representative of the UN Secretary General (SRSG), Sahle-Work Zewde, negotiated a compromise. A somewhat modified code was promulgated on 2 October and pastor Joseph Binguimale was subsequently elected chairman of the commission by a majority of its 30 members. Binguimale worked hard to respect the deadline of the initial electoral calendar, i.e. holding elections in April 2010. Whereas the minister of territorial administration had announced in April that voters' lists would have to be set up entirely anew, because those used in 2005 were said to have been destroyed, Binguimale announced in December that he had 'found' the lists and it was now a simple matter of updating them. This announcement reinforced looming suspicions that the government would use manipulated voter lists.

Former president Ange Félix Patassé came back to Bangui (via Libya) from his exile in Togo in October and met with Bozizé on 9 November. He still enjoyed support within the MLPC, the **main opposition party**, although a party congress had excluded him on 13 June for "not respecting the line of the party". Supporters were not allowed to welcome Patassé at the airport. His return and announcement that he would stand in the 2010 polls challenged the ambitions of Martin Ziguélé, former prime minister and new party chairman, who had been Bozizé's most serious contender in the 2005 elections. However, on 31 December the Supreme Court confirmed an earlier court ruling that Ziguélé was the rightful leader of the MLPC.

On 15 June, the ICC officially confirmed the charges against Jean-Pierre Bemba, DR Congo's former vice president, for **crimes against humanity** committed in CAR in 2002–3 when Patassé had called upon him for help. The 'Fédération Internationale de Droits de l'Homme' continued to demand the issuing of arrest warrants by the ICC against Patassé (and Miskine) for the same crimes. This was clearly not supported by the authorities, because Patassé was an obvious ally of Bozizé against Ziguélé – at least for the moment.

Veteran politician Abel **Goumba** died on 11 May. He was a central figure in national politics in the 1960s and 1990s, but had lost influence in recent years, although he headed a government of national reconciliation under Bozizé in 2003. Goumba held the position of National Mediator until his death. He was succeeded in this position by former archbishop Pomodimo.

Foreign Affairs

The death of the highly influential Omar Bongo Ondimba, President of **Gabon**, had repercussions in CAR. Bongo had time and again brokered agreements between the various conflicting parties of the country. It was not expected that his son Ali, the new president, would be as committed to regional diplomacy as was his father. The local UN peacebuilding office became increasingly active. It was renamed 'Bureau intégré des Nations Unies pour la consolidation de la paix en Centrafrique' under the new SRSG, the experienced Ethiopian female career diplomat, Sahle-Work Zewde.

When the EUFOR Chad/CAR mission was officially terminated on 15 March, the UN Mission in the Central African Republic and Chad (MINURCAT by its French acronym) had to take over. The **UN mission** was – in principle – strengthened in advance on 14 January by UN Security Council resolution 1861 and authorised to total 5,200 military personnel, 25 military liaison officers and 300 police officers. The mandate was extended until 15 March 2010. Finland and Sweden, which had participated in EUFOR, agreed to be part of 'MINURCAT 2'. The EU Council issued statements of satisfaction with the overall success of the EUFOR mission. Because of delays in deployment of additional troops, France agreed to keep its EUFOR contingent in place for some additional weeks. However, like EUFOR, the UN mission was focusing largely on Chad and only superficially on north-eastern CAR, with only about 500 soldiers operating on Central African soil. In April, UN assistant secretary general for peacekeeping, Edmond Mulet, admitted that MINURCAT lacked soldiers and equipment essential to its mission. At the end of the year, UN peacekeepers were deployed to Sam Ouandja in the north-east, when Sudanese rebels threatened to attack that village. The UN's peacebuilding commission remained active in the CAR and concretised its plans with a strategic framework paper adopted on 9 June and a second mission to the country in December. APRD rebels, however, refused the commission's delegation access to Paoua.

CEEAC's MICOPAX, which had taken over from a similar CEMAC force as the subregional complement of peacekeeping troops, operated in the central and western part of the country. The allegedly 'arrogant' Chadian contingent met with suspicion from the population of the capital Bangui (as had been the case with all former regional peacekeeping units of Chadian origin since 1997). The mission built barracks in several cities and partly handed them over to the national armed forces. Under French pressure, the reluctant CEEAC agreed to supply 31 additional military observers to oversee the DDR process. They arrived in mid-December.

Bozizé visited **China** between 9 and 15 September and called on Chinese investors to step up their interests in CAR, notably in communications and mining. Presidents Hu Jintao and Bozizé signed an agreement on technological and economic cooperation.

In January the regime annoyed **France** with the appointment of controversial businessman Saifee Durbar (of Indo-Pakistani origin) to deputy minister for foreign affairs. The move was meant to give Durbar diplomatic immunity in order to escape prosecution in London and Paris. He was dismissed from his position in June, obviously under French pressure, and extradited from the United Kingdom to France on 2 December. He was arrested on charges of fraud.

Socioeconomic Developments

GDP was forecast to grow by only 2%, a slowdown compared with the 2.2% calculated for 2008. The global financial crisis had a direct negative impact on both major **export commodities**. Timber exports dropped by 38%, and the value of exported diamonds, in previous years making up for some 50% of exports, declined by 27%. A long-awaited new mining code, aimed at creating more transparency in the sector, was adopted in April, but fell short of expectations and increased the tax for foreign mining companies. It was feared that it made the investment climate even more unattractive.

The 2009 **budget**, approved by the National Assembly in late 2008, was highly expansionary with a 24% increase in spending. Total revenue was set to increase by 20.3%. The budget was based on an assumption of real GDP growth of 4.5% in the calendar year and could soon be declared unrealistic. The government nevertheless worked on ameliorated domestic revenue collection and improved management of public expenditure. Domestic debt was thereby reportedly reduced by a significant CFAfr 12 bn. The IMF was, on the whole, satisfied with the implementation of the PRGF, particularly with fiscal performance, and extended the facility for a further six months into mid-2010. In July, CAR attained the completion point under the HIPC initiative, the precondition for large-scale **debt** relief. Multilateral debt was, in fact, reduced by $ 578 m and the total debt owed to Paris Club creditors declined from $ 59.3 m to $ 3.7 m in 2009. The IMF expressed its hope that the freed resources would be used to meet some of the MDGs where the CAR was far behind schedule. On 29 December, the National Assembly approved the 2010 budget, increased by 7.9% to CFAfr 184.6 bn, with 42% of the budget planned to be covered by outside support.

Reports multiplied about growing **malnutrition** and a rise in related illnesses in diamond-producing areas around Nola and Boda. The already poor standards of cassava-based nutrition could not be met by dismissed miners. According to UNICEF, 700,000 children below the age of five were severely malnourished. Extreme **poverty** was cited as a cause, with six out of ten people living on less than $ 1.25 a day. Torrential rainfall led to **flooding** in Bangui in July and a substantial loss of housing and property.

The number of IDPs declined to 108,000 by February but, following the numerous new outbursts of violence, rose again to an estimated 162,000 in October. Among these, 73,000 people had earlier returned to their villages of origin, but were not able to build a sustainable basis of subsistence as violence continued. Refugees in neighbouring Cameroon and Chad numbered about 64,000 and 74,000 respectively.

A severe crisis affected the **Catholic Church**. Vatican officials had criticised the local clergy for living a double life, i.e. frequently having a wife and family. The bishop of Bossangoa announced his retirement in May, only to be followed by the country's archbishop Pomodimo. Both resignations were accepted by the Holy See and an apostolic administrator was appointed without consultation with the local hierarchy. This led to the surprising announcement of strike action by the country's priests on 27 May, suspended only the next day.

Andreas Mehler

Chad

On the military front, the year was relatively calm with just one major attack by armed opposition groups in the east of the country. However, the general security situation in the same part of the country remained a major source of concern, hampering humanitarian work to assist the more than 500,000 Sudanese and Central African refugees and Chadian IDPs, despite the efforts of the European stabilization force (EUFOR) and its successor MINURCAT ('Mission des Nations Unies en République Centrafricaine et au Tchad'). Relations with neighbouring Sudan remained precarious despite peace negotiations. Refugees continued to flow in from CAR in the southeast. Following insufficient rainfall, the food security situation became increasingly problematic over the year. The government experienced major budgetary problems, following slackening oil prices and lower oil production than anticipated.

Domestic Politics

The security situation in the east of the country remained a major problem throughout the year. Banditry and attacks on NGOs continued to hamper **humanitarian assistance** to the 254,000 refugees from Sudan and 70,000 from CAR, plus 171,000 IDPs residing in more than 60 camps throughout the region, as well as approximately 150,000 members of the host population heavily affected by the conflict. Between January and October, 192 attacks on humanitarian aid projects were recorded. In some areas, humanitarian activities had to be scaled back temporarily – for example after repeated attacks on camp Koukou Angarana, aid staff were relocated and were only able to return after 120 UN troops were posted there. Security within the camps was also a source of worry, with armed elements present in several of them, especially on the border, and the recruitment of youths by armed Chadian opposition groups. The relocation of the refugee camp Ouré Cassoni, located 7 km from the border with Sudan north of Bahai, was hampered by difficulties in finding a place with sufficient water more inland.

Efforts to improve the **security situation** were stepped up by MINURCAT and a specially trained police force, the 'Détachement Intégré de Sécurité' (DIS). By April, it reached full strength, with a force of 850 to protect 12 refugee camps and six key towns, although its effectiveness was hampered by lack of equipment and infrastructure. Over its first year of operation, the DIS conducted 3,611 patrols and 1,392 security escorts and arrested more than 300 individuals involved in various crimes. It also recovered 27 vehicles belonging to the UN. As a result, the security situation improved somewhat and, for example, the incidence of rape in refugee camps decreased. This improvement was also due to the onset of the rainy season in July, which made roads and tracks impassable for potential intruders.

However, the DIS itself became the object of attacks and security escorts for humanitarian convoys had to be scaled back. A number of DIS officers left the service as a result of low morale and a perceived lack of support for their operations. Consequently, 150 new officers had to be trained by the end of the year. The DIS was also promised 50 all-terrain vehicles to conduct patrols, and better housing and office space. Special emphasis was given to recruiting female officers to improve the gender balance. In order to improve the rule of law, efforts were made to reinforce the judicial system. However, by March, only 37 out of 180 newly appointed magistrates were effectively posted in the east. To fill the gap, 148 civil servants were trained to serve temporarily as judges and justice auxiliaries.

On 18 January, after months of inactivity and five months of negotiations, seven armed opposition groups decided to form a united front, the 'Union des Forces de la Résistance' (UFR), against the government of President Idriss Déby Itno. On January 23, Timan Erdimi, leader of the 'Rassemblement des Forces pour le Changement' (RFC), was put at the head of the coalition and on 20 March the military command headed by General Tahor Odji was put in place. In order to put up a defence against this threat, the Chadian government posted nearly 25,000 troops in the east of the country, together with a number of attack helicopters and jet fighters manned by Ukrainian mercenaries.

On 4 May, elements under the command of the UFR staged an **attack** on the east of the country, with two convoys entering Chad each comprising 60–70 vehicles. The columns regrouped on 7 May in the area of Am Dam, 100 km northwest of Goz Beida. A third column entered Chad in the extreme south and moved towards the Salamat region. On 6 and

7 May, the Chadian air force attacked these columns between Goz Beida and Koukou Angarana. On 7 May, clashes between ground forces ensued, leaving 22 government troops and 225 rebels dead on the battlefield, according to the government. Two hundred rebels were captured, including the deputy commander of the UFR, Mahamat Hamouda Bechir. Remaining elements took refuge in Sudan, though a rebel spokesman claimed they were hiding in Chad. The third column withdrew to Darfur without engaging in battle.

Later in the year, on 25 July, a **peace agreement** was concluded between the Chadian government and three of the armed opposition groups, the 'Front pour le Salut de la République' (FSR), the 'Union des Forces pour la Démocratie et le Développement' (UFDD) and the 'Mouvement National pour la Réforme' (MNR). This pact entailed the integration of the rebel fighters in the Chadian army within three months and a monitoring unit organised by the UNHCR to facilitate the return of refugees. It was never implemented, just as no progress was made during the year with the peace accord between the rebel groups and the government concluded in Sirte in 2007. The political opposition, united in the 'Coalition des Partis Politiques pour la Défense de la Constitution' (CPDC), called for a peace conference.

Internal **political dialogue** advanced slowly, with the CPDC disagreeing with the proposed electoral reform. They claimed that the 'Commission Électorale Nationale Indépendante' (CENI) would lack independence from the state apparatus. Outside legal advice from the OIF was called to help. Agreement was reached over two draft laws regulating the status of the opposition and the charter of political parties. These laws were approved by the cabinet on 4 June, and were adopted by the National Assembly on 16 July. However, there was again protest from the CPDC because one provision in the laws had been removed without their consent.

Between 20 May and 30 June, the government undertook a **population census** in line with the agreement of 13 August 2008 with the CPDC, in order to prepare the electoral process. The results published on 13 October were accepted by all parties as a basis for planning the elections. The 30 members of the CENI, presided over by Gami Ngarmajal, secretary general of the Teachers' Union, were appointed by presidential decree on 13 July.

Over the year, there were two **cabinet reshuffles**. The first, on 23 March, brought no major changes in the responsibilities of the key ministries. The former rebel leader, Yaya Dillo, had to resign as minister of mines and energy, while the total number of ministers was increased to 41. On 5 June, there was also a minor cabinet reshuffle involving the ministry of mines and geology and the ministry of livestock and animal health.

On 12 June, former president Felix Malloum (1975–1979) died in Ndjaména. Another former president, Goukouni Oueddey (1979–1982), returned from exile in Algeria on 18 August. He declared that he wanted to play a reconciliatory role and began with a tour of his home area around Bardai to have meetings with local leaders opposed to President Idriss Déby Itno.

There were several ongoing efforts to improve **human rights** in the country, focused on the problem of rape in and around refugee camps in the east, but also in the rest of the country, where women marched to protest against domestic violence. The government gave free access to 85 child soldiers out of 212 suspected rebels captured after the May attacks. Despite this sign of good will, UNICEF estimated that approximately 10,000 children under 18 were still working for both the army and the rebel forces.

There were **riots** in the capital on 14 January, following a government ban on the use of charcoal in the large cities to protect the environment. This measure made the already hard living conditions in Ndjaména even worse. Later in the month, there were protests over forced evictions and house demolitions affecting 10,000–15,000 people in the capital. The government claimed that these people were illegally occupying state property needed for the construction of public facilities, such as a maternity hospital. The evicted were given no compensation, despite efforts by magistrates to stop the government action.

Foreign Affairs

Relations with **Sudan** remained the centre of attention. At the beginning of the year, there were attempts to begin the implementation of the Dakar agreement of 13 March 2008. The Dakar group, in which Libya, Sudan, Chad, Gabon, the Republic of Congo, Senegal and Eritrea participate, had last met in November 2008. Agreement was reached to set up joint border patrols composed of 1,000 troops each from both Sudan and Chad in order to ensure there were no further incursions by rebels from either side. On 3 May, an agreement was concluded in Doha under the aegis of the Sultan of Qatar to refrain from the use of violence against each other and to cease supporting rebel groups. However, the ink was not yet dry on the agreement when, on 4 May, Chadian rebels staged an attack in eastern Chad. Subsequently, the Chadian government accused Sudan of hosting and helping Chadian rebels and threatened to sever ties with Sudan once again. On 15–16 May, the Chadian army attacked rebel positions in Sudan as far as 40 km from the border inside Darfur. On 17 May, Chad retreated, claiming to have destroyed seven rebel bases. Sudan protested and called for restraint. On 28–29 May, there were reports of bombing by Sudanese aircraft in Bahai in eastern Chad. Relations remained strained and no progress was made with respect to the implementation of the peace accords. Diplomatic efforts by Egypt, Libya and Qatar continued, aimed at bringing the two countries together, and the embassies of both countries remained open. On 29–30 May, Libyan President Muammar Kadhafi met separately with Presidents Déby and Al-Bachir at the margins of the 11th summit of the Community of the Sahel-Saharan States. However, there were unconfirmed reports of Chadian bombing on Sudanese territory and Déby called for the closure of Sudanese schools and cultural centres in Chad, as teachers employed by those institutions were Sudanese potential agents.

On 14 January, the **UN Security Council** adopted resolution 1861, extending the mandate of MINURCAT until 15 March 2010 and permitting the deployment of 5,500 peacekeepers from 15 March until 15 March 2010 to succeed the European peace-keeping mission (EUFOR), which was due to end on the same date. Of these 5,500 troops, 4,900 were to be stationed in Chad and 500 in CAR. Given the short period of time between the adoption of the resolution and the start of its mandate, it was feared there would be a power vacuum if there were not a smooth handover between EUFOR and MINURCAT. MINURCAT was given free access to all but two EUFOR sites for the duration of the mandate, as well as exclusive use of airport facilities in Ndjaména and Abéché. Fortunately, a number of European countries agreed to have 1,877 troops (from Albania, Austria, Croatia, Ireland, Finland, France, Poland and Russia) 'rehatted' as UN troops, with 140 troops from new contributors Ghana and Togo. However, as of 31 March, the strength of the force stood only at 2,079 troops, 40% of those authorised. Deployment was delayed because of limitations on air movement and air freight facilities in Ndjaména. Despite its budget of $ 691 m, the mission lacked critical equipment, such as patrolling helicopters, and engineering capacity to keep the helicopters in the air for day and night patrol availability. This equipment was critical, given its operational area of 1,000 km x 450 km.

MINURCAT continued to provide technical and logistical support for the DIS in executing its task, mediating in finding funding for the DIS and supporting efforts to reform and reinforce the judicial system in eastern Chad. In September, a total of 248 UN police men and women were supporting Chadian security forces in maintaining security. However, military capacity stood at only 2,655 troops on 15 September. Where needed, MINURCAT backed up the DIS in protecting refugee camps and humanitarian convoys but, due to lack of fuel, troops, air medical evacuation capacity and critical engineering capacity, not all demands could be met.

Following the ICC's arrest warrant against Sudan's president and the subsequent expulsion of 13 international NGOs and restrictions on the functioning of UN organisations in Darfur, there were fears of a renewed influx of Darfur **refugees** into Chad. In the southeast, there was a renewed influx of refugees from **CAR**, resulting from banditry and fighting between the government and rebels. Between January and May, more than 18,000 refugees were hosted in six camps near Daha and Haraze, where major operations were also carried out by MINURCAT in order to provide a security umbrella for humanitarian aid. These operations were critical for creating the necessary conditions for providing aid during the rainy season, when most of the area would be inaccessible. In areas deemed safe, UNHCR cut back on assistance to IDPs to give them an incentive to return to their homes. As a result, 20,700 IDPs returned to the Dar Sila region in the areas of Koukou, Tiero, Marena and Loboutique.

In February, **Belgium** filed a lawsuit at the International Court of Justice against former president Hissein Habré, under whose regime about 40,000 people had died in prison. The intention was to exert pressure on **Senegal** to prosecute Habré, while the Senegalese government seemed reluctant to do so, claiming to need an additional CFAfr 18 bn to carry out the trial.

The **World Bank** re-opened its office in Ndjaména on 16 January, after its closure following the rebel attacks in February 2008 and the souring of relations with the government following the latter's unilateral suspension of the oil contract. An eventual expansion of support was said to depend on the performance of the Chadian government in poverty reduction. For the present, only on-going projects in education, the struggle against HIV-AIDS infection, and agriculture were administered by the Bank. The Chadian government declared it was pleased with the World Bank's return, because it considered the Bank to be an important partner in development.

France successfully mediated in the disagreement between the Chadian government and the opposition over the new electoral code. French Foreign Minister Bernard Kouchner visited Chad several times and was present at the handover of command from EUFOR to MINURCAT. However, France was also questioned by its European partners and accused of bias as a result of its unrelenting support for Déby. Paris also faced accusations of doing too little to support the peace process, in their view, and for its policy with respect to the provision of intelligence information to the Chadian government. France claimed it was providing intelligence to all parties involved in the process – Chad and Sudan, as well as EUFOR and MINURCAT. The French foreign minister also said that the solution to the Chadian conflict would rest with Sudan, even though the French were also disappointed that Déby had not done much to implement the 2007 Sirte peace agreement with the armed opposition.

Socioeconomic Developments

In the capital, Ndjaména, life became increasingly difficult following the ban on the use of charcoal, especially for poor residents, who could not afford alternative fuel. The **provision of electricity and water** was also deteriorating because the 'Société Tchadienne de l'Eau et de l'Électricité' (STEE) was not able to improve its performance and produced little more than 20 MW of electricity.

The harvest over the 2008–2009 agricultural season was estimated at 1.8 m metric tonnes. This was 10% down from the record harvest of the previous season, with the most striking shortfall in the Salamat, where most of the country's flood recession sorghum is produced. The **food security situation** was satisfactory overall in January, though prices remained high because of the high demand to replenish the national security stock. Low livestock prices in the Kanem-Batha region depressed the exchange rate between livestock and cereals for the (agro-)pastoral population, who depend on the sale of animals to acquire their staple food. This caused stress on the food market. By March, there was more food insecurity in this area and in parts of the south, which had been stricken by floods in the preceding season. Prices remained above the long-term average during April. Grain markets in the east were disrupted in May as a result of rebel attacks.

In May, there was alarm over chronic food insecurity in the Kanem region, when child mortality rates rose above three per 10,000 per day. Since the 1980s, the region has been chronically food insecure due to a combination of floods, droughts and poor infrastructure. An emergency project was started to work out an integrated strategy of food aid and to provide technical assistance, but long-term funding was not yet secured.

The rainy season started early in the southeast, but the rains were soon followed by dry spells in July, which forced farmers to replant later in the season. In the north the rains were late, leading to a very harsh hunger season because many livestock returned later from the south and did not produce milk for the population. It also led to massive livestock deaths. As there was no market supply, the national reserve could not be replenished and prices were 18%–53% above the long-term average. Later in the season, pasture conditions started to improve, though high cereal prices eroded the exchange rate for livestock. In September, 175,000 people were affected by floods in the west of the country and 1,000 families needed emergency assistance. By the end of the season, rainfall deficits were recorded in most areas. At the first harvest-time, prices fell but remained far above average. Due to the low rainfall, water sources dried up quickly, leading to problems with the flood recession and dry season crops. In November, it was estimated that cereal production was down by 31% compared with 2008 and 34% below the long-term average. Pasture conditions for livestock were poor for the second consecutive year. The forecast for the flood recession crops was also bad and in December it was estimated that a net deficit of 637,000 tons of cereals was developing. Food prices were highest in the subregion and, as the harvests in neighbouring countries were also poor, not much could be expected from cross-border trade and traditional safety nets. In October, the Global Acute Malnutrition rate in the town of Abeché was found to be 20.6%, above the intervention threshold of 15%, and measures were being taken to improve the food supply and health conditions as 19.8% of children were suffering from diarrhoea and 13.3% from respiratory infections. The cost of living rose steeply with the heavy influx of aid agency personnel and foreign troops, though the latter tried to compensate the population by providing free electricity and drinking water.

In May, the W-135 strain of **meningitis** showed up in the west of Chad after a ten-year absence and 102 people died. The authorities vaccinated hundreds of thousands of people in the regions of Chari-Baguirmi, Tandjile and Mandoul, as well as in Ndjaména. In

October, there were six new cases of polio, bringing the total number to 30, with some of them located in the capital. An extensive vaccination campaign was started at the end of October, as less than 50% of all children had been vaccinated.

Economic growth was hampered by a **fall in oil prices** on the global market and also in oil production. Instead of the expected 83.3 m barrels only 52 m barrels were produced and oil prices were significantly lower than in 2008, when a record of $ 1.87 bn of revenue was achieved. Estimated GDP growth was just 1.6% (against the 3.5% initially expected). Non-oil GDP increased by 4.0%, while oil-related GDP fell by 3.4%. The consumer index rose by 4.0%. Total GDP was estimated at CFAfr 2,158.8 bn.

As a result, government revenues were much lower than anticipated at only CFAfr 343.5 bn, instead of the CFAfr 716.2 bn expected. Foreign finance for development investment was also less than expected. Military spending remained higher than normal at CFAfr 205.7 bn. In consultation with the IMF, the **budget** was amended by slowing down investments in priority sectors. The remaining gap of almost 18% of GDP was financed mainly by using Chadian government reserves deposited with the BEAC.

Han van Dijk

Congo

Political discussion focused mainly on the intensification of President Denis Sassou Nguesso's (and his allies') search for control of power. International relations were dominated by .a number of significant bilateral agreements. The economic situation remained unfavourable for most of the population, and a series of strike actions towards the end of the year highlighted the effects of the economic crisis.

Domestic Politics

Three significant events provided the framework for the political year: discussions ignited by the death of President Sassou Nguesso's daughter in the spring, the president's re-election in the summer, and the final establishment of a new regime in the autumn, marked simultaneously by the death of one of the more symbolic opponents of the regime, Bernard Kolélas, the amnesty granted to former president Pascal Lissouba and the effective return of Pasteur Ntumi.

The president's oldest daughter and wife of Gabon's President Omar Bongo Ondimba, **Edith Lucie Bongo Ondimba**, died on 14 March in Morocco and Sassou Nguesso and his wife received messages of condolence from international and national dignitaries.

Many photographs of the funeral, some showing the president in tears, supported by two women, were circulated on the internet with a variety of comments. One comment claimed that, with the death of his daughter, Sassou was going through the same experience as ordinary Congolese during the civil war, while others added that he would have been insensitive to their feelings when they lost their loved-ones. Mrs Bongo was buried on 22 March, in Edou, her father's village, in the district of Oyo (department of La Cuvette). A few days later, a witch-hunt was launched against those who had illegally appropriated and circulated the photographs, which allegedly dishonoured the image of the president.

Although the re-election of Sassou Nguesso could be taken for granted, the imminence of the elections brought with it **widespread fear of potential violence** associated with political transition, and all sorts of social disturbances were envisaged. As a consequence, a seminar on the prevention of electoral conflict was held well in advance. On 8 January, the 'Programme de renforcement des capacités des organisations de la société civile dans la prévention, la gestion et la résolution des conflits en Afrique centrale' organised a workshop on "Conflicts in Congo. What can the civil society expect?" at the premises of the UN information centre in Brazzaville. The participants proposed the development of conflict prevention strategies in the run-up to the elections. They insisted first on the need for politicians and the media to adopt moderate and calm language during the election campaign. They also made a plea for the establishment of accurate and transparent electoral rolls, the application of and respect for existing laws, a sensitization campaign on peace culture, and the reinforcement of police neutrality. On a broader front, participants called for the improvement of living conditions for the population, equal distribution of national revenue, liberalisation of the media, promotion of freedom of thought and tolerance, and the neutrality of civil society with respect to political parties and other organisations. Lastly, they suggested the organisation of services of prayer throughout the country.

Presidential elections were held in July. Since the end of 2008, various political parties had declared their support for the outgoing president and encouraged him to stand for a new seven-year term. Supportive messages came from all over Congo, from both rural and urban areas, and were voiced by all kinds of organisations (parties, associations, etc). However, while information circulated about the imminence of the elections, the exact date was not officially set, leading the Constitutional Court, on 28 April, to ask for a precise date. A decree published by the presidency on 8 May set the election date for 12 July. One week later, on 19 May, Minister of Territorial Administration and Decentralisation Raymond Mboulou fixed the period for the declaration of candidates as 21 May to 12 June. Sassou Nguesso announced his own candidature only on 6 June, claiming he was responding to popular pressure. According to the official results declared on 15 July, Sassou Nguesso won in the first round against 12 other candidates, with 78.6% of the votes. The candidate who came second, Joseph Kingnoumbi Kia Mboungou (independent), lagged far behind with just 7.5%, while Mathias Dzon ('Union Patriotique pour le Renouveau National', UPRN), who was seen by many as the most serious challenger, came fourth with only 2.3%. Various observers, among them delegates of the French National Assembly, AU, CEEAC and OIF, declared the elections free and fair. However, on 17 July, three losing candidates launched an appeal, asking the Constitutional Court to cancel the results. The Court nevertheless rejected their claim and confirmed the results on 25 July. Sassou was sworn in on 14 August in the National Assembly. A month later, on 15 September, a new government of 37 ministers was named. It had one minister fewer than the previous government and Prime Minister Isidore Mvouba retained his position.

The **death of influential elites and well-known opponents** received widespread comment. The first, Jean-Baptiste Tati-Loutard, was minister of state for hydrocarbons when he died on 4 July in Paris. He was a well-known poet and had held ministerial positions in various governments since 1975. His burial took place on 19 July in Ngoyo, department of Pointe-Noire. However, the most significant departure was that of Bernard Bakana Kolélas, MP for the Pool region, unchallenged leader of the 'Mouvement Congolais pour la Démocratie et le Développement Intégral' (MCDDI), and an extremely rebellious and prominent opponent of the regime, who had challenged the ruling 'Parti Congolais du Travail' (PCT) under the one-party system. He died in Paris on 13 November and his burial took place on 22 November at Ntsouéké, a village close to Brazzaville. Lastly, on 5 December, the death occurred of Jacques Mouanda Mpassi, influential member of the 'Union Panafricaine pour le Développement Sociale' (UPADS), the party of former president Pascal Lissouba. Mouanda Mpassi was seen as the most virulent opposition adversary of Sassou. He died in Brazzaville, following a heart attack. The speed and suddenness of his death left room for suspicion that he was poisoned by the president's camp, who allegedly wanted to get rid of this awkward rival.

In addition to these disappearances, Sassou Nguesso's control of political power was also consolidated, on 11 December, by the Senate's adoption of an **amnesty** for former president Pascal Lissouba, who had lived in exile since 1997. The High Court of Justice had condemned him to death in absentia for high treason in 2001. On the instruction of the president, the government had initiated an amnesty bill referring to articles 11 and 118 of the Constitution of 20 January 2002. The amnesty sought to meet concerns about national reconciliation, the search for durable peace and national concord.

Finally, on 28 December, Frédéric Binstsangou alias Pasteur Ntumi, returned to Brazzaville and was officially appointed the president's general delegate, responsible for the "promotion of peace values and war reparation". Pasteur Ntumi continued to control a group of militiamen in the Pool region and controlled the destiny of the '**Conseil National des Républicains**' (CNR). At the beginning of the year, some elements of consensus emerged between the CNR and the government. The *ad hoc* committee for the follow-up of peace negotiations in the Pool department had met on 31 December 2008 in Brazzaville and decided to start the implementation of disarmament and identification of ex-combatants. The *ad hoc* committee had also taken into account the recommendation, resulting from the dialogue between government and CNR representatives, that disarmament, identification of ex-combatants, and social and economic rehabilitation should take place together in order to save time, for which Pasteur Ntumi expressed his support.

Foreign Affairs

Foreign affairs were dominated by the renegotiation of multilateral and bilateral agreements. On 9 January, the government signed a joint programme financing agreement (2009–2013) worth $ 68 m with UNDP, UNFPA and UNICEF. On 9 May, it signed a voluntary partnership agreement with the EU on the application of forestry regulations, governance issues and commercial exchanges of wood and derivative products with the European Community. This agreement, the first of its kind in Central Africa, fixed mutual obligations to provide a joint response to the problem of illegal exploitation of tropical forests and the associated trade by linking good governance in Congo to the internal market of the EU. It established a system for controlling the conformity of exports of timber and derivative products with Congolese forestry regulations. Some bilateral relations improved significantly. On 13 and 14 January, expert delegations of the two Congos met in Brazzaville in order to discuss an economic action plan for the implementation of certain joint development projects, specifically the construction of the road and rail bridge between **Brazzaville and Kinshasa** and the electricity-generation project connecting the Inga III dam (DR Congo), which should feed the towns of Kinshasa, Cabinda and Pointe-Noire. In February, decision-makers from both countries' public and private sectors met to launch a business facilitation network between the two countries. This meeting was organised by the 'Union Congolaise des Petites et Moyennes Entreprises' (UCPME) joinly with the CEEAC. Participants dealt with issues of co-operation between the economic sectors of the two countries. The stakeholders developed tools allowing an effective liberalisation of exchanges between the two Congos. In March, the two countries confirmed their commitment to preserving the trans-border hydro-forest zone by implementing a project that should respond to the comprehensive framework of the strategic programme of UNDP's Global Environment Facility for the management of the Congo basin. On 25 April, an agreement was signed on cooperation in the field of technical and professional education.

On 20 January, the **US** ambassador inaugurated the new premises of the US embassy a few hours before President Barack Obama took office. The new building was presented as an effective guarantee for the reinforcement of mutual co-operation.

Congo's historic support for the anti-apartheid movement in **Southern Africa** was confirmed when, on 23 June, an African National Congress (ANC) delegation visited Brazzaville in order to reinforce relations between Congo and South Africa, as well as between the ANC and the PCT. In addition, Congo and Namibia signed a cooperation agreement for the construction of a technical training centre, the 'Institut de Formation Technique et Professionnelle de Loudima' (IFTPL). The project is a revival of the old centre run by Namibia's ruling South West African People's Organisation (SWAPO) in Loudima, which had been used for the SWAPO executive's political and military training from 1986 to 1991.

The year ended with bilateral agreements with the former colonial power, **France**. On 22 October, seven protocols were signed. The most important aimed at funding the development of social funds in conjunction with Congolese civil society organisations. This project should help to improve living conditions for the rural and urban populations and received support totaling CFAfr 44 m. An agreement to strengthen the programme to fight against poaching in the Nouabalé-Ndoki (Sangha/Likouala) national park was signed with the NGO Wildlife Conservation Society Congo. Further projects concerned a plastic recycling project, the socio-economic integration of people from the Pool region displaced during the 1997 civil war, and health and school projects. In addition, on 5 November, the French government made a grant of CFAfr 31 m for the maintenance and repair of Congolese Armed Forces vehicles in Brazzaville.

Socio-economic Development

The economic situation remained deplorable for most of the population, in spite of the enormous oil resources. To fight against the **effects of the high cost of living**, the government began the year by evaluating and reinforcing the application of measures taken on 12 May 2008 in relation to the sky rocketing of the prices of all consumables, including the reduction and lifting of certain taxes on basic products. Thus, on 9 January, in Pointe-Noire, Commercial, Consumption and Provisioning Minister Jeanne Dambendzet, Security, Law and Order Minister Paul Mbot, and Transport and the Civil Aviation Minister Emile Ouosso, gave a serious warning to economic operators at a working meeting. The government ordered them to lower the market prices of essential products in order to alleviate the suffering of consumers. The government delegation reprimanded importers, wholesalers, distributors and forwarding agents, who had till then obstinately refused to respect the efforts of the government and persisted in their malpractices. On 29 January, again in Pointe-Noire, the prime minister reiterated this call.

On 3 February, the National Assembly adopted the **budget**, which was significantly lower than the previous one, at CFAfr 1,403 bn compared with the revised 2008 budget of CFAfr 2,756 bn. The reduction was part of the strategy implemented by the government to make the country eligible for the next HIPC stages. Government expenditure fell from CFAfr 913 bn to CFAfr 888 bn, while the investment budget rose from CFAfr 455 bn to CFAfr 514 bn. The major difference was in oil revenues, which were forecast to fall from CFAfr 2,373 bn (2008) to CFAfr 975 bn owing to an expected sharp decline in oil prices on the world market. Oil production was actually set to increase slightly, but the income generated related to the volatility of the price of the barrel and the fluctuation of the exchange rate between the CFAfr and the US$. The budget built on significantly higher income from the non-oil sector, predicted to reach CFAfr 386 bn (an increase of CFAfr 57 bn), due mainly to an increase in tax revenue. Public debt servicing amounted to CFAfr 294 bn (slightly up by CFAfr 7 bn).

On 7 March, the Italian government decided to cancel the debt of CFAfr 36 bn owed by the Congolese government. This meant that all **debts** (owed to Italy) in the framework of the Paris Club of creditors had now been cancelled, although an agreement signed in Paris on 11 December 2008 had prescribed a reduction of only 90%. On 10 April, Germany cancelled commercial debts of CFAfr 22 bn and rescheduled non-commercial debts in the framework of its development aid, amounting to almost CFAfr 6 bn.

On 30 November, the IMF's board of directors examined the economic performance of Congo in the framework of its second triennial review of the PRGF. On 4 December, it approved the report and released a further PRGF tranche worth $ 1.95 m. According to the IMF, the government had improved its performance over the past few years with regard to revenue-generation from **the non-oil sector** and had thereby reduced its dependence on oil production. The Congolese authorities aimed at completing the reform of the tax and customs system and initiating changes of the fiscal policy with the technical assistance of the IMF. Likewise, on 14 December, the World Bank expressed satisfaction with efforts to meet the completion point within the HIPC initiative, estimating that all conditions for attaining this goal were fulfilled.

On 20 April, the government and major companies engaged in the oil sector, i.e. the state-owned 'Société Nationale de Pétrole du Congo' (SNPC), PUMA and X-OIL, concluded an agreement on methods of finishing the process of privatising Hydro-Congo and transferring all its assets to various companies. The agreement also aimed at supplementing the framework of contractual relations between the state and the oil companies and agreeing on a division of the sector into four **fields**, namely field A, allocated to Total, field B to be allocated after selection by the state, field C1 to Puma, field C2 to X-Oil, and field D to the SNPC-AOGC (Africa Oil Gas Corporation) consortium. These agreements put an end to the provision of oil products for the national market by the state via SNPC and removed the existing mechanism of quotas, which had frequently resulted in shortages of supply. The new principles allowed the private oil companies to purchase oil directly at the CORAF ('Société Congolaise de Raffinage') refinery and build up stocks to cover 15 days' consumption.

Unusual **commercial interests** emerged when Tunisian and Dutch businessmen explored possibilities for future investment. On 9 June, a meeting took place between multi-sector delegations of Tunisian and Pointe-Noire businessmen on the occasion of the Tunisia-Congo partnership days. Several partnerships were concluded in the areas of painting for construction projects, hotel fitting and furnishing, oil exploitation, and agricultural production, as well as information and communication technologies. On 27 and

28 August, a delegation of Dutch businessmen visited Congo to explore opportunities, particularly in port management and agriculture. They met their Congolese counterparts at the Chamber of Commerce in Brazzaville.

According to UNICEF figures delivered on 15 April within the framework of the launching of a "white paper on the protection of the children in Congo", poverty would affect 54% of children below the age of 15 years, i.e.1.2 m individuals. Children suffer from shortages of money, and poor levels of access to education, nutrition, health, water, sanitation and housing. The main aim of this white paper was to **redefine** the social contract in favour of children and to implement the PRSP.

On 28 August, the National Assembly adopted a set of laws against corruption aimed at raising moral standards in public life. This was a response to a key requirement for attaining the HIPC completion point. Subsequently, a capacity-building seminar was held in Brazzaville on 25 September, attended by the members of the national Commission to Fight Corruption.

The end of the year brought some social **protest action**. In Likouala, a group of non-permanent civil servants took strike action for 15 days from 24 September to protest against salary arrears of seven to nine months. In addition, a teachers' strike in certain schools in the Plateaux region disrupted the beginning of the 2009–2010 school year. On 5 October, the national coordination of workers associated with companies in liquidation proposed a sit-in in front of the ministry of justice and human rights to protest against the non-payment of their salaries. On 20 October, this collective urged the most powerful trade unions to inform the minister of finance about their situation, deploring the administration's lack of action. The group represented the interests of 4,369 workers from 26 companies. On 6 November, more than 90% of employees of Warid Télécom decided to begin an unlimited strike to protest against the dismissal of more than half of the company's 220 employees. In response, at a general assembly on 9 November, the executive director of Warid-Congo announced a company restructuring plan. He claimed that this would improve efficiency and said that staff reductions would be carried out transparently and without discrimination.

For the first time, and only as a result of international aid efforts, the government showed concern about the development of rural areas. Six departments (Brazzaville, Pointe-Noire, Niari, Likouala, Cuvette and Sangha) received funds totaling CFAfr 344.5 m from the 'Fonds de Soutien à l'Agriculture'. This action was aimed at reviving agriculture through the implementation of 25 projects. The announcement was made on 19 April, at the end of the first session of the technical committee for project validation, which met in Brazzaville's Forum for Investment in Regional Agriculture. The EU contributed € 1.5 m in support of these projects.

Rémy Bazenguissa-Ganga

Democratic Republic of the Congo

Celebrating his third year in office after his election victory in 2006, President Joseph Kabila had few achievements to show as peace and reconstruction made slow progress at best. However, political events were dominated by a breath-taking turnaround in relations between Rwanda and Congo, which held the promise of bringing some form of peace to eastern Congo. The rebel movement 'Conseil National pour la Défense du Peuple' (CNDP) struck a deal with the government after its chairman had been ousted. In a closely related development, Kinshasa invited the Rwandan army back to Congo to join the fight against the Rwandan rebels of the 'Forces Démocratiques pour la Libération du Rwanda' (FDLR).

Domestic Politics

The tentative **rapprochement between Rwanda and the DR Congo** of late 2008 came into full relief in 2009. It had a significant bearing on Congo's national politics as well as on the situation in its eastern part. The new Rwandan-Congolese entente triggered a series of unexpected events that dramatically changed the political and military landscape. The first turnaround concerned an outbreak of power struggles within the CNDP, the

North Kivu-based rebel group that over the previous three years had inflicted severe military defeats on Congo's national army, the 'Forces Armées de la République Démocratique du Congo' (FARDC). On 5 January, Jean-Bosco Ntaganda, CNDP's chief of staff, declared that the rebels' high command had removed Laurent Nkunda from the movement's leadership amid accusations of "poor leadership" and "bad governance", although statements by Nkunda insisted that he was still chairman of the CNDP. The second unexpected incident occurred on 16 January, when Ntaganda appeared in Goma, where he held talks with Interior Minister Célestin Mbuyu and Congolese and Rwandan army chiefs. After the meeting, Ntaganda announced a truce and said that he was immediately putting "all CNDP combat forces at the disposal" of the army "for their integration into the FARDC". Roadblocks erected by both the CNDP and the FARDC were removed with immediate effect. On the following day the pro-government militia 'Patriotes Résistants du Congo' (PARECO) also declared an end to hostilities. Four days later (20 January), about 2,000 troops of the Rwandan Defence Forces (RDF) crossed the border into North Kivu north of Goma for joint military operations with the Congolese army against the estimated 5,000 to 6,000 FDLR fighters, a decision that had been taken the previous month. An additional 1,500 to 2,000 RDF troops were deployed to Congo shortly thereafter. Before taking on the FDLR, however, the Rwandan and Congolese soldiers advanced on Nkunda's headquarters in Bunaganga near Rutshuru, forcing the CNDP chairman to flee. The fast-moving events came to a head on 23 January, when the Rwandan authorities announced **Nkunda's arrest** in Gisenyi, thus ending the internal CNDP power struggle in favour of Ntaganda. It thus appeared that, within less than a month, the groundwork for peace in eastern Congo had been laid, a feat that had proved elusive for many years.

The sheer speed of the turnaround was as impressive as it was unexpected and left many observers perplexed, including many of North Kivu's citizens, who could barely comprehend that the former occupying force from Rwanda had been invited back into Congo by President Kabila. With hindsight, the **reasons behind the shifting alliances** seemed to be the convergence of interests of Kigali and Kinshasa. Kabila's evident powerlessness to neutralise the CNDP had become a political and military embarrassment as well as a source of rising opposition to Kabila within the Kivus. Striking a deal with Rwanda that eliminated the problem carried great political risks in view of the resentment that the return of Rwandan troops would spark domestically, but Kabila had few other choices as neither Angola nor the EU, nor indeed the UN Mission in the DR Congo (MONUC), were willing or able to solve the Nkunda problem for the government. Kigali's rationale was most likely informed by the escalating international costs it incurred as a result of its support for the CNDP. A report published in late 2008 by UN experts had detailed Rwanda's alliance with the Congolese rebels. Although the core allegations were hardly novel, the report instigated something of an international outcry. Some observers believed that the UK and the US in particular pressurised Kigali to stop supporting the rebels and to cooperate with Kinshasa. Ntaganda's collaboration in the deal was finally secured through pressure from Kigali and money from Kinshasa. It is also clear that he obtained the (uncertain) promise of the Kinshasa authorities that he would not be handed over to the ICC in The Hague, which had issued a warrant for his arrest in 2008. Ntaganda was accused of the war crime of enlistment and conscription of children, which he allegedly committed while serving as the chief of staff of the 'Front Patriotique pour la Libération du Congo' (FPLC) in Ituri in 2002 and 2003. To gain the broader support in the CNDP for a change of its leadership, Kinshasa offered additional concessions. According to the ICG, these included guarantees against prosecution for all CNDP commanders; de facto political control of North Kivu's 'petit nord' (Masisi, Rutshuru, Walikale territories) by the Banyarwanda ethnic group, which provides the backbone of the rebel movement; and leadership positions for CNDP's political and military leaders in the provincial administration and the army units deployed in North Kivu.

The sudden outbreak of peace in North Kivu was formalised on 23 March, when the Congolese government, the CNDP and various pro-government Mai Mai groups, including PARECO, signed a **peace accord in Goma**. In the presence of the UN secretary general's special envoy in eastern Congo, former Nigerian president Olusegun Obasanjo, the new civilian president of the CNDP, Désiré Kamanzi, signed the agreement. The Goma accord stipulated the transformation of the former rebel group into a political party and the integration of its fighters into the FARDC. Moreover, CNDP members were to deploy in Rutshuru and Masisi territories as part of their integration into the provincial administration. Another element of the deal, an amnesty for "acts of rebellion and acts of war" was formally adopted by the Congolese parliament on 5 May. However, it became clear that some members of the CNDP were not satisfied with the new course of action the group had taken and in mid-June clashes were reported in Goma between Ntaganda supporters and followers of Laurent Nkunda, who appeared to command loyalty within the group. Rumours suggested that Rwanda intervened in an attempt to solve the dispute. On 11 November, Désiré Kamanzi resigned as the president of the movement, officially citing the failure of the government to implement the Goma peace accord, but it was speculated whether internal conflicts were a more pressing reason for his departure.

Unsurprisingly, the deal between Kabila and the CNDP had economic and political ramifications in North Kivu. It marked a power shift away from autochthonous ethnic groups, notably the Nande, who had come to dominate the province in the wake of the 2006 elections. Given the popular perception that the CNDP (and its predecessor, the 'Rassemblement Congolais pour la Démocratie' – RCD) drew its strength from the Rwanda-backed Tutsi community, ethnic tensions were once more on the rise. The settling of scores and long-standing conflicts over land mean that North Kivu will remain a powder keg for many years to come, regardless of the uncertain question of whether the CNDP rebellion has come to a definite end or not. Highlighting the polarised political climate were the reactions to the incremental return of Congolese Tutsi refugees from

Rwanda. An estimated 12,000 refugees (out of some 60,000) were reported to have arrived in North Kivu. Wild rumours from other communities and associated leaders circulated about the illegal immigration of tens of thousands of 'Rwandans' and claims that Kigali and the CNDP were conspiring to change the demography to occupy and control land in Masisi.

The turn of events in eastern Congo had political repercussions on the national level. The invitation to the Rwandan army to return shook Kinshasa's political scene like an earthquake. The National Assembly was in recess, but numerous deputies expressed their irritation and anger at Kabila's decision. Spearheading the protest was **Vital Kamerhe**, the Speaker of the National Assembly, a senior figure in Kabila's government coalition 'Alliance pour la Majorité Présidentielle' (AMP) and a native of South Kivu. Kamerhe attempted to organise an emergency session of parliament to discuss the turn of events and criticised the government for not having notified parliament of its decision. More striking was the fact that not even the chief of staff of the Congolese army, Didier Etumba, had been involved in the preparation of the military operation 'Umoja Wetu' (Our Unity). More than 250 members of parliament signed a petition in favour of an emergency session, including a significant number of deputies from the AMP. The overt challenge to Kabila's gamble had political consequences. Kabila forced four senior members of the Bureau of the National Assembly to resign. Only Kamerhe resisted the pressure, but he eventually quit on 25 March. He was replaced by Evariste Boshab, Kabila's former chief of staff and the parliamentary leader of the 'Parti du Peuple pour la Réconstruction et la Démocratie' (PPRD).

The joint **Congolese-Rwandan operations against the FDLR** were a politically sensitive exercise, but their military and security implications were a quite different matter. As scheduled, the month-long operation **Umoja Wetu** ended on 25 February and the Rwandan army left Congo. The results were mixed at best, though both the Congolese and Rwandan military described the operation as a success. Limited to North Kivu province, the operation targeted FDLR strongholds in Masisi, Rutshuru and Walikale. Relatively few direct clashes occurred as the FDLR withdrew to more remote locations and dispersed into smaller groups in anticipation of the offensive. According to the UN, the operation resulted in the repatriation of more than 6,000 Rwandans from the Congo, but this included former Rwandans in the ranks of the CNDP and a large number of civilians and dependants. Only an estimated 400 FDLR combatants had returned to Rwanda within the first two months of the year. On the negative side, the FDLR conducted reprisals against the civilian population, resulting in at least 75 arbitrary killings and 40 rapes.

Following the end of Umoja Wetu, the Congolese government requested MONUC to assist it in follow-up operations against the FDLR. This permitted MONUC to return to the game; it had been prevented from even monitoring the Congolese-Rwandan military offensive. The new operation, called **'Kimia II'** started in North Kivu on 2 March and was aimed at further weakening the FDLR and preventing it from reoccupying territory it had abandoned during Umoja Wetu, primarily in the territories of Lubero, Masisi and Rutshuru (North Kivu). The UN mission provided logistical and fire support to FARDC, and sought to protect the civilian population. The newly integrated FARDC units that participated in the operation included large numbers of former CNDP and PARECO soldiers. Cooperation with these units posed a problem for MONUC as rumours spread that Ntaganda, wanted by the ICC, was involved in Kimia II, an allegation that the minister of defence denied. In military terms, Kimia II claimed a number of successes. The FARDC took control of several areas, including mining sites, from which the FDLR had been dislodged during Umoja Wetu in Walikale, Lubero, Shabunda and Virunga National Park. In late June, MONUC noted that 624 FDLR fighters had joined its disarmament, demobilisation, repatriation, reintegration and resettlement process, a significant increase over past years. However, the humanitarian costs of the operation increased dramatically as the FDLR fought back or carried out reprisal attacks against the civilian population. In Lubero alone, around 100,000 people were displaced by mid-year. An estimated 125 civilians were killed in North Kivu during Kimia II. Starting on 23 June, the Kimia II operation was extended to South Kivu province, resulting in a dramatic and immediate increase of insecurity, due to fighting, human rights abuses by the Congolese army and reprisals against civilians by the FDLR. The UN special rapporteur on extrajudicial executions, Philip Alston, who visited DR Congo in October, said that since January 2009, the FDLR had committed an average of 50–60 killings per month, compared with less than ten killings per month in 2008.

In due course, national and internal human rights groups expressed their concern about the devastating **humanitarian toll of the military campaign against the FDLR**. Inevitably, the **role (and responsibility) of MONUC**, which supported the campaign, was put under the spotlight. Activists expressed dismay at the mission's failure to protect civilians and stop the abuses committed by the Congolese army. Thus MONUC faced tough questions, especially in view of the fact that the UN Security Council had determined in Resolution 1856 (22 December 2008) that the mission should give the protection of civilians the "highest priority". Implicit to the conundrum, though rarely articulated, was the question of whether the results of the military operation against the FDLR were worth the humanitarian cost or, in other words, whether the long-term benefits in terms of security justified the humanitarian crisis in the short and medium term. The fact that such a crisis existed was beyond doubt. The UN estimated that 900,000 people had been internally displaced and more than 500 civilians were killed during the Kimia II operation, which officially ended on 31 December. Health centres registered more than 8,000 cases of rape, almost double the figure for 2008, though probably only the tip of the iceberg. Organisations such as Human Rights Watch called on MONUC immediately to suspend its support for the Congolese army or risk being implicated in further atrocities. Others, such as Oxfam, described the human cost as "unacceptable and disproportionate to the results it has achieved". The results of Kimia II, as reported by MONUC, included 1,878 Rwandans who were demobilised and returned to their home country (though this included 477 Rwandans who had served in the CNDP) as well as 14,000 Rwandan civilians (official FARDC statistics unconvincingly declared that Kimia II had 'neutralised' 5,000 Rwandan combatants). Assuming that the FDLR had not received significant new numbers of recruits in 2008 and 2009, their strength had thus decreased by around 35%. The head of MONUC, Alan Doss, acknowledged the moral and practical dilemmas and the "unpalatable choice" the mission needed to make. He also emphasised that supporting an army that was frequently accused of human rights violations did not mean that MONUC condoned such abuses, arguing instead that the civilian population would suffer more, not less, if MONUC were to give up and walk away. In early November, the UN announced that MONUC would suspend its support for the 213th brigade of the FARDC due to reports that at least 62 civilians had been killed during operations close to Lukweti in North Kivu. This was a symbolic gesture which did not affect the mission's general support for the army.

Its fledgling reputation was hardly MONUC's only problem. First, reinforcements of soldiers and additional capabilities, as mandated by UNSC Res. 1843 (2008) only started to arrive in the second half of the year. Second, relations with the government were strained as MONUC came under growing pressure to cease cooperation with abusive FARDC units. Following the apparent resolution of the CNDP problem, Kabila, in his annual state of the nation speech, declared that Congo was on the "path to normalisation" and asked the UN to draw up a timetable for the incremental **withdrawal of MONUC**, to be completed in 2011. Despite the mission's difficult relations with the host government, Kabila's demand came as a surprise to many. However, it seemed to reflect his growing confidence that, thanks to much-improved relations with Rwanda, the rebellious situation in the Kivus had become manageable. His rationale was also related to domestic concerns. Congo was set to celebrate the fiftieth anniversary of its independence in 2010. It would not look good at all, especially for Kabila who had been elected on promises of peace and reconstruction, if the country was then still hosting some 19,800 peacekeepers. Even so, Kabila probably reckoned that an early withdrawal of large numbers of blue helmets would be overruled by the UN Security Council, but a small reduction of the force and a roadmap for the eventual drawdown would be good enough a message to Congo's electorate. On 23 December, the UN Security Council extended MONUC's mandate until the end of May 2010 (Res. 1906), suggesting that it was too early to consider a drawdown, but stressed its intention to assess and adjust the mandate in the subsequent resolution.

How tenuous the situation in the country still was, even outside of eastern Congo, became evident on 29 October, when **inter-ethnic fighting in the Dongo area** (Equateur province) broke out, reportedly caused by rows among local communities (Lobala and Boba) over fishing rights. More than 100 people were killed, including 47 policemen, and 50,000 people were displaced, most of them fleeing to nearby Congo-Brazzaville. Other sources said at least 150,000 had been driven from their homes. Riot police took control of the area, but the insurgents captured the town again on 26 November. On 12 December, the army was deployed and recaptured Dongo. The situation remained tense at the end of the year.

Politics in the capital Kinshasa was rather uneventful, with the notable exception of Kamerhe's resignation as speaker of parliament. This raised the question of whether one of the country's best known politicians would leave the Kabila camp altogether and become a serious contender for the 2011 presidential elections. Kamerhe had played a crucial role in delivering South Kivu's popular vote to Kabila during the 2006 elections. Rumours indicated that he might create his own political party. Until the end of the year, however, Kamerhe kept whatever ambitions he had to himself. The political opposition in Kinshasa remained very weak. The country's oldest opposition party, the 'Union pour la Démocratie et le Progrès Social' (UDPS) showed few signs of recovery after having boycotted the elections in 2006. The party's first congress in many years, initially scheduled for February, was cancelled by its leader, Etienne Tshisekedi, amid allegations that the party was experiencing internal rifts. The largest opposition party in parliament, the 'Mouvement pour la Libération du Congo' (MLC), was still leaderless after the arrest of its chairman, Jean-Pierre Bemba, in 2008 and his transfer to the ICC. The MLC was further weakened when the Supreme Court impeached José Makila, the MLC's governor of Equateur, on charges of embezzlement. Fresh gubernatorial elections resulted in the victory of the former deputy governor, an independent candidate (13 November). Thus the MLC lost the leadership over the only province it had governed. In October, a motion of no confidence was also brought by North Kivu's Provincial Assembly against Julien Paluku amid accusations of embezzlement of public funds, but the governor held his ground.

After initial denials, the government admitted in September the existence of a commission aimed at assessing options for **constitutional reform**. According to the government, the commission was composed of ten members representing the Office of the President, the Office of the Prime Minister, the National Assembly, the Senate and the Supreme Court of Justice. Rumours suggested that the reform project might target clauses pertaining to the provinces and the power of the president. More specifically, it was suggested that presidential term limits may be abandoned. However, Article 220 of the Constitution expressly stipulates that the number and length of presidential mandates cannot be subject to constitutional revisions. As for the provinces, the 2005 Constitution stipulates that the number of provinces (11 at present) be increased to 26, an undertaking that has raised questions about the economic viability of the entities. By year's end, the fate and recommendations of the commission were unknown.

Adolphe Muzito of the 'Parti des Lumumbistes Unifiés' (PALU) remained a weak prime minister with little effective leverage over the executive. This was underscored in June when President Kabila decided that all public spending over $ 5,000 would need the approval of the presidency. This unprecedented step came on the heels of a letter from the presidency which castigated substantial and repeated expenditure slippages. On 17 October, opposition parties in parliament launched a motion of no confidence against the Muzito government, which was rejected by the National Assembly.

The government sacked 165 judges and prosecutors on 15 July, accusing them of corruption and other abuses of office This was the first sign of a new anti-corruption policy that Kabila had announced on national Independence Day.

Local elections, initially planned for 2008 and then postponed to 2009, were once more delayed. Only the overall costs of $ 163 m were approved, although the government pledged to disburse a mere $ 31 m and expected the rest to come from donors. Registration for an updated voter registry began only on 3 August in Kinshasa and Bas Congo province and was later extended to the rest of the country. In the absence of foreign funding, the national election commission lacked resources to move preparations forward. Some observers believed that the government deliberately starved the commission of resources, insinuating that Kinshasa had little interest in the polls taking place. In addition, it failed to provide the electoral commission with an authoritative list of local electoral constituencies. Given that the administration had failed to deliver on its 2006 election promises to build infrastructures and provide public services ('les cinq chantiers'), Kabila did not expect a favourable election outcome. It seemed doubtful that local elections would be held in 2010. The likelihood increased that, if ever, they would be held jointly with the presidential and parliamentary elections in 2011.

The **reform of the security sector** and the integration of former rebels (CNDP) and militias (Mai Mai) into the FARDC made only halting progress over the year. Some 5,800 CNDP fighters and some 7,000 Mai Mai elements formally joined the FARDC as part of an accelerated integration process between 26 January and 18 April. In official terms, the closing ceremony of the programme in Goma thus put an end to the existence of armed groups in North Kivu. In reality, however, the process was deeply problematic. Both the CNDP and Mai Mai fighters handed in only a small percentage of their weaponry. The accelerated and unstructured integration produced heterogeneous units composed of former foes that naturally lacked cohesion. Parallel command structures persisted. This was particularly salient in the case of the CNDP, as some observers claimed that a fair number of fighters were still loyal to the ousted Nkunda (still living under house arrest in Rwanda). What is more, the fighters were not vetted and discontent about the distribution of ranks and other benefits was rife. To make matters worse, the government did not provide the units with adequate salaries and equipment, let alone barracks. As a result, a steady stream of mutinies and desertions from the units occurred, with some Mai Mai elements allegedly joining the FDLR. CNDP elements manned roadblocks and continued to extort local taxes in Rutshuru and Masisi, apparently with the connivance of the Kinshasa government, which lacked the will or the resources to sustain the units. The UN's Expert Group estimated that the CNDP collected as much as $ 250,000 per month from these taxes.

On 4 February, the Ministry of Defence published a revised plan for the reform of the army. The plan projected 145,000 troops, with military capabilities on three levels: cover, rapid reaction and principal defence forces. The first phase of implementation would cover the period from 2009 to 2011. The second phase of the national programme for the **disarmament, demobilisation and reintegration (DDR)** of Congolese combatants was launched on 23 April. Scheduled to run until the end of the year, it had a budget of $ 75 m and was expected to process around 78,000 FARDC soldiers and 19,600 non-state combatants. MONUC expected 30,000 of them to opt for demobilisation. The programme aimed at reinforcing its reintegration component to handle some 70,000 combatants, 40,000 of whom were demobilised soldiers who had not yet benefited from reintegration assistance. The government refused to include the approximately 10,000-strong Presidential Guard in the DDR programme.

The **human rights** situation remained poor or even worsened. The US State Department noted that security forces "continued to act with impunity" and committed "many serious abuses, including unlawful killings, disappearances, torture, and rape". The government took some limited steps to bring perpetrators from the army to justice as international protests grew, including by US Secretary of State Hillary Clinton, but this was hardly enough to convince critics that Kabila's "zero-tolerance" policy against human rights abuses and sexual violence by the FARDC was credible. Political rights were severely limited, showing once more the limits of Congo's electoral democracy. According to the UN, "endemic corruption and political interference ensure that anyone with money or connections can escape investigation, prosecution, and judgment". Political activists and journalists were regularly harassed, imprisoned or mistreated. MONUC's human rights section noted an increasing number of politically motivated abuses. The media watchdog 'Journalistes en Danger' documented 23 cases of journalists being arrested or detained and 75 attacks again the press. In July, the government suspended the broadcasting of 'Radio France Internationale' in the country for transmitting news that allegedly threatened national security. Human rights campaigners were also frequently threatened, arrested and abused, including Floribert Chebeya and Dolly Inefo from 'Voix des Sans Voix' and Donat Tshikaya from the civil society organisation 'Réseau National des ONGs des droits de l'homme de la RC Congo' (Renadhoc), who protested against the undemocratic methods through which Kamerhe had been forced to resign. Human rights abuses were also committed by armed groups. A UN report on the massacre in Kiwanja (North Kivu) in November 2008 noted that the CNDP had arbitrarily executed 67 civilians.

Despite the endemic abuses of human rights in the country, a majority of countries in the Geneva-based United Nations Human Rights Council blocked attempts by the EU to reinstate a UN human rights expert for the country (27 March).

Prosecutions and trials against former Congolese rebel leaders by the **International Criminal Court** in The Hague made some progress. On 15 June, the ICC ruled that

Bemba would stand trial on five charges of war crimes and crimes against humanity pertaining to atrocities his troops had committed in the Central African Republic in 2002–3. The trial was scheduled to start in April 2010. Trials against Germain Katanga and Mathieu Ngudjolo, two former Ituri militia leaders, started on 29 November. Both were accused of war crimes and crimes against humanity. Thomas Lubanga's case began on 29 January. Meanwhile, the Kinshasa government resisted calls to hand over Bosco Ntaganda to the ICC. Government spokesman Lambert Mende said such a move, at this time, might threaten peace in North Kivu.

Foreign Affairs

Fast improving relations between Congo and **Rwanda** were the outstanding development of the year. Not only were joint military operations in North Kivu conducted, but it was agreed that normal diplomatic relations, suspended since 1998, would be restored. Consequently, the two countries appointed new ambassadors to Kigali and Kinshasa, respectively. On 6 August, President Kabila and Rwanda's President Paul Kagame held their first ever **summit meeting in Goma**, highlighting the new pragmatist approach that both sides had embraced. However, Nkunda's extradition from Rwanda to Congo had not taken place by year's end, suggesting Rwandan reluctance to hand over a man who might ultimately be a useful token in its dealings with Congo. Economic cooperation was also enhanced. Rwanda and the Congo agreed on the joint exploitation of methane gas in Lake Kivu, requiring an investment of $ 300 m. The countries hoped to produce 200 megawatt of electricity (12 June).

Relations with **Uganda** also improved during the year. This was evidenced by the full restoration of diplomatic ties and the arrival of the new Congolese ambassador in Kampala, Jean Charles Okoto (24 August). Moreover, the Congolese government endorsed the presence of Ugandan army troops in eastern DRC to pursue the rebels of the Lord's Resistance Army (LRA) in Haut Uélé District (Orientale province). The Ugandan army attacked the LRA near Garamba National Park. The operation, which was jointly conducted with FARDC and troops of the (southern) Sudan People's Liberation Army (SPLA), combined with the atrocities committed by the LRA, displaced at least 180,000 people internally. More than 800 civilians were killed and an estimated 1,480 civilians were abducted by the roving rebels. Military operations did not significantly weaken the LRA, which split into several groups and moved several hundred fighters to the Central African Republic and southern Sudan. MONUC estimated that only 100 LRA fighters remained in the Congo.

Another diplomatic turnaround was the normalisation of relations with **Belgium**, the former colonial power, in January. Relations had hit rock bottom in the previous year when Belgian Foreign Minister Karel de Gucht had made sweeping remarks about rampant corruption in DRC and Kinshasa had recalled its ambassador from Brussels. The country's continued importance to Belgium was underscored by the fact that the then ambassador to the US, Dominique Struye de Swielande, took up the job in Kinshasa.

In contrast to the improving relations with its eastern neighbours, Congo's relations with **Angola**, though a key ally of Kabila, deteriorated sharply. The bone of contention was once more a dispute over the border. In March, the Kinshasa government suggested that Angola's oil production was partly taking place in Congo's territorial waters. Kinshasa estimated that it lost out on 450,000 barrels per day, worth around $ 8 bn a year. Following a visit by Prime Minister Muzito to Luanda, both governments vowed to create a commission to settle the dispute. Relations were further strained when Congo started a campaign to expel 20,000 to 40,000 Angolan citizens. The move was widely perceived as an act of retaliation. Since December 2008, more than 160,000 Congolese had been expelled from Angola. Regardless of the rising tensions, both governments pledged to move ahead with plans to build both a road and a pipeline that would connect Angola's Cabinda enclave with the rest of Angola and which would pass through Congolese territory.

On 7–8 September, a **SADC summit** was held in Kinshasa. President Kabila was elected as chairman of the organisation. On 24 October, Kinshasa hosted a **CEEAC summit**, an organisation Kabila currently also chairs. During a visit to Bangui (12 October), Kabila and his Central African counterpart, François Bozizé, pledged to speed up the integration process between CEEAC and CEMAC, pursuant to the CEEAC summit of heads of state and government held in Brazzaville on 30 October.

As in previous years, relations with **China** intensified. Various Chinese officials travelled to DRC during the year. Congolese Minister of Defence, Charles Mwando Nsimba, visited Beijing in October. Details did not emerge, but the Chinese government agreed to intensify its military cooperation with Kinshasa. More significant was the Chinese involvement in the country's economy.

France's President Nicolas Sarkozy visited Kinshasa in late March. He did not reiterate earlier controversial remarks suggesting that regional peace required that DRC share its enormous mineral wealth with its neighbours. On the occasion of the visit, the French company Areva unveiled plans to develop the Shinkolobwe uranium mine in Katanga.

German police arrested the president and the vice president of the FDLR, **Ignace Murwanashyaka and Straton Musoni** (17 November) on suspicion of membership of a terrorist organisation and crimes against humanity. They remained in custody at year's end, awaiting a possible trial in 2010. MONUC officials hoped that the arrest would further undermine the morale of FDLR fighters. On 23 November, the **UN's Group of Experts** published a report in which it claimed that Murwanashyaka had been in regular contact with field commanders. The group also investigated the FDLR's control of mining sites as a prime source of fund-raising, possibly amounting to several million dollars per year.

Additional resources and support, the group said, came from extensive external networks and the Rwandan diaspora. The report was widely quoted in the international media, but not so much for its findings concerning embargo violations and FDLR financing. Rather the report's comments on the Kimia II operation and, by extension, the role of MONUC were highlighted. The group concluded that military operations against the FDLR had "failed to dismantle the organization's political and military structures on the ground in eastern Democratic Republic of the Congo. The increasing rate of FDLR combatant defections and FDLR temporary removal from many of its bases are only a partial success." In addition, it noted that the FDLR continued "to benefit from residual but significant support from top commanders" in the Congolese army. The **UNSC decided to extend the arms embargo and sanctions regime** for another year (Resolution 1896 of 30 November).

US Secretary of State **Hillary Clinton** made a 48-hour stop in DRC (10–11 August) during a seven-nation trip across Africa. The most noteworthy feature of her visit was her insistence on flying to Goma, where she met victims of sexual violence. She held also talks with President Kabila. The US government announced that it would examine options in support of the reform of the Congolese army.

In April, **Britain** announced that it would give $ 131 m in support of DRC's security sector reform. Half of the money was aimed at the police. The British initiative rattled some Western partners as it has long been acknowledged that – besides the lack of a credible Congolese reform plan – the multitude of donors in the security sector and the concomitant lack of donor coordination was an obstacle to substantial progress. It remained to be seen to what extent Britain would liaise with MONUC, which considered the reform of the security sector to be the overriding priority.

The football club 'Tout-puissant Mazembe' brought rare international glory to the country by winning the 2009 **African Champions League** in November with a victory over Nigeria's Heartland FC. Mazembe's President was Moïse Katumbi, the governor of Katanga.

Socioeconomic Developments

Military operations against armed groups and an undisciplined Congolese army had **devastating humanitarian effects** in eastern Congo. In early December, more than 2 m Congolese were internally displaced. This was an increase of 30% on 2008. Equally significant was the fact that displacement in 2009 reached the levels of 2001 and 2000 (with a peak of 3.2 m in 2002 before the number dropped to its lowest of 1.1 m in 2006). The rise in numbers would have been even steeper, were it not for some 500,000 people in North Kivu who returned to their homes during the year.

The Congolese economy remained weak and the effects of the global financial and economic crisis made a bad situation worse. The IMF cut its 2009 economic growth forecast for Congo from an initial 8.8% to 4.4%. In the end, the IMF and government estimated **real GDP growth** at 2.7%, indicating that the economy shrank by well over 4% compared with 2008. However, it recovered in the second half of the year as global demand for mineral resources rose again. Due to the indirect effects of the global recession, Congo's mining sector contracted by 8.5%, partly due to steep falls in output in the first two quarters of the year. As a result, Congo's export earnings during the first six months stood at $ 2.2 bn, compared with $ 4.8 bn during the same period in 2008. Therefore the country incurred a trade deficit of $ 300 m as imports fell to $ 2.5 bn. Throughout the year, the government struggled hard to make ends meet. In May, Budget Minister Michel Lokola Elamba had to revise the budget for the current fiscal year and was forced to impose a budget freeze. This was partly due to the fact that government revenue in 2008 was 68% lower than budgeted. **Inflation** rose dramatically, reaching 53% in December, due to monetary expansion, new incoming donor loans, higher food prices and the depreciation of the national currency, the Congolese Franc (FC). The average yearly inflation rate was estimated at 45%. The Congolese Franc was traded at 910 FC per $ 1 in November, compared with an average of 639 FC in 2008.

The **mining sector** continued to be a pillar of the economy, for good or for ill, accounting for around 70% of Congo's foreign exchange revenues. A leaked Senate commission report in early September explained that not one single statistic about Congo's mineral exports bore any resemblance to reality; nor did mining companies pay proper taxes. Estimating that mining companies should have paid $ 205 m in 2008, the report said that actual tax income was only half that, explaining that massive corruption, fraudulent contracts and other kleptocratic practices on all levels of the state were hardly a thing of the not so distant Mobutist past. As a result, the Congolese state lost $ 450 m in income. One example was the Congolese-American joint venture Tenke Fungurume Mining, which runs what is potentially the world's largest copper mine. Whereas the company claimed to have paid $ 11 m in taxes in 2008, the tax agency 'Direction Générale des Impôts' said it had collected only $ 1.7 m.

To make matters worse, the government failed to conclude its lengthy **review of mining contracts**, launched in 2007. Six companies had outstanding negotiations with the government to revise their concessions, including AngloGold Ashanti, Banro and Freeport McMoRan. Contradictory statements by government ministers suggested either that confusion or tactics to extort more money from the mining companies dominated the process. The most notable case was **Tenke Fungurume**, a leading source of state revenue. After having invested more than $ 2 bn in the Tenke mine, its managing company, Freeport McMoRan, started copper production in March. However, the government insisted that the share of the state-owned company Gécamines in the joint venture be increased from 17.5% to 45%. Freeport McMoRan refused, claiming to have a legally enforceable contract that was re-negotiated between 2003 and 2005. The outcome of the standoff was uncertain. A similar episode had seen Canada's First Quantum mining licence revoked in August. The company (predictably) lost its case in a Congolese court and announced that it would seek international arbitration. Even so, Congo's exceedingly difficult investment environment seemed less repellent to foreign companies than expected. An upswing of global demand for commodities meant that investments and production in numerous mines resumed in Katanga. However, diamond mining continued to suffer from the global crisis. IBHP Billiton and De Beers stopped diamond exploration in Eastern Kasai. In May, the state-owned diamond mining company Société Miniére de Bakwanga (Miba) announced that it would resume production only once international prices for diamonds recovered.

On 10 October, the government presented its draft **budget** for 2010 to the National Assembly, totalling around $ 5.3 bn, compared with almost $ 3.3 bn in 2008. Astonishingly, half of the projected expenditure was expected to come from donors, an unrealistic assumption by any standard. The government also assumed that it would increase its domestic tax revenue by 24%, an optimistic projection in view of the only modest recovery of the mining sector.

The Congolese government concluded a six-month long **review of timber contracts** that had begun in 2008 (19 January). The aim of the review was to fight corruption in the sector and to enforce legal and environmental standards. Officials declared that only 65 out of 165 timber deals were viable, leading to a cancellation of concessions that concerned half of the surface exploited by timber companies.

Increasing international pressure and the unrelenting effects of the global economic crisis grudgingly convinced the government that the terms of its bilateral **mining-for-infrastructure deal with Chinese companies** needed revisions. Under the $ 9 bn deal, Chinese companies would provide a variety of much needed infrastructures in exchange for huge mining concessions in Katanga. Ever since the deal was announced in 2006, the IMF and the Paris Club of Western donors had insisted that it threatened Congo's debt sustainability. As a consequence, these donors had refused to grant Congo significant foreign debt relief ($ 13 bn). Currently, Congo's debt service amounts to about one fourth of total expenditure. The IMF said that, at the end of 2008, publicly contracted or guaranteed external debt was an estimated 93% of GDP, 150% of exports, and 502% of government revenue, excluding foreign aid.

The **Managing Director of the IMF, Dominique Kahn-Strauss**, visited Kinshasa in May to discuss external assistance that would help the country to alleviate its economic crisis, reiterating the IMF's position on the Sino-Congolese barter deal and underlining that a revision of agreement would enable donors to pave the way for debt relief. The same message came from the **President of the World Bank, Robert Zoellick**, who visited DRC on 9–11 August. Then, on 8 October, the Chinese government announced that the Export-Import Bank (Exim) and the participating Chinese companies had signed a revised contract with the government. The volume of the deal had been reduced to $ 6 bn and the role of the Congolese state as the guarantor of the Chinese loan was much reduced. The Congolese government also set itself ambitious economic and financial targets for the next three years, including average real GDP growth of 5.5%, an inflation rate of 9% by 2012 and gross reserves equivalent to ten weeks' of non-aid imports by 2012. The authorities also pledged structural reform aimed at improving domestic revenue mobilisation, restoring the independence of the 'Banque Centrale du Congo' and developing the private sector, including the reform of public enterprises, protecting foreign investment and improving transparency in natural resource management.

Consequently, the IMF approved **a new poverty reduction and growth facility** (PRGF), worth $ 551 m (11 December). It also provided Congo with interim assistance worth $ 73 m under the enhanced HIPC Initiative to reduce the country's debt service payment to the IMF. Congo would be eligible for debt relief in 2010, provided that the administration successfully implemented the PRGF and a Poverty Reduction Strategy.

The compromise on the Chinese-Congolese barter deal brought additional benefits for the country. Its **foreign reserve levels** reached a 25-year high of $ 894 m at the end of the year following the release of fresh donor money. It benefited in particular from the disbursement of $ 600 m by the IMF, money that the IMF provided to bolster African economies severely affected by the global economic downturn. In March, the fund had already disbursed $ 200 m as part of its Exogenous Shocks Facility. In February Congo's foreign reserves had fallen to $ 30 m. Additional assistance came from the African Development Bank ($ 97 m), the World Bank ($ 100 m) and the EU.

Denis M. Tull

Equatorial Guinea

After the overwhelming victory by the pro-presidential camp in the previous year's 2008 legislative and local elections, President Obiang, the longest-serving ruler in Sub-Saharan Africa, was returned to power in a landslide victory in November. He continued to enjoy almost absolute power without any checks and balances. Meanwhile, the human rights record of the regime remained poor. In foreign relations, the regime demonstrated the enhanced importance of South-South cooperation and continued to concentrate on the sub-region. Relations with Spain were given a new start. As a result of much lower oil prices in the first half of the year, growth rates were expected to have turned negative for the first time in years.

Domestic Politics

The country's **fragile security situation** was exposed on 17 February when a group of heavily armed men carried out a boat-based **attack on the presidential palace** in Malabo while President Obiang was in Bata. One of the assailants and a member of the presidential guard were killed in the gunfire. The government accused the Nigeria-based Movement for the Emancipation of the Niger Delta (MEND) of carrying out the repulsed attack. These accusations were quickly denied by MEND. Given the government's inability to provide a convincing version of the events, intense speculation about the true causes began to circulate right after the attack. While it seemed difficult to shed full light on what had happened, the government's action following the attack provided some clues. Although the government's initial accusation had not spoken of an attempted coup, a few days after the attack Obiang stated on public television that the assailants were financed and supported by home-based nationals. Despite dubious evidence – why would attackers go for the presidential palace knowing that the president was elsewhere in the country, and why did the assailants not attempt to take over the radio and television station first? – as in the past, the government used the allegation of a coup attempt to go after the opposition. Nine members of the opposition party, 'Unión Popular' (UP), were arrested and detained. In addition, foreign nationals from neighbouring countries, Nigerians and Cameroonians in particular, were the target of police harassment and arrests and were only released two months after the attack. Expulsions of hundreds of Cameroonians continued throughout the year.

On 24 February, Obiang **sacked the minister of national security**, Manuel Nguema Mba, and replaced him with Nicolas Obama Nchama. Lower ranking officials in the national security apparatus and the army were also dismissed. Despite this internal purge, the country's security apparatus remained firmly in the grip of the president and his immediate family and clan-based support structure.

Contrary to previous years, Obiang's 67th birthday on 5 June was not marked by amnesties or the commuting of political prisoners' sentences. However, ahead of the presidential elections and the day before the visit of South African President Jacob Zuma to Malabo, **Simon Mann**, who had dual British and South African nationality, and four South African nationals, who had been accused and sentenced to 35 years for the attempted coup in 2004, were **released** on 2 November after spending five-and-a-half years in Malabo's notorious 'Black Beach' prison. Although the government claimed that the release was granted on humanitarian grounds, the upcoming presidential elections and the intention to effect an improvement in relations with South Africa were obvious.

In the **presidential elections** on 29 November, Obiang, who had become the longest-serving head of state in Sub-Saharan Africa after the death of Gabon's Omar Bongo in June, was re-elected with 95.4% of the votes, down from 97% in the last presidential elections in 2002. Placido Mikó Abogo, the main opposition candidate from the 'Convergencia para la Democracia Social' (CPDS), who had been re-elected as secretary-general of the CPDS and contender for the presidential election during a congress of his party in Bata in May, retained 3.6% of the vote, according to the final results released by the government on 3 December. However, the electoral roll was not released and AU observers noted the ruling party's tight control of polling stations, limiting any supervision of ballot results by opposition parties. In his statement, Abogo condemned the high-level presence of security forces on election day and at polling stations, pointed to the continuous harassment of rallies organised by opposition parties during the official electoral campaign between 5 and 29 November, and insisted to no avail that the elections were neither free nor fair, but rigged. As a result of the presidential election, Obiang continued to enjoy almost absolute power without any checks and balances in a nominally multi-party system.

As legally required, the **cabinet resigned** after Obiang was sworn in for another seven-year term in office on 8 December. Prime Minister Ignacio Milam Tang was re-appointed but the new cabinet had not been announced by year's end. It was widely speculated, however, that Teodoro Nguema Obiang, the president's eldest son, minister of agriculture and forestry and supposedly the president's heir apparent, would be promoted to one of the key ministries.

Despite pardons and amnesties granted to foreign citizens ahead of the presidential election, the **human rights record** of the regime **remained poor**. AI complained that citizens from Equatorial Guinea, who had also been tried for the attempted coup in 2004, remained imprisoned. Along with TI and AI, HRW judged the regime as one of the most corrupt and brutal in the world, having failed to adopt pro-poor policies and to distribute the oil wealth to all parts of the population. The United Nations Universal Periodic Review, a new mechanism scrutinising the human rights situation of each member state every four years, was outspoken in its report released in December. Widespread violations of human rights and the regular use of torture by security forces were listed in the report. The government reacted in a moderate and non-confrontational way, committing to improve human rights.

In a related move towards the end of the year, UNESCO came under pressure to **suspend a proposed leadership prize** sponsored by Obiang in 2007 to the tune of $ 3 m. The rebranding exercise by the government to establish the annual $ 300,000 UNESCO-Obiang Nguema Mbasogo International Prize for Research in the Life Sciences "in recognition of scientific achievements that improve the quality of human life" drew heavy criticism from the former colonial power Spain, from France and from the human rights organisation Global Witness, which argued in an open letter that the money should better be used to improve life for the country's people. The **heightened sensitivity to the perception of the country abroad**, coupled with a decision to employ consultants in the US to lobby officials in Washington, demonstrated that the government was attempting to become more diplomatic.

Foreign Affairs

Tensions with Cameroon seemed to further escalate when security forces arrested and incarcerated three Cameroonian fishermen in early January. Shortly afterwards, the Cameroonian navy detained and arrested three members of the army of Equatorial Guinea for allegedly entering Cameroon's territorial waters. Since the joint maritime border had not yet been determined in a mutually acceptable way, and against the backdrop of supposedly large numbers of Cameroonian illegal immigrants resident in Equatorial Guinea, such incidents implied the risk of military confrontation. However, on 12 January, a settlement was reached to exchange prisoners. Both sides were apparently willing to avoid further escalation and to return to enhanced cooperation in the gas sector and attempts at deeper regional integration.

In a demonstration of the **enhanced importance of South-South cooperation**, Obiang paid an official visit to **Egypt** in mid-May. Equatorial Guinea also opened an embassy in **Venezuela**. In early April, President Faure Gnassingbé of **Togo** visited Equatorial Guinea, recalling his father's excellent relations with his counterpart in Malabo. The two countries needed each other's support to provide balances against their dominant neighbour, Nigeria. Later that month, **Morocco**'s King Mohammed VI, visited Equatorial Guinea for the first time and signed several bilateral agreements covering activities in security and infrastructure. The excellent relations between the two countries dated back to 1979. Obiang's presidential guard was largely dominated by Moroccan security forces, and infrastructure companies from Morocco built and operated Malabo's newly extended deepwater port. **Ethiopia**'s President Meles Zenawi visited Malabo at the beginning of June. A delegation of businessmen from **Brazil** arrived later that month.

Relations with the former colonial power, **Spain**, which had been difficult and strained at times over the last few years, were given a new start with a three-day visit by Spanish Minister of Foreign Affairs Miguel Angel Moratinos in mid-July. Accompanied by a large delegation of businessmen, Moratinos signed an investment protection protocol for Spanish companies and announced a new direct flight connection between Madrid and Bata. He openly criticised the Spanish media for failing to portray the situation in Equatorial Guinea in a more balanced way. Spanish business interests in the country's oil wealth continued to conflict with the highly critical opinion of the Spanish public and press with respect to the political system and human rights record of Equatorial Guinea.

In August, **Minister of Foreign Affairs** Pastor Micha **visited the US** and held talks with US Assistant Secretary of State for African Affairs Johnnie Carson. Micha requested US technical assistance to improve and reform Equatorial Guinea's justice system. Aside from this intention to demonstrate the country's commitment to improving governance structures, the talks centred on the supposedly deteriorating security situation in the Gulf of Guinea, a concern shared by both countries. Micha continued diplomatic activities along these lines when he visited **Nigeria** in September and held consultations on defence, trade, education and aviation. He signed a memorandum of understanding to improve joint military co-operation and to fight piracy and other illegal activities in the Gulf of Guinea. Shortly afterwards, in September, Equatorial Guinea participated in a joint military exercise with **Gabon, Cameroon and São Tomé** directed at fighting piracy, illegal fishing and clandestine immigration.

South African President **Jacob Zuma** paid a **state visit** to Equatorial Guinea on 3 November. Aside from the release of South African nationals imprisoned in Malabo, the visit centred on the plan to make Equatorial Guinea a regional hub for natural gas exports and joint ventures in agriculture, mining and tourism. From Obiang's point of view, improving relations with South Africa, which had soured towards the end of Thabo Mbeki's presidency, held the advantage of gaining an important regional ally in the periodic disputes with Cameroon and Gabon.

Obiang's inauguration on 8 December was attended by several international heads of state, notably the leaders of Chad, **Liberia, Ghana** and Congo-Brazzaville, and by official delegates from France and Spain. Liberian President Ellen Johnson-Sirleaf signed a bilateral agreement related to closer cooperation in economic, scientific, technical and cultural relations and to the establishment of a joint commission scheduled to meet every two years. Ghanaian President John Atta Mills also attended the inauguration and signed a contract for the supply to Ghana of about 65,000 barrels of crude oil per day from Equatorial Guinea, roughly one sixth of national production. Ghana's national oil production would not start before late-2010, a gap to be covered by imports from Equatorial Guinea. However, by the end of the year, the detailed regulations and requirements of the contract had not been finalised.

Socioeconomic Developments

In 2009, **real GDP growth** was estimated to have contracted, for the first time in years, by 1.8%, as a result of both a fall in output and lower prices for oil and gas, the country's dominant exports. However, it was thought that an expected increase in oil prices and in production in 2010 could mean the country might quickly return to positive growth rates, albeit more modest than the staggering rates of the last decade. The country had become overly dependent on the oil and gas sector and was virtually **a mono economy**. The sector accounted for more than 90% of GDP, 99% of exports and more than 85% of government revenue. **Inflation** was estimated to have declined to 4.5%, although it was still higher than in other CFA Franc Zone countries because of the ongoing effects of the oil-boom.

In April, the **IMF published a new report** warning that the country was following an overly expansionist course in capital expenditure. With the dramatic fall in international oil prices in mind, the IMF calculated that the **2009 budget** would increase the non-oil primary fiscal deficit to 78% of non-oil GDP. Initially, the government insisted that spending on public infrastructure was necessary to meet the ambitious targets of the National Economic Development Plan (Horizon 2020), launched in 2007 to turn the country into an emerging economy by 2020. A month later, the government decided to reduce fiscal spending in line with the expected fall in oil revenue. Public investment was cut by 37% to CFAfr 970 bn. However, in the run-up to the presidential election, budgetary constraints were quickly set aside. In the first half of the year, public-sector salaries rose by 15% and the minimum wage by 17%. And with the upward trend in international oil prices in the second half of the year, the government seemed to have resumed its ambitious plans to become an emerging economy through an expansionary fiscal policy.

In his inauguration speech on 8 December, and again in his annual New Year's message, Obiang reaffirmed his previous statements that the country was overly dependent on hydrocarbons and that activities in the areas of agriculture, livestock and fish farming, tourism and trade needed to be increased. However, the country's **failure to diversify the economy** and to lower its reliance on the exploitation of oil and gas was not a new phenomenon but the result of government policies since the onset of the oil boom in the 1990s. And the dismal record of almost 80% of the population living below the poverty line, and worsening infant mortality and school enrolment was also due to one-sided decisions and ill-conceived government policies. Whereas **real GDP per head** in 2009 stood at $ 15,795 (in terms of US dollars at 2006 constant purchasing power parity), which was over three times higher than in 2000, **health indicators** were extremely poor when compared with countries with a similar income per head. Average **life expectancy** barely increased – from 49 years in 2000 to just over 50 in 2009.

In the **oil sector**, with production in some of the older fields continuing to decline and no new fields scheduled to come on stream before 2012, production was estimated at 394,000 bpd in 2009, declining to 387,000 bpd in 2010. In mid-January and February, **new oil and gas discoveries** were announced. They were found at more than 2,000 m below sea level in deepwater blocks situated east and south-west of Bioko Island. Later in the year, in July, the national gas company, Sonagas, signed a joint venture with a South African gas company to develop gas resources at existing fields rather than to continue the flaring of gas from these older oil fields. These natural gas reserves could be used to feed a second liquefied natural gas (LNG) train at Punta Europa, the northern point of Bioko Island and west of Malabo. Developing gas resources was more complicated than for oil, requiring the co-ordination of different companies for supplying natural gas and for building or expanding the necessary gas-processing facilities. In January, the government announced that a **memorandum of understanding** had been signed between Sonagas, Germany's EON Ruhrgas, Spain's Union Fenosa and Portugal's Galp Energia to create a **new company**, called EP3, responsible **for guaranteeing gas supplies** from different sources to feed new LNG processing facilities in Equatorial Guinea.

Cord Jakobeit

Gabon

This was a landmark year in the history of the political system of Gabon as it marked the end of over four decades of uninterrupted rule by President Omar Bongo Ondimba, who died quite unexpectedly of a heart attack in June at the age of 73. Bongo had been a powerful patrimonial ruler until the very end, so selecting a new president tested the strength of both the ruling party he had created and the large family he had left behind. By the end of summer, presidential elections divided powerful barons of the old regime between those who supported the former president's son, Defence Minister Ali Bongo, and those who opposed him. In the end Ali Bongo won the elections, becoming the country's third president since independence.

Domestic Politics

Senate elections were held on 18 January but held little interest for the electorate. The Senate is elected indirectly by members of municipal councils and departmental assemblies in a two-round ballot. The ruling 'Parti Démocratique Gabonais' (PDG) took 75 out of the 102 seats, giving it an unassailable voting majority. Nine independent candidates were elected, leaving the 'Rassemblement pour le Gabon' (RPG) the most successful opposition party with just six seats. Although only 17% of the Senators were women, the upper chamber did manage to elect a woman, Rose Francine Rogombé, as its president, which enabled her to become acting President of the Republic after the death of Omar Bongo.

On 14 March, First Lady Edith Bongo, who was 27 years younger than her husband, died in a hospital in Rabat, Morocco, after several weeks in a coma for which no explanation was given. She had been a medical doctor by training, and had given President Bongo the last two of his estimated 30 children, Omar Denis 'Junior' and Yacine Queenie, who were thought by some observers to be dangerous potential rivals to Bongo's older children in the deadly dynastic politics of succession in Libreville. Bongo was reportedly overcome with grief at the death of his third and final wife, whose curiously premature departure foreshadowed his own death three months later. Daughter of Congolese President Denis Sassou-Nguesso, Edith Bongo had also been influential in the country's neo-patrimonial regime because of her proximity to the person of its ruler. A few months later, on 7 May, Omar Bongo was flown on a medical aircraft from Morocco to Spain, where he checked into a private clinic in Barcelona. Government spokesman at first declared this a "routine check-up", but as the weeks went by, and President Bongo remained in hospital, the Spanish newspaper *La Vanguardia* eventually leaked that he was seriously ill. Apparently he was suffering from intestinal cancer which had metastasized. Doctors gave him chemotherapy and attempted an operation, but his cancer proved too advanced, and on Sunday 7 June, he went into a coma – a rumour at first denied by Prime Minister Jean Ndong, who said that Gabon's 73-year-old ruler was "alive and well". But that same day, **Omar Bongo died of a heart attack**.

Bizarre denials of Bongo's death for the rest of that week reflected the regime's fear of what could come to pass after 43 years of personal rule, for President Bongo had designated no successor. He had always maintained that his office was not an inheritance, and that Gabon was a republic, and not a monarchy, but the Bongo family had established itself as the predominant informal power structure, and a peaceful transition of power to one of his children had been expected. First there was Bongo's oldest child Pascaline, his chief of staff, and the wife of Finance Minister Jean Toungi. She was the child of Bongo's first wife, a now anonymous Bembe woman from French Congo whom the young Omar had married before converting to Islam. She was considered highly competent, but she was a woman – a serious obstacle to assuming the role of patriarch in a neo-patrimonial system. Next there was his youngest son and namesake, Omar Denis Bongo, born to his third wife Edith. He is still a teenager, so despite his appellation 'Junior' was simply too young to assume real power. Finally there was his oldest son, the Minister of Defence Ali Ben Bongo, who had long been considered as the best placed to succeed his father. Ali is the child of Bongo's second wife, singer Joséphine Kama (today known by her stage name, Patience Dabany), who was of Obamba royal blood. Ali had changed his name from Alain after converting to Islam in 1973, and was named president of the 'Conseil Supérieur des Affaires Islamiques du Gabon', the country's highest Islamic body. For many years he had been groomed for power, but now that his moment had arrived, great uncertainty surrounded the rightful **succession of Ali.**

Fearing an outbreak of civil disorder, the government established a curfew and sent troops to patrol the streets of Libreville and Port-Gentil. On 9 June, the ruling PDG replaced Bongo with the president of the Senate, Rose Rogombé, as 'interim' president. Rogombé – the first female president of Gabon – served ex officio for two months while elections were prepared to designate a permanent replacement.

Presidential elections were scheduled for 30 August. Opposition leaders complained this did not give them adequate time for preparation. Ali Bongo received the endorsement of the ruling PDG (the only party with effective organisation throughout the national territory), facing a total of 23 opponents who presented their candidacies for these historic elections. Among those challenging the late-president's son were powerful former barons of the PDG, including Prime Minister Jean Ndong, former prime ministers Casimir Oyé Mba and Jean-François Ntoutoume Emane, and former interior minister André Mba Obame, who all ran as 'independents'. In addition to these barons there were more genuine opposition candidates, including: Pierre Mamboundou of the 'Union du Peuple Gabonais' (UPG) who formed a strategic five-party alliance; Paul Mba Abessole (RPG); and Pierre-Claver Maganga-Loussavou of the 'Parti Social Démocrate' (PSD). In addition to failing to rally around a single opposition candidate, necessary to win Gabon's single-round presidential ballot, none of the opposition candidates were able to extend their campaigns outside traditional ethno-regional bases of support (e.g., Mamboundou's southern Punu-Eshira, Mba Obame's northern Fang).

Ali Bongo also enjoyed the advantage of access to the state-controlled media, not to mention his vast personal and family fortune, which he used successfully to buy political support. Using helicopters, Bongo was the only candidate able to campaign throughout a national territory which strategically lacks a network of roads – a deliberate policy of divide and rule since the early days of independence that prevents social networks from forming beneath the level of the ruling elites who can travel by air throughout the territory. He also received complicit support from the international community, which turned a blind eye to dynastic succession in favour of stability. While all the other regime barons had been forced to resign their ministerial portfolios after becoming candidates, Bongo remained as minister of defence, a glaring irregularity which resulted in a protest on 7 August, when 10,000 opponents of the regime defied a government curfew and filled the streets of the capital city chanting, "Ali resign!" and "Ali dictator!" before being suppressed by security forces.

On 30 August people went to the polls, using dubious lists with allegedly 120,000 'ghost' electors (out of a total of 800,000 registered voters). Polling booths were manned by PDG loyalists. Soldiers were stationed in the streets. Ali Bongo was quickly declared victor on 3 September. Both leading opposition candidates, Mamboundou and Mba Obame, claimed electoral fraud, and announced that they had in fact received more votes than Ali Bongo. Mba Obame's television station was shut down by the authorities while state-run media proclaimed Ali Bongo the clear victor. According to the Constitution, the winner of presidential elections could only be named after the Constitutional Court had validated the results. This occurred on 12 October, when Chief Justice Marie Madeleine Mborantsuo (named by Bongo's father) confirmed **Ali Bongo as the winner in the first round with 41.8% of the vote**. Mamboundou was credited with 25.6%, and Mba Obame 25.3%.

Immediately after Ali Bongo declared his victory, Mba Obame staged a hunger strike in protest, decrying that Gabon had been the victim of "an electoral coup d'état", but later he ended his action when it became clear to all that the international community would not lift a finger to help to liberate the Gabonese people from over four decades of Bongo family rule. On Friday 16 October, Bongo was sworn in as Gabon's third president in the marble banqueting hall of Libreville's presidential palace, but it was not an entirely peaceful transition, for no sooner had his victory been declared, than **violent protests broke out in Port-Gentil**, the second largest city and oil capital. Port-Gentil is the bastion of the Punu-Eshira opponents who had supported Pierre Mamboundou, and has a history of anti-regime riots going back to 1990, when the mysterious death of Punu opposition leader Joseph Rendjambe had resulted in several weeks of uncontrolled rampage. On 3 September, a massive outbreak of violence was unleashed on the French consulate and several installations belonging to the French oil firm Total and the French oil-service company Schlumberger. The government declared another curfew, defied by the protestors. Angry youths formed mobs up to 250 strong and attacked government buildings, including the police commissariat. Gabonese soldiers were eventually joined by 100 French troops, called in to protect French expatriates and property. After three consecutive nights of riots around half of the city had been sacked. On 4 September, violent government repression resulted in the deaths of several youths when soldiers fired on the crowds.

Despite the crisis of legitimacy surrounding his rise to power, once in office Ali Bongo made several important gestures to consolidate the legitimacy of his rule. First, he named Paul Biyoghe Mba (PDG) as his new prime minister. (By an unwritten tradition the Bongos have always named a Fang as prime minister.) Second, only twelve members of the previous cabinet were re-appointed in his **new government**, most notably Paul Toungui (foreign minister), Jean-François Ndongou (interior minister), and Laure Gondjout (communication). Most of the oldest ministers did not survive the cabinet reshuffle. Over half of the faces in Ali Bongo's first government were new faces. One notable feature of the new cabinet was Bongo's appointment of six women, including Angélique Ngoma (defence) and Anicette Nang Ovinka (justice). Another innovation was Ali Bongo's decision not to hold his cabinet meetings in Libreville, but in other cities around the country, so that cabinet ministers could witness the reality of life in the provinces for themselves.

Foreign Affairs

France remained the most important ally of Gabon, although relations between the two countries had been tense early in the year after TI and Sherpa had filed a civil action against Omar Bongo on 2 December 2008 for embezzlement, misuse of public funds and money laundering in "the acquisition of very substantial property and assets in France". TI had filed suits twice before (in 2007 and 2008) to denounce the Gabonese president's acquisition of luxury homes in France. The second of these had resulted in a police investigation, which revealed that Bongo's family owned 33 properties in France, but since the police had not established the origins of the funds used to purchase these properties, the criminal charges had been dismissed. So TI and Sherpa decided to file a **civil lawsuit**.

Throughout the spring of 2009 a series of articles in the French press continued to spread **scandalous revelations**. The publication of a book criticising the French Foreign Minister Bernard Kouchner, "Le Monde Selon K", written by investigative journalist Pierre Péan, also alleged that Bongo had paid Kouchner for consulting, opening another debate about the shady financial dealings between Paris and Libreville. Then on 27 February, two of Bongo's French bank accounts were frozen after a Bordeaux court ordered him to return an illegal 1996 payment made to him in exchange for the release of a jailed French businessman who had refused to pay bribes.

On 5 March, Bongo denounced the French media for waging an "abject campaign of calumnies and insults orchestrated against his person", and suggested that his government was going to "re-examine in depth the cooperation accords between France and Gabon". Despite diplomatic pressure to get President Nicolas Sarkozy to have the charges dropped, on 20 April the Paris courts declared the TI-Sherpa civil complaint admissible and opened an investigation into the affair – which was closed after Bongo died.

On 11 June, Bongo's corpse was flown back to Libreville for a week of national mourning. Briefly the world's attention was focused on Gabon, when fifteen heads of state flew into Libreville to attend the **official funeral** ceremonies on 16 June. Among those attending were: President Nicolas Sarkozy and former President Jacques Chirac (France), Denis Sassou-Nguesso (Congo), Joseph Kabila (DR Congo), Paul Biya (Cameroun), Abdoulaye Wade (Senegal), Laurent Gbagbo (Côte d'Ivoire), Amadou Toumani Touré (Mali), Blaise Compaoré (Burkina Faso), Idriss Déby (Chad), Mamadou Tandja (Niger), François Bozizé (CAR) Fradique de Menezes (São Tomé and Príncipe), and Obiang Nguema (Equatorial Guinea), who all inclined before the coffin before it was flown for a private burial on 18 June in Franceville. The funeral provided a snapshot of regional alliances, and a family portrait of the system known as 'Françafrique'. The presence of two French heads of state was emblematic of France's deep implication in the country. Chirac's presence was appreciated by powerful insiders in the regime, but when Sarkozy arrived in Franceville, crowds hissed and booed at his presidential limousine. It was not, as some might have believed, a protest against French neo-colonialism. On the contrary, Franceville was Bongo's home town, and those present were Bongo loyalists who were angry that President Sarkozy had not protected their late-patriarch from the scandalous court cases in Paris.

Socioeconomic Developments

The economy of Gabon is export-oriented, with its main exports being oil, manganese and wood. Low oil prices in the beginning of the year, combined with a fall in demand for other raw materials on the world markets, resulted in **negative economic growth**. Nominal GDP fell from $ 14.4 bn to $ 11.3 bn, and real GDP was estimated to have contracted by 1%, because of the world economic crisis. Industrial output fell by 5%, and total exports dropped from $ 9.2 bn to $ 5.9 bn. Oil production declined from 239,000 barrels per day (bpd) in 2008 to 231,000 bpd in 2009, due to the gradual exhaustion of the country's mature fields and the failure to discover any major new reserves. The global economic downturn forced French oil company Total Gabon to re-evaluate its investments in the country. Total had announced that it would invest $ 2 bn in the mature Anguille oilfield, but at the beginning of the year oil prices stood around $ 40 per barrel, and the firm indicated that it could not get a return on its investment at such low prices. Prices started to recover in spring, reaching $ 78 by the year's end, so Total went ahead with its planned investments. Manganese prices dropped 15% over the year, and the Belinga iron ore project has still not begun, despite assurances by the China National Machinery and Equipment Import and Export Corporation.

Although timber only accounted for 5% of total exports, forestry is the most important employer in the formal economy. The sector employs around 10,000 workers. Timber companies, most foreign-owned, have not developed the sector much beyond cutting trees and floating them downriver to port. Only 45% of all logs cut are processed in any way locally. Most logs are not even stripped of their bark, but remain floating in the ports, raw, waiting to be picked up by cargo vessels for processing in Asia. The government had set a target for 75% of timber exports to be locally processed by 2012, but little had been done to achieve it. One of the first dramatic acts of the new government was its announcement on 5 November that it would **ban the export of raw unprocessed timber** as of 2010. This government ban was intended to stimulate more local value added in a forestry sector that is something of a tree farm for foreigners. The need to build saw-mills, not only to strip the logs, but to create true lumberyards and carpentry shops, has long been recognised as an important potential source of job-creation. One in five adult workers in Gabon is currently unemployed. Mining provides few opportunities for employment.

This ban of unprocessed wood was the first concrete step by the Ali Bongo regime to evolve the Gabonese economy from a raw wood exporter to an integrated producer of value-added goods. It was strongly criticised by the French investors' lobby, 'Conseil français des investisseurs en Afrique', who complained that he had not consulted them before imposing it. Ali Bongo promised the logging companies his government would pay them compensation for the losses caused by his decree, but it was not clear how he would find the money needed to do so. Foresters called the ban "brutal" and complained that the short-term effects on exports would burden their sector, which suffered a 15% decline in output in the second half of 2009.

Despite its largely fictional per capita income figures of PPP $ 13,866 the reality for most Gabonese remained abject poverty. The life expectancy has barely changed in two decades. One in two women did not have access to education, and one in five workers was unemployed. The working conditions and salaries of those who do have jobs were so poor that much of the year was interrupted by **strikes**. From January to March strikes by health workers paralysed that sector. On 24 March, workers at the state refinery Sogara went on strike. Then in October, teachers went on strike. At its first cabinet meeting in mid-October the government announced that workers would not receive their salaries for the duration of a strike, and if they failed to comply with a series of new tight regulations, such as getting government approval in advance for a strike, they risked losing their jobs altogether.

Douglas A. Yates

São Tomé and Príncipe

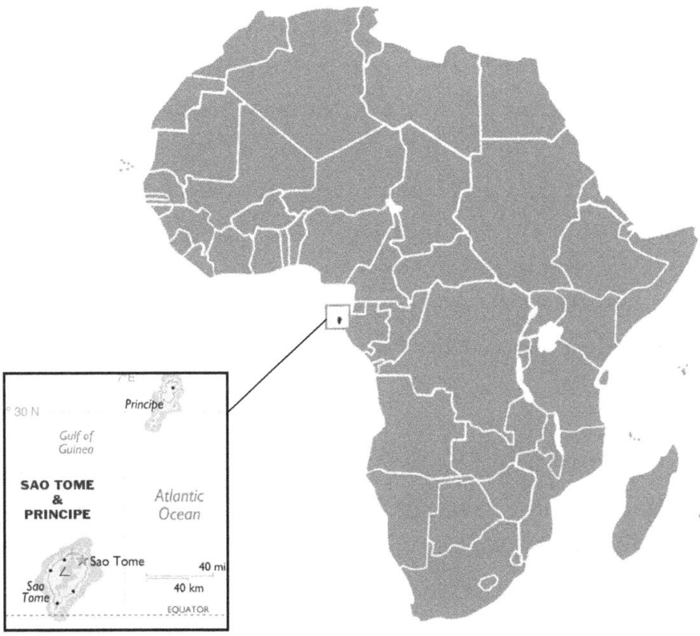

The government strengthened its efforts to attract financial and development aid from the regional powers, Angola and Nigeria, and from new donor countries. At the end of the year President Menezes's election as leader of the 'Movimento Democrático Força de Mudança' (MDFM) provoked a political crisis as its constitutionality was contested on the grounds of the incompatibility of his holding the party leadership while head of state. After three years of inactivity, in the second half of the year, exploratory drilling in the Joint Development Zone (JDZ) with Nigeria was resumed.

Domestic Politics

Judicial-political affairs were a feature of the entire year. On 12 February, the police detained 39 persons, including Alércio Costa, the leader of the small 'Frente Democrata Cristã' (FDC) party, who had allegedly attempted to destabilise public order. Later, a judge charged 29 of the detained, including Costa, a former member of the infamous South African Buffalo Batallion, and one of the leaders of the July 2003 coup in São Tomé, with having threatened state security, while the others were released. On 30 July, a judge ordered the release of another 15 of the detained, of whom four had to report to the police. During the trial that started on 7 October, the 18 defendants faced three charges, including criminal association, illegal possession of weapons and plotting an attack against state security. Costa denied all accusations and blamed President Menezes for having invented a plot because of competing private business interests regarding land at Praia das Conchas and a gambling hall. On 11 November, the court found Alércio Costa guilty of rebellion and illegal possession of weapons and sentenced him to a five-year prison term, and Bonifácio Ramos received a two-year suspended prison term for illegal possession of weapons, while all the other defendants were acquitted.

On 27 March, Diógenes Moniz, the former director of the food aid agency 'Gabinete de Gestão de Ajuda' (GGA), and Aurélio Aguiar, the GGA treasurer, had already been sentenced to nine and seven years' imprisonment respectively. At the trial, which started on 29 October 2008, the two men had been found guilty of forgery and harmful management related to the embezzlement of some $ 4 m of counterpart funds stemming from the **sale of Japanese food aid** in 2004. Previous charges in this case against the former prime-minister, Maria das Neves, and ex-trade minister, Arzemiro dos Prazeres, were dismissed in 2006 for lack of evidence.

On 14 April, the International Court of Arbitration in Paris required the government to pay the Luso-British company Synergie Investment only € 3 m in compensation for having, in 2005, unilaterally declared null and void a contract signed in 2004for the construction of a power plant. Synergie had initially claimed huge compensation payments of € 452 m, later reduced to € 200 m. The Court of Arbitration decided that Synergie Investment should pay the costs of the action – about € 590,000.

Corruption remained an important issue of debate. In early August, seven of the 14 local merchant houses that, in November 2008, had constituted the company STP-Trading, for importing from Brazil basic food stuffs financed by a Brazilian government credit line of $ 5 m, withdrew from the company after having accused its management of corruption, fraud and the import of food products unfit for consumption. The food products that had arrived by ship in May had been purchased in Brazil by SAX Logística Internacional, which in turn had been entrusted with the operation by the legal firm A.W. Galvão & Filhos. From 20 August to 28 October, STP-Trading's director general and advisor to the minister of internal administration, Armando Correia, and the company's commercial director, Osvaldo Santana, were detained on charges of maladministration and financial fraud. On 8 October, following several refusals, which he justified on the basis of parliamentary immunity, STP-Trading's financial director, Delfim Neves, a deputy of the 'Partido da Convergência Democrática' (PCD), finally agreed to be questioned by magistrates.

As already had been the case between 1995 and 2006, the normal process for local elections was not respected. On 6 August, the National Assembly approved a resolution that **postponed local elections** scheduled for that month to 2010. The government blamed financial constraints for the inability to hold the elections in time. On 19 October, the

Assembly approved another resolution, which extended the mandate of the regional government in Príncipe and the six district councils in São Tomé for five months. However, on 28 October, Foreign Minister Carlos Tiny claimed it was impossible to hold elections in February 2010 due to delays in voter registration by the 'Comissão Eleitoral Nacional' and a lack of finance.

President Menezes provoked a **political crisis** when the fourth extraordinary congress of the MDFM elected him as new party leader by acclamation on 19 December. Menezes declared his intention to become elected deputy and to take up his parliamentary seat after the end of his presidential term in September 2011. The two coalition partners, 'Movimento de Libertação de São Tomé e Príncipe/Partido Social Democrata' and PCD immediately accused Menezes of having violated the country's semi-presidential Constitution, which regards the function of head of state as incompatible with any other public or private office. In turn, on 30 December, an angry Menezes ordered the withdrawal of the four MDFM ministers from the government coalition. The departure of the MDFM left the remaining coalition parties with a working majority of 31 deputies out of 55 in the National Assembly.

Foreign Affairs

In search of aid, the government strengthened relations with regional partners and established co-operation links with India. In mid-January, the **Nigerian government** agreed to resume the supply of 30,000 barrels of crude per day to São Tomé for resale on the international oil market, an arrangement that had been suspended in 2007 after former President Obasanjo was succeeded in office by President Yar'Adua. On 25 June, the Nigerian Senate approved a $ 10 m interest-free loan to São Tomé as advance payment of signature bonus payments for oil blocks in the JDZ. On 20 December, during a two-day visit to Abuja, Prime Minister Branco asked Nigeria for another $ 10 m loan to support his country's 2010 annual budget.

On 6 October, Prime Minister Rafael Branco and Foreign Minister Carlos Tiny arrived in Luanda for a two-day visit. Branco thanked the **Angolan government** for the support granted to his country and encouraged Angolan businessmen to invest in São Tomé with a credit line of $ 15 m to be financed by Luanda. In addition, Branco proposed a joint-venture with Angolan oil company Sonangol to develop his country's Exclusive Economic Zone (EEZ). During the visit, the Angolan government promised the release of $ 5 m, the second tranche of a $ 11.5 m loan pledged earlier in the year. In February, Sonangol and the government had already signed an agreement on the construction of a $ 30 m regional naval fuel supply station in Neves.

On 29 November, Foreign Minister Tiny began a four-day visit to **India**, the first ever high-level visit between the two countries. Tiny held discussions with Minister of State for External Affairs Shashi Tharoor and discussed co-operation in the hydrocarbon sector with officials of the ministry of petroleum and the oil company ONGC Videsh. India pledged São Tomé $ 1 m for the establishment of a small industries development centre and conceded a credit line of $ 5 m for priority projects in the areas of agriculture, capacity building and infrastructure. In addition, India granted Rs 10 m ($ 213,000) for the aquisition of pharmaceutical products. In return, Tiny promised to support India's application to become a permanent member of an extended UN Security Council.

Socioeconomic Developments

On 11 October, a fire destroyed two generator groups in the energy utility's 'Empresa de Água e Electricidade' (EMAE) central thermal power station, which reduced its capacity from 13.7 MW to 5 MW. Prime Minister Branco complained that his government had put at EMAE's disposal some $ 10 m, without any results. For months, some 70% of the island was without **electricity**. In late December, Taiwan started the construction of a new $ 15 m thermal power station for five generator groups in Santo Amaro, with a total capacity of 8.5 MW. Taiwan Electrical and Mechanical Engineering Services were entrusted with the management of the plant for the first two years. In the same month, Hidroeléctrica, a company in which the Portuguese construction company Soares da Costa has a 60% ownership, sent six generators, which were installed in Bobô Fôrro and expected to produce 5 MW.

In January, the Portuguese construction company Mota-Engil and the government signed an agreement for the construction of a new **water supply** system for the capital. The $ 5.8 m project was co-financed by the AfDB ($ 2.7 m), the EDF ($ 2.5 m) and the local government ($ 600,000). In February, Portugal approved a € 50 m credit line to finance Portuguese projects included in the archipelago's Public Investment Programme.

In March, the IMF released $ 540,000 as part of a new three-year **Poverty Reduction and Growth Facility** (PRGF) for the period 2009–11, totalling $ 3.8 m, approved only the same month. The new PRGF, the third since 2000, replaced the previous one concluded in August 2008. It aimed at achieving average annual GDP growth of 6.3%, reducing inflation to below 10% until 2011, implementing sustainable public finances and further structural reform of public enterprises, and improving the overall business environment. However, following the first review of the PRGF in September, the IMF expected a drop in GDP growth from around 6% in 2008 to 4% in 2009 due to falling direct foreign investment.

On 28 July, São Tomé and Portugal signed an **exchange rate parity agreement** which allowed the national currency to be pegged to the euro at the fixed rate of € 1 to dobras 24,500 from 1 January 2010. The agreement was supported by a Portuguese credit line of up to € 25 m to reinforce the archipelago's forex reserves whenever necessary. The fixed exchange rate was expected to contribute to macroeconomic and financial stability in order to decrease inflation and attract more direct foreign investment.

Agriculture attracted several foreign investment agreements. On 21 July, the government and the Libyan company Atico – African Investment Company signed a 20-year concession contract for the 239 ha Monte Café estate. Atico promised to invest $ 3 m in the first four years in the revival of the coffee and cocoa plantations and the restoration of the dilapidated infrastructure on the state-owned plantation. On 25 October, the Libyan chargé d'affaires, Salem Milud Alfaqui, donated five tractors to seven small farmers' communities in support of the government's 'Nova Agricultura' programme. Lybia also provided drivers, fuel and maintenance for the tractors. On 21 October, the government and the Belgian Socfinco Group signed an agreement for a 25-year concession on 5,000 ha of plantation lands and investments of € 40 m in palm oil production. The joint output of the restored palm oil factory EMOLVE ('Empresa de Oleo Vegetal') in Ribeira Peixe, and another factory to be constructed on the Sundy estate in Príncipe, was estimated at 5 tons per day. Palm oil production was expected to create 1,000 jobs and to start within three to five years.

In August, the National Air Security Company ENASA disclosed that the government had rescinded by mutual consent the contract for aero-space exploration signed with the Nairobi-based AVC Consultants in 2007. The 11-year contract had come into force in February 2008 and allowed AVC a 95% share in the revenue earned from aero-space exploration. On 26 November, the European Commission included all **airlines** registered in São Tomé on the black list of 228 airlines from 15 countries banned from European airspace for safety reasons. Despite repeated warnings, São Tomé's National Institute of Civil Aviation had not met the international security norms required by Brussels. However, the national company STP-Airways continued operations to Lisbon, since its single plane was owned by the Portuguese EuroAtlantic, a 37%-share holder of STP-Airways, and was registered in Portugal.

As a result of financial difficulties experienced by the French container shipping group CMA-CGM, the beginning of the construction of the **deepwater port** in São Tomé by the group's subsidiary, Terminal Link, announced for 2010 was postponed to 2011. On 25 September, during the official transfer of the 40 ha construction area in Fernão Dias to Terminal Link, Olivier Tretout, the company's director, declared that he expected international financial institutions to participate in financing the $ 570 m project for a 16-metre deepwater port.

Oil production remained the biggest hope for the country. On 27 and 25 August, China's Sinopec and the Swiss Addax Petroleum started exploratory drilling in blocks 2 and 4 in the JDZ, where they are the operators. After having concluded drilling in Block 4, Addax commenced exploratory drilling on 7 October in Block 3, where the company had acquired Anadarko's 51% stake and operatorship on 26 August. In November and

December, Addax drilled another two wells in Block 4. It was claimed that hydrocarbon reserves were tapped, but official drilling results had not been disclosed by the end of the year. On 2 October, Sinopec became the largest stakeholder in the JDZ through its complete takeover of Addax for $ 7.3 bn. Besides drilling rights in the Kurdish area in Iraq, Gabon and Nigeria, Addax had owned stakes in Block 1 (40%), Block 2 (14.3%), Block 3 (66%) and Block 4 (45.5%) of the JDZ, while Sinopec already owned a 28.67% stake in Block 2. This did not immediately affect São Tomé's relations with Taiwan, one of the archipelago's largest donors since 1997.

On 4 November, President Menezes promulgated the new oil operations law. The amendments allowed the government, in certain circumstances, to concede drilling rights in the country's EEZ directly to oil companies, without the obligation to hold a licensing round to sell exploration concessions.

On 23 December, the National Assembly approved the national **budget for 2010**, worth $ 153 m, of which $ 50 m was for current expenditure and $ 103 m for capital expenditure; of the latter, 90% was to be financed by foreign donors. Public works and infrastructure projects represented 19% of the budget, while education, health and agriculture receive 13%, 11% and 8% respectively.

Gerhard Seibert

VI. Eastern Africa

External attention on the sub-region continued to be mainly focused on the increasing threat by Somali pirates to international shipping in the Indian Ocean and the Gulf of Aden and, to a lesser extent, on the continuing armed conflicts in Somalia and in the Darfur region of Sudan. Other conflict zones (Ethiopian-Eritrean border, Djiboutian-Eritrean border) received almost no international attention and were left unresolved, albeit without any renewed belligerent confrontations. The last remnants of many years of armed rebel activities in northern Uganda and Burundi were finally ended. Some conflict configurations along the western borderlines of the sub-region continued to be closely intertwined with developments in neighbouring countries in the Central African sub-region (Chad, CAR, DR Congo). The ICC issued an arrest warrant against Sudanese President al-Bashir and started investigations about the key perpetrators of the post-election violence in Kenya in early 2008.

There were practically no changes in the domestic political situation in the twelve countries in the sub-region. Legislative elections were held in Comoros and new leaders were chosen for the transitional political institutions in war-torn Somalia. However, a total of seven countries were already gearing up for crucial elections that were set to take place in 2010 or early 2011.

The economies by and large proved to be far more resilient to the effects of the global economic and financial crisis than had initially been feared. Most countries experienced some slowdown in economic growth, but nevertheless achieved relatively respectable macroeconomic growth figures, ranging between 1% (Comoros) and almost 10% (Ethiopia). Only tiny Seychelles suffered the consequences of its near-collapse in 2008 and saw a substantial contraction of its GDP. The countries in the Horn of Africa and parts of Kenya were once again severely hit by exceptional drought conditions.

The EAC, after a lengthy and difficult negotiation process, decided to move on to the next integration stage of a common market in 2010, while IGAD's activities remained largely immobilised due to the persistence of antagonistic positions of several member states. Again, no substantial progress was made in the protracted negotiations with the EU over EPAs or in the discussions to find a consensus for the sharing of water resources among all riparian states of the Nile river.

Political Developments

The situation in the **Sudan** remained highly precarious and was again overshadowed by the massive human suffering resulting from the conflict in the country's western Darfur provinces, now in its seventh year, and by recurring uncertainties about the durability of the 2005 Comprehensive Peace Agreement (CPA) that had ended the long civil war in the South and made possible the establishment of a semi-autonomous Government of Southern Sudan (GoSS). The level of outright fighting in Darfur was somewhat subdued compared with previous years, but this did not translate into a substantial improvement in living conditions for the long-suffering civilian population. The build-up of the large hybrid AU-UN peacekeeping force continued throughout the year, but it still remained short of its intended strength and had only a limited capacity to effectively end the violence and protect all civilians. Various ongoing peace talks were complicated by the diverging views of many feuding rebel groups and again proved fruitless, and no political solution to the conflict was in sight. The ICC, after careful investigations, issued a formal arrest warrant for President al-Bashir on charges of crimes against humanity in Darfur, but he received wide solidarity support from African and Arab leaders in gatherings of the AU and the Arab League. Recurring tensions between Khartoum and the GoSS in Juba about the results of the 2008 census and other election preparations led to the delay of crucial nationwide elections, which were postponed to May 2010. Amid increased violence between different groups in the South, growing concerns also started to emerge about the likely dangers of the referendum about Southern Sudanese independence, to be held in early 2011 under the CPA.

In **Eritrea**, there was no change in respect of the long-entrenched political repression and the extremely authoritarian rule of President Isaias Afewerki and his immediate power circle. The all-pervasive militarisation continued to affect all segments of society. No opening-up of the regime appeared to be in sight. There was a constant out-flow of citizens trying to escape from the harsh conditions and look for a better life elsewhere. Political rights and media freedom in Eritrea were again ranked globally at the very bottom. External opposition groups moved toward better cooperation, but generally remained weak and without realistic chances of changing the situation inside the country.

The political situation in **Ethiopia** remained practically unchanged with a continuing sharp confrontation between Prime Minister Meles Zenawi's dominant Ethiopian People's Revolutionary Democratic Front (EPRDF) and various opposition groups. The regime maintained tight control over the public sphere and increased the level of intimidation against perceived political opponents and critics, and no reconciliation between the ruling EPRDF-affiliated elite and the different opposition forces appeared to be in the making. Social and ethnic unrest continued in various parts of the country, particularly in the Ogaden and Somali regions. Ahead of the next elections, scheduled for April 2010, Meles and the EPRDF attempted to further solidify their all-pervasive control and to prevent a repeat of the controversial 2005 elections, when there had been a surprisingly strong showing by opposition parties. A controversial new NGO law strongly curtailed any external support for local civil society groups. Organised opposition forces remained weak and fragmented, and the authoritarian regime showed no indication of moving towards a gradual liberalisation, feeling relatively secure with the continued backing from Western countries due to the perceived geo-strategic importance of the country.

In **Djibouti**, the long-established overwhelming dominance of President Ismail Omar Guelleh and his ruling multiparty alliance remained virtually unchallenged. A meaningful political opposition was practically non-existent, and potentially critical voices were silenced by intimidation and the general authoritarian behaviour of key government agencies. A very early public campaign was started to prepare the ground for a change in the constitution that would allow Guelleh to obtain a third presidential mandate in the next elections in early 2011. Despite its authoritarian nature, the regime was largely spared from external criticism due to the country's position as a strategic base for most international anti-piracy activities and as the location of important French and US military installations.

Somalia continued to be partitioned into three distinct entities with very different political conditions. There was no indication that this situation would change soon or that there might be a return to a unified country. **Somaliland** remained relatively stable, but was nevertheless plagued by increased political confrontations and by disputes about the conditions for over-due elections, which were further postponed into 2010. Again, no break-through was achieved with respect to the country's full international recognition as an independent state, but de-facto external relations were further strengthened. **Puntland** also maintained its semi-autonomous status and managed to stay largely removed from the turmoil in the rest of the country. In January, the local parliament elected a new president, who exerted only very limited authority to control a degree of lawlessness in the territory and particularly to restrain the continued flourishing of the activities of pirates, who operated largely out of small towns along the Puntland coast. The situation in **Southern Somalia** was not markedly improved, despite the installation of new leaders of the transitional political authorities in the aftermath of the 2008 Djibouti Accord, which had brought an agreement with the majority moderate faction of the former Islamist opponents. The Transitional Federal Government (TFG) and the parliament had thus clearly gained a wider political base and were able to become established in Mogadishu. But their effective territorial control still remained very limited and they continued to face strong, violent attacks from several radical Islamist groups who controlled large parts of the countryside and managed to cause havoc even in Mogadishu, despite the presence of an AU peacekeeping mission. The TFG was internationally recognised as the legitimate government, but its internal foundation remained extremely shaky.

The tiny island state of **Seychelles** was mainly occupied with coping with the necessary economic and social adjustments that had become inevitable in the wake of the near-collapse of the economy in late 2008. The introduction of many liberal economic reforms was a clean break with a tradition of long-held welfare-oriented policies. The GDP contracted sharply, but a new optimism to maintain the relatively comfortable Seychellois standard of living soon re-emerged. Despite the hardships experienced by most people, the political authority of President James Michel and the long-ruling government party were never seriously threatened, while an open cooperative political climate was maintained.

Somewhat delayed parliamentary elections were held in the **Comoros**, but did not bring an end to the constant quarrelling between the Union and the island authorities over their respective competencies. Against initial fierce resistance from the three island presidents, Union President Abdallah Sambi eventually managed to obtain a convincing victory in a constitutional referendum in May, which lowered the status of the island presidents to that of governors and generally strengthened the authority of the Union institutions. December elections for the Union parliament and the re-constituted island councils were clearly won by Sambi's camp. But a further conflict remained unresolved, since Sambi insisted on streamlining the complex electoral calendar while his opponents suspected him of wanting to illegally extend his mandate beyond the regular expiry in May 2010.

Kenya continued to be governed by the grand coalition of President Mwai Kibaki and Prime Minister Raila Odinga that had been created in March 2008 in the aftermath of the disturbing post-election violence triggered by fraud accusations after the 27 December 2007 elections. This power-sharing arrangement included all major political players and it persisted throughout the year despite repeated frictions and open conflicts between different political camps and their leading personalities, as well as within the various heterogeneous political alliances. As usual, the public was constantly confronted with rumours of new political manoeuvres and changing allegiances, but in the end the political architecture remained practically unchanged. Many of these moves were already forerunners of the formation of new political groupings for the next elections in 2012. Expert discussions were begun about the promised, and in the past never achieved, production of a new constitution, but they still remained at an early stage. Much public excitement centred around the possible persecution of the main culprits in the post-election violence, whether by local jurisdiction or by the ICC.

In **Tanzania**, the long-acclaimed political stability and the overwhelming dominance of the former single party CCM remained largely unchallenged, but serious frictions between different party wings, confronting the old-style clientelistic and corruption-prone establishment with younger reformers, became more visible than ever before. Various prominent corruption cases continued to be in the public eye, and the population expressed a growing disenchantment with the socioeconomic performance of President Jakaya Kikwete's government. Despite there being no restrictions on their operations, the political opposition remained generally weak. Early political posturing began in anticipation of the next general elections in October 2010. Surprising progress was made towards possibly overcoming the longstanding antagonism between CCM and the main opposition party in semi-autonomous **Zanzibar**. An eventual conciliation with a view even to forming a coalition government seemed possible by year's end, but remained to be confirmed.

Uganda had another relatively uneventful political year, with President Yoweri Museveni and his ruling National Resistance Movement (NRM) remaining absolutely dominant and holding the reins of power largely unchallenged. The various opposition parties were relatively free to express public dissent and to criticise the government in parliament and in the public media, but on the whole were restrained from having a significant impact on public affairs. The major opposition groups attempted both to internally strengthen their profile and leadership and to realign a possible common front against the NRM, while the latter also experienced its internal frictions and was far less monolithic than often assumed. Political discussions were already geared up to the next elections in early 2011, with a new presidential bid by Museveni becoming ever more likely. Old tensions between the central government and traditionalist Buganda forces again became more visible, including over the delicate land issue. The northern parts of the country were no longer affected by the long-standing rebel threat and were slowly returning to normalcy, since the remnants of the LRA rebels had fully retreated into neighbouring countries.

There was absolutely no change to the political situation in **Rwanda**. The country remained stable and peaceful, and all aspects of public life continued to be meticulously controlled by President Paul Kagame and the ruling Rwandan Patriotic Front. There was almost no space for any dissenting political opinions or for expressions of an independent civil society. The authoritarian repression of any dissent continued to be justified by the dangers of a relapse into 'ethnic divisionism' and by the exigencies of a highly-disciplined pursuance of a modernising development path for the country. Various externally-based opposition groups did not succeed in making any visible impact on events in Rwanda.

A hectic political year in **Burundi** was primarily focussed on the run-up to the crucial next series of elections for all levels of the political system in mid-2010. These elections were expected to be the litmus test for whether the country had transitioned into a formal democracy after long years of civil war and the first successful elections in 2005. A major step was accomplished by the long-delayed formal peace agreement with the last remaining active rebel group 'Forces Nationales pour la Libération' (FNL) and by their conversion into a regular political party. President Pierre Nkurunziza's government continued to be dominated by his ruling party, but – in accordance with the power-sharing formula of the 2005 constitution, based on the principles of consociational democracy – it also included ministers from Burundi's two major traditional parties, who otherwise behaved more like an opposition. An intriguing plethora of political parties was preparing the ground for the electoral contest in 2010 in an environment of great uncertainty about the likely outcome. A noticeable increase in acts of intimidation and scattered violence raised fears of further escalations.

In the entire **Eastern Africa sub-region**, there were virtually no changes in Freedom House's annual assessment of **political rights** and **civil liberties** in 2009. For political rights, all country ratings remained absolutely unchanged, whereas on the civil liberties index Eritrea, Kenya and Somaliland each slipped by one point (on a scale of 1 at the top to 7). While none of the twelve sub-regional countries (plus Somaliland as a separate entity) were rated in the top category as 'free', four countries (Eritrea, Rwanda, Somalia, Sudan) remained in the 'not free' category. Eritrea, Somalia and Sudan were among the lowest-rated countries worldwide (with scores of 7 for both political rights and civil liberties), while Rwanda was only slightly better (with scores of 6 and 5, respectively). The remaining eight countries (plus Somaliland) were all categorised as 'partly free' (with both political rights and civil liberties in the 3–5 point range). Among these, Seychelles was again judged the best, followed by Comoros and Tanzania.

TI's **Corruption Perceptions Index** for 2009 once again revealed wide discrepancies between countries of the sub-region. Of the 180 countries listed, Seychelles again easily achieved top position with an overall ranking of 54 and a score of 4.8 points (out of 10), practically unchanged from 2008. By contrast, Somalia was again rated as the worst country (ranked 180 and scoring 1.1), while Sudan was ranked 176 (1.5 points) and Burundi 168 (1.8 points). The remaining countries, similar to most other African countries, ranged somewhere between 3.3 and 2.2 points in the following order: Rwanda (rank 89), Djibouti (111), Ethiopia (120), Eritrea and Tanzania (jointly 126), Uganda (130), Comoros (143) and Kenya (146).

Similar divergences between countries were discernible with regard to **press freedom**, as expressed in the 2009 Press Freedom Index by Reporters Without Borders. Of 175 listed countries, Eritrea for the third year took last position (score 115.5), behind even North Korea. Somalia (rank 164), Rwanda (157), Sudan (148) and Ethiopia (140), with scores ranging from 78 to 49 were also judged to be general offenders against the principle of freedom of the media. Relatively better marks for press freedom were given to Tanzania (rank 62), Seychelles (72), Comoros (82), Uganda (86) and Kenya (96), while Burundi (103) and Djibouti (110) were somewhere in between.

Freedom House's similar Press Freedom Report 2010, covering all events in 2009, showed comparable results, but with some notable variations for specific countries. Out of a total of 196 listed countries, five Eastern African countries appeared in the category 'partly free': Comoros and Tanzania (jointly ranked 102), Uganda (110), Kenya (121) and Seychelles (124). The press situation in the remaining countries was judged to be 'not free', ranking in the following order: Burundi and Djibouti (159), Sudan (165), Ethiopia (169), Rwanda (178), Somalia (181) and Eritrea (192).

Transnational Relations and Conflict Configurations

The ongoing **Darfur** conflict in **Sudan**, although the fighting was considerably less intense, continued to have cross-border effects on the western neighbours **Chad** and the **Central African Republic**. Bilateral Chadian-Sudanese relations remained strained throughout most of the year, but some improvement appeared to be possible towards the year's end, although with no stable agreement as yet. The EU military mission EUFOR, set up in 2008 to protect Sudanese refugees in Chad and the CAR, ended as envisaged on 15 March and its tasks were handed over to the enhanced UN Mission in the CAR and Chad (MINURCAT).

The population in very remote areas in the triangle between **DR Congo, CAR** and **Southern Sudan** was victimised by the remnant rebel groups of the Lord's Resistance Army (LRA), which had for many years waged a civil war and committed horrendous atrocities in northern **Uganda**, but had since been completely driven out of Ugandan territory. A concerted joint military operation against the LRA in December 2008 had been a failure, and this was also true of continuing attempts by the Congolese, Southern Sudanese and Ugandan military to catch the evasive, scattered small LRA groups. Protracted earlier peace negotiations with the LRA had been abandoned and several LRA leaders surrendered after being rigorously pursued, but no complete end of the threat was in sight.

Eritrea continued to be highly isolated in the sub-region and to be at loggerheads with all other governments, with the exception of **Sudan**, with which it had relatively good bilateral relations. Again there was no progress towards a lasting solution of the border conflict with **Ethiopia**, which had remained unresolved since the end of the 1998–2000 war. Despite the 2008 termination of the UN monitoring mission, brought about by strong Eritrean pressure, there were no significant confrontations between the military of the two sides, who were facing each other at close quarters along the border. Similarly, no solution was in sight for the other border conflict, with **Djibouti**, which had broken out in 2008 with the occupation of pockets of Djiboutian territory by Eritrean troops. The Eritrean government simply refused to acknowledge the existence of any problem and to comply with international mediation attempts. The government, in its enmity to Ethiopia, was also suspected of actively supporting (including with the supply of arms) the radical Islamist forces in **Somalia** that were trying to topple the transitional government in Mogadishu. Two UN Security Council resolutions clearly condemning Eritrea's positions had no visible effect. Eritrea's membership in IGAD remained in limbo following its unilateral declaration of suspension in 2007.

All countries in the Horn of Africa continued to be significantly affected by the ongoing insecurity and political turmoil in **Somalia**. Early in the year, the enlarged interim parliament, sitting in **Djibouti**, elected a new leadership of the Transitional Federal Government (TFG) at the conclusion of the lengthy 2008 negotiation process between many Somali factions and groups, including the majority moderate wing of formerly Asmara-based Islamist opponents, which had ended with agreement on the Djibouti Accord. The transitional institutions subsequently relocated to Mogadishu, but were hardly able to exert real authority over large parts of Southern Somalia, despite general international recognition and support. An AU peacekeeping mission (**AMISOM**), with contingents from **Burundi** and **Uganda**, was increased in numbers, but still short of its intended strength and was largely limited to protecting the TFG and some parts of Mogadishu, without much impact on restraining wide-spread violence beyond its own barracks. A discussed supplementation of AMISOM with more troops from other countries did not materialise. Radical Islamist forces opposed to the TFG managed to gain control over large parts of the country, with support from **Eritrea** and Islamist extremists from outside. **Ethiopia** had withdrawn its troops from Somalian territory at the end of 2008, but kept them at the border (with intermittent limited incursions) and remained highly vigilant with regard to the protection of its own strategic interests as self-styled sub-regional hegemon. **IGAD** repeatedly discussed the Somalia problem at ministerial meetings, but was unable to have any significant positive influence.

The scope of the threat by **Somali pirates** to international shipping in the Gulf of Aden and along the East African coast increased markedly during the year, in both geographical coverage (deep into the Indian Ocean) and the number of attacks. Most of the pirates operated from the territory of Puntland, but others acted from places in Southern Somalia. In response, various international anti-piracy activities were greatly extended, with warships from many nations patrolling the sea-lanes to protect regular shipping traffic. The EU had launched its EUNAVFOR operation Atalanta in December 2008; some participating navies operated under NATO command and several Asian countries (China, India, Japan) also joined the concerted exercise. **Djibouti, Kenya** and **Seychelles** acquired special importance as support bases for these operations, and the last two were internationally preferred as suitable territories where apprehended pirates could be prosecuted and imprisoned.

Although the political tension in **Comoros** had subsided somewhat after the 2008 AU-mandated military invasion of Anjouan, the **AU** nevertheless remained diplomatically involved in the ongoing political disputes between the Union and island authorities. This was in pursuance of its decade-old efforts to contribute to the reconciliation of the intricate local antagonisms, seen as a minor test case for the AU's conflict resolution capability.

In **Burundi**, the last active rebel movement, the FNL, finally accepted the terms of a peace agreement with the government and the demobilisation of its fighters. This had to a large extent become possible as a result of enhanced pressure from concerned neighbouring states, with South Africa as official mediator. With the registration of FNL as a fully-registered political party, the armed insurgency became a new political contestant. The repatriation of most remaining Burundian refugees from Tanzania also gained further momentum and was almost completed.

The **Great Lakes region**, with its wide-ranging significance across national borders, continued to witness the complex interplay of many groups and interests from various countries in the region. The year brought surprisingly fast changes in existing power constellations and the emergence of new regional alliances. The most substantial change was a **new entente** between the governments of **Rwanda** and the **DR Congo**. In an amazing move, Congolese President Kabila in January invited the Rwandan army to participate in joint operations with his military against the notorious 'Forces Démocratiques pour la Libération du Rwanda' (FDLR) rebels, the main enemy of the Kigali government, in the North Kivu province. The operation was only partially successful and did not succeed in eliminating the FDLR, and the Rwandan army returned home in February. In the wake of this rapprochement, several thousand Congolese Tutsi refugees were allowed to return to Kivu, thus creating new anxieties among autochthonous population groups. The important Congolese Tutsi rebel leader Nkunda, long perceived as an ally of Rwanda's President Kagame, was arrested by the Kigali authorities, but not extradited to Kinshasa as demanded by Kabila. Full diplomatic relations between Rwanda and the DRC, suspended since 1998, were re-established later in the year. Similarly, bilateral relations between **Uganda** and the **DRC** also improved remarkably, again including the exchange of ambassadors. The Ugandan army was permitted to operate on Congolese territory in their pursuit of the LRA rebels. The Tripartite Plus Joint Commission (Burundi, DRC, Rwanda, Uganda) remained dormant throughout the year, since it was apparently no longer needed in view of improved bilateral exchanges.

UN peacekeeping initiatives in the sub-region again ran up against severe restraints. The continued presence in the eastern Congo of the large UN Mission in the DRC (**MONUC**) had some limited effect in containing the overspill of rebel activities (FDLR, LRA) into neighbouring East African countries and in stabilising the internal situation in the DRC. Preliminary discussions began about a coming reduction of MONUC's strength. The UN Mission in Sudan (**UNMIS**) continued to monitor the implementation of the 2005 peace agreement in Southern Sudan against the backdrop of growing concern about the viability of the whole process and fears about the 2010 elections and the 2011 independence referendum. The hybrid UN-AU Mission in Sudan (**UNAMID**), after substantial gestation problems in 2008, was slowly succeeding in attaining its intended strength and fulfilling its peacekeeping role in the embattled Darfur region.

The **ICC**, after lengthy careful investigations, issued a formal indictment of Sudanese President al-Bashir for crimes against humanity in the conflict in Darfur. This was an unprecedented move against a sitting state president and was heavily condemned by most African and Arab governments. The ICC chief prosecutor also started internal investigations about the chances of indicting some of the key culprits in Kenya's post-election violence in early 2008.

Socioeconomic Developments

The **macroeconomic performance** of countries in the sub-region was again quite divergent, but on the whole moderately satisfactory. Practically all countries experienced a slow-down of their recent growth pattern, but they weathered the effects of the global financial and economic crisis generally better than had been feared at the close of 2008 and gathered new momentum for a resurgence in 2010 and beyond. In the circumstances, the still relatively limited integration of low-income countries into the global economic system, particularly the complex financial networks, had proved to be a blessing in disguise. The sub-regional economies by and large proved to be far more resilient to negative external shocks than had been the case in earlier periods, largely the result of a string of pragmatic reform policies introduced since the 1990s and of a fairly strict adherence to conservative monetary and fiscal policies. The slow-down nevertheless further retarded progress with respect to most poverty reduction goals, since growth rates were well below the scale needed to lay the foundations for a more dynamic economic acceleration and substantial employment creation.

According to preliminary figures in the IMF Regional Economic Outlook for April 2010, the **2009 GDP growth rate** for Sub-Saharan Africa was 2.1% (3.0% when excluding Nigeria and South Africa). This was markedly surpassed by the EAC bloc (five countries) with a GDP growth of 4.5%, although this was clearly lower than in any of the last five years. Of all Eastern African countries, Ethiopia performed by far the best, with 9.9% growth in a sixth exceptional year in a row. Uganda (7.1%), Tanzania (5.5%) and Djibouti (5.0%) also performed surprisingly well, and clearly better than had been projected. Another group of countries achieved at least moderate GDP growth somewhat higher than the population growth rate, thus allowing a very slight improvement of the average per capita income: Sudan (4.5%), Rwanda (4.1%), Eritrea (3.6%) and Burundi (3.5%). Growth in Kenya (2.1%) and Comoros (1.1%) was clearly below this important threshold and unsatisfactory, apparently a lasting after-effect of the political turbulences in both countries during the last two years. The small and highly vulnerable island economy of the Seychelles was an entirely different unique case. Its GDP contracted sharply by 7.6% as a result of the harsh economic remedies that were introduced in late 2008 to prevent complete bankruptcy emanating from an overexposure to the global financial system and from the longer-term effects of pursued welfare-oriented policies. Despite this shock contraction, Seychelles nevertheless remained a middle-income country and was set for a future recovery. As had for years been the case, no reliable figures were again available for Somalia.

Most countries officially proclaimed the pursuance of cautious monetary policies and comparatively modest **inflation** targets, but almost everywhere average consumer prices increased relatively strongly, although the 2008 global surge in food prices and oil costs had considerably receded. The estimated 2009 average sub-Saharan inflation rate (excluding Nigeria and South Africa) was 11.9%, practically the same as in 2008. The EAC as a group was close to this figure with 12.3%, but several sub-regional countries surpassed the average by far. Seychelles, as a result of its shock currency devaluation, again ended up with high 31.8% inflation (after 37% in 2008). Ethiopia too again had exceptionally high inflation (36.4%) as a side-effect of years of determined growth stimulation, while Eritrea (34.7%) suffered from the pervasive shortage of goods in the almost closed economy. Comoros (4.8%) and Djibouti (6.4%) had by far the lowest inflation rates, clearly the effect of the firm institutional tie with the Franc zone or the currency board arrangement, respectively. All other countries were not very far off the continental average.

A good measure for the intensity of domestic development efforts, without simply relying on the inflow of aid funds, is the volume of **government revenue** (excluding grants and expressed as percentage of GDP). Most of the countries in the sub-region remained somewhat below the yardstick of the sub-Saharan (excluding Nigeria and South Africa) 2009 average of 21.5%. The EAC as a group only achieved a ratio of 17.3% and no improvement over the previous two years. On the positive side, Seychelles (34.2%) in continuance of a long, similar record and, surprisingly, Djibouti (28.8%) and Burundi (26.4%) too, were able to demonstrate high domestic revenue-generation. The opposite of disappointingly low ratios was the case for Ethiopia (12.0%), Uganda (12.5%), Rwanda (12.8%), Eritrea (13.1%), Comoros (14.0%), Sudan (14.7%) and Tanzania (16.7%). All these countries relied to a large extent on the influx of external funds (in very different forms) to meet governmental expenditure.

All countries in the sub-region had a considerable negative **current-account balance**, in contrast to the only slightly negative sub-Saharan average of –2.1% of GDP (due to surpluses or only small deficits for major oil and mineral exporters that are severally skewing the average). Seychelles (23.1%) and Djibouti (17.3%) experienced by far the highest current-account deficits, followed by Sudan (12.9%), Burundi (12.1%) and Tanzania (9.4%), while all the other countries had deficits in the range of about 5–7%.

UNDP's 2009 **Human Development Index** (based on 2007 data) clearly highlighted wide variations in the sub-region in respect of general socioeconomic development levels. Only Seychelles attained the high human development category (HDI value above

0.8) and was ranked 57 out of 182 countries. Comoros (ranked 139), Kenya (147), Sudan (150), Tanzania (151), Djibouti (155) and Uganda (157) all appeared in the lower half of the medium human development category (HDI values above 0.5), with index values somewhat above the sub-Saharan average, while the other countries were in the low human development category (HDI value below 0.5): Eritrea (165), Rwanda (167), Ethiopia (171) and Burundi (174), and Somalia was not listed at all.

Sub-regional Cooperation and Sub-regional Organisations

The **EAC**, enlarged by Burundi and Rwanda as new members in 2007, held its 11th summit on 20 November in Arusha and simultaneously celebrated its 10th anniversary in style with many public events. The summit finally endorsed a significant new step in consolidating the regional cooperation venture by signing a protocol for the establishment of an **EAC Common Market**. The new regulatory framework was to become effective on 1 July 2010 after ratification by the member states, but several transitional clauses, safeguarding against various national fears, extended the implementation of the full application of all common market rules until 2015. The signing of the protocol constituted the final conclusion of a lengthy and sometimes controversial process. Formal negotiations in the context of a High-Level Task Force had started in April 2008, but ten rounds of acrimonious meetings, rotating between locations in all five countries, and a postponement of the originally set timeframe, were needed to reach agreement on compromise formulas that allowed for the prevalence of some national laws over standard common market procedures, as had been most vehemently demanded by Tanzania. The Tanzanian government strongly objected to uncontrolled access to land and permanent residency rights for non-citizens and to the use of national IDs as travel documents. This evidence of continued Tanzanian fears of being overwhelmed by more aggressive competitors, particularly from Kenya, had provoked accusations from other EAC member states that Tanzania was out to block the whole process. The 10th EAC summit, on 29 April in Ngurdoto Lodge near Arusha, was deadlocked over these issues and consequently postponed a generally expected decision until November.

The **EAC Customs Union**, in force since 2005, entered its final stage at the year's end with no further extensions of any of the transitional safeguard clauses favouring Tanzania and Uganda for an initial five-year period. Intra-EAC trade had strongly expanded during this period, with high export growth from Tanzania and Uganda to Kenya proving wrong all earlier existing worries. In July, Burundi and Rwanda also formally signed up to the Customs Union and to the validity of its common external tariffs.

In September, discussions were started at the technical level to prepare the ground for moving the EAC to the next integration stage, a **monetary union** tentatively envisaged for 2012. The presidents at both summit meetings also confirmed their determination to further strengthen all existing pillars of the EAC, including a vision to fast-track a political federation. A progress report on the national consultative process in Burundi and Rwanda about the political federation, undertaken in 2008, was submitted to the April summit. A 2nd EAC investment conference, attended by all presidents, at the end of July in Nairobi attempted to promote East Africa as an attractive entity for international investors. In September, over 1,500 military personnel from all five member states participated in the first-ever joint field exercise in northern Tanzania with a view to strengthening defence cooperation and creating the EAC's own stand-by force.

The April summit appointed two new deputy secretaries general from Burundi and Rwanda for the EAC secretariat, thus completing the process to achieve equal representation for all member states. The **East African Legislative Assembly (EALA)**, at its May session in Bujumbura, approved the **EAC budget** for 2009–10 to the sum of $ 54.3 m, an increase of 34% over the previous year. Almost 52% of the budget was expected to be raised by partner state contributions, and the rest by external donors. Early in 2009, the functioning of EAC organs was seriously jeopardised by a cash crisis, because of national contributions being in arrears.

Again, no final agreement was reached in the protracted negotiation process for concluding an **EPA** with the **EU**. The interim framework agreement that had been initialled in November 2007, but had not yet been ratified, technically lapsed in mid-2009, leading to a situation of trading 'free' with the EU in the absence of a formal agreement, albeit without any immediate negative consequences. With items on development cooperation, rules of origin and trade-related issues, agriculture and services, remaining outstanding, expectations for the conclusion of a full EPA were further postponed into 2010.

The 13th **COMESA** summit, originally scheduled for May 2008 in Zimbabwe, but cancelled due to ongoing post-election violence, was held on 7–8 June at Victoria Falls. Kenya's chairmanship had thus been extended by one full year. On this occasion, the much delayed **COMESA Customs Union** was officially launched. During a three-year transition period, all 19 member states were expected to align their national tariffs to a common external tariff, with a three-band structure for primary, intermediate and manufactured goods (similar to the EAC). This was the starting point for the next integration stage, building upon the strong five-fold growth of intra-regional trade that had resulted from the existing FTA, launched in 2001, which currently had 14 participating member states. Burundi and Rwanda were the first countries to receive special financial compensation, financed by the EU, for the revenue losses resulting from their adherence to the FTA and the EAC Customs Union. Ministerial council meetings (in June at Victoria Falls, and in December in Lusaka) deliberated extensively on a wide range of COMESA's cooperation activities and particularly endorsed progress reports from the **tripartite task force** of the COMESA, EAC and SADC secretariats, which had been directed in October 2008 to develop a roadmap for the establishment of a **single FTA** by all 26 member countries of the three blocs. A draft document to that effect was finalised in November and circulated for further discussion. The various overlapping memberships by individual countries in different sub-regional organisations made the intended move extremely difficult, but optimists were aiming for a new grand FTA in 2012.

The **IGAD** council of ministers met for several extraordinary sessions on the current crisis situations in Somalia, Sudan and between Eritrea and Djibouti, and held its much delayed 33rd ordinary meeting on 7–8 December in Djibouti. IGAD expressed full support for Somalia's struggling transitional government and for Djibouti in its border dispute with Eritrea, and attempted to have an attenuating influence on developments in Sudan, but on the whole the impact of its stated positions remained rather ineffectual due to the continued lack of a convincing united strategy by its member states. No real progress was made on the badly needed and long-awaited revitalisation and institutional strengthening of IGAD's secretariat.

Further progress was made with the establishment of the **Eastern Africa Standby Brigade (EASBRIG)** as a component of the AU's envisaged African Standby Force. Over 1,000 soldiers from 11 sub-regional countries participated from 29 November in a five-day field training exercise in Djibouti. With its membership of 14 Eastern African and Indian Ocean countries, EASBRIG was expected to reach an initial operational capacity by mid-2010 and its full strength of 7,000 personnel by 2015, under the direction of its Nairobi-based Coordinating Mechanism (EASBRICOM). The separate intensification of EAC military cooperation appeared likely to form the nucleus of the wider EASBRIG approach.

The **IOC** celebrated its 25th anniversary on 23 March with the opening of its new headquarters building in Quatre Bornes (Mauritius). On 4–5 April, the 25th ministerial council meeting was held in Moroni, when the rotating IOC presidency passed from the Comoros to the French secretary of state for development cooperation, Alain Joyandet, to whose irritation the Comorian foreign minister used the occasion to publicly attack France for holding a referendum about Mayotte's departmental status on 29 March. Other than the continuation of a number of technical cooperation programmes, the IOC's political concerns mainly related to the crisis in Madagascar, the increased threat from Somali pirates, and the conclusion of EPA negotiations with the EU, but with the organisation in all cases only having minor influence.

The **Indian Ocean Rim Association for Regional Cooperation (IOR-ARC)**, although almost moribund for quite some time, held its 9th ministerial council meeting on 25 June in Sana'a (Yemen). Most of its 18 members from Africa, Asia and Oceania had lost interest in this rather disparate regional grouping, which primarily focused on trade and investment promotion, but lacked a political agenda and a clear vision. From Africa, only Mauritius, as host to a minuscule secretariat, still attached some importance to the IOR-ARC, while this was no longer the case for South Africa.

Only limited progress was made to substantively revitalise the **'Communauté Economique des Pays des Grands Lacs' (CEPGL)**, although with the re-establishment of full diplomatic relations between the three member states, prospects now looked somewhat better. The Kinshasa government still failed to fulfil its promised financial and staff contributions to the small secretariat in Gisenyi (Rwanda), thus leaving it entirely reliant on Burundi and Rwanda. External support was primarily given by Belgium and the EU. The presidents of the three national parliaments met on 28–29 September in Bujumbura to initiate regular involvement of parliamentarians in CEPGL affairs. A meeting of governors of all border provinces attempted to facilitate the circulation of goods and persons across borders.

The 11-member **International Conference on the Great Lakes Region (ICGLR)** held its 3rd regular summit on 10 August in Lusaka, with Kenya's President Kibaki handing the chairmanship to Zambian President Banda. The summit had originally been scheduled for December 2008 in Kinshasa, but had to be postponed due to the then prevailing security crisis in the eastern DR Congo. The assembled leaders were now satisfied that there was a considerable improvement in the security situation in the sub-region, but identified three main groups (the LRA, FDLR and ex-Interahamwe) as still constituting negative forces that threatened peace and security. A roundtable conference was convened on 5–6 November in Bujumbura with the support of the AfDB to discuss with a large number of international donor organisations their envisaged support for over 30 development projects to the value of about $ 1.5 bn, but no firm pledges were made, since further viability investigations in the still uncertain political environment were deemed necessary.

The **Nile Basin Initiative (NBI)** of nine riparian states (plus Eritrea as observer) celebrated its 10th anniversary on 7 December in Dar es Salaam without any final consensus being reached on a cooperative framework agreement that would allow the intended establishment of a fully-fledged River Nile Basin Commission. Most of the text had been agreed in 2007, but Egypt and Sudan continued to reject the contentious article 14(b) on water security. This would alter their historical water rights (formulated in colonial-era treaties in 1929 and 1959), which gave Egypt veto powers over water use by other countries. While seven upstream countries had increasingly run out of patience and agreed on a common position, Egypt and Sudan stubbornly maintained their objections in NBI ministerial council meetings on 22 May in Kinshasa and on 27–28 June in Alexandria. The deadlock over conflicting fundamental interests, most pronounced between Egypt and Ethiopia as the major source of Nile waters, thus remained unresolved.

Rolf Hofmeier

Burundi

The year was marked by the successful **completion of the peace process**, with the last remaining rebel movement registering as a political party. Mainly as a result of the **pre-electoral climate**, tensions were on the rise at various levels: within political parties, between the dominant 'Conseil National pour la Défense de la Démocratie – Forces pour la Défense de la Démocratie' (CNDD-FDD) and opposition parties, and between the government and civil society groups considered to be too close to the political opposition and the international donor community. With the active support of local diplomatic representatives, severe political crises were averted over two issues: the composition of the **Electoral Commission** and the adoption of a new **electoral code**. The mandate of the UN Integrated Office for Burundi **(BINUB)** was extended for another year. After reaching the completion point under the HIPC initiative, Burundi benefited from significant **debt relief**.

Domestic Politics

After several years of hesitation, the **implementation of the peace agreement** signed in September 2006 between the government and the last remaining rebel movement 'Parti pour la libération du peuple hutu – Forces Nationales de Libération' (Palipehutu-FNL) was finally completed. In accordance with the joint declaration of 4 December 2008 following the regional summit on the Burundian peace process, the government released hundreds of FNL prisoners under a regime of provisional immunity. Rebel combatants were assembled and either demobilised or integrated into the army and the police force. Some 10,000 persons associated with the rebel movement, but who had not actively participated in regular combat, received a small reintegration package. Leading FNL officials were appointed to 33 (generally relatively minor) positions in the state apparatus. Most importantly, the rebel movement agreed to alter its name (deleting the ethnic reference, which was considered to be contrary to the Constitution) and **registered** as a **political party (FNL)** in April. To symbolise the end of its armed activities, FNL leader Agathon Rwasa, newly appointed as head of the National Social Security Institute, handed in his weapon at a public ceremony three days before his party's official registration.

Compared with the situation that prevailed in 2007 and 2008, the **composition of the government, the National Assembly and the Senate** was marked by a high degree of stability. A minor **government reshuffle** was carried out in January. The most important changes were the replacement of the minister of the interior, Venant Kamana (Tutsi, CNDD-FDD) with former Kayanza provincial governor Edouard Nduwimana (Tutsi, CNDD-FDD) and the replacement of the minister of foreign affairs, Antoinette Batumubwira (Tutsi, CNDD-FDD), who joined the AfDB, with former Burundi ambassador to the UN Augustin Nsanze (Hutu, CNDD-FDD). Vice-ministries were elevated to ministries, much to the satisfaction of the coalition parties 'Front pour la Défense de la Démocratie' (FRODEBU) and 'Union pour le Progrès National' (UPRONA), which had complained of earlier conflicts of jurisdiction. In November, Minister of Mines and Energy Samuel Ndayiragije (Hutu, CNDD-FDD) was dismissed because of "serious shortcomings", after cancelling the debts owed by electricity companies in DR Congo and Rwanda without prior consultation with the government. At the level of **parliament**, only a relatively small number of MPs and senators changed their political party affiliation, leaving FRODEBU and CNDD-FDD and joining the ranks of the FNL and the 'Union pour la Paix et le Développement' (UPD), which thus far were not (or rather, not officially) represented in the National Assembly. They did so in September, shortly before the publication of a new provision in the electoral code stipulating that MPs defecting from their party would no longer retain their seats in parliament. Despite this apparent institutional stability, **major disputes** continued to oppose the CNDD-FDD and its coalition partners UPRONA and, most notably, FRODEBU. While being part of the government, the latter in particular generally presented itself as the main opposition party and distanced itself from official government policy and the dominant party on several occasions. In May, FRODEBU Chairman Léonce Ngendakumana publicly accused CNDD-FDD of establishing an armed militia. With local, parliamentary and presidential elections scheduled for 2010, tensions also increased between CNDD-FDD and two 'new' parties, the UPD and the 'Mouvement pour la Solidarité et la Démocratie' (MSD). Like other opposition parties, the latter complained of what they considered to be a well organised pattern of oppression of political opposition activities (through violent intimidation of their members, attacks on party premises or symbols, arbitrary and discriminatory prohibition of party rallies, abuse of public resources by the dominant party, etc.). The UPD was the party reportedly led, from inside Mpimba prison compound, by the former CNDD-FDD strongman Hussein Radjabu, who had been sentenced in 2008 to 13 years' imprisonment by the Supreme Court for endangering the security of the state. The MSD was the party of the well-known journalist Alexis Sinduhije, who had been arrested in 2008 but, after considerable international pressure, was acquitted and released in 2009. After several months' delay, the MSD was registered in June, bringing the number of official political parties to 43.

More generally, the domestic political scene was dominated throughout the year by preparations of the **forthcoming 2010 elections**. Prospects for the elections were primarily strongly related to internal developments within political parties. In addition, the electoral process was nearly derailed by two political crises, over the composition of the 'Commission Électorale Nationale Indépendante' (CENI) and the enactment of a new electoral code.

As far as internal developments within political parties were concerned, the **CNDD-FDD** party congress in March reaffirmed and consolidated the leadership of President Pierre Nkurunziza (Hutu, from Ngozi) and a group of army generals loyal to him. The party chairman, Jérémie Ngendakumana, considered to be (too) close to a group of more moderate, civilian party officials, saw his powers reduced through the creation of the position of a secretary general (Gélase Ndabirabe) and the establishment of a 'comité des sages', chaired by Nkurunziza himself. However, rather than expelling internal dissidents (as it did in 2007 and 2008), the CNDD-FDD leadership decided to try to keep them on board, thus preventing yet another opposition party emerging from within its own ranks. Somewhat surprisingly, and despite the fact that incumbent President Nkurunziza will in all likelihood run for a second term, the CNDD-FDD has not yet identified its candidate for the forthcoming presidential elections. Throughout the year, the party's youth wing, 'Imbonerakure' ('those who can see from afar'), became much more prominent than before. As a youth division that, according to the party leadership, organised innocent sports activities, they were denounced by others for operating as a militia, intimidating and frightening opposition supporters and the general population.

First to appoint its candidate for the presidential election was **FRODEBU**, the party of the national hero and first democratically elected Hutu president, Melchior Ndadaye (who defeated incumbent UPRONA president, Pierre Buyoya, in June 1993 but was assassinated four months later). Its candidate was Domitien Ndayizeye (Hutu, from Kayanza), who was president of Burundi during part of the political transition period that followed the signature of the Arusha peace and reconciliation agreement in August 2000. Although questions were raised about the procedure leading to his selection, this early nomination nipped internal dissidences in the bud. In response to what it considered to be a provocation by the CNDD-FDD, the party's youth wing renamed itself 'Intakagwa' ('those who cannot be frightened') and became increasingly visible and active. Ten years after an internal split occasioned by divergent views on the Arusha peace negotiations process, the two wings of **UPRONA**, the former single party with a predominantly Tutsi electorate, reunited. At a party congress in August, the reunification was crowned by the election of a new party leadership, with Bonaventure Niyoyankana, a brother of the minister of defence, as its new chairman. Presenting itself as the real alternative for change, the **FNL** was increasingly perceived as the main challenger to the dominant CNDD-FDD party in the forthcoming 2010 elections. FNL leader Agathon Rwasa was in November nominated as presidential candidate. Most probably with the active support of the CNDD-FDD, an internal dissident group, led by the former spokesperson Pasteur Habimana and a former diaspora member Jacques Kenese, unsuccessfully tried to oust Rwasa from the party's leadership. Following their exclusion from the FNL in August, Kenese and Habimana announced the creation of their own political party 'FNL Iragi rya Gahutu' (FNL the legacy of Gahutu), named after the founding father of Palipehutu-FNL, Rémy Gahutu.

The **composition of the CENI** gave rise to a major political crisis. In January, Nkurunziza requested the chairman of the National Assembly and the Senate to convene an extraordinary session of parliament to appoint the members of the CENI. All proposed members, most notably the proposed chairman, Clotilde Niragira (Minister of Civil Service, Labour and Social Security), were considered close allies of Nkurunziza and CNDD-FDD and were therefore strongly contested. With all other parties boycotting the session, the National Assembly failed to reach the quorum of two thirds, and in the Senate the proposal was rejected. After several weeks of informal dialogue, and with important pressure exerted by international diplomatic representatives, an alternative team was agreed upon by the CNDD-FDD, FRODEBU and UPRONA, with the widely respected Pierre Claver Ndayicariye (an independent consultant and former minister and ambassador) appointed as chairman in March. Both the crisis itself and its solution through political dialogue were highly illustrative of the pre-electoral political context. Throughout the year, relations between the CENI and the government, in particular the CNDD-FDD, were relatively smooth, with one major exception. Criticising the CENI for recruiting its staff primarily from among opposition sympathisers, the CNDD-FDD secretary general accused it of a lack of impartiality and transparency and the minister of the interior blocked payments for the working budget of the CENI for a number of weeks.

Another major political controversy was related to the adoption of a new **electoral code**. Among the issues that divided the CNDD-FDD and most of the other important parties, two stood out: the chronological sequence of the elections and the use of a single or multiple ballot paper. The CNDD-FDD wanted to start the electoral marathon with the presidential election, hoping that a victory for the incumbent President Nkurunziza would also contribute to the party's victory in the local and parliamentary elections. The other political parties preferred to maintain the sequence followed in 2005. The opposition parties also insisted on the use of a single, rather than a multiple, ballot paper in order to curb voter intimidation (which had allegedly occurred in 2005). In early July, the five FRODEBU ministers issued a public declaration, protesting against the bill that had been put before the cabinet. In early September, once more following considerable donor pressure, a compromise was found and the new electoral code was adopted in parliament. In December, the CENI announced the electoral calendar. Elections at municipality level were scheduled for the end of May 2010, followed by presidential elections at the end of June and parliamentary elections at the end of July. Multiple ballot papers would be used, but with additional guarantees against voter intimidation.

One of the essential foundations of Burundi's transition from war to peace, the smooth **consolidation of the army**, the 'Force de Défense Nationale', both in ethnic terms as well as between the former (Tutsi dominated) government army 'Forces Armées Burundaises' (FAB) and the former (Hutu dominated) CNDD-FDD rebel force, continued to prevail in 2010. For the first time in the post-colonial history of the country, a Hutu, Godefroid Niyombare, was appointed army chief of staff (obviously with a Tutsi, ex-FAB as second in command). In July, the senate established a commission of inquiry to analyse the ethnic, regional and gender balance in the composition of the national police, and the progress made towards ethnic parity in the security forces, as required under the Constitution.

Repeated criticism of the poor **human rights** record of the government and the security forces (in particular the intelligence service, 'Service National des Renseignements' (SNR) gave rise to considerable tension between the government and civil society. Throughout the year, the use of political violence, politically motivated arrests and intimidation against perceived political opponents and civil society activists were strongly denounced by both international and local human rights organisations. In April, Ernest **Manirumva**, a well-known civil society activist and vice president of the anti-corruption 'Observatoire de la Lutte contre la Corruption et les Malversations Économiques' (OLUCOME) was assassinated. According to local NGOs and independent media, the murder was linked to Manirumva's investigation into major financial scandals involving senior government and party officials. The killing followed an earlier pattern of harassment and intimidation of OLUCOME. Throughout the year, the local civil society movement continued campaigning for truth and justice for the Manirumva assassination. Against that background, the NGO umbrella organisation 'Forum pour le Renforcement de la Société Civile' (**FORSC**) was temporarily suspended by the minister of internal affairs and its newly elected chairman fled the country amidst death threats. Once again after strong pressure by international diplomatic representatives, FORSC (itself a beneficiary of donor support) was rehabilitated soon after.

A new **criminal code** was adopted in April. Widely applauded for abolishing the death penalty and for incorporating crimes under international law (genocide, crimes against humanity, war crimes and torture) into the national criminal legislation, the code was also strongly opposed by the human rights movement for criminalising homosexual acts between consenting adults.

From July until December, after several months of delay, national consultations were held, under the auspices of a tripartite steering committee (including representatives of the government, the UN and civil society), on the proposed establishment of a truth and reconciliation commission and a special tribunal for Burundi. The report on the national consultations was expected for early 2010. In the public debate, however, the issue of **transitional justice** was largely overwhelmed by the prospect of the 2010 elections. Discussions about the establishment of a **National Human Rights Commission** (in particular regarding its composition, functioning and independence) continued. A report in September by the UN secretary general on children and armed conflict noted that, despite improvements in the overall security situation (with the entire country under UN security phase III after the end of the civil war), a climate of impunity for violators of the **rights of children** persisted in Burundi.

Foreign Affairs

On 17 December, the **UN Security Council** extended the mandate of **BINUB** (UN Integrated Office in Burundi) until 31 December 2010, requesting it "to play a robust political role in support of all facets of the peace process, in full coordination with subregional, regional and international partners", in particular the leaders of the regional peace initiative and the AU (resolution 1902). Two reports were presented to the UN Security Council by the UN secretary general, in May and November respectively. Partly because of the critical tone of these reports, the government requested, in December, the departure and **replacement of the UN executive representative**, Youssef Mahmoud.

UN Security Council resolution 1902 (2009) also welcomed the progress by the Tripartite Commission comprising Burundi, Tanzania and the UNHCR in handling the residual **Burundi refugee caseload**. In the first quarter of the year, the return movement slowed down considerably, partly as a consequence of the lack of Burundian absorption capacity, which was particularly related to the settlement of land disputes involving returnees. The number of returnees increased from April onwards and by the end of November around 31,600 refugees had returned to Burundi, including some 29,000 from neighbouring Tanzania.

At the end of May, the mandate of the South African facilitation came to an end. It was replaced by the **Partnership for Peace** in Burundi. All elements of the **AU Special Task Force**, including the Close Protection Unit (in charge of providing protection for some senior FNL members) left the country by the end of December.

Although, in 2008, the government had indicated it did not want any UN support for the electoral process, Nkurunziza called for **electoral assistance** in May. International partners of Burundi responded positively and established a twin mechanism for the coordination of international (financial and logistic) support for the elections: a consultative strategic committee (chaired by the UN executive representative, also head of BINUB) and a technical coordination committee (chaired by the UNDP country director). A needs assessment mission, led by the under-secretary general for political affairs visited Burundi in July. Of the total estimated budget of $ 43.7 m needed for the elections, the government committed to contribute $ 6.1 m, leaving some 85% to be financed through a donor basket fund. By the end of the year, around half of the budget had been pledged to this basket fund.

In July, a biannual review was conducted of progress made in the implementation of the **Strategic Framework for Peacebuilding** in Burundi and the new chairman of the Burundi configuration of the UN Peacebuilding Commission, Ambassador Peter Maurer, visited the country in November. A component of the Peacebuilding Fund programme was the strengthening of anti-corruption mechanisms. One of the most visible steps in the fight against corruption was the arrest of Burundi's ambassadors to Kenya and Italy on allegations of embezzlement of public funds.

In November, the **UN Group of Experts on the DR Congo** reported to the UN Security Council that the 'Forces Démocratiques pour la Libération du Rwanda' (FDLR) maintained a relationship with General Adolphe Nshimirana, head of the SNR, and senior police officers. The Group of Experts reported that it had received several credible testimonies that Burundi was being used as a rear base for FDLR recruitment, support networks and arms deliveries – an allegation that Burundi firmly denied.

Nevertheless, Burundi's external relations with neighbouring countries remained generally friendly. On 1 July, at the same time as neighbouring Rwanda, Burundi joined the **Customs Union** of the **EAC** (also comprising Kenya, Tanzania and Uganda) and adopted its common external tariff. A Burundi Revenue Authority ('Office des Recettes') established as part of that process, also in July, was not expected to be operational before early 2010. In November, a protocol was signed by EAC member states, including Burundi, on the creation of a common market, replacing the customs union. Ratification by the Burundian parliament, necessary for the protocol to come into force, was scheduled for 2010.

In September, 12 Burundian military, including a deputy commander of the force, were killed in a suicide attack against the headquarters of the **AU Mission to Somalia** (AMISOM). In August, a third battalion of 850 troops was sent to join the military contingent in Somalia.

Socioeconomic Developments

Burundi's macroeconomic performance was marked by a decline in real **GDP growth** from 4.5% in 2008 to 3.2% in 2009. While export earnings related to **tea** production reached a historical peak, the **coffee** harvest for the year 2008–09 dropped to 6,500 tonnes (compared with 30,000 tonnes the previous year). In an effort to simplify the coffee production and marketing chain, the 'Office Industriel du Café du Burundi' (OCIBU) was replaced by a new regulatory authority, the 'Autorité de Régulation de la Filière Café du Burundi' (ARFCB) in November.

Consumer price **inflation** fell to 11% (compared with 24% in 2008). As in previous years, Burundi's **currency** remained relatively stable. The **current account deficit** slightly decreased to 13.2% of GDP (compared with 14.2% in 2008).

In January, the IMF completed the first review of Burundi's economic performance under the new three-year **PRGF arrangement** approved in July 2008. The IMF commended Burundi's performance and announced the disbursement of an additional $ 10 m. A similar amount was announced after the second review under the PRGF, completed in July. The IMF visited Burundi for a third review in November. In March, the annual progress report on the **PRSP** was published. Despite this reported progress, acute food insecurity struck the population in a number of provinces as a result of extended drought conditions.

At the end of January, the World Bank and the IMF announced that the conditions for completion under **HIPC debt relief** had been met. In March, the Paris Club of Burundi creditors announced the cancellation of the whole $ 134 m debt.

In August, a **revised 2009 budget** was presented to parliament for approval. Revenue estimates for 2009 decreased by 7.5%, and expenditure estimates increased by 2.5%. Increases in wages and salary scales for **civil servants** were agreed upon in September, following recurrent periods of strikes. The **2010 budget** was passed on 28 December by the National Assembly, reducing defence spending and increasing social spending, particularly on education. Expected expenditure for 2010 was set at 1.5% above the revised 2009 expenditure.

In October, the government and the World Bank organised the first **Consultative Group meeting** with donor countries and organisations, in Paris. An important focus was put on investments in agriculture, energy, infrastructure and tourism as a way to promote the general objectives of macroeconomic stability and sustainable and equitable growth.

Stef Vandeginste

Comoros

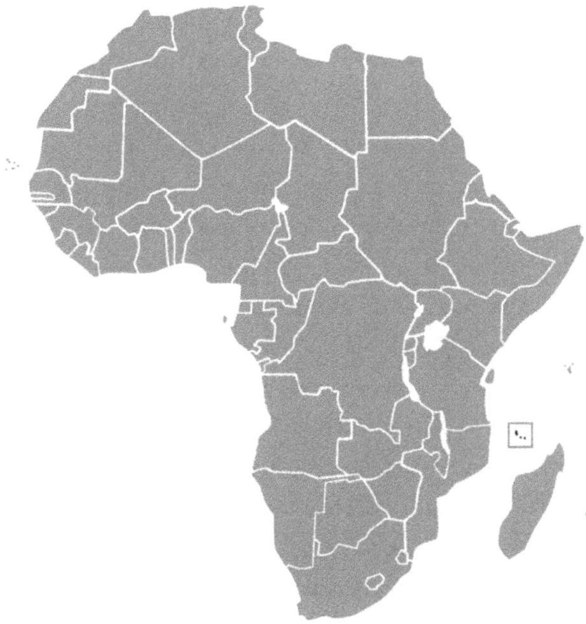

The political scenery continued to be dominated by the tensions emanating from the delicate politico-institutional structure of the 'Union des Comores' and by constant quarrelling over the respective competencies of the Union authorities and the leaders of the three semi-autonomous islands. President Sambi finally succeeded in bringing about changes to the complex federal constitution by way of a referendum, against fierce opposition from the island leaders and other opponents. Delayed legislative elections in December further strengthened the presidential camp, but the crucial question of the length of Sambi's mandate remained contentious and mistrust among leading politicians continued unabated. There was no noticeable improvement in social conditions for the population, but some modest progress in the government's economic policy performance.

Domestic Politics

Union President Ahmed Abdallah Sambi started the year by reiterating his often expressed conviction of the need to change some elements of the overly complex federal Fomboni constitution, in force since December 2001. His ideas centred around a clearer division of competencies between Union and island authorities, a substantial reduction of the costly parallel public service structures and a harmonisation of the differing election schedules, as an essential cost-saving measure. All this had always been met by suspicions about Sambi's ambition to centralise power in the Union government and to extend the length of his own presidential mandate. Sambi met the island presidents of Anjouan, Ngazidja (Grande Comore) and Mohéli on 23 January to discuss the framework of an intended constitutional referendum, subsequently outlined his intentions in a large public meeting in Moroni on 9 February and decreed 22 March as the date of the referendum. An **'inter-Comorian dialogue'** conference to discuss all contentious issues was at first boycotted by the opposition and only got underway after the constitutional court had, on 2 March, annulled the referendum on procedural grounds. The dialogue on 2–7 March brought together over 100 prominent members of the political class under the aegis of AU envoy Francisco Madeira, but there was no consensus between two clearly opposing camps.

Sambi nevertheless insisted on the need for **constitutional changes**. In a speech to the nation on 15 April, he outlined the key elements and gave **17 May** as the new **referendum** date. According to the proposed new provisions, the island presidents would be downgraded to governors and the island ministers and parliamentarians similarly to commissioners and councillors, thus rebalancing the division of powers in favour of the Union and more clearly demarcating the respective responsibilities. The electoral period would be extended to five years and the president would be given the right to dissolve the legislature. In an immediate reaction, the island presidents and other opposition politicians called for a boycott of the referendum, accusing Sambi of dictatorial tendencies and of illegally trying to extend his mandate (although the future harmonised election schedules were only to be decided by the congress, a combined sitting of the next Union and island legislatures). The referendum was eventually held without incident and acclaimed as a success by Sambi and his followers and also by most outside observers, including the AU. The official results showed an overwhelming majority, 93.9% of those who voted, agreeing to the referendum measures, but there was a low level of participation – 51.8% of the 335,000 registered voters. However, the outcome was strongly contested by the opposition and some independent observers, who claimed the low turnout indicated widespread indifference.

The referendum outcome provided a clear boost for Sambi's goals of **streamlining** the top-heavy **administrative structures**, an immediate result being the creation of a unified public service with common pay scales. Nevertheless, the island rulers tried to resist the inevitable changes and to mobilise protests against Sambi's alleged dictatorial authority. In June, an opposition 'Union pour l'Alternance Démocratique en 2010' was launched and **protest demonstrations** were held. Opposition was particularly vigorous on Mohéli, since the island elite feared to lose their constitutional right to provide the next Union president in May 2010 (in accordance with the regular election schedule and the principle that the presidency should rotate between the islands). The conflict about changed responsibilities further escalated on Ngazidja in early August, with the arrest of ten island leaders (including four commissioners and three police officers) for forceful resistance against Union authorities over the control of the police. They were quickly sentenced to three to six months' imprisonment and only released on probation in mid-September after a mediation initiative by AU envoy Madeira. For several months, a tug-of-war about public appointments was played out between the Union authorities and the island governors, until the latter had eventually to accept their new lowered status.

On 24 June, Sambi appointed a **new cabinet** composed of two vice presidents and ten ministers. His fifth cabinet in three years was enlarged by two new posts and included no women; five former ministers had to relinquish their posts. The most notable feature was the new appointment of an interior minister, who was to become mainly responsible for monitoring the power clashes with the island governors. A further small reshuffle on 31 July was necessitated by the resignation of the justice minister. Mohéli Governor Mohamed Ali Said finally acknowledged his changed role with the appointment of a new island executive of six commissioners on 8 October, while Ngazidja Governor Mohamed Abdoulwahab continued to pursue a confrontational stance against the Union authorities. Anjouan Governor Moussa Toybou proved to be the most conciliatory, since he had been elected in 2008 with strong support from Sambi, himself originating from Anjouan.

As a consequence of the lengthy disputes over the referendum, the mandates of both **Union and island legislatures** had run out in April (in accordance with a conveniently extended five-year cycle due to the 2008 Anjouan invasion crisis), without any concrete election date in sight. It was only in June that preparations for a revision of the electoral roll got underway. The elections were initially expected to be held in August, but after several rather impromptu postponements the **legislative elections** were eventually held on **6 and 20 December**. The electoral contest was clearly a confrontation between two opposing sides, pitting the presidential camp (under the banner of a baobab) against the combined anti-Sambi forces. Despite the continued existence of a multitude of small political parties, their individual profiles hardly mattered during the fierce election campaign. The 'Convergence Nationale pour Mai 2010' represented about 25 parties and militated for strict adherence to the statutory holding of an election in 2010 with candidates from Mohéli. Said Larifou, a franco-comorian lawyer and leader of 'Rassemblement pour une Initiative de Développement pour une Justice Avertie', was particularly vocal in his attacks on Sambi and was temporarily put in custody on 17 November. The 'Convention pour le Renouveau des Comores' (CRC) of Sambi's predecessor, Azali Assoumani, tried to make a come-back during the campaign after years of lost influence. In January, the CRC had held its second national congress, advocating a balance between modifications of the constitution and preserving the principle of the rotating presidency.

The official **election results** brought a landslide victory for Sambi and his camp. The calm conduct of the elections was generally acclaimed as satisfactory both by a national observer group and by about 40 international observers, while the opposition strongly criticised a number of alleged irregularities. The low participation rate of only around 40% expressed a general level of voter apathy with regard to the quarrelling of the politicians, but was no sign of support for the opposition cause. Of the 24 constituency seats in the Union parliament (11 Ngazidja, 9 Anjouan, 4 Mohéli), only four were won by the opposition, while an additional nine MPs were subsequently to be nominated by the island authorities (three from each island). In the first round on 6 December, only three baobab candidates secured an outright victory, whereas all the other main contenders were forced into a run-off on 20 December. On Anjouan, the Sambi camp made a clean sweep of all the constituencies, and on Ngazidja the opposition only obtained one seat (with seven for the baobab and three for a closely associated group). Only on Mohéli did the opposition win a majority, taking three of the four seats, although the popular votes were almost equal. The Mohéli result was a clear popular expression of the fear on this smallest island of being left out by Sambi's alleged manoeuvres to extend his mandate. The contest for the island councillors (23 seats Ngazidja, 19 Anjouan, 9 Mohéli) was decided in just one round on 6 December and brought a similar pattern of clear majorities for the baobab on Ngazidja and Anjouan and for the opposition on Mohéli. Some violent post-election unrest in the Sima region on Anjouan was sparked by the announcement of an extremely tight constituency result in which Sambi's rival in the 2006 elections, Mohamed Djanfari, was declared the loser.

The year thus ended with a **clear consolidation of Sambi's powers** and a mandate for the consistent implementation of the many reform measures that he had for long been advocating. No clarification had, however, been reached about the harmonisation of the next (presidential and gubernatorial) election dates, with the opposition attempting to regain strength for their resistance to Sambi's alleged dictatorial regime.

Foreign Affairs

Throughout the year, **Sambi** had a busy **international travel schedule** in continued pursuit of his goal to secure both diplomatic recognition (including support in the conflict with France over Mayotte) and concrete socioeconomic assistance for his weak government. He thus personally attended both semi-annual AU summits, the 21st Arab League summit in Doha on 29–31 March, the 11th CEN-SAD summit in Tripoli on 29–30 May, an extraordinary AU summit about conflicts in Tripoli on 30–31 August, the UN General Assembly and the 2nd Africa-South America summit in Venezuela in late September, the 4th Africa-China summit in Sharm-el-Sheik, an OIC economic summit in Istanbul and the FAO food summit in Rome in November, and also the UN climate summit in Copenhagen in mid-December.

The visit of **Iranian President Mahmud Ahmadinejad** on 25–27 February confirmed the close bilateral links that had been established under Sambi's presidency, largely due to his own close connections with Iran and background as a Shi'ite cleric. Four protocols about economic cooperation were signed during the visit, with Sambi appealing for more Iranian investment. The next prominent visitor, on 24–26 March, was **Tanzania's President Jakaya Kikwete**, who was warmly welcomed on the occasion of the first anniversary of the Anjouan invasion by an AU military mission under Tanzanian leadership. Kikwete was warmly praised and thanked for his crucial role in the exercise. A TanzaCom Forum in mid-August was also proof of increasingly close economic cooperation between the two countries. The prime minister of **Kuwait** visited Moroni in July with the intention of further enhancing their good bilateral relations and announced the intended opening of a Kuwaiti diplomatic mission. This was quite in line with the Sambi government's general efforts to strengthen relations with countries in the Arab world, and particularly in the Gulf region.

The **AFRICOM** commander, General William Ward, during a visit on 21 January, stressed US concern to strengthen regional capabilities in the fight against international terrorism. With that intention, the Comorian military continued to participate in the build-up of the East African Standby Brigade. On 4–5 April, the 25th ministerial council of the IOC was held in Moroni. **French Prime Minister François Fillon** paid a brief visit on 11 July, mainly in commemoration of the 152 victims who died when a Yemenia Airways plane crashed close to landing in Moroni on 30 June.

Bilateral relations with **France** continued to be rather ambivalent and delicate, as had been the case for many years, due to the conflict over **Mayotte**, the fourth island of the archipelago. A long-expected referendum was held there on 29 March and brought an overwhelming 95% approval vote (with a 61% turnout) for giving Mayotte the full status of France's 101st département in 2011. This had long been demanded by the majority of the island population, while all Comorian politicians were united in insisting that Mayotte was still part of the Comoros in accordance with international law. The referendum triggered several protest demonstrations against France, and Sambi used all possible international forums to solicit declarations of support in protest against France's behaviour. In the UN General Assembly on 24 September, Sambi proposed a model of 'one country, two administrations' as a possible solution, but without much reaction. Despite the Mayotte issue, the government had to be careful not to jeopardise the continued crucial support of its former colonial power and major aid donor. France supported the government in its dealings with the IMF, backed up the currency and provided financial resources. In reaction to the Mayotte referendum, Moroni nevertheless suspended further deliberations of the French-Comorian 'Groupe de Travail de Haut Niveau' that had been initiated in 2008. In consequence, a vaguely envisaged visit by French President Sarkozy did not materialise and relations remained ambiguous.

Socioeconomic Developments

Despite the positive effects of a stabilised political situation and of government efforts to initiate long-overdue economic policy reforms, the general **economic performance** remained very poor and unsatisfactory. For the vast majority of the population, no improvement of living conditions was in sight. GDP growth in 2009 was expected to have stagnated at 1% (as in 2008), thus leading to a further decline in per capita income for a fourth consecutive year. The average inflation rate of 2.3%, lower than in both preceding years, was largely due to the restraining effect of membership of the franc zone, whereby the franc comorien remained pegged to the euro. Remittances from the large Comorian diaspora (estimated at 150,000–200,000 people) remained essential for the national current account (amounting to around 50%), as well as for many individual families; remittances had accounted for about 25% of GDP in 2008. An investment forum in February in Marseille was specifically targeted to attract new investments from Comorians residing in France. No improvement of the enormous structural trade deficit was in sight, with exports (mainly cloves and vanilla) suffering from low prices and traditionally not even matching 10% of the ever growing import needs (including a 70% import dependency on staple cereals). The 2009 current-account deficit was expected to reach almost 10% of GDP. The accumulated total external debt of $ 260 m in 2008 had clearly become unsustainable, although relatively stable foreign-exchange reserves of over $ 100 m did provide a safety cushion. Public finances remained extremely precarious and perpetuated the almost habitual situation of many months of payment arrears for public sector employees. The IMF nevertheless observed some positive tendencies, with a revenue ratio of 13.5% of GDP and a budget deficit of about 2.4% of GDP. Despite many years of economic stagnation and social problems, the Comoros were nevertheless ranked 139th in the HDI for 2009 and placed in the medium development category. A lowered rank (162) in the World Bank's 2009 Doing Business clearly indicated the deficiencies with respect to the development of a more dynamic economic environment.

IMF missions in March and June reviewed the performance under the Emergency Post-Conflict Assistance (EPCA), approved in 2008, and were broadly satisfied that most structural benchmarks had been met and that progress had been made with regard to reform strategies for major public utilities (hydrocarbons, telecoms, water, electricity). This made it possible for the IMF to approve, on 21 September, a three-year PRGF to the tune of $ 21.5 m (with the immediate disbursement of $ 6.7 m) to assist in poverty alleviation and towards an achievement of the MDGs. Another IMF mission in November concentrated on discussions about a reform budget for 2010 and on preparations for an expected interim HIPC debt relief arrangement in mid-2010. In February, relations with the **AfDB** had also again been normalised after a break of 16 years due to loan defaults: all old debts were cancelled and a new credit of € 20 m was granted, followed by another $ 11.3 m grant for institutional strengthening in mid-July. On 19 November, the Paris Club agreed to a cancellation of 80% of all debts falling within its responsibility. In connection with the PRGF application, the government had finally, in September, after a lengthy process, approved its full PRSP ('Document de Stratégie de Croissance et de la Réduction de la Pauvrété').

On 23 February, Sambi inaugurated the premises of the 'Banque Féderale de Commerce', a new bank with **Kuwait capital** and linked with Comoro Gulf Holdings (**CGH**), owned by influential businessman Bashar Kiwan. However, banking operations did not start until the end of July, since the 'Banque Centrale des Comores' had suspended the formal authorisation due to suspicions about alleged illegal offshore activities. Some of Kiwan's other business ventures were also rumoured to be somewhat suspect, but he was apparently protected by presidential benevolence. In mid-September, CGH started construction works on four secondary ports that Kiwan had promised as part of a deal for a licence for mobile phone operations.

In May, hospital staff went on **strike** and, in June, teachers threatened to boycott all examinations at the end of the school year in response to the recurrence of the habitual Comorian problem of many months of non-payment of public sector salaries. In August, Sambi publicly claimed not to have known that salaries had not been paid since January; upon his personal request, Libya helped out with a $ 2 m grant to cover the arrears (as France had already done in March with a similar amount). Another cause of popular dissatisfaction was the problem of constant **power shortages**, with the failure of Sambi's promise to restore regular electricity supplies to all homes by August.

Rolf Hofmeier

Djibouti

President Ismail Omar Guelleh and his long-ruling **'Rassemblement Populaire pour le Progrès' (RPP)** continued to fully control all aspects of political and public life in an undisputed fashion, leaving practically no space for the expression of dissenting opinions. Alleged critical opposition voices were subjected to intimidation and harassment and risked losing their jobs. A forceful early campaign was started to allow Guelleh to obtain a third mandate in the next presidential elections, due in 2011, by way of a constitutional amendment. The 2008 border conflict with Eritrea remained unresolved despite two UN Security Council resolutions condemning the continued Eritrean occupation of pockets of Djiboutian territory. Its strategic geographical situation gave Djibouti increased international recognition as an indispensable hub for concerted efforts against the escalating threat of Somali pirates in the Indian Ocean and the Gulf of Aden, thus muzzling any open criticism of the authoritarian nature of the regime. The IMF judged that there had been some improvements with regard to fiscal policies, the implementation of structural reforms and the overall macroeconomic performance, but severe food security problems and widespread poverty remained pertinent for large segments of the population.

Domestic Politics

In the unchanged absence of an open political environment, the domestic political scene was tightly controlled by the governing **'Union pour la Majorité Présidentielle' (UMP)** coalition and dominated by the highly personalised rule of President Ismail Omar Guelleh (widely dubbed IOG) and his extended family network, including the business interests of his wife. After the February 2008 elections, the UMP held all 65 seats in the National Assembly. Within the coalition, Guelleh's **RPP** wielded the real power and was generally perceived to represent the interests of the Somali Issas, the country's major population group (about one third of the total). Four other political parties were clearly relegated to subsidiary positions as junior partners in the coalition, including the **'Front pour la Restauration de l'Unité et de la Démocratie' (FRUD)** as representatives of the Afars (about one fifth of the population).

A special **RPP congress** on 4 March celebrated the 30th anniversary of the party and passed a resolution that called for a constitutional amendment to allow **Guelleh** to stand for a **3rd presidential term** in the next elections, due in early 2011. This was further reinforced by organised mass demonstrations on 9 April on the occasion of the 10th anniversary of IOG's assumption of the presidency. Since Guelleh had been a key political figure for more than three decades and was deemed indispensable by his inner power circle, an orchestrated early campaign was started to prepare the ground for his continued retention of the presidency. Despite the generally prevailing climate of suppression of dissenting voices, the move to extend Guelleh's mandate was faced by some guarded and even openly expressed resistance, even from the UMP coalition members FRUD and 'Parti Nationale Démocratique' (PND) and including the parliamentary speaker. The issue eventually lingered on until the end of the year without a formal decision being taken. Two alternative ways of formalising the desired change were discussed: a vote in parliament or a referendum. In an apparent precautionary measure, the president of the constitutional court, a known opponent of the amendment and an alleged ally of the prominent exiled businessman Abdurahman Boreh, was replaced by Guelleh in November by an elderly long-term supporter of the president. It was clear that the constitutional change was imminent in early 2010. PND leader Aden Robleh Awaleh announced that he might run against Guelleh in the election, thereby potentially jeopardising PND's continued participation in the UMP.

On 1 March, Prime Minister Dileita Mohamed Dileita opened the new parliamentary session with a general outline of government policies, focusing mainly on education, health, defence and foreign relations. In the following debate in late March, **FRUD leader Ali Mohamed Daoud** criticised Dileita's outline surprisingly harshly, thus provoking the prime minister to respond with an open letter in the government newspaper "La Nation" on 30 March. He took issue with Daoud's criticism in view of FRUD's co-responsibility as a UMP coalition partner, but at the same time claimed it was proof that democracy was functioning. The exchange was highly indicative of the delicate structure of the UMP and of the strict limitations placed upon the junior coalition partners, while the legally tolerated opposition bloc **'Union pour une Alternance Démocratique' (UAD)** was practically prevented from playing any meaningful role at all. In early May, a week-long 'reflection seminar' on government activities during the period 2002–2009 was intended to present a sort of performance balance to a wider public audience, with the key message of the vastly improved economic situation and of a focus on the 'Initiative Nationale de Développement Social' (INDS), launched in 2007 as Djibouti's own PRSP.

The undercurrent of growing discontent about the extension of Guelleh's mandate led to a **wave of intimidation and harassment** against critical individuals and their relatives. A popular singer was imprisoned in June, and a poet was jailed for six months in July for speaking against the regime. A manager of "La Nation" and a director of the state radio/TV service were sacked for not being sufficiently supportive. The PND leader's son and daughter were harassed in response to his disobedience. A prominent businessman and former supporter of the regime, Abdurahman Boreh, fell out with Guelleh and was forced into exile in Dubai; his assets were confiscated and licences withdrawn. Reports about talks between Boreh and Eritrea's President Isaias Afewerki fuelled suspicions of a renewed strengthening of **armed rebel activities** in the north by the **minority FRUD wing** that had all along kept up Afar resistance against the regime. The FRUD rebels claimed to have repulsed an army operation on 31 August, killing four soldiers and wounding 20 others. The regime clearly feared continued rebel activities, even though they remained at a low level, and kept various Afar dignitaries under close surveillance. There were also reports about latent tensions between Afar and Issa soldiers in the army, indicating a hidden persistence of animosities that had in the past led to years of civil war. The regime's ruthless suppression of any legitimate opposition and its unfettered patronage were responsible for the country's very low scores in various indices of governance.

Foreign Affairs

The unresolved 2008 **border conflict** with **Eritrea** continued to be the centre of attention, although it had almost no concrete impact on the rest of the country. Eritrean troops still occupied the strategically important Ras Doumeira promontory along the Red Sea, while Djibouti had withdrawn its troops from the frontline in 2008 and there were no armed confrontations throughout the year. A UN Security Council (UNSC) resolution on 14 January called for the withdrawal of Eritrean troops from Djibouti's territory within five weeks, but to no effect. On 7 April, the UNSC declared Eritrea's failure to comply with the resolution, but took no action and called for more mediation efforts. Both Djibouti and Ethiopia subsequently criticised the UN for lack of energetic action. On 20 May, the IGAD ministerial council called on the UNSC to impose sanctions against Eritrea for its interference in Somalia, while there was a continued stalemate on the Djibouti-Eritrea border and no progress regarding UN mediation. In September, a UN fact-finding mission was welcomed in Djibouti, but was simply refused entry into Eritrea. IGAD and the Djibouti government again expressed their disappointment about the international failure to act strongly against Eritrea. On 23 December, the UNSC finally unanimously passed resolution 1907, which called for the imposition of sanctions in the case of Eritrea's continued non-compliance with demands for the withdrawal of its troops. By year's end the conflict remained unchanged.

Djibouti continued to take a close active interest in the evolving political developments in its crisis-ridden neighbour **Somalia**, following on from its crucial role as facilitator of the lengthy discussions that had led to the signing of the Djibouti Agreement in August 2008. Elections for Somalia's new Transitional Federal Government (TFG) by the enlarged new parliament took place in January/February in Djibouti. Subsequently, full support was given to the TFG in its difficult task of restoring some governmental authority. On 11 November, the UNHCR protested against the forced repatriation of 40 Somali asylum seekers to Mogadishu. A strategic partnership was officially declared to exist with the self-declared Republic of **Somaliland**, but remained short of full diplomatic recognition.

Relations with **Ethiopia**, the weighty neighbour and sub-regional hegemon, remained as usual somewhat delicate, but on the whole without open friction. Ethiopia repeatedly criticised the poor handling services and high costs for its essential external trade, which depended on the port of Djibouti; on 13 November a new bilateral agreement was signed on this issue. No concrete progress was made again in regard to the long-stalled plans for a major rehabilitation of the dilapidated railway line from Djibouti to Addis Ababa. In February, a concession was signed by both foreign ministers, which gave Djibouti access to 5,000 hectares of arable Ethiopian land for growing needed food crops.

Various political and economic activities were pursued to further strengthen the links with **Yemen**, the United Arab Emirates (particularly **Dubai**), **Qatar** and **Saudi Arabia**, which had gained greatly in importance in recent years. Several cooperation agreements were signed with **Iran** during a visit of President Mahmoud Ahmadinejad on 24 February, and with **Kuwait** during a July visit by a high-level Kuwaiti delegation led by the prime minister.

Guelleh's foreign travels during the year included state visits to **Malawi** in April, where he obtained a concession for 55,000 hectares of arable land, and to **Burundi** in December in connection with the participation of Burundian soldiers in the AMISOM mission in Somalia. In January, Guelleh attended an Arab economic and social summit in Turkey and visited Kuwait, and at the end of March he attended the 21st Arab League summit in Doha. On a visit to Paris in mid-October, Guelleh spoke at the UNESCO general conference and opened a Djibouti forum at the Franco-Arab chamber of commerce.

The somewhat ambivalent and partially strained past relations with **France** saw a marked improvement due to strong French support in the border conflict with Eritrea and after a ruling by a French court on 28 May that seemingly brought to an end the almost endless Borrel affair, going back to the alleged murder of a French judge in Djibouti in

1995 and the alleged involvement of Guelleh in his then capacity as security chief. In 2008, in relation to this incident, two close associates of Guelleh had been sentenced in absentia to prison terms by a French judge and were threatened with international arrest warrants. The new ruling now quashed the verdict and withdrew the arrest warrants. A high-level Franco-Djiboutian business forum in mid-March was given prominence as a sign of renewed intensification of French interests. By the year's end there were hints of a possible forthcoming visit by French President Sarkozy.

Both **France** and the **US** maintained their substantial **military installations** almost exactly as in previous years. In 2008, official payments for these military camps had accounted for 38% of the government's revenue, quite apart from other indirect economic benefits, thus testifying to the overriding importance of the foreign military presence for the country's economy. A visit by AFRICOM commander William Ward on 9 February underscored the value of Djibouti's strategic location for Western interests in the volatile Horn of Africa and over large parts of the Indian Ocean, including the adjoining countries on the Asian continent.

Djibouti's strategic value was further enhanced by its still expanding role as the **key sub-regional hub** for all combined international efforts to contain the escalating massive threat of **Somali piracy activities** along the Somali coast, in the Gulf of Aden and in far-off parts of the Indian Ocean. Apart from the EU's joint Operation Atalanta, several other navy units (including Japan, India, China and others) participated in the anti-piracy campaign and all used Djibouti as by far the most convenient supply base in the entire sub-region (followed by Mombasa in Kenya and Victoria in Seychelles). In late January, a sub-regional meeting with participants from 17 countries was held under the auspices of the International Maritime Organisation (IMO), which concluded with a code of cooperation in the fight against piracy.

Other outstanding events were: a sub-regional conference on the role of Islam in Eastern Africa in May; the 3rd COMESA ministerial conference on infrastructure on 28 October; a conference of the forum of intellectuals of the Greater Horn of Africa with a focus on Somalia in early November; and a massive week-long military field training exercise of the Eastern Africa Standby Force (EASBRIG) with over 1,500 participants from ten countries, which began on 29 November.

Socioeconomic Developments

The substantial transformation of the economy and the relatively strong growth performance of the last few years were again largely continued, despite some minor effects of the global economic and financial crisis. The **GDP growth rate** of 6.4% in 2009 was the highest ever achieved (after 5.9% in 2008) and was again mainly driven by a continuing influx of foreign direct investments into capital-intensive projects related to the port and in the construction and tourism sectors. **Inflation** was brought down to an average of around

6% for the year, largely due to lower international prices for oil and food imports. The Djibouti franc remained pegged to the dollar under a currency board arrangement (at a rate of 178 Dfr to the $). **Foreign reserves** continued their gradual build-up and reached a healthy volume of $ 208 m by mid-2009. Exports (in fact mostly re-exports to neighbouring countries) were slightly up at $ 78 m, while imports decreased considerably to about $ 435 m as a result of a levelling-off of the huge port construction activities and a fall in Ethiopian demand for imported goods. This allowed a sharp contraction of the traditionally highly **negative current-account** balance from 24% of GDP in 2008 to around 10% in 2009. The extremely skewed structure of the economy saw no change, with over 80% of GDP derived from services (mostly linked with international transit trade) und only about 3%–4% from agriculture. On 28 December, the parliament approved the 2010 **government budget** with a volume of Dfr 83.2 bn, an increase of 8% over the revised 2009 budget.

Djibouti's position in the **2009 HDI** (based on 2007 data) fell slightly to rank 155 (down from 149), almost at the bottom of the category of countries with a medium human development score. The GDP per capita (in PPP terms) was calculated to have been $ 2,061, but this was to a large extent boosted by activities around the port and did not genuinely reflect the income situation of the majority of the population. In the World Bank's latest 2010 Doing Business Report, Djibouti scored very badly (ranked 163 out of 183 countries), thus confirming its image as one of the worst countries in respect of the business environment for private entrepreneurs.

In March, the **IMF** conducted the first review of the $ 20 m three-year PRGF arrangement that had been approved in September 2008. The generally positive assessment of the government's adherence to the agreed policy goals enabled another disbursement of $ 2.3 m in mid-June, bringing the total disbursed to $ 8.2 m. Nevertheless a large fiscal slippage in 2009, driven by spending related to social and security pressures facing the country, was subsequently noted by the IMF, as was the need for more consistent fiscal and structural reforms. It was evident that the high macroeconomic growth, centred around a few enclaves, had not been accompanied by a noticeable reduction in poverty and unemployment. In April, the **World Bank** outlined a new country assistance strategy for the period 2009–2012 as a basis for a renewal of activities in Djibouti after a lapse of several years. Generally in support of the INDS, three strategic themes (economic growth, human development and access to basic services, governance and public sector management) were identified as priorities for the coming years.

Food insecurity continued to be a serious problem after five years of drought and near-famine conditions for large parts of the population. At the start of 2009, about 340,000 people had been estimated to be seriously at risk, and many pastoralists had lost most of their livestock. After temporary hopes for a good rainy season, the situation again became highly precarious toward the year's end. Poorer urban groups were threatened by steeply rising staple food prices and the World Food Programme was concerned about a lack of resources for adequate emergency supplies. There was continued criticism of the government for the inadequacy of its programmes to face the recurring food crisis. Djibouti's crucial **livestock exports** were seriously threatened in November, when Saudi Arabia lifted a nine-year ban on livestock imports from Somalia and Somaliland. Exports of cattle, camels, sheep and goats to Saudi Arabia had significantly grown in recent years and become a major source of income, but were now faced by strong competition.

The big new **Doraleh container terminal**, a $ 400 m investment with a capacity of 1.2 m TEU, was belatedly inaugurated on 7 February in the presence of many dignitaries from Dubai, since it was managed under a 20-year concession by Dubai Ports World. It was the biggest port along the entire East African coast, able to handle the latest giant vessels. High expectations were raised about Djibouti becoming a major transhipment hub for this part of the world in the near future, although the immediate traffic build-up remained somewhat subdued. In November, the port lost a major contract when the leading French shipping company CMA-CGM decided to transfer its container transhipment business to Salahah in Oman, where port charges were considerably lower. Operational problems also continued to exist at the old port, which was highly dependent on serving the transit traffic for Ethiopia.

On 27 November, Djibouti's national **Daallo Airlines** was banned from operating in any EU country due to concerns about safety standards. During the year several new **commercial banks** were opened by foreign banks based in Malaysia, Yemen, etc., a welcome addition to the two long-established French banks and an indication of promising business expectations.

Rolf Hofmeier

Eritrea

The country's autocratic political system persisted, while its economic performance weakened further and a hunger crisis loomed. The Warsay-Yikealo Development Campaign, which forces hundreds of thousands of national service recruits to work without pay for unspecified periods, continued. The human rights record remained extremely worrying. The EU Commission nevertheless made a grant to the government of $ 122 m for the period 2009–13. Eritrea's border conflict with Ethiopia was not solved. In December, the UN Security Council imposed targeted sanctions on Eritrea because of its alleged military involvement in Somalia and its refusal to enter into negotiations with Djibouti over the unresolved border conflict.

Domestic Politics

The autocratic political system remained unchanged and **President Isaias Afewerki** showed no intention of holding elections or introducing even minimal reforms. The **People's Front for Democracy and Justice** (PFDJ) was the only party allowed and no elections were planned for the future. Around mid-March, the president **reshuffled his cabinet**. Health Minister Saleh Meki was moved to the Ministry of Fisheries, and Tesfai Gebreselassie from the Ministry of Mining to the Ministry of Land, Water and

Environment. Labour and Social Welfare Minister Askalu Menkerios was transferred to the Ministry of Tourism, former Tourism Minister Amna Nurhussein was appointed minister of health, and Ahmad Hadji was moved from the Ministry of Fisheries to the Ministry of Mining. The former minister of land, water and environment, Michael Ghebremariam became minister of local government, a post that had been vacant since the arrest of Minister and Vice President Mahmoud Sherifo in 2001. Salma Hassan, former administrator of the Anseba region, was appointed minister of labour and social welfare. The ministers of agriculture, defence, education, finance, foreign affairs, information, justice, as well as transport and communication retained their positions. The national media did not report the cabinet reshuffle. It was unlikely that the reshuffle made any difference to the weak position of the cabinet in the political decision-making process. Saleh Meki died of heart failure on 3 October at the age of 62. The military commanders maintained their powerful positions.

The **judicial system** remained in the poor state that had characterised it during previous years. It was based on a weak modern court system that was unable to act independently from the government, on 'special courts' dominated by military lay judges, and on community courts that were supposed to adjudicate on the basis of customary law in cases of minor importance. The **political dissidents** (G 15) arrested in 2001 remained in solitary confinement without formal charges; the same was true for 30 journalists held behind bars. When the president was asked about the fate of the G 15 by a journalist from the 'Financial Times' on 21 July, he replied: "It has nothing to do with the domestic politics or the political reality in the country. That is history." Reporters Without Borders ranked Eritrea last in world **press freedom** for the third consecutive year. The organisation stressed that Eritrea had meanwhile reached parity with China in the absolute number of detained journalists. Dawit Isaac, a journalist with dual Swedish-Eritrean nationality and reportedly in poor health, was not released despite of international efforts, including those of EU Commissioner for Development Louis Michel. President Isaias even asserted that he would never be tried. The European Parliament nominated Dawit Issac as one of three finalists for the 2009 Sakharov Prize for Freedom of Thought in early October. In January and February, six journalists of Radio Brana, a station controlled by the Ministry of Education were arrested on allegations that they had passed information to diaspora-based news websites.

Religious persecution continued unabatedly throughout the year. The government built a camp in Meiter, a remote area in the desert, which was said to serve exclusively for the detention of religious prisoners. On 11 January, 15 members of the **Kale-Hiwot Church** in Keren were arrested, and on 28 June the state security detained 22 female **Jehovah's Witnesses**, whose husbands or fathers had been arrested earlier. In January, 60 **influential Muslims** were jailed countrywide, accused of being 'radical Islamists'; in May, 24 of them were released, while the others remained in prison without charge. In early August, about 50 Muslims from different walks of life, some of them teachers and students, were rounded up in Asmara by security officers and taken to undisclosed prison locations. Among them was Sheikh Abdella, an elderly graduate of Al-Azhar University in Cairo. On 5 December around 30 Christians, many of them elderly women, where detained while praying in a private house. According to International Christian Concern, they belonged to the Methodist **Faith Mission Church**, which had been operating in Eritrea for half a century.

The **Warsay-Yikealo Development Campaign**, a military and national service programme obliging people from 18 to 50 years to work without salary, continued. The 2009 Military Balance Report of the International Institute for Strategic Studies ranked Eritrea the **second-most militarised country** in the world. As during previous years, people had to work for PFDJ-owned construction companies, on military-controlled farms and on various infrastructure projects. The 30th anniversary of the **National Union of Eritrean Women** (NUEW) was celebrated on 30 November at Sawa military camp, which served both as a military training centre and a boarding school for those undergoing their 12th school year under military surveillance. Mothers of students were invited to join the celebrations, thus giving them the possibility to see their children, from whom they had been forcibly separated. The 30th anniversary of the **National Confederation of Eritrean Workers** (NCEW) was commemorated from 21–25 November at various locations. Both NUEW and NCEW were founded as grass-roots popular organisations during the liberation struggle.

The **exodus** of young people in reaction to unlimited conscription into the national service intensified further. According to the UNHCR, 1,800 Eritreans crossed the border to **Sudan** monthly, while Sudanese media reported up to 100 daily arrivals at Sudanese refugee camps. Many Eritreans who managed to escape did not register with the authorities in order to avoid living in a refugee camp, but tried to find employment in Sudanese cities or to reach Libya in an attempt to make their way to European countries such as **Italy** or **Malta**. On 20 August, the Italian coast guard rescued a boat which had been carrying 78 Eritrean refugees from Libya; only three of them had survived three weeks at sea, during which many vessels had passed by without aiding the desperate passengers, who were dying of thirst and hunger. In mid-December, the entire **Eritrean national football team** absconded in Kenya after a football match against Tanzania. The government at first denied the defections and claimed that the reports were propaganda by ‘enemies of the country’, but had to concede the fact after the head of Cecafa (Council of East and Central Africa Football Associations) confirmed that 12 players had stayed in Nairobi, where they were later granted refugee status.

On 16 April, the president held a meeting with the cabinet, regional administrators and military operation zone commanders for planning infrastructural programmes to overcome dependence on rain-fed agriculture. On 2 September and 18 December, he held two more meetings with the cabinet without the participation of the military commanders, who had regularly taken part in previous cabinet meetings. No open tensions were apparent between the president and the influential **military leadership**, namely the four commanders of the operational zones, but it was likely that underlying tensions persisted. There were various rumours concerning **assassination attempts** against the president carried out by middle-ranking officers. One such story reached the international media through a diaspora-based opposition website: according to asmarino.com, a lieutenant and former combatant tried to shoot Isaias on 13 August in the vicinity of a place called Mai Atal, near the port city Massawa and was reportedly shot by the president's security personnel. Foreign diplomats in Asmara were unable to assess the reliability of these reports due to the complete absence of freedom of information. Other rumours circulated concerning an uprising by a group of 70 **rebel soldiers** in the Southern Region (Zoba Debub). The incident was related to the attempt by a military commander to force a young female recruit living in the region to serve as his concubine, which was common behaviour among high-ranking officers. A captain from the woman's home region objected and provoked an uprising by part of the battalion. After various **armed clashes**, the president was said to have personally mediated in the conflict and made an apology for the incident in the presence of regional elders. In early October, three Eritreans working for the Australian Chalice Gold Mines Ltd, which intended to start gold production in 2011, were ambushed and shot in a remote area 35 km north-west of Keren. The government denied that the deaths were related to the company's mining activities, an opinion shared by Chalice officials, who were interested in downplaying the event. It was, however, not unlikely that the killings had been an act of sabotage.

In May, four **opposition groups**, namely the Eritrean Liberation Front (ELF), Islah, AlKhalas and the Eritrean Federal Democratic Movement, formed the **Eritrean Solidarity Front** or 'Tadamun'. In mid-June, the Red Sea Afar Democratic Organization (RSADO) and the Democratic Movement for the Liberation of the Kunama founded a **Democratic Front of Eritrean Nationalities** (DFEN). Both organisations opted for armed struggle against the regime and called on all opposition organisations with military wings to coordinate their efforts. On 1 August RSADO claimed they had carried out a **successful attack** on an intelligence post near Senafe, close to the Ethiopian border, killing 13 military personnel and capturing five, who were brought to Ethiopia. They reported that the post was used to capture national service recruits trying to flee to Ethiopia. The attack had been a joint operation with the Eritrean Salvation Front (ESF). On 31 December, the Eritrean People's Movement (EPM), the Eritrean Democratic Party (EDP) and the Eritrean People's Party (EPP) held a conference in Frankfurt (Germany) and merged into one single party, the **Eritrean People's Democratic Party** (EPDP). The unification process had taken more than a year. The EPP (formerly a part of ELF-RC) and the EDP (founded by PFDJ dissidents) were probably the most influential opposition parties within the Eritrean Democratic Alliance (EDA), an umbrella organisation made up of 13 organisations, and expected to gain more efficiency and impact through the merger. The EPDP elected an executive committee with 24 members, headed by Woldeyesus Ammar.

Foreign Affairs

The **stalemate** between **Eritrea** and **Ethiopia** remained unresolved, but the border area was calm throughout the year, despite the removal of UN troops observing the situation on the ground and the lapse of the Temporary Security Zone on Eritrean territory. After the termination of the UN Mission to Eritrea and Ethiopia in 2008, the international community had not started new initiatives to bring the conflict to an end and implement the Algiers peace agreement of 2000. The border remained undemarcated; Eritrea claimed that the conflict was solved by virtual demarcation and stated that Ethiopia occupied sovereign Eritrean territory, while Ethiopia insisted that a dialogue was needed prior to demarcation. Libyan leader **Kadhafi** was the only one who made a new **attempt at mediation** in his position as AU chairman. After attending an AU meeting in Addis Ababa, he visited Eritrea from 6–8 February and held talks with President Isaias who, however, called the initiative a "wicked ploy" by Ethiopia. The **Eritrea-Ethiopia Claims Commission**, a body established in The Hague with the task of deciding through binding arbitration all claims for loss, damage or injury sustained during the 1998–2000 border war, awarded $ 174 m to Ethiopia and $ 161 m to Eritrea for war-related damages. It stated that both sides had committed atrocities against civilians and prisoners of war.

Eritrea's border **conflict with Djibouti** also remained unresolved. On 14 January, the UN Security Council urged both countries to solve their conflict peacefully and demanded that Eritrea withdraw its forces and military equipment within five weeks from Ras Doumeira and Doumeira Island, where fighting had broken out in June 2008. It commended Djibouti which had withdrawn its forces to the status quo ante. The Ministry of Foreign Affairs rejected the resolution, claiming that Eritrea had not occupied any land belonging to Djibouti, and stressed that Ethiopia had been occupying Eritrean territory with impunity since August 2002. In a speech to the diplomatic corps on 20 February, Isaias said that the conflict had been "deliberately masterminded by external forces" to provoke Eritrea and to please the Ethiopian government. On 15 May, the **UN Security Council** expressed concern about Eritrea's breaking of the UN arms embargo on Somalia. On 20 May, **IGAD** called upon the Security Council to impose **sanctions** on Eritrea, following an emergency meeting on Somalia in Addis Ababa; the sub-regional organisation accused Eritrea of supporting 'criminal elements' in Somalia by financing, training and supplying them. On 22 May, the **AU** joined the initiative, opting for sanctions against one of its members for the first time in its history. It adopted a resolution to pressure for UN sanctions during an AU summit in Sirte, Libya on 3 July. Eritrea had always strongly denied supporting the Islamist al-Shabaab militias and other insurgency groups opposed to the Transitional Federal Government (TFG) of Somalia and again dismissed such allegations as baseless in a press release by the Ministry of Foreign Affairs on 15 June. The Security Council expressed its readiness to consider the AU-proposed sanctions on 9 July. On 8 October, the **British Ambassador** to the UN said that the Security Council should give 'serious consideration' to the AU sanction request, a suggestion supported by representatives of both the **US** and **Russia**. The position of Russia came as a surprise, as it had usually been reluctant to support sanctions.

Russian-Eritrean relations had not been very close, as the USSR had been a strong supporter of the Ethiopian government during the time of Eritrea's independence struggle, but diplomatic relations were established immediately after independence in 1993. On 28 November, a Russian delegation, headed by actress and MP Yelena Drapeko, took part in the inauguration of a monument to Alexander Pushkin in Asmara, created by Russian artists. Some scholars have suggested that the great-grandfather of the poet, who had African roots, was born in Eritrea. Isaias used the opportunity to give his support to stronger ties between the two countries and emphasised the prospects for investment in Eritrean fisheries, agriculture and industry.

When **Djibouti's representative to the UN** urged the Security Council in September to "use all means at its disposal" to solve the conflict between his country and Eritrea, the Eritrean delegate repeated his government's standard argument, that Eritrea did not occupy Djiboutian territory and had no ambitions to do so, ignoring the incompatibility of the two countries' positions in this regard. Ali Abdu, acting minister of information, repeated in an interview on 14 October that the allegations against his country were completely baseless and "of no concern at all to Eritrea". On 23 December, the **UN Security Council** passed **resolution 1907 (2009)**, imposing **sanctions** in response to Eritrea's role in Somalia and its refusal to withdraw troops following its conflict with Djibouti. The sanctions included an embargo on arms and associated materials to and from Eritrea, travel restrictions and an asset freeze for the political and military leadership of Eritrea, including an asset freeze to "governmental and parastatal actors and entities privately owned by Eritrean nationals living inside or outside Eritrean territory". The persons and entities affected were to be designated by a committee. China abstained from the vote; Libya was the only council member that rejected the sanctions.

The government called the sanctions "unjust and illegal" and a covert act of conspiracy. It claimed that the **US** was the mastermind behind the resolution, repeating its allegations that there had been a deliberate conspiracy by the US against Eritrea. The new assistant secretary of state for African affairs, Johnnie Carson, said on 4 July that the Obama government wanted to "return to a more normal relationship with Eritrea", but demanded cooperation in key issues related to the Horn of Africa. As the Eritrean government was not ready to modify its policies, relations between the two countries did not improve under the Obama administration. After the adoption of sanctions, US Ambassador to the UN Susan Rice remarked that her government had tried for many months to start a constructive dialogue with Eritrea in an attempt to persuade it to change its policy with regard to Somalia and Djibouti. She said that the US did not see the sanctions as "the door closing on Eritrea" but as an opportunity for the country to play a more constructive role in the sub-region, and stressed that the US was standing with the people of Eritrea who had fought hard for their independence.

Relations with **Sudan** remained positive. Sudanese President **Omar al-Bashir**, against whom the ICC had issued a warrant for alleged crimes against humanity, made a one-day visit to Eritrea on 24 March. It was his first trip abroad following the ICC decision. Isaias had invited him in order to express his solidarity, because he considered the verdict as a "defamatory conspiracy on the parts of external forces". The president of the Government of Southern Sudan, **Salva Kiir Mayardit**, visited Eritrea on 15 September and discussed bilateral relations with the president. They also agreed to strengthen strategic relations between the PFDJ and the Sudan People's Liberation Movement (SPLM). In May, Isaias had criticized the SPLM for being corrupt. From 15–16 November the president visited the Sudanese Red Sea Region and Port Sudan, where he discussed with al-Bashir the enhancement of cooperation with the Sudanese Red Sea Zone and Eritrea's Northern Red Sea Region. On 17 September, EU special envoy to Sudan Torben Brille held talks with Isaias in Asmara, discussing the situation in Darfur and the risks of destabilization of relations between Northern and Southern Sudan.

Eritrea's relations with **Iran** were close, but very little concrete information was available as to the specific character of their cooperation; rather, there was a lot of unconfirmed speculation that the Iranians were using their presence in the port of Assab for **arms smuggling** activities. On 25 November, the Yemeni foreign minister claimed that there was increasing evidence that Iran was arming the Shi'ite Huthi factions in Saada Province, using Assab port as a base. Other rumours said that Iran was transporting arms to the Palestinian Hamas in Gaza via Assab. These rumours were, however, not confirmed by the US or French governments, both of whom had a strong military presence in nearby Djibouti.

Relations with **Libya** and **Qatar** were close. Isaias made an official visit to Doha from 4–6 October, where he held talks with the Emir of Qatar. The PFDJ and the Libyan Revolutionary Committees decided to hold a joint conference titled 'Democracy in Africa', organized by the Libyan Green Book Society and the Eritrean Research and Documentation Centre. It took place from 21–23 May in Asmara, and focused on topics such as 'western democracy and its negative impact on African societies'.

Socioeconomic Developments

The economic situation deteriorated further and **basic consumer goods** were **scarce**, while prices for imported goods rose continuously. Limited rations of kerosene were available, unlike the previous year without any supply for several months. The government did not pass information regarding the **nutritional situation** to the international community. In an interview with the Nigerian newspaper 'Sunday Trust' on 7 June, Isaias explained that his government had ceased communication with UN agencies because they were feeding the African continent on "expired foods" instead of financing programmes for food security and because he objected to his country being categorised as one of the neediest. The 2009 Global Hunger Index ranked Eritrea 82 out of 84 countries affected by malnutrition (84 being the worst). On 8 September, the president directed his regional administrators to put in place infrastructure that would improve agricultural output. Infrastructural projects were usually carried out by national service recruits who were absent from their own land and thus unable to cultivate it. Isaias declared during a meeting with regional administrators in Massawa on 10 November that there would be no food shortages in 2010. The reality on the ground gave a different picture. During the summer months, hundreds of people from the countryside migrated to Asmara to beg for food in front of religious buildings and from private houses, which had been uncommon in previous years. The beggars were reportedly rounded up and deported to their home villages, while those who originated from Asmara were only released after their relatives had signed guarantees that they would not engage in begging again. According to aid workers, it was difficult to determine the severity of the **food crisis** due to lack of information and travel restrictions on foreigners. UNICEF reported in June that in some regions rates of acute malnutrition had passed **the emergency threshold** of 15%, and that in February admission rates to therapeutic feeding had been six times higher than in 2008. The government insisted that the country would not need food aid, in spite of poor rains and rejected direct food distributions, because they created dependency and "lethargy".

The government initiated various **resettlement programmes** to enhance agricultural production. In June, entire villages in the **Southern Region** were moved to places along the Sudanese border in **Gash-Barka**. According to state media, 1,300 families from Senafe sub-zone and 553 families from Adi Keyh sub-zone were resettled in Goluj and Tessenei sub-zones, respectively. However, these programmes suffered from very poor planning and the affected communities were only provided with limited food rations and left without shelter or agricultural tools. As a result, many of them were said to have fled to Sudanese refugee camps, while others returned to their home villages without the permission of the authorities.

The availability and reliability of statistical data was poor in the absence of transparency and independent financial monitoring of party and military-owned enterprises, which dominated the economy. Data from different sources often showed significant differences. The Economist Intelligence Unit estimated **inflation** at 15%, while the IMF predicted 34.7%, the latter figure probably being more realistic in view of exorbitant increases in consumer prices. The **GDP growth rate** was expected to be between 2.5% and 3.6%. The current account balance decreased to minus $ 283.8 m, and foreign exchange reserves were at a low of $ 33.8 m. The **IMF** held consultations with Eritrea in December and stated that the economy had further weakened as a result of severe drought and the international food and oil price crisis. It noted that low growth and high inflation had undermined poverty reduction, and that domestic and external **debt levels** were **unsustainable.** The IMF criticised the conduct of monetary policy for being determined by the government's large financing needs and recommended re-engagement with the donor community and the restoration of an independent monetary policy. Eritrea's HDI ranking was 165 out of 182.

On 1 April, the **EU approved € 122 m** in funding for Eritrea for the period 2009–13 from the European Development Fund under the Cotonou Agreement. The decision had been controversial because of Eritrea's appalling human rights record. The European Parliament had asked the EU Commission to reconsider its strategy following unsuccessful appeals for the release of journalist Dawit Isaac (see above). The Commission decided that continued engagement was the best response, although it admitted that the human rights situation was of great concern. Out of the total funds, € 70 m were supposed to be channelled to projects aiming at achieving **food security,** with emphasis on land and water development. A second priority was **road maintenance and safety**, with a sum of € 34 m. According to the EU Commission's office in Eritrea, the aim of the Road Maintenance and Safety Programme was to increase access to economic and social services and "generating employment by using a labour-intensive road maintenance approach". Taking into consideration that the construction sector was completely monopolised by PFDJ-owned firms employing unpaid national service conscripts, this EU decision seemed to be **highly problematic**, as it allocated aid to projects based on **forced labour** and to an economic sector in which all private licences had been withdrawn in 2006. Another € 10 m were to be provided for the governance sector and € 5 m for the preservation of cultural assets in Asmara.

The **Chinese** Ambassador to Eritrea announced in May that there were plans to increase cooperation in the fields of health, education, trade and culture. The bilateral trade volume had reached $ 31 m in 2008. There was no increase in **Japanese** investments throughout the year.

The **Kuwait Independent Petroleum Group** took Eritrea to the Court of Arbitration in London to claim unpaid bills of $ 65 m in mid-September. The Petroleum Corporation of Eritrea and the government acknowledged the claim but said they were unable to pay due to the international financial crisis.

The **Bisha gold project**, a joint-venture of the government and the Canadian Nevsun company, was supposed to start operations in late 2010, while the Zara project, managed by Australia-based Chalice Gold Mines, was expected to start production in 2011 or 2012. The Ministry of Energy and Mines issued eight **new exploration licences** during the year. Canada-based NGEx Resources won licences to search for sulphide in northern Eritrea and the Australian company, South Bolder, announced it would start drilling for potash in the Danakil desert in October. Other mining companies that won licences were based in the UK, India and China. It remained unclear whether the imposed sanctions would have a negative impact on mining activities in Eritrea that were yet to start.

The **education system** retained its militarised character and the 12th school year for all students continued to be held at the Warsay-Yikealo School in Sawa. There were rumours that hundreds of students had managed to escape while being transported to the facility from their home towns by bus at the beginning of the school year.

Nicole Hirt

Ethiopia

All public life continued to be strongly dominated by the Ethiopian People's Revolutionary Democratic Front (EPRDF). The country started to gear up for the May 2010 elections, with the government becoming nervous about opposition parties and trying to restrict their expansion. EPRDF party organisation was given priority in an effort to co-opt as many people as possible, particularly those in economic and administrative key positions. This was in line with the EPRDF's mission to prevent a repeat of the 2005 elections, which were nearly lost. Prime Minister Meles Zenawi declared himself ready for another term in office. A new opposition coalition, 'Medrek' or Forum for Democratic Dialogue, was formed by eight parties and gained support by having a broad spectrum of leaders from various backgrounds. The building of their support base in rural areas was hindered by the EPRDF, which was afraid of competition. Overall, there was little evidence of real progress in democratic consolidation. The human rights record was as disappointing as in 2008 – no fundamental improvements were seen with respect to the rights of opposition political activists, journalists and other media agents. Police and army behaviour was unsatisfactory in many cases. Arbitrary arrests, extra-judicial procedures and abuse were regularly reported. Internet access remained restricted, despite a false announcement in March that access was to be free.

The stalemate in relations with Eritrea continued as before, with on-going reciprocal negative propaganda and no dialogue on any subject. No negotiated solution was in sight, mainly due to Eritrea's refusal to enter into any talks before the 2002 Eritrea-Ethiopia Boundary Commission (EEBC) border decision was implemented to the letter, which Ethiopia refused. Ethiopia's armed forces left Somalia in January, with AMISOM troops from Uganda and Burundi being augmented as a stabilisation force in Mogadishu. Ethiopia's relations with other neighbouring countries were uneventful. Meles Zenawi took a prominent role as Africa's representative at the UN climate change conference in Copenhagen.

There was economic growth resulting from infrastructural investment and modest growth in the agrarian sector, apart from coffee. Benefits of growth accrued mostly to the well-established political-economic elite. Substantial uncritical donor-country support was again provided to the tune of almost $ 2 bn. A slight decline in poverty incidence was reported, although the rural masses and urban poor saw little improvement; they remained strongly dependent on government/ruling party inputs and had no access to independent media information. Conditions remained dismal for most rural people and social inequality increased. Again the threat of famine loomed and international humanitarian aid was requested for an estimated 5–6 m people in dire need. The process of concessioning large tracts of allegedly unused or vacant land to foreign investors and governments – without consulting local peasants – continued, with major financial benefits for the federal government, but as yet unforeseen consequences for the local society and economy.

Domestic Politics

The **political scene** was strongly **dominated** as before by the **EPRDF**, the former insurgent movement that came to power in 1991 and proceeded to solidify its autocratic single-party rule under the leadership of **Prime Minister Meles Zenawi** by extending its influence into all spheres of the bureaucracy, administration, press, education system and economic life. **Opposition parties**, while permitted and represented in parliament since the controversial 2005 elections, were repeatedly **obstructed, marginalised and harassed** throughout the year in the context of preparations for parliamentary elections in May 2010. Opposition parties remained divided but succeeded in forming a **new alliance**, the Forum for Democratic Dialogue, or in Amharic 'Medrek', in anticipation of the upcoming elections. The alliance included major political figures from various ethnic backgrounds, including former president Negaso Gidada and former Tigray People's Liberation Front (TPLF) defence minister Siye Abraha, as well as other prominent personalities. Former judge and major opposition leader Birtukan Mideqsa of the United Democratic Justice Party (UDJ) was also a leading member, but she remained in prison. Medrek united eight parties. Apart from the UDJ, which had emerged from the Coalition for Unity and Democracy (CUD) upon its collapse as a result of external interference and internal squabbles after a good showing in the 2005 elections, these were: Arena Tigray for Democracy and Sovereignty (led by former TPLF member Gebru Asrat), the Oromo People's Congress, the Coalition of Somali Democratic Forces, the Ethiopian Social Democratic Party, the Oromo Federalist Democratic Movement, the Southern Ethiopian People's Democratic Coalition, and the Ethiopian Democratic Unity Movement. This coalition represented major groups or parties with an alternative programme for the country, but they were reportedly unable to build up mass support due to harassment of rural activists and frequent party office closures. They also had some internal problems. On 3 November, the opposition parties stated that 450 of their members and candidates had been jailed by the government. The government's message to the public was often voiced in threatening language, perhaps in the belief that a show of force expressed authority; there was little if any appeal to harmony and consensus building.

Opposition politics was generally difficult in a climate of distrust, harassment (especially in rural areas) and complete domination of the state and its resources by the ruling party. Dubious accusations were levelled against opposition figures, including a 'plot to overthrow the government', for which 40 people were arrested on 24 April. They were mostly opposition party members and associates. This 'plot', soon called the 'Ginbot 7' plot after the opposition group in exile led by Berhanu Nega, the Addis Ababa mayor-elect in 2005, allegedly involved a few army officers and opposition party figures, but the octogenarian father of Andargatchew Tsige, an opposition party figure in exile, was also accused. As in previous similar cases in recent years, no credible evidence was presented and, according to many Ethiopians, spite and intimidation by the government seem to have dominated this case. In August, the Federal High Court found 13 of the defendants guilty and one not guilty *in absentia*. In November, the court found another 27 guilty and sought the death penalty for the 40 defendants. It ignored testimonies by some of the accused of abuse and torture in prison and it was hard to conclude that justice was done.

UDJ leader Birtukan Mideqsa had had no trial before being imprisoned again in December 2008 for her alleged 'violation of pardon', and no trial took place during the year. She was held in solitary confinement until June and her health suffered. She remained popular and admired among the Ethiopian public, and the government did not consider legitimate demands, including by donor countries, for her release. Her case remained a point of conflict between the ruling party and the opposition groups, symbolising the lack of progress in democratisation, fair election campaigning, and trust-building in the political process.

On 30 September, an electoral 'code of conduct' for the 2010 elections was signed by the EPRDF and a number of opposition parties (the Ethiopian Democratic Party, the remnant Coalition for Unity and Democracy, and the All-Ethiopia Unity Party), but it had limited value because it did not include the Medrek coalition. No agreement was reached between the government and opposition parties on a reform of the EPRDF-dominated National

Electoral Board. Some diaspora-based parties proceeded to voice their opposition to the EPRDF by stating that even armed struggle might perhaps be justified to replace the current government.

On 22 June, in an interview for 'The Times', Meles Zenawi floated the idea that he might step down after the 2010 elections, but this proved to be empty words. It soon appeared that, as all observers and opposition leaders had predicted, he would stand again for election as party leader and prime minister. The **EPRDF** exerted major efforts to extend its **societal hegemony** via the educational and administrative systems. There were reports that people were pressured to become members of the party, and obliged to participate in monthly party meetings to be instructed in the party ideology of 'revolutionary democracy'. Carrying a party card was also a practical necessity for appointment to any public sector job, e.g. for higher education graduates. In addition, the women's and youth wings of the party were expanded, reminiscent of old-style Communist parties. People working in the state administration (from local 'k'ebeles' up to ministries) could not be members of an opposition party, on pain of dismissal. The civil service became even more politicised.

Reports of **corruption** regularly surfaced. The government Ethics Commission arrested 203 suspects for corruption. In some court cases, e.g. on 24 December, officials found guilty of corruption were sentenced to long terms in prison and high fines. On 29 October, an EPRDF member and MP, Bekele Etana, defected to the UK after giving a press release on corruption and unaccounted spending within the federal government, based on his experience as a member of the parliamentary Public Account Standing Committee.

Internal EPRDF party control was maintained by evaluation sessions ('gimgema'). One such a 'fundamental self-evaluation' was announced by the EPRDF on 16 August. An earlier round had already led to the arrest and sentencing (to 10–23 years in prison) of six army officers who had allegedly 'conspired' with and collected arms for the CUD opposition party in 2005.

On 13 February, the House of Peoples' Representatives (parliament) formally approved the new **Charities and Societies (CSO) law**, restricting funding from abroad of any civic organisation to 10% of the budget of local NGOs, limiting the legitimacy of their work in many fields of human rights and social advocacy, and stipulating stiff penalty clauses. It forced many NGOs to scale down or close. On 7 July, the parliament passed a new **'Anti-Terrorism Proclamation'**, with a very broad definition of 'terrorism' that bore no resemblance to its core meaning of armed violence towards non-combatant civilians with the aim of intimidating, creating fear and killing. The new law designated peaceful political demonstrations, property crimes and disruption of public service (and even "intentions to influence the government") as terrorism, in a rather ludicrous extension of the concept. Experts noted that the law, with draconian prison terms and death penalty clauses, appeared to be an effort to outlaw or criminalise any criticism, even peaceful, of the regime. The law was another missed opportunity to build confidence and enhance public security, and while 'innovative' in the judicial sense, observers noted that it left all proportionality behind.

Security problems were evident throughout the year, but remained outside the purview of the national press (silenced by the new Media Law, harassment, newspaper closures and arrest of journalists) and foreign journalists. The main trouble spot was the Somali-inhabited Ogaden, where the government's harsh campaign to suppress the Ogaden National Liberation Front (ONLF), a violent insurgent movement with a similarly bad record, continued. Interviews with local people and eye-witnesses revealed disproportionate violence and gross abuse of civilians in the region and adverse effects on food security. Thousands fled the area. Criticism voiced in human rights reports was, however, dismissed by the government, which said that killings had occurred but were the result of inter-clan fighting. There were also sporadic clashes between government forces and Oromo Liberation Front (OLF) units in the east and west of Oromiya Region.

Several major **'ethnic' clashes** also occurred, e.g. in the south, continuing a recurrent pattern of conflicts about borders, land and water sources between ethno-linguistic groups. They led to hundreds of people being killed and tens of thousands displaced. The two major incidences were the Garri-Boran conflict in the south, in which in February and later in September around 300 people were reported killed and more than 70,000 displaced, and clashes on 20 May between members of the Afar, Oromo and Argobba ethnic groups in northern Ethiopia, which caused the death of 14, with at least 18 seriously injured. Another incident resulting in death was the conflict between the Konso and Dirashe groups on 2–4 January (18 killed). On 24 August, the Federal High Court issued its judgement in a 2008 case of 'ethnic cleansing' which had led to death and destruction in the Oromo-Gumuz area in western Ethiopia, with 101 of the defendants declared guilty. Six were sentenced to death and 95 to prison terms of six years to life.

Religious tensions were recorded between Orthodox Christians and Muslims as well as between Orthodox Christians and Pentecostal-Evangelical Christian groups, which increased in number, but this did not lead to major violent conflicts. Mainstream relations were peaceful. Struggles for influence on the local level were more visible between Orthodox and Pentecostal believers, with many of the latter having entered local administrations in the countryside, which made several of them into arenas of competition. Polemics between Orthodox, Pentecostal and Muslim spokesmen continued in various media but were less confrontational than previously, due to government monitoring. Tensions were, however, always present under the surface. On 2 October, a mob of Muslims reportedly attacked evangelical churches in Western Arsi zone, injuring at least three Christians. On 11 September, the Mulu Wongel Evangelical Church and Qale Hiwot churches in Senbeté town were ransacked and church property burned, due to a false rumour about Christians having 'desecrated' the Qur'an. On 21 January, criminal charges were brought against 18 members of a radical-Islamic Wahhabist group called 'Kwarej' because of their suspected violation of the Ethiopian Penal Code by organising Muslim youths and preparing them to carry out terrorist acts. On 6–10 January, religious clashes between young Christians and Muslims in Dire Dawa resulted in one dead and 20 injured.

Human rights did not substantially improve compared with previous years. Constitutional clauses about civic freedoms and free expression were 'flexibly interpreted', and were contravened by recent legislation, as in the new civil society law and in the new anti-terrorism law. The political system in place was prone to allow arbitrary and unpredictable repression, although not against all opponents or opposition spokesmen. There was a trend towards impunity for the armed forces and police when abuses were committed and reported: only a few perpetrators of misdeeds were apprehended, let alone tried in courts of law, including in respect of cases related to previous years. Nevertheless, some opposition figures and activists arrested while campaigning were cleared of police charges in court. Popular singer Teddy Afro, imprisoned in 2008, was released on 13 August after his sentence was reduced.

In general, the government showed little concern to respond to criticisms by **human rights organisations** and Western countries, which called for national dialogue, cooperation and respect for the constitutional rights of citizens. The independent Ethiopian Human Rights Commission was thwarted in its fact-finding missions and its researchers were harassed. Several of its chief officers fled the country in the course of the year. The same applied to the well-respected Ethiopian Women Lawyers' Association.

In the local (Amharic, Tigrinya, Orominya) press and some diaspora media, discussions emerged on the early history of the TPLF, the core of the ruling party, with eye witness accounts about tense internal relations and the violence used by the Front during its struggle for power. Several books with memoirs of former participants and victims appeared, including sensitive accusations of abuse and repression. In addition, one former Front member contended that the $ 100 m in Band Aid money given to the TPLF in 1985 to ward off famine in the north was largely used for procuring arms. This debate continued into 2010.

The **press** and other **media** continued to face serious restrictions, with arrests and court cases against journalists for alleged defamation. One of the most important independent news magazines, 'Addis Neger', was forced to close in December due to harassment, and its chief editor fled the country. In June, the private Sheger-FM radio station was also ordered to close. **Internet access** (available to only 0.5% of the population) was not free, with many sites again blocked. Compared with other African countries, Ethiopia had a very low record on numbers of Internet users as well as user freedom, thus slowing down the ITC revolution. Control of the only Internet server, the state-owned ETC, was a prime means of restricting the free flow of information. In smaller towns and rural areas particularly, there was no access to independent information from any source.

Foreign Affairs

The issues of Eritrean-Ethiopian relations, the Somali problem, and Ethiopia's changing place in the global order (relations with donor countries and with new investor countries) remained the primary concern. On the first issue, no progress was registered, with the

stand-off between Ethiopia and Eritrea fully confirmed and no new international initiatives in sight. More young Eritreans, both army personnel and civilians, slipped across the border into Ethiopia. Their number grew by around 900–1,000 per month, and Ethiopia opened several new camps in the north to house them. Propaganda from both sides continued as usual, e.g. via radio and TV programmes aimed at 'the enemy'. In August, the Eritrea-Ethiopia Claims Commission in The Hague published its final rulings on the damage claims by the two countries regarding their 1998–2000 war, with Eritrea having slightly more to pay than Ethiopia. But this did not lead to any rapprochement between the feuding countries; on the contrary, they supported some of each other's opposition groups.

In January, Ethiopia withdrew all of its military forces from **Somalia** under an agreement negotiated between Somalia's Transitional Federal Government (TFG) and Somali opposition groups. The troops had been there for more than two years in support of the TFG, which made too little headway and exasperated the Ethiopians. The AMISOM forces (reaching 5,200 during the year) partly 'replaced' the Ethiopians in protecting the TFG. However, Ethiopian units stayed close to the border and worked to support the TFG and its allies against the militant Islamist insurgent fronts, which were seen as a security risk to Ethiopia too. Later in the year, there were rumours that Ethiopia made occasional forays into Somalia to support local allies and that it sent them shipments of arms. The new TFG President Sheik Sharif Sheikh Ahmed, a former Islamic Courts Union leader and enemy of Ethiopia, visited Addis Ababa for the AU summit and an IGAD meeting in February, when he also consulted with Ethiopian leaders. He was in Ethiopia again in November to attend the Saudi-East Africa Forum. In the UN and in IGAD, Ethiopia tried to further incriminate and isolate Eritrea, which it accused (with reference to plausible UN evidence) of continuing military support for Islamist radicals in Somalia.

On 1 June, the **Nile riparian countries** reached agreement on many elements of a new treaty on Nile water utilisation and development, despite the persistent refusal of Egypt and Sudan to negotiate any alteration in the status quo, but two controversial key clauses were put in an appendix for a decision to be taken at a later stage, thus keeping the creation of a Nile River Commission on hold.

Ethiopia maintained relatively good relations with the **US** under its new President Obama, who operated cautiously and slowly fell back into the foreign policy pattern of his predecessor towards the Horn of Africa. For Ethiopia, this meant that Washington perceived Ethiopia to be 'stable', a partner in anti-terrorism campaigns, and in need of more foreign development assistance. The US State Department and various US human rights agencies stated that human rights and political conditions were not good in Ethiopia, but this did not prompt the US government to act. For example, the US did not respond to the Ogaden campaign, where no one could deny that gross human rights abuses and cruelty were perpetrated against civilians accused of supporting the ONLF.

The **EU** played a low-key role in Ethiopia, or at least a rather invisible one, showing a measure of indifference to the country and its people. No EU statements were issued on controversial issues such as the CSO law or the Anti-Terrorism law. Aid funds were kept flowing as usual, with little open critique on the country's record or socio-economic policies. The UK was again an eager contributor, with about $ 180 m of aid provided.

At the **UN climate conference**, on 6–18 December in Copenhagen, Meles Zenawi acted as the main spokesman for Africa, a move strongly criticised by the Ethiopian diaspora. He led a call for hundreds of billions of dollars to be paid to Africa as compensation for the effects of global warming.

Relations with **China** were strengthening and were dominated by economic interests and resource acquisitions by China. Trade soared again and reportedly reached a value of $ 1.376 bn, although with China exporting much more to Ethiopia than it was importing from it, despite China encouraging the latter by special quota and tariff arrangements. The Chinese post-Communist, state-capitalist model and its dominant-party governance system continued to appeal to the Ethiopian leaders, who faced no criticism on politics, governance or human rights issues from the Chinese.

Ethiopia's relations with **neighbours** Kenya, Djibouti, Sudan and Somaliland remained stable and friendly overall. With Kenya, more efforts toward security cooperation were made in view of the southern Somalia problem. With Djibouti, some tension existed over impending price rises for the use of port facilities, on which Ethiopia has been dependent ever since it had made itself landlocked in 1991 by ceding its ports to Eritrea. Sudan and Ethiopia held talks on border issues, with Ethiopia reportedly ceding some contested land to Sudan. Sudan supplied about 80% of Ethiopia's oil needs.

Socioeconomic Developments

Ethiopia registered growth, but poverty characterised the lives of most people and socio-economic insecurity remained serious. Overall social inequality increased, with a top layer of elite-related business people, officials, cadres and civil servants safe in their jobs and income, and the large mass of peasants and workers in vulnerable, dependent conditions, struggling to make ends meet and retain their dignity.

As usual, there was again controversy, or at least great divergence, over the estimated **GDP growth** figures, based on a variety of divergent figures. The government claimed 10%–11% growth, and more neutral observers some 5%–6.5%. The IMF (in April 2010) gave the 2009 growth rate as 9.9%, in continuance of the solid performance of the last five years. Population growth of about 3%, however, qualified the importance of this GDP growth figure. Ethiopia's per capita GDP was estimated to be ca. $ 330, up slightly compared with 2008. According to official government figures, total GDP rose to an estimated $ 33.9 bn ($ 75.9 bn. in PPP terms), as a result of growth in agriculture, infrastructural works and services. While GDP is a limited measure of how the overall economy of a country fares, let alone of well-being or wealth distribution, donor countries, in their often superficial and clueless policies toward African development, were satisfied with the outward picture of growth and kept on disbursing the usual aid flows to Ethiopia. The central government budget reached $ 4.67 bn, but expenditure was $ 5.36 bn. The country's external debt rose to $ 4.2 bn, some 25% higher than in 2008, perhaps due to increased Chinese borrowing.

Despite the GDP growth figures, some 5–6 m people were again in need of **food aid**, and many more (about 7 m) were undernourished or food insecure under the National Productive Safety Net Program. On 22 October, the government officially asked for emergency food aid for 6.2 m people. The reason given was again 'failure of the rains'. While many people died of hunger or hunger-related diseases, a famine disaster was averted by recourse to domestic and foreign food aid supplies.

In agreement with the **IMF,** a **new macroeconomic package** was drawn up. Domestic borrowing by the government was to be reduced to zero. A first, a 'no strings attached' disbursement of $ 50 m was given in January, after the National Bank of Ethiopia had asked for emergency loans. Thereafter, the government requested a 14-month IMF loan arrangement under the **Exogenous Shocks Facility** (ESF), to "help the country cope with the adverse effects of the global recession" on its balance of payments. Again, on August 26, a loan of $ 240.6 m was granted – 115% of the country's quota. In total, Ethiopia received almost $ 1.8 bn in development aid and loans in 2009, bringing the total sum received since 1991 to just under $ 26 bn.

In February, the Birr (local currency) was **devalued** by 10% and the rate to the dollar was 12.4 in December. **Inflation** went down from a staggering 45.6% in January to about 11% in December. The year's average was about 15%, and was felt notably in the domain of staple food items, weighing heavily on the urban masses. Inflation was fuelled not only by the rising prices of imports (notably fuels), but also by unproductive government spending in the expanding bureaucracy and in party activities (massive membership drives, party cell organisation, propaganda meetings, party and civil service trainings, etc.). The EPRDF claimed to have 5 m members.

Agriculture saw some growth but no major changes, with productivity low, irrigation used on only 3% of the land, and small-scale peasants (numbering about 13.3 m) forced to eke out a living on tiny farm plots, with the government in legal possession of all land. EPRDF-affiliated companies supplied all fertilizers to the peasants. In one respect the land produced a lot – on plots leased by foreign companies and governments, provided by the government with low costs and no legal problems. The phenomenon of **foreign land acquisitions** (critics called it 'land grabbing') gained further momentum during the year, with more land going to these foreign operators. In November, the government announced that it would lease out 3 m hectares of (allegedly unused, empty) land to domestic and especially foreign investors over the next three years, and advertised large tracts on the Ministry of Agriculture website. Controversy emerged among experts over who would gain and whether these schemes would benefit Ethiopian agrarian producers. While it was too early to fully evaluate the results, so far few visible benefits that might uplift Ethiopian rural producers were seen. Saudi Arabian state media waxed lyrical about the 'first harvest' of Ethiopian (Saudi-owned) farms to arrive in the country, while displaced Ethiopian subsistence farmers were less enthusiastic. At $ 0.75–$ 1.0 a day, salaries of farm workers were very low. Some of the new land exploitation schemes might also threaten nature reserves or protected areas, as with plans announced in October that Ethio-Saudi business tycoon Mohamed al-Amouddin was to build a rice farm inside the Gambella National Park.

Industry, with a share of 13% of GDP, did show some growth but saw no major take-off. EPRDF's 'Agricultural Development-Led Industrialisation' (ADLI) strategy remained in place, despite its lack of success so far. Mining (gold, salt) remained limited, and natural gas reserves of an estimated 24.9 bn m^3 were known but not taken into production.

Infrastructural works continued throughout the year, with major projects in road building and hydro-electricity plants. On 13 November, the new 300 MW Tekkeze Hydropower Plant was officially opened. The Gilgel Gibe II dam on the Omo River also neared completion. A third Gilgel Gibe dam in the lower Omo was in preparation but was causing uproar due to its foreseen negative effects on the livelihoods and settlement areas of hundreds of thousands of people (smaller ethnic groups) living downstream along the Omo River. The government denied all negative effects and proceeded, but no adequate impact assessment studies appeared to have been made, certainly not with the cooperation and input of local people. Italian firms had a major role in building these dams. Road construction also continued, with Chinese contractors building about 70% of them. **China** also supplied very substantial loans (over $ 1 bn) to Ethiopia, with about 70% going to state/party-owned companies. About 120 private Chinese companies were active in Ethiopia, alongside over 800 Chinese projects. A study by the African Economic Research Consortium published in November showed that many of them were engaged in business and investment ventures for which they were not licensed and that only a few were willing to engage in joint ventures with Ethiopian companies.

Remittances from Ethiopian communities overseas amounted to an estimated $ 970 m and provided a lifeline to many impoverished families, and much was used as start-up capital to form small businesses by people without political connections.

Socioeconomic development was marked by an **increase in social inequality**, showing staggering class differences between the peasants and workers as compared with the business and political elite. People with income and benefits from external aid schemes were popularly known as 'the developmental wealth owners' (in Amharic 'lematawi balehabt'), i.e., a kind of rent-seeking class. They were seen by the population at large as owing their comfortable position to foreign support. **Youth unemployment** remained high (50%–60%).

Other developments in the economy again signalled the efforts of the state/ruling party to expand their power. After warnings were given to **coffee exporters** about 'hoarding' (in the expectation of international price rises), the government in late March revoked the licenses of six main coffee exporters. It then **confiscated** some 17,000 tons of coffee stocks from some 90 traders and began exporting coffee via the state-owned Ethiopian Grain Trade Enterprise. This indicated that the government was ready to intervene in the free operation of the market and also wanted more direct access to export revenue. Coffee accounted for about 10% of GDP and about $ 376 m in sales, down from $ 525 m in 2008, an exceptionally good year. Total exports rose, however, to $ 1.6 bn, while imports were over $ 7 bn with 16.3% of Ethiopia's total imports coming from China, followed by Saudi Arabia at 12%.

According to the UN, Ethiopia's **population** in 2009 reached 82.8 m, indicating that the country was continuing its unprecedented **demographic explosion**. The annual growth rate remained around 2.7%–3%, despite high maternal and disease mortality figures. The infant mortality rate, for instance, was high at about 93 per 1,000 live births, but this still represented a drop over previous years. **Health issues** remained a critical concern. Common diseases were still widespread. In August, there was a cholera outbreak in Addis Ababa (caused by poor sanitation and contaminated food and water), with at least 34 people dead and more than 4,000 hospitalised; in September, 18,000 people were reported infected. The government forbade use of the word 'cholera' ('acute watery diarrhoea' was the approved term), but the UN humanitarian agency sent six mobile cholera treatment centres for training purposes and drugs for treatment. The number of health extension workers expanded to more than 30,000, but the number of physicians was only about 2,100. There was a significant brain drain due to the attractions of jobs abroad.

Several NGOs in the **health sector** were adversely affected by the new NGO law, which restricted their activities. Even those with a programme geared to maternal healthcare or care for the disabled were barred from operating if their income from foreign donations reaching more than 10% of their budget. At a conference on the occasion of World Mental Health Day in Addis Ababa, it was said that several million people in the country suffered from mental health problems, with only 95,000 treated during the year. While the **HIV-AIDS** epidemic still remained a significant public health problem, the number of people dying from the disease dropped by about 20% to an estimated 80,000–90,000. This was due to increased awareness of the disease, more available medication, and behavioural changes, notably among the urban population. Over the past six-seven years, more than half-a-million Ethiopians have probably succumbed to the disease.

Out-migration from Ethiopia to the industrialised world and to Middle Eastern countries continued, both by people seeking employment and by journalists, civil servants, opposition politicians, etc., escaping repression. It was suspected that about 30,000 of these migrants (mostly females) were victims of human trafficking, mainly to Middle Eastern countries. Some 45,000 Ethiopians entered Yemen through Somali ports.

There were about 110,000 **refugees** in Ethiopia, with new influxes continuing to arrive from Eritrea (ca. 11,000) and Somalia (c. 13,000). The UNHCR estimated that the country also had almost 250,000 **IDPs**, mainly in Oromiya, Gambela and Somali Regions as a result of 'ethnic' clashes and the conflict in the Ogaden. There were also those still displaced by the Ethiopian-Eritrean war of 1998–2000.

Resettlement efforts continued to be made throughout the year, serving the dual purpose of settling populations affected by drought and erosion in new areas, as well as changing the socio-political balance between population groups. Conflicts around **resettlement schemes** occasionally arose, when indigenous people were pushed out or driven from their land by newcomers or disagreed about land and resource use. The attitude of the authorities in such cases was often ambiguous. Locals also regularly refused to accept (large numbers of) resettled immigrants from the north and pressured them to go elsewhere. In one instance in July in the Southern Region, about 5,500 people of northern origin, resettled in the Bench-Maji Zone, were forced from their homes after serious problems between them emerged.

Environmental problems were worrying. Deforestation and land erosion were serious ongoing problems and were combated only in selected areas with tree planting, bunding, etc. Population growth placed continued pressure on the environment, as did pollution in urban industrial areas, including the massive random disposal of plastic bags and batteries from radios, recorders, etc. across the country, visible to any visitor. Environmental awareness increased, especially as a result of NGO reports, government information and academic research, but policies matching this were not making significant headway.

Jon Abbink

Kenya

The fallout from the **'Kenyan post-election crisis'** of **2007/8**, when civil strife resulted in the deaths of over 1,000 people and the displacement of over 300,000 more, continued to dominate social and political life in 2009. Media coverage and political gossip focussed on two main questions: which individuals would face **prosecution** for their involvement in the violence, and which leaders would emerge from intra-party struggles as likely presidential candidates ahead of the 2012 elections. The process of national reconstruction and reconciliation was hindered by slow economic growth, a dysfunctional power-sharing government, and a lack of political will to engage in serious reform of the constitution and security services.

Domestic Politics

Following flawed elections in December 2007, a range of international mediators including then US Secretary of State, Condoleezza Rice, Tanzanian President Jakaya Kikwete, and former UN Secretary General Kofi Annan, persuaded Kenya's main political parties in February 2008 to form a **government of national unity** in order to restore political stability. Although ministerial positions were shared evenly between a bloc led by Mwai Kibaki's Party of National Unity (PNU) and a bloc headed by Raila Odinga's Orange

Democratic Movement (ODM), the PNU and its allies retained many of the most powerful positions, including president, vice president, home affairs, finance, foreign affairs, defence, and justice and constitutional affairs. By contrast, the ODM had to be content with Odinga's promotion to the newly created post of prime minister, and a series of less prestigious infrastructure ministries, such as land, roads, agriculture, and water.

The poorly defined **power-sharing arrangement** continued to be a source of political instability as the main parties disagreed on how the deal should be interpreted in both procedural and substantive terms. Following a series of skirmishes in 2008 over the election of the speaker, controversy over the duties and responsibilities of the prime minister came to the fore this year. In April, a dispute over who should fill the post of **leader of government business**, a role with considerable influence over the parliamentary process, brought legislative proceedings to a standstill. Odinga argued that, as prime minister, he was the natural leader of government business and should be allowed to co-ordinate the legislative programme in the spirit of the power-sharing deal. PNU hardliners countered that, as Kenya remained a fundamentally presidential system of government, the post should be filled by President Kibaki's nominee, Vice President Kalonzo Musyoka. Responsibility for resolving the dispute fell on the **speaker of the National Assembly**, Kenneth Marende, who wisely refused to rule in favour of either bloc. Rather, in a landmark ruling on 28 April, Marende declared that the post could only be filled when both factions of the government had 'consensually agreed' on a candidate, and pledged to personally chair the House Business Committee so that government business could continue during negotiations.

When parliament finally got down to business, a number of divisive policy issues exacerbated **tensions** both between and within the ODM and PNU. Factionalism plagued the ODM all year, as Odinga struggled to persuade his 'pentagon' of regional leaders and their constituencies to fall into line behind his leadership. Throughout 2008 and 2009, many ODM voters criticised the prime minister for 'selling out', first by accepting inferior positions in a government dominated by the PNU, and subsequently by not doing enough to reward the efforts of party supporters. The biggest challenge to ODM unity was the controversy over the fate of around 20,000 families living as 'illegal' settlers in the **Mau Forest** in Rift Valley Province. The squatters were widely blamed for having destroyed the forest to the point where it was incapable of storing rainwater, resulting in flooding during the wet season and **drought** thereafter. The problem for Odinga was that many of the settlers were from the Kalenjin ethnic group and had typically voted for the ODM in the 2007 election under the leadership of William Ruto. Odinga's decision to order the removal of the settlers in July 2008, and his subsequent refusal to reconsider his position ahead of evictions scheduled for November 2009, deepened the growing rift within the ODM leadership. In response, Ruto openly campaigned against his own party leader, arguing that many squatters had a legitimate claim to the land and so deserved compensation. During the tenure of President Daniel arap Moi (1978–2002), land grabbing was common as parts of the forest were parcelled up and sold by political fixers in a bid to raise funds and build support; consequently, many 'settlers' felt they had both a legal and moral right to remain. Under pressure from a vocal group of Kalenjin MPs, parliament debated the appropriate compensation for the estimated 1,962 people with land titles, and whether or not it was appropriate to extend compensation packages to all settlers. Odinga's refusal to back Ruto's campaign ultimately led to a number of ODM MPs from Rift Valley publicly rejecting his leadership, including Isaac Ruto, Magerer Langat, Benjamin Langat, Elijah Lagat, Julius Kones, Moses Lessonet, and Sammy Mwaita.

ODM unity was also undermined by a series of **corruption** scandals, the most significant of which served to further strain relations between William Ruto and the rest of the party. In the context of a severe drought that resulted in widespread food shortages, allegations emerged in January that officials in Ruto's Agriculture Ministry had contributed to the problem by illegally trading **maize**. An independent audit by PricewaterhouseCoopers (PwC) later confirmed these rumours, finding that the government had lost more than $ 26 m when a government company sold subsidised maize to ghost companies in corrupt deals that it had not been authorised to make. The revelations caused considerable embarrassment for Odinga, who had sought to present himself as a 'clean' alternative to Kibaki during the campaign for the 2007 elections. However, exactly who was to blame for the scandal was unclear. While Odinga's supporters sought to divert the blame onto Ruto, the prime minister's rivals pointed out that a permanent secretary from his own ministry had been a signatory to the maize allocations. Odinga later suspended a personal aide heavily implicated in the incident, but appeared to have emerged relatively unscathed from the episode; according to opinion polls carried out by the Steadman Media Group, he remained the leader Kenyans trusted most to act against corruption. However, the scandals did undermine the public image of the ODM as an alternative to the corrupt practices of previous administrations, and played into the growing rift at the heart of the party.

Of course, corruption was not the sole preserve of the ODM, and a number of scandals involving senior PNU leaders eroded public and donor confidence in the government throughout the year. Most dramatically, in January the state-owned **Kenya Pipeline Company** (KPC) was accused of illegally selling oil worth $ 100 m. The KPC's managing director, George Okungu, was fired on 11 February, but opposition supporters claimed that the scam could not have been perpetrated without the knowledge of those further up the chain. However, even though the KPC fell within his remit, PNU Energy Minister, Kiraitu Murungi, claimed to be 'in the dark' and kept his job. Later in the year another scandal broke over allegations that $ 1.4 m had gone missing from a fund for the government's flagship **free education** project. The reports undermined public confidence in the education ministry, led by Sam Ongeri, a close ally of Kibaki and a representative of the Kenya African National Union (KANU) that was part of the PNU faction within the legislature. Donors, fatigued by the constant reports of endemic corruption, responded swiftly. In December, the UK announced a freeze on support for education programmes, and the US soon followed suit, suspending $ 7 m of funding.

While neither policy challenges nor corruption scandals proved to be as divisive for the PNU as Mau Forrest and the maize scandal were for the ODM, intra-party tension was intensified by the battle to succeed Kibaki as **presidential candidate** in 2012, when constitutional term limits will render him ineligible to stand. Kibaki was believed to have endorsed fellow Kikuyu heavyweight and PNU Deputy Prime Minister Uhuru Kenyatta, son of independence leader Jomo Kenyatta, as his successor. In February, rumours began to circulate that Kenyatta, in turn, had engaged in talks to establish an **electoral pact** with ODM's William Ruto, whose relationship with party leader Raila Odinga deteriorated throughout the year. Such an alliance was remarkable for bringing together representatives of the Kikuyu and Kalenjin communities, which were at the forefront of the inter-communal violence in early 2008. The Kenyatta/Ruto coalition owed much to the fear of both leaders that they would be prosecuted as a result of investigations into corruption and post-election violence, and represented a complex **realignment** of anti-reform forces under the cover of the unity government. By forming a cross-party alliance, the two leaders secured enough votes within parliament to effectively control the reform agenda and insure their interests. While grassroots sentiment among both the Kikuyu and Kalenjin communities appeared to reject the pact, and many predicted that it would collapse before the next election, it had instant ramifications at the elite level. On the ODM side, Ruto's willingness to engage with PNU leaders undermined the position of Prime Minister Odinga, who risked being marooned as the leader of a party over which he could exert only nominal control. On the PNU side, Kenyatta's ascension marginalised a number of other presidential hopefuls, prompting former Kibaki ally and Justice Minister Martha Karua to **resign** from the government on 6 April to pursue her own presidential ambitions.

Throughout the year, continued uncertainty over prosecutions relating to human rights abuses before and after the election of 2007 kept the political temperature close to boiling point. When the Commission of Inquiry on Post Election Violence, better known as the **Waki Commission**, reported its findings in October 2008, it placed the names of high-profile suspects in an envelope. The envelope was then handed over to Kofi Annan, who was tasked with making the names public when a process had been agreed for prosecuting those concerned, or handing over the envelope to the **ICC** if Kenya's leaders failed to make progress. Although the government did put forward legislation that would have established a domestic tribunal, Kenyan lawyers argued that it contained a number of loopholes and would not have insulated the process from political manipulation. At the same time, civil society leaders feared that the right of the president to pardon prisoners would be abused to protect Kibaki's allies. Consequently, both those fearful of prosecution, and those strongly in favour of ending the country's culture of impunity, had reasons to vote against the proposals. On 12 February, the **Special Tribunal for Kenya Bill, 2009**, was rejected by 101 votes to 93, making it impossible for the government to meet Annan's 1 March deadline for the creation of a domestic tribunal. In frustration, Annan handed over the envelope to the ICC, who ultimately stated an interest in prosecuting the case if the Kenyan government failed to meet a fresh deadline of August 2010 to begin proceedings.

Concern among the political elite about the contents of the 'envelope' was exacerbated by domestic and international probes into a range of other human rights abuses that threatened to expose the police and army to prosecutions. In the run-up to the last elections, a series of grisly murders raised the profile of the controversial **Mungiki** gang, a largely Kikuyu organisation that had slowly morphed from a cult into a criminal protection racket. The government responded by unleashing a crackdown in the slums of Nairobi throughout December 2007. Human rights organisations and the BBC alleged that the tactics used by the security forces included the execution of hundreds of suspects without trial, a claim that was later supported by the Special Investigator of the UN, Philip Alston.

Events following Alston's visit in February revealed just how dangerous Kenya's political environment had become. On 5 March, two **human rights activists**, Oscar Kamau Kingara and John Paul Oulo, were shot and killed while on their way to a meeting at the Kenya National Commission on Human Rights (KNCHR). They had been working for the Oscar Foundation Free Legal Aid Clinic, which had previously accused the police of having killed over 8,000 people during its investigations into Mungiki. In response, figures within the security forces had alleged that the Oscar Foundation was a front for Mungiki, and had warned them to cease their activities. Coming just days after the release of Alston's report and hours after a government spokesman had denounced the Oscar Foundation, the **assassinations** were interpreted by the domestic media and human rights groups as a warning not to investigate the security services. The shameless and audacious nature of the attack, committed in broad daylight just a few streets from Parliament, sent shock waves through Kenyan opposition parties and civil society.

Perhaps unsurprisingly, **militia-related violence** continued throughout 2009 and took both inter- and intra-ethnic forms. In Central Province, ordinary Kikuyus rejected Mungiki demands for protection money, sparking Kikuyu on Kikuyu clashes in the Kirinyaga West and Nyeri East districts. In April, an estimated 42 people lost their lives in the violence, the worst single attack being the murder of 29 Mathira residents by suspected Mungiki members on 21 April. At the same time, poor rains, escalating food prices, disease, and displacement all contributed to an increase in inter-communal tension.

One of the worst **droughts** for years affected many parts of the country, placing 10 m people at risk of starvation according to the Kenyan government, which declared a **state of emergency** on 9 January. The Red Cross estimated that average walking distances to water doubled in pastoral areas, putting vulnerable communities under even greater strain. Combined with the continued ethnic tension throughout the country, rising **food insecurity** contributed to increased competition among pastoralist communities with deadly consequences. From May onwards, stock theft incidents inspired inter-clan fighting between the Bwirege and Nyabasi, as well as between these groups and the Maasai and Kipsigis, who reside in Trans Mara District, and the Kuria, who hail from Tarime District in Tanzania. The clashes, which peaked in mid-July, resulted in more than 700 homes being burnt down and around 6,000 individuals being displaced. Meanwhile, Kenyans throughout the country were alarmed at a perceived rise in **violent crime**. Reports of kidnappings and armed robberies were common in 2009, and on average one police officer was killed in the line of duty every month. High-profile attacks, such as the murder of Kinuthia Murugu, a senior civil servant who died of a gunshot wound inflicted during a carjacking on 9 July, called into question the ability of the police to maintain basic law and order.

Frustration with the poor performance of the police inspired student groups to join protests calling for Police Commissioner Hussein Ali to step down on 10 March. The **demonstrations** quickly turned violent as around 5,000 people blocked traffic and looted shops. The government responded by creating a **National Taskforce on Police Reforms** on 8 May to hold public hearings on how to strengthen the legitimacy and capacity of the force, but the stipulated timetable suggested that real reform would be unlikely before 2012. In the absence of immediate progress, pressure for the removal of Hussein Ali continued to build. Although Kibaki finally agreed to transfer Ali to head-up the postal service on 8 September, his choice of successor, Mathew Iteere, failed to inspire public confidence. In his former position as head of the paramilitary **General Service Unit** (GSU), Iteere had played a central role in securing government buildings during the post-election crisis and was said to be close to the president. Consequently, reformers complained that his appointment reflected a policy of continuity rather than change.

The mounting evidence of the human rights abuses committed by the military and police in the recent past exacerbated the pressure to launch a **Truth, Justice and Reconciliation Commission (TJRC)** as promised in the text of the power-sharing agreement. On 29 November 2008, the Truth, Justice and Reconciliation Commission bill had been signed into law, despite criticism from civil society groups that it was a deeply flawed state-owned process and that the inclusion of an amnesty clause would undermine any attempt to end the culture of impunity. On 23 July, Ambassador Bethuel Kiplagat, a diplomat and Executive Director of the Africa Peace Forum, was appointed to head the TJRC, which was tasked with making specific recommendations to the Attorney General on which cases should be brought to court. The TJRC was expected to hear evidence on all cases of potential human rights abuse dating back to independence in 1963, which was likely to generate an unfeasible amount of work. The impact of the Commission rested largely in the hands of the Attorney General, who was given the ultimate say on which cases brought to the TJRC should be prosecuted, and whether recommendations for amnesty made by the TJRC should be upheld. This seriously compromised the independence of the Commission and the likelihood that opposition parties and human rights groups would be satisfied with results, as the **Attorney General**, Amos Wako, has been one of the main barriers to reform since his appointment in May 1991.

In late August, civil society groups expressed concern that a national **census** would reignite civil strife by asking questions concerning the ethnic identity of respondents. Because the 1999 census was widely believed to have exaggerated the size of the Kalenjin population to enable then-President Moi to create more constituencies in his 'home areas', the 2009 census was expected to be controversial. Donors and local commentators feared that the new census would record lower numbers of Kalenjin, further antagonising communities that supported the opposition in 2007 and continued to believe that they were robbed of election victory. However, while the publication of the final figures may yet cause unrest, the data collection process passed largely without incident; the only real flashpoint occurred when close to 2,000 IDPs in Uasin Gishu refused to be counted until they had been appropriately compensated by the government for loss of property as a result of the post-election crisis.

As the year drew to an end, the **Committee of Experts** tasked with drawing together a **draft constitution** by merging the strongest aspects of Kenya's previous constitutional review processes into one document delivered their verdict. The 'harmonised draft' that was presented on 19 November echoed many of the recommendations of the Bomas Constitutional Conference in 2004, which sought to devolve power away from the executive by strengthening parliament and disbanding the notorious Provincial Administration. Key provisions of the harmonised draft included: a cap on the size of the **cabinet** to 15–20 ministers; a permanent post of **prime minister**, to be held by the leader of the largest political party or coalition in parliament; eight **regional parliaments** without tax-raising power, sitting on top of a devolved system of government featuring county assemblies with tax-raising power; the addition of a second chamber (Senate) that would enhance regional representation.

While the harmonised draft was largely welcomed by civil society, lawyers pointed out that many provisions were poorly defined. For example, the exact financial powers that would devolve to the regional assemblies were not clearly specified. Furthermore, many commentators identified a number of flaws in the extremely complicated electoral system designed to ensure that women and representatives of the disabled community would be represented within parliament. Civil society activists were also quick to express their fear that, as had occurred during previous review processes, provisions to reduce the power of the president would be watered down before the final draft is put to a national **referendum** in 2010.

Foreign Affairs

Relations with Western donors remained strained due to the slow pace of reform and rumours of systematic corruption. During the presidency of George W. Bush, **US** foreign policy had been broadly supportive of the Kibaki government, which was an important ally in the war on terror by virtue of its proximity to Somalia. Although security concerns remained the primary determinant of US policy under the Obama regime, the new administration was quick to signal that it would take a tougher line on democratic backsliding. The appointment on 7 May of **Johnnie Carson**, a former Ambassador to Kenya, as Under-Secretary of State for African Affairs suggested that in future Kenya would be a higher priority in American thinking, and that US engagement would be based on greater expertise. Barack Obama's decision to visit Ghana in July, rather than Kenya, the country of his father, was widely interpreted by the Kenyan media as further evidence that the country had fallen out of international favour.

American concerns were relayed first by Ambassador Ranneberger and then by Secretary of State **Hillary Clinton** during her visit on 6 August. The public criticism of the limitations of the unity government was poorly received by the political elite; even Odinga, who potentially stood to gain from the creation of a more level political playing field, retorted that, "We don't need lectures on how to govern ourselves." Shortly after, on 18 September, Carson sent letters to 15 Kenyan officials, warning them that personal sanctions would be introduced if they did not cease to act as **barriers to reform**. Although the US did not publicly release the names, it was widely reported that they included the joint chief whips George Thuo and Jakoyo Midiwo, along with Environment Minister John Michuki and Internal Security Minister George Saitoti. In October, Carson followed through with his promise, issuing a travel ban to an anonymous senior government official, sparking weeks of rumours regarding the identity of the individual. On 4 November, the speculation was ended by the Attorney General Amos Wako, who took the unusual step of publicly announcing that he was the official concerned, claiming that he had been falsely accused and would sue the US accordingly.

Although less explicitly critical than the US, actors from within the **EU** also sought to use their positions to advance the reform agenda. In March, representatives of the British DFID expressed frustration that offers of assistance to restructure the electoral commission and the police force were being ignored. On 1 October, similarly slow progress in dealing with the post-election violence prompted the presidency of the EU to express its concern "that the Government of Kenya has been unable to establish a credible, independent, constitutionally protected local special tribunal to end the impunity of perpetrators of the post-election violence within the agreed timeframe". Tension between donors and the Kenyan government led to an increasing amount of international financial assistance being channelled through **non-state actors** (NSAs) working in the areas of human rights and good governance. The European Commission reported that in 2009 over KSh 350 m was directed to Kenyan NSAs – more than any other African country bar Sudan.

Engagement with **China** was more harmonious, if tentative, in part because the Chinese policy of 'non-interference' stood in particularly strong contrast to the more challenging strategies adopted by many Western donors. In mid-October, the two governments announced plans to construct a new transport 'corridor' and a new port in Lamu in order to enable Sudan to export oil through Kenya, and to better connect the country to Rwanda and

Ethiopia. Odinga visited China on 13 October, and stated that Kenya preferred to partner with China because "they offer the full package". The Chinese government responded by offering a $ 7 m grant to fund 'infrastructure development projects'.

The government found it significantly more difficult to keep the **UN** on side in 2009. A visit by the Special Investigator, Philip Alston, to investigate extra-judicial killings by the police and security services resulted in a war of words between the Kenyan government and the UN in February. Alston's report found that the Kenyan police "frequently executes individuals and that a climate of impunity prevails". At a press conference in Nairobi on 25 February, Alston went further, claiming that "Kenyan police are a law unto themselves. They kill often, with impunity." Alston's undiplomatic language and recommendation of sweeping resignations and reforms within the security system drew a hostile response from a number of ministers, who argued that he had overstepped his remit and impinged upon Kenyan **sovereignty**. Alfred Matua, the official government spokesman, expressed "deep displeasure" with the report, and called into question the "approach, conduct, and method of work".

Regionally, the conflict in **Somalia** continued to destabilise northern Kenya. Fleeing drought and fighting, 32,000 Somali refugees entered Kenya in the first six months of the year alone, increasing the number of refugees in camps in the Dadaab area to over 300,000. The influx placed international aid agencies under even greater pressure, and increased tensions between the refugees and their host communities. Of greater concern to Kenya's Western donors was the possibility that the **al-Shabaab** Islamist militia, which the US government believed to have links with al-Qaida, would take the opportunity to permeate the border in order to radicalise Kenya's large Somali population. Members of al-Shabaab were said to have crossed into Kenya on 16 July on a recruiting mission that targeted school pupils and refugees. Just a day later, three foreign aid workers were abducted from a hotel in Mandera town, prompting the government to increase the numbers of army personnel deployed along the border. Although Kibaki was quick to blame al-Shabaab and the influx of small arms from Somalia for the increase in violent crime during 2009, Vice President Kalonzo Musyoka rejected suggestions that Kenyan troops should be deployed in Somalia, preferring to call upon the **AU** to help return the country to political stability.

Fears over the potential expansion of al-Shabaab also impacted on Kenyan-**Eritrean** relations. On 7 August, Kenya deported an Eritrean diplomat for 'security reasons', the second such expulsion in as many months. The government refused to explain its reasons, but as the expulsions came immediately after the visit of Hillary Clinton, who had used her time in the region to warn Eritrea against "meddling" in Somalia, the deportations were widely interpreted by local media as retaliation for alleged Eritrean support of the al-Shabaab insurgency. Shortly after Clinton's visit, Eritrean Foreign Minister Osman Saleh Mohammed travelled to Nairobi in a bid to normalise relations, but failed in his mission to set up a meeting with President Kibaki.

Although Kenya generally enjoyed more positive regional relations with members of the EAC in 2009, a squabble between Uganda and Kenya over **Migingo Island**, a tiny piece of land about the size of a football pitch located in Lake Victoria and mostly populated by the Luo community, threatened to undermine regional stability. Although the island was officially controlled by Kenya, **Uganda** had frequently questioned Kenyan ownership, largely because it was frustrated that Kenya made more revenue from fishing for the valuable Nile perch despite having rights to a smaller proportion of the lake. International relations deteriorated in early March when Uganda, having moved a small number of troops and police officers onto the island, raised the Ugandan flag and announced that forthwith Kenyans would have to apply for permits in order to operate businesses. However, a meeting of government ministers on 13 March led to new surveys, which showed the island to be 510 m within the Kenyan portion of the lake. On 11 May, Uganda's President Yoweri Museveni accepted that the islands were Kenyan and withdrew Ugandan troops, although his government continued to argue that Kenyans were fishing illegally throughout the year.

Attempts by regional leaders to strengthen the infrastructure of the **EAC** in order to prevent a recurrence of the Kenyan post-election crisis, when political instability closed crucial ports and roads thus undermining the ability of the whole region to import and export, enjoyed mixed fortunes. Although the incorporation of Rwanda and Burundi in 2007 made it more complicated than ever before to build consensus within the EAC, Rwandan President Paul Kagame devoted considerable energy to promoting the integration process. Despite this, stated plans for a common president and currency remained little more than a pipe dream, and the inability of the EAC's conflict resolution mechanisms to manage the spat between Kenya and Uganda over Migingo Island provided further evidence of the organisation's limitations. Furthermore, although the members of the EAC signed a deal with the UK that made up to $ 3 m a year available to support regional development and **integration**, little had been achieved by the end of the year.

Socioeconomic Developments

The combined impact of the post-election political crisis, drought and the global economic downturn continued to hurt Kenya's economic performance and contributed to an intensification of food insecurity throughout the country. Throughout 2008 and 2009 unusually poor rains caused crops to fail and undermined the ability of cattle herders to keep their animals alive. Although aid agencies believed that the worst affected areas were the semi-arid south-east region and parts of central Kenya, the drought had severe consequences for standards of living throughout the country; in some areas, maize prices were reported to have increased by 130% in less than a year. On 20 August, the Kenya Food Security Steering Group revised its estimate of the number of people requiring emergency **food assistance** to 3.8 m, a 32% increase on February 2009. The report also identified 2.5 m **'chronically food insecure'** individuals in urban areas, 100,000 of whom remained displaced following the post-election violence. Widespread starvation was only averted by an increase in support from the **World Food Programme** (WFP), which increased the number of people receiving food distributions from 1.2 m to 2.5 m and sought to provide school meals to an additional 1.5 m children affected by the drought, at a cost of $ 475 m. Anecdotal evidence suggested that, despite the intervention by the WFP, many farmers responded by abandoning the rural areas and relocating to urban areas where they often ended up in already overcrowded slums.

However, in general terms 2009 represented something of a **stabilisation** of Kenya's economic fortunes. The **GDP growth rate** improved marginally from a low of 1.7% in 2008 to 2% in 2009, and the Economist Intelligence Unit predicted that growth would rise to 3% in 2010 and over 5% in 2011. In part due to a fall in public spending, the government managed simultaneously to exert greater control over **inflation**, and the consumer prices index declined from 21.9% to 17.9%. Towards the end of the year, the government decided to revise the index for calculating inflation, using a new methodology and a larger basket of goods. On the basis of the new system, inflation averaged 9.3% in 2009, a revelation that encouraged the government to relax monetary policy from November. Despite continued political uncertainty, the **Kenyan Shilling** remained remarkably stable, trading at between 74.70 and 80.26 to the dollar all year. From March onwards, growing investor confidence, improved assessments of emerging market risk, and a weaker dollar saw the Shilling gradually gain value, reaching a high of KSh 75.8:$ 1 in January 2010.

Economic stabilisation owed much to the release of **IMF** emergency funding worth $ 207 m in May. IMF support enabled the government to ride out the global economic downturn without drastic cuts in public services. The **budget** speech of 11 June outlined Finance Minister Uhuru Kenyatta's vision of 'overcoming today's challenges for a better Kenya tomorrow', and identified five main priorities: macroeconomic stability; infrastructure and public works; equitable regional development; food security; and public service delivery. Specific infrastructure projects included a promise to extend rural electricity to all major trading centres at a cost of KSh 7 bn, KSh 1.3 bn to purchase mobile computer laboratories for each constituency, and a range of investments in roads and railways projects designed to strengthen the position of the Mombasa port as a regional hub. At the same time, Kenyatta provided a stimulus to local economic activities across the country by offering an additional **economic stimulus or resilience package** worth KSh 105 m to each consistency, on top of existing allocations such as the Constituency Development Fund. Fearful of causing a further retraction in the economy, the government sought to avoid large **tax** increases and instead opted to rely on greater domestic and international borrowing to finance the budget. Treasury officials pledged that half of the planned KSh 109 bn of new borrowing would be ring-fenced for the purposes of accelerating the process of economic recovery. As a result, the total public debt increased from 37.2% of GDP in 2008/2009 to an estimated 40.2% in 2009/2010, and was expected to rise further to 42.9% in 2010/2011. While shying away from tax increases, the accuracy of the government's economic forecasts depended on whether the rejuvenated Kenya Revenue Authority (KRA) would collect existing taxes more efficiently. The budget projected that the KRA would collect KSh 523 bn in 2009/2010, a jump of 30% from the year before.

However, despite Kenyatta's stated intention to kick-start the economy through the adoption of a fiscal stimulus plan, the final **budget deficit** for 2009 was expected to be lower than was initially estimated (3.9% rather than 5.1% of GDP) as a result of governmental underspending. Weak procedures for planning and implementing projects consistently delayed the release of funds, undermining development efforts. Consequently, capital spending amounted to 7.1% of GDP rather than the planned 8%, and many important **infrastructure** programmes were behind schedule by the year's end. Remarkably, despite the considerable cost of the government of national unity and the demands of national reconciliation, recurrent expenditure fell from 20.6% of GDP in 2007/08 to an estimated 19.3% in 2008/09, lower than the corresponding pre-violence level of 19.7% in 2006/2007.

On 22 December, the IMF announced its approval of the country's strategy for dealing with the global economic downturn at the conclusion of the latest Article IV consultations, praising the "prudent" economic course plotted by the government. However, the IMF remained critical of the slow pace of **structural reforms**, which it argued were essential to change the way that the Kenyan economy was run, most notably with regard to financial management and bank regulation. Although many prominent politicians agreed that these measures were important for the country's long-term economic growth, they faced pockets of entrenched opposition because they promised to curb corruption and so restrict the patronage opportunities for senior political leaders and civil servants.

Kenyan **supermarkets** continued to lead domestic business activity. The year began tragically for Nakumatt, Kenya's most successful supermarket, currently valued at KSh 5.4 n, when a fire in one of its Nairobi stores on 28 January resulted in 29 deaths. Soon after the fire, rumours began to circulate that security guards had contributed to the disaster by deliberately locking the exits in order to prevent looting. Despite a police investigation and damage to its reputation, **Nakumatt** continued to thrive and now had 18 stores and over 3,000 employees. Having established its first store outside Kenya in Kigali (Rwanda) in August 2008, the company planned to open four more stores in Kenya, one more store in Rwanda, and its first in Uganda in 2010. Bosses spent much of 2009 attempting to finance this expansion by securing a KSh 4 bn syndicated medium-term loan from a consortium of banks including Stanbic and Barclays. Nakumatt was also understood to have made a 30% stake in the company available to selected investors in an attempt to raise a further KSh 1.8 bn. On 16 December, rumours began to circulate that Satya Capital, a private investment firm associated with Sudanese magnate **Mo Ibrahim**, had emerged as Nakumatt's favoured partner, although talks were ongoing at the end of the year.

The prospects for one of Nakumatt's main rivals, **Uchumi**, also took a turn for the better. Having been placed in administration in 2006, Uchumi finally began to show signs of recovery after outstanding debts worth around KSh 150 m were rescheduled. The combination of lower debt repayments and a return to profitability enabled the company to pay back KSh 708 m of an estimated KSh 900 m debt to suppliers. Although the company still had heavy debts, and was forced to concede a 15% stake to the government, it emerged from a period in receivership and announced plans for trading in Uchumi shares on the Nairobi Stock Exchange to resume in 2010.

After a terrible 2008, the **tourist sector**, one of Kenya's main sources of foreign exchange, recovered strongly in 2009. According to Tourism Minister Najib Balala, the number of visitors fell 30% from 2007 to 2008, but then rose by 90% in 2009. The return to pre-crisis levels reflected renewed confidence among European tourists, demonstrated by an increase in the average number of charter flights heading to Mombasa from Belgium, Holland, Germany and France, from 20 to 30 a week. However, the news was not all positive. When an increase in **air passenger duty** for long-haul flights leaving from the UK came into effect on 1 November, it raised the cost of flying to Kenya by between £ 90 and £ 100, providing an incentive for holidaymakers to choose destinations closer to hand. On 8 October, Balala responded by asking the British government to create exemptions for developing countries, pointing out that because more tourists travel to Kenya from Britain than from any other country, the duty could significantly undermine Kenya's economic development plans.

Following a bumper year for **remittances** in 2008 as the Kenyan diaspora rallied round to ease the impact of the political crisis on families and friends, the amount of money sent home rose again in 2009, according to official figures compiled by the Central Bank of Kenya. Responding to drought and continued economic hardship, Kenyans living abroad transferred KSh 47.1 bn in 2009, a KSh 4.8 bn increase on the year before. After horticulture, tea, and tourism, remittances were Kenya's fourth largest source of foreign currency. As in previous years, more than half of all remittances came from North America.

Nic Cheeseman

Rwanda

Political life remained relatively unchanged from 2008. The Rwanda Patriotic Front (RPF), under President Paul Kagame, continued to govern the country with an iron fist. Political freedoms for Rwandans from all walks of life remained limited. The government further curtailed the activities of opposition politicians, journalists and human rights advocates while peasant Rwandans experienced the double-shock of strict government policy on agricultural production and the economic downturn precipitated by the global financial crisis. Domestic political violence remained minimal, affirming Rwanda's reputation as a stable and peaceful country. Relations with members of the international donor community warmed up again in early 2009, following a brief period of tension after the release of a UN report in December 2008 that identified Rwanda as a prominent actor in the conflict in eastern DR Congo. Diplomatic relations were restored with both DR Congo and France. In November Rwanda was admitted to the Commonwealth. Donors, notably Germany, the UK, the US, and the EU, affirmed their commitment to support the development vision of the RPF, despite their growing concern about the lack of domestic political freedoms. In October, the World Bank named Rwanda as among the top 20 reformers around the world in its Doing Business survey. Despite the global economic meltdown, the authorities remained committed to market-oriented reform policies. The country registered economic growth of 5% despite higher-than-forecast inflation. Urban poverty decreased but poverty remained widespread and chronic in rural areas.

Domestic Politics

The **ruling Rwanda Patriotic Front (RPF)** continued to dominate all levels of socio-political life, from the lowest levels of the administrative hierarchy up to **President Kagame**'s inner circle of advisors and aides. Formally a multi-party democracy following parliamentary elections in 2008, Rwanda was *de facto* a **one-party state**. The electoral gains of the RPF in the 2008 elections gave the semblance of political pluralism while masking the fact that six of nine political parties existed only in alliance with the RPF. These parties did not have their own platform or policies, and had to clear all candidates through the RPF party executive. Parliamentarians had little power to legislate on behalf of their constituents.

To assure its **prominence in political life**, the RPF had also introduced in late 2008 an "oath-of-oneness" that required all civil society leaders, university staff and student leaders, and local administrators to publicly pledge an oath of allegiance to the RPF. Those individuals who decided not to take the pledge were harassed and intimidated into submission. Government ministers and other senior representatives of the government also took the oath, but did so directly with the Office of the President which recorded the pledge as evidence of its commitment to good governance and accountability. Kagame also circulated the political elite through frequent cabinet shuffles in an apparent attempt to control the ruling class while assuring individual loyalty to the RPF. **Cabinet shuffles** in July, October and December kept the ruling class on its toes, and resulted in the consolidation of political power in the hands of the RPF as Kagame promoted party loyalists and demoted or ejected perceived or real critics from cabinet. In September, Kagame announced that presidential elections would be held in August 2010 and took the opportunity to remind political elites of the importance of loyalty to the RPF. In December, Kagame was re-elected as RPF chairman with 95% of the vote, affirming his nomination as the party's presidential candidate.

The government maintained its **tight rein on free and open political expression**. It continued to ban any public expression of "ethnic divisionism" (between Tutsi and Hutu) or "promoting genocide ideology" (against Hutu) or of "preaching genocide negationism" (meaning those who questioned that only Tutsi died in 1994). These laws were vaguely worded and arbitrarily applied to anyone who made public statements that the government perceived as critical of its policies. The government continued to target journalists as the purveyors of divisionist opinion, and consequently sought to control the media as much as possible. In February, a law aimed at maintaining high standards of journalism was introduced in parliament. It meant that only those individuals with a Bachelor of Journalism degree were eligible for press accreditation. This new law followed on the heels of the 2008 genocide ideology law, which had been widely criticised by international and domestic human rights organisations as a tool of social intimidation. Taken together, the **new media law** (signed in August), meant that anyone who neglected information that the government considered essential to understanding or interpreting its post-genocide reconstruction and reconciliation policies was subject to demotion, dismissal or imprisonment.

The new media law also meant that only those **media outlets that expressed views in line with the government** were able to operate successfully. A good example of this was the government's crack-down on the BBC Kinyarwanda service in April. The service was shut down for two months for giving airtime to genocide negationists and others critical of the government. A BBC interview with representatives of the **'Forces Démocratiques de Libération du Rwanda'** (FDLR, a Hutu-led anti-government rebel group based in eastern DR Congo) and members of the political opposition living in exile led to the ban. The ban could in part be linked to the timing of the interview, as the government designated every April as a month of mourning for all Rwandans to commemorate Tutsi lives lost during the genocide. The ban was also likely to have been partially linked to the arrival of more than 3,000 Rwanda Defence Force (RDF) troops in eastern DR Congo at the invitation of the Congolese government in January. The government did not want to be seen as engaging in public dialogue with its sworn enemy, the FDLR.

The government also maintained **strict control over civil society organisations**, including Tutsi survivor groups. Civil society organisations and other forms of associational life existed at the behest of the government. There were strict regulations, instituted in 2008, about which groups were allowed to register. Any group or organisation that criticised or challenged government policy was not allowed to register and those that had registered before the new regulations came into effect were closely monitored. There were no major disciplining incidents involving civil society in 2009. This was not to be interpreted as a sign of peace and stability but was better understood as an indicator of the extent to which government controlled civil society.

Two notable examples were emblematic of the close relationship between civil society and the RPF. The most prominent **civil society** organisation, IBUKA ("to remember"), the umbrella body of all survivor organisations in the country, **appeared independent of government**. In practice, senior staff were all RPF loyalists. In November, two long-standing staff members, Benoit Kabgayi and Ange Mukaremera, were suspended by IBUKA president Theodore Simburudari for no substantive reason. Their suspension may have been the result of their failure to take the "oath-of-oneness". It was common practice for individuals who were unwilling to take the oath to be accused of corruption, embezzlement or immorality, including sexual impropriety and adultery. In July, HRW submitted an open letter to the **International Criminal Tribunal for Rwanda** (ICTR) asking it to uphold standards of international justice in trying members of the RPF for the crimes against humanity and war crimes it committed between 1990 and 1994. Not surprisingly, the RPF reacted to the letter negatively. IBUKA also denounced the letter in identical terms to the government with its own open letter, detailing the many positive steps that the government had taken to try its own officers for crimes allegedly committed during the 1994 genocide. Some **outspoken Tutsi survivors** resident in Kigali took issue with IBUKA's reaction, noting their wish that the RPF be held to account for its alleged crimes in 1994 as the basis of peace and reconciliation for all Rwandans. These individuals were not imprisoned, as would be the government's usual reaction to such public criticism, perhaps highlighting the impact that the HRW letter had on domestic politics.

HRW and other international human rights and advocacy groups continued to highlight the **government's lack of commitment to basic human rights**. Kagame continued to highlight the importance of state security for lasting peace in Rwanda and the Great Lakes Region to justify his government's heavy-handedness in controlling its population. Some organisations accepted this, stating that they saw Rwanda's poor human rights record as a result of its special circumstances since the 1994 genocide, an explanation that the government has repeatedly invoked since 1999. For example, in September, the government aggressively argued against its low ranking in the **Mo Ibrahim Good Governance Index**, which analyses good governance in Africa across four sectors: safety and rule of law; participation and human rights; sustainable economic opportunity; and human development "as proxies for the quality of the processes and outcomes of governance". The 2009 index was released in September, and ranked Central Africa as the lowest performing sub-region on the continent, and Rwanda as the best in the sub-region and a respectable 18th out of the 48 countries surveyed. Rwanda's rank was seen as too high by international observers on the basis of its human rights record, repression of political opposition and freedom of speech, and its continued harassment of journalists. The government, however, perceived its Ibrahim ranking as too low and launched an aggressive domestic and international media campaign to illustrate how Ibrahim staff had manipulated statistical data or relied on out-dated evidence. In particular, the government cited its **strong record of good governance** and **zero-tolerance policy on corruption** as justification for deserving a higher ranking. In October, Kagame made a speech to diplomats in Kigali that questioned the credibility of the index, while noting that Australia's Institute for Economics and Peace named Rwanda "the 13th most peaceful country in Africa". Domestic and international human rights analysts opined that Kagame's involvement in denouncing the findings of the Ibrahim Index was evidence of the government's efforts to disguise the purge of politically disloyal elites from the RPF. By November, the government had released seven directors-general, four permanent secretaries and six secretaries-general from both government and civil society in the name of anti-corruption and good governance.

The **'*gacaca*' neo-traditional courts** remained a site of insecurity for many Rwandans – Hutu and Tutsi alike – as the government stepped up its efforts to ensure that the trials ended no later than December. The government initially hoped that all *gacaca* trials would end in June but this proved impossible in light of changes to the *gacaca* law in 2007 that allowed the courts to try individuals accused of rape. The courts were a central part of the government's post-genocide national unity and reconciliation tool-kit and emphasised legal retribution over social reconciliation. Participation in *gacaca* trials was mandatory for all Rwandans, and those that did not attend were subject to intimidation until they presented themselves to fulfill their legally-mandated role as perpetrators (read Hutu) who had to tell the truth of what they had done during the genocide and survivors (read Tutsi) who had to forgive those who had killed their loved ones. Human rights organisations continued to criticise the *gacaca* process throughout 2009, stating that the government was **sacrificing sincere reconciliation between Hutu and Tutsi for judicial expediency**. The government argued that it was costly in both financial and human terms to have the trials continue much longer, as the cost to society was too high. At the level of the ordinary Rwandan, the courts remained controversial, as any discussion of RPF war crimes or crimes against humanity committed before, during or after the 1994 genocide remained taboo. By the end of December, an estimated 2,200 cases remained to be heard.

The **mandate of the ICTR** had been set to expire in 2008. In June, the ICTR asked for an extension of its mandate from the UN Security Council. In July, the open letter from HRW questioned **chief prosecutor Hassan Bubacar Jallow's** credibility as the ICTR had so far failed to prosecute anyone from the RPF. In response, Jallow officially argued that he could only prosecute suspects on the strength of the legal evidence against them, thereby implying that there was not sufficient evidence to try RPF crimes. Behind closed doors, Jallow noted that the court had yet to do so because of the lack of political will from the international community to prosecute RPF crimes and because of RPF harassment and intimidation of witnesses and other actors who were willing to testify before the ICTR. Pro-Hutu individuals and groups living in the diaspora, particularly in Belgium and Canada, used the debate between HRW and Jallow as evidence that the RPF had organised and implemented the 1994 genocide (it did not) because there was not sufficient evidence to prosecute the accused. The ICTR used this opportunity to assert its judicial independence and argued for the importance of being able to establish a truthful record of what happened in Rwanda between 1990 and 1994 (the temporal jurisdiction of the court). Further buoying the work of revisionists using the decisions of the ICTR to promote their own political agenda, the **ICTR acquitted Protais Zigiranyirazo** (the brother of the wife of former president Juvenal Habyarimana) in November on a technicality, not on substantive evidence. In December, the UNSC extended the ICTR mandate until 2012.

Foreign Affairs

Once again, Rwanda's foreign affairs were dominated by the country's presence (critics would say interference) in eastern DR Congo. A December 2008 UN panel of experts report had linked the Rwandan authorities to the **'Congrès National pour la Défense du Peuple'** (CNDP, a Tutsi-led anti-Congolese government militia). The report provided evidence that **Rwanda provided support to the CNDP** and its Tutsi leader, Laurent Nkunda, despite vigorous denial from the RPF. DR Congo authorities worked with the UN Security Council to provide evidence not only of the relationship between Rwanda and the CNDP but also of Rwanda's plan to eliminate the FLDR. Rwanda responded, saying its troops were not present in the northern Kivu region, and that the DR Congo was only trying to cover up its inability to deal with the conflict. The RPF believed that the FDLR was responsible for the 1994 Tutsi genocide and was using the Kivu region as base from which to attack Rwanda to finish the genocide. The FDLR claimed it did not participate in the 1994 genocide (current evidence showed that members of the FDLR participated in but did not plan the genocide) and that its current interest was to return to Rwanda to represent ordinary Hutu who it believed were currently oppressed by the ruling RPF. In an atypical show of public bravado, Kagame publicly stated in January that if the RDF had been present in northern Kivu, the conflict would have ended because of the superior discipline and tactical skill of its soldiers. **FDLR combatants** were to voluntarily return to Rwanda throughout 2009 in a **disarmament and demobilisation** exercise spearheaded by MONUC. By the end of 2009, approximately 1,500 FDLR fighters (out of an estimated 6,000) had begun the disarmament process.

In January, in a surprise turn of events, DR Congo's president Joseph Kabila invited the RDF to assist the Congolese army (FARDC, 'Forces Armées de la République Démocratique du Congo') in its drive to root out the FDLR from its positions in northern Kivu. The invitation was probably precipitated by the calls of the UN and some of Rwanda's bilateral donors for an urgent settlement between DR Congo and Rwanda, as well as the December 2008 reactivation of the **Joint Verification Mechanism (JVM)** between the two countries. The RDF declared its joint military operation with FARDC a success as it flushed FDLR rebels out of their positions in rural and remote areas of the north Kivu (along the border with northern Rwanda and southern Uganda), including its liberation of a coltan mine near the Congolese town of Goma. RDF troops were withdrawn in February at Kabila`s request. About the same time, Kagame requested a meeting with CNDP leader Nkunda in Kigali, where he was detained without charge. DR Congo requested that Nkunda be returned for trial there for mass human rights violations committed by soldiers under his command; Kagame, however, did not comply, despite the **formalisation of diplomatic relations between DRC and Rwanda** in March, more than a decade after they were severed.

In March, the **UN Mission in the DR Congo (MONUC)** reported that FDLR rebels had returned to their positions in the hills bordering Rwanda and had failed to win over the support of the civilian population. The joint operation opened age-old wounds in the region, where the predominantly Hutu population – local elites and peasants alike – feared the dominance of ethnic Tutsi. The demobilisation of FDLR rebels of Rwandan origin failed to result in significant numbers of returnees. A **humanitarian crisis** resulted as the ill-disciplined and poorly-paid FARDC personnel wrought havoc in the Kivu region. The UN and international organisations, such as 'Médecins sans Frontières' and Oxfam, alleged that all armed groups in northern Kivu – FARDC, FDLR and the RDF – were guilty of human rights abuses against civilians. Combatants from both sides in the conflict were responsible for an estimated **160 rapes of women and girls every day**. Men and boys were reportedly sometimes raped by enlisted men as a form of cruel and unusual punishment against them (and the local population) on the orders of their commanders.

The governments of DR Congo and Rwanda had reactivated the **Tripartite Plus Joint Commission (TPJC)** in Kigali in December 2008. The purpose of the TPJC was to monitor the conflict in eastern DR Congo and to maintain a common military strategy of participating governments (Burundi, DR Congo, Rwanda and Uganda) against the various militias at large in the region. Throughout 2009, the TPJC remained dormant, perhaps because of a warming of diplomatic relations between Kigali and Kinshasa throughout 2008 and 2009. Kagame had appointed a new **Great Lakes Region envoy** in December 2008, **Joseph Mutaboba**. Mutaboba had a reputation in the region as a practiced and thoughtful diplomat, in stark contrast to his predecessor, the aggressive and unforgiving Richard Sezibera. Mutaboba's appointment was seen by the international community and political leaders in Burundi, DR Congo and Uganda as a positive sign and possible statement of Rwanda's willingness to find a solution to the seemingly endless crisis in eastern Congo. Mutaboba reached out to political and military leaders from all sides in the conflict to discuss its peaceful resolution. No official meetings between the various actors were held in 2009, but rumours circulated in both Rwanda and northern Kivu that Mutaboba would host a regional peace summit in early 2011.

In November, the **Congolese ambassador to Rwanda** presented his diplomatic credentials in Kigali; the Rwandan ambassador to DR Congo followed suit in December, thereby affirming the full restoration of diplomatic relations between the former adversaries. In November, **France** and Rwanda agreed to restore diplomatic ties. Other significant diplomatic gains included the restoration of full diplomatic ties with **Angola**, which also promised to assist Rwanda in its efforts to root the FDLR out of eastern Congo. During the fifteenth annual commemoration of the genocide in April, Kagame awarded "hero medallions" to President Yoweri Museveni of **Uganda**, further improving relations between the two countries. Rwanda acceded to the **EAC Customs Union** in July. Kagame acted as chair of the EAC heads of state throughout 2009. The RDF continued to supply peacekeeping troops to the **AU/UN peacekeeping mission** in Darfur throughout 2009. It also continued to partner with the US department of defence. US President Barack Obama honoured all military commitments made to Rwanda under his predecessor, meaning that the **US provided an estimated $ 20 m in annual support to the RDF**.

The government's belief that the **ICTR** was a **product of bad international politics**, rather than providing justice for Rwandans, continued throughout 2009. The RPF linked the failure of the ICTR to prosecute Protais Zigiranyirazo, a man many human rights observers believed to be at the heart of a cabal of extremist Hutu power that organised the genocide, to the arrest of the RPF's chief of protocol, **Rose Kabuye**. Under an international arrest warrant issued by French judge Jean-Louis Bruguière, which accused nine senior RPF officials, including Kagame, of downing the plane that killed former president

Habyrimana, Kabuye had been arrested in Germany in November 2008 and in late January was turned over to France, where the indictment was issued, to enter her plea of not guilty. By the end of 2009, the **Kabuye case had yet to go to trial**, and sources resident in Rwanda reported that, with the warming of diplomatic relations between France and Rwanda late in the year, she would probably not appear in a French court. There was speculation among international diplomats that the RPF had scapegoated Kabuye (traveling on official government business with a non-diplomatic passport) in order to survey Bruguière's indictment and assess the evidence against those named, and to plan its strategy to avoid negative donor reaction to its perceived role in downing Habyarimana's plane (the event that most analysts agreed triggered the start of the 1994 genocide). The **downing of Habyarimana's plane** remained one of the most contested political issues in post-genocide Rwanda, with some pro-Hutu groups arguing that the RPF downed the plane in order to seize political power (rather than continuing to negotiate at the Arusha peace negotiations) and others arguing that it was the French government that downed the presidential plane to assist its Francophone ally.

World Bank president, Robert Zoellick, was one of Rwanda's prominent visitors. Other visiting dignitaries included **Chinese** foreign minister Yang Jiechi, the UN Secretary General's Special Envoy for the Great Lakes Region Olusegun Obasanjo, President Horst Köhler of Germany, and US Deputy Secretary of the Treasury Neal Wolin. **Kagame** received **numerous international accolades and awards**, including the 2009 Clinton Global Citizenship Award for Leadership in Public Service and the International Medal of Peace.

Rwanda was admitted as a member of the **Commonwealth** at its November summit meeting in Trinidad and Tobago, despite a damning report issued by the Commonwealth Human Rights Initiative in July, which concluded that the economic success of the government was built on its repressive human rights record. Senior British diplomats argued that the UK, and other members of the Commonwealth such as Australia, could better assist the RPF with its human rights record from within the Commonwealth. The government had for years, without success, pursued the goal of joining the Commonwealth. This was also in line with the 2008 decision to make English, rather than French, the second official language of the country.

Socioeconomic Developments

The government continued to **promote social reconciliation** among Rwandans through its policy of national unity and reconciliation. The policy made any discussion of ethnicity – of Tutsi, Hutu or Twa identity – illegal (articles 13 and 33 of the revised 2003 Constitution). The policy was the basis of national peace and security. Adherence to the policy by all government bodies was paramount and was monitored by the **National Unity**

and Reconciliation Commission (NURC). RPF loyalists staffed the NURC at all levels of its administration.

The government also continued to implement its development and poverty reduction policy, **Vision 2020**. This was the foundation of the government's economic development plan and was funded by the IMF and World Bank. The implementation of the Vision 2020 policy was mixed, with urban areas benefiting significantly more than rural areas. The quality and availability of infrastructure, including roads, bridges, schools, water, sanitation and health clinics, varied across the country. The northern regions beyond the town centres of Gisenyi and Ruhengeri lacked basic infrastructure. The situation was similar in the south and west where basic infrastructure was limited and only close to town centres such as Butare, Byumba, Cyangugu, Gitarama, and Kibungo. Individuals who did not live within walking distance of principal towns remained among Rwanda's **most vulnerable citizens**, notably widows, orphans and female-headed households. Rural poverty was also shaped by the government's **policy of mono-cropping**, which made it illegal to grow crops for subsistence needs; instead small-holder farmers were told by local authorities to grow coffee, tea and other foreign-exchange producing crops. Heavy rains in some regions and persistent drought in others, along with poor soil quality, meant that Rwanda remained vulnerable to nutritional shortfalls for much of its population. Average prices for the tea and coffee produced by Rwanda fell in 2009, while the cost of exporting their finished product to America and Europe increased. Rwanda's land-locked and hilly terrain meant that the cost of getting products to foreign markets was prohibitive. The government therefore focused its efforts on producing high quality coffee and tea to offset export costs. Some of the costs were foisted through the mono-cropping policy onto peasant farmers, many of whom openly resented the policy. Peasant farmers who resisted or subverted the directive were subject to fines of at least Frw 5000 (rural incomes averaged Frw 100/day) or imprisonment for failure to pay. **Agricultural output continued to drive the economy** with the government announcing an expected 2009 increase in GDP of 5%–6% (much reduced from the 11% growth of 2008). Coffee earned 56% more over 2008 ($ 47 m) while tea revenue was up 24% ($ 42 m).

Rwanda remained on track to meet most of its **MDG targets**, notably in primary school enrolment rates, gender equality in primary and secondary education, a reduction in HIV and malaria prevalence, and women's participation in parliament (56%, the highest ratio in the world). An estimated 5,000 laptops were distributed to primary students through the One-Laptop-per-Child Initiative. Approximately half of the population lived within 5 km of a health clinic. The government remained **unlikely to meet other targets**, especially the goal to eradicate extreme poverty and hunger and the equitable use of land, most likely because of increasing population pressures. Almost 50% of the population lived on an income insufficient to meet basic food needs. Of this percentage of the population, 85% were women. Rural poverty increased across the country while **urban poverty decreased**.

This was probably due in part to the government's mass eviction of people living in low-cost housing in Kigali in late 2008 and early 2009. These individuals were not adequately compensated, and most were returned (in some cases forcibly) to their rural communities of origin.

In October, the government also imposed a **ceiling on prices for vacant land** in Kigali, which limited the value of such land to just 6% of its market value. The government justified the decision, saying it had a right to reduce prices to ensure national security and development. Donors remained mute on the matter, despite the obvious anti-free market quality of the diktat. Donors commented negatively on Kagame's foray into economic policy following the dismissal of finance minister James Musoni in December. Musoni's replacement had been little known hitherto, and donors perceived his elevation from permanent secretary to minister as a sign of **Kagame's interest in controlling economic policy**. The national airline, **Rwandair**, signed a code-share agreement with Virgin Atlantic (to London) and another with Belgium's Brussels Airlines, while Kenya Airways cancelled the existing code-share agreement for fear of endangering its security rating by its association with Rwandair. **High-speed internet** access came on-line in August through the privately owned SEACOM fibre-optic undersea cable connection in Mombasa. By November, the cost of internet access had dropped from $ 2,000 per megabyte to just $ 200. The government lauded both the Rwandair and internet cable deals as evidence of its commitment to market liberalisation and ease-of-access for foreign investors. In October, the World Bank named Rwanda as a **leading reformer** in its Doing Business survey. The country jumped from 139th place in last year's survey to 67th. The survey noted the ease with which businesses can be started, as well as improvements in the hiring and firing of workers and investor protection.

The government continued with its **policy of home-grown solutions** to domestic problems. In January, it announced an **11-year industrial plan** to open up the manufacturing sector to the foreign competition afforded by Rwanda's accession to the EAC. The ministry of agriculture was planning to establish new small-scale agro-industries to add value to products prior to export. Also in January, the government announced that the **Rwanda Revenue Authority** had successfully increased tax-payer compliance to collect $ 619 m. In December, parliament approved a mini-budget covering the first six months of 2009 with the purpose of aligning Rwanda with the fiscal year of the EAC (July–June). In June, the ministry of finance tabled an **expansionary budget** that projected an increase in domestic revenue despite the global economic downturn. Donor funding remained on target, providing Rwanda with a much-needed buffer against external market forces. The government upheld its commitment to improve infrastructure and social spending with a 24% increase in the budget over the mini-budget of December 2008. The IMF spoke positively about Rwanda's mid-year budget, calling it a "necessary stimulus".

Economic growth remained steady at 5%, despite the global credit crunch, because of the agricultural, manufacturing and tourist industries. Inflation remained high, averaging

12% over the course of the year. **Foreign investment** was strategically situated in the energy and telecommunications sectors, both of which were relatively unaffected by the domestic liquidity squeeze that plagued the economy in the middle part of the year. By the end of 2009, the economy was again showing signs of growth as domestic interest rates stabilised at approximately 14%.

Susan M. Thomson

Seychelles

A relatively uneventful year politically was completely dominated by the socioeconomic adjustments that followed from the shock economic reforms introduced in November 2008 to prevent a complete collapse of the national economy. Despite unaccustomed hardships for large parts of the population, there was no noticeable social unrest and the country returned surprisingly quickly to a new situation of economic and financial stability with positive prospects for the future. This impressive recovery was widely praised by international institutions as exemplary. The long-ruling government party continued to dominate the political scene. Somali pirate activities became a major threat and necessitated agreements with several foreign countries for the presence of their navy units in joint anti-piracy action.

Domestic Politics

There were no significant changes in the country's political situation during the year. On 2 June, the long-governing **Seychelles People's Progressive Party (SPPF)** held its 24th national congress in celebration of its 45th anniversary and used the occasion to change its name to **People's Party (PP)** – or **Parti Lepep** in the local Creole language. This move was intended to present a new image in line with the radically changed new policy directions, while at the same time adhering to the old ideals of national unity and social cohesion and creating a link to the original founding name, Seychelles People's United Party (SPUP). **President James Michel** became the first chairman of the new party and was thus able for the first time to assume full political authority; his predecessor, France Albert René, as SPPF chairman, had remained a powerful figure after 2004 and only now withdrew to an honorary position as founder leader. The post of secretary general, previously held by Michel, was handed to Finance Minister Danny Faure. The party's name change did not lead to any substantial alterations, apart from René's exit, and the 25-member executive committee of the PP remained largely the same. Michel and the SPPF/PP successfully managed to ensure unchallenged continuity in the exercise of administrative power throughout the year, while showing a high degree of pragmatism and flexibility in terms of policy reforms that would not have been conceivable a few years earlier. Foreign Minister Patrick Pillay resigned in September and, in the absence of an immediate replacement, his portfolio was added to the president's responsibilities. Despite intermittent rumours of a possible cabinet reshuffle, and even of early elections (not due till 2011), to benefit from the remarkable economic recovery and the surprisingly widespread acceptance of harsh reform measures, nothing of the sort materialised. Increased public attention was turned to the Jj Spirit Foundation, an allegedly non-political youth organisation, but rumoured by the opposition to be a disguised support group for Michel.

The main **opposition** leader, **Wavel Ramkalawan**, and his **Seychelles National Party (SNP)** were faced with the dilemma of opposing the new market-oriented reform policies of the government that they had been demanding for years. The SNP now claimed that the government had converted too radically to a neo-liberal approach and stressed the need for the protection of social security. The SNP experienced several defections, and some senior members reacted positively to cooperation offers from the government and accepted appointments in public institutions; in early March two MPs from the proportional list had to be replaced. In parliament, the SNP generally abstained from voting for economic reform bills. Ramkalawan refused to take part in the regular high-level forum meetings that Michel had proposed on 26 February in his state-of-the-nation address to discuss key national issues between himself, the parliamentary leader of government business and the official leader of the opposition. He felt that his support for the rescue measures in the crisis situation in late 2008 had been misrepresented by government and he saw no value in regular talks, unless some clear conditions were met and concrete government actions were taken. The SNP also boycotted the opening, on 3 December, of the new parliament building, constructed by China, in objection to the use of foreign funds to build a key national symbol.

The small **Democratic Party (DP)**, not represented in parliament, had to find a new leader upon the mid-January resignation of Paul Chow, who wanted to concentrate on his business interests. On 4 March, Ralph Volcere pledged to revive the dormant party. During a DP convention on 27 June, he was confirmed as leader and announced an intended name change to New Democratic Party (NDP). He also explained that the previous alliance with the SNP had ended and that the NDP would field its own candidate in future presidential elections. The DP founder and first Seychelles president (1976–77), James Mancham, remained absent, since he had in January launched his non-partisan Seychelles Foundation for National Reconciliation and Prosperity as the first national think-tank.

Throughout the year, Michel went to great lengths to create a more open and **transparent political climate** than had been the case in the past and also to initiate **reform processes** in several non-economic areas. A special committee was formed to organise activities under the year's national theme '*Koste Seselwa*' (come together Seychellois). In addition to several high-level forum meetings (in SNP's absence just with government business leader Marie-Louise Potter), Michel also launched a new series of public consultations with the people in all districts. Several appointments for leadership positions in public institutions were given to private sector representatives and to members of the political opposition as a clear gesture to promote more national unity. The retirement of five senior police officers in April signalled the start of a thorough reform of the police force, with the help of four Irish police officers. In February, review processes of both the constitution and the criminal justice system got underway, and members of a new human rights commission were appointed. On 21 August, Frederick Egonda-Ntende from Uganda was sworn in as new chief justice in the Supreme Court. The Liaison Unit of NGOs of Seychelles was repeatedly given the opportunity to exchange views with international organisations. Seychelles obtained quite high scores in relation to governance issues in various international indices.

In late March, Seychellois sailors, in two separate incidents, became victims for the first time of the increased geographical range of **Somali pirate activities**. Seven hostages were only released after almost three months of difficult negotiations, and another three hostages only in September in apparent exchange for the highly controversial release of 23 captured pirates, although this was officially denied, with the pirates' release being explained as due to insufficient hard evidence.

Foreign Affairs

The **piracy threat** also became a major foreign policy concern, after Somali pirates had extended their operational range far into the Indian Ocean and near to the Seychelles, since this had immediate strong negative repercussions on the economy with respect to the fishery and tourism sectors. The country emerged as an important sub-regional hub and basis for coordinated international anti-piracy activities and several **"status of forces agreements"** were signed (inter alia with the EU, France and the US). The temporary presence of navy personnel from many different countries in the port of Victoria also had a welcome economic side-effect. Navy units from China, India and Japan also participated in the joint international exercises. A visit by Africom commander William Ward on 19 August highlighted a strengthening of surveillance cooperation with the US, including the use of drones from a base in the Seychelles. Apart from Kenya, Seychelles was the only other sub-regional country where it was possible to legally prosecute and incarcerate suspected pirates. An initiative was started to create a special tribunal for handling such trials. A visit to the United Arab Emirates by Michel in early September mainly centred on increased military cooperation with a view to the UAE becoming a key partner in patrolling the territorial waters with joint naval units, and for setting up a special anti-piracy naval force.

Michel quite successfully continued to pursue an active **outward-looking policy**, which he had started upon assuming the presidency in 2004. This largely paid off, not only with general international praise for the government's determined reform efforts, but also with concrete financial support from various international bodies. An international forum on 18 May in Victoria brought together all the country's main economic partners, appraised the strong local ownership of the reform agenda and confirmed continued international goodwill for the policies being pursued.

Michel used various **international forums** (such as the UN General Assembly in September, the FAO food summit in October and the UN climate conference in Copenhagen in December) and several state visits, to repeatedly stress the particular vulnerability of the Seychelles and the dangers of global climate change. In this context, during a UNESCO conference in October in Paris, Seychelles was entrusted with the co-chairmanship of the grouping of Small Island Developing States. In addition to his attendance at international conferences, Michel was several times in the UAE and visited Japan (April), South Korea and China (October), Lebanon and Cuba (November) with a view to enhancing the country's global visibility.

In April, the Seychelles appeared on an **OECD "white list"** of countries that fully complied with international tax standards. This was in stark contrast to previous years, when the country had long been black-listed and suspected of being a haven for covert money operations. The Seychelles International Business Authority (SIBA), on its 15th anniversary in December, was consequently in search of a new strategy under the changed international finance regime, since SIBA's original creation as a (somewhat dubious) offshore financial centre and an expected third pillar of the national economy had proved to be no longer sustainable.

Socioeconomic Developments

The tiny import-dependent economy recovered surprisingly well from the effects of the near collapse and subsequent introduction of shock reforms in November 2008 and from the repercussions of the global recession. Although **GDP contracted by 7.6%** (substantially less than the initially projected 10.7%) after a preceding small 2008 decline of 0.9%, renewed growth prospects showed potential for a growth rate of 4% for 2010. As a result of both the implementation of a determined governmental reform strategy and strong external support, the **macroeconomic picture** was dramatically **stabilised**. Despite some inevitable hardships resulting from the reform measures that had been introduced, the population by and large accepted the new more market-friendly policies, which initiated a remarkable reversal from the previous welfare-oriented SPPF policies. The quickly recognisable positive results thus led to a renewed climate of confidence, since the PP government was careful not to cut drastically the benefits of the socially-oriented programmes pursued hitherto.

While **inflation** had peaked at 63.3% in December 2008 after the shock devaluation, consumer prices fell continuously from March onwards until November (nevertheless averaging a 31.8% rise for the entire year) and thus recouped some of the initial purchasing power losses. A similar picture was true for the **exchange rate** of the Seychelles Rupee (SR). From a low of SR 16.8 per $ in February, it appreciated to a rate of 10.3 in October and stabilised at around SR 11.3 per $ at the end of the year. This strong recovery of the SR was a clear reflection of new confidence on the part of international and local markets. **Interest rates** similarly fell dramatically from an extreme 29.3% in January to just 3.6% in December. Gross **external reserves** of around $ 190 m by end-2009 were equivalent to about two months' import coverage, a far cry from the extreme shortage just one year earlier. Foreign direct investments slumped considerably from $ 366 m in 2008 to about $ 200 m, due to a slow-down of several large planned projects, but nevertheless maintained a remarkable absolute volume. According to provisional estimates, the **current-account deficit** was practically halved from 45% of GDP (in 2008) to 23% as a result of a 15% decline of exports to $ 428 m (primarily due to reduced canned tuna and lower oil re-export earnings) and a much sharper 30% fall of imports to $ 708 m. The structural **merchandise trade deficit** was thus greatly compressed to $ 280 m, compared with $ 516 m in 2008. With a positive services and transfer account, this enabled the overall balance of payments to turn into a modest surplus ($ 23 m), after a huge deficit ($ 210 m) in 2008.

The government's strong **fiscal discipline** made it possible to exceed the original targets and to achieve a **budget surplus** of 2.9% of GDP, compared with a deficit of 3.3% in 2008. The domestic revenue was estimated to have attained a quota of 35.9% of GDP, a very impressive figure by any account. External grants contributed another 2.3%. With strict control measures, total government expenditure was slashed to 35.4% of GDP. A substantial primary budget surplus (excluding interest payments) of 13.4% of GDP allowed a partial repayment of the huge accumulated external and domestic debt. As a core element of the state's austerity measures, about 2,500 public servants (out of a total 17,000) were dismissed with compensation, and more efforts to outsource public services were underway. Unemployment figures rose from 2% to 4%, but remained manageably low, with a continued need for foreign workers for certain types of jobs.

Several **IMF** missions during the year reviewed the economic performance under the IMF two-year stand-by arrangement, approved as emergency support in November 2008. The assessment was generally very positive and the government was praised for its good compliance with the agreed reform goals. This led the IMF on 22 December to approve a new three-year arrangement under the extended fund facility to the tune of $ 31 m and to cancel the stand-by arrangement prematurely. After many years of conflicting views, this was clear evidence of the government's acceptance of the standard IMF advice. In pursuance of this line, the **AfDB** and the **World Bank** also approved new programme loans to support the economic reforms, in the latter case after an absence of 17 years from the Seychelles. In July, the UAE gave a grant of $ 30 m for building houses and infrastructure over a ten-year period.

A crucial relief for the economy was the exceptional **debt treatment** granted by the Paris Club of official creditors on 16 April: 45% of the nominal outstanding debt stock was to be cancelled in two phases (cutting the debt by $ 70 m to $ 93 m), with the remainder rescheduled over 18 years with five years' grace. This very generous step took care of a substantial part of the clearly unsustainable debt burden. According to the government, by end-2009 the external debt had been reduced from 170% of GDP (at end-2008) to a more sustainable level of 84% of GDP. In December, the government launched a promising proposal for a debt-restructuring deal with commercial creditors to convert their outstanding debts (over $ 300 m) into new discount notes.

As part of a vigorous **public sector reform exercise**, the seven most important parastatal enterprises were screened by a London-based company and a new monitoring unit was created in the finance ministry. A new foreign exchange bill in late June confirmed the total liberalisation of currency dealings already in practice and even stipulated the return to its owners of foreign currency confiscated in 2000/2001 as part of the draconian control measures. The 2010 budget, with emphasis on a wide-ranging overhaul of the tax system and on a second generation of reform measures, was approved on 11 December by the PP majority, with the SNP opposition abstaining. In the World Bank's 2009 "Doing Business" report, the Seychelles dropped six places to 111th, indicating that, despite all the government reforms, there was still need for major improvements in the business environment. In August, the government signed an interim EPA with the EU, since no general conclusion of the lengthy process was in sight.

The key **tourism** sector suffered some decline early in the year, but then experienced a remarkable recovery in the second half. Final visitor numbers for the year were 157,500, just 0.9% lower than in 2008. Tourism earnings probably fell by about 12% in dollar terms, but grew very substantially in local currency terms. An international campaign was mounted under the slogan "affordable Seychelles". The **fisheries** sector, the second pillar of the economy, was badly affected by the increased pirate activities, since probably about a quarter of the regular foreign fishing vessels stayed away. Exports of canned tuna declined by 8% to $ 198 m. On 17 September, a national **university** was inaugurated, with an initial intake of just 55 students.

Rolf Hofmeier

Somalia

Somalia remained effectively divided into three main political zones: the Republic of Somaliland in the north, the autonomous region of Puntland in the northeast, and state-less southern Somalia, where the Transitional Federal Government (TFG) struggled to survive against an increasingly ruthless and uncompromising Islamist insurgency of two radical-Muslim resistance fronts, who refused negotiations for any kind of political deal.

Somaliland maintained relative stability and, despite socioeconomic problems and deeply contested preparations for (delayed) national elections in 2010, was marked by a wide consensus on the political order. The autonomous Puntland government stayed in place but slid more towards authoritarianism and criminality. It could not control either the growing piracy along its shores or the continued influx of thousands of Ethiopian and Somali migrants converging on its ports. High levels of violence, including terror attacks by the Islamist fronts in the south, were evident throughout the year, aggravating the human rights situation and the staggering humanitarian crisis. No political progress was achieved. The TFG, while gaining some ground, remained dependent on protection by AU Mission in Somalia (AMISOM) peace-keeping troops in Mogadishu, and the Islamist fronts were supported by outside forces. In January, the last troops from Ethiopia, ally of the TFG, retreated from Somali soil. The new TFG president was Sheikh Sharif Sheikh Ahmed, and the transitional parliament was enlarged to accommodate most of the former opposition to the TFG when led (until December 2008) by Col. Abdullahi Yusuf. Repeated calls by the TFG and the UN for national dialogue and reconciliation were not heeded by the extremist Islamist fronts, who established themselves in southern parts, e.g. Kismayo. Prospects for southern Somalia remained bleak in view of the weakness of the TFG and the authoritarian and violent agenda of the Islamist resistance fronts, which consistently used intimidation, targeted killings and terror attacks in attempts to dislodge the TFG. Relations of Somaliland and Puntland with neighbouring states were low-key, but piracy endangered the stability of Puntland and also engaged a large international naval force. The Islamist fronts, repeating previous threats to Kenya and Ethiopia, entertained relations with Eritrea, radicalised Somali diaspora groups, several Muslim countries and international Islamist organisations.

Domestic Politics

Somalia remained **divided in three separate regions**, with no signs of any re-integration. While the two autonomous regions Somaliland and (to a lesser extent) Puntland remained stable, southern Somalia continued to be bogged down in violent conflict, instability, chaos and a deep humanitarian crisis. The TFG, in place since 2004, was based in Mogadishu and acquired a **new president** on 31 January: Sheikh Sharif Sheikh Ahmed, the former leader of the defeated Islamic Courts Union (ICU) of 2006. He had been part of the Islamist opposition that regrouped in Asmara in 2007 under the name 'Alliance for the Re-Liberation of Somalia' (ARS). During the year, the ARS split, with the majority of 'moderates' entering the TFG following the 2 June 2008 power-sharing agreement, reached in negotiations in Djibouti. The **TFG** was **broadened** and the **parliament extended** from 270 to a staggering 550 members, enforced by donor countries allied in the Somalia Donor Group. The elections for the presidency in January in Djibouti were narrowly won by Sheikh Sharif against, surprisingly, Masleh Mohammed Siad, son of former dictator Siyad Barre. On 14 February, a candidate from Puntland was appointed as prime minister: Omar Abdirashid Ali Shermarke. The 'transitional charter' was extended until 2011. While the new TFG enjoyed some support in Somalia and its legitimacy and international recognition were confirmed, no stability was reached and no significant moves towards efficient administration were seen. The remnant ARS stayed in Asmara, persisting in rejection and allying itself to the violent Islamist fronts in Somalia, **al-Shabaab** and **Hizbul-Islam**. The latter was a coalition of four militant groups: the Mu'askar Ras Kamboni, the ARS-Asmara, the Mu'askar Anole and the 'Islamic Front', all with a regional or clan basis and regularly at loggerheads. The well-known Salafist radical and enemy of the TFG, Hassan Dahir 'Aweys' of the ARS-Asmara, became a leader, together with ideologue Umar Iman Abubakr and his rival Mohammed Hassan Ahmed. Aweys had returned to Somalia from Asmara on 23 April but refused to meet President Sheikh Sharif. There were reports of talks between them in early September, but they led to nothing.

The **TFG**, which included well-qualified people from Somalia and the diaspora, was still based on a conglomerate of various groups with a clan basis, and could neither significantly extend its influence nor build its institutions. Internal divisions between various army units also remained a problem. In the course of the year, the new president appeared indecisive and lacking in ideas. Few if any policy documents were prepared. The president made foreign trips to ask for funds, but somewhat neglected to build his support in Somalia itself. The TFG was weak in presenting a 'counter-narrative' against the Islamists. However, on 27 March, Sheikh Sharif stated his anti-Al Qaida position: "Al Qaida has never helped Somalis reach a peaceful solution and has never wanted Somalis to have a government.... Al Qaida did not teach us the Islamic religion and has not given us any support so I urge them to leave us alone."

An important development was the growth of the Sufi-oriented, mainstream Muslim movement **'Ahlu as-Sunna wal-Jama'a'** (founded in 1991) into a fighting force, potentially the greatest threat to the Islamist fronts because of its wide community support and the broad appeal of its mainstream 'moderate' version of Islam. Sheikh Sharif, however, remained hesitant to take the movement's advice, and only after tenuous negotiations did the two conclude an agreement to cooperate. The movement held its ground in central Somalia. There were unconfirmed reports that it received some of its weapons from Ethiopia. The 'Ahlu as-Sunna', not being originally a military movement, only reluctantly took up arms in self-defence of Somali Islam and their way of life.

Continuous **armed conflicts and shifting alliances** between members and leaders of the warring groups were evident throughout the year, adding to the proverbially unpredictable and in many ways apocalyptic political landscape of southern Somalia. A notable case was the 'defection' to the TFG of the former warlord Yusuf Mohammed Siyad 'Indha'adde', known for his record of abuse and destruction in southern Somalia in the 1990s. He had been a member of the ICU before December 2006 and later of one of the radical groups in Hizbul Islam. Behind the violence, the shifting membership and the group rivalries were clan politics, but in a less transparent way than before. Several top TFG members were killed in terror attacks by al-Shabaab and Hizbul Islam, including the senior army general Ali Said on 15 June, Umar Hashi Adan, a former security minister, on 18 June in Beledweyn, and Ubyad Ali Fidow, member of the prime minister's security team, on 11 March in Mogadishu.

In the south, **al-Shabaab** and **Hizbul-Islam** took over local administrations, e.g. in Kismayo and Merca, and imposed their authoritarian theocratic politics, including the banning of elections and NGO activities, introducing strict Shari'a punishments (e.g., amputations, stonings and beheadings), restricting the public role of women, imposing dress codes, limiting international food aid programmes, and dishonouring clan elders. They also kept agitating against Sufi Islam, as evident in their continued destruction of the graves of Sufi sheikhs, condemnation of 'non-Islamic' days and festivals, and the prohibition of dancing and singing at weddings, music on the radio, football, the use of the stimulant *qat*, etc.

After protests and even some public demonstrations, as in Kismayo on 9 January, some measure of pragmatism was shown in the actual control of local communities, but more out of temporary expediency than out of conviction. Al-Shabaab also tried to restyle education on a religious basis, in what amounted to religious indoctrination. A dominant motive in their campaigns was a systematic effort to disempower women by prohibiting them from having jobs, being present in public life, or following education. The aim was to force them into a separate sphere from men and relegate them to the home.

Somaliland, the self-declared independent republic of about 3.8 m people, took its own course and refused to be drawn into the quagmire of the south. Its own 2001 Constitution and political institutions were working relatively well. President Dahir Riyale Kahin, however, caused controversy by his attempt to change the Constitution and go for a third term and by delaying the parliamentary and presidential elections originally scheduled for March 2009. The process led to demonstrations and political wrangling with opposition parties, causing unrest. Somaliland's economy grew, but remained fragile. While on the whole peaceful, there were also violent incidents, as in November when a top military commander, Osman Yussuf Nur, was shot and killed in Las 'Aanod in Sool region.

The autonomous region of **Puntland** (ca. 1.9 m inhabitants) saw many problems in the economic and political sphere, with growing authoritarian rule, security problems and entrenched criminality due to the corrosive effect of piracy, organised and supported with the help of several key Puntland figures, and of other criminal groups. Presidential elections were held in January in the 26-member unicameral parliament, resulting in Abdirahman Mohammed Farole replacing Mahmud Muse Hirsi 'Adde' (who was of the same ruling party). The election had limited value as a democratic exercise. In June, a new constitution was promulgated to replace the Puntland Charter of 1998, but it was not the product of broad societal discussion. Puntland experienced a lack of effective law enforcement. President Farole's promise in February to eradicate piracy "within a matter of months" came to nothing. Clan elders and community leaders worked to discourage youngsters in the coastal areas from getting involved in piracy, but with mixed results. Unemployment and the profitability of piracy proved strong incentives to recruitment.

There were no developments in the **low-intensity border conflict** in the Sanaag-Sool and eastern Togdheer regions between Puntland and Somaliland, with the latter still in effective control of the disputed regions.

Especially in southern Somalia, **suicide bombings** by Hizbul Islam and notably al-Shabaab continued throughout the year, accompanied by a jihadist discourse glorifying the criminal violence as Islamic virtue. The idiom of 'martyrdom' surrounding these actions was, however, rejected by a majority of Somalis. None of the perpetrators of unlawful killings were apprehended. Recruitment by the extremist fronts of youths from the US, UK, Gulf States and other diaspora communities continued. A number of foreigners and diaspora Somalis participated in terror missions. In March, there were US congressional hearings about the problems of jihadist recruitment in the US Somali community.

Al-Shabaab and **Hizbul Islam** aimed to install an Islamic state with Shari'a as the only law, and systematically **refused to deal with the TFG** or any other foreign party. They kept on receiving their own support from several foreign governments (according to the UN Monitoring Group on Somalia, Eritrea was amongst them), as well as from elements in several Arab/Muslim countries and from radicalised parts of the Somali diaspora. On several occasions they also publicly claimed loyalty to the Al Qaida agenda, and also continued their attacks on the **AMISOM stabilization force**, which some of their spokesmen equated with the 'Ethiopian occupier troops' – an accusation meant to rally Somalis to their alleged 'Somali nationalist' insurgency. AMISOM, although it caught civilians in cross-fire, tried to assist the TFG and to protect civilian areas as much as possible from ongoing battles and sabotage acts by the Islamist fronts. On 17 September, there was a terrorist attack on an AMISOM compound which killed 21 people, including the Burundian AMISOM deputy force commander.

From 8–14 May, a new **'battle for Mogadishu'** was started by al-Shabaab against the TFG, ending in the Islamists' conquest of more urban territory. There were hundreds of civilian casualties, many of them used as human shields in the fighting. A TFG counter-offensive was not successful. Further heavy fighting followed in July and late August. The aim of al-Shabaab was to dislodge the TFG but, despite some gains, this was not achieved.

After the killing of other al-Shabaab radicals and Al Qaida operatives in 2007 and 2008, **Saleh Ali Saleh Nabhan** (who had also participated in the 1998 attacks in Dar es Salaam and Nairobi and in 2002 on a tourist hotel and an Israeli plane in Kenya), was eliminated in a well-planned US Navy Seals action on 14 September. This left two of the five unit members still alive: Fazul Abdullah Mohamed and Issa Osman Issa.

As a result of the ongoing violence and insecurity created by the Islamist fronts, **human rights and civil liberties** were in very bad shape, with no improvements observable in the areas controlled by al-Shabaab and Hizbul Islam. The TFG record improved, and there were no reports of TFG involvement in targeted killings of civilians or torture. Al-Shabaab and Hizbul Islam rejected the entire concept of human rights and civil liberties, because they thought them 'un-Islamic'. The use of civilians as human shields was common among the Islamist militants, as was the recruitment of children and youngsters by force. Targeted **assassinations of TFG and TFG-affiliated persons** was seen as a legitimate tactic and had dozens of victims, most of them innocent bystanders. A few examples are: the killing of Abdullahi Abdi Egal on 1 January in Baidoa, of Abdillahi Isse Abtidon, an MP, in Mogadishu on 15 April, of Ali Ahmed 'Irro', a Hawiye clan elder, on 7 September, and of *ugaz* Adan Nur Matan, also on 7 September (he was beheaded). The most dramatic case was an al-Shabaab attack on a medical school graduation celebration on 3 December in Hotel Shamo in Mogadishu. A joyous event turned into a massacre when bombs killed more than 22 people (and wounded over 50), including three TFG ministers and many students, parents, teachers and hotel staff. This attack led to an outpouring of rage among the Somali public and later to one of the few public demonstrations against al-Shabaab.

In the course of the year, nine **Somali journalists** were **killed** and several wounded. Some 150 Somali journalists were in exile. The Islamist fronts closed down virtually all private media in the southern areas they controlled and did not allow independent news gathering, let alone foreign journalists.

Al-Shabaab and Hizbul Islam recruited local youngsters and the unemployed, providing them with regular monthly 'salaries' of up to $ 200 and giving them 'authority' to lord it over civilians, especially women. A number of radical Islamist clerics and self-appointed sheikhs or imams, often trained in foreign Islamic institutions, were the increasingly vocal ideologues of the movements. While the young recruits might not have been fully committed to the hardcore ideology of the fronts, these radical clerics became increasingly influential among the young generation.

According to local informants and UN monitors, **Eritrea**, despite its denials, continued to supply arms and training to Islamist fighting forces inside Somalia, but less obviously than in previous years. Al-Shabaab was well-funded by jihadist circles from overseas (private and diaspora sources) as well as by sources in some Middle Eastern states.

Piracy along the southeastern Somali coast increased, becoming a major international concern and threatening relief supply vessels and regular commercial shipping. Towards year's end, 12 of a total of 47 ships captured were still in the hands of pirates. An estimated $ 60 m–$ 80 m in ransom money was paid by shipping companies. The number of vessels attacked (217) was also higher than in the previous year. The policy of the shipping lines and national governments was not effective: paying ransom instead of holding out and improving on-board security measures and arrest rates led to continued growth of pirate ventures, allowing the business to become more professional and more ruthless. Pirates were better organised and better equipped with the latest technology, and operated on a larger scale. Cases of hostage abuse and killing were reported. The naval force present in the area did not act pre-emptively but only in a reactive manner, responding to the pirates when they attacked. The lack of efficient international judicial responses (few courts and countries were ready to put the pirates on trial, although the necessary international law was in place) helped this trend.

The role of the **Somali diaspora** in the civil conflict was significant. Somalia could be said to be a 'diaspora state' in more than one sense. With huge amounts of remittances paid and also with personnel for the TFG (many ministers and parliament members came from outside Somalia) as well as fighters for the Islamist insurgents coming from abroad, Somalia lost its grip on its own domestic political dynamics.

Somaliland was in better shape than southern Somalia and expressed no desire to unite with the rest, but it had its share of problems – notably a limping economy, unemployment, lack of educational facilities, social problems, and a political stalemate between President Dahir Riyale Kahin and the opposition parties about the election delay. There was also a low-key presence of Islamist opponents.

There were no developments in Somaliland's quest for international recognition, necessitating the country's reliance largely on its own (and diaspora remittance) resources, while the collapse of the political order could make the country more susceptible to Islamist sabotage and violence.

Puntland, while having a semblance of order, did not register progress in building its political system or tackle its economic and security problems, including piracy. The proceeds of piracy were invested locally in property and businesses, and many politicians profited from it. Puntland's small coast guard made a few arrests but was no match for the well-organised pirates. Bosaaso port remained the transit point for migrants and refugees trying to reach Yemen and Saudi Arabia. Puntland was also marred by growing corruption and clan group tensions. Respect for human rights deteriorated. In November, two suspected pro-Ogaden National Liberation Front (ONLF) men were arrested on flimsy evidence and died in jail.

Southern Somalia remained hell for humanitarian aid workers, civil society activists, journalists, women's groups and, increasingly, clan elders. The Islamist insurgents used systematic intimidation, threats, abductions and terror attacks against members of these groups. Al-Shabaab militants assassinated elders, women's leaders and sheikhs who opposed their policies and their ban on most NGOs and foreign aid. They proceeded to intensify the recruitment of young men by force, threatening family members. They also used force and abuse to recruit children as combatants. The TFG added its share of abuse, extortion, etc. and occasionally killed civilians in cross-fire, but their record was much better than that of the Islamists.

The **AMISOM force** increased in numbers to some 5,250 (Ugandan and Burundian) soldiers, not yet the projected strength of 8,000, but a significant increase. They protected the presidential compound, government buildings, the port and the airport, and guarded certain checkpoints and main roads in Mogadishu. AMISOM made little difference to the overall domestic military situation. Its mandate did not allow it to forcefully extend its range.

The **civilian population** was again the main victim of the ongoing violence, although many of them also supported specific parties or armed groups in the conflict. An estimated 1,000 to 1,300 civilians were killed during the year in Mogadishu alone.

Foreign Affairs

Foreign policy was conducted by the separate Somali entities. The **TFG** continued to receive support from the UN, Western donor countries and neighbouring countries such as Ethiopia and Kenya (e.g. via IGAD), although no major all-out effort was made to prop up the regime. The TFG's performance was seen as very poor, and its disunity prevented foreign partners from supplying it uncritically with funds and other support. Several training programmes (e.g. for the Somali police) were started, and some arms shipments for the TFG army were sent, but international donors, united in the Somalia Donor Group, withheld support in an attempt to put pressure on Sheikh Sharif's administration to forge unity and come up with a different formula to expand power. The Somali political system, traditionally based on localised, decentralised power units, did not cooperate to form a state administration from above, and Sheikh Sharif did not show enough vigour to pursue a strong federal agenda and engage the local power blocks in coming together.

Somaliland, which had declared independence in 1991, still found no recognition internationally but enjoyed good political and economic relations with Ethiopia, Djibouti, Yemen and a number of other countries, including in the West. Its relations with Puntland saw no marked improvement due to the lingering border problem.

Puntland was largely absorbed by its internal political problems and by piracy. It was under international pressure to tackle the latter, but due to capacity problems and the complicity of leading figures in the piracy, it did not register much progress. Puntland's foreign relations were low-key and informal. Cooperation with Ethiopia (in economic and security matters) and with Yemen was maintained.

Ethiopia fully withdrew its troops from Somalia in January. They had assisted the TFG in the offensive against Islamist radicals. However, Ethiopia's forces remained present just across the border to monitor developments and were reported to have given occasional support to pro-TFG forces in northern areas and to be closely monitoring the field situation. An earlier TFG request to the UN for international **peacekeepers** in southern Somalia was not met.

Socioeconomic Developments

No official and reliable figures on socioeconomic indicators were available on GDP, government budgets, tax revenues, imports and exports, health developments, debt, etc. With the Somali economy being largely an informal one, driven by private initiative and often semi- or illegally organised, all figures were guesswork. Since the UN estimate of 2006 of per capita GDP at $ 283, no new figures became available. Agriculture (production of tropical fruits, charcoal, hides, and fish and livestock for export) accounted for an estimated 40% of GDP and about 65% of export earnings, the rest being from foreign trade. The chief imports remained sugar, sorghum, corn, the stimulant *qat*, machinery, including electronic equipment, and weapons.

Somalia had virtually **no productive economy** outside agriculture or animal herding – i.e., no mining or industry, except for some small-scale artisanal enterprises, sugar refineries and textile businesses. There was again lack of rain during the year, leading to crop shortages, price rises and famine conditions. Somalia's main income consisted of overseas **remittances** from the Somali diaspora, which reached an estimated $ 1 bn. Many Somalis were dependent on these remittances for survival, investment, education, etc.

The **Somaliland** 2009 budget was only a projected $ 50 m, with half of it destined for the security forces, the executive and public sector salaries. The country's economy, surviving with virtually no foreign aid or direct investment due to its unrecognised status, registered growth but was severely hurt by drought, affecting livestock herds and water supplies. Somaliland's exports were predominantly livestock, hides, skins, myrrh and frankincense. Self-reliance slowed down overall growth but avoided the pitfalls of donor dependency. Trade with Ethiopia, Djibouti and Saudi Arabia increased. Hargeisa port grew, chiefly due to Ethiopian import and export business. Somaliland's main revenue, however, came again from diaspora remittances, estimated to be at least $ 300 m. On and offshore oil and gas fields remained unexplored. During the year, the Djiboutian 'Banque pour le Commerce et l'Industrie – Mer Rouge' opened a branch in Hargeisa, the first bank other than the National Bank of Somaliland.

Puntland's budget was about $ 17.6 m, dwarfed by the income from piracy ransoms, estimated to have reached about $ 60 m–$ 80 m. While it did not all remain in Puntland but flowed to operators in Kenya, some Gulf states and other countries where organisational hubs of the piracy networks were located, much of the money was locally invested in real estate and other ventures. Puntland's exports apart from livestock were fish (lobster, dried fish and tuna), sea salt, frankincense, gum arabic and some manufacturing products. Agriculture and livestock herding suffered greatly from the drought, with an estimated 195,000 people facing acute food and livelihood crises.

Somalia's economy overall saw much **private and informal activity** in trade, import-export, contraband and telecom networks, but the level of development and production was very low, and poverty was rampant. There was no central bank in southern Somalia. The economy was marked by versatile informal entrepreneurial activities, but was unregulated and provided no reliable tax base. Telecoms, transport, arms sales, crime and contraband flourished. Somalia's internationally well-connected business elite was an important political player behind the scenes, with some members supporting the Islamists and others the TFG.

Food scarcity and **high food prices** were registered across Somalia. Crime rates – theft, raiding, land grabs, rape, abduction, etc. – remained high, in addition to the violence of the Islamist fronts. Corruption was an endemic trait of Somali economic and political life.

The physical **environment** suffered further as a result of the unregulated depletion of the natural habitat, erosion, and substantial pollution. Game animals were shot for local consumption as well as export, and the few remaining forests continued to be used for unrestricted charcoal burning. The resource base of Somalia's economy, notably in the south and in Puntland, declined, and competition over land and water increased, leading regularly to local ('clan') conflicts. Somalia's mineral resources were not explored or exploited, due to the absence of security and law. Contracts given earlier by the TFG to several foreign companies could not be implemented.

Public health problems in the wake of the civil war and the absence of an adequate health infrastructure were appalling. While no reliable statistics were available, there was a continued scarcity of hospitals, doctors, nurses and supplies, and little investment due to the dismal security and humanitarian situation. In Somaliland, the health situation was somewhat better, but still far from satisfactory. Somalia's last recorded ranking on UNDP's HDI of 2001 had been 161 (out of 163).

Some **foreign NGOs** continued to assist the health sector, but several left in the course of the year due to continued harassment and death threats from al-Shabaab and Hizbul Islam. The NGOs and UN agencies working in medical and emergency aid sectors paid regular 'protection' money and were also subject to extortion, intimidation and threats. UN agencies spent several hundred millions of dollars on humanitarian programmes, serving an estimated 3 m people in need.

Educational structures remained underdeveloped and were only kept running with large private inputs. Somaliland had primary schools serving more than 108,000 children and also had five universities. In the south and in Puntland, many schools were run by Islamic charities with foreign or diaspora funding. Most children received no formal education or only went to Qur'anic schools. Universities and colleges had very limited places and were underdeveloped as centres of learning due to lack of funds, poor academic culture, Islamist intimidation and the persistent insecurity notably in the south. Most promising were those in Somaliland and Puntland (four universities), supported by diaspora funding and academic alliances abroad.

Migration flows were due to refugees and IDPs moving from place to place and to neighbouring countries. They related to conflict patterns and went in several directions: Somalis into Kenya, Ethiopia, Djibouti to escape violent clashes, Ethiopians and southern Somalis moving to Bosaaso and entering Yemen or Saudi Arabia for work or asylum. This led to human trafficking and illegal migration. Hundreds of people were again drowned in the Gulf of Aden in accidents or were forced overboard when Yemeni coast guards were sighted. Hundreds of Somalis also reached Europe or the Middle East to take refuge and ask asylum.

The number of **IDPs** grew by several hundred thousand to 1.5 m at the end of the year, notably due to the fighting in Mogadishu, which was emptied of more than 60% of its population compared with 2004. Refugee flows continued to Kenya, Ethiopia, Djibouti and overseas. Some 40,000 people fled to Kenya. A similar number fled to Ethiopia, despite insecurity in the Ogaden. Puntland and Somaliland remained hospitable to tens of thousands of refugees and IDPs from the South.

Jon Abbink

Sudan

It was a year of growing tensions, which began with the ICC indictment of President al-Bashir for the government's part in the conflict in Darfur. This was rejected by the government, though fears that it would lead to the expulsion of the UN were not realised. Meanwhile, the level of violence in Darfur dropped, though general insecurity for many of the population continued. There were several rounds of Darfur peace talks in Qatar, but no agreement by the year's end. In contrast, violence flared up in a number of places in the South. Much of it appeared to be south-south fighting of a largely ethnic character, though there were accusations of outside interference. The preparations for the 2010 elections continued, though there were difficulties. The census figures on which constituencies were to be based brought dispute, especially in the South. Voter registration at the end of the year also brought some further tension, again in the South in particular. The economy slowed at the start of the year as world oil prices fell, but picked up in the later months. In foreign relations, the major development was the formulation by the Obama administration of a new US Sudan policy, which was energetically pursued by its new envoy.

Domestic Politics

The political pace accelerated during the year towards the presidential, parliamentary and state **elections** originally scheduled for 2009, but which had been **postponed to 2010**, as well as the referendum on the future of the South in 2011. However, the first major political event of the year was not directly concerned with either of these events, but involved the investigation of **President Omar Hassan al-Bashir** by the **ICC** at The Hague with regard to his personal responsibility for the violence in Darfur from 2003. In particular, it was claimed that it was his deliberate policy, after the initial success of a rebel attack at the start of 2003, that had led to the establishment and arming of local militia, which became internationally known as the 'Janjaweed'. The case had been referred to the ICC by the UN Security Council, and it was the first investigation by the court of a serving head of state. On 4 March, the ICC Prosecutor, Luis Moreno-Ocampo, announced that he was indicting al-Bashir and two others, Ahmed Haroun (ironically the minister for humanitarian affairs) and Ali Kushayb (a 'Janjaweed' leader) on charges of crimes against humanity and war crimes, though a charge of genocide, which some had thought possible, was not included.

The charge against al-Bashir was not unexpected and, predictably, the Sudanese government, which had not signed up to the ICC, rejected it vehemently. Indeed it went on the attack, depicting the charge as a hostile Western act against an Islamic country and staging popular demonstrations to denounce the court and its backers. Other political groups in the country, however, took different views. Hassan al-Turabi, the eminence grise behind the coup that brought al-Bashir to power in 1989 but who had broken with him ten years later, announced that al-Bashir should be arrested and sent for trial. For saying this, al-Turabi was imprisoned though soon released once more. However, the Sudan Peoples' Liberation Movement (SPLM), the southern-based partner of al-Bashir's National Congress Party (NCP) in the Government of National Unity (GNU) since the Comprehensive Peace Agreement (CPA) of 2005 that had ended the civil war in the South, was more ambiguous, siding outright with neither al-Bashir nor the ICC.

There had been speculation that the indictment would lead to a break between the GNU and the UN, and that the latter, which was heavily involved in the country following the CPA and the conflict in Darfur, might be expelled. However, the government decided not to isolate itself to that degree and instead contented itself with expelling 13 international NGOs, a move which in the end made little difference to the delivery of aid in Darfur. Nor, in spite of al-Bashir's threats, did the indictment have much impact on the **implementation of the CPA**. Nevertheless, though an immediate crisis was avoided, the issue of the ICC indictment was to rumble on for the rest of the year. One immediate impact was on al-Bashir's foreign travels, which were substantially curtailed and mainly confined to Arab states, where he felt in no danger of a possible arrest.

In May, al-Bashir announced his acceptance of the results of the **2008 national census**. The results themselves were the subject of dispute, especially in the South, where the population figure of 8.2 million, 21% of the country's total population, was lower than expected by the Government of Southern Sudan (GoSS), which felt it should have been closer to one third of the national total of 39 million. The census results also had implications for the preparations for the 2010 elections, since they would form the basis for the constituencies for the national parliament that the National Election Commission (NEC) was preparing. With progress on the elections proving slower than originally hoped, the NEC announced in July that they would be put back from the already delayed date of February 2010 to April of the same year.

With the elections in sight, there was also work on a **new press law**. The opposition parties had long complained about the restrictions on the press imposed by the security forces. These had included security officials closely monitoring newspapers as they came off the presses and, on occasions, suspending licences to publish. Such censorship had long been criticised and, in June, a new press law was introduced. This was seen as only a partial concession, and indeed the habit of interfering with the press persisted in practice.

As part of his assertion of authority in the face of the ICC charge, at the end of June, al-Bashir led the country in **celebrations** of his **20 years in power**. Having seized power in a coup in 1989 and survived a number of challenges to his position, he was reminding both Sudan and the international community that he had held power for longer than any of the country's rulers since its independence in 1956. However, there was still a good deal of speculation about tensions within the ruling party and, in August, one of its leading insiders, Director of the National Intelligence and Security Service Salah Gosh, was sacked. The reasons for his dismissal were not announced, but there had been embarrassment when Chad released a recording of a telephone conversation in which Gosh appeared to be encouraging the Chadian opposition movement, which had in recent years launched two major attacks on the capital Ndjamena.

With the first competitive multi-party **elections** since 1986 **fast approaching**, the opposition parties spent much of the year trying to strengthen their positions, particularly vis-à-vis the NCP. Some claimed that, since July marked the time when elections should have been held according to the CPA, the transitional period was over and the GNU was therefore no longer legal. In its place they called for a national government made up of a broader range of parties. Predictably, this call was swiftly rejected by the NCP and the SPLM.

Nevertheless, the **SPLM** was in a somewhat ambiguous position with regard to the postponed elections, since it was the junior partner in the GNU and might have been expected to enter a continuing power-sharing pact with the NCP in the election campaign. However, the SPLM was by no means happy about its relationship with the NCP in the GNU, often feeling that the NCP asserted the right to speak as the government without reference to its junior partner. Partly due to this discontent, the SPLM decided that it would compete with the NCP in the national elections, including the presidency itself, as well as standing in the elections in the South. Meanwhile the NCP was preparing its electoral machine throughout the year. The party had set aside a substantial amount for the campaign, rumoured to be $ 500 m, and was increasing its activities especially in the towns, where the census revealed that nearly half the population now lived, and in central areas of the country, where it believed there had been sufficient economic expansion for it to hope for significant support.

In addition, having been in power since 1989, many of its supporters had been appointed to state positions at all levels and could use state resources to build support.

One important issue related to the elections was whether other parties would compete individually, or work together as a **national alliance against the NCP**, as they had done in the years before the signing of the CPA, when they had been known collectively as the National Democratic Alliance. In October, the SPLM hosted an All Political Parties Conference in Juba, attended by the main opposition parties, but not the NCP, which resulted in the Juba Declaration whereby all the parties called on the NCP to lift the restrictions on their freedoms of expression, organisation and political activity. In the following month, the SPLM even withdrew from the seats it held in the nominated national parliament established under the CPA; while all the opposition parties threatened to boycott the forthcoming elections. Faced with this threat to the legitimacy of the elections, the NCP did make some concessions with regard to the existing restrictive laws, but there were still incidents with regard to the press and public meetings that gave rise to concern. By the end of the year, some progress had been made towards a more level playing field for the elections, but the opposition parties still found cause for complaint and continued to threaten to boycott the elections if they were not satisfied with the conditions in which they would eventually be held.

The developments around the Juba conference led to speculation about **possible new electoral alliances**. There was talk of the NCP coming to an arrangement with the Popular Congress Party, which had been set up by al-Turabi after he left the NCP as a result of his split with al-Bashir in 1999. Al-Turabi, a wily politician, was still an appealing figure to many Islamists, amongst whom he had built a personal following ever since the 1960s, and there was speculation that his new party could be a direct threat to the NCP amongst the Islamists. There was also speculation that the SPLM might align with the Umma Party, led by Sudan's last elected prime minister, Sadiq al-Mahdi, who was overthrown by al-Bashir's coup in 1989. Sadiq, an energetic leader, was endeavouring to re-unite his party and re-awaken its support in the north, though its traditional areas of strength such as Darfur and Blue Nile appeared changed as a result of the conflicts. However, in the event, neither of these possible alliances came to pass, although there was clarification about presidential candidates, around which subject there had been much speculation. As expected, the NCP declared that al-Bashir would be its candidate. The NCP had also hoped that the SPLM would not put up a rival candidate for the national presidency, and made it clear that, in return, the NCP would not nominate a candidate of its own for the presidency of the South. When the SPLM announced that it would after all compete with al-Bashir, it was thought at first that the candidate might be the GoSS president, Salva Kiir, but he decided to run for the leadership of the South again and the SPLM nominated instead Yasir Arman, its leader in the north, to challenge al-Bashir.

By November, interest had moved on to the issue of **voter registration**. This was only possible once the census had been completed and the constituency boundaries adjusted accordingly. It had been intended that voter registration would be completed by the end of November, but it was decided that, because of problems of registration in parts of the South and Darfur, it would be extended into early December. It was generally regarded as quite successful and recorded a figure nationally of 71% of the eligible population. However, critics argued that the NCP had been able to influence registration, especially in those central areas of the country where it was hopeful of good support. In the South, registration was put surprisingly high at 94% and it was noted that, with the SPLM in disagreement with the census figures, high registration was seen as a form of compensation. In at least one area, the number of voters registered was higher than the figure returned in the census.

In August, the Permanent Court of Arbitration (PCA) in The Hague gave its long-awaited **ruling on Abyei**, the border area between north and south, which is important for the oil wells in the area, amongst other things. In 2005, Abyei was administered as part of Western Kordofan, in northern Sudan, but in the early years of British rule it had been in Bahr al-Ghazal in the south; the population is a mixture of peoples who regard themselves as northerners and southerners and both had claims on Abyei. Under the CPA, there was to be an international panel of experts to decide on the boundaries of Abyei in the light of the area's history and, following that settlement, there would be a referendum in 2011, at the same time as the referendum on the south's independence, to decide if the people of Abyei would remain in the north or become a part of Southern Sudan. The international Abyei Boundaries Commission subsequently produced a report generally seen as favouring the south, but although under the CPA it was to be accepted by both sides, the NCP rejected it. It was then agreed by the NCP and the SPLM that the whole matter would be referred to the PCA. The PCA ruling reduced the size of Abyei, excluding many of the northerners and most importantly putting two more oilfields, Heglig and Bamboo, outside Abyei and definitely in the north. The South was now likely to gain the support of Abyei in the 2011 referendum, but had lost its share of the revenue of the two oilfields.

However, work on demarcating the whole of the **border between the north and the south** continued to be slow. It was intended that the new border would accord with the one in place at independence in 1956, but the record from that time was not entirely clear. It was a crucial issue for both the GNU and the GoSS in terms of the peoples who would be eligible to take part in the referendum and, if there was to be separation, its precise position could affect both oil and the movements of the border region's many pastoralists. It was thus understandable that progress has proved slow and difficult; though meanwhile the SPLM has been trying to assure the Rizeigat pastoralists on the northern side of the likely border that, in the event of separation, they will still be able to migrate south of the border as they have done for centuries in the dry season.

In the South, politics took on a different character. The **SPLM** was clearly the dominant party and although a number of other parties emerged, they were quite small and not expected to mount a major challenge. However, there was still talk of divisions within the SPLM. Riek Machar, a Nuer leader who had once broken from the SPLM and then re-joined, was seen as an emerging leader, though he took care not to be seen openly to challenge the president of the GoSS, Salva Kiir, who comes from the Dinka, the largest ethnic group and the core of the SPLM and the army (SPLA) behind it. Instead, Riek was expected to run for the vice presidency of the GoSS. Another prominent Nuer was Paulino Matip, who had led a rival force to the SPLA, known as the Southern Sudan Defence Force, which had had the support of the NCP in the civil war. After the signing of the CPA, Salva Kiir had won Paulino over to the SPLM side, but there was still concern that Paulino continued to harbour his own ambitions. In October, there were clashes between his men and SPLA forces in the oil-producing area of Bentiu, which required intervention by troops of the UN Mission in Sudan (UNMIS). Lam Akol, the former foreign minister, was another prominent figure who had support among the Shilluk of Upper Nile and appeared increasingly likely to split from the SPLM and launch his own party as the year progressed. There were even rumours in June that Lam and two other prominent Shilluk were plotting to oust Salva Kiir, forcing the latter to nip this move in the bud; this was followed shortly afterwards by the widely expected emergence of a new breakaway party led by Lam Akol and called SPLM-DC (Democratic Change). It came a month after a group of small Southern political parties opposed to what they saw as the dominance of the SPLM met for a conference in Kenana in the north. The venue encouraged accusations that the meeting was sponsored by the NCP with the intention of undermining the SPLM's strength in the South. Such political manoeuvres contributed to rising tensions within and between ethnic communities in the region. The Dinka are the largest group and dominate in the SPLA/M, yet amongst them there were strains between the Bor Dinka and other groups from further north. In the far south in Equatoria, there were not only fears of domination by the Dinka from the north, but that within Equatoria itself the Toposa might be seeking domination.

The GoSS found itself running into financial and administrative problems as well, with reports that both the Bank of Southern Sudan and the Nile Commercial Bank, the major private bank, were running short of cash. With the fall in global oil prices reducing revenues, the GoSS was hard put to maintain the limited services it provided, while there was also mounting criticism of maladministration, which was resulting in intermittent failures to pay salaries and pensions. In addition, there were charges of corruption, some of which the GoSS recognised, and in an effort to address them Salva Kiir announced a number of prominent dismissals. However, the charges did not go away but re-appeared intermittently throughout the remainder of the year.

June also saw an announcement by SAB Miller of South Africa that a new brewery in Juba, the first anywhere in Sudan since the introduction of Islamic law in 1983, would be producing White Bull Lager. However, this was an exceptional development and private international investors overwhelmingly avoided the region, concerned about stability and security in uncertain times regarding the South's future.

However, the greatest concern in the South was the **rising level of violence**, with the UN recording approximately 2,500 people killed in various clashes, with particularly bad fighting in the major town of Malakal in Upper Nile. The nearby state of Jonglei also saw a fresh outburst of ethnic fighting in April between the Murle, the Bor Dinka and the Lou Nuer. In July, there were further bloody clashes between the Lou and Jikany branches of the Nuer. As well as those who were killed, the UN estimated that a further 350,000 were displaced during the year. It was claimed that, overall, the level of violence in the South in 2009 was higher than that in Darfur. Much of the fighting was attributed to ethnic clashes, often associated with land disputes and cattle raids, which have sometimes been intensified by the return home of soldiers and displaced people following the ending of the war. It was also suspected that the drop in international food aid after the war was increasing local struggles over land: on the Ugandan border it was noted that former Dinka refugees, now deprived of outside food supplies, had been seizing land from local Mardi. Efforts by state governments to implement policies of disarmament were also sometimes met by violent resistance. However, it was a mark of the suspicion of the two parties in the GNU that the SPLM accused the NCP of being behind some of the clashes with the aim of trying to destabilise the South. It was also reported that in some of the clashes the fighters included uniformed men with modern weapons, and though there was no clear evidence of the original sources, rumours abounded.

Throughout the year, the GoSS was becoming increasingly focussed on the **referendum in 2011**, and frustrated by the NCP's reluctance to make progress on the referendum law that would outline the arrangements and conditions for the biggest decision on Sudan's future since independence in 1956: would it be one country or two separate states? Such was the level of frustration that, by September, various Southern leaders were starting to threaten that the region should make a unilateral declaration of independence if there was no progress. The NCP, concerned about continuing access to the South's oil revenues in particular, wanted to set the bar for separation high and initially proposed that it would require a 75% turnout and then a 75% vote in favour of the South's independence. It also wanted to include as many people of southern origin living in the north as possible, believing that they would be likely to vote against separation. For its part, the SPLM wanted the referendum to be based on a simple majority of the voters, with the latter restricted to people of southern origin living in the South. After much haggling, an agreement was reached in December, under which southerners living in the South would vote, together with southerners in the north who had moved there after independence in 1956. A decision for separation in the referendum would require a 60% turnout, and a 60% vote in favour. While the referendum law was finally agreed, the Referendum Commission would have many further issues to address before the decision is finally taken in January 2011, though it was widely believed that the trend in public opinion amongst southerners was clearly towards choosing independence.

The overall picture of **Darfur** was quieter than in earlier years. The joint UN-AU force in Darfur (UNAMID) was approaching its target of 26,000 military and police and better able to offer some form of protection to civilians, though there were still violent outbreaks throughout the year. In May, however, there was a fresh confrontation between people on both sides of the border between Darfur and Kordofan immediately to the east, with the suggestion that it may have been over control of land that it was rumoured might contain new oil finds. According to the UN, some 2.6 million people, a third of the region's population, remained in IDP camps, with few feeling able to return to their homes. Humanitarian agencies continued to provide relief, though there were a number of incidents of NGO staff being kidnapped for ransom during the course of the year. It was an indication of the rising scale of banditry in parts of the region. For those still in the countryside, there was better news, with improved harvests. Much of the political attention centred on the continued search for peace. Qatar had sought to take the initiative in peacemaking, supported by the UN-AU joint mediator, Djibril Bassole, and there were successive rounds of talks in Doha between the government and the Justice and Equality Movement (JEM), which increasingly appeared to be the major force in the region. However, the Sudan Liberation Movement (SLM), which was said to speak for the large Fur population, chose not to participate and its leader, Abdel Wahid, remained in Paris. Libya also continued to seek to play a role and, in October, it hosted talks aimed at bringing a number of small factions together, very much in line with its general disposition of trying to work with grassroots community representatives.

One new element in the situation was the establishment by the AU of a high-level team under the leadership of former president of South Africa, Thabo Mbeki. Its recommendations at the end of the year were not confined to Darfur but, in view of the time and attention it gave to the region, it was largely seen in that light. It suggested that peace talks be more inclusive, including civilian groups as well as parties to the conflict. While not going against the ICC's investigation of Darfur, the team recommended that hybrid courts be established, including local and international judges. This was swiftly rejected by the NCP, which claimed that Sudan's courts were perfectly capable of trying any cases arising from Darfur, though few other observers of the independence of the judiciary shared that confidence. Critics also suggested that, with the recommendation of hybrid courts, the AU panel was seeking to bypass the question of the ICC's indictment of al-Bashir. With the example of South Africa in mind, it also spoke of the need for a commission to address issues of truth, justice and reconciliation as an additional measure to contribute to conflict resolution.

Foreign Affairs

Darfur also contributed to the continuing problems of relations with **Chad**. In May, there were new talks between the two governments, but little was achieved that stabilised the situation, with more clashes in the border area and accusations by Chad that Sudan was supporting a new opposition movement in eastern Chad, called the Union of Resistance Forces. The relationship between Chad and Sudan was important for both countries. Both President Idriss Déby and his predecessor, Hissène Habré, had launched their takeovers of power from Darfur; while the JEM in particular had received significant support from Chad. By the end of 2009, the importance of the relationship was growing, but a stable agreement had yet to be achieved and may require wider international pressure.

Following the announcement of the ICC indictment, al-Bashir underlined his rejection of the move by visiting a number of neighbouring countries that were not signatories to the ICC convention. His travels focussed on **Arab League members** in particular, since that organisation had specifically denounced the indictments. The AU was also generally hostile, with the notable exception of Botswana, though al-Bashir was more circumspect in his African travels, fearing that Western powers, including the US (though not itself a signatory to the ICC), might pressurise African hosts to make an arrest.

In April, Sudan received the first visit from the new **US special envoy**, Scott Gration, at a time when the new Obama administration was discussing a fresh policy for the country after a period of drift in Washington following its involvement in the CPA in 2005. In June, Gration visited China for talks with his Chinese counterpart, Liu Guijin, an indication of US acceptance of the importance of China in international engagement with Sudan. This was followed by an invitation for a Sudanese delegation to go to Washington, where talks were held with representatives of both the NCP and the SPLM on the problems of implementing the CPA. Throughout these contacts, the US deliberately avoided any direct dealing with al-Bashir because of his indictment by the ICC.

In September, the **US** finally clarified its policy on Sudan. The GNU had hoped that progress on the CPA would lead to the normalisation of relations between the two countries, but this was not to be the case. There were people in the new Obama administration who had a very critical view of the Sudan, going back to their earlier experience in the Clinton years, notably Susan Rice, the influential new US ambassador to the UN. Thus the policy review did not lift US sanctions or take Sudan off the list of states giving support to terrorism. Normalisation would not be possible without a settlement on Darfur and continuing progress on the CPA, which would not be complete until the referendum in the South in 2011. The new policy also had an annex indicating measures that the US might take if Sudan did not proceed on Darfur and the CPA, but this was kept secret. However, with a peace settlement in the South and Darfur less violent than in recent years, the level of interest in Sudan amongst the American public was diminishing.

As Sudan's closest ally amongst the permanent members of the UN Security Council, **China** continued to strengthen bilateral relations. In November, a new agreement was signed by which China would assist in the doubling of Sudan's oil-refining capacity. China had large investments in Sudan, and Sudan's oil made a significant contribution to China's oil imports. It had concern for the stability of the country and sought to win the friendship of the GoSS as well as the GNU, including making loans to the former to help it through revenues lost due to the fall in oil prices. To a lesser extent, India also had oil and other interests in Sudan, and favoured stability.

In September, the Nile Basin Initiative (NBI) meeting brought about a major difference of approach between Sudan and Egypt on one side and the other seven African member countries on the other. Egypt and Sudan had signed a legal agreement in 1959 to share the Nile waters between them, and no other international agreement relating to the river was currently in place. At that time, the Nile waters were of less concern in Africa, but rising populations and environmental decay had produced new demands for a share of the waters, which Sudan and Egypt, with their large populations and irrigation schemes, were reluctant to concede. However, the issue will not go away and the demands on the Nile from all countries will grow in the years to come.

It was also notable that the GoSS was starting to develop its own external relations and its president, Salva Kiir, visited first **Libya** and then **Egypt**, where there was concern about the possible implications of the South opting for secession in the 2011 referendum. Libya's leader, Muammar Kadhafi, had in the past appeared to take different positions with regard to the possible independence of the South, but he was concerned about the future of Sudan as a whole, especially as it affected Darfur, with which Libya has a common border and from where many thousands of people have moved to Libya seeking work. Egypt was particularly concerned that, if the South chose independence, it might ally with the African countries that are putting pressure on Egypt in the NBI.

African states also had varying approaches to Sudan. **Ethiopia** continued to benefit from Sudan's oil boom and had concern for its future stability. Were it to become more unstable, it would have consequences both for western Ethiopia and the provision of oil and power affecting the country as a whole. **Eritrea** remained hostile to Ethiopia, with its border dispute unresolved, and sought an active regional policy in response to what it believed were Ethiopia's hegemonic ambitions. Thus Eritrea continued to keep a watch on eastern Sudan, where it had been involved in the making of the Eastern Sudan Peace Agreement in 2007, and also had links to the JEM in Darfur. Both Eritrea and Libya had military observers on the Darfur border. **Uganda** may have been less concerned about Sudan as a whole and some of its businessmen had profited from links both during the war years and afterwards. Their main concern was likely to be with the South, and the opportunities that might be created there if it chooses independence.

International organisations continued to be important in 2009. In addition to **UN** support for UNAMID, UNMIS continued with its large-scale countrywide activities even after the ICC indictment of President al-Bashir was announced. These included major operations in the South, though it was increasingly recognised in UN circles how complex the problems of the region actually were. The main **AU** activity in 2009 was the delegation to Darfur led by Thabo Mbeki. His panel's report, however, sought to put Darfur in a wider perspective; it was entitled "A Global Political Agreement", and referred to "the Sudanese crisis in

Darfur". The report was accepted by the AU, which then set up a High-Level Implementation Panel, but it remained to be seen whether it would be capable of much impact with only a short time left before the elections and the South's referendum. The IGAD, the body that had officially managed the CPA, also continued to keep watching developments and was preparing to step in to support the implementation of the CPA right through to July 2011, when the interim period was finally scheduled to end and Sudan would be either one country or divided into two.

Socioeconomic Developments

The **US sanctions** on Sudan contributed to isolating the country from much of the effects of the global credit crunch. The economy continued to grow, with GDP estimated at $ 92.8 bn, though the rate of growth slowed down considerably to 3.8%. Nevertheless, there were still a number of local problems, central amongst which was the fall in oil prices in the first half of the year, which reduced government income, and there was relief when prices picked up again in later months. Some 65% of the revenue of the GNU was derived from oil exports, and the figure for the GoSS was even higher, so, while Sudan's recent economic growth continued, it remained heavily influenced by international prices. In particular, the falling oil price had tipped **Sudan's trade into deficit** for the first time since there had been significant oil exports, though by the end of the year the picture improved, with total exports estimated at $ 8.5 bn, exceeding imports of $ 6.8 bn. Largely due to oil, government revenues totalled just over $ 9 bn, while expenditure was $ 10.8 bn. There were also inflationary pressures, though inflation remained at an average of around 9%, which was less than in 2008. The combination of lower oil revenues and concerns about security, as well as Sudan's political future more generally, tended to hold down the level of international investment during the course of the year. In August, the IMF recommended a policy of tighter fiscal regulation and a flexible exchange rate for the coming 18 months.

There were reports throughout the year of the continuing **high level of expenditure** on **armaments** by both the GNU and the GoSS, in spite of repeated assertions by both that they did not intend to return to conflict. Meanwhile, comparatively little was being spent on the kinds of social welfare, health and education projects that might have convinced rural communities in particular that there was a peace dividend from the CPA. Few areas saw much improvement, while both the GNU and the GoSS criticised delays by the international community in distributing the large amounts that had been pledged following the signing of the CPA for reconstruction and development, especially in the South. In this, they appeared to have a case, for the World Bank, which had responsibility for the distribution of much of this money, appeared to encounter blockages that often left the bulk of it unspent.

There were a number of notable developments. It was announced in April that there were to be new trade links with Turkey, which already had a growing presence in Sudan's economy in both commerce and infrastructural projects. In addition, the Kuwait Fund announced a new $ 52 m loan to raise the level of the Roseires Dam, on the Blue Nile near the border with Ethiopia. Together with the new dam at Meroe, built by the Chinese and now fully completed, this was a further fulfilment of Sudan's ambitious plans to make greater use of both the Blue and White Niles. Sudan maintained that its first priority was to generate power, which does not in itself reduce the volume of water in the rivers, but other riparian states were concerned that there would be an expansion in irrigation without international agreement on water allocation by all nine states involved. In July, Sudan also announced a significant industrial advance of its own. It had long been expanding its industrial sector, especially in armaments and transport vehicles, and it had now added the manufacture of small aircraft and helicopters at a new facility at Wadi Sedna, north of Omdurman.

In the same month, two foreign oil companies, ONGC Videsh of India and Lundin Oil of Sweden, announced that they were pulling out of their exploration projects due to poor results. There was also disappointment that the French company Total still appeared reluctant to begin work on its Block B concession in the South, which was thought to be a very promising area. The main reason appeared to be continuing doubts over security there. Greater confidence was shown by a small company from Moldova called Accom, which did sign up to explore a concession area in Block B. Overall, there were a number of uncertainties over oil related not only to security and the fluctuating price of exports, but also to the quality and quantity of the reserves. In an unexpectedly cautious comment in December, the minister responsible, Zubeir Ahmad Hassan, spoke of his expectation that oil output would fall by some 10% over the coming decade.

The 2011 referendum on the future of the South also added to speculation during the year concerning the future of oil. At present, most oil originated in the South and was piped north for refining for local consumption near Khartoum, with most continuing to the Red Sea coast for export, mainly to China and other parts of Asia. It was widely hoped at the time of the CPA that this pipeline connection and the heavy dependence of the revenues of both the GNU and the GoSS on oil would make unity more attractive than separation. However, the political tensions in both the north and the South have contributed to the expectation of separation in 2011, leading to **repeated speculation about the oil sector**. In the South, this has led to talk of seeking investment for a new pipeline to Mombasa on the Kenyan coast. Meanwhile, in the north, the NCP spoke confidently of expected new discoveries there. Areas for which it had hopes included Darfur, where China already had a concession and was starting surveying, which, if successful, would have a major impact on the politics of the area.

A number of Asian countries in particular have been involved in metals in the past and there was renewed interest in prospecting for gold. As its value reached new highs on international markets, a number of new contracts were signed for concession areas in the Red Sea Hills.

In the field of agriculture, the giant sugar-growing business at Kenana announced that it was diversifying into the production of ethanol with the aim of encouraging the use of a hybrid fuel mixed with petrol. By the end of the year, the first export of ethanol was reported. In June, there was an announcement of the removal of the state monopoly on gum Arabic, once Sudan's second largest agricultural export after cotton. It was hoped that this new move would free up prices and encourage farmers to expand their output.

Peter Woodward

Tanzania

In a year without major political changes or excitement, political discussions mainly centred on several allegations of high-level corruption, ever clearer signs of deepening rifts between quarrelling factions of the ruling party CCM, and the continuing confrontation between the two leading parties, CCM and CUF, in semi-autonomous Zanzibar. The overwhelming dominance of CCM was not in serious jeopardy, while internal cracks were partly a forerunner of infighting for a rearrangement of power positions in the election year 2010. Local government elections were convincingly won by CCM, while all opposition parties remained relatively weak as opponents of the long-dominant governmental forces. Despite some reluctance, Tanzania finally accepted the next step in deepening the EAC into a common market. The economy remained surprisingly resilient to the negative effects of the global economic recession, but some fall in the growth trend of recent years was unavoidable. International financial institutions continued to support the government's economic policies, while the majority of the population became increasingly dissatisfied with not seeing any direct tangible improvements.

Domestic Politics

One year before the next general elections, the **ruling party 'Chama cha Mapinduzi' (CCM**/Revolutionary Party) maintained its dominant position despite severe internal rifts and the first signs of infighting about the nomination of candidates. Support for opposition parties, namely 'Chama cha Demokrasia na Maendeleo' (CHADEMA/Party of Democracy and Progress), increased slightly but without posing a serious threat to CCM's political dominance. Several opinion polls conducted throughout the year indicated a still significant but decreasing and by no means compelling degree of sympathy for **President Jakaya Kikwete**, and massive dissatisfaction with the performance of his government and the CCM. Public discontent resulted mainly from a perception of continuous and increasing hardship for the majority of Tanzanians while a small minority among the elite were seen to be benefiting excessively from government policies, mostly through corrupt practices, and – despite all the official anti-corruption rhetoric – without being prosecuted.

The campaign against **corruption** remained one of the hot issues. Numerous cases involving accusations against high-ranking politicians and civil servants had been revealed in previous years, but hardly any visible measures had been taken against the alleged culprits. Former prime minister Edward Lowassa, who had to resign in February 2008 in the wake of corruption allegations, creating the severest government crisis in more than 25 years, was never legally taken to task and also retained his powerful position on the CCM Central Committee. Two other former ministers, who had allegedly been involved in the same scandal – known as 'the Richmond-Saga' – and had stepped down with Lowassa, also got off scot-free. During the parliamentary budget session (June/July), Deputy Minister for Energy and Minerals Adam Malima submitted a government report that cleared three senior civil servants (former attorney general Johnson Mwanyika, former permanent secretary in the Ministry of Energy and Minerals Arthur Mwakapugi, and Director-General of the Prevention and Combating of Corruption Bureau Edward Hosea) of any wrongdoing in the scandal. Parliament firmly rejected the report and demanded clear answers to the outstanding questions, which, however, had not been provided before end-2009. Shortly after the parliamentary debate, the state house issued a detailed response to rumours that Kikwete had been directly involved in the scandal. The statement elaborated four areas in which the president had played a role in the deal, but rejected any involvement in corrupt practices.

In July, the government cleared **former president Benjamin Mkapa** of any accusation of misuse of political power regarding his purchase of Kiwira coal mine at the end of his presidency in 2005. The mine had been sold at a give-away price to a company co-owned by Mkapa, then energy and minerals minister Daniel Yona and some of their closest family members. In June, the Energy and Minerals Ministry announced it had taken over the mine, but a heated dispute emerged between the ministry and a parliamentary committee of enquiry about whether the owners would be required to refund to the government about TSh 17 bn, disbursed to the company for investing in the mine. The ministry, on the contrary, announced that it would have to reimburse the company for its investments.

Accused of corruption in another case, Yona had been arrested in November 2008, together with former finance minister Basil Mramba and former finance permanent secretary Grey Mgonja, over charges of abuse of office and having caused the loss of over TSh 11 bn to the government. The full hearing of the case started in September, when both ex-ministers accepted the allegations. Public opinion remained sceptical about the seriousness of **anti-corruption efforts** and visible actions such as prosecution of culprits were expected. It was feared that prominent politicians and civil servants in particular would be spared prosecution. In early September, Kikwete explained in an unprecedented question-and-answer-session with the general public on TV and radio that 578 corruption cases were currently in the courts, compared with 58 when he came to office, although he acknowledged that there were delays in prosecution due to the heavy caseload and a shortage of judges and magistrates. According to TI's 2009 Corruption Perception Index, Tanzania performed better than most other EAC member states (apart from Rwanda), but nevertheless dropped 24 places as compared with 2008 to rank 126 out of 180.

The fight against corruption also revealed **deep rifts within the CCM**. Rumours of factions and a probable split in the party had been discussed for years, especially prior to elections, but the party had always been able to reconcile these tensions internally. Together with the media, **parliament** had become the driving force in the fight against corruption. A group of CCM MPs constantly used parliament as a forum to criticise corruption in the government and in their own party and to demand that more vigorous measures be taken against the accused. This had apparently caused a defensive reaction among some other parliamentarians, who appealed to parliament speaker Samwel Sitta to discipline the critics. However, the speaker, known for his strong anti-corruption stance, allowed the outspoken MPs to continue. During a CCM National Executive Committee (NEC) meeting in mid-August, some CCM MPs tried to unseat Sitta, claiming that his way of dealing with the corruption allegations would harm the party. The attempt failed but unveiled a deep internal rift in the party. Immediately, an **ad-hoc committee of 'three wise men'** was set up, comprising former president Ali Hassan Mwinyi, former speaker of the East African Legislative Assembly Abdulrahman Kinana and ex-parliamentary speaker Pius Msekwa. The team was tasked with reconciling the conflicting groups and looking into ways that CCM parliamentarians could air their views and grievances without harming the party, but fears were expressed that the committee had only been established to discipline and silence the critics.

The deliberations conducted by the 'three wise men' revealed that the **conflict** was between a **reformist group**, including Sitta, Harrison Mwakyembe (chairman of the parliamentary committee on the Richmond Affair in 2007/08 that had forced Lowassa to resign) and some other MPs on the one hand, and a **group of influential politicians facing corruption allegations** on the other. The core of this group seemed to comprise Lowassa, former CCM treasurer Rostam Aziz, who was suspected of having played a major role in the Richmond Affair, former attorney-general and minister Andrew Chenge, who had to step down in 2008 following corruption allegations, and CCM Secretary General Yusuf Makamba. They were accused of trying to gain control of the party and sideline the reformers, who had attracted much public sympathy for their crusade against corruption. Despite the efforts of the 'three wise men' and CCM's long-standing experience of reconciling internal rifts, this conflict posed a severe **threat to the unity of the party** and its ability to continue to rule the country almost unchallenged. It appeared unlikely that a split would occur before the next elections in 2010, but it was nevertheless an indicator of the internal power struggles taking place in the run-up to the usually fiercely contested nomination processes for the party's parliamentary candidates, and thus the composition of the next CCM parliamentary faction. President and CCM chairman Kikwete remained remarkably silent in this important dispute. Observers argued that his position in the CCM was apparently too weak to enable him emphatically to support the reformers and intervene in the struggle between the factions battling for control of the party.

Despite this intense infighting in the ruling party, the **opposition** was hardly able to capitalise on the situation. **CHADEMA**, the main opposition party on the mainland, was also mired in a leadership conflict, indicating the existence of rival factions in the party. In late August, deputy Secretary General Zitto Kabwe, an aspiring and very popular young MP, announced that he wanted to challenge party chairman Freeman Mbowe in the party's forthcoming leadership elections. This came as a surprise, since Mbowe (chairman since 2000) had been generally credited with CHADEMA's growing importance over the previous few years. Mbowe welcomed Kabwe's candidacy as a sign of the party's political maturity, but party elders persuaded Kabwe to abstain from challenging the incumbent in order to maintain the unity of the party. Kabwe was reminded that, at 32, he was still very young and had ample time for a political career. Mbowe was re-elected unopposed with 93% of the votes. Kabwe had explained his move as arising out of a desire to strengthen the party in order to prepare it to play a leading role in the country. Despite the 'cease-fire' between the rival leaders, elections to the youth wing and elders' committees showed that their supporters were still divided. Allegations of bribery were made, Secretary General Wilbroad Slaa announced the suspension of the elections, and the national anti-corruption agency PCCB was called in to investigate. Apart from partisan support for either Mbowe or Kabwe, the conflict was mainly between a more conservative wing on the Mbowe side and a rather leftist wing on Kabwe's side. Furthermore, the latter attracted younger party members, while Mbowe's power-base were the well-established networks of party elders and business people, mostly from Kilimanjaro Region. On 25 February, party elections in the **Civic United Front (CUF)**, the strongest opposition party in Zanzibar, went smoothly. The two leading politicians, chairman Ibrahim Lipumba and Secretary General Seif Sharif Hamad were easily re-elected.

Several parliamentary **by-elections** were seen as a litmus test for the general election in 2010; elections in Mbeya Rural, Busanda (Mwanza Region) and Biharamulo-West (Kagera Region) on the mainland and in Magogoni in Zanzibar were all won by CCM. The Mbeya elections on 25 January were overshadowed by the disqualification of the CHADEMA candidate on formal grounds; voter turnout was extremely low at 35% and the CCM candidate won by 73%. Campaigns for the elections in Busanda (24 May) and Biharamulo-West (5 July) were tense, with some violent incidents. No major incidents occurred on polling days, but voter turnout was again very low (36% and 41%, respectively). CCM was able to win the polls against CHADEMA, its main rival – albeit by slim margins. While CHADEMA accepted defeat in Busanda, they complained about irregularities in Biharamulo, but refrained from filing a petition with the electoral commission, stating that the general elections were to be held in slightly more than one year anyway. The peacefully conducted and well organised by-election to the Zanzibar parliament in Magogoni constituency on Unguja Island (23 May) was won by the CCM candidate as expected.

In September, political parties began preparations for the **local government elections** held on 25 October. Voter registration took place from 4 to 10 October and candidates were allowed to campaign between 15 and 24 October. As in the by-elections, voter registration and turnout was very low. Various problems occurred during selection of candidates, voter registration and the voting process. Voters had to write the names of their preferred candidates on the ballot, a tiresome procedure which also allowed party agents to manipulate voting by 'assisting' voters who could not read or write. Although the government had increased the funds for the elections from TSh 1.4 bn in 2004 to TSh 13 bn, the electoral process was unsatisfactorily managed. Instances of bribery and manipulation and a few minor violent incidents were reported. In some cases, campaigns were dominated by incumbent MPs or individuals who wanted to stand for a parliamentary seat in the 2010 general election. **CCM** was the only party with a nationwide presence and easily won the poll by securing 93.9% of the votes. Only CUF (2.9%) and CHADEMA (2.3%) were able to win a somewhat significant number of seats; other parties got less than 1%. Despite this landslide victory, CCM had to accept a small loss in comparison with the 2004 elections, when it received 96% of votes.

A civic-education booklet by the **Catholic Church**, which was distributed to all Catholic parishes in May, caused a great controversy. The booklet was part of the church's comprehensive civic education project to raise citizens' awareness about the general election and the importance of identifying and electing committed leaders who were not corrupt. The church used the project and the booklet to criticise the growing gap between rich and poor and advocate a change of policies. The booklet caused outrage and numerous critics with various standpoints accused the church of influencing people to vote for the church's preferred leaders and of creating disunity in the country, as well as hostility between religious groups. The church entirely rejected these accusations and its booklet also received warm support from a number of popular politicians. A few weeks later, the **Council of Imams** ('Shura ya maimamu') launched its own booklet of guidelines in response. It called upon believers to elect candidates who loved Islam and would end the alleged suppression of Muslims in Tanzania. However, the Muslim Council of Tanzania (Bakwata), regarded as the official Muslim representative organisation, distanced itself from the text, stating that no religious body should produce such a political document.

In April, remarks by Zanzibar's Minister for Water, Works, Energy and Land, Mansoor Himid, brought **tensions between Zanzibar and the mainland** back to the surface. In a speech before the Zanzibar House of Representatives, he declared that his government would seek to remove the clause on oil and natural gas from the list of issues falling under the jurisdiction of the Union government. A British consulting company had been assigned by the Union government to ascertain how best to deal with potential oil revenues, if oil were found in Zanzibar waters. The company suggested sharing the potential incomes, but Zanzibar's government and parliament rejected the recommendation and insisted that all revenues from any oil found in Zanzibar would not be shared by any means. Representatives of the Union government gave a relatively relaxed reaction, probably owing to the fact that, despite more than 55 years of exploration, no oil had yet been found, and stated that any Zanzibari wishes could be discussed. These remarks should probably be understood in the context of the 2010 elections, in which the Zanzibar wing of CCM will have to compete not only with strong opposition from CUF, but also with internal divisions about who would have the final say in choosing the next presidential candidate for the islands, since the incumbent Amani Karume was constitutionally barred from standing again.

The highly sensitive issue of **voter registration** in **Zanzibar** led to chaos and violence. In February, the Zanzibar Electoral Commission (ZEC) announced that it would only accept Zanzibar ID cards as proof of identity for the registration process, although other official documents had been accepted for registration purposes in the past. The main opposition party, CUF, protested against this regulation, saying that many Zanzibaris did not hold ID cards and would be denied them by the local authorities because of their political affiliation. CUF alleged that CCM intended to use this as a means of reducing the number of people voting for the opposition in order to redesign constituencies in CCM's favour. CUF also suspected the government of planning to issue Zanzibar ID cards to their supporters on the mainland, with a view to shipping them to the islands in great numbers on election day. Registration started on 6 July on Pemba Island, the CUF stronghold, and was expected to conclude there on 14 December. Registration on the larger Unguja Island was meant to begin in September. Refusals to register numerous voters soon led to **violence** on Pemba. The media reported the planting of landmines, and some exploded, albeit without causing injury. Houses and offices were torched. Police opened fire and, on 3 August, injured two CUF protesters. On 7 August, the ZEC finally reacted by suspending the registration process. In a joint statement, the representatives of the major donor countries expressed serious concern about these developments and the obstacles Tanzanians on Pemba were facing to obtain Zanzibar ID cards, the principle means of registration. However, the ZEC resumed the registration process on Pemba on 12 September and started on Unguja the same day. Turnout on Pemba was very low and violent incidents were reported from Pemba as well as from a few areas on Unguja.

Amidst this highly charged atmosphere of conflict between the two rival parties, it came as a major surprise when it was revealed on 5 November that **CUF Secretary General**

Seif Shariff Hamad and **Zanzibar President Amani Karume** had met behind closed doors. It was the first meeting between the two leading politicians since the controversial 2005 elections, when CUF had refused to recognise Karume as president. Both politicians said that they had agreed to **end the hostilities** between their parties and to cooperate in future for the benefit of the people of Zanzibar. However, it remained unclear what practical consequences this meeting might have with regard to the outstanding problem of voter registration and the likelihood of the establishment of a government of national unity. While Karume indicated that he did not rule out the idea of a CCM-CUF coalition government, two influential Zanzibar ministers spoke clearly against this option. This indicated that Karume's move was not supported by the whole of Zanzibar CCM, which was divided into at least two rival factions, namely the Karume camp and supporters of former Zanzibar chief minister Mohamed Bilal, who was among those tipped to succeed Karume in 2010. CUF followers also responded ambivalently to the agreement. In a number of gatherings immediately after his meeting with Karume, Hamad was booed and even called a traitor. The CUF leadership had, after all, long portrayed CCM and Karume much more as enemies than simply as rivals, and all the agreements that had previously been reached between the two parties had ultimately been blocked by CCM. These experiences had caused deep frustration among CUF supporters and their willingness to trust in new agreements was therefore very limited. Nevertheless, the temperature cooled significantly after CUF leaders had toured the islands and explained to their supporters their new policies regarding the government. Although the international community, as well as the Union government, praised the two leaders for their agreement, both insisted that there had been no involvement by anyone from outside Zanzibar. CUF even called upon the mainland CCM to stay out of the reconciliation process.

As in previous years, several violent clashes occurred in various parts of the country, in most cases caused by **land conflicts** between pastoralists and farmers. Clashes caused the deaths of several people and left many injured, and property including houses and farms was destroyed. Pastoralists were also in conflict with government authorities, whom they accused of violating their rights, complaining of detentions, expulsion from their land and the forced sale of their cattle. Land conflicts also arose between villagers and commercial investors. In June, hundreds of villagers invaded the land of a MP in Arusha Region, who had intended to establish a hotel there. They destroyed his property and blocked roads to prevent security forces from intervening. Six hours of fighting between villagers and police left one woman killed, and two other villagers and six policemen injured. Almost 400 villagers were reported to have fled to the forests of Mount Meru. The villagers declared that they were angered by government policies to allow rich people to own large tracts of land while poor villagers did not have enough land to farm. International attention was drawn to a conflict in parts of the Loliondo Game Controlled Area (Arusha Region), where in early July Maasai villagers were violently expelled from an area that the government had leased for game hunting to a company from the United Arab Emirates in 1992. The police field force unit conducted an operation in eight villages, torching about 200 homesteads, including food stores and maize fields. As a result, some 3,000 people were left without shelter, food or water and more than 50,000 cattle were pushed into areas hit by extreme drought with no water or grass. The authorities denied that any houses had been burnt, but justified the operation by stating that the villagers were illegal immigrants and were damaging the environment. The incident provoked an outcry from Tanzanian and international NGOs. The Danish ambassador, who travelled to Loliondo with four other ambassadors, called upon the government to stop evictions and to investigate what he described as inhuman acts. Denmark had just handed over a 15-year development project in the area. The African Commission on Human and Peoples' Rights also requested Kikwete to intervene. Parliament decided to investigate the issue through one of its committees. In mid-September, Minister for Natural Resources and Tourism Shamsa Mwangunga announced in Ngorongoro that fresh demarcations of land in Loliondo Game Controlled Area were planned in order to avoid property conflicts in the future.

Severe clashes between **conflicting clans** of the **Wakurya** in Mara Region had been causing loss of life and property for about two decades, and this continued in 2009. According to Home Affairs Minister Lawrence Masha, 136 people were killed between 2001 and April 2009, 336 people were wounded and 2,421 houses burnt down. Theft of cattle, conflicts about land and cultivation of cannabis were seen as the main causes of the conflicts. Former minister Philemon Sarungi accused rustlers from Kenya of having caused the problems and demanded compensation from Kenya for 3,500 cattle and the deaths of 40 people. In late March, a 44-member committee was formed, including representatives from the warring clans. It was the first time members of the two clans had held peace talks without the presence of senior central government leaders. The elders, who were held responsible for triggering the conflicts, promised to preach peace instead of hatred. However, in May the situation escalated again and more than 60 people were killed. In July, the government declared Tarime and Rorya districts special regional police zones and deployed a large number of police officers and since then reports of violence have decreased dramatically.

The government continued its endeavours to repatriate **refugees** from Burundi. On 30 September, all refugee camps in Kagera Region were officially closed. Only two camps in Kigoma Region were still operating, hosting fewer than 100,000 refugees for the first time in 15 years. According to reports from human rights organisations, the authorities exerted considerable pressure on the refugees, enforcing repatriation by allowing degrading living conditions in the camps. Tanzanian officials were accused of denying about 37,000 refugees in Mtabila camp access to basic services such as medical care and primary education, and also of routinely harassing, beating and threatening refugees who declined to return to Burundi. In contrast to this heavy-handed approach to refugees who had fled Burundi in the 1990s, 3,568 Burundian refugees who had escaped from Burundi in 1972 were granted Tanzanian citizenship on 4 August. They were the first of a total of 162,000

Burundian refugees who had accepted Tanzania's offer of naturalisation. This was the first large-scale naturalisation of this kind in Africa and was expected to be completed by early 2010.

Foreign Affairs

On 2 February, Kikwete completed his one-year term as **AU chairman**, during which he had earned international commendation for efforts in various conflict-resolution exercises in Africa (specifically Kenya, Comoros and Zimbabwe). However, during the hand-over ceremony to Libya's leader Kadhafi, he criticised the weak position of the AU chairman and suggested reforms.

Despite some minor disputes, peaceful and cordial international relations were generally maintained. **Western aid donors** were pleased by the government's commitment to curbing corruption, although more decisive action against culprits was expected. Finance Minister Mustafa Mkulo expressed dismay at a public statement by the World Bank that Tanzania was not doing enough to fight grand corruption. Minor rows occurred over several incidents, such as Western concerns about manipulation in the voter registration process in Pemba and the violation of human rights in Loliondo. In July, the Dutch government threatened to withhold $ 42 m of direct budget support, following a commercial dispute between the Tanzanian government and a Dutch investor. However, by November the conflict was resolved and Finance Minister Mkulo declared that the support had been released.

The generally high standing of the government's reputation in the Western community was also reflected by the fact that, on 22 May, Kikwete became the first African head of state to be received by the new **US** President Barack Obama. According to the White House, the two presidents exchanged ideas about intensifying bilateral cooperation, improving development policies in the fields of health, education and agriculture, and solving conflicts in Africa. During his week-long working trip to the US, Kikwete visited various organisations, companies and financial institutions.

On 10–11 March, Dar es Salaam hosted an international conference on the impact of the global financial crisis on African states, organised by Tanzania and the **IMF**. More than 300 high-ranking financial sector delegates from all over Africa adopted a joint declaration calling for enhanced support to help Africa cope with the effects of the crisis. Kikwete and Foreign Minister Bernard Membe were among the few African leaders invited by British Prime Minister Gordon Brown to participate in the Pre-G20 Summit Africa Outreach Consultative Meeting in London on 16 March. The meeting was intended as a forum to discuss African leaders' views concerning the world economic crisis and have them reflected in the G20 Summit on 2 April.

Over 45 years of cordial relations between **China** and Tanzania were celebrated during a visit by Chinese President Hu Jintao on 15–16 February. Tanzania was one of four

African countries Hu toured on his "journey of friendship and cooperation". The Chinese president attended the official launch ceremony of the Chinese-built national stadium in Dar es Salaam. He announced a new $ 22 m aid package and invited Tanzanian students to China, offering more scholarships.

Tanzania remained a somewhat reluctant supporter of the **EAC integration process**. During the final round of lengthy negotiations about the EAC Common Market Protocol in April, the Tanzanian delegation delayed the signing because of its continued concern about three main issues, namely the use of ID cards as travel documents between member states, the right to permanent residence for all East African citizens, and access to land. Access to land appeared to have been the most contentious issue because of already existing land conflicts in Tanzania and differences in land ownership laws compared with those in other EAC countries. Furthermore, there was fear that sparsely populated Tanzania could witness a massive influx of migrants from its neighbours, especially Uganda, Rwanda and Burundi, which were among Africa's most densely populated countries. Although the disputed issues were not resolved, the protocol was finally signed on 20 November, allowing future free trade and movement of people in the EAC common market, to be effective from 1 July 2010.

On 6–23 September, Tanzania hosted an **EAC field training exercise** conducted by military units from all five EAC countries and fully funded by the member states. The exercise was meant to train a Combined Joint Task Force of 1,556 personnel in planning and conducting combined joint operations and civil-military cooperation activities in the three areas of peace support operations, counter-terrorism and disaster management.

On 12 August, Tanzania deployed an advance party of 200 soldiers to the **UN/AU peacekeeping mission in Sudan (UNAMID)** in Darfur. They joined some 60 Tanzanian military observers, staff officers and police advisers who had been deployed earlier. In a change of attitude, the government promised to contribute a total of 875 personnel, although it had in the past been reluctant to participate in UN peacekeeping exercises.

Socioeconomic Developments

The global economic and financial crisis had a destabilising effect on Tanzania's economy, mainly due to reduced foreign investment, trade and tourism, but in the end the **slowdown** turned out to be much less pronounced than had initially been feared. Most economic activities proved to be surprisingly resilient, and the financial sector was affected very little because of its limited exposure to the toxic elements of global financial markets. The 2009 **GDP growth rate** was forecast to finally attain 5.5%, better than projected earlier, but below the 7% average for recent years (7.4% in 2008). Consumer price **inflation** was persistently high, with monthly rates hovering around the year's average of 12%. This was largely due to elevated food prices, partially the effect of adverse weather conditions (drought in northern regions early in the year) and substantial exports to neighbouring countries. The **exchange rate** experienced normal fluctuations throughout the year, but on balance remained relatively stable (vis-à-vis the dollar). The structural **trade deficit** narrowed somewhat, with exports (over 40% gold) growing slightly by 6% to $ 3,227 m and imports, as a result of a slackening of new investments and lower oil prices, even contracting by 2% to $ 6,294 m. Thus, roughly half of Tanzania's import bill was covered by its own exports, the highest ratio for many years. This improved situation enabled a reduction of the (provisional) current-account deficit to about 9.4% of GDP (down from 11.4% in 2008). Gross **foreign reserves** reached a new high of $ 3.2 bn at year's end (compared with $ 2.8 m at end-2008), partly the effect of an injection from the IMF; this was sufficient for an astounding import coverage of about six months. While the **external debt** had in previous years, through concerted debt cancellations, been substantially reduced to a low of $ 4.2 bn in 2006, this continued to rise again and the debt stock attained a volume of $ 7.1 bn at year's end.

Several **IMF** missions reviewed Tanzania's macroeconomic performance in the framework of the **Policy Support Instrument (PSI)** that had been in effect since February 2007 (and was extended until May 2010) as a form of monitoring government's financial and economic policies aimed at sustained broad-based growth, but without the need for IMF financial assistance. All the agreed benchmarks were by and large met, thus gaining for the government the IMF's positive stamp of approval, which was in turn crucial for maintaining the confidence and support of the many other donor countries and institutions that provided various forms of aid programmes for the country. On 29 May, the IMF approved a new 12-month $ 336 m arrangement under its **Exogenous Shocks Facility (ESF)**, intended to bolster Tanzania's foreign reserves and to support its balance of payments, which were assessed to have reached a precarious status. The ESF was specifically meant to cushion from the effects of the global crisis countries that were in principle eligible for the PRGF, but did not currently have a PRGF-supported programme. Under the ESF, $ 244 m were made available immediately, and a second disbursement of $ 63 m on 24 November upon the completion of a first review. Earlier plans for issuing a sovereign eurobond to raise funds for public investments were dropped in the prevailing financial circumstances, as a precautionary measure against the dangers of new commercial borrowing.

Despite its praise for Tanzania's strong macroeconomic performance, the IMF nevertheless noted that progress on **poverty reduction** was mixed. In its assessment, there were substantial improvements in education and health outcomes, but the incidence of income poverty had declined only modestly. It was evident that Tanzania would not be able to achieve the MDGs by 2015. Despite all the macroeconomic successes and positive acclaim from the donor community, Tanzania still remained one of the poorest countries in Africa. In UNDP's 2009 HDI (based on 2007 data), Tanzania was ranked 151 (out of 182), near the end of the medium human development category. GDP per capita was only $ 400 and in PPP terms it was given as $ 1,208, a considerable upward revision over previous calculations.

The **fiscal outturn** for the financial **year 2008/09** (July–June) was characterised by a shortfall in revenue collection and under-spending in foreign-financed development expenditure. Total domestic revenue collection of TSh 4,293 bn was 18% higher than in 2007/08, but a shortfall of 10% against the original budget estimate, mainly caused by the impact of the global financial crisis and the resulting slowdown of domestic economic activities. To compensate, the government had resorted to higher domestic borrowing. Recurrent expenditures were broadly in line with budget estimates and showed a marked improvement in budget execution. Development expenditures were, however, 14% lower than budgeted due to non-disbursement of foreign project funds. The overall effect of this situation was a sharp widening of the fiscal deficit to 4.4% of GDP (against 0.8% in 2007/08).

Faced with somewhat gloomy economic prospects, just prior to the release of the new budget, Kikwete announced an ambitious **economic stimulus plan** with a financial volume of about $ 1.3 bn (roughly 6% of GDP). The main components entailed large infrastructure programmes, financial support for crisis-affected ailing companies and help for small farmers. It was, however, not altogether clear to what extent these programmes were included in the state budget or were to be handled by public financial institutions. A concurrently released new government document (**medium-term public investment plan**) outlined a public investment strategy with a focus on the agricultural sector and on strengthening Tanzania's role as a sub-regional logistical hub, wherever this was feasible in the form of public-private partnerships.

On 11 June, Finance Minister Mkulo presented to parliament the **2009/10 budget**, with an overall 30% volume increase. The key focus was a substantial increase for agriculture, raising its share of the budget from 4% to 7%. This was in line with the government's new 'Kilimo Kwanza' (agriculture first) strategy, officially launched by Kikwete on 4 August, to give much more energetic support to small farmers, but to also pursue opportunities for more large-scale farming (including irrigation) and to initiate a dynamisation of agriculture over the medium term, the agricultural sector having long been grossly neglected. Other sectors receiving priority attention were education, health and infrastructure. Domestic revenue was rather conservatively projected to grow only from 15.9% to 16.4% of GDP, thus lowering earlier more ambitious forecasts and effectively relying on a further rise in donor funds, thereby quietly dropping all plans for a reduction of ingrained aid dependency. About 12.5% of the budget volume was expected to come under the general budget support scheme, supported by eleven bilateral and three multilateral donors. A reduction of VAT from 20% to 18% was intended as a stimulus to economic activities, but created obvious budget risks. The projected total revenue of TSh 9,513 bn was expected to be generated from domestic revenue (56%), foreign loans and grants (33%) and domestic borrowing (11%). By the middle of the financial year at end-December, it emerged that domestic revenue was 10% lower than targeted and that there might be a need to look for supplementary funding.

The World Bank in its 2010 Doing Business report assessed that there had been a considerable slippage in respect of further improvements in the **general business environment**. No significant reform measures were recorded in the preceding year and Tanzania was consequently downgraded by five places to rank 131st. Several government spokespersons expressed concern and pledged to remain on track in the pursuance of favourable market-friendly conditions. For most of the year, intensive discussions were held in parliament and government about revising the existing **mining legislation** with the aim of raising more government revenue in royalties from the international mining companies, whose activities had increased tremendously over the last decade, but the new mining bill was not ready by year's end. The volume of **foreign direct investments** was expected to have declined by about 10% compared with 2008 (with a record $ 744 m, mostly for mining ventures) due to delays of several new projects as a result of the global crisis. Apart from gold, new prospects for uranium mining appeared to be very promising. **Tourism**, the second foreign-exchange earner after gold, also experienced a set-back, with visitor numbers declining by about 10% compared with 2008.

Weaknesses in key parastatal service institutions continued to be a burden on the economy and to create hardships for the population. **Electricity** supply remained insufficient to meet the growing demand, due to maintenance problems in existing facilities and delays in planned new power projects, thus necessitating the repeated introduction of power cuts. On 10 December, the power cable from the mainland to Zanzibar broke, causing an electricity blackout on the island well into 2010, with strong negative effects on the local economy, especially in the tourist sector. Operations of **Tanzania Railways Ltd**, operated and 51% owned by RITES from India since 2007, continued to be very poor and workers protested vehemently against management in November, while the government was contemplating looking for a new arrangement. The **TAZARA railway line** to Zambia similarly continued to be in deep operational trouble and in permanent deficit; discussions were underway to obtain new assistance from China for a major rehabilitation. The future of **Air Tanzania** was also uncertain, with a sharp reduction of staff in December and government efforts to find new investors.

Climatic conditions were unfavourable for most of the year. The northern and central regions as well as the coast were hit by exceptional drought, causing severe problems for agricultural production and for the provision of an estimated 1 m needy people with food and water. The government supplied food from southern regions, which had produced a surplus, and duty on imported food was temporarily waived. Heavy rains in December flooded several areas in various regions and led to loss of life and severe damage to infrastructural facilities (including the closure of the central railway line for several months), houses and agriculture.

Kurt Hirschler & Rolf Hofmeier

Uganda

A diplomatic highlight of the year was when President Yoweri Kaguta Museveni took Uganda's seat in the UN Security Council chambers in New York in September. Uganda being one of the ten current non-permanent Council members, he participated in the high-level meeting chaired by US President Barack Obama. However, US-Uganda bilateral relations were not as cordial as during the presidency of George W. Bush. The country was severely reprimanded by Western politicians, NGOs and media over a backbencher's parliamentary motion on homosexuality. On the African scene, Uganda maintained its opposition to AU Chairman Kadhafi's schemes for express unification of the continent. At the same time, it kept up its commitment to peacekeeping in Somalia. Relations with neighbouring countries were mostly smooth. The country sailed surprisingly unbothered through the world economic crisis. Much interest was generated by recently-discovered crude oil deposits. Domestically, the confrontation with traditionalists in Buganda – the country's central region – intensified and led to acts of violence not seen there for many years. The alliance of major opposition parties posed no serious challenge to the president and his ruling party. The Lord's Resistance Army (LRA) left a bloody trail in neighbouring countries, but no longer had an effect on events in Uganda itself.

Domestic Politics

President Museveni continued to keep his firm grip on the ruling party, the **National Resistance Movement (NRM)**, and the 50,000-strong Uganda Peoples' Defence Forces (UPDF). In a mid-February **cabinet reshuffle**, a number of ministers were dropped, most casualties happening in the lower echelons of ministers of state. Among those losing their positions, the most prominent was the minister of finance, planning and economic development, Ezra Suruma, who had been blamed for the Temangalo scandal over the sale of some tracts of land to the marked advantage of Amama Mbabazi, the security minister. Mbabazi himself not only retained his position, but even found it strengthened, since some of his supporters were given ministerial posts. His most vocal critic, local government minister Kahinda Otafiire, was transferred to the less weighty trade ministry. Suruma was followed by Syda Bbumba as the country's first female finance minister. Caleb Akandwanaho, aka Salim Saleh, the president's brother, lost his position as minister of state for microfinance. Suruma and Akandwanaho were appointed senior presidential advisors for finance and defence respectively. A most notable newcomer was Ankole's Ruhaama county MP, Janet Museveni, who was made minister of state for Karamoja. This highlighted the plight of the people in the semi-arid northeast, but at the same time served to embed the First Lady in government solidarity, since she had become a politician in her own right, with her own largely Christian fundamentalist following, and was at times at variance with positions taken by her husband. A former Uganda People's Congress (UPC) stalwart and one-time presidential candidate, Aggrey Awori, was given the portfolio for communications and ICT. Former army commander Jeje Odongo returned, this time as state minister for defence. Altogether, there were 70 ministers, 26 with full cabinet rank and 44 ministers of state. Of the six **top political positions** (president, vice president, prime minister and his three deputies), Western Uganda and Buganda provided five, the sixth being a politician from Busoga, which is geographically and culturally close to Buganda. Of the 26 cabinet ministers (including the prime minister and his deputies), ten hailed from Western Uganda and seven came from Buganda. Only two had their constituencies in the north: lands minister Omara Atubo in Lango, and energy minister Hilary Onek in Acholi. The composition of the cabinet reflected Museveni's policy to reward the regions that supported him most strongly, but the west and Buganda were in any case the most populous parts of the country, accounting jointly for roughly three-fifths of all inhabitants.

Allegedly more narrow in its composition was the top brass of the **UPDF**, consisting largely of 'Bahima generals' who shared with the president the history of the struggle against the 'Obote II' regime and the same ethnic background. In August, a group of lawyers petitioned the constitutional court to redress the situation with regard to the army leadership, claiming it was not in line with the Constitution, which stipulates that the armed forces "shall be non-partisan" and "national in character". The army established a Military Aviation Academy in Nakasongola and an Engineering Brigade College in

Magamaga, near Jinja. In line with the increment for all public servants, payments to all ranks rose by 5%, with a private now receiving a minimum of Shilling (USh) 210,000 per month (about $ 109 at year's end). On 16 January, the government agreed with a UN task force on an action plan aimed at ending and preventing the association of children under the age of 18 with the military. Verification visits by the task force confirmed that there was no evidence of recruitment of children by the UPDF or its auxiliary Local Defence Units (LDUs) since August 2007. The government asserted that the LDUs were in the process of being disbanded, their members being integrated into the UPDF and the police force or being demobilised. In the year's largest multinational exercise of the US Africa Command (AFRICOM), named 'Natural Fire 10', in which about 550 US personnel and 650 soldiers from Burundi, Kenya, Rwanda, Tanzania and Uganda took part for ten days in October in Kitgum district, humanitarian assistance and disaster relief capabilities were to be enhanced, but skills to be improved by training also included convoy operations, weapons handling, fighting techniques and crowd control. Former UPDF commander James Kazini, who had been notorious in the Congo campaign in the 1990s and had been named in the UN report on the plundering of the DR Congo's natural resources, was free on bail whilst facing a general court martial for disobedience, when he was killed on 10 November by his girlfriend. His two wives and the public doubted that she had acted alone.

The anti-**corruption** division of the high court meted out the first jail sentences in connection with the scam over money from the Global Fund to Fight AIDS, Tuberculosis and Malaria. Two senior politicians were still under investigation. The Anti-Corruption Act, 2009, passed by parliament on 14 May and signed by the president on 19 August, strengthened the existing mechanisms, called for the confiscation of property acquired directly or indirectly through corruption, and offered protection for witnesses and whistleblowers. The 2007 Commonwealth Heads of Government meeting (CHOGM) in Kampala was followed by parliament investigating reports of massive misappropriation of funds.

Relations between the government and the traditionalists in **Buganda** took another turn for the worse. The Baganda people, living in the country's heartland and accounting for nearly 18% of the population, had seen their kingship restored as a solely cultural institution in 1993. Their king, the Kabaka, and his advisory body, the Lukiiko, both unelected, stepped up their campaign for a greater political role under the banner of federalism (*federo*) and for the preservation of a land ownership arrangement once established by the colonial power. In the face of the government's intention to extend the limits of Kampala city, the Lukiiko demanded the relocation of the capital. In order to curtail the reach of 'Mengo' (the seat of the kingdom), the government continued to support the aspirations of two small groups that had formerly been incorporated into the Buganda kingdom, but who were already listed separately in the 1926 colonial register of Uganda's 56 indigenous communities, namely the Banyala and the Baruli, who live in the districts of Kayunga and Nakasongola. Apparently intended to reassert Buganda's claims, a trip to Kayunga by the Kabaka, who had been prevented from visiting the area of the Baruli in 2008, was planned, though opposition from at least part of the local population was expected. When the Mengo prime minister set off on 10 September to prepare the visit, the police blocked his way. Word of this immediately spread, leading to seemingly spontaneous **demonstrations against the government**, but also aimed at non-Baganda. People with "long noses", i.e. supposed Banyankole or Banyarwanda, were beaten up, women wearing trousers were undressed and a number of Asians, some of them injured, had to seek refuge with the police after their shops were looted. In Kampala, a police station was set ablaze. Apart from the capital, some other major cities in Buganda were also affected. The brutality that characterised the protest by mainly unemployed, desperate youths was unexpected and the army, which soon re-enforced the police, used lethal force even in cases where it was not warranted. The **violence** on 10 and 11 September left at least 27 people dead, of whom 20 were suspected rioters, according to the internal affairs minister. The government closed four radio stations, including Mengo's Central Broadcasting Service (CBS), for inciting ethnic hatred and contributing to the outbreak of violence. At the end of September, the president and the king met in state house in Entebbe in an attempt to defuse the precarious situation. It emerged that for two years Museveni had tried in vain to contact Kabaka Ronald Muwenda Mutebi, his phone calls having remained unanswered. The Entebbe meeting touched on the various underlying conflicts, but did not lead to a new beginning. Three of the radio stations were allowed to operate again, but CBS did not have its licence returned since Mengo refused to meet conditions set by government.

Another major conflict with Buganda traditionalists was linked to the proposed amendments to the **Land Act**. Whilst, in the view of its proponents, these were intended to put an end to the illegal eviction of tenants, the Kabaka and other landowners feared for their property rights. On 26 November, the Land (Amendment) Bill, 2007, was passed, though not yet signed into law by the president. In the 325-member parliament, 112 MPs voted in favour, 55 against (amongst them three NRM MPs from Buganda), and three abstained. The main features of the new law will be the criminalisation of evictions not ordered by a court and the safeguarding of interests of registered owners (who frequently receive only a nominal rent) by giving them the right of preemption if a *bibanja* holder, i.e. tenant, wants to sell the entitlement to occupancy. Conversely, a tenant will have the first option when an owner intends to sell the land. Mengo reacted fiercely by announcing its unremitting opposition. Critics pointed out that the law would not be sufficient to counter rampant evictions and to address the general problems of land tenure.

The other **monarchies**, restored in 1993, sought to consolidate their status. The king of Bunyoro, Omukama Solomon Gafabusa Iguru, hosted a Forum for Kings and Cultural Leaders in Masindi in November. The traditional leaders backed the government's 'regional tier' proposal for closer cooperation between districts as opposed to Mengo's demands for *federo*. The Kabaka neither attended nor sent representatives because the heads of the Banyala and Baruli were among the participants. In Busoga, where there was no tradition of automatic hereditary succession, two rivals claimed to have been selected as the new Kyabazinga. On 19 October, a monarchy that formerly had not been recognised by the state received presidential blessing in a ceremony in Kasese, at the foot of the Mountains of the Moon. This was Rwenzururu kingdom, headed by Omusinga Charles Wesley Mumbere, the son of Isaya Mukirane, who in the 1960s had led a rebellion against the king of Toro. However, the authority of Mumbere, who belonged to the Bakonjo ethnic group, was disputed by the Baamba living on the other side of the Rwenzori mountain range. Museveni's approval of the new kingdom was also a gesture towards the people of Kasese, who had voted for the opposition in 2006. In anticipation of the next elections, the ethnic card was played by various political players. In Bunyoro, the conflict between Banyoro and immigrants (*bafuruki*) from Kigezi, also Ugandans, over land and political positions turned bitter. Bunyoro, having been humbled in the colonial period by the British and their Baganda collaborators, came into the spotlight as the area where most oil exploration takes place. Fears of losing control over these resources were easily exploited. The president's plan to safeguard the interests of the Banyoro by reserving certain political positions in their region for their ethnic group ('ring-fencing') was widely criticised.

While the NRM was fairly successful in by-elections to local councils held in May, even in Acholiland and Teso, the opposition **political parties** made little headway. However, on 14 December, the Inter-Party Co-operation consisting of the Forum for Democratic Change (FDC), the UPC, the Conservative Party (CP) and the Justice Forum (JEEMA) declared their intention to field joint candidates in the 2011 presidential and parliamentary elections. The Democratic Party (DP), the country's oldest party, remained aloof. On 20 January, FDC leader Kizza Besigye scored a major success when the supreme court decided that his court martial was illegal, but his treason case in the high court remained pending. The UPC and the DP continued with their internal squabbles, being unable to hold their delegates' conferences, both planned for November. In August, Olara Otunnu, foreign minister of the short-lived 1985 putsch government, returned to Uganda from 23 years' exile after an international career that had taken him to the position of one of the UN's under secretaries general. He toured the country and was given a party card by UPC president Miria Obote, although the Obote family denied him access to Milton Obote's grave. Some UPC diehards remained suspicious of his role in the 1985 coup that had toppled president Obote for the second time. The re-appointment of the chairman and most members of the electoral commission who had administered the 2006 elections was sternly criticised by the opposition.

In January, the **police** force established its Anti Human Sacrifice and Trafficking Task Force. During the year, 29 people (15 of them juveniles) were the victims of suspected ritual murder, compared with 25 reported cases in 2008. The Prevention of Trafficking in Persons Act was approved by parliament on 2 April and later assented to by the president. The **Domestic Violence** Bill, aimed at the protection of victims and the punishment of perpetrators, was passed in parliament on 11 November. On 10 December, a bill was endorsed seeking to outlaw female genital mutilation (**FGM**), providing for prison sentences for perpetrators including life imprisonment in the case of aggravated FGM, i.e. if the act was followed by death or the infection of the victim with HIV. Neither bill was signed into law before year's end.

On 21 January, the supreme court determined that the **death penalty** was legal, stipulating at the same time that, if execution had not taken place within three years of sentence being passed, it should be commuted to life imprisonment. Prior to the ruling, the president pardoned former Amin minister Brig. Ali Waris Fadhul and Chris Rwakasisi, state minister for security under 'Obote II', both of whom had been on death row for more than 20 years.

The final country review report under the **APRM** was launched in Kampala on 23 March. A governing council with 13 members from stakeholder groups was set up under the chairmanship of Anglican Bishop Zac Niringiye to monitor independently the implementation of the APRM national programme of action.

After the limited success of the December 2008 'Lightning Thunder' military operation against Joseph Kony and his **LRA** followers in their hideout in the Congolese Garamba National Park, and the subsequent 'Christmas massacres' perpetrated by the LRA, the population in the northeastern parts of the DR Congo continued to experience extreme suffering. LRA activities spread to Southern Sudan and the Central African Republic. The assignment of the UN Secretary General's special envoy for the LRA-affected areas, former Mozambican President Joaquim Chissano, was suspended with effect from 30 June. Chissano, in his last briefing to the UN Security Council on 15 July in informal consultations, advocated a twofold strategy of simultaneously offering a return to negotiations and pursuing military action. The military option prevailed; the UPDF received permission from the Bangui government to pursue the LRA in its territory. On 17 November, the members of the Security Council expressed their "deep concern at the direct and serious threat the activities of the LRA pose to the civilian population, the conduct of humanitarian operations and regional stability". In northeastern DR Congo, tens of thousands of civilians were uprooted and in December alone several hundred were reportedly killed. In Uganda, there was no longer a LRA presence, and the closure of IDP camps continued. By mid-year, the camp population was given as 388,000, down from 1.84 million in 2006. Most of the 1.4 million who left the camps did so of their own accord. Upon returning to their home areas, they often were faced not only with a lack of infrastructure, particularly access to clean water, but also with land disputes.

Though there was talk about a shadowy **new rebel force** called the Popular Patriotic Front (PPF), allegedly created by former LRA sponsors from the diaspora, the era of numerous armed anti-government groups, large or small, in Uganda may well have come to an end. Since 2000, as announced by the chairman of the **Amnesty** Commission, 23,526 former combatants from 28 different rebel groups had benefited from the pardon regulations. Among them were 12,645 former LRA fighters; next in numbers came the West Nile

Bank Front (WNBF) with 4,316 ex-fighters, the Uganda National Rescue Front II (UNRF II) with 3,115, and the Allied Democratic Forces (ADF) with 1,907.

The remote **Karamoja** region was still plagued by food insecurity, but the security situation was somewhat improved. Karimojong leadership was passed to another age set.

Foreign Affairs

On 1 January, Uganda achieved the lead position on the 'honour roll' of the UN's Committee on Contributions, being the first of all 192 member states to pay the regular budget assessment promptly and in full. On that date, Uganda's two-year tenure as a non-permanent member of the **UN Security Council** commenced and, on 17 February, Uganda's new permanent representative, Ruhakana Rugunda, presented his credentials to UN Secretary General Ban Ki-moon. He became the chairman of the Council's ad-hoc working group on "conflict prevention and resolution in Africa". On 5 May, following a Ugandan initiative, the Council expressed "its deep concern over the resurgence of unconstitutional changes of government in a few African countries". Rugunda also co-headed the Council mission for the consultative meeting with the AU Peace and Security Council in Addis Ababa on 16 May. In July, Uganda assumed the rotating presidency of the Council, the highlight being the thematic debate on post-conflict peacebuilding chaired by Foreign Minister Sam Kutesa. At the 24 September Council summit on nuclear non-proliferation and disarmament chaired by President Obama, Museveni emphasised that "nuclear energy is of great interest to Africa".

Up to the Commonwealth summit in Trinidad and Tobago at the end of November, Museveni held the position of chairperson-in-office of the Commonwealth. Of more relevance was the role he played on the African stage, opposing current AU chairman Kadhafi's intention to put through his idea of a single government for Africa. Instead, he advocated a three-level approach: regional political federations, a common African market and areas of joint action. During the **AU summit** in early February, he clashed with one-time republican revolutionary Kadhafi, now laying claim to the title of 'king of kings' of Africa, over his use of traditional rulers to advance his unification scheme. Shortly before the Addis Ababa summit, the Uganda government barred a Libya-sponsored gathering of some 200 kings, princes, sultans, sheikhs and other traditional leaders from East Africa, which had been planned to be held in Kampala on 13 January. Later, AU chairman Kadhafi did not attend the special AU summit on refugees, returnees and IDPs, held in Kampala on 22–23 October. It was graced by the presence of only three heads of state, among them Zimbabwe's Robert Mugabe, apart from Museveni, who took the chair. The summit adopted the AU Convention for the Protection and Assistance of IDPs in Africa (**Kampala Convention**), a legal instrument which aimed at ensuring assistance for IDPs and reiterated the AU's right to intervene in cases of "war crimes, genocide, and crimes against humanity".

Uganda persevered in its **Somalia** commitment, providing 2,700 troops for the AU Mission in Somalia (AMISOM), which had a strength of 4,300 by mid-year. It later rose to 5,200, still only 65% of the mandated numbers. The force was tasked to support the Transitional Federal Government in Mogadishu and the soldiers operated in an extremely difficult environment with little success, in addition to having their allowances delayed for months by the AU. Maj. Gen. Nathan Mugisha took over as force commander from Maj. Gen. Francis Okello. On 17 September, a suicide attack resulted in the death of 17 AMISOM peacekeepers, among them the Burundian deputy force commander and five UPDF soldiers, plus four civilians, and Mugisha was slightly injured.

Inter-state relations in the **Great Lakes Region** improved further when Museveni met his DR Congo counterpart Kabila on 4 March at the common border near Kasese. Diplomatic relations between the two countries were re-established and in August a new Congolese ambassador arrived. The US-facilitated Tripartite Plus Joint Commission, composed of Burundi, DR Congo, Rwanda and Uganda, did not meet during the year, but security cooperation between these countries continued at least to a certain extent. On 10 August, Museveni attended the third ordinary summit of the International Conference on the Great Lakes Region (ICGLR) in Lusaka. The ICGLR chair will pass to Uganda in 2011.

The rapport with Southern Sudan, also a partner in flourishing formal as well as informal cross-border trade, remained on the whole cordial. Cooperation with the other **EAC** member states continued smoothly, apart from a conflict over the tiny Migingo island in Lake Victoria claimed by both riparian states of the northern part of the lake, after **Kenyan** fishermen were obliged to pay for Ugandan permits. In late April, Uganda lowered its flag, but a police presence remained with the approval of the Kenyan government. Some sections of the Kenyan public took a hostile attitude towards Uganda. Slum dwellers in Nairobi's Kibera area removed part of the railway track to Kampala. The dispute was to be resolved on the basis of the colonial boundaries by a joint survey. Eventually the Ugandan and then the Kenyan team withdrew for consultations with their respective governments and the joint work was not resumed thereafter.

While the issue of traditional rulers had already spilled over onto the African scene to some extent, a quite different domestic issue had international implications that threatened Uganda's global standing and donor support. In parliament on 15 April, Minister of State for Ethics and Integrity Nsaba Buturo castigated UNICEF and a number of human rights organisations for having "been in the forefront of a campaign to legalise homosexuality". He was outdone by the opposition's shadow minister of information and national guidance, who said, "We must exterminate homosexuals before they exterminate society." Independent Uganda had inherited the criminalisation of "carnal knowledge against the order of nature" from the colonial power, and the legislation had lain dormant in the statute books. In the contemporary debate, religious and political leaders vied with each other in defence of African values against Western permissiveness. In October, David Bahati, an NRM

MP from Kigezi, tabled the **Anti Homosexuality Bill**, 2009, which defined homosexual acts in almost clinical detail. The bill was aimed at "strengthening the nation's capacity to deal with emerging internal and external threats to the traditional heterosexual family" and introducing protective measures "against the attempts of sexual rights activists seeking to impose their values of sexual promiscuity on the people of Uganda". The existing legislation, which already made provision for a maximum penalty of life imprisonment, was to be expanded to include the offence of "aggravated homosexuality", committed e.g. against a person under the age of 18, or with a disability, or perpetrated by an offender with HIV, the culprit being subject to capital punishment. Any "person in authority" failing to report an offence within 24 hours would be liable to a fine or up to three years' imprisonment. Bahati's draft promptly became the subject of an international campaign criticising Uganda for widespread homophobia. Moreover, it was seen by civil rights organisations as an infringement of personal liberties, including with regard to the reporting obligations, and was judged to represent a setback to AIDS prevention by placing gays and lesbians outside society. It was alleged that the drafting of Bahati's private member's bill had been facilitated by US Evangelical circles. The international outcry was most prominently manifested in the pressure exerted upon Museveni by British Prime Minister Gordon Brown and Canadian Premier Stephen Harper during the Commonwealth summit.

Socioeconomic Developments

Following a staff mission to Kampala in March and April, the **IMF** completed its fifth review under the three-year Policy Support Instrument (PSI) of end-2006. The IMF's assessment criteria were met, including ceilings related to government debt. It was pointed out that the country's economic activities were now under constraint from the global financial crisis. The sixth review in October, however, found that Uganda had been doing remarkably well, weathering the impact of the crisis "better than expected". On 22 December, when the IMF Executive Board concluded the sixth review, it approved an extension of the PSI for one year in order to bring a successor PSI into line with the budget cycle and the National Development Plan that was in preparation. Uganda was praised for its "prudent economic management and strong fundamentals".

Real **GDP growth** was 7.1% during the 2008–09 financial year, against the 8.7% reached in 2007–08. Total export earnings amounted to $ 2.8 bn in 2008–09, an 8.2% increase from the previous year's $ 2.6 bn. Ugandan food exports were in high demand in the region. The boost contributed to considerable price rises for consumers at home, the annual headline **inflation** rate for the year ending December 2009 being 11.0%. The rate of underlying inflation, excluding food crops, fuel and electricity, for the same reference period was markedly lower at 7.4%. In the 2008–09 financial year, the share of private investment in real terms stayed constant at 20.4% of GDP. Between September 2008 and

May 2009, the value of the USh declined by 34.7% against the dollar. During the second half of the year it gained strength against a weakening dollar, appreciating by nearly 20%. At the end of May the external debt amounted to $ 4 bn.

Finance Minister Syda Bbumba read her first **budget** speech on 11 June. For the 2009–10 financial year, the catchphrase was once more "prosperity for all", to be achieved through "enhancing strategic interventions to improve business climate and revitalize production". The previous emphasis on infrastructure in the fields of transportation – mainly building and upgrading roads – and energy was maintained. Rural electrification was to be intensified and the inter-connectivity of the entire country completed, which meant laying more than 1,500 km of optical fibre to link most major towns and the provision of connectivity with the East African sub-marine cable via Kenya. Works and transport was allotted the largest share of the budget with 17.4%, followed by education (16.2%), health (10.2%), public sector management (9.2%), energy and minerals (8.8%) and security (7.6%). Spending on agriculture was to increase, albeit only from 3.8% in the previous financial year to 4.4%. Though the budget grew by about one fifth in local currency to USh 7,334 bn, in dollar terms, at roughly $ 3.3 bn on budget day, it was even lower than the 2008–09 level of about $ 3.8 bn, thus reflecting the sharp depreciation of the currency. According to Bbumba, 32.6% of expenditure was to be financed by external budget support and project aid (higher than in the preceding year, when the projected rate of support from donor partners stood at 30%). As "a measure to stimulate the economy", the minister resisted proposing increases in duty and taxation, but expected improved proceeds from the work of the Uganda Revenue Authority. A number of exemptions were to be introduced or continued: house sales to be VAT-exempt (the 5% rate being scrapped), further exemption of new agro-processors from income tax and, in order to encourage local barley growing, the 60% excise duty on beer produced from grain grown and malted in the country was to be reduced by a third. Peace consolidation and reconstruction was to be effected through the three-year Northern Uganda Peace, Recovery and Development Plan (PRDP). On a much smaller scale, rehabilitation programmes were foreseen for the Luwero Triangle (scene of the 1981–85 bush war) and Rwenzori area (where the ADF had been active). The minister noted a "marked decline in remittances from Ugandans working abroad" and in transfers to NGOs.

Oil reserves were estimated to amount to 2 bn barrels. Though this accounted for only 2% of Africa's confirmed deposits, it put Uganda on a par with Equatorial Guinea or Gabon. Commercial exploitation was not likely to begin before 2012. The production-sharing agreements concluded by the government with international oil companies were not made public. Museveni insisted that refinement would take place within the country.

The 2009 TI **Corruption Perceptions Index**, released in November, ranked Uganda at 130, a further fall (from 126 in 2008 and 111 in 2007). Of Uganda's EAC partners, Rwanda (89) and Tanzania (126) did better, Kenya (146) and Burundi (168) worse.

A new campaign of **AIDS** prevention messages encouraged married people to be faithful, acknowledging that they currently belonged to the most-at-risk population and taking into account that a major proportion of new HIV infections appeared to be attributable to multiple partnerships. There was a shortage of antiretroviral (ARV) drugs for people living with AIDS, with ARV programmes almost entirely dependent on funding by donors. In general, the health infrastructure was found wanting; most government-run hospitals were in bad shape, as was acknowledged by a parliamentary committee.

Volker Weyel

VII. Southern Africa

Zimbabwe remained among the top 'hot spots' that kept the sub-regional body, SADC, busy, although Madagascar emerged as a strong contender, albeit more from a distance, as a result of the overthrow of the government and the subsequent international non-recognition of the new president. The frequency of SADC meetings was also related to the situations in Zimbabwe and Madagascar, but did not produce any visible and concrete results.

A similar lack of progress characterised efforts towards integration in the socioeconomic sphere. Plans advanced in rhetoric but hardly in practice. SACU faced its most serious test as a result of a decline in revenue income caused by the effects of the financial crisis, and South Africa's willingness to agree to a generous distribution of the duty income among the junior partners seemed more limited than ever. Negotiations cast a shadow of doubt over SACU's future. Disagreements over the strategy for dealing with the contested interim EPAs emerged as another divide among SADC countries and resulted in a deep rift between the EU and Angola, South Africa and Namibia, which refused to sign up.

Elections in several of the SADC countries brought no unexpected results but rather consolidated the dominant parties in power. While some of the results were disputed, the sub-region continued to benefit from relative peace and little unrest. Political differences between the SADC member states remained obvious, however, over issues such as the ICC indictment of Sudanese President al-Bashir and the continuing conflict in Zimbabwe.

Elections, Democracy and Human Rights

Several elections during the year – in almost half of the countries in the sub-region – testified to the phenomenon of the **dominant party syndrome** as a common feature. Parliamentary and presidential elections followed the established procedures and allowed the registered electorate a relatively free vote, at least with regard to the direct election process during the day(s) of voting. As is often the case, election observers, on the ground for a limited period of time, tended to neglect the long periods of preparation for elections and the nature of the election campaigns, when they presented their generally positive conclusions. Looked at in relative isolation, the elections in the five countries of the sub-region (Botswana, Malawi, Mozambique, Namibia and South Africa) that took place during the year did indeed seem quite free and fair, with only minor queries concerning suspected irregularities and little doubt that the outcomes were a rather true reflection of the will of the electorate, who, in the absence of meaningful alternatives, were often left without choices.

Parliamentary and provincial elections in **South Africa** took place on 22 April. They drew widespread international attention due to the fact that the Congress of the People (COPE) had split from the African National Congress (ANC) and formed a new political party. While COPE had been the decisive factor leading to the ANC's loss of its two-thirds majority in the national parliament, the latter's dominance remained unchallenged after it received 65.9% of the vote (3.8% less than 2004), resulting in 264 out of the 400 parliamentary seats. COPE failed to meet expectations. With 7.4% of the vote (30 seats), it became the third relevant political party, but was unable to replace the Democratic Alliance (DA), which secured 16.6% of the vote, as the official opposition. The Inkatha Freedom Party (IFP) lost further ground, taking 4.6% of the vote. In its stronghold of KwaZulu-Natal, the ANC, with Jacob Zuma as its presidential candidate, received a record 66.1% of the vote – an indication that in this province the Zulu identity, which Zuma cultivated in his public appearances and the controversial cultural traditions he adhered to, had an impact and mobilised support. Voting patterns suggested that the ANC had lost its appeal as a 'rainbow coalition' and moved towards being more an African nationalist party. Along similar lines, the DA's profile reinforced the impression that it was mainly attracting voters who were distancing themselves from the African nationalist image of the ANC. This was illustrated by the DA's success in the Western Cape province, where it took 51.5% of votes cast, securing a mandate for party leader Helen Zille to govern with an absolute majority. With the inauguration of Jacob Zuma as the new president on 9 May, he became the fourth head of state in the first 15 years of democratic South Africa.

Parliamentary and presidential elections in **Malawi** took place on 19 May after initial controversies over the nomination of candidates. President Bingu wa Mutharika managed to defend his position as leader of the Democratic People's Party (DPP) and its presidential candidate. With 50.7% of the votes, he could claim to have obtained the best result of any elected president in 15 years. His main challenger and former president Bakili Muluzi was stopped in his attempt to make a come-back by a verdict of the constitutional court, which ruled that no one who had already held two terms in office was entitled to compete again. With the DDP securing 114 out of the 193 electoral constituencies, it joined the club of dominant parties in the sub-region. Competitors from other parties for both the presidency and parliamentary seats found little reason to question the credibility of the results.

On 16 October, **Botswana** held its ninth parliamentary elections since independence. Once again, the governing Botswana Democratic Party (BDP) defended its uninterrupted political reign in the sovereign state. Its 53.3% share of the vote was an increase of 2% and one seat, to 45 out of 57 seats. The translation of the proportional vote into such dominance in parliament indicated the skills of the party, over time and by means of several reforms, to translate the demographic and regional realities into electoral districts that provided a favourable result for the party's candidates, thereby skilfully mastering (if not manipulating) the electoral process without risking Botswana's image as an exemplary African democracy. Neither was Botswana's reputation dented by the fact that it was among the countries where the head of state was not elected by the voters but appointed by the governing party. President Ian Khama, who had succeeded Festus Mogae in 2008, was automatically confirmed in office.

In **Mozambique**, the 28 October elections for parliament, the president and new provincial parliaments presented the ruling Frelimo with another landslide victory, which firmly consolidated and entrenched it as the dominant party at all levels and in all spheres. Armando Guebuza was re-elected president with 75% of the votes, while his Frelimo party took 191 parliamentary seats, more than two-thirds of the total of 250. It also won majorities in all tne provincial assemblies, taking altogether 703 of the 812 seats. Since independence, Frelimo has re-established firm control over the country, not without dubious practices, and evidence of attempts at manipulation provoked criticism among international election observers. However, despite the emergence of a new political alternative with the formation of the Mozambique Democratic Movement (MDM), which broke away from the declining Renamo, no short-term alternative was in sight.

Last but not least, the parliamentary and presidential elections in **Namibia** on 27–28 November completed this year's cycle of consolidating the political rule of dominant parties. The extension of the elections to a two-day period caused raised eyebrows, not only domestically among those suspicious of vote rigging, but also among SADC observers, who suggested that the country should return to one polling day in conformity with the SADC election guidelines. While the election results, and particularly some actions of the electoral commission, were a matter of legal dispute and court proceedingss were in full swing by the end of the year, there were no serious doubts among observers that the reigning South West African People's Organisation (SWAPO) had retained its dominant status. With 74.3% of the votes, it secured 54 out of 72 seats in parliament. The new Rally for Democracy and Progress (RDP), which was formed by long-standing SWAPO politicians when they lost an internal power struggle, emerged as the new official opposition with 11.2% of the votes and eight seats, although this was below expectations. Seven other parties shared the remaining ten seats in parliament, often mandated by a regional, ethnically-defined electorate. President Hifikepunye Pohamba secured another prestige success by securing his re-election to a second (and last) five-year term with 75.3% of the vote, a higher percentage than his party received in the parliamentary election. His most serious contender, former foreign minister Hidipo Hamutenya, of the new rival party RDP, trailed with 10.9%.

All five elections during the year were examples of the latent ambiguities contained in the assumption that **elections and democracy** are congruent, provided that the election results meet certain minimum standards of transparency and accountability. Four of the countries represent the dominant party syndrome, which implies that the authority with which political rule is exercised often leads to practices that show little regard for democratic behaviour and values. Rather, the dominant parties managed to exploit their hegemonic status to further entrench their power to define the rules of the game and use their access to state property (and not least over state-owned media) to create a comparative advantage.

Events took a dramatically different turn in **Madagascar**, where the legitimate though increasingly controversial President Marc Ravalomana was ousted from office, after several weeks of public unrest, by supporters of his rival, Andry Rajoelina, who on 18 March was declared by the country's constitutional court to be the new head of state. This coup-like seizure of political power was, however, not recognised by the international community and Rajoelina was denied any legitimacy, even by the member states of SADC, which suspended Madagascar's membership. Throughout the year, efforts to bring a solution to the impasse were unsuccessful.

The hangover from the previous year's disputed election results in **Lesotho** kept SADC and its mediators busy without any concrete results. A failed, somewhat amateurish coup attempt on 22 April created confusion and illustrated the tense atmosphere, which was a threat to the country's political stability. SADC mediator and former Botswana president Ketimule Masire, who presented a report on 8 July, admitted that he was unable to contribute to a sustainable compromise that would lead to a way out of the political impasse. Lesotho's domestic politics remained a contested arena, with emotions running high and no promising perspects.

Similarly shaky and tense was the political situation in **Swaziland**, the only country in the sub-region where political parties were not allowed to operate, by decree of the king. A new act to suppress terrorism provided the instrument to prosecute and clamp down on any form of dissent. In particular, the media and their journalists were among the targets, and the country's human rights record deteriorated further.

In **Zimbabwe**, the impasse between the three parties competing for political influence over the country's affairs continued unabated. While the negotiated Government of National Unity (GNU) was inaugurated on 11 February as a power-sharing arrangement, power struggles and intrigues were the order of the day, with President Mugabe resenting any power-sharing in the true sense of the word. Frustrations arising from bullying and disrespect caused the new Prime Minister Morgan Tsvangirai of the Movement for Democratic Change (MDC-T) to announce on 16 October the disengagement of his party from the GNU. This decision was retracted on 5 November and a joint press conference given by the three party leaders on 23 December stressed their political will to keep the GNU operational despite 'minor' differences. It very much looked as if the GNU was indeed providing the Zimbabwe African National Union – Patriotic Front (ZANU-PF) with a lifeline to stay in power, despite its loss of popular support.

Less spectacular was the daily political business in the other countries of the sub-region. **Angola** postponed the presidential elections originally announced for this year, while President Eduardo dos Santos quietly concluded his 30th year in office on 21 September. He was re-elected as the 'Movimento Popular para a Libertacao de Angola' (MPLA) party leader at a congress in December. The MPLA elite was able to continue its autocratic rule in the absence of any meaningful and credible political alternative. In **Mauritius**, the coalition government was much occupied with business as usual, while some attention was drawn to efforts to modify electoral laws for the forthcoming national elections. The relative political stability was evidence of why the country regularly ranks among the top performers in any survey on good governance on the continent. Domestic politics in **Zambia** were also much affected by initial preparations for the elections in 2011; disputes around the appointment of President Banda were brought to an end and initiatives for nominations for the next elections dominated political agendas. Competition between the bigger parties and conflicts over electoral reform absorbed much energy, as did internal power struggles and rivalries within the parties and the strategic positioning of individuals competing for nomination as presidential candidates.

More than half of the sub-region's countries were under the political control of *de facto* one-party regimes, which had sole control of political affairs, with the governments in Angola, Botswana, Mozambique, Namibia, South Africa and (with modifications) Zimbabwe being composed by the very same party that had assumed political power at independence or (as in South Africa) at the first democratic elections. This is not necessarily a failure of so-called 'good governance' practices. According to the latest **governance rankings** in the 2009 Ibrahim Index of Governance, presented by the Mo Ibrahim

Foundation on 5 October in Cape Town, the Southern African sub-region scored the best aggregate with 58.1 (out of 100), ahead of North Africa. Central Africa was ranked last with a score of 40.2. The overall sub-regional score was lowered by the ranking of Zimbabwe, which was categorised as the third-worst-governed country on the continent (above Somalia and Chad). The survey included five countries from the sub-region (Mauritius, Botswana, Namibia, South Africa and – surprisingly – Lesotho) in the top-ten list of best-governed countries. A parallel Index of African Governance, launched on 1 October in Johannesburg by the Kennedy School of Government at Harvard University (responsible for the first two surveys of the Mo Ibrahim Foundation), presented similar results. Only Lesotho did not feature among the ten top countries in terms of governance. Both surveys once again ranked Mauritius first and Botswana second in the sub-region.

Socioeconomic Developments

The SADC ministers with the finance and investment portfolios held an extraordinary meeting in Cape Town during February in an effort to stress the need for urgent and innovative strategies to respond to the challenges of the **global recession**. The reduced demand and subsequent lower world market prices for some of the major natural resources exports (minerals, oil, base metals, as well as agricultural commodities) led to sluggish economic growth and fiscal problems in several of the countries in the sub-region. Most prominently affected was Botswana, with its almost exclusive dependency on diamond exports. The tourism industry, another major income-generating sector in the sub-region, was also negatively affected by the the financial crisis, which manifested itself in a decline in overseas visitors. According to the Regional Economic Outlook presented by the IMF in October, SADC's real GDP growth was 5.1% in 2008. It projected a decline of 0.9% in real GDP for the year.

SADC issued reports on the impact of the **economic crisis** in March and September. It differentiated between three types of economies negatively affected. The global recession hit South Africa because its financial system was most integrated with the global one; Angola suffered from the lower price it received for its oil; and countries such as Botswana and Namibia struggled because of the dependence of their commodity-producing economy on the export of raw materials. Easing oil prices and increased food supply contributed to a decline in inflation, with Botswana, Lesotho, Malawi, Mauritius, Namibia and South Africa recording single digit figures by July. Average inflation in the sub-region was expected to slow down to 12.6% during the year. As from June, capital markets in Botswana, Mauritius, Namibia, South Africa and Zambia improved again, but current accounts and fiscal matters remained under pressure and household savings in the sub-region generally dwindled. Negative growth rates were forecast for Botswana (-10.3%), South Africa (-2.2%), Lesotho (-1.0%), Namibia (-0.7%) and Madagascar (-0.4%). The

African Economic Outlook prognosis for the year expected a decline in exports of 1.8%, with a corresponding (lesser) decline in import volumes of 0.4%. The SADC current account deficit was expected to average 10.5%, with a tendency to widen further.

According to the **SADC Food Security** Early Warning System update in September, cereal production had increased by 6% from 29.62 m tonnes to 31.26 m tonnes. Only Lesotho, Namibia and South Africa recorded lower production than during the previous year. A cereal surplus of 476,000 tonnes was expected, compared with a deficit of 1.78 m tonnes in 2008. Food security also improved due to a fall in the benchmark FAO Food Price Index by one-third measured against its peak in June 2008.

Initiatives to further promote a cost-effective **trans-boundary infrastructure** network continued. According to the SADC secretariat, about $ 20 bn were required in support of trade facilitation measures and an upgrade of the sub-regional infrastructure (roads, rail and ports) through targeted development corridors. A sub-regional master plan for infrastructure development focussed on five priority sectors: energy, transport, telecommunications, water infrastructure, and tourism.

The effects of the **HIV/AIDS** pandemic continued to weaken the societies in the subregion, with nine countries having an adult HIV prevalence above 10%. According to the latest figures presented by UNAIDS, Swaziland continued to have the most severe level of infection in the world with 26% (2007 data), while Lesotho's epidemic stabilised at 23.2% prevalence (2008 data). South Africa continued to be the country with the world's largest absolute number of people living with HIV, estimated at 5.7 m (2007 data). Figures for HIV incidence dropped among women in Zambia between 2002 and 2007, and Zimbabwe registered a steady fall in HIV prevalence due to changed sexual behaviour. In South Africa, adults reportedly using condoms during their first sexual encounter rose from 31.3% in 2002 to 64.8% in 2008. These latest data suggested that the pandemic had reached its peak in most countries.

Sub-regional Organisations

With the Seychelles rejoining the sub-regional configuration the previous year, **SADC** comprised 15 member states (including the DRC and Tanzania, as well as all countries considered in this sub-regional overview) with an estimated combined GDP of $ 430 bn, which accounted for more than half of GDP in sub-Saharan Africa. The dominant subregional player remained South Africa, with Angola emerging as a second viable subregional powerhouse and continuing to seek a competing hegemonic role. During the year, the latent rivalry between the two dominant states remained mild, however, not least because of the good relations cultivated by the South African President Zuma (representing the South Africa government under the ANC) with the MPLA government, as likeminded erstwhile liberation movements now in political power. Zuma, who also succeeded

Thabo Mbeki as SADC-appointed mediator in the Zimbabwe conflict, kept a low profile in this task and, unlike his predecessor, did not seek to play any prominent role in international affairs.

An extraordinary SADC summit held in Pretoria on 26–27 January officially welcomed and supported the efforts towards a power-sharing agreement in **Zimbabwe** as a united SADC position. It soon after emerged, however, that neither Botswana nor Zambia approved of this reconciliatory approach. Instead, and in contrast to the official communiqué, they demanded new elections. **Zambia** and **Botswana** also spearheaded demands for adherence to defined standards of legitimacy and good governance by neighbouring governments.

On 30 March, SADC suspended **Madagascar**. On 9 August, a Maputo Accord proposed a consensus government, to be composed of Rajoelin, the ousted Ravalomanana and the two former presidents Didier Ratsiraka and Zafy Albert, as a compromise solution. But it was difficult to understand the rationale for this and, not surprisingly, no progress was made, suggesting that it might not be established before year's end. Rajoelina was denied permission to address the UN General Assembly on 25 September after SADC intervention. Efforts to mediate a sustainable and lasting power-sharing solution for **Zimbabwe** and to end the simmering political conflict following the previous year's elections in **Lesotho** ran parallel to the initiative to restore a legitimate political regime in Madagascar. All the ongoing activities, which were at the centre of several mediation efforts and extraordinary meetings at the highest level, produced no visible results during the year.

The regular annual **SADC Summit** of Heads of State and Government was the 29th of its kind. It took place for the first time in the DRC's capital Kinshasa on 7–8 September. The hosting President Kabila succeeded President Zuma as new SADC chairman. At the summit inauguration, Zuma commented on the challenges that had resulted from the impact of the global financial crisis on the economies of the sub-region. While acknowledging the need for expanded relations with industrial countries in the North, especially ties with Europe, he emphasised that the SADC community should embrace and enhance its viable and feasible partnership with the newly emerging economies in the southern hemisphere. Thomas Salamao, former Mozambican transport minister, was re-elected for a second term as SADC executive secretary.

On 5 November, a summit of the troika of the **Organ on Politics, Defence and Security Cooperation** in Maputo considered and summarised the political and security situation. The heads of state of Mozambique, Swaziland, South Africa and Zimbabwe, jointly with high-level representatives from Zambia and the DRC and in the presence of representatives of the two MDC factions of Morgan Tsvangirai and Arthur Mutambara as the other political partners in the GNU, urged the Zimbabwean parties to "fully comply with the spirit and letter of the GPA and SADC Summit decisions of 27 January", and "not allow the situation to deteriorate any further", thereby implicitly recognising that hardly any progress had been made. The communiqué nonetheless appealed to the international community "to lift all forms of sanctions on Zimbabwe". The summit asked the Zimbabwean parties to resume dialogue within 15 days, or 30 days at the most. No results followed this appeal during the year, despite the announcement of the MDC-T that it had suspended its partial disengagement from the GNU. The summit also noted progress by the Joint Mediation Team on Madagascar, led by former Mozambican president Joaquim Chissano as SADC facilitator, which promoted dialogue between the four political leaders "to restore the constitutional normalcy". The summit also appreciated the role of the Christian Council of Lesotho in facilitating dialogue between the Basotho political stakeholders to find a lasting solution to the post-electoral conflicts that characterised the domestic situation in the kingdom. At the end of the year, all three countries remained a challenge for mediating efforts and seemed no closer to lasting solutions.

The judgment passed in 2008 by the Windhoek-based **SADC tribunal**, which had ruled that land invasions in Zimbabwe were illegal, was rejected by the Zimbabwean high court on 3 March with the argument that the protocol establishing the tribunal had not been ratified by parliament. It was announced in early November by a local newspaper close to ZANU-PF that Zimbabwe had withdrawn from the tribunal until the protocol had been ratified by two-thirds of SADC member countries.

Fears grew during the year that **SACU** might come to an end because of conflicts in the EPA negotiations and the options pursued by its member states. The definition of parties put the SADC-EPA group, which is not a legal entity, at odds with SACU, which, as a customs union, embraced countries that had signed up to the interim EPA as well as others that had refused to do so. The oldest existing customs union also went through some turbulence over the distribution of the reduced revenue income to be shared among South Africa, Botswana, Lesotho, Namibia and Swaziland. While South Africa contributed most to the pool, the other members benefited more under the revenue-sharing formula, deriving considerable proportions – in the case of Swaziland as much as 60% – of their national budgets from the pool. Pretoria had indicated it wanted to see changes to this arrangement.

A proposed further integration of the three overlapping **sub-regional economic communities** of SADC, EAC and COMESA into one FTA would attend to matters of harmonisation and cooperation among the diverse member states in the areas of trade and customs, as well as joint coordination of infrastructure development programmes to overcome the 'spaghetti bowl' of diverse and potentially mutually exclusive memberships in different unions. Almost two-thirds of the 26 states that make up the three communities were either already in a customs union and negotiating with an alternative customs union or were in the process of negotiating membership with two separate customs unions. As a paper presented to the African Economic Conference 2009, organised by the AfDB and the ECA on 11–13 November in Addis Ababa, warned: "Without an appropriate way to effectively incorporate business and civil society interests into the negotiations, subordinating 'the national interest' to the common good, and responding to the needs of smaller economies, the dream of a tripartite free trading area may prove difficult to realize."

Skirmishes around the signing of an interim **EPA** did not ease this potentially complicated situation and continued throughout the year. Angola, Namibia and South Africa refused, despite increasing pressure – if not threats – from Brussels, to sign the agreement, which the other countries of the SADC-EPA configuration had entered into for fear of losing preferential access to the EU market. Zambia, Madagascar, Mauritius and Zimbabwe signed the interim EPA as members of the COMESA configuration on 29 August. Mozambique, Botswana, Lesotho and Swaziland signed a separate interim EPA as the so-called 'SADC minor' group. Namibia in particular was taking a serious risk, but maintained an uncompromising position. The main bone of contention was the most favoured nation (MFN) clause, which required the countries to extend any future trade preferences with parties representing more than 1.5% of global trade to the EU. Namibia and South Africa argued that this reduced their policy space and hampered South-South trade – just at a time when SACU was negotiating a trade deal with India. The European Commission argued that the MFN clause formed part of most trade agreements. By the end of the year no solution to the impasse was in sight.

Henning Melber

Angola

The consolidation of the government was only marginally affected by the ongoing debates about the long-outstanding constitutional reform. While presidential elections were scheduled for this year, technical reasons were cited as causing the delay in resolving the constitutional debates, and both the constitutional project and the date of the next presidential election remained unresolved issues. Instead, the ruling elite extended its grip on political and economic power. On 21 September, President José Eduardo dos Santos silently marked his 30 years in power, making him the second-longest-serving head of state in Sub-Saharan Africa. The human rights situation and media freedom improved only marginally, and the low-level guerrilla war in Cabinda simmered on. Although the world economic crisis, and especially the drop in crude oil prices, impacted adversely on economic growth, economic indicators were showing signs of recovery towards the end of the year. Economic and political ties with the most important partner countries were strengthened and in line with the country's growing ambitions as a regional power. Social conditions also improved slightly, but for the vast majority of the population the situation remained difficult.

Domestic Politics

The most important non-event was the absence of **presidential elections**, regularly scheduled for one year after the 2008 parliamentary elections. The government stated that the long-overdue constitutional reforms were necessary preconditions for presidential elections, and initiated extensive parliamentary and media debates about the adoption of a 'semi-presidential' model.

In January, parliament elected a new **constitutional commission**. The parliament, where the ruling 'Movimento Popular para a Libertação de Angola' (MPLA) has a comfortable majority, with 191 of the 220 seats, appointed MPLA MP Bornito de Sousa as chair of the Parliamentary Constitutional Commission. The two vice-presidential posts were given to the majority party and the largest opposition party, 'União Nacional para a Independência Total de Angola' (UNITA), the MPLA's former wartime opponent, which held 16 seats in parliament. Of the 45 members of the commission, 35 were from the MPLA and six from UNITA, while the remaining seats were given to minor opposition parties represented in the national assembly: 'Partido de Renovação Social' (PRS) (two members), and 'Frente Nacional para a Libertação de Angola' (FNLA) and Nova Democracia (one member each).

On 26 October, Bornito de Sousa announced the launch of a major **constitutional debate**, even though, with the parliamentary opposition reduced to all but irrelevancy, the MPLA was in a position to change the constitution without any form of meaningful political negotiation. The MPLA presented a draft charter for a constitution, proposing three variants for the future government model and the role of the president. The favoured option appeared to be a 'presidential-parliamentary system', which would continue to see the president as head of government, head of state and commander in chief (as was the case before), but he would be automatically elected by nomination of the majority party in parliament. This move could delay presidential elections until 2012, when the mandate of the current parliament ends.

UNITA president Isaias Samakuva insisted the president should honour his promise and hold elections in 2009. However, as his party was defeated at the last elections, his protests remained ineffective. Other **opposition parties**, such as the historic FNLA and the PRS, protested forcefully and threatened to walk out of the commission, but were weakened by internal disputes and their lack of a popular base. Thus, instead of elections being held, debates over constitutional reform thrived in parliament and the (independent) media, with the president keeping his plans very much to himself. It appears that, although the MPLA had a comfortable parliamentary majority, there were internal tensions within the party. This, together with a number of independent presidential candidates – some from within the party – announcing their ambitions publicly, seemed reason enough for the president to decide to play it safe.

On 21 September, dos Santos silently marked his **30 years in power**, making him effectively the second-longest-serving ruler in Sub-Saharan Africa. He came to power in October 1979, one month later than Equatorial Guinea's Teodoro Obiang. Interestingly, and quite contrary to its usual front-page celebrations of the president, the state-owned newspaper 'Jornal de Angola' made no reference to the event. Independent media, opposition parties and activists claimed that he was purposely delaying the **presidential elections** as a means of retaining his hold on power. Critical voices described the state as a monarchy, where the president ruled by decree and through powerful patronage networks of relatives, ministers and generals, with little or no accountability to parliament, the judiciary or the population.

Between 7 and 10 December, the sixth MPLA congress was held in Luanda, which not surprisingly re-elected dos Santos as head of the party, with 1,964 out of 2,080 votes. In his acceptance speech, he proclaimed his intention to work "harder and better in order to defend the rights of [the] party" and stressed the government's commitment to implementing the reforms and improvements it had promised during the previous year's electoral campaign.

The effects of the cabinet reshuffle after the elections of September 2008 were felt positively in the economy. A new **economic policy team** under Economy Minister Manuel Nunes Junior, with a team that included the governor of the National Bank (BNA) and Finance Minister Eduardo Severino de Morais, seemed to have more impact on the state of affairs than the previous team. The BNA managed to stabilise the Kwanza at about Kz 86 to the $, although concerns about the sustainability of these measures were voiced. However, the prevailing popular view was that the new government was keeping precious few of its electoral promises – such as the provision of housing and jobs – and levels of dissatisfaction were on the rise. The numerous improvement works hastily conducted before the elections were seen as inadequate and already disintegrating, and the lack of economic opportunities and persistent social problems continued to frustrate the broad population.

Typically for Angola's opaque **system of patronage**, where state oil revenues are siphoned away in the notorious 'Bermuda Triangle' of the oil parastatal Sonangol, BNA and the treasury, the promiscuity between political and economic power continued to dazzle foreign observers. Numerous business interests were held by the president's family, and the highest-ranking generals of the Angolan armed forces engaged in lucrative joint-ventures, such as diamond production and the private security sector. An especially prominent example was the case of Sonangol chairman Manuel Vicente, whose business links came under scrutiny by foreign oil companies. Besides his appointment as Sonangol chairman, Vincente held board and executive posts with other private oil companies, banks and Unitel, Angola's largest mobile phone operator, as well as being the vice president of dos Santos's charity, the 'Fundação Eduardo dos Santos' (FESA). Fostered by this culture of promiscuity and the highly untransparent business interests of the political elite, **corruption** remained a major problem, despite repeated public statements in which the president expressed his opposition to corrupt practices and his determination to tackle the issue: TI's 2009 Corruption Perception Index ranked Angola as the 18th most corrupt state in the world, four places lower than the previous year.

A major domestic event was the March **visit of the Pope**, Benedict XVI, who was received by enthusiastic crowds of believers. In his sermons, the pontiff raised, amongst other things, the issue of corruption, which was echoed later in a speech by the president of the republic as one of his government's top priorities (an irony not lost on most of the few outspoken critics of the government in the country). While the pope's praise of the post-war spiritual and material recovery certainly helped improve the country's image, his visit was overshadowed by the death of at least two people trampled in the stadium where he spoke to the masses – 1 m followers attended his last service. However, his reluctance to address persistent human rights violations and the spread of HIV/AIDS was criticised by activists, European governments (most notably Germany) and international advocacy organisations.

On an unrelated note, the recent **growth of Islam**, not a religion that was historically rooted in Angola, apparently created enough anxiety for Minister of Culture Rosa Cruz e Silva to issue a warning statement on 31 March. A study of the expansion of Islam and its consequences for society was to be conducted by the National Institute of Religious Affairs. According to the minister, this investigation was not hostile to Islamic doctrine, but was concerned with practices, habits and acts that were harmful and alien to Angolan society and culture, specifically the 'enslavement' of wives.

The accountability and transparency of state institutions remained low: in March, the building of the Directorate for Criminal Investigation collapsed, leading to the death of 30 detainees and injuries to another 145. An official inquiry was conducted, but its results were never made public. Although Amnesty International reported some improvements, the overall **human rights situation** has only marginally improved. Despite outspoken condemnations by international human rights organisations, forced evictions of poor tenants from informal inner-city neighbourhoods in Luanda continued, with residents being evicted to make way for new property developments. The evicted people were relocated to peri-urban zones, in most cases without adequate compensation, where they lived in improvised houses or tents. More crucially, these new settlements were established over 20 km outside the city centre, behind the municipality of Viana, with no access to employment, informal business or schooling. Crime, drug abuse and prostitution were said to be on the rise in the affected communities. Advocacy organisations addressing these issues were threatened or harassed. Most notably, Luis Araújo, the director of SOS Habitat, an NGO fighting these forced evictions, barely escaped a plot to assassinate him under cover of a mock robbery in August.

The enclave province of **Cabinda**, where over 60% of Angola's oil production was located and the site of a long-standing separatist insurgency, remained in a state of unrest. Although the government claimed that the war in Cabinda was over, and the separatist forces were said to number only a few hundred men, sporadic attacks on government forces and oil company personnel continued. The local human rights situation also remained worrying. According to Human Rights Watch, numerous residents of the province were arrested during military raids attributed to the Liberation Front of the Enclave of Cabinda, and charged with "crimes against the security of the state". Many were held in unofficial military detention centres for more than the 90 days permitted under Angolan law without being charged with any offence. Reports indicated they were held in inhumane conditions and tortured to obtain unlawful confessions.

Media freedom remained severely restricted. Despite the emergence of a new privately owned television channel, 'TV Zimbo', and the opening of a new radio station, 'Rádio Mais', in Huambo, the only national daily 'Jornal de Angola', as well as most television and radio broadcasters remained in the hands of the state or individuals affiliated to the ruling party. Beyond this one-sided media structure, which fostered a climate of self-censorship, journalists were still regularly harassed. On 9 May, William Tonet, editor of the independent weekly 'Folha 8', was apprehended by security forces when he tried to cross the border into Namibia. His passport was seized and he was banned from travelling outside the country. Independent reporters were repeatedly detained and intimidated by the police, particularly in Cabinda. In July, independent broadcaster 'Rádio Despertar' was suspended for 180 days jointly by the ministry of posts and telecommunications and the ministry of media, on the grounds that it had exceeded the broadcasting range allowed by its operating license.

Foreign Affairs

Bolstered by its oil wealth, Angola sought to further improve its standing as a regional superpower. Spurred into activity by China's increased investments in the Angolan oil and construction sectors, most foreign partners actively courted the government with promises of credits, investments and trade agreements, without any political conditionalities attached.

Relations with **South Africa** have steadily improved since Jacob Zuma took over the presidency from Thabo Mbeki. South Africa's hunger for Angolan energy, coupled with Angola's interest in South Africa's expertise in developing infrastructure, presaged a mutually beneficial alliance of the two regional powers. A visit by Zuma and his delegation to Luanda in August – his first bilateral state visit – underlined Angola's regional importance and took place in a spirit of felicitation and satisfaction over diplomatic and commercial successes. Zuma also visited a former ANC guerrilla camp in Pango, recalling the historical alliance between the two current governments. Questions about Angola's democratic and human rights record were staved off by reference to NEPAD's peer review mechanism, and by emphasising new bilateral agreements in the areas of transport, communication and trade. Furthermore, both countries pledged to revitalise the development of the sub-region through **SADC**, and to contribute to stability in Zimbabwe and the DRC through peacekeeping missions.

Relations with the **DR Congo** were tenser than in previous years, as the two countries engaged in a disastrous campaign to mutually expel each other's nationals. These expulsions were said merely to mask deeper economic disagreements over border and territorial water delineations (i.e. oil fields), diamonds and hydroelectric power, but they still resulted in waves of displaced people crossing the border. Up to 200,000 Angolan refugees from the DRC, as well as an equal number of illegal Congolese immigrants, mainly *garimpeiros* (artisan miners) working in the diamond-rich Lunda areas of Angola, were forcibly driven out. This resulted in a humanitarian crisis only alleviated by the rapid intervention of the UNHCR, who provided temporary shelters for the repatriated. The Angolans in DRC, who in most cases had been living there for many years, said their perfectly legitimate residence permits had been taken away and destroyed. Both Angolans and Congolese claimed to having suffered severe human rights abuses at the hands of the security forces. Congolese women expelled from the Cabinda enclave stated that they were systematically raped by Angolan soldiers, and many of the returnees showed marks of torture. A provisional agreement between the two countries drafted in October was confirmed at a bilateral meeting in November with the intention of reviving a tripartite mechanism for repatriation under the auspices of the UNHCR. However, as in previous years, Angola displayed its military strength and influence over DRC in another troop incursion at Tshela on 17–18 October.

Ties with **Portugal** and **Brazil** remained strong. In March, dos Santos made his first state visit to Portugal, the former colonial power. More important than the long-standing, historical political ties, however, were Angola's growing investments in Portuguese and Brazilian companies, which led some commentators to speak of 'reverse colonialism'. Indeed, according to financial consultants AT Kearney, Sonangol and Isabela dos Santos, the president's daughter, held between them 3% of Portugal's capital quoted on its stock exchange index PSI20, totalling shares to the value of € 1.8 bn. Similarly, Portuguese investments in Angola tripled from 2008, amounting to € 634 m. Portugal was also Angola's largest import partner, accounting for 17.6% of total imports. As a result of this increased financial entanglement, political relations were friendlier than ever, with Portugal often acting as Angola's advocate on the international stage.

The growing importance of **China** as an economic and political partner was reflected in the attribution of further oil-backed credit lines without political conditionalities. Chinese credit lines were estimated to exceed $ 5 bn in total by 2009, and China overtook the US as Angola's main trading partner, accounting for 33% of total exports, and 15.7% of total imports. In return for credits and loans, Chinese food products and consumer goods were imported into Angola, and Chinese companies played a major part in the ongoing infrastructural reconstruction and development activities. However, in an effort to minimise economic dependency on China, Angola rejected some Chinese direct investment proposals. Allegations of assaults on Chinese workers were made in the area of Luanda. These reports, as well as wild rumours about Chinese cannibalism circulating among the population, could be seen as indicators of growing popular resentment against the very visible Chinese presence. Despite these added strains on the bilateral relations, overall diplomatic ties with Beijing remained friendly and constructive.

On the occasion of a visit by **US Secretary of State** Hillary Clinton to Angola on 9 August, six prominent civil society activists sent her an open letter, denouncing the monopolisation of the banking and telecommunications sectors by the president's children, ongoing human rights violations, and the unconstitutional practices of dos Santos' government. While promoting closer co-operation in the energy sector, Clinton did raise the issue of human rights at her news conference. She also lauded the peaceful 2008 parliamentary elections and called for "timely, free and fair" presidential elections according to schedule. However, as the US was Angola's second most important trading partner, accounting for 28.7% of Angolan exports, and remained critically dependent on oil imports, this political criticism remained subtle at best. Military relations between the two countries also became closer, as the US sought to secure oil from the Gulf of Guinea, but the US also, through USAID, increased its support in the areas of agriculture, healthcare and economic reform.

Russia's increasing interest in reviving its Cold War ties with Angola was reflected in Russian Prime Minister Dmitri Medvedev's visit to Luanda in June. The first visit of a Russian leader since the 1980s was seen as an effort to balance the growing influence of China and the West in Africa, and to secure a share of Angola's mineral wealth for Russia. The meeting between the two heads of state took place in an atmosphere of friendship and trust – especially as dos Santos speaks fluent Russian, having studied in the Soviet Union in the 1960s – and saw the signing of several bilateral agreements on economic cooperation, natural resources and education. Bank credits of over $ 300 m from Vneshekonom–bank, VTB Group and Roseximbank were granted for investment in telecommunications and the construction of hydroelectric dams on the Kwanza River, but would possibly also include exploitation rights for oil, natural gas and diamonds, as well as lucrative railway contracts. Furthermore, Medvedev promised support for Angola's AngoSat satellite programme. After strong military and political collaboration in the 1970s and 1980s, bilateral relations between the two countries had been weakened in the 1990s. Medvedev's visit thus marked a new high point in renewed trade and education links.

In July, **Cuba**'s President Raúl Castro arrived in Luanda for his second visit in five months. Angola's former Cold War ally agreed to send 230 doctors to Angola (in addition to the 200 already working there) to help address the shortage of doctors and the underdeveloped state of the health sector. The Angolan health minister also announced that the two countries would jointly develop a vaccine against cholera. Like relations with Russia, the long-standing partnership with Cuba had waned during the 1990s, when popular resentment against the presence of Cuban military advisors was high, but it is now being renewed.

Relations with **France** remained fraught and overshadowed by spectacular corruption scandals. In October, the main accused in the so-called 'Angolagate' affair, Pierre Falcone and Arkadi Gaydamak, were sentenced *in absentia* in Paris to six-year terms of imprisonment for organising illegal arms sales to Angola in the 1990s. Former French interior minister Charles Pasqua was sentenced to one year, and Jean-Christophe Mitterrand, the son of the late French president, to a two-year suspended sentence. Not only were the shipments illegal, but the $ 790 m deal also involved millions of dollars in kickbacks, allegedly to dos Santos and his entourage. Although no Angolan officials were indicted, the trial strained relations between the two countries considerably. Less well-known publicly was a joint venture signed in April between French defence company Thales and a relatively unknown Angolan company, Sadissa. According to Angolan investigative journalist Rafael Marques, Sadissa is owned by Manuel Vicente, chairman and chief executive of state oil company Sonangol, and Miguel da Costa, Angola's ambassador in Paris. The deals to supply the Angolan armed forces with equipment and arms were said to be worth a total of € 141.6 m.

In May, dos Santos was invited by a representative of Italian President Silvio Berlusconi to participate for the first time in the July **G8 Summit** in Italy. This invitation was issued in recognition of Angola's role as an oil producer and its ever-growing business ties with China. Dos Santos' participation was highlighted by US and EU officials, most notably by European Commission President Manuel Durão Barroso, who voiced his hope that Angola would contribute to solving the world financial crisis. Finally, the 155th Extraordinary Meeting of the Conference of OPEC convened in Luanda on 22 December, under the chairmanship of Minister of Petroleum José Maria Botelho de Vasconcelos. Angola's **presidency of OPEC** also underlined its increased international importance.

Socioeconomic Developments

Despite its massive economic growth in the last years, Angola suffered from the global economic crisis. Early in the year, the government had to revise its GDP growth projections to 11.9%, due to falling oil prices and oil production cuts imposed by OPEC. More realistically, however, the recession led to the first **contraction in GDP growth** since the end of the war. Various sources estimated real GDP growth at between 0.2% and -3.6% (down from 13.2% in 2008). Facing such adversity, the government entered into negotiations with the IMF, resolving a long-standing feud with the Bretton Woods institutions.

In November, the IMF announced its approval of a $ 1.4 bn loan to rebuild Angola's international reserves and alleviate immediate cash-flow pressures. The deal was hailed by Economy Minister Manuel Nunes Junior as a victory, marking the improvement of relations with the IMF, and a token of trust in the country's financial credibility. Earlier, international corruption watchdog Global Witness had urged the IMF not to pursue the arrangement, as it risked condoning corruption by so doing, and called instead for the IMF to use its leverage to press the Angolan government for greater transparency.

Despite earlier government promises, the economy was still largely dependent on the **oil industry**, with production peaking at 2.015 m barrels/day. Together with subsidiary industries, oil accounted, according to Oil Minister Botelho de Vasconcelos, for almost 95% of total export revenue – Sonangol's total profit for the year was announced at $ 2.4 bn. In order to address this dependency, state-owned Sonangol embarked on a risky expansion course, investing in natural gas exploitation, construction and banking, but also acquiring exploitation rights for oil fields in the Gulf of Mexico, Algeria and Iraq, and, through the newly-formed joint venture China Sonangol, buying assets in Africa, Asia and Latin America. Paradoxically, parliament voted in March to exempt companies exploring for natural gas from taxes in order to stimulate investment in this area. Nevertheless, Angola was overtaken by Nigeria as the largest oil producer in Africa.

Diamonds continued to be Angola's other major source of income and, according to statal diamond producer Endiama, output remained high at around 9 m carats per year. Alluvial diamonds are mined artisanally in the north-eastern provinces of Lunda Norte and Lunda Sul. Despite this wealth, these provinces are generally viewed as being exploited and underdeveloped, and were described by their inhabitants as "the land of diamonds, without electricity, water, schools or roads". Furthermore, the proximity to the border with DRC, coupled with a number of private security companies operating in the area, made for a volatile and potentially explosive situation. Many of these companies, owned by generals and ministers, were again accused of severe human rights violations. The indiscriminate use of force against 'illegal' miners, and the arbitrary, forced dispossession of local landowners without adequate compensation, were the most frequent allegations. On 28 June, the Dubai Multi Commodities Centre announced its intention to strengthen ties with Angola in the area of the diamond trade. Interestingly, some members of Angola's elite put forward the idea of making Angola Africa's Dubai, so the visit of an Angolan delegation to Dubai might be seen as concerned with more than diamond-mining and processing alone. A deal on uranium exploration was signed with Romania, but generally other mining resources, such as iron, copper, and uranium remain to become more developed.

A number of large-scale **infrastructural development projects** were completed and inaugurated towards the end of the year, most notably the road bridges over the Catumbela River, between Benguela and Lobito, and the Cunene River Bridge, on the major north-south road leading to the Namibian border. Four football stadiums for the 2010 African

Cup of Nations were (almost) completed, together with some investment in transport and accommodation infrastructures in the host cities of Luanda, Benguela, Lubango and Cabinda. In fact, the whole country resembled an extensive construction site, the most visible improvements being the road network and impressive property developments in Luanda (especially in the new business/residential area of Luanda Sul). The railway network, redeveloped with the help of Chinese contractors, was also rehabilitated, although regular services were not yet available outside Luanda. In May, the Brazilian construction giants Odebrecht and Andrade Gutierez – usually known for warm and very close links with the government – hinted that their coordination of construction works was hampered by complicity between the ministry of public works and General Kopelipa's 'Gabinete de Reconstrução Nacional' (National Reconstruction Cabinet) and intimated that there was a conflict over the 'blue bag' (i.e. kickback) expected from the private companies.

The **manufacturing and industrial sector** remained marginal, operating far below its potential because of an unfavourable business environment characterised by high costs, rampant corruption, Byzantine legislation, an overvalued currency and poor infrastructure. The Doing Business Project ranked Angola at 170 out of 183 economies for ease of setting up and running a business. According to this index, registering property, for example, would take 185 days, compared with the OECD average of 25 days. Nonetheless, some industries experienced increasing success, mainly those producing beverages and cement. On 10 July, London-based brewery giant SABMiller announced its intention to invest $ 125 m in a new brewery and soft drinks plant to satisfy the growing local demand for beverages – Angola has become the third largest beer consumer in Africa. It also announced that it had trained 200 graduates on its apprentice scheme. As a result of the construction boom and limited supplies, cement became even more profitable than beer, with a 50 kg bag selling for $ 30. These revenues were mostly racked up by the two local producers, Nova Cimangola and Secil, who virtually constitute a politically-connected duopoly: the Angolan state is the majority shareholder in Secil, while Nova Cimangola is, through a web of holdings, largely owned by the president's daughter, Isabela dos Santos (popularly know as 'the princess').

Angola's other major resource, its abundance of rich arable land, remained underdeveloped and 90% of the **agricultural sector** was still at subsistence level. Probably impelled by the drop in crude oil prices, the government announced a stimulus plan to reduce the country's dependence on food imports and incentivise people to leave the overcrowded cities (mainly Luanda) to take up farming in rural areas. The years of war had left large swathes of land mined and uncultivable. By investing in schools and health centres in the countryside, the government pledged to support rural communities socially and economically, reduce poverty and boost production levels. NGOs active in rural development remained sceptical that these top-down programmes would lead to reversing the migration flows from the cities back to the rural areas. Nevertheless, this policy met with some success as Angola saw a dramatic increase in its production of staple cereals, including maize. Output during the 2008/09 period grew by 42% to 1.052 bn tonnes, according to Agriculture Minister Afonso Pedro Canga. Furthermore, London-based multinational Lonrho announced in January that it had secured 25,000 hectares of rice paddy in Angola. Although a large part of this production was meant to feed the local market, the company conceded that some small farmers might have to be 'relocated' to make way for their business development. In February, heavy rains and floods in the provinces of Huíla, Cuando Cubango and Cunene forced more than 20,000 people from their homes. This raised fears of food shortages in the already under-supplied provinces, but the WFP still phased out its assistance operations in August, shifting its emphasis to capacity-development.

The **lack of jobs** and a skilled workforce continued to hamper economic development. Infrastructural development projects carried out by Chinese and Brazilian/Portuguese contractors employed only small numbers of Angolans, partly because there were not enough trained workers, but even more because Chinese labour was cheaper than national labour. This was possible because of the favourable conditions enjoyed by Chinese companies, namely tax and tariff exemptions on imported materials and their ability to house their workers on-site, thus effectively bypassing the local economy and resulting in the 'insular nature' of these capital flows. Only in the oil industry, where laws stipulate that a certain percentage of the workforce must be Angolan, could some improvements be seen; a small number of young Angolans were sent to study abroad on Sonangol scholarships and bursaries. Otherwise, most Angolans were left to look for an income in the informal sector, engaging in trade or services, but this was made more difficult by the government's crackdown on 'illegal' street vendors. In a bid to 'regularise' their trade, the *zungueiras* were assigned to newly constructed, formal market places, which in fact threatened their income base. The **education sector** is still recovering from years of neglect. Despite the opening up of new, private higher education institutes in Luanda, many schools are yet to be rebuilt and staffed; the literacy rate remained low at 67.4%.

Despite its oil wealth and improved international and regional standing, **development indices** remained alarmingly low, an indicator that these revenues were perhaps not put to the most efficient use. The HDI ranked Angola at 143 out of 182 countries, up from 162 in 2008. According to the IMF, GDP reached an estimated $ 113.9 bn, with a per-capita income of $ 8,800 but, of an estimated 19 m people, two thirds continued to live on less than $ 2 a day, and this in a country whose capital has been named the most expensive city in the world for the second consecutive year (a 5 kg bag of rice cost $ 200). The city continued to be crippled by daily traffic congestion, with road infrastructure nowhere near sufficient for a population now estimated at over 5 m. Furthermore, water and power cuts were still almost as frequent as during the war, and basic sanitation was lacking in the majority of *musseques* (shantytowns).

In addition, **health delivery** was still in a dismal state. Health Vice Minister José Van-Dúnem admitted in July that health services did not match the needs and expectations of the population and that infrastructures were inadequate to cope with demands, especially in Luanda. He promised improvements after cameras of the state television station TPA recorded the death of a young man who had been refused treatment at Luanda's Americo Boavida hospital. A campaign was launched in the province of Kwanza-Norte in the same month with the aim of vaccinating over 89,400 children against polio. The same campaign would also immunise some 74,000 women against tetanus. Furthermore, USAID announced the release of $ 6 m for basic health service projects during the year. Despite these efforts, life expectancy at birth stood at about 38.2 years, and the infant mortality rate remained the world's highest, at 180 deaths per 1,000 live births. The population kept growing at a rate of over 2%, resulting in over 50% of the population being under the age of 25. The official HIV adult prevalence rate was given as 2.1%, comparatively low for the region, but this was largely the result of outdated information and under-reporting. In fact, it appears that the virus was spreading fast, especially along the transport corridors in the south of the country. Other widespread diseases included malaria, sleeping sickness, cholera, bilharzia, hepatitis A and typhoid fever. An outbreak of Ebola in neighbouring DRC led to the borders being closed in the north-eastern part of the country in January.

Jon Schubert

Botswana

Despite internal rifts, the Botswana Democratic Party (BDP) won a sound victory in the ninth election after independence. Botswana remained the Southern African region's most vocal critic of Zimbabwe's President Mugabe. Notwithstanding relative macroeconomic stability, dependence on diamond exports proved problematic as reduced demand and a decreasing GDP followed the international financial crisis.

Domestic Politics

During preparations for general elections in October, factional infighting within the ruling **BDP** intensified. The launch of the BDP election manifesto on 29 March was overshadowed by a fierce argument between state and party president Ian Khama and BDP party chairman and minister of presidential affairs and state administration Daniel Kwelagobe. Khama's suggestion that politicians holding national office should not also sit on the party's central committee was opposed by Kwelagobe. Kwelagobe declared that, if forced, he would remain party chairman rather than stay in the cabinet. On 3 April, Kwelagobe was replaced as minister by Margaret Nasha, the former minister for local government. Inner-party division increased further when, at the party congress from 17 to 20 July, Khama announced his support for the former minister Tebelelo Seretse as candidate for

Kwelagobe's post as party chairman. However, Kwelagobe secured a narrow victory over Seretse at the congress (with 508 votes to 469). Kwelagobe's 'Baratha Phati' faction (literally 'those who love the party') also won all other committee posts. In his capacity as BDP president, Khama rushed to appoint his supporters (the 'A Team') to unelected posts on the central committee and various party sub-committees, without the usual consultation. On 18 August, Khama suspended the BDP's newly elected secretary general, Gomolemo Motswaledi, after the latter's criticism of Khama's inner-party policies.

The leading opposition party, the Botswana National Front (**BNF**), proved unable to exploit the turmoil in the BDP. Inner-party strife about the leadership qualities of BNF party president, Otsweletse Moupo, persisted. Despite calls for reconciliation when the party launched its manifesto in mid-April, Moupo's purge against 'dissidents' continued. On 11 May, Tlhomamiso Kebaswele, parliamentary candidate for Moshupa constituency, was expelled from the BNF following an argument with Olebile Gaborone, the BNF chairman and Moupo's ally. In June, Robert Molefhabangwe, long-standing MP in Gaborone West South, was also expelled. Internal strife dominated the BNF congress in July. In mid-August, a court ruled invalid the 2008 suspension of Akanyang Magama, a MP and fierce critic of Moupo. It also found that Magama was the party's legitimate candidate in the Gaborone South constituency. The party leadership accepted this ruling only reluctantly and was able to finalise its list of election candidates just weeks before election day.

The Botswana Congress Party (**BCP**), the second opposition party, represented with only one MP in parliament, fared well compared with both the BDP and BNF. In mid July, the BCP and the Botswana Alliance Movement (BAM), another, smaller opposition grouping, held a joint party conference and declared an agreement to merge formally after the general election. The two parties formed an electoral alliance, fielding candidates in different constituencies so that they did not stand against each other.

While the BDP's election campaign centred around Khama and his 'four D's' (democracy, development, dignity and discipline), the opposition focussed on **criticism of Khama**'s allegedly authoritarian leadership style and also exploited the implementation of the controversial Media Practitioners' Act, passed by parliament in December 2008. At the heart of the legislation was the establishment of a government-appointed media appeals committee to replace the current self-regulating council. Two prominent lawyers, Dick Bayford and Duma Boko, both close to the opposition, turned down an invitation to serve on the committee, questioning its credibility. The two lawyers also represented the family of John Kalafatis, who had been shot dead by military intelligence in Gaborone on 13 May. The shooting had caused an outcry in the private media. Kalafatis, a 'most wanted' listed criminal, was shot eight to 15 times while apparently unarmed. The government failed to explain the circumstances of the shooting and Vice President Mompati Merafhe appeared to trivialise the incident. Human rights groups and the Law Society of Botswana joined the criticism and, of all the political parties, the BCP took issue with the shooting most strongly and effectively.

On 30 July, when the parties stepped up their **electoral campaigns**, the Kgalagadi Breweries announced a P 2 m ($ 290,000) donation to help political parties finance their election campaigns. There is no public funding of political parties in Botswana and, although the donation was allocated according to the parties' share of the vote at the last election, giving more than 50% to the BDP, the opposition parties in particular welcomed the move. On 21 August, parliament was dissolved, starting the final phase of the election campaign. The Independent Electoral Commission (IEC) published the final electoral roll, showing that 724,000 people had registered, clearly above the targeted 650,000 and 30% more than the 553,000 who registered for the previous elections in 2004.

On polling day, 16 October, fears of voter apathy proved unsubstantiated: 555,308 Batswana, around 76% of registered voters, cast their votes (compared with 412,379 in 2004). The balloting went smoothly and international observers judged the elections free and fair. Once again, the **election results** secured a sound majority for the BDP, with 45 of the 57 parliamentary seats, which automatically confirmed Khama in office. Despite the internal rifts, the BDP even increased its vote share by around 2% compared with 2004 to 53.3% and gained one more seat than in the 2004 election. As expected, the BNF suffered a severe defeat and lost half of its 12 seats in parliament, including all seats in the capital, its former stronghold. Yet, on closer inspection, the heavy loss was also due to the British-style 'first-past-the-post' system. The BNF's 21.9% of the vote share was only 5% less than in 2004 and the BNF retained its position as the official opposition party. Nevertheless, the BCP took advantage of the BNF's weakness and secured four seats (with 19.2% of the vote), three seats more than in 2004. Its ally, the BAM (with 2.3% of the vote) gained the first parliamentary seat in its history. A remarkable development was the rise of independent candidates; 146 stood in the parliamentary elections (compared with 14 in 2004) and one candidate, the former BNF MP Nehemiah Modubule, even made it to parliament. Results of the local elections, held on the same day, were fairly comparable to the national elections.

While the election results prompted calls for BNF leader Moupo to step down, the relative success of the BDP strengthened Khama's position. It was apparently mainly Khama's huge popularity with ordinary and rural Batswana, alongside with opposition blunders, that had guaranteed the party's success, despite the infighting. Having a strong mandate for his **first full presidential term** – he had succeeded Festus Mogae 18 months ahead of elections – Khama avoided open confrontation with his opponents within the party. Though Kwelagobe did not return to the cabinet, the newly elected president made pragmatic choices for the 'specially elected' MPs the head of state is allowed to appoint. Khama reappointed Merafhe as vice president, but the cabinet also saw a number of new faces after four cabinet ministers lost their seats or retired from politics. As expected, Kenneth Matambo was appointed minister of finance and development planning. He had been acting in this role since 1 August after the long standing incumbent, Baledzi Gaolathe, left the cabinet due to 'ill health'. It therefore came as a surprise that Gaolathe was appointed minister for trade and industry. Khama may have been forced into this after the previous minister, Neo Moroka, unexpectedly lost his parliamentary seat to the BNF. In his inauguration speech on 20 October, Khama reiterated his commitment to the 'four Ds' and added a new one, 'delivery'; he also promised to promote economic diversification, poverty alleviation and youth empowerment.

The now 'five D's' were also at the centre of the **State of the Nation address**, delivered on 13 November. Khama particularly stressed the need to overcome the country's dependence on diamonds, after a decline in demand on Botswana's primary export commodity had resulted in recession (see socioeconomic developments). The speech was well received by ordinary citizens. In the following public debate, however, the issue of Khama's leadership style came once more to the fore. The debate centred on the case of BDP secretary general Motswaledi, whose original suspension (60 days) had been drastically extended (to five years) on October 23. Khama's immunity as state president had prevented Motswaledi from appealing against his suspension from the party by Khama in his capacity as party president. Some BDP MPs were concerned that the court ruling gave Khama a licence to run the BDP as he pleased and called for a revision of the constitution. Opposition speakers, such as BCP president Gilson Saleshando and independent MP Modubule, strongly questioned Khama's democratic credentials in connection with his handling of BDP factionalism. Following pressure from BDP party elders, however, Khama's official website reported on 23 November that Motswaledi had been reinstated as secretary general and to all other party functions unconditionally, further maintaining that Khama had at all times acted within his powers.

Foreign Affairs

The crisis in neighbouring **Zimbabwe** continued to be one of the key concerns of Botswana's foreign policy, with the country being the strongest critic of President Robert Mugabe in Southern Africa. The Ministry of Foreign Affairs officially welcomed a deal brokered at the extraordinary summit of SADC on 27 January, which resolved to implement the stalled power-sharing agreement in Zimbabwe between the Zimbabwe African National Union-Patriotic Front (ZANU-PF), led by President Mugabe, and the opposition Movement for Democratic Change (MDC). Botswana only reluctantly accepted this resolution, given the fact that, together with Tanzania and Zambia, it had earlier argued for fresh presidential elections in Zimbabwe.

As a result of an extraordinary summit of SADC heads of state on 30 March, Botswana, together with the DRC, South Africa and Zambia, even assumed responsibility for seeking international financial support for Zimbabwe. At the SADC summit in Kinshasa (2–8 September), the government finally voted in favour of dropping sanctions against senior Zimbabwean officials. However, the Ministry of Foreign Affairs insisted that the softening of its policy stance on Zimbabwe was dependent on further progress being achieved.

Accordingly, when Zimbabwe's Prime Minister Tsvangirai withdrew for some weeks from the power-sharing agreement with President Mugabe on 16 October, Botswana immediately repeated its call for fresh elections to be held under international supervision.

Botswana continued to enjoy cordial relations with most of its peers and was a widely respected member of the **AU**. However, at the same time Botswana's government explicitly criticised the continental body. Following the summit of the AU heads of state from 24 June to 3 July, Vice President Mompati Merafhe maintained that Muammar Kadhafi had abused his position as chairman of the AU to force acceptance of the Libyan position, which includes the establishment of the African Defence Council and a resolution of non-cooperation with the ICC indictment of Sudanese President Omar al-Bashir.

Being a landlocked nation, Botswana sought closer ties with its neighbour **Namibia** in order to build a railway line to gain better access to the Namibian port of Walvis Bay. This should allow Botswana to more efficiently export mineral products – mainly coal from the Mmamabula and Morupule coalfields and soda ash from Sua Pan – and to import mining equipment more cheaply. On 4 June, Botswana and Namibia signed an agreement to construct a railway line, which would significantly lower transportation costs. The project commenced with a feasibility study in July, which was financed by the World Bank and the governments of both countries.

On the global stage, Botswana was still criticised for its treatment of the **Basarwa/San minority**. Organisations such as the London-based Survival International maintained that the government still discriminated against the group and was not adhering to the High Court decision from December 2006 allowing them to return to the Central Kalahari Game Reserve. In general, Botswana benefited on the global level from its reputation for political and economic stability. In this respect, President Khama's meeting with US President **Barack Obama** at the White House on 5 November was the most notable event. President Obama praised Botswana for its "extraordinary" achievement since independence.

Socioeconomic Developments

The world economic crisis was severely felt in Botswana as global demand for **diamonds**, the country's main export commodity, plunged. Debswana's diamond mines, which were all shut down in December 2008, remained closed until mid-April. Two of them, the No. 2 plant at Orapa and the Damshaa operation, remained shut down throughout the year. The crisis also resulted in significant job losses. At the end of September, Debswana employed 5,809 people, a reduction of 1,384 since December 2008. In the diamond cutting industry, 26% of staff were made redundant (with numbers falling from 3,226 to 2,391) between November 2008 and August.

Before delivering his **annual budget** on 2 February, the then minister of finance and development planning, Baledzi Gaolathe, spoke about the need for belt-tightening as a result of falling government revenues. Government in turn introduced cost-saving measures, which included cutting the development budget by 5% and the recurrent budget by 7% across the board. However, the government maintained an expansionary fiscal stance in order to cushion the world economic crisis' effects on the domestic economy and, in December, parliament approved additional expenditure. For the fiscal year 2009/10 (April–March) a budget deficit of P 13.39 bn, approximately 14% of expected GDP, was projected. The **deficit** was financed by savings that had accumulated over several years of fiscal surplus and additional borrowing. Following the government's request in May, the AfDB on 2 June approved a record loan of $ 1.5 bn to support government finances in 2009/10. Botswana borrowed from the bank for the first time in 17 years.

Due to the uncertain economic outlook, government in March deferred the commencement of the new **National Development Plan** (NDP 10) for one year until April 2010. The country continued to focus on development projects that had already started under the NDP 9. Yet, in contrast to widespread expectations, the recession was not catastrophic. In real terms, GDP showed a decline of 4.6% over a one-year period up to September, with signs of recovery and increasing international demand for diamonds already apparent in the second half of the year.

On 23 August, the anniversary of the day when the Pula replaced the South African Rand as Botswana's currency in 1976, the Bank of Botswana (BoB) launched a series of **new banknotes**, including a newly introduced P 200 note (around $ 30), the first higher denomination note to be issued in ten years. At 8.2%, annual inflation was lower than the 12.6% recorded in 2008, but still remained above the BoB 3%-6% medium-term target range.

Efforts to diversify the economy showed no progress. Despite the government's drive to revive the economy under the banner 'Botswana Excellence Strategy for Economic Diversification and Sustainable Growth', the attempt to diversify the economy appeared even gloomier following the announcement in November by Caratex, the main textile manufacturer, that it would close its six textile factories with the **loss of 5,000 jobs**.

In June, ignoring objections by South Africa, Botswana, together with Lesotho and Swaziland, signed an **Interim EPA** with the EU. Botswana's decision hinged on the need to safeguard access to the EU market for its beef exports, and to make the country more attractive to international investors. In this respect, Botswana plans to act as a hub for international investment in Africa, and Southern Africa in particular.

Despite the recession, Botswana continued to exhibit comparatively strong macroeconomic fundamentals and received favourable governance ratings. For instance, it was once again rated the least corrupt country in Africa on TI's 2009 Corruption Perceptions Index. The socioeconomic record was more mixed, however, as in the years before, with pronounced levels of poverty and unemployment. Regarding **HIV/AIDS**, measures undertaken by the authorities, such as the country-wide rolling out of antiretroviral medicine (ARVs) and regular testing, had a significant effect on halting the spread of HIV/

AIDS in one of the countries with the highest HIV prevalence rates in the world. Of those eligible for ARV treatment, 86% were enrolled on the national programme at the end of September and infection among the critical younger generation was on the decline. The Botswana AIDS Impact Survey (BAIS III) of 2008 indicated that the prevalence rate for 15–24 year-olds fell from 15% in 2004 to 8% in 2008. Nevertheless, life expectancy in 2009 was still nearly ten years lower than in 1995.

Matthias Basedau & Christian von Soest

Lesotho

An **armed attack** upon the Makoanyane Barracks and the prime minister's official residence in Maseru on 22 April indicated that the controversies caused by the 2007 election, which had seen the return to power of the Lesotho Congress for Democracy (LCD) in alliance with the small National Independence Party (NIP), continued to run deep. Although unsuccessful and conducted largely by foreign assailants, the attacks appeared to have links with members of the Lesotho Defence Force (LDF) and possibly with the parliamentary opposition. The attempted coup (for that is what it appears to have been) was badly bungled, and various assailants were either killed or captured by security forces on both sides of the Lesotho-South Africa border.

Domestic Politics

An **attempted coup** took place on 22 April against the background of Pakalitha Mosisili's consolidation of his authority as leader of the LCD, the entrenchment of the LCD's dominance through disputed means, and indications of growing intolerance of political challenge by opponents and elements of the media. An armed attack took place on the prime minister's official residence and the Makoanyane Barracks. The attack on the prime minister's residence was beaten off and, after a chase, three of the attackers were killed and two captured, while another was killed attempting to cross the river to South Africa, and others arrested when they arrived there. At a press conference a few days after the attack, a senior police officer named Makotoko 'Mashai' Lerotholi, as the mastermind of the assault. Lerotholi, a former warrant officer in the LDF, had a history of involvement in shadowy opposition activities. Further, it later emerged from court proceedings in Ladybrand, that seven Mozambicans and one South African had been arrested by South African police between 22 and 25 April in connection with the attack. They were detained until such time as the Lesotho government requested that they be deported to Lesotho.

Meanwhile, Lerotholi, who been charged with an array of serious offences in absentia in court proceedings in Maseru on 1 May, had also fled to South Africa, where on 8 May he turned himself over to the police for protection from someone who, he alleged, was hunting him down to kill him. The following day, however, he was formally arrested following a request from the Lesotho director of public prosecutions for his extradition. Meanwhile, his LDF colleagues continued to be held in a police station, from which they were sprung after an armed attack on 7 July, only to be swiftly recaptured by the LDF. Lerotholi contested his extradition and was released on bail.

Further **details of a murky story** were revealed – first, by the Mozambican high commissioner to Lesotho, who indicated that the Mozambicans involved were former soldiers who had been recruited to South Africa to work as security guards, but later stated that they had been hired to participate in a mission in conjunction with the LDF and security forces; and second, by an affidavit put before a court in Bloemfontein on 9 September, in which a South African told of his recruitment in Soweto and the leadership of the mission by a man who claimed to have trained the LDF for 30 years, and who was referred to as 'the general'. The affidavit goes on to tell of the capture of seven LDF soldiers in the attack on Makoanyane and the theft of arms, an armoured vehicle and a jeep, only for the attackers to encounter vigorous resistance by the LDF as they left the barracks. After a dramatic chase through Maseru, they abandoned their vehicles and attempted to make their way back across the border river to South Africa.

If the good news for Mosisili was that the attempted attack had been thwarted, the bad news was that it seemed that at least some of his opponents, some of them with linkages to the LDF, were prepared to resort to violence. If this was so, it was perhaps because of widespread **frustration amongst the opposition** about the futility of appealing through the legal and political processes, with the courts apparently searching for legal devices to help them avoid confrontation with the government, and the latter stubbornly determined to give no ground on key issues that threatened the country's political stability. The seriousness of the political impasse was demonstrated by the visit to Maseru by Ketumile Masire, former president of Botswana, on 8 July, and the intemperate response to his report by the government.

Masire's Report on his efforts to negotiate a solution to the political impasse during the previous year concluded that his attempt to promote dialogue had been blocked by the government. A seminar scheduled for late 2008 that would have involved the ruling party, government, opposition and other stakeholders, and would have been addressed by electoral experts, had ultimately not been held because the government had withdrawn its agreement to call in the experts and, in December 2008, had written to SADC stating that it saw no need to continue with the dialogue. Masire now indicated that he felt unable to continue as mediator, but would report back to SADC that the spirit of Mixed Membership Proportionality (MMP) had been undermined by both the major parties, the LCD and the All Basotho Convention, forming alliances with smaller parties without formally merging with them. This had distorted the result and rendered the MMP electoral model ineffectual. Accordingly, the electoral laws should be reformed to prevent this happening again – presumably by requiring coalescing parties to merge to prevent their abuse the of proportional representation (PR) list; the jurisdiction of the High Court and Appeal Court to determine appeals from election petitions should be placed beyond doubt; and the law governing the recognition of a leader of the opposition should be clarified. But none of this was acceptable to the government. Mosisili accused Masire of seeking to set the country on fire by dousing it with petrol, while the government's official response to the report denied that it had blocked the seminar, arguing that, while it had wanted expert advice, the opposition had wanted the distribution of PR results reviewed; that the formation of electoral alliances had been legal; and that an attempt to amend the Constitution to give full authority to hear cases concerning election results had been defeated in the Senate (where opposition forces were stronger). Masire, it said, had been appointed as a facilitator of dialogue, not an arbitrator.

Encouraged by the Masire Report, the major opposition parties joined together in July to form an **Opposition Parties Forum** which presented a petition to the Independent Electoral Commission and parliament. This called for mass action, including a 'stay away' on 3 August. The stay away proved ineffective, but the government conceded to talks, which took place under the chairmanship of the retired Anglican bishop, Philip Mokuku. The talks succeeded in drawing up an agenda for further talks about MMP, while in September SADC appointed a three-man mediation team, composed of the foreign ministers of Mozambique, Swaziland and Zambia, to see if they could succeed where Masire had failed. The danger remained that no resolution of the issue would be reached in time for 2012, in which case the LCD might be even more ruthless in resisting the challenge from a potentially more united opposition.

The high drama in the political sphere was minimally reflected in a summary of the **APRM report** on Lesotho published in June (the full report still awaited presentation to the AU Heads of Government and States' summit in 2010). While the report included extensive coverage of and recommendations concerning economic governance and management, corporate governance and socio-economic development, its principal paragraph concerning the political situation was woefully bland, declaring simply that "the lingering threat of internal conflict that is fuelled by intraparty and interparty tensions could distract from normal operations". Its conclusion, that Lesotho has taken steps in the right direction to becoming a stable democracy and a united and prosperous country, is belied by the evidence provided during the year.

Foreign Affairs

Lesotho continued to source major budgetary support from **Great Britain**, but its ties with the former colonial power were weakening. The closing of the British High Commission in 2007 was supplemented by a decision from London that, along with nationals from other countries in the region, Basotho would need to apply for a visa to visit the UK, which they would have to acquire from the British High Commission in Pretoria.

Increasingly dependent upon **South Africa** for political as well as economic security, Lesotho appeared bent on strengthening its ties with other countries in SADC. In his budget speech, the minister of finance indicated that there was a possibility that the Lesotho Highlands Water Project would supply water to Botswana, while in order to avoid winter shortages, a power purchase agreement had been signed to source electricity from Mozambique, which had a power surplus. A further development recorded what was probably Lesotho's first foreign aid donation – a grant to **Zimbabwe** of M 10 m (the Maluti is a currency linked to the South African Rand), pledged at the 29th SADC summit in September, to help with that country's economic collapse.

Socioeconomic Developments

Indicators pointed to an alarming state of **social crisis**. The summary report of the APRM pointed out that Lesotho had a declining rate of population growth on account of out-migration, falling fertility rates, decreasing life expectancy and the HIV-AIDS pandemic, Lesotho having the third highest prevalence of HIV in the world (23.2% of the population, or approximately 1.8 m people). There was further evidence of the desperate state of the hospital system, an appalling shortage of doctors (5.4 per 100,000 compared with 13 per 100,000 in Sub Saharan Africa and 279 per 100,000 people in the USA), massive backlogs in the judicial system, extensive corruption and poor public financial accountability, and so on. The rather desperate state of affairs was symbolised by the **state of the university**, where the vice chancellor was suspended on charges of corruption, the bursar had been suspended but untried for fully seven years, and the acting bursar declined to continue in his position after being injured in an attack by students rioting in protest against delayed payment of government allowances.

In his **budget speech**, presented to parliament on 18 February, Minister of Finance Dr Tim Thahane identified five serious consequences of the global economic crisis: first the reduction in orders for Lesotho's clothing exports, putting at risk the jobs of the industry's 42,000 workers (with 200,000 dependants); second, the impact of the crisis upon banks in Hong Kong, Singapore and Taiwan, which provided export-import financing and letters of credit for the textile firms; third, the fall in commodity prices for diamonds and platinum, causing retrenchments from South African mines and Lesotho's own small diamond mining industry; fourth, reduced demand for capital and consumer imports in the SACU, reducing the revenue pool (so that Lesotho might find itself returning SACU payments it had already received; and fifth, the prospect that 'development partners' would scale down their support.

Overall, the **budget** proposed a total expenditure of M 11,652 m, of which M 8,237 m would be recurrent and M 3,414 m would be capital expenditure. M 8,883 m would be sourced from government revenue, M 1,078 m from development partners and M 383 m from soft loans from multilateral development institutions. This would leave a deficit of M 1,307, or 8% of GDP.

Roger Southall

Madagascar

A coup d'état was the dominant event that marked the year. The combined impact of the political unrest, the concomitant fragility of the private sector, and the sudden loss of donor funds made for a year of precipitous economic decline. Many institutions, charged with such tasks as protecting natural resources and combating corruption, experienced a diminished capacity to perform their functions. The relative strength of Malagasy technocrats saved Madagascar from state collapse. There was little violence on the streets, but progress with resolving the political conflict was nil. Dwindling foreign exchange reserves raised fears of currency collapse.

Domestic Politics

On 16 March, President **Marc Ravalomanana was overthrown** by Andry Rajoelina after two months of violent street protests. Ravalomanana attempted to hand power over to a group of military officers led by Vice-Admiral Hyppolite Ramaroson, but this failed, as another military faction, led by Colonels Noël Rakotonandrasana and Ndrianarijaona André, arrested the would-be junta members, claiming the hand-over was an unconstitutional change of power. The military leaders promptly installed Rajoelina as President of the High Authority of the Transition (HAT). An arrest warrant was issued for

Ravalomanana, who fled to self-imposed exile in South Africa. On 18 March, Madagascar's High Constitutional Court (HCC) confirmed Rajoelina as president even as he dissolved the National Assembly and the Senate. The view of the HCC was that Ravalomanana had been the first to abrogate the constitutional process, which would have been for him to step down and hand power over to the president of the senate, forcing elections within 60 days. While the constitutional basis for the HCC's position on Ravalomanana's actions was clear, what was far less clear was how this led to the legitimation of the rise of Rajoelina. The HCC presided over his investiture on 21 March. At 34 years of age, Rajoelina's total public leadership experience had been one year as mayor of the capital. He took power with no clear agenda, no clear domestic policy, no clear international policy, no clear economic experience, and no clear network (political, clientelist, or otherwise), and he had no clear way of routing Ravalomana's deeply rooted networks in political, economic and church cirlces. Most importantly, his strategy for winning the support of the regions outside of the capital was to create a large tent. He created the HAT, comprised of 44 leaders from around Madagascar, to run the country. Unlike those surrounding Ravalomanana in 2002, this was not a team of loyalists but a grouping of people involved in disparate political networks, often in conflict with one another. All this made for a dangerous, fragile moment in Malagasy history.

There were four primary reasons for Ravalomanana's ouster: the new presidential plane, the Daewoo Logistics land deal, the perceived curtailment of freedoms, and the growing gap between development and poverty alleviation. "Air Force II", as it was called in English, was the new plane Ravalomanana ordered for himself at a cost of $ 60 m. It was perceived as a gross extravagance and aroused popular revulsion. Early in the year, Ravalomanana finalised a deal with Daewoo Logistics, a subsidiary of the Korean Daewoo conglomerate, for a 99-year lease of 1.3 m hectares (13,000 sq km) of mostly arable land for biofuel production. This was a far from transparent process, speedily carried through. Ravalomanana and Daewoo argued that the project would bring an estimated 45,000 jobs to Madagascar and $ 2 bn in infrastructure investment. However, the popular perception was that only the president and the mining sector benefited from the deal.

These events were symbolic of a deeper concern about centralisation and the **curtailment of freedoms** under Ravalomanana. The events of 16 March actually began on 13 December 2008, when Ravalomanana closed Rajoelina's television station, Viva, for "public order and security" reasons. It had broadcast an opposition message from former president Didier Ratsiraka (in self-imposed exile). Tempers simmered until 17 January when, in direct opposition to a presidential order, Rajoelina installed the 'Place de la Democratie' in the Ambohijatovo *commune* of Antananarivo. Attending the installation was a panoply of opposition leaders from across political and demographic groupings, including all the challengers in recent presidential elections or their representatives. Rajoelina demanded a general opening up of the media, while calling for the firing of Budget and Finance Minister Haja Nirina Razafinjatovo and Minister of Territorial Management Marius Ratolojanahary by 21 January. On 24 January, he stepped up his rhetoric, calling for the removal of Ravalomanana on the grounds that he had violated the public trust and used his public office to gain public contracts for his companies illicitly, and was leading the country in a downward slide towards authoritarianism. On 26 January, the dynamics of demonstrations in the capital changed. The number of Rajoelina supporters in the streets dropped precipitously and protests became significantly more violent.

The **political crisis** was complex, involving the Protestant Church, of which Ravalomanana was lay-vice president, the Catholic Church, followed by Rajoelina, important families of *merina* ethnicity, and, often parallel, the new business elite, which accused Ravalomanana of improperly using his office to advance his company, the Tiko Group, at their expense. Opposition, long divided, was working together. The military was present but, following the norm, not a critical player in the complex web of Malagasy clientelism.

On 3 February, **Ravalomanana sacked Rajoelina** as mayor of the capital Antananarivo. This was a constitutionally questionable action. Rajoelina was the *de facto* opposition leader, not because of his stature but because, after a cycle of elections challenged at each level, he was the only opposition leader to win a significant office. In removing him, Ravalomanana appeared to do exactly what Rajoelina accused him of: act autocratically. Rajoelina took his demand for the removal of Ravalomanana to the Malagasy HCC. On 4 February, the HCC ruled that the removal of the president was outside its jurisdiction. The turning point came on 7 February. Dozens were killed when the presidential guard opened fire on unarmed protestors in front of the presidential palace. It is far from clear that Ravalomanana gave the order, and he distanced himself from these events, but it served to significantly erode what was left of his authority. For his part, Rajoelina declared himself to be in charge, though he had neither the political power nor the military support to back such a statement.

Rajoelina's opportunity came on 9 March, when Army Chief of Staff General Edmond Rasolomahandry ('General Dina'), frustrated with the political gamesmanship, told Ravalomanana and Rajoelina that they had 72 hours to resolve the crisis or he would take power. However, Colonel Noël Rakotonandrasana, commander of the 'Corps d'Armée du Personnel et des Services Administratif et Technique' (CAPSAT), decided to back Colonel André Ndriarijaona in taking over before General Dina had the chance. The events that followed were extraordinary. The military split, but with few supporting Ravalomanana. The gendarmes quickly joined the military in saying they would no longer take orders from the president. The military was positioned to take over but did not. The **military role** began late in the conflict, with Noël Rakotonandrasana recruited into action only in mid-February by retired General Rasolosoa and Andry Rajoelina's father, Colonel Rajoelina. At the time, discussion in the international community referred to the CAPSAT 'mutiny'. It was indeed a mutiny, but perhaps the better question would have been how one small base in the capital could act with impunity outside of the vertical military command structure. It is clear that the military was already fractured in the face of a weakening institutional centre. Broadly reported but not well evidenced is that CAPSAT was also financially supported by the French, who had made their frustration with Ravalomanana clear for some time and had both received Rajoelina and offered him protection. The role of the military appeared to devolve into armed security. Rakotonandrasana frequently appeared at Rajoelina's side. Other military units began hiring themselves out to those looking for additional personal security – on both sides of the conflict – needing to ensure their own safety. Guns became prevalent but militarism did not spread. Instead, the change of government brought out an army of businessman. Prey Group, led by Rajoelina supporter Edgard Razafindravahy, OpsmosisBusiness Solutions, Imperial Tobacco, and the ailing Savonnerie Tropicale, suddenly had new currency. Rajoelina's company, Injet, was poised to grow. Magro, a subsidiary of Ravalomanana's Tiko Group, came under intense political and legal fire and began being dismantled. Just weeks on from the change of power, it was clear that Rajoelina was governing following Ravalomanana's example. New political networks were displacing old networks and the private sector began lending political capital to the public sector.

Rajoelina's **new government** was based on an HAT comprised of 44 members from across the political, ethnic and geographic spectrum. Monja Roindefo Zafitsimivalo was made prime minister. The son of famed Malagasy opposition leader Monja Jaona, Roindefo was a technocrat who brought with him much support from the south. The rest of the HAT members, and particularly those with ministerial appointments, were experienced politicians who had served in previous administrations or represented critical regional powerbases. While there were subsequently two modest shake-ups in the HAT, it appeared to remain surprisingly unified in light of the challenges the members faced and the differences they felt.

Two issues dominated from April to December: internationally sponsored **reconciliation** talks, and how to prevent the economy from collapse. Street protests ended. Calls for Ravalomanana's return were at first muted and then virtually disappeared. Instead, a general malaise began to grip Malagasy political culture. Both Ravalomanana and Rajoelina are *merina* (a historically privileged ethnicity from the central highlands of the country's capital) and the entire conflict was popularly viewed as a war between houses. Fears of unrest in the majority rural populace were ultimately unfounded, but the anomie that gripped the country was stoked by the contagious failure of government institutions to perform basic functions in such areas as education, health and protecting Malagasy rainforests from illicit logging.

At the end of the year, Ravalomanana's key **policy initiatives** such as the Madagascar Action Plan (based on using extractive industry revenues to pay for development), Madagascar Naturally (a sweeping, donor-supported environment programme), and leadership reform were all moribund. A political party system reform law was passed in January to much criticism, but the momentum for change, so critical after the challenges apparent in the last electoral cycle, had dissipated. There was no clear path by which a much talked-about new constitution could come to fruition. Key concerns between Malagasy elites, such as federalism, decentralisation, and even the design of regional and local government, were topics of debate, not actionable items. Rajoelina had called for elections, but none were scheduled. Rent seeking was on the rise in Madagascar even while institutions were on the wane.

Foreign Affairs

The international community was uniform in its **condemnation of the overthrow** of the president. France called for the rapid return of constitutional order. President Nicholas Sarkozy demanded in May that elections be held within a year. Others, such as the United States, called for Ravalomanana's return Early conflict resolution efforts by the AU, led by former Burkina Faso foreign minister Ablassé Oudragogo, appeared to move towards supporting a rapid call for elections. However, 9 August saw the signature of the Maputo Accord. This agreement, led by the AU and joined by SADC, the UN, and the International Organization of La Francophonie, was based on a new approach focused on bringing Rajoelina, Ravalomanana, and the two living former presidents of Madagascar, Didier Ratsiraka and Zafy Albert, to the negotiating table. The diplomatic community rallied around this effort, but the 'Four Movements' led to few results, as Rajoelina was not convinced that there was value in his buying into the talks.

The reaction of the international **donor community** had a more significant impact on the country. By 2008, nearly 70% of Madagascar's expenditure came from donor funds. The two leading donors, the World Bank and the EU, accounted for more than half of Madagascar's budget. The US acted decisively to suspend all non-humanitarian assistance to Madagascar. However, the World Bank, the EU and other bilateral donors were less decisive, freezing new aid flows but not suspending their lending programmes. Ravalomanana had been popular amongst foreign leaders and under him donor aid had risen to unprecedented levels. By December 2008, aggregate aid accounted for nearly 70% of receipts. That month, however, the EU and the World Bank expressed their first significant concerns about the quality of public sector governance under Ravalomanana, freezing direct budgetary support (at approximately $ 100 m).

On 17 March, the **World Bank** invoked its Operational Policy (OP) 7.30, 'Dealing with de facto Governments', jeopardising its over $ 1 bn Madagascar portfolio. OP 7.30 allows for a continuation of aid on a project-by-project basis. In practice, the World Bank did not suspend operations (which would entail closing its office and halting all activities), but rather froze new funding streams. Project monies already in place continued, albeit at a trickle. Over the course of the year, the Bank spent $ 52 m (or about 15% under OP 7.30). The EU, UNDP, UNICEF and many bilateral donors followed a similar course of action. The US suspended all non-humanitarian aid coming from both USAID and its Millennium Challenge Account. The exception was France, which continued foreign aid. Foreign aid receipts totalled around $ 150 m, about $ 21.5 m dispersed through UN agencies, though many of the project disbursements came before March.

Madagascar was suspended from participating in **AU activities** on 20 March and from SADC activities on 30 March. However, it was not until the signing of the Maputo Accord of 9 August that there was a common international vision. The approach of the accord was to seek a consensus government with Rajoelina, Ravalomanana and the two former living presidents Ratsiraka and Albert. While the goals were clear, the working relationships between the movements, the triggers for the re-engagement of the international community, and the path to constitutional order were not. Moreover, the 'Four Movements' approach did not resonate in Madagascar. Ratsiraka had been voted out of office and pushed out of the country by Ravalomanana in 2002 and Albert had been impeached in 1996. Their involvement was therefore questioned locally. More critically, it was far from clear to many that these four combined could represent the Malagasy interests that brought about the crisis in the first place. The International Contact Group, as the negotiating group led by AU Commission Chairman Jean Ping came to be called, involved summits with the 'Four Movements', but it did not engage in a process that included civil society, historically embedded powerful families from the capital region, private sector actors, the military, or the plethora of regional politicians with growing sway.

Within a month of signing the accord, Rajoelina was successfully using it to keep Ravalomanana far from power and the three other movements were building an unlikely coalition against him. This came to a head with the allocation of the post of prime minister. The international community disapproved of Monja Roindefo. Rajoelina refused to return to the negotiating table on 4 September, but made an effort to create a **unity government** under Roindefo with a change of cabinet on 8 September. SADC, led by former Mozambican president Joaquim Chissano, in turn barred Rajoelina from addressing the UN General Assembly on 25 September as a sign of rejection of his right to rule. The problem for SADC, the international community and the three other movements was that, with the passage of time, Rajoelina's domestic authority had grown. The new agreement negotiated by the International Contact Group on 6 October focused on a change of prime minister. Ravalomanana stated that he would sign only if Rajoelina would be refused the right to run in presidential elections to be held in 2010. Rajoelina did not agree to this proviso but did change prime ministers and appointed Eugene Mangalaza, a former university leader close to Ratsiraka.

The three movements continued under the auspices of SADC's Joaquim Chissano and the AU's Jean Ping but, on 12 December, Rajoelina stated that it was "impossible and no longer conceivable to collaborate (with the three movements)". Rajoelina replaced the consensus prime minister with Colonel Vital Albert Camille and released an **elections schedule**. He argued that this was a return to constitutionality, but simply not through a transitional process as the international community demanded. The International Contact Group did not budge, making it clear that it would reject any efforts towards elections or a constitutional convention that did not directly involve the 'Four Movements' sharing power.

Socioeconomic Developments

According to a 2005 household demographic study, 78.3% of subsistence farmers lived in **poverty** with an intensity rating of 31.4%. In all, some 68.7% of Malagasy live in poverty: 52% of the urban population and 73.5% of the rural population. The Gini coefficient of 0.47 indicated a wide gap between rich and poor. World Bank indicators demonstrated a modest reduction in poverty for the majority rural population, but the benefits of high real GDP growth of 9.5% in 2008 had disproportionately advantaged a new urban elite.

The political tumult created a tremendous economic shock. As shown, foreign aid dropped precipitously, and strategic areas supported by donors lost support. The **anti-corruption** bureau, Bianco, lost approximately one third of its budget. Many local NGOs playing critical roles with community based organisations for health, education, environmental protection and other areas saw these efforts come to a halt. Efficiency losses in tax and customs administration saw revenues drop by a quarter. According to the World Bank, energy and petroleum products consumption was down by 15% in real value (a sign of great hardship in the population). Credit declined in real terms. Imports declined by 22%. Job losses, mostly in urban areas, were estimated at around 220,000 – a dramatic figure in a country with chronic unemployment.

Nevertheless, the **fiscal gap** remained under control. VAT revenues increased. The rice harvest was good, protecting both those involved with the large rice industry and the rural subsistence farming population that dominated the economy. In all, the World Bank estimated that GDP grew at 0.6%. While outpaced by the 3% population growth rate, this was not too bad, given both domestic pressures and the global economic crisis.

Extractive industries were a growing segment of the economy. QMM, fundamentally owned by mining giant Rio Tinto, invested nearly $ 1 bn to build an illemnite mine and a port in the southern region of Anosy. Canadian mining company Sherritt invested in building nickel-mining operations in the Tamatave region on the east coast. Both these operations provoked protest as local benefits did not meet expectations for jobs or revenue sharing. Riots in Anosy were not over macro-political change but rather against the perceived opacity of QMM. Revenues began to come in from QMM operations for the first time. The mining law governing the distribution of revenues continued to draw ire:

transparency in the sector was challenged both locally and internationally, a dramatic fall in global nickel prices destabilised Sherritt's prospects, and, at less than 4%, extractive industries were still far too small as a part of the economy to drive change.

Richard R. Marcus

Malawi

Dr Bingu wa Mutharika's landslide victory in the presidential elections of 19 May caused a major transformation of the political landscape. The regional voting mainly determined by ethnic identities that had characterised the three previous multi-party elections was virtually absent. The dramatic swing of the political pendulum to a parliament dominated by the Democratic People's Party (DPP) ushered in a totally new political climate in the National Assembly. This was yet another year of international awards for Mutharika for his performance in various spheres of governance. The year also saw tobacco and cotton sales attracting lower prices, largely due to a decline in demand for these crops in Western markets, which were suffering from the global financial crisis. This resulted in a serious foreign exchange crisis, which haunted the country for a good part of the year. There were also some fuel shortages and a few labour disputes in major cities.

Domestic politics

Parliamentary and presidential elections took centre stage in Malawi's domestic politics. **Registration of voters,** which had commenced towards the end of the previous year, spilled over to 10 January; 5.8 m voters registered, as compared with 5.7 m in 2004. An inspection of the electoral roll should have been carried out twice but, on 7 May, the chairperson of the Electoral Commission (EC), Anastanzia Msosa, announced the cancellation of the inspection for lack of time.

The domestic political scene was generally characterised by both **intra- and inter-party conflicts**. Most primary elections for the ruling and opposition parties ended in chaos, with the losers rejecting the results and alleging irregularities, vote-rigging, favouritism and candidate imposition, which created a sense of frustration among candidates. In most cases, parties were not able to hold re-runs. Consequently, many DPP members withdrew their party membership and stood as independent candidates, a move described by many as "unfortunate" and "killing the party". It was alleged that, in some cases, bona fide popular-choice DPP candidates were asked to withdraw their candidacy so that they could be replaced by others, whilst being promised diplomatic posts and a refund of their campaign expenses. In one incident, a DPP hopeful was thrown out of a DPP convention after he had won the primaries in his area. This shows that it was the party that largely dominated in the choice of candidates in the general election, against the will of the people. It is no wonder that, in some cases, the imposed candidates lost to independents, both in the general elections and in the by-elections that followed later. Such malpractices were not peculiar to the DPP.

Intra-party conflicts were also conspicuous in the **opposition parties**, such as the Malawi Congress Party (MCP), whose parliamentary hopefuls who lost in primary elections formed an alliance and resolved to stand as independents, claiming that the party had not addressed their queries on the election process. Because of these problems in the primaries, over 33% of the 1,141 registered parliamentary candidates stood as independents, the largest number since the beginning of the country's multiparty democracy.

By January, it was clear that political parties were reducing the number of their candidates because of the EC's high nomination fees of K 1 m for aspiring MPs and K 500,000 for presidential candidates, refundable to those who obtained at least 5% of the total vote. The DPP convention did not reveal the identity of the president's running mate, but only endorsed Bingu wa Mutharika as the party's presidential candidate. Between 2 and 6 February, **presidential and parliamentary candidates** submitted their nomination papers and on 6 February, Mutharika presented his own nomination paper alongside the first female candidate for the vice presidency, Joyce Banda – ending speculation about his running mate. The choice of Joyce Banda was hailed by many, not least by women, who make up 52% of the population. Her nomination was perceived as the most surprising move in the electoral process and a smart vote-winning tactic. The choice was also a response to advocates of the 50–50 campaign, started in January, which aimed at ensuring equal representation of women in parliament.

Inter-party conflicts were inevitable in an election year, with the presidential candidates challenging one another. In January, the DPP leadership accused the opposition of buying voter registration certificates from voters as a ploy to rig the elections. Former president

Bakili Muluzi challenged Mutharika to a one-on-one debate, in which Mutharika refused to participate. Further inter-party conflicts resulted in a degree of violence between members of various parties.

In fulfilment of his ambition, **Bakili Muluzi** handed in his nomination papers as presidential candidate, but was frustrated by the EC, which declared on March 20, three days after the official campaign period started, that he could not run for president, although the United Democratic Front (UDF) senior leadership urged the party's area, branch constituency and district officials to support their rejected presidential candidate. On 16 May, three days before the elections, the constitutional court ruled that presidents who had held office for two consecutive terms could not stand again. This confirmed the EC's ruling that Muluzi was therefore disqualified. On 24 March, less than two months before the elections and while the case was in court, Muluzi and MCP leader John Tembo met to discuss a possible coalition. An MCP/UDF electoral coalition was announced on April 9 with John Tembo as coalition presidential candidate.

On 20 March, **parliament** stood down, paving the way for the election of new members. Analysts attacked the conduct of MPs, saying the scars left by political battles in the 'august house' should serve as lessons to the electorate to choose legislators with a sense of vision and commitment to service. The performance of the last parliament was described as dismal because, instead of serving as a national forum for dialogue, reconciliation and development, it had degenerated into a partisan battleground where politicians settled scores, irrespective of the national interest.

On the day of the **elections** (May 19), poll materials had reportedly not yet been delivered to some districts, including Nsanje and Karonga. Despite such impediments, which delayed the voting process in some districts and polling centres, the elections were described as peaceful, with the majority having voted. On 22 May, the EC declared Bingu wa Mutharika the winner with 2,946,103 votes (50.7% of the total cast), markedly higher than the 36% he obtained in 2004 and the best result in a presidential poll since 1994. In second position was MCP/UDF coalition leader John Tembo, with 1,370,044 votes (24%). In third position was Kamuzu Chibambo of the People's Transformation (PETRA) with 35,167 votes, and in fourth position was Stanley Masauli of the Republican Party with 33,887 votes. Loveness Gondwe, a former Alliance for Democracy (AFORD) legislator, came in fifth position and James Nyondo, an independent presidential candidate, came sixth. Finally, Dindi Gowa Nyasulu of AFORD trailed at rank seven. In terms of parliamentary seats, the DPP scooped 114 out of the 193 constituencies, making it the dominant party. Bakili Muluzi was the first of the political elite to congratulate Bingu wa Mutharika before the official announcement.

On 25 May, the MCP fired Ishmael Chafukira as publicity secretary for openly rebelling against the leadership by attributing the MCP's weak performance in the election to party president John Tembo's poor leadership. Chafukira asked Tembo to step down to pave the way for a new leadership. The High Court in Lilongwe upheld Chafukira's dismissal. On 27 May, the elected MPs were sworn in, marking the beginning of a new era in Malawian politics. In the 41st session of parliament, a number of issues dominated the political scene. Chafukira moved a motion proposing an amendment to standing order 3(3) so that the leader of the opposition would be elected by all MPs present in the house. The standing order had previously stipulated that a "leader of opposition means parliamentary leader of the largest party elected by the parliamentary membership which is not in government or in coalition with government party and who is recognised as such". In June, Parliament waived standing orders on the election of the **leader of the opposition** after two MCP factions disagreed on Tembo's nomination and blocked his automatic return to power. The opposition was asked to nominate individuals to compete in the election for the leader of the opposition. On 27 August, the High Court in Mzuzu ordered parliament to recognise the MCP president as leader of the opposition in the interim until the parliamentary Legal Affairs Committee made their decision on the matter. On 17 November, the National Assembly adopted new standing orders allowing the whole house to vote in a secret ballot for candidates nominated by the opposition benches. Only two hours after adopting the new standing orders, the once mighty John Tembo, who based on the election results and the former regulations would have been the designated leader of the opposition failed to obtain this status when Henry Chimunthu Banda declared 36-year-old Ephraim Abele Kayembe to be the new leader of the opposition in parliament. Kayembe was supported by 15 of the MCP's 26 MPs. On 21 September, **Ishmael Chafukira** died mysteriously on his return from South Africa, putting into disarray the motion to change parliamentary standing orders on the election of the leader of the opposition.

On 18 June, Bingu wa Mutharika released the list of names of a 43-member **cabinet**, with several expected names missing. It included 11 women (26% of the cabinet) up from seven (17% of the previous 42-member cabinet) and had 29 newcomers. The opposition and other civil society organisations expressed mixed reactions over the DPP-dominated parliament; some fearing it had the potential to stifle democracy, as little debate on bills was expected. The passing of **16 bills in six weeks**, most of which took less than five minutes, illustrates the point.

By October, the date for the **local government elections** was still not known, though it had previously been announced for May 2010. Towards the end of November, the minister of local government and rural development announced that elections would be held before the end of 2010. However, on 1 December, a **constitutional amendment bill** was passed in parliament empowering a sitting president to set the date for local government elections without consultation. The passing of the bill meant that Mutharika had the last word on whether the country could go ahead with the polls.

Also during the year, lawyers in a case in which members of parliament challenged procedures laid out in Section 65 of the constitution on crossing the floor agreed to withdraw the matter. The Anti-Corruption Bureau (ACB) pressed the former president on issues to do with **corruption**. Muluzi has a case to answer for diverting donor money amounting to K 1.7 bn into his personal accounts when he was president between 1994 and 2004. Because of ill-health, Muluzi was abroad for most of the year for medical treatment – first in the UK, and later in South Africa – and this has delayed the case. The ACB has been active in the investigation of several alleged cases of corruption in government departments and by individuals, but there were no major convictions during the year.

Foreign Affairs

Malawi continued to enjoy good relations with the international community, and donor confidence led to offers of **aid and loans**. On 22 April, Germany granted Malawi K 5 bn for budgetary support, asserting that they now had confidence in the government. On May 4, Mutharika was praised at a US summit for achieving food security and standing up to pressure from the World Bank and the IMF against continued subsidies to fertilisers. The US was also impressed with Malawi because of the political will shown by Mutharika, and was willing to support Malawi even in the face of the global financial crisis On 27 May 27, the AfDB approved a $ 36 m loan for the improvement of road networks in the country. In the middle of the year, Japan pledged to double aid to Malawi over a five-year period up to 2012. On 17 October, the Saudi Fund for Development pledged $ 12 m for the Thyolo-Bangula road project in Southern Malawi. Talat Salem Radwan, Saudi Arabian Ambassador to Malawi, told local journalists that he was in the country to strengthen ties between Malawi and Saudi Arabia. This was seen as an opportunity for Malawi to make a break-through into Middle East countries. On 23 October, the UK pledged continued support for Malawi and, in the same month, the UN increased its financial assistance for development projects by 9% from $ 110 m to $ 128.5 m, arguing that Malawi was on the right track for achieving its MDGs.

When President Ismail Omar Guelle of Djibouti was on a three-day state visit in April, he took a keen interest in the Shire-Zambezi Waterway project, saying he was ready to offer technical support so that the port would be ready by December. Mutharika attended the 15th Non-Aligned Movement Summit held in Egypt (11–16 July). On 25 June, Malawi received free fertiliser from China for winter cropping and, on 30 June, the WHO provided Malawi with drugs to treat 19,000 cases of swine flu if there should be an outbreak. The EU also pledged to support Malawi in combating foot and mouth disease.

Mutharika attended the World Food Summit in Rome (15 November), before proceeding to Trinidad and Tobago to attend the Commonwealth Summit. There, Italy pledged continued support to develop the country's agriculture and education sectors. In addition, Australia pledged to give Malawi K 4 bn over three years as development aid, while the Irish envoy launched a K 110 m basic education programme in the same month. In mid-September, Mutharika went on a state visit to Brazil, which intensified its bid to establish partnerships with African countries, and signed a cooperation agreement with Malawi under which it would share its expertise and experience in a number of economic sectors. Malawi's minister of foreign affairs, Eta Banda and her Brazilian counterpart, Celso Amorimo, signed the agreement on 16 September in the Brazilian capital at a ceremony witnessed by the presidents of the two countries.

Mutharika attended the UN General Assembly in New York (20–27 September). During the same period, the Vice President Banda went to Venezuela, where she attended the second Africa-South America heads of state summit. Towards the end of September, the SADC meeting of foreign affairs ministers endorsed Mutharika as chairperson of the African Union to succeed Libya's Muammar Kadhafi in January 2010. Within **SADC**, Malawi continued to enjoy friendly relations with countries such as Zambia and Mozambique. The president received **awards** from the international community, including, in September, the Medal of Glory Award from the US-based Foundation for Democracy in Africa for democratic governance in Africa. He received the award, among other reasons, for his economic reforms, as evidenced by the high growth rate of 9.7% in 2008, up from 1% in 2003. On 29 October, he was awarded the 2009 Drivers of Change Award by the Southern Africa Trust, and, on 27 November, FAO Director Jacques Diouf came to Malawi to honour Mutharika with an Agricola medal for his efforts in maintaining food security in the country.

Socioeconomic Developments

On 31 March, an **IMF** team concluded a two-week visit to Malawi with a statement that the Malawi economy continued to do well, even in the face of the global financial crisis. The mission conducted the first review of the government's economic programme, which is supported by the Fund under the Exogenous Shocks Facility (ESF) and 'held' the 2009 Article IV consultation discussions on economic prospects and policies. This was meant to ease the foreign exchange crisis Malawi had experienced since the beginning of the year. In March, the IMF disbursed $ 80 m to Malawi from its contingent allocation of SDRs to help the country reduce its foreign currency shortages. Further discussions were held on new credit facilities to replace the PRGF that had ended in 2008 and the ESF that ended in December. The IMF resident representative in Malawi, Maitland MacFarlan, also promised continued support from international partners, despite the global economic crisis.

The year started with good **agricultural production** triggered by the government's Targeted Input Programme coupled with good rains, which resulted in the country registering a real GDP growth rate of above 7% over the past three years, as well as helping bring down inflation to single figures at 8.4%. The exchange rate was generally stable during the year. According to the Ministry of Agriculture, tobacco output was expected to jump to 250 m kg (from 194 m kg produced in 2008). The year's maize harvest increased to 3.7 m metric tonnes. Following a bumper harvest, maize prices fell to around K 40 per kg (from about K 70 per kg the previous year). Private traders were banned from buying maize from farmers to ensure food security. In addition, sugar fetched higher prices on the international market.

When Mutharika opened the **tobacco** season on 16 March, he fixed the minimum price for burley tobacco at $ 2.15 per kg and flue cured tobacco at $ 3.09 per kg to ensure that farmers benefited from tobacco sales. Despite the president's announcement, tobacco sales started below the set prices and were as low as $ 1.15 and $ 0.94 for burley and flue cured tobacco respectively. This was attributed to low demand for the leaf as a result of the global financial meltdown. It was feared that the poor prices would have an effect on Malawi's economic growth for 2009/10, which is largely dependent on agriculture. The low prices led to the suspension of sales pending talks between buyers and government. On 8 April, Mutharika warned that he would deport buyers who were offering below the set minimum prices for tobacco and, by 24 April, things had improved as farmers were paid better prices. On 22 April, leaf of the highest quality as was selling for $ 2.45 per kg and, by 22 June, tobacco prices had moved closer to the official rate. Overall, revenues from tobacco dropped by 9% from $ 472 m in 2008 to $ 432.9 m. On 9 September, the government deported officials of three major tobacco buyers for offering low prices.

Tobacco was not the only cash crop that suffered from the global financial crisis. **Cotton** prices were probably the lowest in the last ten years. From K 60 per kg in 2008, buyers were willing to pay only K 32, compared with farmers' expectations of K 120 and government minimum prices of K 75. In the second week of November, it was learnt that, in an effort to bail out the cotton farmers, the government had given the Agriculture Development and Marketing Corporation (ADMARC) money to buy cotton from farmers who had been struggling with private buyers over poor prices since April.

In his **State of the Nation address** during the opening of the 41st parliament in June, Mutharika expanded the list of development priorities, including agriculture and food security, integrated rural development, irrigation and water development (to include greenbelt irrigation), transport and communication infrastructure, energy, mining and industrial development, management and prevention of HIV/AIDS, education, science and technology, climate change, natural resources and environmental management, youth development and empowerment.

On 28 July, parliament passed without any amendments the 2009/10 **national budget**, amounting to K 256,769,062,591. The budget, among others things, subsidised fertiliser at K 500 to benefit 1.8 m farmers and continued funding the development of the Shire-Zambezi Waterway. In contrast to the two previous budget years within an opposition-dominated parliament, where Section 65 created a lot of tension, this was the first budget to be passed without any controversy.

In addition to the low prices fetched by tobacco and cotton, a **foreign exchange crisis** haunted Malawi, with many forex bureaus being closed down in August for not partnering with authorised dealer banks. Businessmen were accused of hording and illegally exporting foreign currency. Chinese nationals were caught red handed at airports trying to smuggle currency, in contravention of Malawi's Foreign Exchange Act. On 24 June, for example, a Chinese national was arrested at Chileka international airport trying to fly to Hong Kong with $ 39,151.

For the first time in many years, the Malawi Regulatory Authority reduced the price of **fuel** by 15%. This was a result of the stable exchange rate of the Malawi Kwacha and the reduced prices for crude oil caused by a temporary decline of demand due to the global financial crisis. Towards the end of the year, the foreign exchange shortage started affecting fuel supplies, and this paralysed the transport sector. In November, the fuel crisis cost Malawi an estimated K 111 bn as a result of lost economic activities due to transport bottlenecks and, in December, it was learned that the transport industry was on the verge of collapse due to the shortage of fuel.

The cost of living in the country's major cities, Blantyre, Lilongwe, Mzuzu and Zomba, fell in October, mainly due to the decline in the cost of basic food items. However, lack of money continued to haunt many Malawians in the cities, making them unable to access minimum basic needs. Consequently, there were **strikes** in Blantyre and Lilongwe, in particular at Shoprite, the Blantyre Water Board and Electricity Supply Commission of Malawi (ESCOM). The minister of labour visited various hotspots and intervened in the bargaining processes between employers and employees. It was reported that 40% of Malawians lived below the **poverty line**, 25% down from 2004. The year also saw an urban poverty drop from 24% to 11%.

On 11 September, Malawi registered its first case of **swine flu**. The year ended on a sad note as a series of earthquakes, and earth tremors shook most parts of the northern region, specifically Karonga, from 6 December. On 20 December, a fourth major **earthquake** occurred, measuring 6.2 on the Richter scale, which resulted in Karonga being declared a disaster area. Many individuals, civil society organisations, private companies, international organisations and friendly governments helped with donations including money, tents and food items.

Lewis B. Dzimbiri & Tiyesere Mercy Chikapa-Jamali

Mauritius

Despite being a vulnerable small island state, Mauritius fared better than anticipated in this crisis year and recorded economic growth of 2.1%. The government and the central bank responded appropriately to the global financial crisis by easing macroeconomic policies. While the crisis halted the expected decline in public debt, the IMF considered the public finances to be fundamentally sound and external debt sustainable. In the light of flexible exchange rates, the country's current reserve position was comfortable, and banks remained liquid and profitable. With these strong economic fundamentals and an effective institutional policy and stability framework, Mauritius succeeded in weathering the challenges. Domestic policy was characterised by initial struggles for position within the political elite ahead of the general elections due in 2010. Mauritius ranked first in the Mo Ibrahim Index of African Governance.

Domestic Policy

Prime Minister Navinchandra Ramgoolam led a Social Alliance **coalition government** consisting of the Mauritius Labour Party (MLP), the Mauritius Social Democratic Party of Xavier Duval (PMXD) and four smaller parties. He was the dominant political figure in his fourth year in office, followed by Ramakrishna Sithanen, the vice prime minister and minister of finance and economic empowerment. The two large **opposition parties**, the Mauritius Militant Movement (MMM) and the Militant Socialist Movement (MSM), presented a rather fragmented image and were not generally perceived by the public as viable alternatives to the office holders. Paul Bérenger of the MMM had some popular support as leader of the parliamentary opposition, but Pravind Jugnauth of the MSM, who had lost his parliamentary seat in the 2005 election, was only able to develop a public profile after he won a by-election on 1 March in constituency No. 8, where he stood against his uncle, Ashock Jugnauth, of the National Union party. The by-election was called after a decision by the Supreme Court to annul the election of Ashok Jugnauth, the brother of President Sir Anerood Jugnauth, for having unduly influenced and bribed the electorate in the 2005 election. Labour did not field a candidate but implicitly supported Pravind Jugnauth against his uncle, who was supported by Bérenger. Pravind Jugnauth was elected by a narrow (less than 1%) margin of 950 votes and managed to re-enter parliament, which gave him a voice and the stature of national MSM leader and counterbalance to Bérenger of the MMM. Mauritian domestic policy then once again acquired the 'tri-angular' profile of three major political blocks – the Labour Party, MMM and MSM – and some small political parties, requiring coalitions and compromises to be worked out for electoral purposes. Domestic policy discussions centred around the question of whether Ramgoolam would set a date for the anticipated 2010 elections, and around the issue of who would ally with whom in 2010.

Despite a long-standing demand for change in the **electoral laws**, the government of Ramgoolam did not succeed in bringing this about. On 14 August, the Mauritius Creole Federation proposed a reform such that every constituency should command four seats in parliament in order to facilitate fairer representation for the Creole electorate and other minorities. With the current provision for 'best losers' being declared un-constitutional, everyone called for a more proportional electoral model. On 10 November, the Electoral Boundaries Commission submitted a report to the prime minister and the leader of the parliamentary opposition suggesting a re-drawing of the existing constituency boundaries. Constituencies had been adjusted in 1966 and 1976 in response to demographic developments and migration, but a further change had been rejected by Ramgoolam in 1999; boundary changes had an impact on electoral outcomes and the political parties calculated the likely gains and losses and acted accordingly. A final decision for the 2010 election was not taken. Since the present boundaries would be valid up to 16 August 2010 and a boundary change would entail far-reaching judicial and administrative decisions, Ramgoolam postponed the government's decision and called for a thorough judicial examination. The 2010 elections will therefore take place under the current majority system. A particularly controversial law enabling the government to keep permanent records of DNA and other personal data was passed by parliament in a drive to combat international terrorism. The **SADC-Gender Agreement**, aimed at ensuring women would hold 50% of political positions by 2015, was not approved by the Ramgoolam government.

On 13 December, James-Burty David, Minister for Local Government, Rodrigues and the Outer Isles, died unexpectedly of heart failure at the age of 64. He had been a central political leader in Mauritius for decades, holding the posts of Labour Party chairman 1977–82 and Labour's secretary general since 1983. During the budget discussion in December, Jaya Cutteree of the MMM, long-serving minister of foreign affairs and international economic cooperation (2000–2005), and the architect of Mauritius' integration into the global and African regional economies, announced that he would resign from active political life in parliament at the end of his term in the legislature.

Foreign Policy

Foreign policy was influenced by the **Malagasy developments**. After improved political relations with Madagascar since 2003, the plot by which Andry Rajoelina ousted President Ravalomanana in March led to frustration. In particular, economic ties suffered and the textile industries and other joint ventures recorded financial losses. If Madagascar's status in the AGOA preferences, which expired in December, is permanently suspended, the Mauritian textile industry must re-adjust its marketing to the US.

In a general move, Ramgoolam raised the **Chagos issue** in the UN General Assembly on 25 September in New York, asserting that Chagos and Diego Garcia belonged to Mauritius. It is therefore not surprising that, in parliament on 20 November, Ramgoolam linked the international issue of Chagos to domestic policy: the Electoral Boundary Commission had decided that Chagos, Tromlin and St Brandon would come under its mandate and would consequently be integrated into Mauritian constituencies under reform and consideration. The project for a maritime farm and reserve around the Chagos islands re-animated the international debate in Mauritius' government, opposition and civil society. On 5 December in London, Ramgoolam rejected the British proposal to negotiate a maritime reserve with officials of the British Indian Ocean Territory Administration. Ramgoolam indicated that only the restoration of the rights of the Chagossian population (who are substantially refugees in Mauritius), their resettlement of the islands, and the establishment of their fishing rights in their waters, including the right to economic exploitation, could lead to the establishment of a maritime reserve. In December, Bérenger argued in parliament that negotiations with the British authorities would be a waste of time and that only American President Obama would be in a position to change the territorial and judicial stalemate on Chagos. On 5 October, the chairman of the Chagos Refugee Association, Olivier Bancoult, who had not been consulted by the British authorities on the project, went to Washington to plead with the American administration to restore the rights of the Chagossian population in their territory. At this time, the Chagossian Social Council also declared that it would call on the UN Nuclear Non-Proliferation Agency to declare whether there were US atomic arsenals on Diego Garcia. Since the Penadaba Treaty on the African nuclear-free zone stipulated that any member of the AU could call for transparency in the region, Mauritius and the Chagossians had the right to question the US military commitment and equipment on Diego Garcia. The Chagos question was also a central issue in the 10 December presentation by former foreign minister Jean-Claude de l'Estrac of his book 'Passions Politiques: Maurice 1968–1982', when he recalled the excision of the Chagos islands on the eve of Mauritian independence in 1968, when the British Indian Ocean Territory should have been transferred to Mauritius.

The **People's Republic of China** continued to be one of Mauritius' strategic partners. Chinese President Hu Jintao visited Mauritius and on 16 February signed three financial contracts in the order of $ 300 m provided partly by Exim-Bank, with a concessionary interest of 2%, for extension work at Sir Seewoosagur Ramgoolam Airport. Minor credits or grants went to road construction and other infrastructures. The Chinese government also agreed to speed up the 'Tianli' industrial project north of Port Louis. China supported Mauritius' territorial claims on Chagos and Tromlin, while Ramgoolam assured the Chinese leadership that Mauritius would support a peaceful solution to the Taiwan question. In the aftermath of this visit, the Chinese-Mauritius Investment Project 'Tianli' in Riche-Terre, Terre-Rouge, on the northern outskirts of Port Louis, was re-designed and was set in motion with the laying of the foundation stone for construction and buildings on 16 September. This project initially began as a private initiative of the Tianli group of companies from Shanxi province, and was restructured with the participation of the Taiyuan Iron and Steel Company and the Shanxi Coking Company as the largest shareholders. After the visit of the Chinese president, this project became a cornerstone of the official **Chinafrique strategy** with a more public 'state-to-state' profile. In consequence, the China-Africa Development Fund will be the fourth capital group engaged in the project, which was renamed the Jin Fei Economic Trade and Cooperation Zone. Given the lack of transparency in figures and conditions, approval for this 'Peking high-tech showroom' – as the project is branded in Mauritian society – was (and is) not unanimous.

The privileged bilateral foreign relations with **India** were put under stress by the Satyam Computer Services scandal. The Indian Central Intelligence Board closed its investigations into fraudulent management practices by the chairman of this company on 26 October. About $ 130 m must have been siphoned off via bank accounts, using Mauritius as an on- and offshore laundering platform. In consequence, the Indian administration posted a senior tax supervisor with the Indian High Commission in Port Louis on 11 November to monitor the application of the Double Income Tax Avoidance Treaty between the two countries. In December in New Delhi, Sir Anerood Jugnauth defended the offshore banking companies in Mauritius, assuring Indian press critics that his country was not a tax paradise. In an Indian Ocean rim cooperation move, an Indian surveillance vessel with a helicopter on board was invited by the authorities to assist the Mauritius coast guard to patrol in its territorial waters and prevent piracy.

In a move to honour Mauritius' long-standing commitment to the world economy and regional integration, COMESA decided to locate its Development Fund in Port Louis and, in parallel, the IMF decided to base its African Regional Technical Assistance Centre (Africtac) for the SADC countries in Port Louis too.

Socioeconomic Developments

Despite the global **economic and financial crisis**, Mauritius resisted the general downturn. According to the World Bank, real GDP growth was 2.1% and consumer price inflation was in the order of 6.4%. The crisis did, however, have an impact on **investments**. Preliminary figures suggested that foreign direct investment dropped by 80%. Unemployment rose from 7.8% in December 2008 to 8.2%. Massive local retrenchments in the textile industry were avoided by the re-deployment of Bangladeshi expatriate textile workers to their home country, which even created a slight additional demand for low-skilled workers. Despite the economic crisis, tourism remained surprisingly stable: 850,000 tourists visited Mauritius in comparison with 900,000 in 2008 (about 5% fewer for mainland Mauritius, but about a 12% fall for Rodrigues). Tourism Minister Xavier-Luc Duval labelled Mauritius as a "terrorism and porcine flu free" tourism destination in an up-market area for well-being, health and pleasure.

Although massive redundancy in the textile sector was avoided, employment fell continuously in the **sugar sector** following a decade of restructuring and shrinkage – from 40,000 employees in the 1990s to 17,000. Industrial restructuring in the sector succeeded as the first integrated production line became operational, processing sugar cane straight through to the final, exportable sugar product. At the same time, product diversification continued with the production of ethanol and bio-energy on a sugar cane bio-masse. The government relied on revenue from the sale of luxury mansions and residences on the resettled sugar cane plantations to expatriate investors.

Growth sectors were still banking, financial (offshore) and IT services. Growth potential was seen in the Sea Food Hub in Port Louis, although the fisheries industry did not create the expected employment openings. While the Malagasy port of Toamasina was eliminated as a potential competitor as a result of political events in Madagascar, the Mauritius fishing industry was jeopardised by foreign fleets and unauthorised fishing in its territorial waters, albeit clear-cut acts of piracy and fishing were rarely reported.

With respect to **social development**, the new Employment Rights Act and Empoyment Relations Act came into force in February after a painful legislative process. The introduction of flexible working hours and a stronger right to dismiss workers were intended to attract new industries by modernising Mauritian labour laws, which dated back to the 1970s in the form of their Industrial Relations Act and Labour Act, and were considered outmoded. The reform was fiercely criticised by trade unions. After a year, it could be said that neither trade union fears of significant deterioration in working conditions, nor government expectations of attracting new investors, materialised. On the whole, the introduction of this new package of social laws was interpreted as a success for Ramgoolam, who managed to implement overdue reform and at the same time not lose popularity. He benefited from the input of new Labour Minister Jean-François Chaumière, who succeeded in creating good relations with trade unions and using his communication skills to destroy the population's fears. The easing of the labour laws and a generally business-friendly environment made Mauritius a top competitive economy: in the World Bank "Doing Business Report", Mauritius climbed to 17th out of 181 countries, seven places higher than before.

In order to combat external shocks from the world financial and economic crisis, the government had enacted an **Additional Stimulus Package Bill** in December 2008. This was again strongly supported by Sithanen in his intermediary budget speech on 22 May, but criticised by the opposition as ineffective and an uncontrolled transfer of taxpayers' money to private companies, channelled through a special governmental fund agency. When it became apparent that funds in this stimulus package were earmarked for the private firm of a Labour parliamentarian, the criticisms seemed justified.

Port Louis reached a point of traffic saturation. The government decided to ban heavy vehicles from 6.00 to 9.30 hours, but this measure was decried as discriminatory because it impeded supply to the economic centres. Neither a light tram project nor an electric bus system found majority support in parliament. The World Bank was to provide finance for a **Port Louis ring road**.

By African standards, Mauritius continued to be considered a model country with respect to its social achievements: free health service and schooling, free bus transport for retired people and school-age children, cooperative and low-cost housing schemes, etc. These were not questioned by any political party or social grouping. This was partly due to the still strong position of **trade unions**, although they were anachronistically fragmented with as many as 130 of the 350 trade union organisations having fewer than 50 members. Out of a labour force of 535,000 formally employed people, 105,000 were organised in trade unions. After introducing new labour laws in 2008, Jean-François Chaumière was in charge of implementing the reforms: According to the new law, a minimum number of 30 employees was necessary to form a trade union, as compared with only seven previously. At the same time, the right to strike was restricted: according to the new provisions, strike action is permitted only after collective settlement negotiations have failed and a two-month period of reflection has expired. Moreover, the prime minister has the right to appeal to the Supreme Court to suspend the strike if economic and social functions in the country are considered to be in jeopardy. During the year, the labour minister also had to enact the gradual raising of the age of retirement to 65 years and implement social reforms with respect to creating a fund for unemployment, retraining and venture capital for creating new enterprises.

The lack of direct foreign investment was partly balanced by **World Bank loans**. On 3 December, Finance Minister Sithanen signed a $ 50 m loan agreement for a general budgetry support package for infrastructure development projects (in the context of the fourth Trade and Competitiveness Development Policy Loan, which supported the transition budget from July to December). In the context of international discussion on monetary and currency turbulence, Mauritius officially bought 2 metric tonnes of gold (worth $ 71.7 m) from the IMF in order to strengthen its long-term financial stability. With respect to fiscal policy, two budgets were presented to parliament. In a move to **synchronise the financial and calendar years**, the government presented a second half-year budget for June to December on 22 May and another for 2010 on 18 November. In the June-December budget, Sithanen announced, in particular, measures to maintain the reputation of Mauritius as an OECD white-listed jurisdiction and to promote the development of new financial products. Following up on the Additional Stimulus Package, the budget reflected three priorities: saving jobs, protecting the people and preparing for recovery.

The new budget, presented in parliament on 18 November, focussed on recovery, social progress and 'Green Mauritius' ('Maurice Ile Durable'). In justifying the budget, Ramgoolam stressed that his government had contributed to the democratisation of the economy during his tenure. Economic observers qualified the budget as conservative and prudent, but noted at the same time that a 3.5% salary increase announced for April 2010 for the low-paid in the public sector was already Ramgoolam's play to the electorate with the forthcoming general elections in prospect.

Klaus-Peter Treydte

Mozambique

Frelimo's landslide victory in national elections confirmed its position as the predominant political party. Traditional opposition party Renamo continued its collapse, but a new third party made a strong showing. Donors withheld aid because of electoral misconduct and manipulation. Mozambique was not seriously affected by the global economic crisis. Economic growth continued, but poverty was not decreasing.

Domestic Politics

President Armando Guebuza was re-elected and the ruling Frelimo party won a landslide victory in the 28 October **elections**. However, the elections were controversial and tainted. EU observers concluded that "Frelimo's overwhelming victory suggests that the results reflect the choice of a vast majority of Mozambican voters." But the EU went on to say, "The broader electoral process was weakened by the insufficient measures of transparency shown by the country's electoral authorities, by an unlevel playing field during the electoral campaign and by limitations with regard to voter choice at local level." The lack of a level playing field and the growing role of Frelimo as the dominant party led the group of 19 budget support donors to withhold some aid late in the year in an attempt to force changes in Mozambican law.

There were three elections the same day, for president, national parliament and new provincial parliaments. Guebuza was re-elected, having received 75% of the vote; Renamo president Afonso Dhlakama, standing for the fourth time, gained 16%; Daviz Simango for the Mozambique Democratic Movement (MDM) had 9%. For the national parliament (Assembly of the Republic [AR]), Frelimo won 191 seats (more than a two-thirds majority), Renamo 51, and the MDM eight. Frelimo won majorities in all ten of the new provincial assemblies, gaining 703 of 812 seats; Renamo won 83, the MDM 24, and the 'Partido para a Paz, Democracia e Desenvolvimento' (PDD) two. Turnout was 45% of registered voters, similar to 2004 and much below the high levels of 1994 and 1999; 9.9 m, people registered to vote – over 90% of voting age adults. The MDM was a new party, formed in 2009. Simango had been the successful Renamo mayor of Beira, but was not chosen by Renamo to stand again; he had stood as an independent in the 2008 local elections and was overwhelmingly re-elected, but was then expelled from Renamo. Still tightly controlled by Dhlakama, who seemed to be losing interest and failed to organise effective election campaigns, Renamo seemed in terminal decline. Simango created the new party, the MDM, which largely attracted the more dynamic people from Renamo, plus some younger urban voters (it took one parliamentary seat for Maputo city from Frelimo). It was widely considered that with less than a year to organise, the MDM did well to gain 9% of the vote and eight AR seats, and could represent a much bigger challenge to Frelimo in the 2013 and 2014 elections.

Mozambique had been tinkering since 1994 with its **elections laws**, which were now confused and contradictory. A further law passed on 8 April clarified some problems, but also created new contradictions, particularly in the electoral calendar, and unexpectedly increased to six the number of documents that candidates for parliament had to present. Mozambique's election laws have always given the National Elections Commission (CNE) total freedom to act in secret, and even to change the results without explanation. This had been repeatedly criticised by domestic and international observers, but was never changed. The election procedure was an odd mixture of transparent and secret. Each polling station had a single register of up to 1,000 voters, the count was carried out in the polling station in the presence of observers and press as soon as polls closed, and the results were posted on the polling station door. This allowed parallel counts, and three were carried out – an accurate sample survey by a local NGO, the Electoral Observatory; a reasonably close tally taken by Radio Mozambique simply by reading out results all day during the day after polling; and a parallel count by election officials themselves. These parallel counts prevented the CNE from tampering too much with the results in secret, but other actions caused growing discontent. For example, full lists of candidates and of polling stations were never published.

Observers estimated that polling station staff were guilty of misconduct or **fraud** in at least 6% of polling stations. Ballot box stuffing in favour of Frelimo and Guebuza occurred in Tete, Niassa and Gaza provinces – in many cases polling stations claimed a 100% turnout with nearly everyone voting for Frelimo. The CNE (in secret and without comment) excluded 104,000 votes – 16% of the votes in Tete and 9% of the votes in Niassa – apparently because of impossibly high turnouts. The other widespread fraud took the form of polling station staff adding an extra ink mark or fingerprint to ballot papers for the opposition, making is seem as if the voter selected two candidates, thus invalidating the vote. The second ink mark was often in different coloured ink and the difference was obvious to journalists and observers when invalid votes were being reconsidered by the CNE. At a few polling stations, more than 30% of the votes cast were invalid, compared with a national average of 4%. Although ballot box stuffing and nullifying ballot papers is a crime, no action was taken against polling station staff and the evidence was destroyed by the CNE.

Although Frelimo's overwhelming victory was unquestioned, there were growing complaints by observers, diplomats and the local independent press of the lack of a '**level playing field**'. The CNE was seen as being biased toward Frelimo, and it excluded MDM parliamentary candidates lists for seven out of 11 provinces on the grounds that the MDM had not completed the new, more stringent conditions for its candidates in those provinces. Again, detailed reasons were kept secret. The issue went to the Constitutional Council, which ruled in favour of the CNE on the basis of secret CNE documents not disclosed to the MDM – but which were later shown to contain errors. During the campaign, there were widespread media reports and complaints about Frelimo using state cars in the campaign, and of teachers, health workers and other civil servants being put under heavy pressure to campaign for Frelimo. This followed a period when civil servants complained about growing pressure to join the party, and administrators were being pushed to favour Frelimo members for jobs, grants, licences and other forms of preferential treatment. Mozambique's First Lady, Maria da Luz Guebuza, was given increasing prominence, playing a part in her husband's election campaign, speaking at various international meetings, and being given prizes by obscure international organisations.

Mozambique's Central Office for the Fight against **Corruption** (GCCC) and the 11 provincial attorney's offices investigated 534 allegations of corruption and theft of state funds and property, according to GCCC director Ana Maria Gemo. Of these, 27 came to trial, 40 were shelved, and charges were laid in 155 cases; 111 people were arrested. The figures show a significant rise since the shake-up in mid-2007, when Augusto Paulino was named attorney general and named Gemo to head the GCCC. The trial of former transport minister Antonio Munguambe and Diodino Cambaza, former chair of the Mozambique Airports Company, began in November. They were accused of stealing $ 3 m. Former interior minister Almerino Manhenje remained in detention awaiting trial on corruption charges. A range of other corruption cases also became public. In Cabo Delgado province, $ 3.5 m were stolen from the government in at least seven different cases. Former provincial director of planning and finance Paulo Risco and four other finance officials were arrested. Tete provincial Director of Planning and Finances Jose Joao, and three senior officials, were arrested in August for stealing $ 5.4 m. Five staff members from the Manica planning and finance directorate were arrested and several provincial directors were dismissed; two civil servants in the education department were dismissed for stealing $ 38,000. Jose Carlos Amade, who had been administrator of Angoche, and before that of Muecate district, was expelled from the civil service; he had been publicly criticised in both districts for giving contracts to businesses owned by his family. The former permanent secretary of the ministry of health, Filomena Zimba, was arrested for corruption. In Matola, four officials were suspended for stealing $ 58,000 – 17% of the municipality's entire revenue for the year.

Mozambique still ranked 130th out of 180 countries in TI's Corruption Perception Index. A British construction firm, Mabey and Johnson (M&J) pleaded guilty in a London court to systematically bribing officials around the world to win lucrative contracts. One official of M&J said it had bribed Carlos Fragoso, who at the time was national director of roads and bridges in the ministry of public works. M&J said it paid £ 287,000 into his Swiss bank account between 14 October 1997 and 10 April 2000. Fragoso denied he had taken bribes and there has been no follow-up in Mozambique, where it is widely believed the money went to the Frelimo party rather than to Fragoso personally. The dropping of charges in May meant that no one was tried over the ruinous management of Banco Austral in 1998–2000 by people with important links in Frelimo, nor was anyone charged with the 11 August 2001 assassination of Antonio Siba-Siba Macuacua, the Bank of Mozambique head of banking supervision, who tried to clean up Banco Austral. However, Anibalzinho, the convicted killer of investigative journalist Carlos Cardoso, who was allowed to escape (for the third time) from a high security jail on 7 December 2008, was recaptured in South Africa in August.

In order to reduce conflicts of interest within the AR, it passed regulations requiring MPs to declare any personal or family interests they had in matters under debate, including cases where an MP or a close relative of an MP was involved in any business that would be affected by a law or resolution passed by the AR. However, MPs were still permitted to vote on matters in which they had an interest, and the AR did not establish a register of members' interests.

At the swearing-in ceremony for his second term, Guebuza said he was "launching a centralised mechanism to drive a successful **decentralisation** for local government, where the district serves as our development pole". In December, the government had already announced a series of changes to speed decentralisation. The Local Initiative Investment Budget (OIIL) had, since 2006, given each of the 128 districts at least $ 300,000 per year for locally decided projects to improve food security, create jobs and generate local income. This was money that was meant to be repaid, but the repayment rate had been low, both because of recipients' difficulties in making payments, and also because district administrations had no means to administer such funds. Formal District Development Funds had therefore been established to replace the OIIL. These were to be rotating loan funds, using both the $ 300,000 annual grant and repayments of previous loans. Funds were managed by the provincial governments, but the District Consultative Councils continued to play a key role in decision making. As further support, the existing Economic Rehabilitation Support Fund was redirected to work with micro-credit and banking institutions to expand financial services in the countryside. In July, as part of its programme to raise the quality of local administration, the government began raising by 25%–45% the salaries of state employees with high or mid-level education who were not working in the cities.

A new 2.4 km bridge over the Zambezi River linking Sofala and Zambezia provinces was opened in July. The $ 113 m bridge replaced an erratic ferry service. The bridge finally made it possible to drive from the north to the south of the country. As well as the psychological importance of physically linking the north and south, it was likely to increase internal trade.

Social **violence** continued in the poorest areas, reflecting a distrust of the better off and outsiders. Lynching of suspected criminals continued in urban neighbourhoods. Mobs attacked police stations near Maputo and Beira to try to take out and lynch an alleged murderer and a kidnapper. In Nicoadala district of Zambezia, local people accused the government of locking up the rain and giving it only to better off people; in February, 25 houses were burned down, three people were killed and six injured, accused of diverting the rain. Cholera is endemic, but in the poorest areas local people blamed the government and the better-off for spreading cholera to kill the poor, particularly through the use of a white powder. In northern Cabo Delgado province, mobs attacked cholera treatment tents, health workers and community leaders in January and November; on 11 November, police shot and killed four people in a crowd attacking a treatment centre in the village of Muadja, in Ancuabe district. In Quinga, Mogincual district, Nampula, a very poor area with high levels of malnutrition, a Red Cross volunteer was beaten to death in March. Three days later, health workers were attacked and, when the police defended them, the mob attacked the police with knives and spears, disembowelling and killing a police sergeant and seriously injuring two other policemen. A Red Cross activist was assaulted, buried up to her neck, and nearly murdered, when a mob demanded that she hand over "the cholera" she was allegedly keeping in her house. She was rescued by the police, who were attacked by the mob. Frightened police arrested 29 people and packed them into a tiny police cell in Mogincual, where 12 suffocated to death in the early morning of 17 March. Two police officers were each sentenced to one year in jail for actions leading to the deaths.

Foreign Affairs

Mozambique is one of the most **aid**-dependent countries in the world, so foreign relations are dominated by aid. OECD DAC figures for 2008, released during the year, showed that Mozambique received $ 1,994 m in aid (19% of GDP). The largest donors and lenders were the World Bank ($ 280 m), the United States ($ 227 m), the United Kingdom ($ 198 m), the EU ($ 161 m), Sweden ($ 120 m), the Netherlands ($ 106 m), Norway ($ 97 m), Denmark ($ 87 m), Canada ($ 77 m), Spain ($ 78 m), Germany ($ 75 m), and Ireland ($ 74 m).

Mozambique has been in the forefront of the donor shift to **budget support**, in which money is given directly to the government budget in exchange for detailed donor involvement in policy making and the writing of the budget. A quarter of aid is budget support ($ 465 m in 2008, which was 29% of government current expenditure). The group of 19 budget support donors, known as the G19 or Programme Aid Partners, had become the major interlocutor with the government on policy issues – to the annoyance of the United States and Japan, who are not members. A new agreement between the G19 and the government was signed on 29 April, but there were signs of tension. The government failed to keep its promises on justice and governance issues, and the G19 chair and Irish Ambassador Frank Sheridan warned that the conduct of upcoming elections would be an important test. On 28 May, the G19 pledged $ 472 m in budget support for 2010. The World Bank and Canada promised significant increases, but Sweden, which had supported Frelimo since before independence, made a token 3% cut in budget support as a protest at what it saw as the government's unwillingness to combat corruption. At the announcement press conference, G19 chair Sheridan said that several more of the donors had decided not to increase their budget support because of poor performance by the Mozambican government on governance issues. Donor tolerance on this had been partly due to Mozambique's rapid economic growth and claimed substantial reductions in poverty. On 15 September, the G19 issued an unusually strong statement criticising the exclusion of the MDM from standing in many provinces in the October elections, and then demanded and held angry meetings with CNE President Joao Leopoldo da Costa and Guebuza. Finally, in mid-December, the G19 stopped dispersing budget support (although continuing to disperse other aid). The **aid moratorium** was not solid – two large budget support donors, the World Bank and the EU, had released their money earlier, while three southern European countries who only made token budget support contributions (Portugal, Spain and Italy) did not adhere to the withholding of funds, which had the full backing of other influential donors, including the Nordics, Britain, Ireland, Switzerland and the Netherlands. The G19 demanded government commitments to rapid electoral law reform, tighter conflict of interest legislation, improved governance, and a reduction of the party's role in the state, particularly a ban on party cells in ministries. The government responded by taking a hard line, and the stand-off continued.

Mozambique was elected chair of the **SADC** Troika for Politics, Defence and Security in September, and was involved in unsuccessful negotiations in Maputo to try to resolve internal conflicts over disputed elections and governments in Lesotho, Zimbabwe and Madagascar. Former Mozambican transport minister Tomas Salomão was elected on 9 September for a second term as executive secretary of SADC.

Links with Brazil, Portugal and China all increased during the year, although China remained a relatively small player. Agreement was reached with **Brazil** on a number of projects, including the $ 100 m conversion of the former military air base at Nacala into a commercial airport. In September, Portugal signed agreements to the value of $ 1 bn with Mozambique, half for the creation of an investment bank. Guebuza visited Brazil in July.

Mozambique controversially signed an **interim EPA** with the EU on 16 June. The signing split SADC, as only Botswana, Lesotho and Swaziland signed, while others continued to negotiate. EPAs have been criticised because, although they allow duty-free and quota-free access to the European market, signatories must grant the EU access to their markets.

Socioeconomic Developments

Economic growth remained high, but fell to 6.1% compared with 6.7% in 2008 and an average of 7.8% in the five years up to 2007. Growth was significantly above earlier IMF projections of 4.5%, suggesting Mozambique had not been badly hit by the global economic crisis. Tax collection was $ 1.7 bn, which was 17.8% of GDP, up from 12.4% in 2004, reported Finance Minister Manuel Chang. The inflation rate in 2009 was 4.2%, the lowest recorded in the past ten years, according to the Bank of Mozambique. This compared with an inflation rate of 6.2% in 2008. The money supply grew by 34.3% over the year, partly because of increased credit to the private sector, and partly because of state financial operations. In December, net international reserves stood at $ 1.8 bn. Over the year the metical depreciated by 9.6% against the dollar. The IMF approved a credit for MZN 114 m Special Drawing Rights (SDRs) under the Fund's Exogenous Shocks Facility, and MZN 100 m in SDRs were disbursed. Subsidies kept fuel prices pegged at March levels despite large rises in oil prices, and cost $ 34 m. The G19 publicly criticised the subsidy in September, claiming it largely benefitted the better-off, who had big cars, and the subsidy was to be ended in early 2010.

Energy and mining played a central role in the economy. Exports for 2008, announced on 2 April, totalled $ 2,650 m. $ 1,450 m were from the Mozal aluminium smelter, which used Mozambican electricity but contributed little to the economy or tax base. Statistics were unclear, but 'other', most of which was titanium, came next at $ 442 m. Next was Cahora Bassa dam electricity, at $ 221 m, followed by gas at $ 152 m, both exported to South Africa. So the mineral-energy sector accounted for 85% of Mozambican exports. Agriculture and fishing exports included tobacco ($ 132 m), sugar ($ 71 m), cotton ($ 48 m), prawns ($ 45 m), and cashews ($ 23 m). Titanium mining in the north was highly successful, but BHP Billeton cancelled a proposed titanium heavy sands mine in Chibuto, Gaza.

New developments also took place in energy-linked sectors, notably **tree planting and biofuels**. Potential investments of $ 6 bn were approved, but Mozambique did not publish lists of how many were actually carried out. More than half were for three huge forestry projects in the north. Norwegian-owned Lurio Green Resources said it would invest $ 2.2 bn in 126,000 hectares of eucalyptus trees in Nampula province. The Portuguese-owned Portucel planned a 173,000 hectares eucalyptus plantation in Zambezia province. Both planned to set up paper mills. At least 14 biofuel projects were approved. In August, Enerterra, a Portuguese company, was granted 18,920 hectares in Cheringoma, Sofala, for the production of jatropha. Zambezi Grown Energy, with Mozambican, Asian and South African interests, was granted 15,000 hectares in Chemba district, Sofala, for sugar cane for energy. Both planned to export 90%, particularly to Europe, and sell 10% locally. Principle Energy was given 18,000 hectares in Manica province for sugar cane for ethanol. The Portuguese Galpenergia was developing sunflower and jatropha production in Sofala. British-owned Sun biofuels had 5,000 hectares in Manica province on which it was growing jatropha, and profitability was dependent on carbon credits. Meanwhile, a project for a 30,000-hectares sugar plantation for ethanol in Gaza province was cancelled; despite approval in 2007, work had not started, probably because lower oil prices made biofuels less attractive. The project was controversial because it diverted water from potential rice production.

Large natural gas reserves were found off the coast of northern Mozambique in the Rovuma basin, increasing the expectations that **oil** would be found there. Ten multinational oil companies carrying out oil exploration had spent $ 330 m sincc 2006. Development of huge **coal** mines in Tete moved forward. The Australian Riversdale Mining planned to start mining and processing coal in 2011. Its Benga mine would initially produce 5.3 m tonnes of raw coal a year, to be processed into about 1.7 m tonnes of top quality hard coking coal, plus 0.3 m tonnes of thermal coal per year for export. Coal that could not be exported would be burned in a 2,000 MW power station to be built next to the mine. The Brazilian mining giant Vale hoped to produce 8.5 m tonnes of coking coal and 2.5 m tonnes of thermal coal a year; low quality coal would be burned in a 600 MW power station. The rehabilitated Sena railway line from Tete to Beira port did not have the capacity to move all the coal that would be mined so, in October, Vale signed an agreement for a new railway line to Nacala port; 100 km of this line would run though Malawi. Meanwhile, the Sena railway itself, after four years of rehabilitation, was opened as far as the sugar mill at Marromeu, and Mutarara on the north bank of the Zambezi, and should reopen to serve the coal mines in 2010. The Sena line was destroyed in the war in the

1980s; in some areas Renamo rebels forced local people to pull up many kilometres of track by hand.

In May, Mozambique was accepted as candidate country for the Extractive Industries Transparency Initiative (**EITI**), and a coordinating committee was set up, consisting of four representatives of the government, four from civil society, and four from mining and oil companies. Under the EITI, all revenue received by governments, and all payments made by companies resulting from mining and hydrocarbon exploitation, are made public.

Huge investments in the minerals-energy sector and substantial GDP growth did not reduce **poverty**. The self-evaluation report of the National Forum for the APRM, published in March, asserted that the principle beneficiaries of growth were a tiny group and "the most credible indicators show an increase in absolute terms in the number of people below the minimum subsistence line". The National Forum is an establishment body of 58 people, including three provincial governors, the governor of the Bank of Mozambique, university rectors and representatives of eight parliamentary commissions, civil society and the private sector, and it explicitly rejected government and donor claims of dramatic reductions in poverty. "Mozambique's present development model, based on free individual initiative and the principles of a economic liberalism", was seen as creating unemployment and leaving many families without even enough to survive, especially in urban areas. This was polarising society, and created "serious risks" of conflict. In a survey, half of the respondents saw unemployment as the most serious threat to peace, stability and security, the peer review domestic forum noted. Towards the end of the year, internal government evaluations of the poverty reduction strategy programme 2006–2009 (PARPA II) showed that median incomes were falling and poverty was actually increasing. In particular, the goal of increasing rural incomes by improving agricultural technology had been a complete failure; over 90% of Mozambican farmers are peasants using only a hoe and no fertiliser or improved seeds. Most did not grow enough to feed themselves adequately for the entire year. A measure of this was that the number of children with chronic malnutrition (stunting, measured as height for age) only fell from 48% in 2003 to 44% in 2008, still "very high" by WHO standards, according to the 2008 Multi-Indicator Cluster Survey, published in 2009. Meanwhile, the under-five mortality rate was falling slowly, from 201 per 1,000 live births in 1997, to 153 in 2003, and to 138 in 2008, as announced in October. Zambezia province had the highest under-five mortality rate with 205 deaths per 1,000 live births, while the rate in the capital, Maputo city, with the best health services in the country, was 103.

Health Minister Ivo Garrido reported that, at 4,000 deaths, **malaria** death rates were 25% lower than in 2008, but with 4 m cases per year, malaria remained the main public health problem, more serious than HIV/AIDS. Malaria was responsible for 40% of outpatient consultations and 60% of paediatric hospital admissions. The malaria death rate was falling as a result of household spraying, better testing available at the local level, and the use of insecticide-treated bed nets; 2 m insecticide-treated bed nets had been distributed, and over the coming three years 6 m more would be made available – still not enough for the entire population. The **HIV** prevalence rate in Mozambique was 15% for people aged between 15 and 49, down from 16% in 2007, meaning that "the stabilization plateau has been reached," said Garrido. These figures indicated that about 1.6 m Mozambicans were infected with HIV, and that over 120,000 new infections occurred annually. Antiretroviral drugs were available in every district in the country, and about 160,000 Mozambicans were taking such drugs. The HIV prevalence rate was highest in the south, at 21%, followed by 18% in the centre. In the three northern provinces (Nampula, Niassa and Cabo Delgado) it was 9%; rates were lower than in neighbouring countries. The method used to estimate the prevalence rate was testing the blood of pregnant women for HIV antibodies at 36 sentinel sites located in all 11 provinces. Cholera continued to be endemic, with 20,000 cases and 155 deaths during the year. At least 103 people died of hunger in the year ending 31 March, according to Deputy National Director of Agricultural Services Marcelo Chaquisse.

Poor rainfall in the south and centre of the country in the first half of the rainy season (October to December) caused widespread crop failure; the south is already traditionally dryer and was predicted to be more affected by climate change. The more productive northern provinces had a normal rainfall. Tobacco became Mozambique's biggest **agricultural export**, rising to 43,000 tonnes, compared with 39,000 tonnes in 2008. Mozambique Leaf Tobacco employed 4,000 workers in their processing factory in Tete, and had 120,000 contract farmers in Tete, Zambezia and Niassa provinces.

The electricity grid reached 94 of the 128 districts; 42 districts had been linked to the grid since 2003. Minimum wages were agreed on 28 April, ranging from $ 55 per month for agricultural workers to $ 114 per month in the financial sector. The banking network was slowly expanding. There were 352 bank branches, but 56% were in the three largest cities – Maputo, Beira and Nampula. Half of all Automatic Teller Machines (ATMs) were in Maputo, and 71% of establishments that accepted payment by bank debit or credit card were in Maputo.

In a bid to encourage tourism and raise taxes, parliament approved a law relaxing restrictions on gambling and allowing **casinos** throughout the country, with the proviso that they be linked to hotels rated at least four-star. The law also legalised on-line gambling and slot machines in places that were not part of the casinos.

Education expansion continued, with 1,200 new classrooms built in 2009, of which 1,137 were for first level primary schools. This was below the target of 1,400 classrooms per year; and an early target of 6,000 per year had already been abandoned because of shortages of building materials and skilled labour. The teacher-pupil ratio was 1:65. Managing director of Mozambique's National Prison System, Joao Zandamela, said in August that most of the 119 jails in the country were overcrowded. There were 13,453 detainees at that time, 4,704 of whom were awaiting trial.

Results were announced for the August 2007 national **census**. The resident population then was 20,226,296, up from 16.1 m in the 1997 census – an increase of 28%. Mozambicans did not seem to be moving to cities – the urban population was 29.8% of the total, almost identical to the 28.6% in 1997. Nampula remained the largest province, with 4 m people, followed by Zambezia with 3.8 m, and Tete with 1.8 m. The census found that 46.9% of the population were under 15 years old, 50.1% were between 15 and 64, and only 3.1% were 65 or older. The fertility rate remained unchanged at an average of 5.8 children per woman. Illiteracy fell from 60.5% of the population aged 15 and above in 1997, to 50.4% in 2007; 34.6% of men were illiterate compared with 64.2% of women.

Climate had been changing for the past 45 years, according to a detailed study by the National Disasters Management Institute. Between 1960 and 2005, temperatures rose by an average of between 1.1 and 1.6 degrees (centigrade). The rainy season was starting later than it used to. In some parts of northern Mozambique the rains began 45 days later than was the case half a century ago. Cyclones were becoming more frequent and more intense. Between 1980 and 1993, Mozambique was hit by four cyclones, one of which had wind speeds in excess of 100 km an hour, while between 1994 and 2007, there were 11 cyclones, six of which were more devastating than any in the preceding period.

Joseph Hanlon

Namibia

The year was dominated by domestic politics in preparation for National Assembly and presidential elections held in late November. Despite speculation to the contrary, the former liberation movement, the South West African People's Organisation (SWAPO), maintained its overwhelming dominance over the new Rally for Democracy and Progress (RDP), which had been formed in late 2007 in a break-away move following earlier internal power struggles, and emerged as the official opposition. The election campaign took place in a tense atmosphere and the election results were contested in court. The country's foreign policy continued to shift towards newly emerging partners. The collapse of the diamond industry as a result of the global financial crisis, and reduced income from the customs union, took their toll and contributed to a markedly weaker economic performance.

Domestic Politics

The parliamentary and presidential elections cast their shadow over domestic politics during the year and campaigning for votes was a dominant feature of the local political scene. Faced with growing militancy between party activists, which since 2008 had at times turned political competition and rivalry into a violent affair, the leaders of the Namibian churches issued a "Declaration on Elections" on 31 March. A delegation officially handed a copy to the country's president on 28 April. On 4 June, as a follow-up to this, a church-based steering committee on **churches and elections** in Namibia, appointed on 19 February by church leaders from about 57 different churches and chaired by the former president of the Council of Churches in Namibia, issued an open letter to President Hifikepunye Pohamba and Founding President Sam Nujoma. It expressed concern over political statements made towards the end of May by both leaders at different public political rallies and appealed to them to honour the constitutional provisions "so that all of us may go about our daily lawful activities without feeling excluded or being vilified and harassed".

Namibia's first head of state, **Nujoma**, celebrated his 80th birthday (12 May) in the usual style: the Founding Father of the Republic of Namibia (an official title bestowed upon him by parliament when he left State House) appealed to children at a birthday party in a park in Windhoek's city centre to chase away imperialists and colonialists. This militant rhetoric continued with statements at public rallies in his home region in the north. In mid-June, he attacked the Namibian German Evangelical-Lutheran Church for having collaborated with the enemy prior to independence. The church would be tolerated, but any members who asked German friends for help would be shot in the head. Namibian church leaders of several denominations united in the Council of Churches responded by meeting Nujoma on 14 July to share their concerns with the elder statesman. The SWAPO majority dismissed an enquiry by the opposition parties in the National Assembly, since Nujoma was no longer an MP. On 19 September, the founding father, in another speech in the northern region, lashed out against Western imperialism and whites, whom he accused of being as dangerous as black mambas. In a 20 September press release, the National Society for Human Rights (NSHR) quoted Nujoma as saying in his Oshiwambo vernacular: "If you see an English person club (him or her) to the head." During the year, the anything but diplomatic language of the elder statesman also had its impact on the country's foreign relations.

On 22 July, Pohamba announced the suspension of the chief of the **Namibian Defence Force**, Lieutenant General Martin Shalli. He was accused of taking kickbacks dating back to his alleged involvement in arms deals for the Namibian army with Chinese companies while he was ambassador to Zambia, where he had been posted after being relieved of his post as army commander following disagreements with former president Nujoma. When Pohamba took over from Nujoma, he restored Shalli to the highest position in the defence force. The announcement of his suspension came as a bombshell and not only caused unrest within the higher ranks of the army but also provoked intense political speculation as to Pohamba's motives. It was implied that Shalli was the victim of political manoeuvres ahead of the elections. A close ally of former president Nujoma was appointed as acting chief of the defence force.

2 September marked a year since the '**struggle kids**' started public protests demanding compensation for the disadvantages they had suffered as a result of their upbringing in exile. Most of them had been born in Angola. From April, they camped in front of the SWAPO headquarters in Windhoek. On the occasion of the first anniversary of their ongoing protest, a large contingent of the 269 members of the group marched to parliament and handed over petitions. They also demonstrated outside the Angolan embassy.

After a long period of waiting, the Electoral Commission of Namibia (ECN) finally announced on 1 September that **parliamentary and presidential elections** would be held on 27 and 28 November. The announcement was preceded by a long period of deliberation around a revised electoral law. For the first time, votes were to be counted and results announced at local polling stations so that sealed ballot boxes would no longer be transported to Windhoek for centralised counting. In addition, the voting period was extended to two days. While the counting at voting stations was welcomed, those afraid of manipulations and vote-rigging criticised the extended voting period, concerned that it might create temptations to manipulate the votes during the second day.

The SWAPO electoral college, whose members were tasked to compile the **list of candidates** for the parliamentary election, took place on 5–6 September. It was preceded by weeks of speculation and positioning. The expected changing of the guard, however, did not ultimately take place. The candidate list offered hardly any surprises or indications of any major political shifts. Likewise, the list of candidates nominated by the RDP on 20 September had few surprises to offer, with no new defectors from SWAPO. Most notably, former minister of agriculture Anton von Wietersheim – a member of the German-speaking minority – attracted most votes from the delegates and was ranked fifth (after the first four places on the list, which were allocated to the party leadership). Like the SWAPO list, the RDP list sought to offer ethnic and cultural pluralism, even though most of the 72 candidates held only symbolic positions, given the likely outcome of the elections.

In October and November, the final stages of the **election campaign** resulted in several violent clashes between the two dominant rival parties, i.e. SWAPO and the RDP. Police at times had to intervene and disperse crowds by using tear gas. Verbal abuse was common, even among leading political office bearers. At a political rally in the harbour town of Lüderitzbucht in mid-November, former prime minister and current minister of trade and industry Hage Geingob accused the RDP of having a "Savimbi syndrome". The RDP protested that this was a form of hate speech.

The first **election results** reported were from the diplomatic missions abroad, surprisingly, before the elections took place in Namibia. While irrelevant in terms of actual numbers, the vote cast in New York, Gaborone and Cape Town indicated a surprisingly high degree of support for the RDP. In response to the result in New York, where SWAPO obtained half of the votes, the leaders of the SWAPO Youth League and the National Union of Namibian Workers demanded at a press conference on 20 November that the head of state recall Namibia's permanent representative to the UN, since the result was considered proof of his disloyalty to the party.

For the first time, the Namibian electorate voted over two consecutive days (27 and 28 November). The reform of the electoral law provided for a count at polling stations in the presence of observers. However, the results were then transmitted to the headquarters of the ECN in Windhoek for final verification before they were officially announced. This resulted in a considerable delay, so that the **official end result** was made known only on 4 December, after days of speculation. Given the relatively small number of votes counted (just over 800,000), this added to the irritation of those already afraid of attempts at manipulation. Beyond all the party arithmetic, which follows below, **women** were the biggest losers. The number of women parliamentary representatives fell from 18 to 16 out of 72, a mere 22% and a far cry from reasonably equal representation.

In spite of these concerns, **election observers** from various African constituencies remained largely satisfied. The SADC observer team recommended a return to polling on a single day in line with the other SADC countries and that equal airtime should be allocated to all parties during the election campaign by the state-owned broadcasting company. The AU observer mission combined its approval of the elections with a reference to "minor problems", which included a "painstakingly slow" counting process. The observer mission of the Pan African Parliament recommended that "the State media in Namibia be insulated from direct Government control by the establishment of an independent media institution" and raised concern over the printing of 1.6 m ballot papers (for a registered electorate markedly below one million) as a potential recipe for vote rigging. Although the mission concluded that the elections took place within the constitutional and legislative framework, it felt that Namibia could do much better.

For the first time in Namibian elections, **local civil society institutions** had formed their own election observation teams. The Namibian Institute for Democracy declared in a statement that it had noted several minor flaws but had not observed any grave irregularities and therefore trusted that the results were by and large credible. The Institute for Public Policy Research, which had created an election watch website, also refrained from any fundamental criticism and seemed largely satisfied that the results reflected the will of the voters. However, the NSHR, generally most critical of the government, was denied observer status after some quarrels with the ECN. Eight of the opposition parties also felt betrayed. They announced in a joint statement on 4 December that they would bring a list of irregularities before the Namibian justice system to **challenge the election results**. On 24 December, the High Court admitted the case.

The results confirmed the **hegemonic status of SWAPO**, with 602,580 votes or 74.3%, thereby retaining 54 of their previously held 55 seats out of 72 seats in parliament. The loss of one seat was anything but a defeat. Some 'pockets' of dissenting votes cast in some of the urban centres and in the central and southern parts of the country were, however, noteworthy. Chief Garoeb's United Democratic Front (UDF) remained the most popular force among the Damara, securing two seats. Chief Riruako drew considerable support for the National Unity Democratic Organisation (NUDO) among the Herero and also took two seats. SWAPO's majority in the southern and eastern regions was reduced. More than ever since the first elections for independence, it again relied on its stronghold in the so-called four O-regions of the former Ovamboland (Oshana, Omusati, Oshikoto and Ohangwena), where for historical reasons it is firmly rooted among more than half of the country's electorate. In these areas, despite the RDP challenge (with its leaders coming from some of these regions), it remained not only by far the biggest, but in most areas still the only, fish in the pond. Even SWAPO – like most of the smaller parties – has some ethnic aspects.

As the **new official opposition**, the RDP, with 90,556 votes (11.16%) and eight seats out of 72, had little reason to celebrate. While it originally boasted of having a database of close to 400,000 supporters, it only attracted 90,556 votes (11.16%). Four of their eight MPs had previously represented SWAPO. The top loser among the **smaller parties** was the Congress of Democrats (CoD), which fell from official opposition status to irrelevant marginality. Two of the small parties' founders managed to survive with one seat each, under flags of the CoD and the newly established All People's Party (APP). The latter testified to the party's ethnic-regional dimension, with most of its votes secured in the Kavango capital of Rundu. A similar pattern of ethnic-local support characterised the Republican Party (RP) and the Democratic Turnhalle Alliance (DTA), which drew most votes from a white electorate and secured one and two seats respectively. Their declining influence can be seen as indicating the further political marginalisation of the white minority, which was now hardly represented in the National Assembly. The taking of the one seat held by the Monitor Action Group (MAG), the conservative Afrikaans-speaking advocacy group, by the South West African National Union (SWANU), the oldest anti-colonial organisation, was a remarkable symbolic shift.

The results of the **presidential election**, conducted in a parallel ballot with separate ballot papers, showed – as in all previous elections – that the votes for SWAPO's candidate exceeded those for the party. Pohamba received 75.25% of the votes, almost 9,000 votes more than the party list, which underscored his status as a respected leader entrusted by the electorate with running the affairs of the Republic as the head of state, while his new RDP challenger and former comrade Hidipo Hamutenya trailed with 10.91% (88,640 votes). This was a remarkable vote of confidence for Pohamba after a number of internal disputes during his first term in office, when party factions challenged his policy of reconciliation towards some party members accused of being 'unreliable'.

Foreign Affairs

Despite his retirement from political office, former president **Nujoma** remained active and continued to make his mark not only in domestic politics. As the Zimbabwean newspaper 'The Herald' reported, he visited Harare (7–8 July) "to appraise himself on the situation on the ground". Interestingly, this did not make the news in Namibia, though the state media cover the activities of the founding father extensively. This fuelled further speculation about the the identity of the real policy makers behind the scenes. On several occasions at public political rallies, he got carried away making xenophobic statements. Nujoma's explicit reference to the German-speaking minority and their church in Namibia resulted in a **diplomatic note from Germany** seeking an explanation from the foreign ministry. The German parliament discussed the matter on 1 July. Notwithstanding these irritations, Namibian-German bilateral government negotiations on 28–29 July resulted in German financial commitments of € 116.5 m for the next two years. Relations with the **United Kingdom** were also put under strain by one of Nujoma's outbursts during a rally on 19 September. As a result of his insults – he called British and US-Americans and their governments "criminals" – the British High Commission asked the Namibian foreign ministry for an explanation.

Relations with **China** were strained as the result of a series of financial scandals, in which Chinese companies were involved, and by Namibia's decision not to take up a preferential loan offer, which in its view was not really a bargain. Two Chinese news websites, which had reported on the involvement of the Chinese president's son in one of the scandals, were temporarily offline on 21 July and had the news removed. At the end of July, after the Chinese involvement in the Namibian fraud case became international news, the Chinese authorities deleted from search engines all references to 'Namibia' and to the names of the Chinese individuals and companies involved, thus preventing them from being accessed on the Internet and *de facto* eliminating Namibia from the Chinese map of the world.

Some of Namibia's closest allies from the struggle days consolidated friendly relations at the highest levels and also included meetings with Nujoma in their tight schedule. President Dmitry Medvedev of **Russia** arrived for a state visit on 25–26 June, accompanied by a huge delegation, and several agreements were entered into, mainly on economic cooperation, including the involvement of Gazprom in the further exploration and exploitation of the offshore Kudu gas field for local energy production, and Russian participation in the further exploitation of the extensive uranium deposits, even incorporating an option to generate nuclear power.

On 19–20 July, Raul Castro came on a state visit, during which he also met Nujoma, to underline Namibia's friendly relations with **Cuba**. His brother Fidel had never made more than a short stop-over of a few hours, despite Cuba's very prominent role in the final stages of decolonisation, not least through military engagement with the South African army in Angola. Almost 150 Cuban medical doctors and nurses play an essential role in Namibia's public health system, while some 130 Namibian students are studying in Cuba.

Southern African bonds were reinforced on 19 August in the diamond-mining town of Oranjemund, when nine SADC member countries promoted their joint football World

Cup-related tourism agenda. The heads of state of Namibia, Zimbabwe and Botswana, as well as the prime ministers of Lesotho and Swaziland, participated in the public relations offensive, which marketed a 'boundless Southern Africa' for visitors to seven transfrontier conservation areas and 30 national parks and nature reserves. Bilateral links with **Botswana** were srengthened at a meeting on 17 August, when delegations led by Namibia's Prime Minister Nahas Angula and Botswana's Vice President Mompati Merafhe met in Windhoek mainly to discuss new infrastructure investments in the Walvis Bay harbour and a railway line to link Botswana with the Namibian port.

At the AU summit in Sirte on 3 July, Namibia was among the countries that endorsed the dismissal of the ICC extradition order for **Sudan's President** al-Bashir. Upon his return, Foreign Minister Hausiku stressed that al-Bashir would be a welcome guest in Namibia. On 9 July, the director of the Legal Assistance Centre, a local human rights agency already active under the South African administration, criticised this as a violation of legally-binding international treaties signed by the government, such as the Treaty of Rome (which established the ICC). He declared that the endorsement of the AU decision suggested that Namibia could not be trusted with its international treaty obligations and was in defiance of its own Constitution, saying: "Considering our recent history of violent oppression under Apartheid, of all nations, we are expected to side with victims of mass murder, rape, mutilation and torture; not with their tyrants and persecutors."

In contrast to the government's dubious stance in solidarity with al-Bashir, the country's permanent representative at the UN, during the UN General Assembly debate at the end of September, vehemently demanded the strict implementation of the AU principle that governments that seized power by means of coups should not be recognised. He led an initiative which ruled on 25 September that the new government of **Madagascar** would not be admitted to participate in the 64th session of the assembly's high-level segment.

Following the state visit by Liberia's President Sirleaf Johnson in 2008, Pohamba reciprocated with a visit to **Liberia** from 28 to 30 July. During a five-day state visit to **India**, Pohamba signed a number of agreements on 30 August, notably for stronger economic cooperation in the diamond polishing sector and with respect to Indian licences for uranium prospecting.

Namibia's international image was damaged by the government's decision to continue with the annual **seal cull** during July. Despite widely organised international protests, the ministry of fisheries granted two seal rights holders a quota of 85,000 seal pups at the seal colonies of Cape Cross and Wolf/Atlas Bay. Two South African journalists who tried to document the cull were arrested and sentenced for contravening the law prohibiting filming without prior permission. Permission was subsequently requested by a local newspaper but was refused. The government's official justification for the criticised practice was that the seals were reducing fish stocks.

Socioeconomic Developments

Major **financial scandals** made headlines during the year. Following investigations by the Anti Corruption Commission, three arrests were made in early July. Those detained included a member of the influential Public Service Commission and a locally resident Chinese businessman, who had links to Nuctech, a Chinese company co-owned by the son of President Hu Jintao. Suspect transactions had allegedly secured the locally based trio over $ 4.3 m for non-existent services after the ministry of finance transferred an advance of $ 12.8 m to the Chinese company in anticipation of the delivery of x-ray equipment for scanning cargo containers and airline baggage. The main costs were to have been covered by a concessional loan from China. On 20 July, Calle Schlettwein, permanent secretary of the finance ministry, confirmed that the government had suspended the $ 100 m credit lines for preferential export buyers credit with the Export-Import (Exim) Bank of China, which had been the main financer of the scanner deal. The reasons given were high interest rates, a tough repayment schedule, the need to limit the purchase of Chinese goods and services, and costly insurance obligations, which made the credit facility unattractive. A **decline in public morale** was reflected in Namibia's further slide on the scale of indicators compiled by the World Bank in its "Doing Business 2010" report released in September. While Namibia had ranked 48th in 2008 and 51st in 2009, it fell to 66th in the prognosis for 2010.

The **annual budget** was presented on 20 March. Finance Minister Saara Kuugongelwa-Amadhila stated that the fiscal tide had turned. The Medium Term Expenditure Framework (MTEF) projections foresaw massive budget deficits for the years to come and an expected increase in the national debt from 20.5% to 29.3% of GDP by the end of the MTEF period in 2011–12. It was estimated that revenue for 2009–10 would fall from N$ 22 bn to N$ 21.8 bn, while total expenditure was increased by 13.1% to N$ 25.4 bn, of which N$ 4.5 bn was allocated to the development budget, an increase of more than half on the previous year. Again, education received the biggest allocation (21.3%), while defence (10.6%) continued to receive more than health (9.5%). The estimated budget deficit was 5.2% of GDP. As a budget analysis of the local Institute for Public Policy Research concluded, renewed international demand for the country's natural resources would be necessary to avoid a national debt crisis and major expenditure cuts in the future.

Diamond production, essentially the country's greatest single source of revenue, suffered major setbacks due to the collapse of the world market. After record sales until mid-2007, production by Namdeb, a joint venture between De Beers and the state, was dramatically cut from the beginning of the year. Shifts were reduced from January to March and a 'production holiday' declared for April to June. Over the first six months of the year, some 400,000 carats were produced, a 60% decline compared with the 1 m carats during the first half of 2008. The government assisted the company, which was confronted with cash flow problems and laid off some 2,000 miners, by permitting it to sidestep the existing diamond trade regulations and sell a significant portion of its stockpile directly to an Indian consortium. This did not prevent Namdeb from ending the year with a net loss of N$ 414 m in contrast to net profits of N$ 598 m the previous year. The government provided damage control with a tax breather of N$ 141 m; the state coffers had received taxes of N$ 1.4 bn from Namdeb in 2008.

It was expected that increased **uranium** production would compensate for the fall in diamond revenue, but output increased insignificantly compared with the previous year. Namibia nevertheless overtook Russia to end as the fourth biggest uranium producer worldwide with an 11.8% share over the year. In September, new prospecting results for the Rössing South site adjacent to Rio Tinto's big Rössing uranium mine and Paladin's Langer Heinrich suggested that the area ranked among the top five known uranium deposits in the world. This caused some commotion among global players in the uranium mining business and resulted in speculation about who, of the British, Australian, French, Canadian, Chinese, Indian, Russian and other competitors, would manage to secure the investment opportunity to exploit this attractive potential. Government plans to use the uranium resources to embark on **nuclear energy** production were cultivated further through an agreement signed with India on 30 August to seek collaboration in the peaceful uses of nuclear energy. Russia expressed similar interests in collaboration and offered know-how to establish a nuclear energy plant.

During the year, dissonances over the signing of an **interim EPA** increased and the Namibian ministry for trade and industry refused to give in to pressure from Brussels. Together with Angola and South Africa, Namibia did not sign because of unresolved differences. Considerable benefits to the vulnerable, export-oriented economy would be put at risk by the possible loss of preferential access to the EU market. Local producers, especially in the meat sector, which supplied a beef quota to the European market, were concerned about the future.

Henning Melber

South Africa

On 9 May, Jacob Zuma was inaugurated as South Africa's fourth post-apartheid president. After a tumultuous election campaign and peaceful polls, Zuma's first months in office passed fairly smoothly. In his budget speech in February, Minister of Finance Trevor Manuel predicted growth of 1.2%, but by the time of Zuma's State of the Nation address on 3 June, South Africa was officially in a recession, after a 6.4% contraction in the first quarter.

Domestic Politics

In the **national and provincial elections** on 22 April, the ruling African National Congress (ANC) again won an overwhelming victory with 65.9% of the vote. This was a fall of 3.8% compared with the 2004 elections, but the party still obtained an impressive majority in spite of competition from a new party, the Congress of the People (COPE). The ANC's closest rival, however, remained the Democratic Alliance (DA), which polled 16.6% of the vote. After a fierce contest, the DA won the Western Cape Province, where party leader Helen Zille became the premier. COPE, which split from the ANC in 2008, claiming to be the true guardian of its legacy of people-centred politics and non-racialism, came in third with 7.4% of the vote, bringing it 30 seats in parliament. Support for the

Inkatha Freedom Party (IFP) declined further to 4.6% of the vote. The prospect of a Zulu president, Jacob Zuma, persuaded a substantial number of IFP voters to back Zuma with their national vote, giving the ANC a record 66.1% of the vote in KwaZulu-Natal.

In spite of Zuma's controversial candidacy and the entry of COPE, the campaign was conducted without serious disturbances and the polls passed off peacefully. The Independent Electoral Commission (IEC) registered a voter turnout of 77.3% and received few complaints. However, the DA, the IFP and the Freedom Front Plus challenged the constitutional validity of certain sections of the Electoral Act of 1998. The DA reported that 20,000 citizens living abroad had contacted them to make inquiries, but only 5,170 South Africans overseas had registered with the IEC. On 12 March, the Constitutional Court decided that expatriates who had registered had the right to vote.

The ANC's majority remains very comfortable but it is increasingly seen as a party with an African identity, and no longer as a rainbow coalition. The ANC obtained 264 of the 400 seats in parliament, three seats short of the two-thirds majority needed to alter the Constitution. The smaller parties were nearly obliterated. The United Democratic Movement, the Freedom Front Plus and the Independent Democrats each gained four seats. The African Christian Democratic Party was represented by three seats and the United Christian Democratic Party by two seats. The Panafricanist Congress, the Minority Front, the Azanian People's Organisation and the African Peoples Convention all won one seat in parliament.

In the provincial elections, the ANC retained control of all provinces except the Western Cape, where the DA won an outright majority of 51.5%. In this hotly-contested province, the ANC obtained 31.5 % of the provincial votes.

Some observers hailed **COPE's results** as a relative success for an untested newcomer, but the overall sense was that the outcome fell below expectations. COPE had benefited from the massive wave of media attention and publicity that accompanied its breakaway from the ANC. When COPE leaders claimed to speak for the 40% of ANC members who voted for then president Thabo Mbeki at the ANC's Polokwane conference in 2007, it was suggested that the new party might succeed in shaking the ANC hegemony. At the same time, this history was COPE's albatross: the new party was widely perceived as a bunch of losers and associated with Mbeki's unpopular presidency. In analysing the poor showing, the 'Mail&Guardian' suggested that COPE had targeted the disgruntled middle class while neglecting the townships and the countryside. Moreover, the lacklustre performance by COPE's presidential candidate, Bishop Mvume Dandala, raised questions as to whether he was in fact an appropriate choice.

Dandala, former head of the Methodist Church of Southern Africa, emerged as presidential candidate after being nominated by the provincial COPE structures. His nomination on 20 February came as a surprise, as the leadership contest seemed to focus on the two high-profile candidates, Mosiuoa 'Terror' Lekota and Mbhazima Shilowa. COPE profiled Dandala as a clean and trustworthy leader, presumably in contrast to the corruption-tainted image of Jacob Zuma. However, his lack of experience showed in the campaign when he failed to inspire the crowds. He had the right moral image, but little to attract millions of poor voters.

In March, the premier of Limpopo Province, Sello Moloto, resigned and joined COPE, after a bruising battle with Julius Malema, chair of the ANC Youth League. Former Deputy President Phumzile Mlambo-Ngcuka appeared as a COPE member on 4 March, next to Bishop Dandala. While Mbeki has publicly denied any involvement with COPE, some tripartite alliance leaders accused him of being the midwife of the new party. Many COPE leaders consulted Mbeki before resigning from the ANC and Mbeki himself was conspicuously absent from the ANC's election campaign. After these high-profile defections, COPE appeared set to become a challenge to ANC hegemony.

While COPE did not manage to build a solid party organisation throughout South Africa, it did succeed in reinvigorating the ANC. Challenged by this split from its ranks, the ANC overcame the factional divisions and bitter feuding that had characterised the party in recent years and, once galvanized into action, ran a highly professional campaign. In the Eastern Cape, Northern Cape, Limpopo and the Free State, COPE became the official opposition with 13.7%, 16.7%, 7.5 % and 11.6 % of the vote respectively.

After the disappointing election outcome, COPE was plagued by **internal wrangling**, brought into the open by the leaking of a confidential memo by Simon Grindrod, the head of COPE's election campaign. Grindrod complained about the damaging consequences of an informal parallel structure within COPE, with one faction aligned to COPE president Lekota and another to his deputy, Shilowa, with presidential candidate Dandala being mostly invisible, although he was supposed to head the parliamentary party. Grindrod resigned a month after the publication of his leaked memo. Second deputy president and MP Lynda Odendaal also quit, fuelling speculation that the second biggest opposition party was imploding.

In November, the youth wing of the **Inkatha Freedom Party** (IFP) chose Zanele Magwaza-Msibi as its preferred candidate to succeed Mangosuthu Buthelezi as IFP president. Magwaza-Msibi is currently national chairwoman of the IFP. Buthelezi's term expires in April 2010.

Nelson Mandela made a rare public appearance at a political rally on 15 February in the Eastern Cape, joining Zuma on the platform. He did not speak. In April, he appeared at Zuma's final election rally in Ellis Park Stadium in Johannesburg. Mandela's appearance at Zuma's side was seen as an endorsement of Zuma's candidacy, an important gesture in this pre-election period when the ANC had to deal with the perception that its primary concern was to prevent Zuma going on trial for corruption, fraud and money-laundering.

The election campaign had been overshadowed by **Zuma's court case**. On 4 February, a judge postponed a hearing on Zuma's corruption case to 25 August, which meant that the case would continue to overshadow not only the election campaign but also the first phase of Zuma's presidency. On 6 April, the National Prosecuting Authority (NPA) announced that it had dropped corruption charges against Zuma, clearing his way to the presidency. Addressing a media conference in Pretoria, acting NPA head Mokotedi Mpshe said that tape recordings provided evidence of political interference and abuse of power by Leonard McCarthy, the former head of the elite Scorpions anti-crime unit. The NPA had therefore concluded that it was neither possible nor desirable to continue with the prosecution of Zuma. The opposition DA deemed the decision unacceptable, believing that the NPA had buckled under political pressure. Analysts said that the charges had been dropped on a technicality and that Zuma's name had not been cleared in court. Zuma has always denied allegations of graft, racketeering and money laundering related to a multibillion 1999 arms deal. On 9 June, the DA's urgent application to overturn the decision by the NPA was postponed indefinitely in the High Court in Pretoria.

With the shadow of the corruption charges finally gone and comfortable election results, Zuma struck a conciliatory note in his victory speech. The inauguration of the new president on 9 May in Pretoria attracted a massive crowd of over 30,000 people to the Union Buildings, as well as many dignitaries from Africa and other continents. The most notable feature of **Zuma's cabinet**, announced on 10 May, was the shifting of the respected former finance minister Trevor Manuel to a new influential post as the head of the National Planning Commission (NPC), responsible for planning and coordinating between government departments. New Minister of Finance Pravin Gordhan previously headed the Internal Revenue Service (SARS), which was credited with being the most efficiently run government service. Since Gordhan's appointment as commissioner of SARS in 1999, revenue collection had improved dramatically. The NPC is a new organ and will be responsible for strategic planning to ensure one National Plan to which all spheres of government would adhere.

Former interim president Kgalema Motlanthe continued as deputy president. Among the prominent **left-wingers** in the cabinet are Minister of Higher Education Blade Nzimande, who is also general secretary of the South African Communist Party (SACP), trade unionist Ebrahim Patel at economic development, and Rob Davies at trade and industry. Patel, a former general secretary of the Southern African Clothing and Textile Workers Union, has extensive experience in the world of labour. The foreign ministry went to Maite Nkoana-Mashabane. As part of his balancing act, Zuma appointed Pieter Mulder of the Freedom Front Plus as deputy minister of agriculture. In his election campaign, Zuma had tried to reassure the largely Afrikaner white farmers.

Barbara Hogan moved from health to public enterprises. The new minister of health is Aaron Motsoaledi, a medical doctor who previously served as acting premier in Limpopo as well as provincial minister of education. Former Gauteng premier and millionaire Tokyo Sexwale made a dramatic return to politics as the minister of human settlements, previously known as housing. Sexwale left politics in 1998 to pursue business interests. A new ministry for mining is headed by Susan Shabangu, who was previously deputy minister of safety and security.

With four key ministries and three deputy ministers, the Congress of South African Trade Unions (COSATU) and the SACP were satisfied that their support for Zuma's campaign had paid off. COSATU president Sdumo Dlamini called for changes in government policies that thus far had failed to make a meaningful impact on the lives of poor South Africans. Zuma's cabinet had an overall positive reception both in business circles and among trade union leaders. Business had been wary of populist and left-wing preponderance following on from the election campaign, in which Zuma gained the vociferous support of labour and youth.

On 11 May, 'Business Day' commented that Zuma had put together a powerful, diverse cabinet to tackle one of South Africa's biggest challenges, service delivery, and the line-up should be welcomed by financial markets. Some financial experts expressed concern about the splintering of the economic cluster, with considerable overlap between the newly created departments and commissions and thus a potential for conflict.

The NGO Gender Links noted an increase in **women's representation** in the National Assembly, with 43% of seats now occupied by women MPs, up from 27% in the first democratically elected parliament in 1994. It noted that the increase was almost entirely due to the ANC, with other parties giving low priority to gender parity. Gender Links singled out DA leader Helen Zille for her all male Western Cape cabinet, in which Zille herself was the only woman. Moreover, the Western Cape cabinet was 75% white. Women's representation in Zuma's cabinet remained on a similar level as before, with 14 out of 34 cabinet posts allocated to women. Gender Links welcomed the fact that several of these 14 ministries were in 'non-traditional' areas, such as correctional services, defence, home affairs, international relations and cooperation, public enterprises, mining, and science and technology. Noting that the representation of women in the National Council of Provinces had dropped from 40% to 30%, Gender Links called for a legislated quota of 50% that would be binding on all parties. Gender Links was critical of grouping women's interests in the same ministry as children and youth, asserting that women were "adults who should be empowered to exercise their agency while children need to be cared for by both women and men".

The new premiers of the **ANC-ruled provinces** are Nomvula Mokonyane (Gauteng), Zweli Mkhize (KwaZulu-Natal), Ace Magashule (Free State), Noxolo Kiviet (Eastern Cape), Cassel Mathale (Limpopo), David Mabuza (Mpumalanga), Hazel Jenkins (Northern Cape) and Maureen Modizelle (North West). The Polokwane resolutions committed the ANC to attempt to achieve gender parity. Appointing the premier is no longer the president's prerogative. Provincial parties are asked to put up three candidates, from whom the ANC's National Executive then makes its choice.

After the inauguration, Zuma enjoyed some months of **honeymoon**. With the charges against him withdrawn, many South Africans seemed willing to give him a chance. Zuma's personal warmth and attention to all kinds of concerns was a welcome relief from Mbeki's aloof, intellectualist style of government. In an analysis, 'Africa Confidential' characterised

Zuma as a shrewd operator, who made several astute appointments. While remaining in touch with his working class constituency, he took care not to alienate big business and Afrikaners.

However, in July, with record unemployment and an unusually cold winter, South Africa entered a season of violent **protests and strikes**. Service delivery protests have long been a feature of post-apartheid South Africa, but the scope and violence of this season of protest was unusual. By the end of July, the media had reported widespread violent protests in the provinces of Mpumalanga, Gauteng, North West and Western Cape over inadequate access to housing, electricity, water and health care. In spite of Zuma's proclamations against corruption and poor performance, it remained particularly difficult to improve the performance of local government, which was in many instances seen as inherently corrupt and self-serving. Although Zuma put service delivery at the heart of his election campaign, performance has not visibly improved. When protests broke out, police fired rubber bullets and tear gas in a crackdown on protesters.

Winter is traditionally the strike season as this is the period of bargaining over new collective labour contracts. Over 70,000 construction workers labouring on **World Cup** stadiums began a strike on 8 July to press for a 13% increase. Fears that the work would not be completed in time for the World Cup in 2010 proved unfounded as the building projects remained on schedule. A new wage deal between South Africa's biggest union, the National Union of Mineworkers, and the gold and coal mine employers forestalled a strike in the critical mining industry.

Strikes by municipal workers coincided with the upsurge of **township protest** against the poor state of service delivery. While condemning the violent protests, Zuma quickly arranged visits to appease the residents. Housing Minister Tokyo Sexwale expressed concern over the squalid conditions at Diepsloot, where he spent the night. Minister of Cooperative Governance and Traditional Affairs Sicelo Shiceka also lost no time in touring the townships where outbreaks of protest were reported. He instructed a task force to investigate the protests in Mpumalanga, where disgruntled residents had taken to the streets in no fewer than 20 towns. In a preliminary report, they reported instances of financial mismanagement, fraud and corruption, as well as tensions between the political and administrative sections of some municipalities. In a number of cases, local government was not responsive to issues raised by communities, due to ill functioning ward committees. In Gauteng, where violent protests remained limited to a few areas, the provincial government blamed 'criminal elements' for 'hijacking' community concerns over service delivery. In KwaZulu-Natal, 90 people were arrested for looting shops in Durban. The South African Unemployed People's Movement defended the storming of Shoprite, Checkers and Pick 'n Pay outlets as a last-ditch attempt to ask for help after pleas for grants for the jobless went unanswered: "Taking food from the shops was a way of showing government that unemployed people are hungry."

In August, the strike spread to the army, with soldiers demanding a 30% pay increase. While the government was negotiating with the military trade unions, soldiers – some with arms – marched to Union Buildings in Pretoria. The march had been prohibited by the Gauteng High Court and, when the about 2,000 soldiers clashed with police, the police opened fire, resulting in some two dozen solidiers being injured. The incident raised concern about discipline in the **South African National Defence Force** (SANDF). Defence and Military Veterans Minister Lindiwe Sisulu condemned the soldiers' actions as the "severest form of criminality in a democracy". She dismissed some 1,300 soldiers for taking part in the protest, but this decision was blocked by the High Court in Pretoria. Subsequently, the dismissals were backed by the cabinet. On 17 September, Zuma, who is commander-in-chief of the armed forces, questioned the right of soldiers to belong to trade unions, as this could put the country's security at risk. He believed that labour grievances should be resolved by the planned Military Service Commission.

On 31 May, the government appointed Anwa Dramat as head of the Directorate for **Priority Crime Investigation**, the successor to the Scorpions, the elite unit disbanded in 2008. Dramat has a history as an underground operative for the ANC in the 1980s. As a police official since 1995, he had been involved in combating drugs trafficking, taxi violence and gangsterism. Zuma appointed Bheki Cele as head of police, replacing Jackie Selebi, who has to defend himself against corruption charges. Cele, who has the image of a tough crime fighter, aroused controversy when he asked parliament to ease the restrictions on police use of lethal force against suspects. In August, Zuma nominated Constitutional Court Judge Sandile Ngcobo to replace retired Judge Pius Langa as chief justice.

In October, Minister of State Security Siyabonga Cwele announced the appointment of Mzuvukile Jeff Maqetuka as the director general of a new umbrella structure, known as the **State Security Agency** (SSA). Cwele stated that the creation of a single department would centralise command and control of the civilian intelligence structures. With the SSA, the National Intelligence Agency (NIA) and the South African Secret Services will continue to operate in terms of their respective mandates. Cwele appointed Mo Shaik as head of the Secret Services and Lizo Gibson Njenje as head of the NIA.

On 18 July, Nelson Mandela's 91st birthday was celebrated as **'Mandela Day'**, an initiative by the Nelson Mandela Foundation in Johannesburg. The Foundation called on people around the world to volunteer 67 minutes of their day for community service, representing the 67 years Mandela had devoted to the struggle for justice and equality. On 10 November, the UN General Assembly by consensus declared 18 July 'Nelson Mandela International Day' and called for commemorations every year starting in 2010 to recognise his contribution to resolving conflict and promoting race relations, human rights and reconciliation.

The annual **crime statistics** for the year ending in March were published belatedly on 22 September. Overall crime rates increased slightly by 0.3%, after steady decreases in the preceding four years. The murder rate continued its downward trend with a 3.4% fall. However, other categories of crime showed a significant increase, notably house robberies (up by 27.3%), sexual offences (up by 10.1%) and commercial crime (up by 18.7%). The increase in serious crime was a nationwide phenomenon. One of the few areas where police achieved their crime reduction target was in crimes against children, which dropped by 9.3%. Conviction rates remained low, at 11% for murder cases, 36% for common assault and 10.7% for sexual offences. King Buyelekhaya Dalindyebo, the traditional ruler of the AmaThembu in the Eastern Cape, was sentenced to 15 years in jail for a variety of crimes, including homicide, kidnapping, arson and assault.

Veteran anti-apartheid activist and celebrated poet **Dennis Brutus** died on 26 December at the age of 85. Brutus became a banned person in 1961. After his escape from South Africa, he became a key actor in the campaign to bar South Africa from international sporting events and in 1964 succeeded in getting South Africa expelled from the Olympic Games. After the end of apartheid, he remained a champion for social justice, environmental justice and apartheid reparations.

Foreign Affairs

After the demise of President Thabo Mbeki, South Africa's leading role in African and international affairs was moved onto the back burner somewhat. Zuma's priorities during his first year in office were on the domestic front. Nevertheless, he succeeded in improving relations with Angola, although he did not seem to have any impact on the crisis in Zimbabwe.

Since the privatisation of the energy sector in Uganda, the state-owned South African electricity company **Eskom** has become a major player in the sector, raising concerns about its growing political clout. Eskom Enterprises, an offspring of Eskom South Africa, runs Umeme, a joint venture company with the Commonwealth Development Corporation. In February, Umeme was granted powers to prosecute electricity thieves and given leeway to increase the cost of new connections. These measures should enable Umeme to recover part of its $ 65 m annual loss. Umeme has concentrated on power thefts in the poorer areas of Kampala, known as hotbeds of the political opposition. Prosecuting power thieves resulted in the closure of a third of the small businesses in these areas. Apart from the possible spin off of hurting opposition strongholds, the Ugandan government is keen to help Umeme succeed, since Uganda's privatisation of the energy sector has been heralded by the World Bank as a model for the rest of Africa.

On 13 February, Defence Minister Charles Nqakula and his **Ethiopian** counterpart Arto Siraj Fegesa signed a memorandum of understanding in Addis Ababa on working together towards procedures for military cooperation in the context of peace efforts under the auspices of the AU. The envisaged cooperation includes exchange and training of military personnel, instructors and observers, and promoting technical cooperation.

After the military coup on 17 March in **Madagascar**, South Africa's interim president, Kgalema Motlanthe, condemned the takeover, saying, "South Africa and SADC will never countenance the unconstitutional transfer of power from a democratically elected government in one of our member-states." SADC sent a mission to the island, led by minister Nqakula. Meanwhile, the ousted president, Marc Ravalomanana, based himself in South Africa. In late June, South Africa hosted an extraordinary summit of SADC, after talks between the two rival parties sponsored by the AU and the UN broke down. Foreign Minister Maite Nkoane-Mashabane stated that there was no solution for Madagascar except a political , thus distancing SADC from an earlier pronouncement by COMESA. The COMESA summit resolved to support military intervention to restore Ravalomanana to the presidency and called for the total isolation of the regime of Andry Rajoelina. Although there is considerable overlap between COMESA and SADC membership, the SADC summit urged rival parties to commit themselves to an all-inclusive dialogue aimed at restoring peace and security.

On 23 March, after pressure from **China**, Pretoria decided to bar the Dalai Lama from a peace conference to be held there. The Tibetan spiritual leader was to join other Nobel Peace Prize laureates, including Archbishop Desmond Tutu. Tutu was sharply critical of the exclusion, which came a week after the signing of a memorandum of understanding between the Department of Trade and Industry and the China-Africa Development Fund (CADF). Areas covered in the memorandum are mining, energy, infrastructure, and information and communication technology. The CADF, with the China Development Bank (CDB) as its sole shareholder so far, had opened its representative office in Johannesburg on 16 March. Speaking at the opening ceremony, ANC Secretary-General Matthews Phosa indicated that South Africa was quickly learning to look to the East for economic partners. He praised the willingness of the CDB to invest in Africa at a time of global economic meltdown. CDB Chief Governor Chen Yuan, stated that CADF had made investments of nearly $ 400 m in Africa. These investments would facilitate a further $ 2 bn of further investments in the future by Chinese companies. Standard Bank of South Africa strengthened its relationship with China with the signing of a $ 1 bn loan facility with four major Chinese banks, believed to be the largest South African transaction in the Chinese market.

The **navy** announced in March that it had decided to design an "indigenous, non-sophisticated offshore patrol vessel" that could be constructed locally in Durban or Cape Town. The locally-built frigates would be a substitute for the German-built frigates previously ordered by the navy. In terms of the controversial 1999 arms deal, the navy operates four Valour-class frigates, with an option to purchase a fifth frigate. Instead, the navy now wants six locally-constructed vessels, a combination of both inshore and offshore patrol vessels. They placed the costs of an inshore patrol vessel at around R 100 m, but declined to put a figure on an offshore vessel. Naval Forces Commander Mark Fitzgerald insisted that South Africa had the capacity to lead in the fight against **piracy** off the

African continent. Rear Admiral Robert Higgs said they were prepared to help in operations off the Somali coast but that the decision was up to political leaders. Parliament's portfolio committee on defence called for an increase in the annual budget from the current 1.2% to 1.7% of GDP over the next four years. It considered the current budgetary allocation inadequate, particularly for border operations.

On 19 August, Zuma, accompanied by no fewer than 11 cabinet ministers, began a three-day state visit to **Angola** to strengthen ties between Africa's biggest economy and one of its top oil producers. Over 150 South African and Angolan business representatives used the opportunity to hold a gathering in Luanda to explore trade and investment opportunities. The delegation returned to South Africa with a broad range of deals, covering everything from industry to sports, of which the most significant involved a cooperation agreement between South Africa's state-owned oil and gas company, PetroSa, and its Angolan counterpart, Sonangol, to work together in oil exploration, refining and distribution. The two heads of state also discussed cooperation in military assistance to other African countries. During a follow-up visit to Cape Town by Angolan Minister of Energy Vieira Lopes, the two countries finalised an agreement for the upgrading of Angola's weak electricity infrastructure. South Africa expressed an interest in Angola's large potential hydroelectric capacity. Under Zuma's presidency, relations with Angola have improved markedly, after the cooling of relations under Mbeki. The chill left South African companies cut off from lucrative construction jobs following the end of Angola's civil war in 2002.

In July, President Francois Bozize of the **Central African Republic** (CAR) applauded the South African military for helping to rebuild the CAR's army. The SANDF has trained some 400 soldiers, expected to rise to 1,000 by 2010. Earlier, mission commander George Sibanyoni said that about 60 members of the SANDF had been deployed to the CAR. Bozize came to power in a military coup in 2003.

On 27 August, Zuma began a two-day visit to **Zimbabwe** to discuss the progress of the power-sharing deal between President Robert Mugabe and Prime Minister Morgan Tsvangirai. Zuma's trip was watched with interest, since his predecessor Mbeki had been frequently accused of being 'soft on Mugabe'. Zuma stressed that full implementation of the power-sharing agreement was essential for Zimbabwe's economic recovery. He also called for the lifting of sanctions and other restrictive measures against Zimbabwe. ANC Secretary-General Gwede Mantashe said that the party's policy on Zimbabwe had not changed, but added that Zuma would be "more vocal in terms of what we see as deviant behaviour in our neighbours". As examples of 'deviant behaviour', he cited the 2008 presidential election, the reappointment of the discredited Central Bank governor, Gideon Gono, and the continuing arrests of opposition MPs. Earlier, at an extraordinary summit of SADC in Swaziland in March, member states promised to contribute funds to the economic recovery of **Zimbabwe**. South Africa pledged about R 800 m.

On 27 November, South Africa and Zimbabwe signed a **bilateral investment protection** agreement, but the protection will not extend to already expropriated land. According to the 'Sunday Times' in Johannesburg, Zuma's government had been under pressure from local companies and South African farmers to secure their investments in Zimbabwe. South Africans who have already lost their land in Zimbabwe will have to rely on the 2008 landmark ruling by the SADC Human Rights Court when claiming compensation, but Harare has openly flouted this ruling and Pretoria has done nothing to force compliance. Business circles in South Africa doubted whether the new agreement would inspire confidence that investments in Zimbabwe would be safe.

Kenya has become an important processing transit point for **refugees from the Horn of Africa** to South Africa, according to an IOM (International Organisation for Migration) report published in September. The report 'In Pursuit of the Southern Dream: Victims of Necessity' describes how some 17,000 to 20,000 men are smuggled annually to South Africa. This figure includes Ethiopians and Somalis fleeing conflict and insecurity, and Kenyans, who are largely classified as economic migrants. Corrupt immigration officials in Kenya are a vital link in the chain, clearing immigration papers in exchange for bribes. The migrants are processed by brokers stationed along the route from Kenya to South Africa. The trip takes seven to eight weeks for Ethiopians and Somalis, but only four weeks for Kenyans. Unlike the Ethiopians and Somalis, the Kenyans interviewed did not report experiences of harassment in South Africa.

In early November, Zuma visited **Equatorial Guinea** for talks with President Obiang Nguema Mbasogo. His visit was preceded by the pardoning and release of four South African mercenaries being held for plotting to overthrow the government. Pretoria denied intervening in their release.

Congo-Brazzaville offered up to 10 m hectares of farmland for lease to South African farmers willing to grow maize and soya beans and set up poultry and dairy farms in the Republic of Congo. According to Theo de Jager, deputy president of Agriculture South Africa, some 1,300 South African farmers are keen to take up the opportunity. According to De Jager, the land was offered at no cost, with additional tax benefits. For the coming years, a steep rise in food prices is anticipated and Asian and Middle Eastern countries have already made huge land deals with African countries to ensure food supplies.

Socioeconomic Developments

The 2009 budget sought to counter the economic slowdown with an extensive stimulus package and lower taxation rates. In his **budget speech** to parliament on 11 February, Minister of Finance Trevor Manuel listed "the five enduring principles" of the budget: "protecting the poor; sustaining employment growth and expanding training opportunities; building economic capacity and promoting investment; addressing the barriers to competitiveness that limit an equitable sharing of opportunities and maintaining a sustainable debt level so that actions today don't constrain development tomorrow". He delayed the introduction of mineral royalties until 2010 to spare the mining sector, which had been hard hit by a slowdown in demand since 2008. Manuel said that the delay meant a boost for the mining industry of about R 1.8 bn, which would help to minimise job losses. Nevertheless, Anglo-Platinum announced on 9 February that 10,000 contract mining jobs would be cut. Mining companies have argued against the royalties, warning that it could force the shutdown of marginal mines.

In a press briefing after the presentation of the budget, Manuel reiterated that South Africa's economy was not in recession. He said the growth in GNP for 2008 was estimated at 3.1% (based on three quarters) and that, despite the recession in the worlds' major economies, the forecast for 2009 was still for growth, although at the much lower rate of 1.2%.

The **budget deficit** would rise to 3.8% of GDP but debt service costs would remain moderate at about 2.5% of GDP. Manuel called the deficit "reasonably comfortable". Total government spending would amount to R 834 bn, including the second tranch of the R 60 bn facility to Eskom. The largest adjustments in spending were made in support of **poverty reduction**: R 25 bn was added to the budgets of the provinces, mainly for education and health care, in addition to R 13 bn for social assistance grants and their administration, R 4 bn added to the school nutrition programme and R 2.5 bn allocated to municipalities for improvements to basic services. The massive R 787 bn investments in infrastructure were seen as a cornerstone of the pact between government, business and labour. Spending on social grants has increased from 4.6% of GDP in 2005/2006 to 4.8% of GDP in 2009/2010. **Welfare grants** for the elderly, for foster care and for child support were raised by R 50 to R 100 per month. Spending on education has grown by an annual 14% for the past three years and is forecast to grow by 10% annually over the next three years. The budget for land reform and land restitution for the period 2009–2012 totalled R 20.3 bn. South African Airlines (SAA) would receive a cash injection of R 1.6 bn to support its restructuring exercise, which included reducing costs and improving efficiency. Manuel warned that this should not be a recurring allocation.

Amid signs that **inflation** pressures were ebbing, the Reserve Bank cut interest rates several times between December 2008 and February. Since June 2006, South Africa has found itself in an inflationary cycle, which reached an average rate of inflation of 11.3% in 2008 but slowed down during 2009.

In April, Standard Bank reported a rapid fall in **household expenditure**, with a decline of up to 20.1% in the purchase of durable goods. For the first time since 1992, the survey also marked a contraction in sales of services to households, with a fall of 0.1%. Expenditure on durable goods contracted for five consecutive quarters, while sales of non-durable goods contracted for the second consecutive quarter. New vehicle sales in December 2009 showed a massive decline of 21.7% compared with the previous year. The most visible sign of the recession is perhaps the rate of return of new cars to dealers. Each month, between 6.000 and 7.000 cars are repossessed. BMW, the favoured car of the black elite, has reduced its production for the domestic market by 2,000 vehicles. Apart from cars, houses are also repossessed if the owner cannot meet the bond payments. One of the biggest auction houses, Alliance Group, said it auctioned off more than 1,500 mostly middle-class houses in the first quarter.

In his **State of the Nation** address on 3 June, Zuma promised 500,000 new jobs by the end of December, as well as more accountable public services to be achieved through performance instruments, using targets and measures that would begin on 1 July. Among the targets set by Zuma were cutting new HIV infections in half by 2011, increasing enrolment rates in secondary schools to 95% by 2014, and an expanded public works programme destined to create four million jobs by 2014. Zuma also announced the introduction of a national health insurance scheme He insisted that fighting poverty remained the cornerstone of his administration, but at the same time sought to temper expectations.

At the time of the State of the Nation address, South Africa was officially in **recession** after a 6.4% contraction in the first quarter and a 1.8% contraction in the previous quarter. It is South Africa's first recession since 1992. According to Statistics South Africa, there was a contraction of 23% in mining and agriculture, a 15.5% decline in manufacturing and a 0.5% decline in the services sector.

In July, the state-owned **Land Bank** told parliament that hundreds of South Africa's emerging black commercial farmers face eviction because or their inability to service government loans granted under the land reform programme for the purchase of the properties. The Land Bank, which provides financing and advice to black farmers, said it was losing R 100 m a month as a consequence of unpaid loans and had already repossessed 25 farms in the second half of 2008. A moratorium on repossession had been lifted in July 2008 when oversight of the Land Bank, mired in financial scandals, was moved from the Department of Agriculture and Land affairs to the Department of Finance.

In his **medium-term budget statement** on 27 October, Finance Minister Pravin Gordhan noted that tax revenue had dropped dramatically and was now expected to amount to R 70 bn less than budgeted for in February. As a consequence, the government would need to borrow more heavily, with the fiscal deficit extending to 7.6% of GDP. Government debt would increase from 23% of GDP in March 2009 to 41% of GDP by March 2013. He pointed out that government spending was mainly targeted on job-generating projects, not on bank bailouts. Local economists and consultants generally reacted favourably to Gordhan's budget plans.

The European Investment Bank (EIB) allocated over € 100 m to the growth and employment facility for South Africa, which is sponsored and financed by the European Commission and managed by the EIB. The facility provides risk bearing funds to black empowerment enterprises and targets a broad spectrum of economic sectors, including social housing and municipal infrastructure projects.

Black Economic Empowerment (BEE) deals slowed down due to the credit crunch, although many deals were put on hold rather than cancelled. The mining sector continued to dominate empowerment transactions, with a total of 69 deals, worth R 82.7 bn, between January 2007 and August 2009. Andrew McGregor, managing director of Who Owns Whom, said that of the 20 deals done in the mining sector in 2009, four were initiated by foreign investors, three based in Australia and one from Canada. Other notable deals were made by Vodacom, MTN and ABSA Bank. According to McGregor, the trend in 2008 and 2009 was a move away from empowerment deals to more broad-based shareholdings, such as in the deals concluded by SABMiller and Tongaat. The deal initiated by the huge brewery SABMiller set an important precedent, as it included white employees below management level, thus shifting participation criteria from race to income. Research by another South African company, Empowerdex, on companies listed at the Johannesburg Stock Exchange showed that 13 BEE deals worth R 20 bn were concluded in 2009, compared with 80 worth R 61 bn in 2008 and 111 worth R 105 bn in 2007.

Eskom, which supplies over 90% of South Africa's power, went through a managerial and funding crisis. In November, both CEO Jacob Maroga and Chairman Bobby Godsell stepped down after a bruising leadership battle. Meanwhile, Eskom faced a R 30 bn funding shortfall in its R 385 bn expansion programme. Thus Eskom had to delay the construction of its second new power station Kusile, near Emalahleni, which is expected to meet 10% of South Africa's electricity demand. Earlier in the year, Eskom increased its **tariffs** by 31%, causing an outcry over the impact on the rising cost of living. After two years of higher than inflation price increases, Eskom has asked for 45% tariff hikes each year over the next three years, which would result in a trebling of electricity charges. The gold mining sector and the textile industry have already warned that many struggling industries in these sectors may not be able to pay the bill. The National Consumer Forum pleaded with Eskom to reduce the application for a tariff increase to 11% at the most.

Speaking in Johannesburg at the release of climate scorecards, Richard Worthington, climate change manager of the World Wide Fund for Nature, said that South Africa's **greenhouse gas emissions** per capita were similar to those of industrialised countries, partly because of its strong reliance on coal. South Africa's current carbon emission of 11 tonnes per person per annum was way above other emerging economies, with China and India standing at six tonnes, Brazil at five tonnes and Mexico at two tonnes – this while 73% of South Africa's population has access to electricity, compared with 99% in China, 95% in Brazil and Mexico and 43% in India. To be carbon neutral by 2050, emissions in South Africa need to be one tonne per person per annum, said Worthington.

In September, arms parastatal Denel announced it was joining forces with a private company, Advanced Technology & Engineering, in the Unmanned Aerial Vehicles (UAV) Forum, established to conquer a bigger share of the international market for UAVs. This market was estimated at R 2 bn per annum and the South African UAV Forum aimed to capture in excess of 20%, or an estimated value of R 400 m a year. The announcement came after the opposition DA had revealed that government was planning to supply a wide range of countries with armaments. Parliament's **arms sales** monitoring committee has failed to report to parliament for some years now. In August, the DA had warned that the committee had authorised the sale of glide bombs and multiple grenade launchers to Libya and of multiple grenade launchers to Syria and Venezuela, while the committee was considering the sale of thousands of aviator G-suits to Iran, thousands of sniper rifles to Syria and millions of rounds of ammunition to Zimbabwe. Moreover, it had authorised a company to exhibit and demonstrate radar-warning receivers for submarines in North Korea.

Denel stated that the demand for UAV's has increased globally as a result of lessons learnt by allied forces in Iraq and Afghanistan. Beyond national security, UAV's would also be useful in crime fighting, disaster management, election monitoring, search and rescue, and policing poachers on the coastline, and could also provide benefits to the agricultural, mining, health and environmental sectors.

On 28 September, state-owned **South African Airways** reported a R 398 m profit for the year ending March 2009, after years of losses. Flights to South America and Australia compensated for the downturn in flights to Europe and North America. South Africa's airports improved their facilities to handle the expected massive inflow of tourists for the 2010 World Cup. Airports expect half a million visitors for the World Cup, with arrivals of up to 78,000 passengers a day. In December, Minister of Defence Lindiwe Sisulu announced the cancellation of the R 47 bn order for the A400m Airbus because of production delays and escalating costs.

According to Business Report, 484,000 **jobs** were lost in the third quarter, more than in the first two quarters combined, with most being shed in manufacturing and trade. With 4.2 m officially unemployed, the unemployment rate stood at 24.5%, but it is estimated that there are a further 1.6 m people who have given up looking for work. Minister of Trade and Industry Rob Davies noted that unemployment was structural rather than cyclical and that, once economic recovery took off, job creation would not necessarily follow. He pointed to the need "to place the economy on a new growth path". A new industrial policy, including a combination of support and regulatory measures, would be released. Research conducted by his department showed that the manufacture of medium-technology products, such as automotive components, had the most potential to create decent, sustainable work.

In May, South Africa eased **immigration rules for Zimbabweans** by issuing them with special work permits allowing them to stay in the country legally for six months. An estimated 2–3 m Zimbabweans have fled to South Africa, where they are regarded as economic migrants, not as political refugees. The action followed a surge of refugees to the centre of Johannesburg after the closure of a reception centre in the border town Musina. The permit allows Zimbabweans access to basic health care.

Minister of Home Affairs Nkosazana Dlamini-Zuma admitted at a parliamentary briefing in November that the department had no information on the numbers of **undocumented migrants**. According to the 2008/2009 annual report of the South African Police Service, estimates of undocumented migrants vary from between 3 m and 6 m people. A survey published by the Institute of Race Relations on 13 November referred to estimates of between 500,000 and 2 m undocumented migrants. Large-scale violent attacks on foreign Africans did not occur, but in November some 3,000 foreigners, mainly Zimbabweans, fled their homes in De Doorns, a farming area in the Western Cape. They came under attack from South African workers who claimed that wages were depressed because foreigners worked for lower rates. The Red Cross issued an urgent appeal for R 2 m for assistance to the displaced foreigners. Local farmers who helped them received threats for aiding foreigners.

In November, Gill Marcus took over the position of governor of the **Reserve Bank** from Tito Mboweni, who had served for more than ten years and has been praised for his efforts to fight inflation. Marcus previously served as deputy governor.

On 1 December, **World Aids Day**, Zuma announced new and ambitious plans for earlier and expanded treatment for HIV-positive babies and pregnant women. The changes are in line with new guidelines issued by the WHO. By treating all HIV-infected babies, survival rates should also improve for the youngest citizens in South Africa, one of only 12 countries where child mortality has worsened since 1990. In August, a government-appointed committee reported that over 60,000 children aged between one month and five years die in South Africa each year. Major causes of childhood deaths included diarrhoea, lower respiratory tract infections, conditions associated with HIV/AIDS and malnutrition. The committee, set up by the former health minister Tshabalala-Msimang, suggested that South Africa had the correct healthcare policies and guidelines in place, but struggled with implementation. New Health Minister Aaron Motsoaledi told the Maternal, Child and Women's Health Summit in Boksburg that he was shocked by the figures, stating that a third of deaths among women and children were avoidable. He noted that many countries poorer than South Africa had much better health systems.

With an estimated 5.7 m HIV-positive people out of a population of about 50 m, South Africa ranks in absolute numbers top of the world's AIDS crisis list. The policy changes would take effect by April 2010. AIDS lobbyists heralded Zuma's announcement as a welcome change from the AIDS denialism that existed during Mbeki's presidency. According to a Harvard study, Mbeki's refusal to provide anti-retroviral treatment led to more than 300,000 premature deaths. Mark Heywood, executive member of the **Treatment Action Campaign**, a social movement that was often at odds with Mbeki's AIDS policies, lauded Zuma's speech as a departure in thinking that would have a global impact. The US responded with an extra $ 120 m for the provision of AIDS treatment drugs over the next two years.

It is estimated that 500,000 **rapes** are committed annually in South Africa. The conviction rate is low, with only one out of every 25 accused being convicted. Research conducted by the Medical Research Council indicated that more than 25% of South African men have raped. Of those interviewed, 70% were under 30 years old and nearly half said they had raped more than one person.The report 'Understanding Men's Health and Use of Violence: Interface of Rape and HIV in South Africa' found that "men who are physically violent towards their intimate partners are more likely to have HIV".

On 16 December, the former health minister, **Manto Tshabalala-Msimang**, widely known as 'Dr Beetroot' for her promotion of beetroot, lemons and garlic to treat AIDS, died at the age of 69. The minister's disastrous policies on HIV made her the most unpopular minister in post-apartheid South Africa. She was ridiculed in South Africa and abroad, but had a loyal defender in the then president, Mbeki. She was only replaced after Mbeki's fall from power in September 2008.

Ineke van Kessel

Swaziland

From a human rights perspective, this was another bleak year. Repressive practices continued unabated, as did the voluptuous lifestyle of the king and his family, while the majority of the population lived in poverty. The HIV/AIDS pandemic continued to take its toll and the socioeconomic situation deteriorated further.

Domestic Politics

Despite widespread international criticism and only minimal internal opposition, in late 2008 King Mswati III promulgated a **Suppression of Terrorism Act** (STA). Defining terrorism in broad terms, the legislation gave the minister of justice power to ban organisations, and place individuals under banning orders, if they were alleged to be involved in any activity regarded by the state as threatening. Within days, four opposition groupings or associations (political parties have been banned in Swaziland since 1973) were banned and the leader of one of them, Mario Masuku, was arrested on terrorism and sedition charges. Held for ten months, Masuku was allowed visits from his family and lawyers but in circumstances that, according to the latter, denied them attorney-client privilege. When the trial finally began on 21 September, the state's case collapsed on day one when the court found that the state's evidence was both inadmissable and unconvincing.

Shortly thereafter, a crowd of about 50 supporters and members of the media awaiting Masuku's release from prison were baton-charged without warning by security officials. Journalists and photographers were singled out and their cameras and reporting equipment seized, while a prominent activist, Wandile Dludlu, was severely assaulted, arrested and tortured, before being released without charge. With severe injuries to his head, face and other parts of his body, Dludlu was hospitalised for over two weeks. The attack was condemned by **Amnesty International** (AI), which called on the government to institute a judicial inquiry into the attack. It did not. This criticism followed on from two earlier statements by AI (on 9 January and 10 June), which had commented critically on provisions of the STA. On 3 June, a member of Masuku's legal team and the coordinator of the local NGO Human Rights Swaziland, Thulani Maseko, was arrested on sedition charges. He was later released on bail and his case was pending at year's end.

The STA has also adversely affected the media. Press freedom has for many years been under threat in Swaziland, but **media repression** intensified in 2009. After publishing several critical columns in late 2008 in the independent 'Times of Swaziland', Mfomfo Nkambule, a former MP and cabinet minister, publicly apologised to the king on 12 January for criticising the monarchy, and paid a fine of several cows. This came after Prime Minister Sibusiso Dlamini had threatened to charge him under the STA. On 27 April, the 'Times' stopped publishing Nkambule's column. On 12 May, 'Times' editor Mbongeni Mbingo and several fellow journalists were summoned to appear before a Senate sub-committee and reprimanded for publishing an oral exchange between two senators. They were warned that internal parliamentary discussions were private and the committee threatened to charge journalists with contempt for any further such reports. On 30 June, journalists were evicted from a public workshop on HIV/AIDS when some MPs complained of their presence. In August, the prime minister threatened to close any media outlet that reported negatively on a scheduled royal visit abroad in which the king was to be accompanied by a huge entourage, including several of his wives. There was no domestic coverage.

While there were no instances of politically-motivated killings of citizens, there were, according to the US State Department's country report, several instances of **security forces** being responsible for deaths while in the process of apprehending suspects. As with similar killings in 2007 and 2008, no action was taken by the authorities. The torture of suspects by police is routine and, according to the Swaziland Coalition of Concerned Civic Organisations (SCCCO), is "an accepted part of the culture".

There were reports during the year of extra-judicial **mob killings**. On 12 February, the press reported that seven residents of a village in the Shiselweni region had attacked and killed a man suspected of stealing bags of cement, while on 4 March another group of villagers from Shiselweni killed a traditional healer suspected of stealing cattle. In neither case was there any police action.

During the course of the year, the government established a **Smart Partnership National Dialogue** aimed at creating a national vision in collaboration with a range of civil society organisations. This included labour, the private sector and several NGOs. The initiative was greeted with scepticism. Secretary General of the Swaziland Federation of Trade Unions (SFTU) Jan Sithole alleged that Prime Minister Dlamini had set a condition that no demands should be made during the Dialogue and that participants with dissenting views risked being imprisoned under the STA.

In June, approximately 500 people attended the launch of a **Swaziland Democracy Watch** group at a function in Copenhagen, Denmark. The meeting was dedicated to Mario Masuku, then under detention.

In its 2010 country report on the **human rights situation**, the US State Department catalogued a host of human rights violations. These included "the inability of citizens to change their government; extra-judicial killings by security forces; mob killings, police use of torture, beatings, and excessive force on detainees; police impunity; arbitrary arrests and lengthy pretrial detention; arbitrary interference with privacy and home; restrictions on the freedoms of speech and press and harassment of journalists; restrictions on freedom of assembly, association and movement; prohibitions on political activity and harassment of political activists; discrimination and violence against women; child abuse, trafficking in persons; societal discrimination against members of the gay, bisexual and transsexual community; discrimination against white and mixed-race and white citizens; harassment of labour leaders; restrictions on worker rights; and child labour."

Foreign Affairs

Swaziland is a member of COMESA, SADC, and SACU. Mswati served a one-year term as chair of the **SADC Organ for Defense, Politics and Security**, ending in September. In March, he presided over a meeting of the SADC troika, or executive, to discuss political developments in **Madagascar**, and for a brief period the ousted leader of Madagascar, Marc Ravalomanana, was given refuge in Swaziland. After his term as chair, Mswati remained a member of the Organ's troika.

Swaziland and the **US** continued to enjoy good bilateral relations, despite the change in the US administration and the US's frequent criticism of the Swazi political order. Apart from continuing to provide aid in the areas of education, military and human resource training, the US stepped up its assistance with regard to the **HIV/AIDS** pandemic. In June, the US and Swaziland finalised a partnership framework agreement under the President's Emergency Plan for AIDS Relief (PEPFAR), increasing US assistance to approximately $ 28 m per year. The US and Swaziland also finalised a memorandum of understanding expanding the duties of the Peace Corps mission in Swaziland. The Peace Corps/Swaziland programme, known locally as the Community Health Project, focuses on HIV/AIDS and provides assistance in the execution of two components of the HIV/AIDS national strategy – risk reduction and mitigation of the impact of the disease.

Swaziland remained one of only three African governments continuing to recognise the **Republic of China/Taiwan**.

Socioeconomic Developments

Swaziland used to be a lower middle-income country, but it is estimated that over two-thirds of the population were living in poverty in 2009. In 2007, the population stood at just over 1.1 m but, significantly, the annual **population growth rate** fell by nearly 0.5% per year over recent years. This was largely the result of an HIV prevalence rate among Swazi adults of close to 40% – the highest in the world. The infant mortality rate in 2007 was 70/1,000, while life expectancy had dropped to 40 years, reduced by one third since independence in 1968.

In November, an **IMF** team visited Swaziland, reviewed development and discussed the impact of the global recession on the economy. The country was warned of the need to step up domestic revenue mobilisation in the face of sluggish economic growth, with GDP growth estimated at only 0.4%. It was also noted that a significant drop in revenues from SACU transfers was likely. Income from SACU has in recent years constituted approximately 60% of the country's revenue, but in 2008 it was considerably less than estimated and further shortfalls in the SACU income pool were expected. The mission noted with concern "the emerging large fiscal deficits" and warned that this could result "in unsustainable debt levels". It also described public sector pay increases as unsustainable in the light of the "unprecedented deterioration" of the economy.

Food insecurity remained a major problem. The country has been dependent on food aid for a number of years. A severe drought in 2008 was followed by heavy rains and the worst flooding in 25 years during November. Damages in the region of $ 6.7 m were caused to roads and highways, while the damage to crops and loss of livestock was severe.

Compounding Swaziland's economic woes was **endemic corruption** at all levels of the state. Legislation existed to combat corruption but was rarely implemented. According to the Swaziland Coordinating Assembly of Non-Governmental Organizations, officials engaged in corrupt activities with impunity and the result was a loss to government of revenue in the region of $ 6 m every month. An Anticorruption Commission (ACC) established in 2008 was toothless and had not secured a single conviction in the 20–30 cases it had investigated since then.

On a more positive note, in March, the Swaziland High Court ordered the government to adhere to the constitution by providing **free education** for primary school children. In February, Mswati had noted that while free education was desirable, it was not feasible due to budgetary constraints. In response, the 'Times of Swaziland' asserted in an editorial that the government could afford free education if it shelved unnecessary and expensive luxury projects and excessive expenditure on the royal family. As of year's end, the government had not implemented the High Court order.

In recent years, evidence has grown that Swaziland is being increasingly used as a source, destination and transit site for **trafficking in women and children**. In December, the king assented to the People Trafficking and People Smuggling (Prohibition) Act. While the law provided stiff penalties for convicted traffickers, no government agency was set up to lead the drive against trafficking.

The state budgeted E 130 m (the Emalengeni is pegged to the South African Rand) for Mswati and his family, with E 95 m allocated for their travel costs. In August, five of the king's wives undertook an international shopping spree costing at least $ 6 m. **Expenditure on the royal family** exceeds the amounts allocated to education (E 113 m) and social security and welfare (E 73 m). In April, the king bought 20 top-of-the-range armour-plated Mercedes Benz S600 cars for his wives at an estimated cost of E 2.5 m (about $ 250,000) each.

John Daniel & Marisha Ramdeen

Zambia

Domestic politics in Zambia were already overshadowed by the presidential and parliamentary elections due in 2011. The ruling Movement for Multi-party Democracy (MMD) was bickering about its leader and presidential candidate, while two major opposition parties, the Patriotic Front (PF) and the United Party for National Development (UPND) formed an electoral alliance, although it remained fragile. Despite a deep slump in the copper price and major job losses, the economy recovered surprisingly well from the world economic crisis and continued to grow at an average rate of more than 5% for the seventh consecutive year. Under the new president, foreign policy remained unchanged with a clear stance against Mugabe's rule in Zimbabwe and the military take-over in Madagascar.

Domestic Politics

Serious **divisions within the MMD** characterised the year. A first sign was the postponement of an MMD convention, which was required to elect the new party president. This position had been vacant since the death of the former president Mwanawasa in August 2008. In January, acting party president Mabenga surrendered the position to Rupiah Banda. This move sparked serious criticism by opponents within the party, who claimed that Banda was circumventing party regulations. Article 36(1) of the MMD constitution stipulated that the party's president should be elected by a convention. The debate became so heated and publicly damaging that the party secretary banned all public statements by party officials. On 7 February, the National Executive Committee (NEC) finally endorsed Banda as the party's president.

On 26 February, Banda **sacked two deputy ministers**, Deputy Minister of Science, Technology and Vocational Training Jonas Shakafuswa, and Deputy Minister of Energy and Water Development Lameck Chibombamilimo, for lack of allegiance to him. They were also expelled from the party – an action against which they successfully sought an injunction at the Lusaka High Court. Both had criticised Banda in the opposition newspaper 'The Post' and were suspected of maintaining close links with the PR, the strongest opposition party. Banda explained that his action was aimed at instilling 'discipline' in the party and government. The deputy ministers were allies of the late president Mwanawasa and, together with a number of other politicians, they felt sidelined by the new president. However, they formed only one of many factions within the MMD; in 2008 there were 20 aspirants to become the party's presidential candidate, among them former finance minister Ng'andu Magande and national party secretary Katele Kalumba.

Magande became the next target of Banda's fight against his rivals. The former finance minister was accused of financial irregularities with Zambian Airways while he was in office. The vague allegations and the investigation by the Drug Enforcement Commission, the Anti-Corruption Commission and the Zambia Police Service suggested that the issue was primarily an attempt to discredit the politician publicly and expel him from the party.

In April, Kalumba, was accused of corruption – a case that dated back to his time as minister of finance (1999–2002) under former president Chiluba, for which he had been arrested in 2003. The resurfacing of the allegations at this particular time suggested political motives. Shortly before, the internal debate about the MMD's presidential candidate for the 2011 elections had started. While Local Government Minister and MMD spokesman Ben Tetamashimba claimed that only the current party president could be a viable candidate, Kalumba argued that there would be a number of suitable MMD leaders; he himself had failed to win the nomination for the 2008 elections. Finally, Banda and his faction within the party pushed his own nomination through. On 14 June, the NEC nominated Banda as the presidential candidate and as the "sole candidate" for the party presidency, to be elected at the party's convention 2010.

The early nomination of the **presidential candidate** was a reaction to Michael Sata's self-nomination as a presidential candidate for the PF in May. This move had put the MMD under considerable pressure and played into the hands of Banda and his faction. The MMD leadership was faced with the choice of either sticking to Banda as the incumbent and MMD leader with an established presence in the country, or allowing a fierce internal competition that could damage the reputation of the incumbent or produce a new candidate who would then have little time to establish him- or herself as an acknowledged leader, while the ruling president might become powerless.

On 7 July, Minister of Defence George Mpombo resigned. Although the reasons for his resignation remained somewhat obscure, it appeared it was in reaction to Banda's nomination as MMD's presidential candidate. Mpombo explained that he did not agree with the NEC's nomination process and called it undemocratic2. The decision regarding the candidacy was also criticised by a number of other senior MMD-leaders, who demanded that the nomination should be open to other candidates. The dispute not only signalled deep rifts within the party, but also showed that the party's leading organ, the NEC, was under Banda's control. Towards the end of the year, MMD leaders, probably orchestrated by Banda's supporters, called again for the postponement of the convention until 2016. While the critique of the MMD's undemocratic culture continued over the rest of the year, the MMD leadership tried to silence the internal critics by charging Magande and Mpombo with 'indiscipline' in an attempt to kick them out of the party; in December, Mpombo's membership of the MMD was suspended.

During the first half of the year, the **opposition parties** exhibited mixed behaviour. PF President Sata abandoned the petition for a recount of the ballot papers that he had instigated against Banda's election in October 2008. The Supreme Court rejected the application on 11 March because the applicant was not able to provide any evidence to justify a recount. Sata explained that he did not accept the election result, but discontinued the case because he said he could not expect a different judgment from a biased Supreme Court. At the same time, the divisions within the party continued. On 6 February, PF Secretary General Edward Mumbi was forced to resign. Sata claimed that Mumbi had taken bribes during the previous election campaign and was responsible for the party's defeat. A few days later the Supreme Court reserved its ruling in the case of 18 PF MPs who had filed an injunction against the party for expelling them; disregarding Sata's policy, these MPs had joined the National Constitutional Conference (NCC) in 2007 and were therefore sacked from the party. On 11 May, notwithstanding the internal troubles, Sata opened up the electoral competition for 2011 by declaring his intention to contest the presidential elections. This very early move put pressure on all the other parties to present their candidate. With this single-handed move, Sata again provoked criticism of his leadership style and lack of accountability. The former secretary general of the party explained that Sata was keeping all donations to the party not in a bank account but at his private home; he also blamed him for causing the defeat in the last elections by neglecting rural areas in the electoral campaign. In fact, since its formation in 2001, the PF had never held a party convention or proper leadership elections and, in addition, was operating under a draft constitution, which dissident MPs called "undemocratic and despotic".

On 4 June, in further preparation for the next general and presidential elections, Sata and his UPND counterpart Hakainde Hichilema declared an **alliance**, asserting that the parties would work together "on all matters of national importance". The issue of who would lead the alliance into the elections as the joint presidential candidate – either Sata or Hichilema, who contested the last elections – remained open until the end of the year. Measured by the election results and the number of MPs, Sata and the PF were clearly the stronger partner within the alliance and a more national party than the regionally restricted UPND, but Sata was not in control of at least 18 rebels, and probably even more, among the 43 PF MPs. On the UPND side, the pact was formally endorsed on 27 June by an extraordinary general assembly, the party's convention as the highest decision making body.

In contrast to similar exercises conducted previously, the two opposition parties were able to maintain their unity through three **by-elections** that took place before the end of the year by fielding joint candidates and winning two of the elections. On 13 August, the Chitambo by-election (Eastern Province) was won by the MMD with a majority of 56%, while on 15 October the Kasama (Northern Province) and on 19 November the Solwezi (Northwestern Province) by-elections were won by the alliance, with 69% for the joint PF candidate and 56% for the joint UPND candidate respectively. This victory of the alliance in two by-elections, which were usually won by the ruling party because of superior government resources, was taken as a most promising precedent for the coming elections.

PF and UPND also cooperated in an ill-conceived attempt to bring an **impeachment motion** against Banda for "failing to protect the Constitution". The alliance was not only unable to give any reason for the allegation within the given timeframe of 14 days after notifying the speaker of the national assembly of the impeachment plan, but they also were not in a position to gain a two-thirds majority in support in parliament, which was required to bring an impeachment motion, let alone the three-quarters majority necessary to pass it.

The hope that the next elections would be run under a new **constitution** faded away. By July it had become clear that the NCC would not be able to finalise its constitutional review process, and in September the process was extended for another four months. Only four out of the 11 NCC committees had presented their reports to the 600-member assembly, leaving seven committee reports to be discussed. Local political analysts expected that the timeframe had become so tight that the new constitution would not be ready for the 2011 elections, which, at best, would be run under an amended constitution. The reason for this final delay would be one of the most controversial issues: the proposed 50%-plus-one vote for the election of the president remained unresolved and was rejected by members of the ruling party and the government. The ruling party's argument was that this formula would be too costly, since electoral behaviour in Zambia would most likely lead to the need for a second round in the presidential election. The current first-past-the-post system had kept the MMD in power for three consecutive elections since 2001. Parts of the opposition parties and many civil society organisations were in favour of the 50%-plus-one formula.

In a further attempt to curb the opposition, the government introduced the 2009 **Non Governmental Organisation (NGO) Bill**, which was passed by parliament and finally signed by the president on 27 August. The same bill had been withdrawn in 2007 after widespread protests by civil society organisations and opposition parties. The legislation aimed at "the registration and co-ordination of NGOs, to regulate the work, and the area of work, of NGOs operating in Zambia". Many civil society organisations and human rights activists feared that the new law would be used by the government to silence critical voices and destroy civil society activities. Information Minister and Government Speaker Ronnie Shikapwasha left no doubt as to what the new law was all about: "NGOs should not become like the opposition".

After a seven-year trial, the **corruption saga of former president Frederick Chiluba** came to an end. The case reverberated beyond Zambia because it was among the first in Africa that involved the trial of a former head of state on corruption charges. On 17 August, Chiluba was finally cleared of charges on six counts that while in office he had embezzled $ 500,000. The magistrates' court judged that the prosecution had failed to provide sufficient evidence. However, two co-defendants, former Access Financial Services directors, Faustin Kabwe and Aaron Chungo, were convicted on three counts of theft. Surprisingly, the government decided not to appeal against Chiluba's acquittal. When the chief of the Task Force on Corruption (TFC) filed an appeal, he was fired and the appeal was withdrawn; the government later dissolved the TFC. Most donors had already stopped funding the TFC, which had been formed to investigate crimes under the Chiluba government, for lack of any substantial results. Many corruption cases had dragged on for a number of years without convictions, and a number of corruption charges against well-known politicians had been dropped without an adequate explanation. Subsequently, these circumstances gave rise to the suspicion that the judgement on Chiluba was to the result of high-level government intervention and it was a severe blow to the credibility of the government's anti-corruption policy; it also kick-started a public debate about the independence of the judiciary. In fact, several other factors contributed to the widespread doubts. While in May 2007 a London High Court was able to find sufficient evidence that the trio were guilty of fraud, plundering Zambia of $ 46 m, the Zambian investigations seemed not to have exercised due diligence and had perhaps had inadequate tools at their disposal in an obviously difficult case. Apart from these 'technical' issues, it was obvious that Chiluba, who was thought still to have considerable influence in the MMD, had become a close ally of Banda; Chiluba had campaigned for him in the 2008 elections and supported him publicly in the MMD power struggle.

All this nurtured the old argument that the fight against corruption was not very serious, but mainly a tool that the government could use against political opponents. This perception was strongly re-enforced when old and new, and often not very substantial, corruption charges emerged publicly against Banda's rivals within his party. On the surface, the **anti-corruption policy** continued. A number of state officials, particularly of the Chiluba era, were jailed for graft, among them a number of military officials. In early March, Regina

Chiluba, wife of the former president, was sentenced by the Lusaka magistrates' court to three-and-a-half years' imprisonment, she appealed against the sentence and was released on bail. On 21 April, Transport and Communication Minister Dora Siliya finally resigned after a tribunal investigation found that she had contravened formal tender procedures; in June, she was reappointed, as minister of education, after the Lusake High Court found her innocent of breaching the constitution. Banda's son, Henry, was linked to the case, but no further investigation followed; the same happened in a case in which James Banda, Henry's older brother, was allegedly involved in the illegal importation of genetically modified maize. In May, several donors suspended aid to the health ministry after it was discovered that senior government officials had embezzled about $ 5 m of donor funds.

Foreign Affairs

Zambia had in Rupiah Banda a president who was an experienced foreign affairs politician who had served as Zambian ambassador to several states and the UN and as minister of foreign affairs (1975–76). One crucial problem to be addressed was the strained relationship with **Zimbabwe**. During the extraordinary summit of SADC heads of state and government in Pretoria on 26–27 January, Banda continued with his predecessor's tough stance towards Mugabe. While the official SADC communiqué noted 'unanimous' support for the formation of a unity agreement between the rival parties in Zimbabwe – with the consequent power-sharing government of Mugabe and Tsvangirai – it was soon leaked to the media that the Zambian president, together with his counterparts from Botswana and Tanzania, had voted against a unity deal and were in favour of fresh elections. On his state visit to Zimbabwe from 29 April to 2 May, Banda tried to repair the relationship with Zambia's neighbour. Official statements by the Zambian side emphasised that Zambia would continue to support Zimbabwe's economic recovery. On political issues, Banda reminded Mugabe to uphold and not to flout the global political agreement he had signed in 2008 with the leaders of the Movement for Democratic Change, who now formed part of the government, and to stick to the promises he had made to SADC concerning the inclusive government. Banda also confessed that he could offer "little help within our means" and donated 9,000 tonnes of maize – which was criticised in Zambia. In line with the pro-democracy policy, Zambia was the first AU member to call for the suspension of **Madagascar** from SADC in reaction to the military take-over of the country's government.

For one of his first bilateral visits, Banda chose a stop-over in **Angola** at the invitation of his counterpart, José Eduardo dos Santos, on 30 January en route to attend the 12th ordinary session of the AU in Addis Ababa. The year before, a 'new era' in the Zambian-Angolan relationship had been inaugurated after almost three decades of strained relations. The meeting of the two heads of state paved the way for further technical meetings of ministerial staff to continue with the re-opening of the Benguela railway line, which had been disrupted during the 27-year civil war in Angola. The rehabilitation of the line would provide Zambia with additional access to a deep-sea port, allowing for cheaper and faster exports.

On 10 August, Lusaka hosted the third summit of the **International Conference on the Great Lakes Region** (ICGLR) of which Banda took over the chairmanship from his Kenyan counterpart Mwai Kibaki. The ICGLR was formed in 2004 in Dar es Salaam with 11 core members (Angola, Burundi, the CAR, the DRC, Kenya, Republic of Congo, Rwanda, Sudan, Tanzania, Uganda and Zambia). At their second summit in 2006 the members of the ICGLR had agreed on the Pact on Security, Stability and Development for the Great Lake Region, which came into force in June 2008. As UN Secretary-General Ban Ki-moon diplomatically stated in his message to the conference, the region still faced 'profound' security, humanitarian, developmental and environmental challenges for which the organisation sought to find lasting solutions, in particular the ongoing problems in the eastern Congo. One result of the conference was the proposal that the regional Centre for Democracy, Good Governance and Civic Education Programme of the ICGLR should have its headquarters in Zambia and should be named after late president Levy Mwanawasa.

On his diplomatic **trip to the Americas**, Banda attended first the 64th regular assembly of the UN, where he reiterated in his speech on 25 September the call for Africa to have two permanent seats with veto powers and two additional non-permanent seats on the Security Council. He continued his trip by going to Venezuela, where he participated in the second African-South American summit (26–27 September), which was attended by 20 African and eight South American heads of state and government. The aim of the summit was to boost cooperation between two continents facing food, financial and environmental crises. In order to improve trade, investments and a new international financial architecture, Zambia supported the proposal by seven South American countries to establish a 'Bank of the South'. From Venezuela, Banda travelled for a three-day visit to Cuba to meet his counterpart Raul Castro Ruz. Banda also honoured the former president Fidel Castro with the award of the Order of the Eagle of Zambia, first class.

On 7 June, Banda attended not only the 13th **COMESA** summit but also the official launch of the COMESA customs union. Zambian officials underlined the importance of COMESA by emphasising that 70% of Zambia's economic growth was generated through exports to the regional free trade zone. While Tanzania, for example, had left COMESA to avoid double membership in different regional economic organisations, Zambia retained its membership of the SADC customs union. Later, on 29 August, Zambia again lined up in Mauritius with five other COMESA members (Comoros, Madagascar, Mauritius, Seychelles and Zimbabwe) to sign an **interim EPA**, which granted the six countries full access to the EU market with temporary exceptions for rice and sugar, while the six African countries would liberalise in phases and partially over 15 years.

In May, the voluntary repatriation of Angolan **refugees** was restarted, the official programme having ended in 2007. Of the remaining 27,073 Angolan refugees registered in Zambia by the UNHRC, almost 7,000 expressed their wish to return home; some had been in Zambia for almost four decades. The repatriation programme for the 45,000 Congolese refugees was also resumed after being stopped in 2008. In January, about 18,000 had expressed the desire to repatriate, and by the end of November a total of 16,400 refugees had returned to the Republic of Congo.

Socioeconomic Developments

While the world economic crisis did not spare Zambia, the country's economy was hit surprisingly less than expected. With an estimated **GDP growth** of 6.3% the country achieved a growth rate of more than 5% for the seventh consecutive year. This was clearly beyond the projection of the national budget, which was presented by the minister of finance and national planning on 30 January with an estimated growth rate of 5%, and on 9 October, when the minister of finance presented the national budget for 2010, growth was still estimated at only 4.3%. The presentation of two national budgets within one year was an historic event caused by a change of the budget cycle enabled by a constitutional amendment in August, in order to allow for the presentation of the national budget to parliament in advance of the financial year.

The relatively positive development in growth was explained by the IMF mission in February and March as resulting from improved **macroeconomic management** during previous years, which had provided a solid basis for a better adjustment policy. In fact, Zambian economic development compared very well with the 1.3% growth projection for Sub-Saharan Africa and -1.1% for global growth. The strong performance of the economy was based on growth in the mining, agriculture and construction sectors. With an estimated growth of more than 13%, the mining sector performed particularly well. The improvement was due to a strong recovery in international **copper** prices, which more than doubled over the year, reaching about $ 5,900 per tonne; in 2008 the copper price had fallen from $ 8,980 in July – one of the highest for decades – to $ 2,812 in December. Mining output continued to grow and was expected to reach more than 660,000 tonnes compared with 575,000 in 2008 and the little more than 200,000 at the beginning of the decade. While a number of mines were threatened by closure at the end of 2008, the government contributed to the recovery by granting various tax reliefs, especially scrapping the 25% windfall tax, increased capital allowances and the reduction of custom duties for the mining sector. However, due to the crisis and despite the improvements the mining industry recorded a loss of at least 8,500 jobs, of which only 1,500–2,000 were recovered during the year. Two mines, the Luanshya Copper Mine and Munali Nickel Mine were placed under care and maintenance, and the former was reopened during the year.

The **agricultural sector** grew by more than 5%, to which a bumper maize harvest of 1.9 m tonnes, the largest harvest for a decade, contributed. The government linked the growth to its Farmer Input Support Programme for small scale farmers and promised to continue with this programme. According to the government's budget, spending on agriculture was increased by 37%. Growth in the **construction** sector of about 10% was attributed to increased public and commercial investment in the infrastructure as well as demand for housing. Closely related to this development was the expansion of cement production by local manufacturers.

Total **government spending** was also affected by the global crisis. Government expenditure was projected to decline by more than 8%, while income (revenue and grants) decreased by more the 13% compared with original budget projections. Due to falling imports and exports, whose value declined by 26% and 19% respectively, and because of a generally poor level of business transactions, revenue collection was significantly reduced. According to official statistics in October, excise duty had declined by 40%, import VAT by 29%, and customs duty by 23%.

The **inflation** target of 10%, envisaged to be down from 16.6% in 2008, was not achieved, although it fell to 12%; this was partly due to increasing food prices and also to higher transportation and energy costs. During the first half of the year, the kwacha continued to depreciate against major foreign currencies but, with the recovery, started to appreciate slightly during the second half, climbing from ZK 5,665 to the dollar in April to ZK 4,657 in November.

The **health sector** was negatively affected when major donors, among them the Netherlands and Sweden, suspended aid in May following the embezzlement by senior government officials of about $ 5 m of donor funds from the health ministry. Donors provided 55% of the health budget, and most of the funds went into promoting rural healthcare and preventing malaria, TB and HIV, as well as training medical staff. The suspension of aid therefore had a major effect, especially on the rural population and in places with high HIV prevalence. Although the government allocated more domestic funds to the health sector, it was not able to bridge the financial gap. While the government and the donors agreed on a joint action plan to deal with the critical situation and to effect better control of resources, aid was not resumed by the end of the year. As an indication of the huge financial difficulties faced by the health sector as a result of the suspension of aid, the health budget declined by one-third from ZK 1.83 trn once projected for 2009 to ZK 1.36 trn for 2010.

The government announced its intention of selling at least 75% of the highly indebted **telecommunication** company Zamtel, which runs the sole fixed telephone line service in the country. The state-owned company had run up liabilities of more than $ 90 m; its staff costs of 58% of total revenue were considered to be too high with the consequence that job losses were expected with the privatisation of the company. By the end of the year, three foreign companies out of the eight original bidders short-listed by the government to acquire a major stake had submitted their bids to the Zambia Development Agency; the companies were the Indian Bharat Sanchar Nigam Ltd, Unitel of Angola and LAP Greencom from Libya. In a different move, the Zambian government bought back the Indeni Petroleum Refinery from the French oil company Total Fina Elf, which dumped its 50% shareholding after long quarrels with the government over fuel prices and crude oil imports. The government paid about $ 5.5 m for Total's share with the intention not to retain the company under state control but to resell it to a new partner.

On 5 March, Zambia was the first country to sign the **MDG Contract** with the EU. The EU will provide the Zambian government a grant of € 225 m for the next six years to accelerate the fight against poverty programmes; the grant is not linked to any specific donor project but is general budget support for the government.

Gero Erdmann

Zimbabwe

The year witnessed some fundamental changes in domestic politics and the economy. The formation of the Government of National Unity (GNU) and the consequent overhaul of economic policy led to some improvements in the political and economic situation. The economy markedly improved as runaway inflation was dramatically contained. Despite persistent discord within the GNU, political violence noticeably declined after its formation. There was no major shift in foreign relations.

Domestic Politics

On 30 January, Morgan Tsvangirai, leader of the larger Movement for Democratic Change formation (MDC-T), announced that his party and the smaller MDC faction led by Arthur Mutambara (MDC-M) would enter into a **power-sharing government** with President Robert Mugabe's Zimbabwe African National Union-Patriotic Front (ZANU-PF). On 11 February, Tsvangirai was sworn in as prime minister in the GNU, along with two deputy prime ministers: Thokozani Khupe, deputy leader of the MDC-T, and Arthur Mutambara, leader of the MDC-M. In the GNU, Mugabe retained his executive position. He was chairman of the cabinet with Tsvangirai as his deputy. The **cabinet** was made up of 31 ministers, 15 from ZANU-PF and 16 from the MDC factions (13 MDC-T and

3 MDC-M). It was sworn in on 13 February. Mugabe also chaired the National Security Council, a body comprising security services chiefs and Tsvangirai. Tsvangirai chaired the council of ministers, which would oversee the work of cabinet. Its members included all cabinet ministers. Contention regarding the ministry of home affairs, under which the police falls, was resolved by having two 'co-ministers', Kembo Mohadi from ZANU-PF, who was also the sitting minister, and Giles Mutsekwa from the MDC-T. The ministry of finance, another contentious issue, was given to MDC-T secretary-general Tendai Biti. The GNU established the Joint Monitoring and Implementation Committee to monitor the implementation of the power-sharing agreement. The 12-member committee (with four members from each of the three parties to the agreement) would have three chairpersons, one from each of the parties.

There were persistent doubts as to whether the GNU would work. Critics considered the MDC to be a junior partner. Mugabe retained control of the judiciary as well as the military and security apparatus, with the MDC-T having charge mainly of the development and service ministries. The GNU was seen as no more than a transitional arrangement leading to a new constitution and new election at some point in the future. It was characterised by **disputes**. On 25 February, Tsvangirai 'cancelled' the previous day's unilateral appointment of permanent secretaries by Mugabe. On 10 April, Mugabe, again unilaterally, moved the communication portfolio from the MDC-T – controlled ministry of information communication technology to the ZANU-PF – controlled ministry of transport, which would become the ministry of transport and communication. Tsvangirai swiftly declared the unilateral move "null and void". Mugabe uncharacteristically backed down. By the end of the year, there were still some **unresolved issues**, including the appointment of provincial governors, the swearing in of Roy Bennett as deputy agriculture minister, and contention over the attorney general and governor of the Reserve Bank of Zimbabwe (RBZ), whom the MDC-T wanted dismissed. On its part, ZANU-PF insisted that no concessions would be made unless the MDC-T successfully called for the lifting of the 'illegal' sanctions imposed by its Western partners. In addition, ZANU-PF supporters continued **farm invasions**. By the end of the year, mounting violence was reported against the remaining 400 white-owned commercial farms. It came as no surprise when Tsvangirai admitted on 30 May that the GNU had made little progress.

On 16 October, Tsvangirai announced that the MDC-T had disengaged from the GNU over the treatment of **Roy Bennett**. The MDC-T treasurer had been appointed to the position of deputy minister of agriculture, but was arrested on 13 February hours before the ministers in the unity government were to be sworn in. He was initially charged with treason; the charges were later changed to attempting to commit terrorism, banditry and sabotage. While the police insisted the arrest was not politically motivated, the charges were widely interpreted as political persecution and an expression of Mugabe's contempt for the GNU. Tsvangirai said all the issues outstanding with regard to the power-sharing agreement had to be dealt with before the MDC would work with ZANU-PF. He described ZANU-PF as "an unreliable and unrepentant partner in the transitional government". The party embarked on a nationwide **consultation process** on the future of the GNU, which amounted to a veritable referendum on the GNU. On 5 November, Tsvangirai announced that he had suspended the disengagement from the GNU, adding that ZANU-PF had 30 days to meet the issues still outstanding from the 2008 Global Political Agreement (GPA). This did not happen. On 23 December, Mugabe, Mutambara and Tsvangirai held a joint press conference. They admitted that they still had minor differences, but insisted that the GNU was not going to collapse.

Controversies about **politically motivated violence** dogged the GNU. On 24 February, the MDC released a statement criticising the arrest and detention of its members and civil society activists. On 2 March, Jestina Mukoko, the director of the Zimbabwe Peace Project, and several other MDC-T supporters were granted bail after spending three months in detention; they still faced treason charges. On 28 September, the Supreme Court ruled in their favour, quashing all charges against them because they had been tortured by state security agents. After his inauguration, Tsvangirai had called for an end to human rights abuses and political violence. Levels of violence dropped, though violence reportedly increased in rural areas in the second half of the year. It was speculated that ZANU-PF tried to whittle down the MDC's parliamentary majority by causing the arrest of seven MDC-T MPs to enforce by-elections in rural constituencies with the aim of regaining a parliamentary majority by having its own candidates elected. This strategy might not have been successful, as an **opinion poll** taken in May by the Zimbabwe Mass Public Opinion Institute, showed support for ZANU-PF among voters was less than 10%, while the MDC-T commanded 57%.

On 12 April, in line with the GPA, the GNU set up a 25-member parliamentary select committee to spearhead the drafting of a new **constitution** within 18 months. The constitution was to be completed by February 2010 and followed by a national referendum five months later. The process ran into problems as sections of civil society, led by the National Constitutional Assembly, denounced the move and called for a people-driven constitution-making process. Even the pro-MDC-T Zimbabwe Congress of Trade Unions (CTU) warned against restricting the process to politicians. On 22 April, two legislators, one from ZANU-PF (Paul Mangwana) and the other from the MDC-T (Douglas Mwonzora), were appointed to co-chair the select committee. There was some uncertainty about the positions of the 'Kariba Draft', secretly negotiated between the MDC formations and ZANU-PF in September 2007, with ZANU-PF insisting it was to be the basis of the new constitution, a position rejected by the MDC-T national executive on 23 June. On 13 July, a conference to draw up the new constitution descended into chaos as riot police broke up clashes between rival delegates. ZANU-PF supporters were blamed for violently disrupting the meeting. This underscored the tensions within the GNU. Interviews for

constitutional commissions were conducted by the parliament's Committee on Standing Rules and Orders (CSRO). Interviews for the Zimbabwe Media Commission (ZMC) were held on 12 August; for the new Independent Zimbabwe Electoral Commission on 28 September; and for the Human Rights Commission on 12 October. Controversy was not lacking concerning the interview procedure and the final shortlists submitted to Mugabe. On 22 September, the CSRO announced they had been advised of a constitutional clause indicating that members of the Anti-Corruption Commission would be appointed by the president "in consultation with" the CSRO.

On 1 October, the state daily reported that George Charamba, secretary for Media, Information and Publicity (MIP), had announced a list of board members for six **media institutions** that fell under the ministry. The boards concerned were the Broadcasting Authority of Zimbabwe, Zimpapers, Zimbabwe Broadcasting Holdings, Transmedia, Kingstons and New Ziana. The appointments were made "unilaterally" by MIP minister Webster Shamu. On the boards were Charles Utete, former secretary to the cabinet, and Tafataona Mahoso, notoriously known as the media hangman, who had muzzled the media during his tenure as the Media and Information Commission (MIC) chairman. Tsvangirai and Mutambara, as well as deputy MIP minister Jameson Timba, dismissed the appointments as illegal, unprocedural and invalid.

There was some relaxation of **media restrictions**. On 29 July, Shamu announced that CNN and the BBC were permitted to return to live broadcasting from Zimbabwe after an eight-year ban. There were calls on the government to lift the ban on newspapers such as the 'Daily News', 'Daily News on Sunday', the 'Tribune' and 'Weekly Times' by speedily processing their licenses as agreed under the GPA. There were also calls to repeal repressive legislation such as the Access to Information and Protection of Privacy Act and Broadcasting Services Act to allow the entry of new players in both the print and broadcasting sector. In July, a special committee, set up in September 2008 to review the MIC's refusal to grant a licence to the banned 'Daily News' and 'Daily News on Sunday' newspapers, said it was satisfied that Associated Newspapers of Zimbabwe (ANZ) had complied with the provisions of the Access to Information and Protection of Privacy Act. The chairman of the committee wrote to ANZ's lawyers on 30 July advising them "to contact the relevant authority for their licence". However, ANZ would have to wait for an unknown period for its licence as the successor body to the MIC, the ZMC, was still to be constituted.

On 12 December, Mugabe was re-elected as leader at a depleted **ZANU-PF party congress** in Harare. He had already been endorsed as the ZANU-PF candidate for the 2013 presidential elections. The congress almost failed to take place as the party struggled to raise funds for the event. The Mujuru faction outflanked the rival Mnangagwa faction, which had been widely expected to eclipse its rival, by securing most of the influential positions. Jonathan Moyo, the former information and publicity minister who had been re-admitted into ZANU-PF, was elected to the central committee. On 30 June, former finance minister and presidential candidate Simba Makoni launched a **new political party**, Mavambo.Kusile.Dawn, insisting it was an alternative to the GNU. It was believed he would draw moderates from ZANU-PF, but this did not materialise.

All three parties in the GNU had their own **internal problems**. ZANU-PF was still riven by splits between the factions rallying behind Mujuru, Mnangagwa and Mugabe. The power struggles apparently intensified following the death of Vice President Joseph Msika on 4 August. The MDC formations had their fair share of problems: the MDC-T was not united on how to deal with their frustrations with the GNU and the MDC-M had no less than three factions claiming leadership of the party.

On 2 October, the Swiss multinational **Nestlé** announced it would stop buying milk from a farm owned by the president's wife, Grace Mugabe. Nestlé apparently made the decision because of negative attention and boycott threats. The decision prompted a backlash from ZANU-PF loyalists, including senior party and government officials, among them Minister of Youth Development, Indigenisation and Empowerment Savior Kasukuwere. On 23 December, Nestlé suspended operations, citing harassment and the security of its employees.

Foreign Affairs

Relations with most African countries and organisations remained largely friendly, with the majority of leaders supporting the GNU. This is not surprising as SADC and the AU are the original guarantors of the GPA. Throughout the year, the MDC-T continued to refer unresolved matters about the GNU and GPA to SADC and the AU, with little success.

SADC continued its efforts to make the GNU work. On 24 March, it was announced that the venue for a SADC extraordinary summit of heads of state, which was set to discuss possible financial aid to help steer Zimbabwe's economic recovery, had been changed to Mbabane, Swaziland and would take place on 30 March. The meeting had originally been scheduled for Cape Town. When it finally took place, the summit, which Mugabe attended, noted the GNU's Short Term Emergency Recovery Programme (STERP) to guide efforts towards economic and social recovery. Among the resolutions, the summit urged member states "to support Zimbabwe to implement STERP, in the form of budget support, lines of credit, joint ventures and toll manufacturing"; developed countries "to lift all forms of sanctions against Zimbabwe"; donors, international financial institutions and the international community in general "to support Zimbabwe and provide it with the necessary financial support for its timely economic recovery"; and "established a Committee comprising the SADC Troika of Ministers of Finance to coordinate SADC support to Zimbabwe['s] recovery process". In response to Zimbabwe's request for an $ 8.5 bn economic recovery package, SADC agreed to support Zimbabwe, but without any firm pledges except from South Africa. On 30 October, following a SADC foreign ministers' **review of the GPA**, Mugabe was forced to accept the January SADC summit communiqué, which had eventually led to the formation of the GNU, as a binding document. The communiqué, which he had originally refused to recognise as part of the GPA, stipulated among other things that the appointments of the RBZ governor and the attorney general would be dealt with by the inclusive government after its inauguration. On 5 November, Mugabe, Tsvangirai and Mutambara attended a **SADC summit** in Maputo, which sought to prevent the collapse of the GNU. It was organised by SADC's Politics, Defence and Security Troika (Mozambique, Swaziland and Zambia) and was chaired by Mozambican President Armando Guebuza.

In a judgement made available on 3 March, high court judge Justice Anne-Mary Gowora ruled that the 2008 judgment of the **SADC Tribunal**, declaring the land invasions illegal did not apply and could not be enforced in Zimbabwe unless parliament ratified the protocol that set up the tribunal. On 2 November, the official 'Herald' newspaper announced that Zimbabwe had formally withdrawn its membership of the tribunal, throwing into disarray pending cases in which white farmers challenged the legality of the country's land reform programme. Zimbabwe announced it had withdrawn from any legal proceedings by the tribunal until the establishment of the court was ratified by at least two-thirds of the bloc's membership, as required under SADC rules and procedures. Reacting to the move, SADC Executive Secretary Tomaz Salamao said the repudiation had been referred to the ministers of justice of the regional bloc's member nations, who had been asked to provide legal guidance to SADC heads of state.

It was widely anticipated that the appointment of Jacob Zuma as president of **South Africa** would change former president Thabo Mbeki's controversial 'quiet diplomacy'. Although Zuma actively sought to resolve the problems in the GNU, he was later criticised for being pro-ZANU-PF. On 27 August, Zuma made his first official visit to Zimbabwe, where he officially opened the 99th Harare Agricultural Show. He urged the GNU partners to get along with each other, but the visit appeared to have little impact. At the summit in Maputo on 5 November, SADC leaders gave the GNU coalition partners 15 to 30 days to sort out their differences, but the deadline passed without any meeting between the negotiators. On 23 November, it was announced that Zuma had postponed his visit to assess Zimbabwe's troubled power-sharing agreement, as his advisors had expressed impatience over delays in concluding the talks. The South African government stated that it now expected the issues to be dealt with by 5 December, but that 'deadline' also passed. Apparently in an effort to reduce waves of Zimbabwean asylum seekers, South Africa announced on 4 May that Zimbabwean citizens could travel there on free 90-day visitor's permits and apply to do casual work during their stay.

In what was interpreted as an attempt to win over SADC leaders, **Tsvangirai** visited the DRC, South Africa and Angola in October. On 23 October, he announced that DRC President and SADC Chairman Jospeh Kabila would visit Harare to mediate the crisis bedevilling the GNU. Kabila, seen as a Mugabe ally, visited on 1 November without significant results. On 19 November, Tsvangirai left for Morocco and Libya. He briefed the Libyan leader, then chairman of the AU, who had invited him.

Relations with **Botswana** remained tense. While the MDC-T had good relations with the country, ZANU-PF remained hostile as Botswana remained critical of the Mugabe administration. On 15 March, Botswana's foreign affairs minister said no evidence of terrorist training camps had been presented to Gaborone to support the allegations made by Mugabe's government in September 2008. Botswana rejected "the unsubstantiated allegations which were made and are clearly nothing more than an exercise to engage in acts of intimidation and harassment of the innocent people of Zimbabwe".

Other international visits included a state visit by President Rupiah Banda of **Zambia**, who was invited to open the Zimbabwe International Trade fair in Bulawayo on 2 May. He donated 9,000 tonnes of maize. In July, Mugabe visited Zambia. He was guest of honour at a ceremony to commemorate the establishment of the Mukuni Ng'ombe dynasty. In mid-November, a delegation from **Brazil** visited and met Vice President Joice Mujuru on 17 November. Led by Brazil's under secretary for Africa and Asia in the ministry of external affairs, the delegation stated that Brazil wanted to strengthen economic ties with Zimbabwe and to partner the country in development projects. On 13 August, the deputy minister of foreign affairs of **Iran** began a five-day official visit as part of the two countries' move to implement agreements signed during Mugabe's visit to Iran in 2006.

Relations with the West hardly improved. Mugabe and ZANU-PF officials continued to blame Zimbabwe's woes on 'illegal' western sanctions and the MDC-M seemed to agree with this position. Tsvangirai and his MDC-T labelled the sanctions "restrictive measures", which did not go down well with ZANU-PF. Significantly, on 5 March, Tsvangirai called for the "restrictive measures" to be lifted.

Zimbabwe actively sought **international aid** to revive the ailing economy. On 11 January, Mugabe dispatched Foreign Minister Simbarashe Mbengegwi to Tripoli to deliver a letter to the Libyan leader. This was seen as part of a begging campaign to help Zimbabwe out of its economic meltdown. Paul Mangwana, the acting information minister, confirmed that Harare was seeking an economic package from "friends in Southern Africa and other parts of the world who are sympathetic". The 'friends' included Russia, Iran and China. On 5 June, Tsvangirai started a three-week tour of Europe and the United States, ostensibly to drum up financial aid for his unity government. The visit took him to the Netherlands, France, Sweden, Britain, Belgium, Germany, Denmark and the US, where he met President Obama. The visit did not bring significant financial aid from the largely sceptical Western governments. Tsvangirai raised $ 150 m in fresh aid pledges to be disbursed through NGOs. The 'Herald' newspaper ridiculed and condemned the visit. A rival ZANU-PF mission, let by Defence Minister Emmerson Mnangagwa visited Asia and Russia. At the end of June, Tsvangirai announced that **China** had extended credit lines amounting to $ 950 m.

On 30 January, the new **United States** administration voiced scepticism over the power-sharing agreement, stating that US aid would be given only when a representative government was in place. In contrast to the Bush administration, however, State Department spokesman Robert Wood did not call for Mugabe's removal. Throughout the year, the US government focused on humanitarian aid rather than development aid and lifting sanctions. On 5 March, Obama announced that US 'targeted' sanctions aimed at Mugabe and members of his government would continue for another year.

On 26 January, EU **sanctions** on Zimbabwe's leadership were tightened. The EU condemned Mugabe's government for its "ongoing failure to address the most basic economic and social needs of its people". The EU's General Affairs Council extended the restrictions for another year. Added to the list were more than 60 other "persons and entities that are actively associated with the violence or human rights infringements of the regime". According to a letter made public on 28 May, the EU was not yet ready to establish normal ties with Zimbabwe or resume aid, despite a "positive evolution" in politics. The letter was addressed to John Kaputin, secretary general of the ACP. Sanctions were also renewed by Australia, New Zealand and Switzerland. On 15 September, Australia announced it was considering easing a ban on high-level contacts with Zimbabwe, but Foreign Minister Stephen Smith added that it was too soon to end the targeted sanctions. Australia would, however, contribute an extra A$ 8 m in aid to Zimbabwe to fund emergency food supplies, agriculture projects and education.

Zimbabwe's relationships with regional and multilateral **financial institutions** did not change significantly. As of April 2009, Zimbabwe owed an estimated $ 1.24 bn in debt arrears to the World Bank, the AfDB, and the IMF. On 9 March, in response to a request from Zimbabwe, the IMF sent its first delegation to Zimbabwe in two years. The two-week mission was meant to assess the situation and to meet senior officials of the GNU, including Finance Minister Tendai Biti. Zimbabwe's IMF arrears were estimated at $ 130 m, making the prospect of anything coming out of the Article IV consultation slim. The AfDB was owed some $ 460 m and had stopped lending to Zimbabwe until the debt was repaid. On 22 May, the World Bank announced that the right conditions had not yet been created for the institution to re-engage on a fully-fledged economic development programme with Zimbabwe. By then Zimbabwe owed $ 673 m to the World Bank in debt arrears. Humanitarian assistance provided to help the poor was being channelled through NGOs and aid agencies.

Mugabe attended the 13th Ordinary Session of the **AU**, which took place in Sirte, Libya, from 24 June to 3 July. This was interpreted as a clear indication that it was still he who held the power in the GNU. Mugabe also attended the 64th Ordinary Session of the **UN**. In his address on 26 September, he underlined the need for the UN to truly serve the interest of all states and predictably condemned sanctions on Zimbabwe and the embargo on Cuba.

Socioeconomic Developments

There were some dramatic improvements in **key economic indicators**. Consumer price inflation closed the year at about 92.3%. Economist Intelligence Unit estimates put the nominal GDP at $ 1.63 bn, down from $ 1.5 bn in 2008. The official 2010 budget estimated the GDP as at October at $ 5.179 bn. GDP grew by 4.7%. The current accounts balance marginally deteriorated from -$ 584 m to -$ 590 m, while international reserves declined from $ 96 m in 2008 to $ 91 m. As at 31 December, the grand total of all external debt stock, including $ 4.244 bn of arrears, was $ 5.670 bn. Domestic borrowings for the year amounted to a cumulative total of $ 53.9 m.

On 19 March, the GNU launched an interim economic blue print to resuscitate the battered economy. At the launch of the plan, dubbed **STERP**, Finance Minister Biti stated that Zimbabwe's economic recovery was predicated on increasing production capacity. The general idea behind the programme was to boost capacity in agriculture and other key sectors such as mining, tourism, construction and public works. Biti said the biggest hurdle to implementing the recovery programme was that it required outside financial assistance, which unfortunately had not yet started coming. Over $ 5 bn were required. The emergency short-term stabilisation programme would run from February to December.

Two budgets were produced for the year. One, the Z$ 66.5 quintillion ($ 1.7 bn) 'ZANU-PF budget', was presented by the then acting finance minister, Patrick Chinamasa, on 29 January. The second, which became the official GNU budget, was presented on 18 March by Biti, the new finance minister. Slashing the 'ZANU-PF budget', Biti revised spending and revenue estimates to $ 1 bn. The currency had been redenominated in January. Hyperinflation at well over 1 bn% made the local currency worthless. In the new budget, the Zimbabwe dollar ('Zimdollar') was dumped as the trading currency and replaced by a **multiple currency regime.** The country started trading mainly in the US dollar, the South African rand and the Botswana pula. The move appeared to cause some discord in the GNU. On several occasions Mugabe hinted that the Zimdollar would be reintroduced. In November, he said, "The use of multiple currencies is not helping our people much as the money is difficult to secure. We will be re-introducing our own currency by end of the year." The RBZ governor at times favoured the return of the local currency. Biti, the MDC-T finance minister, said he would resign if the Zimdollar returned.

The dumping of the Zimdollar has been largely credited with bringing sanity to the economy. Goods that had vanished from stores became available. The improvement in the general **macroeconomic environment** and the consequent increase in capacity utilisation contributed to price stability, which characterised the economy for the rest of the year. Inflation was dramatically reduced. According to RBZ figures, by November monthly price increases (annualised) had dropped to -1.19%.

On 2 December, Biti presented the **2010 budget** to parliament, proposing expenditure of $ 2.25 bn against revenues of $ 44 bn for an $ 810 m deficit, which would have to be filled by drawing down IMF credits or through loans or grants. Biti projected a 2010 economic expansion of 7%, with inflation for 2010 projected at 5.1%. He also proposed a budget deficit equal to 14.6% of GDP. Total funding requested from ministries and government departments totalled some $ 12 bn, against the projected revenue of $ 1.44 bn, indicating the scale of need.

Despite some decline in the downward slide, the **education and heath** delivery systems continued to experience problems of staffing, equipment and funding. As in recent years, health and educational personnel made up a substantial part of the brain drain to countries such as Australia, the United Kingdom and South Africa. Industrial action and threats of industrial action arising out of salary disputes, particularly by doctors, nurses and teachers, were a constant feature throughout the year, further compromising these sectors. In March, the Zimbabwe CTU demanded a national minimum wage of $ 454 a month from June. At the same time, teachers demanded a monthly wage of $ 2,300. The government's wage package for civil servants was $ 100.

Zimbabwe continued to lose skilled manpower through **migration**, mainly to Commonwealth countries. In its 2009 Migration Initiatives Appeal, the International Organization for Migration claimed that Zimbabwe was "a source, transit and destination country for trafficking in persons for the purposes of forced labour, sexual exploitation and domestic servitude". The country was home to "mobile and vulnerable" populations. The relaxation of visa requirements for Zimbabwean citizens travelling to South Africa was expected to have significant effects. This would hardly reduce the number of Zimbabwean migrants, but the anticipated dramatic increase in the flow of Zimbabweans crossing into South Africa did not materialise.

The **cholera epidemic** continued to spread at the beginning of the year. WHO figures released on 2 February showed that more than 62,000 people had been infected in the outbreak, which led to more than 3,200 deaths. Throughout the year, **electricity and water shortages** became widespread in urban areas. Power cuts were attributed to Zimbabwe being cut off by South African and Mozambican suppliers for failing to settle outstanding debts. Water shortages, a contributory factor to the cholera epidemic, were attributed to shortages of power and purifying chemicals, and ageing plant and equipment, all of which were explained as being the result of a lack of foreign currency and sub-economic tariffs.

In September, new estimates released by the ministry of health and child welfare showed that Zimbabwe's adult **HIV** prevalence rate was continuing its downward trend with a fall from 14.1% in 2008 to 13.7%. Earlier, in August, Zimbabwe had received $ 37.9 m from the Global Fund, which decided to bypass Zimbabwe's National AIDS Council as the principal recipient of existing and future grants after the RBZ had admitted in 2008 to diverting over $ 7 m from the Global Fund's Round 5 grant earmarked for scaling up the national antiretroviral programme.

According to the treasury, after the introduction of stable multiple currencies and supportive measures such as cash budgeting, prices of goods and the services – and with them the **cost of living** – stabilised considerably during the year. From January to October, month-on-month inflation had been oscillating between -3.1% and 1%.

There were marginal improvements in **food security**. However, the WFP reported that recent hyperinflation, an acute shortage of basic supplies and a series of very poor harvests had led to serious food shortages and acute food insecurity. Increasing levels of vulnerability were compounded by the collapsing economy, very high unemployment (estimated at over 80%), and a high HIV/AIDS prevalence rate. This situation necessitated large-scale humanitarian food assistance operations. The maize harvest amounted to 1.14 m tonnes, more than 1.3 times the 2008 level. But Zimbabwe still faced a cereal shortfall of around 677,000 tonnes. A FAO/WFP assessment estimated that around 2.8 m people, mostly in rural areas, might need humanitarian assistance before the 2010 harvest.

Zimbabwe's **diamond industry** faced problems. In June, HRW published a report detailing military activity in the diamond fields. In July, a sensitive report by the Kimberly Process (Diamond) Certification System (KPCS) gave details of atrocities committed by the army that by then had left about 200 dead in the contentious Chiadzwa diamond field in the Marange district of Manicaland Province. The report noted "unacceptable and horrific violence against civilians by authorities in and around Chiadzwa" and recommended a six-month suspension of the import and export of rough diamonds. The government ignored the recommendations and did not release the report. In September, Zimbabwe Lawyers for Human Rights demanded the official release of the report, which was already freely available on the internet, and the government's compliance with its recommendations. On 26 November, the Rapaport Diamond Trading Network (RapNet), the global network of companies that supports the development of free, fair and competitive global diamond markets, announced it had banned trading in diamonds from the Marange fields because of reported human rights violations.

In a move that spread anxiety among investors, the government seized assets of the stock exchange-listed **Meikles group** under a controversial anti-corruption law. An Extraordinary Government Gazette published on 11 September, announced that the government had frozen the assets of four companies linked to the Meikles family – Kingdom Meikles, Tanganda Tea Company (Private) Limited, Thomas Meikles Centre (Private) Limited and Murlis Investments (Private) Limited – and commenced investigations into allegations of externalising huge sums of foreign currency levelled against these entities.

Amin Y. Kamete

List of Authors

Jon Abbink, Researcher, African Studies Centre, Leiden, Professor of Anthropology at the Free University of Amsterdam, The Netherlands, abbink@ascleiden.nl

Michael Amoah, former lecturer, Middlesex University, UK, michael.amoah1@ntlworld.com

Matthias Basedau, Senior Researcher, Institute of African Affairs, German Institute of Global and Area Studies, Hamburg, Germany, basedau@giga-hamburg.de

Rémy Bazenguissa-Ganga, Lecturer, University of Lille, France, remy.bazenguissa-ganga@ehess.fr

Alice Bellagamba, Associate Professor, Cultural and Social Anthropology, Department of Human Sciences for Education "Riccardo Massa", University of Milan-Bicocca, alice.bellagamba@unimib.it

Linnea Bergholm, Post-doctoral researcher, School of Global Studies, Gothenburg University, Sweden, linnea.bergholm@gmail.com

Heinrich Bergstresser, Media Consultant, Freelance Research Associate of the Institute of African Affairs in Hamburg, of the Friedrich Naumann Foundation and of InWent, Germany, heinrich.bergstresser@web.de

Nic Cheeseman, Lecturer in African Politics and Hugh Price Fellow of Jesus College, University of Oxford, UK, niccheeseman@gmail.com

Tiyesere Mercy Chikapa-Jamali, Lecturer at the Department of Political and Administrative Studies, University of Malawi, Tiyeserec@yahoo.com

John Daniel, Academic Director of the School for International Training's programme in Social and Political Transformation in Durban, South Africa, john.daniel@sit.edu

Lewis B. Dzimbiri, Professor of Public Administration, Chancellor College, University of Malawi, dzimbiri2002@yahoo.co.uk

Gero Erdmann, Senior Researcher, Institute of African Affairs, German Institute of Global and Area Studies, Hamburg, Germany, gero.erdmann@t-online.de

Vincent Foucher, Researcher at the Centre d'Etudes d'Afrique Noire, Bordeaux, France, v.foucher@sciencepobordeaux.fr

Mark Furness, Research Fellow, German Development Institute, Bonn, Germany, Mark .Furness@die-gdi.de.

Lansana Gberie, Senior Researcher, Institute for Security Studies (ISS), Addis Ababa, Ethiopia, lagberieJ@yahoo.com

Eric Komlavi Hahonou, Economist & Social anthropologist, Assistant Professor and Postdoc fellow, Department of Society & Globalisation, Roskilde University, Denmark, komlavi@ruc.dk

Joseph Hanlon, Senior Lecturer, Development Policy and Practice, Open University, Milton Keynes, UK, J.Hanlon@open.ac.uk

Kurt Hirschler, Freelance Political Scientist, Hamburg, Germany, kurt_hirschler@web.de

Nicole Hirt, Freelance Research Associate, Institute of African Affairs, German Institute of Global and Area Studies and Senior Consultant at HACOS – "Horn of Africa Consultancy Service", Hamburg, Germany, nicolehi2001@yahoo.de

Rolf Hofmeier, Former Director, Institute of African Affairs, German Institute of Global and Area Studies, Hamburg, Germany, hofmeier@giga-hamburg.de

Cord Jakobeit, Professor of International Relations, University of Hamburg, Germany, cord.jakobeit@uni-hamburg.de

Amin Y. Kamete, Lecturer, University Bangor, Wales, UK, a.kamete@bangor.ac.uk

Christoph Kohl, Ph.D. Candidate at the Max Planck Institute for Social Anthropology, Halle/Saale, Germany, Kohl@eth.mpg.de

Dirk Kohnert, Deputy Director, Institute of African Affairs, German Institute of Global and Area Studies, Hamburg, Germany, kohnert@giga-hamburg.de

Bruno Losch, Senior Economist, Centre de Coopération Internationale en Recherche Agronomique pour le Développement, Montpellier, France, blosch@worldbank.org

Richard R. Marcus, Director and Assistant Professor, International Studies Program, California State University, Long Beach, USA, rmarcus@csulb.edu

Mike McGovern, Assistant Professor of Anthropology, Yale University, USA, michael. mcgovern@yale.edu

Andreas Mehler, Director, Institute of African Affairs, German Institute of Global and Area Studies, Hamburg, Germany, mehler@giga-hamburg.de

Henning Melber, Executive Director, Dag Hammarskjöld Foundation, Uppsala, Sweden, henning.melber@dhf.uu.se

Claes Olsson, Political Scientist and Editor at Global Publications Foundation, Uppsala, Sweden, claes.olsson@globalpublications.org

Helena Olsson, Communication Officer on a project 'Swedish Workplace HIV/Aids Programme (SHWAP)', Stockholm, Sweden, helenarlolsson@hotmail.com

Krijn Peters, Lecturer, Centre for Development Studies, University of Wales, Swansea, UK, k.peters@swansea.ac.uk

Fanny Pigeaud, Journalist, Agence France-Presse, France, Fanny.pigeaud@gmail.com

Marisha Ramdeen, Freelance worker and Masters Graduate in Political Science at the University of Kwa Zulu Natal, South Africa. mramdeen2004@yahoo.com

Jon Schubert, Doctoral Student at the Centre of African Studies, University of Edinburgh, UK, and freelance analyst/consultant, JonSchubert@gmx.net

Gerhard Seibert, Researcher at the African Studies Centre (CEA), ISCTE, Lisbon, Portugal, mailseibert@yahoo.com

Roger Southall, Professor of Sociology, University of the Witwatersrand, Johannesburg, South Africa, Roger.Southall@wits.ac.za

Alexander Stroh, Research Fellow, Institute of African Affairs, German Institute of Global and Area Studies, Hamburg, Germany, Stroh@giga-hamburg.de

Susan M. Thomson, Five Colleges Professor, Hampshire College, Amherst, USA, susanm .thomson@gmail.com

Klaus-Peter Treydte, Economist, Dr. rer. pol., Former country representative Friedrich-Ebert-Foundation Madagascar and Mauritius, kp3t@gmx.net

Denis M. Tull, Senior Research Fellow, German Institute for International Affairs, Berlin, Germany, Denis.tull@swp-berlin.org

Stef Vandeginste, Postdoctoral Fellow of the Research Foundation – Flanders (FWO) at the Faculty of Law, University of Antwerp, Belgium, stefvandeginste@ua.ac.be

Han van Dijk, Researcher, African Studies Centre, Leiden and Professor of Law and Governance in Africa, chair Law and Governance group, Dept of Social Sciences, Wageningen University and Research Centre, The Netherlands, dijkh@ascleiden.nl

Ineke van Kessel, Researcher, African Studies Centre, Leiden, The Netherlands, Kessel@ascleiden.nl

Klaas van Walraven, Researcher, African Studies Centre, Leiden, The Netherlands, Walraven@ascleiden.nl

Martin van Vliet, Institute of Multiparty Democracy at The Hague, The Netherlands mvanvliet_imd@yahoo.com

Christian von Soest, Research Fellow, Institute of African Affairs, German Institute of Global and Area Studies, Hamburg, Germany, soest@giga-hamburg.de

Volker Weyel, Former Editor-in-chief 'Vereinte Nationen' (1977–2004), specialised journalist and consultant, Bonn, Germany, vweyel@gmx.de

Peter Woodward, Professor, School of Politics and International Relation, University of Reading, UK, p.r.woodward@reading.ac.uk

Douglas A. Yates, Assistant Professor of Political Science in the Department of International Affairs, The American University of Paris, France, douglas.yates@aup.fr

www.ingramcontent.com/pod-product-compliance
Lightning Source LLC
LaVergne TN
LVHW082345011026
849160LV00024B/1093